DIGITAL GOVERNMENT

E-Government Research, Case Studies, and Implementation

INTEGRATED SERIES IN INFORMATION SYSTEMS

1.1 Series Editors

Other published titles in the series:

E-BUSINESS MANAGEMENT: *Integration of Web Technologies with Business Models/* edited by Michael J. Shaw
VIRTUAL CORPORATE UNIVERSITIES: *A Matrix of Knowledge and Learning for the New Digital Dawn/* Walter R.J. Baets & Gert Van der Linden
SCALABLE ENTERPRISE SYSTEMS: *An Introduction to Recent Advances/* edited by Vittal Prabhu, Soundar Kumara, Manjunath Kamath
LEGAL PROGRAMMING: *Legal Compliance for RFID and Software Agent Ecosystems in Retail Processes and Beyond/* Brian Subirana and Malcolm Bain
LOGICAL DATA MODELING: *What It Is and How To Do It/* Alan Chmura and J. Mark Heumann
DESIGNING AND EVALUATING E-MANAGEMENT DECISION TOOLS: *The Integration of Decision and Negotiation Models into Internet-Multimedia Technologies/* Giampiero E.G. Beroggi
INFORMATION AND MANAGEMENT SYSTEMS FOR PRODUCT CUSTOMIZATION/ Thorsten Blecker et al
MEDICAL INFORMATICS: *Knowledge Management and Data Mining in Biomedicine/* edited by Hsinchun Chen et al
KNOWLEDGE MANAGEMENT AND MANAGEMENT LEARNING: *Extending the Horizons of Knowledge-Based Management/* edited by Walter Baets
INTELLIGENCE AND SECURITY INFORMATICS FOR INTERNATIONAL SECURITY: *Information Sharing and Data Mining/* Hsinchun Chen
ENTERPRISE COLLABORATION: *On-Demand Information Exchange for Extended Enterprises/* David Levermore & Cheng Hsu
SEMANTIC WEB AND EDUCATION/ Vladan Devedžić
INFORMATION SYSTEMS ACTION RESEARCH: *An Applied View of Emerging Concepts and Methods/* Ned Kock
ONTOLOGIES: *A Handbook of Principles, Concepts and Applications/* edited by Raj Sharman, Rajiv Kishore, Ram Ramesh
METAGRAPHS AND THEIR APPLICATIONS/ Amit Basu and Robert W. Blanning
SERVICE ENTERPRISE INTEGRATION: *An Enterprise Engineering Perspective/* Cheng Hsu

DIGITAL GOVERNMENT

E-Government Research, Case Studies, and Implementation

edited by
Hsinchun Chen
Lawrence Brandt
Valerie Gregg
Roland Traunmüller
Sharon Dawes
Eduard Hovy
Ann Macintosh
Catherine A. Larson

Springer

Hsinchun Chen
University of Arizona
Tucson, AZ, USA

Lawrence Brandt
Consultant
Potomac, MD, USA

Valerie Gregg
Alexandria, VA, USA

Roland Traunmüller
Johannes Kepler Universität
Linz, Austria

Sharon Dawes
University of Albany, SUNY
Albany, NY, USA

Eduard Hovy
University of Southern California
Marina del Rey, CA, USA

Ann Macintosh
Napier University
Edinburgh, United Kingdom

Catherine A. Larson
University of Arizona
Tucson, AZ, USA

Series Editors:
Ramesh Sharda
Oklahoma State University
Stillwater, Oklahoma, USA

Stefan Voß
Universität Hamburg
Germany

Library of Congress Control Number: 2007932235

ISBN-13: 978-0-387-71610-7 e-ISBN-13: 978-0-387-71611-4

Printed on acid-free paper.

9 8 7 6 5 4 3 2 1

springer.com

TABLE OF CONTENTS

Preface xvii
Editors' Biographies xxi
Authors' Biographies xxix

UNIT I. FOUNDATIONS OF DIGITAL GOVERNMENT AND PUBLIC POLICY

Chapter 1. Foundations of Digital Government **3**
By Stephen Coleman
1 Governance and/as Technology 4
2 Digitising Governance 6
3 Barriers to e-Governance 9
4 Governing the e-Public 11
5 Regulating the Behaviour of e-Citizens 12
6 Cultivating the Skills of e-Citizenship 13
7 Managing Interactivity 15
8 What Can Be Expected from e-Governance? 16
References 17
Suggested Readings and Online Resources 18
Questions for Discussion 19

Chapter 2. Discipline or Interdisciplinary Study Domain? Challenges and Promises in Electronic Government Research **21**
By Hans J. (Jochen) Scholl
1 Introduction 22
2 Would EGR Pass as a "Legitimate" Discipline? 23
3 Neighboring "Incumbent" Disciplines: Pub Admin and ISR/CS 27
4 Challenges and Opportunities for Cross-disciplinary EGR 29
5 EGR on the Continuum between Discipline and Transdiscipline 32
6 Concluding Remarks 36
References 37
Suggested Readings and Online Resources 40
Questions for Discussion 41

Chapter 3. An Outline for the Foundations of Digital Government Research 43
By Eduard Hovy
1 Introduction: A New Field of Research 44
2 A Tripartite Model of ICT in Government 45
3 Related Work 49
4 Assumptions behind DG Research in Light of the Model 50
5 The Character of DG and Similar Research in Different Applications 52
6 Digital Government Research in the USA and EU 52
7 What Makes a Good DG Research Paper? 53
8 DG Education 55
9 Conclusion 56
References 57
Suggested Readings and Online Resources 58
Questions for Discussion 58

Chapter 4. Lost In Competition? The State of the Art in e-Government Research 61
By Åke Grönlund
1 Introduction 62
2 Research and Practice 62
3 A Research Maturity Model 66
4 Findings 74
5 Conclusions and Discussion 80
References 81
Suggested Readings and Online Resources 82
Questions for Discussion 83

Chapter 5. e-Democracy and e-Participation Research in Europe 85
By Ann Macintosh
1 Introduction 86
2 Current Research and Practice 88
3 The Research Landscape 94
4 Conclusion and Future Research Direction 98
References 100
Suggested Readings and Online Resources 101
Questions for Discussion 102

Chapter 6. Introduction to Digital Government Research in Public Policy and Management 103
By Sharon S. Dawes
1 Introduction 104
2 Case Studies 107
3 Discussion: Six Public Policy and Management Considerations for Digital Government 109
4 Conclusion 122
References 122
Suggested Readings and Online Resources 124
Questions for Discussion 125

Chapter 7. Privacy in an Electronic Government Context 127
By Priscilla M. Regan
1 Introduction 128
2 Overview 129
3 Conclusions 136
References 136
Suggested Readings and Online Resources 138
Questions for Discussion 139

Chapter 8. Accessibility of Federal Electronic Government 141
By Shirley Ann Becker
1 Introduction 142
2 Types of Disabilities 143
3 Government Involvement 145
4 Section 508 Accessibility Standards 146
5 Web Assessment Guidelines 147
6 e-Government Compliance 150
7 Conclusion 151
References 152
Suggested Readings and Online Resources 154
Questions for Discussion 155

Chapter 9. The Current State of Electronic Voting in the United States 157
By Paul S. Herrnson, Richard G. Niemi, Michael J. Hanmer, Benjamin B. Bederson, Frederick G. Conrad, and Michael W. Traugott
1 Introduction 158
2 Literature Review 159

3 Usability Studies 165
4 Conclusion 174
References 175
Suggested Readings and Online Resources 178
Questions for Discussion 180

Chapter 10. e-Enabling the Mobile Legislator 181
By Angus Whyte
1 Introduction 182
2 European Elected Assemblies and e-Governance 184
3 e-Representative: Mobilising the Legislator? 187
4 Conclusion 193
References 197
Suggested Readings and Online Resources 198
Questions for Discussion 199

UNIT II. INFORMATION TECHNOLOGY RESEARCH

Chapter 11. History of Digital Government Research in the United States 203
By Lawrence E. Brandt and Valerie J. Gregg
1 Introduction 204
2 Literature Review and Overview of the Field 206
3 Case Studies 208
4 Conclusions and Discussion 211
References 214
Suggested Readings and Online Resources 215
Questions for Discussion 217

Chapter 12. Data and Knowledge Integration for e-Government 219
By Eduard Hovy
1 Introduction 220
2 Overiew of the Field 221
3 Two Examples 224
4 Conclusion 228
References 229
Suggested Readings and Online Resources 230
Questions for Discussion 231

Chapter 13. Ontologies in the Legal Domain **233**
By Tom Van Engers, Alexander Boer, Joost Breuker, André Valente, and Radboud Winkels
1 Introduction 234
2 Ontologies and Meaning 236
3 Legal Knowledge 237
4 Ontologies as Knowledge Management Tool 239
5 Ontologies Versus Epistemological Frameworks 242
6 Quality of Ontologies 253
7 Conclusions 256
References 258
Suggested Readings and Online Resources 259
Questions for Discussion 260

Chapter 14. Public Safety Information Sharing: An Ontological Perspective **263**
By Siddharth Kaza and Hsinchun Chen
1 Introduction 264
2 Literature Review 264
3 Case Studies 272
4 Conclusion 276
References 278
Suggested Readings and Online Resources 281
Questions for Discussion 282

Chapter 15. Collaborative Cyberinfrastructure for Transnational Digital Government **283**
By Maurício Tsugawa, Andréa Matsunaga, and José A. B. Fortes
1 Introduction 284
2 Overview and Review of Relevant Approaches 285
3 Application of Machine Virtualization to TDG and a Case Study 292
4 Conclusions 299
References 301
Suggested Readings and Online Resources 303
Questions for Discussion 304

Chapter 16. Semantics-Based Threat Structure Mining for Homeland Security **307**
By Nabil R. Adam, Vandana P. Janeja, Aabhas V. Paliwal, Vijay Atluri, Soon Ae Chun, Jim Cooper, John Paczkowski, Christof Bornhövd, and Joachim Schaper

1 Introduction 308
2 Semantics Driven Data Mining 310
3 Enhanced Semantic Graph 312
4 Threat Structure Mining 317
5 Semantics-Based Threat Structure Mining (STM) Prototype System 320
6 Related Work 324
7 Conclusion and Discussion 326
References 327
Suggested Readings and Online Resources 328
Questions for Discussion 329

Chapter 17. Identity Management for e-Government Services 331
By Fabio Fioravanti and Enrico Nardelli
1 Introduction 332
2 Status of National Electronic Identity in Europe 334
3 A Cooperative Federated Architecture for Identity Management 344
4 Conclusion and Discussion 350
References 350
Suggested Readings and Online Resources 351
Questions for Discussion 352

Chapter 18. Feature Integration for Geospatial Information: A Review and Outlook 353
By Peggy Agouris, Arie Croitoru, and Anthony Stefanidis
1 Introduction 354
2 Spatial Integration 355
3 Spatiotemporal Integration 359
4 Spatial and Spatiotemporal Queries 363
5 Concluding Remarks 370
References 370
Suggested Readings and Online Resources 374
Topics for Additional Discussion 375

Chapter 19. Geoinformatics of Hotspot Detection and Prioritization for Digital Governance 377
By G.P. Patil, Raj Acharya, Amy Glasmeier, Wayne Myers, Shashi Phoha, and Stephen Rathbun
1 Introduction 378
2 Literature Review: Fundamental Methodologies and Computational Techniques 378

3 Illustrative Applications and Case Studies 387
4 Conclusion 392
References 393
Suggested Readings and Online Resources 393
Questions for Discussion 394

Chapter 20. Geoinformation Technologies to Support Collaborative Emergency Management 395
By Sven Fuhrmann, Alan MacEachren, and Guoray Cai
1 Introduction 396
2 Overview of the Field 397
3 Case Studies 402
4 Discussion 413
Acronym Table 415
References 415
Suggested Readings and Online Resources 419
Questions for Discussion 420

Chapter 21. Sustainable Cross-Boundary Information Sharing 421
By Theresa A. Pardo, J. Ramon Gil-Garcia, and G. Brian Burke
1 Introduction 422
2 Interorganizational Information Integration 422
3 Study Methodology 426
4 Informational Integration in Criminal Justice and Public Health 427
5 Main Lessons 429
6 Taking Action 432
7 Conclusion 435
References 435
Suggested Readings and Online Resources 436
Questions for Discussion 438

Chapter 22. UrbanSim: Using Simulation to Inform Public Deliberation and Decision-Making 439
By Alan Borning, Paul Waddell, and Ruth Förster
1 Introduction 440
2 The UrbanSim Project: A Case Study 446
3 Conclusion and Future Work 460
References 461
Suggested Readings and Online Resources 462
Questions for Discussion 463

UNIT III. CASE STUDIES

Chapter 23. Taking Best Practice Forward 467
By Helene Gieber, Christine Leitner, Gerti Orthofer, and Roland Traunmüller
1 The eEurope Awards: Promoting Best Practice 468
2 The eEurope Awards Process 468
3 The eEurope Awards Process e-Government 2005 469
4 The Selection Process 470
5 Themes and Winners of the e-Government Awards 2005 471
6 Lessons Learned from the e-Government Awards 2005 475
7 The Challenge of Using Good Practice 478
8 Finding Suitable Model Cases 478
9 A Framework for Evaluating Feasibility 479
10 Collective Learning Processes and Transfer Mechanisms 481
11 The Future: Proceedings to Higher Order Model Solutions 483
References 484
Suggested Readings and Online Resources 485
Questions for Discussion 485

Chapter 24. ePetitioning in the Scottish Parliament 487
By Ann Macintosh, Nick Adams, Angus Whyte, and Jim Johnston
1 Introduction 488
2 Literature Review 489
3 ePetitioning in Scotland 491
4 Conclusion and Discussion 498
References 499
Suggested Readings and Online Resources 500
Questions for Discussion 501

Chapter 25. Citizen Access to Government Statistical Information 503
By Alan F. Karr
1 Introduction 504
2 Broad Access 506
3 Researcher Access 515
4 Distributed Data 524
5 Conclusion: Thoughts about the Future 525
References 527
Suggested Readings and Online Resources 528
Questions for Discussion 528

Chapter 26. Infectious Disease Informatics and Syndromic Surveillance **531**
By Daniel Zeng, Hsinchun Chen, and Ping Yan
1 Introduction 532
2 Infectious Disease Informatics and its Major Technical Components 533
3 Syndromic Surveillance Systems 538
4 IDI and Syndromic Surveillance System Case Studies 547
5 Concluding Remarks 552
References 553
Suggested Readings and Online Resources 557
Questions for Discussion 558

Chapter 27. Supporting Domain-Specific Digital Libraries in Government: Two Case Studies **561**
By Mathew Weaver, Lois M. L. Delcambre, Marianne Lykke Nielsen, Susan Price, David Maier, and Timothy Tolle
1 Introduction 562
2 Literature Overview 565
3 The Metadata++ Digital Library 566
4 The Software Architecture for Metadata++ 571
5 Our Current Project 576
6 Discussion 577
References 580
Suggested Readings and Online Resources 582
Questions for Discussion 583

Chapter 28. Business-Technology Alignments in e-Government: A Large-Scale Taiwan Government Electronic Record Management Systems Study **585**
By Fang-Ming Hsu, Paul Jen-Hwa Hu, and Hsinchun Chen
1 Introduction 586
2 Background Overview 588
3 Literature Review and Motivation 589
4 Research Framework and Propositions 593
5 Study Design and Data Collection 599
6 Analysis Results and Discussion 601
7 Summary 608
References 610
Suggested Readings and Online Resources 612
Questions for Discussion 613

Chapter 29. Research and Development of Key Technologies for e-Government: Case Studies in China **615**
By Chunxiao Xing, Jijiang Yang, Wei He, Yong Zhang, and Chen Chen
1 Introduction 616
2 GIA: Government Informatization Architecture 621
3 Government Information Catalog and Exchange System 626
4 MEDW: Macro-Economy Data Warehouse 632
5 MEANS: Model of Examination and Approval on Network 637
6 Conclusions 643
References 643
Suggested Readings and Online Resources 644
Questions for Discussion 645

Chapter 30. New Zealand's 2006 Census Online: A Case Study **647**
By Rowena Cullen
1 Introduction 648
2 Literature Review 649
3 Setting up the Project 652
4 Managing the Project 658
5 The Public Response 664
6 Lessons Learned, Changes Advocated 665
References 668
Suggested Readings and Online Resources 669
Questions for Discussion 670

Chapter 31. Multidisciplinary e-Government Research and Education as a Catalyst for Effective Information Technology Transfer **671**
By Bienvenido Vélez-Rivera, Manuel Rodríguez-Martínez, Walter Díaz, Mario Núñez-Molina, and Pedro I. Rivera-Vega
1 Introduction 672
2 Some Socioeconomic Barriers to the Deployment and Utilization of e-Government Initiatives in Mayagüez, Puerto Rico 673
3 Methodology 675
4 Results 676
5 Discussion 681
6 Deployment of e-Government Information Systems to the City of Mayagüez 682
7 Description of Specific e-Government Systems 688
8 Summary 693

References 693
Suggested Readings and Online Resources 694
Questions for Discussion 695

Chapter 32. A Hybrid e-Government Model: Case Studies in Shanghai 697
By Pengzhu Zhang, Xiaoning Mao, Xieping Tang, and Daniel Zeng
1 Introduction 698
2 Shanghai and its e-Government Initiatives 700
3 Case Study I: "China Shanghai" 701
4 Case Study II: Qingpu's Administrative Service Center 706
5 Case Study III: A G2C "Letters-and-Visits" Information System 712
6 Concluding Remarks 715
References 717
Suggested Readings and Online Resources 717
Questions for Discussion 718

Author Index 719

Subject Index 721

PREFACE

Digital government can be defined as the application of information technology to government processes in order to improve services to constituents. The roots of digital government lie in the late 20th century, but digital government initiatives (also called *electronic government* or *e-government*) are a 21st century phenomenon, and new information technologies are being applied swiftly to all levels of government service: local, county, regional and even national and international. Information technology (IT) is being used to improve data management and data sharing, planning and decision support, service delivery, and more. Application areas represent a cross-section of government mandates: healthcare and safety; law enforcement, security, and justice; education; land use; and many others. Not only in the United States but throughout the world, IT is being used to increase public access to information, to provide more convenient and timely transaction services, and to increase citizen participation in the establishment of government regulations and other processes. In so doing, digital government also supports the larger goals of streamlining processes and increasing efficiency, sustaining and strengthening democracy, and improving government accountability and transparency. The study of digital government thus involves not only the information technology used to create e-government tools and services, but also the factors that promote or inhibit successful application, as well as the concomitant public and social policy issues.

Given recent advances in digital government initiatives, this is an excellent and most opportune time to make available a textbook that places the application of such initiatives squarely within the context of the broader goals that are being achieved. The goal of this book is to present a current, comprehensive, and comprehensible review of recent IT research of particular importance to digital government, explorations of current and future policy implications, and case studies of successful applications in a variety of government settings. The intended audience is thus quite broad. Academic readers would include students and faculty in a wide variety of graduate level courses such as, for example, information systems; information, library, and computer sciences; the social sciences including social systems, digital government, and public policy; and business. The student reader will benefit from learning the concepts, techniques, and practices of digital government. Researchers will benefit by being exposed to the interdisciplinary literature of this merging and fast-changing field, and will be able to use the work as a reference guide. Practitioners who would be interested include anyone engaged, or about to be engaged in, planning or implementing new digital government initiatives as well as those concerned with public policy issues. The practitioner audience includes IT and public service managers, decision makers, consultants, and others; they will benefit by gaining knowledge of sound, practical and proven IT strategies for successful digital initiatives, and will be able to better evaluate the strategies that are most likely to be successful in their own settings.

SCOPE AND ORGANIZATION

This book has been grouped into three major units. Unit I focuses on the foundations of digital government and public policy. Unit I has been designed to answer such questions as: why is electronic goverment being used? What are its benefits? Which disciplines are central to the study of digital government, and which research methdologies best support advances in the field? It also addresses broader questions, such as: how is democracy being served? How is society benefitting? Are there trade-offs in, for example, confidentiality, security, or trust issues? Unit I chapters address the following topics and concepts:

- Foundations of digital government
- E-government concepts and approaches
- The state of the art for digital government research
- E-government in and for public policy and management
- Participation and democratization, including electronic voting
- Privacy and accessibility

Unit II spotlights current IT research that is having a major impact on the advancement of digital government aims. These technologies include, but are not limited to, novel techniques for data collection, management and sharing, and information access and retrieval; advances in geographic information systems (GIS) and image storage and retrieval; web services; system architecture and integration; and the related issues of scalability, sustainability, and security. Unit II is intended to provide a comprehensive inventory and overview of state-of-the-art technologies and techniques that show the most promise for e-government initiatives. Topics addressed include:

- The history of digital government research in the United States
- Data and knowledge integration
- Data mining
- Ontologies for the legal domain
- Collaborative processes

- Information sharing
- Electronic identity management
- Geospatial information and GIS technologies and techniques
- Egovernment for public decision making

Unit III presents case studies of successful e-government initiatives from around the world that have lessons of broader context. High impact U.S. and international digital government initiatives are explored. Applications include innovative e-voting initiatives, improved knowledge-management and information sharing, and new means of transaction services and citizen involvement. How the specific technologies were selected and applied is often a primary focus, along with project management, organization development issues, and lessons learned. Unit III case studies report on the following:

- The eEurope Awards for eGovernment
- ePetitioning in the Scottish Parliament
- Citizen access to government statistical information in the U.S.
- Information sharing and collaboration for public health in the U.S.
- Supporting domain-specific digital libraries in government
- A large-scale government Electronic Record Management Systems study in Taiwan
- Key technologies for egovernment in China (Beijing)
- New Zealand's online census
- Technology transfer in Puerto Rico
- A Hybrid E-Government Model in China (Shanghai)

In addition to its primary subject content, each chapter also includes Suggested Readings, Online Resources, and Questions for Discussion to stimulate and guide the reader's interest.

EDITOR BIOGRAPHIES

Dr. Hsinchun Chen is McClelland Professor of Management Information Systems at the University of Arizona and Andersen Consulting Professor of the Year (1999). He received the B.S. degree from the National Chiao-Tung University in Taiwan, the MBA degree from SUNY Buffalo, and the Ph.D. degree in Information Systems from New York University. Dr. Chen is a Fellow of IEEE and AAAS. He received the IEEE Computer Society 2006 Technical Achievement Award. He is author/editor of 13 books, 17 book chapters, and more than 130 SCI journal articles covering intelligence analysis, biomedical informatics, data/text/web mining, digital library, knowledge management, and Web computing. His recent books include: *Medical Informatics: Knowledge Management and Data Mining in Biomedicine* and *Intelligence and Security Informatics for International Security: Information Sharing and Data Mining*, both published by Springer. Dr. Chen was ranked eighth in publication productivity in Information Systems (CAIS 2005) and first in Digital Library research (IP&M 2005) in two recent bibliometric studies. He serves on ten editorial boards including: *ACM Transactions on Information Systems, ACM Journal on Educational Resources in Computing, IEEE Transactions on Intelligent Transportation Systems, IEEE Transactions on Systems, Man, and Cybernetics, Journal of the American Society for Information Science and Technology, Decision Support Systems,* and *International Journal on Digital Library*. Dr. Chen has served as a Scientific Counselor/Advisor of the National Library of Medicine (USA), Academia Sinica (Taiwan), and National Library of China (China). He has been an advisor for major NSF, DOJ, NLM, DOD, DHS, and other international research programs in digital library, digital government, medical informatics, and national security research. Dr. Chen is founding director of the Artificial Intelligence Lab and Hoffman E-Commerce Lab. The UA Artificial Intelligence Lab, which houses 40+ researchers, has received more than $20M in research funding from NSF, NIH, NLM, DOD, DOJ, CIA, DHS, and other agencies over the past 17 years. The Hoffman E-Commerce Lab, which has been funded mostly by major IT industry partners, features one of the most advanced e-commerce hardware and software environments in the College of Management. Dr. Chen is conference co-chair of

ACM/IEEE Joint Conference on Digital Libraries (JCDL) 2004 and has served as the conference/program co-chair for the past eight International Conferences of Asian Digital Libraries (ICADL), the premiere digital library meeting in Asia that he helped develop. Dr. Chen is also (founding) conference co-chair of the IEEE International Conferences on Intelligence and Security Informatics (ISI) 2003–2007. The ISI conference, which has been sponsored by NSF, CIA, DHS, and NIJ, has become the premiere meeting for international and homeland security IT research. Dr. Chen's COPLINK system, which has been quoted as a national model for public safety information sharing and analysis, has been adopted in more than 200 law enforcement and intelligence agencies in 20 states. The COPLINK research had been featured in the New York Times, Newsweek, Los Angeles Times, Washington Post, Boston Globe, and ABC News, among others. The COPLINK project was selected as a finalist by the prestigious International Association of Chiefs of Police (IACP)/Motorola 2003 Weaver Seavey Award for Quality in Law Enforcement in 2003. COPLINK research has recently been expanded to border protection (BorderSafe), disease and bioagent surveillance (BioPortal), and terrorism informatics research (Dark Web), funded by NSF, CIA, and DHS. In collaboration with Customs and Border Protection (CBP), the BorderSafe project develops criminal network analysis and vehicle association mining research for border-crosser risk assessment. The BioPortal system supports interactive geospatial analysis and visualization, chief complaint classification, and phylogenetic analysis for public health and biodefense. In collaboration with selected international terrorism research centers and intelligence agencies, the Dark Web project has generated one of the largest databases in the world about extremist/terrorist-generated Internet contents (web sites, forums, and multimedia documents). Dark Web research supports link analysis, content analysis, web metrics analysis, multimedia analysis, sentiment analysis, and authorship analysis of international terrorism contents. The project was featured in the Discover magazine, Arizona Republic, and Toronto Star, among others. Dr. Chen is the founder of the Knowledge Computing Corporation, a university spin-off company and a market leader in law enforcement and intelligence information sharing and data mining. Dr. Chen has also received numerous awards in information technology and knowledge management education and research including: AT&T Foundation Award, SAP Award, the Andersen Consulting Professor of the Year Award, the University of Arizona Technology Innovation Award, and the National Chaio-Tung University Distinguished Alumnus Award.

Lawrence E. Brandt is Program Manager for Digital Government in the Information Integration and Informatics Cluster of the Division of Information and Intelligent Systems within the NSF Directorate for Computer and Information Sciences and Engineering. Larry joined NSF as a management intern in 1976 shortly after completing his undergraduate degree (San Diego State University, Anthropology). In 1983 he joined NSF's nascent Office of Advanced Scientific Computing as a manager for supercomputing centers where he was responsible for budget and oversight, for tri-annual reviews of the centers' performance, and for justification for continued funding exceeding $100M in aggregate. In 1993 Larry completed a Masters in Computer Science from the Whiting Engineering School at Johns Hopkins University. In 1994 Larry funded the software development at the University of Illinois that lead to the first popular Web browser (Mosaic) and Web server (Apache). In response to the interest of Federal agencies in these early Web technologies, Larry brought into being and chaired a group of 12 agencies (the Federal Web Consortium) to provide additional funding for Mosaic, giving the agencies entré and input to the further development directions of Mosaic. The Consortium developed sample policy for agencies and the Office of Management and Budget, and sponsored 3 Federal Webmasters Workshops with annual attendance over 500. Larry chaired the first of these workshops. In 1997, following the Mosaic experience, Larry convened a workshop to explore the opportunities for a broad program in computer science research and development in Federal information Services. Based on the advice of this workshop report, NSF created the Digital Government research program under Larry's direction; first awards were made in 1999. Over the last 7 years over 100 awards have been made.

Valerie Gregg is Assistant Director for Development at the University of Southern California/Information Sciences Institute's Digital Government Research Center. She is Secretary of the North American Chapter of the Digital Government Society. Valerie serves on a National Research Council-Computer Science and Telecommunications Board study panel assessing the Social Security Administration's E-Government Strategy. She is Co-PI on a National Science Foundation funded 4-year award entitled "Building and Sustaining an International Digital Government Research Community of Practice". Prior to working in academia, she had a 30-year career in public service at the Federal level. For eight years, she was Program Manager for the Digital Government Research in the Division of Information and Intelligent Systems at NSF. She has been on the conference committee for the annual International Conference for Digital Government Research (dgo) since its inception in 2000. Prior to NSF, Valerie worked for twenty-two years at the United States Census Bureau as a program manager in various aspects of the decennial census. She was a member of the Joint Ventures Project with the Census Bureau, and her work included involvement with the 'Tiger Mapping Service', a Coast-to-Coast digital map base that was designed and implemented to demonstrate cost efficient delivery of public data and research and development of the Census Bureau applications on the Internet. Valerie also served as Chair for the Interagency Task Force responsible for design, development and management of the award winning "one-stop" shopping for Federal statistics Internet site (http://www.fedstats.gov).

Prof. Dr. Roland Traunmüller is Professor Emeritus with the Institute of Informatics in Business and Adminstration at Linz University, Austria. Prof. Dr. Roland Traunmüller studied Chemistry and Physics at Vienna University and joined the Max-Planck-Institute in Mühlheim (Ruhr) working on his Ph.D. in calculating quantum-models of chemical reactions. In the year 1970 he went back to Austria becoming head of a DP-department within Public Administration. After three years he joined the Technical Faculty of Linz University (Senior Lecturer with Habilitation 1977, University Professor with tenure 1983). Teaching and research concern now Information Systems, Electronic Government and Knowledge Management. Earlier work concerned Systems Analysis and Design, Tele-cooperation and Semantic Modelling. There is a continuous thread of research work, projects and consulting in applications of information technology in Government for more than three decades. Prof. Traunmüller is the (co)author of 4 books and 140 contributions. His editorial work spans more than 20 books, two journals and one book-series. He has accepted several invitations for visiting professorships (Amsterdam, Bangkok, Bonn, Budapest, Chengdu, Graz, Heidelberg, Krems, Paris, Prag, Speyer, Zaragoza). Within IFIP (International Federation of Information Processing Societies) Prof. Traunmüller has served several functions and was awarded the IFIP Silver Core in 1996. So he was founder and chairman of the working group "Information Systems in Public

Administration" (IFIP 8.5) and served as deputy chairman of IFIP Technical Committee 8 "Information Systems". For two IFIP World Congresses he chaired the respective conference about e-Business so 1998 in Vienna/ Budapest and 2002 in Montreal. In Austria Prof. Traunmüller heads the Forum e-Government, in Germany he is member of the steering body e-Government within the German Computer Society (GI, Bonn). In addition he is involved in various consulting activities and boards on the national and international level (Ministries, EU, UNO, UNESCO). Regarding the main activity of Prof. Traunmüller in recent years, this is the building up of a network on e-Government research on the international level. As one pillar for this he serves on the Academics Board of the e-Forum Association. Further on he founded the EGOV conference series: This means an annual international five day conference that is scientific-oriented and solely targeted on e-Government. It has become a focal point of reuniting researchers: EGOV 2002 in Aix, EGOV 2003 in Prague; EGOV 2004 in Zaragoza, EGOV 2005 in Copenhagen, EGOV 2006 in Krakow. Besides he has initiated and co-chaired four conferences on the particular topic of Knowledge Management in e-Government (KMGOV). In recognition of founding the e-Government R&D Community he got 2006 the "Prometheus" – an Award dedicated by the North-American Society on Digital Government and by the European Society for e-Government. A recent activity is spreading e-Government to countries on the way of developing e-Government – an action that includes several visits and seminars: Brazil, Chile, China, Iran, Syria, Lithuania, Thailand. For this aim Prof. Traunmüller chaired the e-Government part of the First World Information Technology Forum of UNESCO and IFIP (WITFOR 2003 in Vilnius and WITFOR 2005 in Botswana.August).

Sharon Dawes is the Director of the Center for Technology in Government and Associate Professor of Public Administration and Policy at the University at Albany, State University of New York. Her main research interests are cross-boundary information sharing and collaboration, international digital government research, and government information strategy and management. Most of this work has been supported by the National Science Foundation, US Department of Justice, the Library of Congress, and State of New York. Her work is published in such journals as the *Journal of Public Policy and Mangement*, the *American Review of Public Administration*, *Public Performance and Management Review*, and *Government Information Quarterly*. From 1987 to 1993, Dr. Dawes was Executive Director of the

NYS Forum for Information Resource Management, a network of state government organizations and public officials interested in information management, policy, and technology. She also has a dozen years experience in the Executive Branch of New York State government. From 1977 to 1984, she was an Associate Commissioner with the NYS Department of Social Services, a position with responsibilities for the state's multi-billion dollar intergovernmental public assistance programs. A fellow of the National Academy of Public Administration, Dr. Dawes was honored with the Government Technology Conference *Rudoph Giuliani Leadership Award* in 2005 and was named a "Public Official of the Year" by *Governing Magazine* in 1997. An experienced teacher and author, she has presented on information policy and management in the public sector before numerous professional, academic, and government audiences in US an international venues. Dr. Dawes holds a Ph.D. in Public Administration from the Rockefeller College of Public Affairs & Policy University at Albany/State University of New York.

Dr. Eduard Hovy currently holds several positions: *Director of the Natural Language Group at ISI.* The NL Group, which currently contains about 40 people, consists of several related projects, conducting research in various aspects of natural language processing, including text summarization, machine translation, text parsing and generation, question answering, information retrieval, discourse and dialogue processing, and ontologies. *Deputy Director of the Intelligent Systems Division of ISI*, which performs Artificial Intelligence research. In this capacity Dr. Hovy helps administer the division, which currently contains about 150 people. Research Associate Professor of Computer Science at USC. Dr. Hovy regularly co-teaches a graduate course and advises Ph.D. and M.S. students. *Director of Research for the Digital Government Research Center (DGRC).* The DGRC is one of three NSF-supported centers in the US that perform research in various aspects of Digital Government. The DGRC focuses on Information and Communications Technology (ICT), housing several projects at any time. One of Dr. Hovy's principal research areas includes digital government, and currently includes a project to study the development of systems to *automatically find alignments or aliases across and within databases* (2003–06). The SiFT system uses mutual information technology to detect patterns in the distribution of data values. Current government partners in this NSF-funded project are the Environmental Protection Agency (EPA), who provide databases with air quality measurement data. (This work with

Mr. Andrew Philpot and Dr. Patrick Pantel from ISI). Another project is researching the development of *sophisticated text analysis of public commentary*, such as emails, letters, and reports (2004–07). Government staff who have to create regulations regularly face tens or hundreds of thousands of emails and other comments about proposed regulations, sent to them by the public. Funded by the NSF, the eRule project is a collaboration between Prof. Stuart Shulman (a political scientist at the University of Pittsburgh), Prof. Jamie Callan (a computer scientist at CMU), Prof. Steven Zavestoski (a sociologist at the University of San Francisco), and Prof. Hovy. Government partners providing data are the Environmental Protection Agency (EPA) and the Department of Transportation (DOT). Research at ISI focuses on technology to perform opinion detection and argument structure extraction. This research relates to the analysis of text for psychological profiling. The development of *text analysis of public communications with city government* via email began in 2005. The NSF funded a one-year project to collaborate with the QUALEG group, a European consortium of businesses, researchers, and three cities funded by the EU's eGovernment program to develop ICT for city-to-citizen interaction. Work at ISI focuses on the development of a system to classify emails and extract speech acts, opinions, and stakeholders, in German, and possibly French and Polish. Dr. Hovy's previous work included the development of *systems to access multiple heterogeneous databases* (1999–2003). Funded by the NSF, the EDC and AskCal systems provided access to over 50,000 table of information about gasoline, produced by various Federal Statistics agencies, including the Census Bureau, the Bureau of Labor Statistics, and the Energy Information Administration. The system includes a large ontology and a natural language question interpreter (this work in collaboration with Dr. Jose-Luis Ambite and Andrew Philpot at ISI). Partners in this project were the DGRC team at Columbia University, New York, headed by Dr. Judith Klavans. Dr. Hovy's Ph.D. work focused on the development of a text generation program PAULINE that took into account the pragmatic aspects of communication, since the absence of sensitivity toward hearer and context has been a serious shortcoming of generator programs written to date. In general, he is interested in all facets of communication, especially language, as situated in the wider contextintelligent behavior. Related areas include Artificial Intelligence (work on planning and learning), Linguistics (semantics and pragmatics), Psychology, Philosophy (ontologies), and Theory of Computation.

Professor Ann Macintosh is Professor of E-Governance and Director of the International Teledemocracy Centre at Napier University in Scotland. Since joining Napier University, she has established herself as an internationally recognised research leader in eDemocracy. She is actively involved with parliament, government, business and voluntary organisations concerned with the research and development of eDemocracy systems in the UK, Europe and the Commonwealth. She has been working with the Scottish Parliament since 1999, researching the design and management of an electronic petitioning system for the Parliament and has recently undertaking similar work the German Bundestag. She has provided consultancy to the Canadian and Australian governments on eDemocracy. In 2003 she conducted a research study on behalf of the OECD into e-consultation within policy-making. In 2005 she was an expert advisor on the evaluation of eDemocracy projects in UK public authorities funded through the UK Office of the Deputy Prime Minster. Ann has participated in major EU research projects on eDemocracy and is currently the Strategic Research co-ordinator for Demo-Net, a network of Excellence on eParticipation research. She has strong US research connections and was co-chair of the 2006 Digital Government Research Conference in California. She has published widely in this area.

Catherine A. Larson is the Associate Director of the Artificial Intelligence Lab at the University of Arizona (Director: Dr. Hsinchun Chen). Prior to her position at the Lab, she served as the University of Arizona's first data services librarian as well as the fine arts/humanities team leader. Catherine's background also includes several years as a preservation librarian and a bibliographer. Her areas of interest include digital government, digital libraries, and user evaluation. Catherine received the B.A. degree from the University of Illinois at Urbana-Champaign (UIUC) with Spanish and Anthropology majors, and the M.S. in library and information science, also from UIUC.

AUTHOR BIOGRAPHIES

Raj Acharya obtained his Ph.D from the Mayo Graduate School of Medicine in 1984. Since then, he has worked as a Research Scientist at Mayo Clinic and at GE (Thompson)-CGR in Paris, France. He has also been a Faculty Fellow at the Night Vision Laboratory in Fort Belvoir in Washington D.C. and has been a NASA-ASEE Faculty Fellow at the Johnson Space Center in Houston, Texas. He is currently the Department Head of Computer Science and Engineering at the Pennsylvania State University. His main research thrusts are in the general area of Bioinformatics and Biocomputing. He is the prime architect of the PCABC Cancer Bioinformatics Datawarehouse project. He works on using information fusion techniques for genomics and proteomics. He is also developing fractal models for the DNA replication and transcription sites. His research work has been featured among others in *Businessweek, Mathematics Calendar, The Scientist, Diagnostic Imaging Biomedical Engineering Newsletter, and Drug Design.*

Nabil R. Adam is a Professor in the Department of Management Science and Information Systems, the Founding Director of the Center for Information Management, Integration and Connectivity (CIMIC), Director of the Meadowlands Environmental Research Institute, and the Director of the Laboratory for Water Security at Rutgers University (Newark, NJ). Dr. Adam has published numerous technical papers in such journals as *IEEE Transactions on Software Engineering*, *IEEE Transactions on Knowledge and Data Engineering*, *Communications of the ACM*, and *Journal of Management Information Systems*, and has also co-authored/co-edited several books. Dr. Adam's research work has been supported by various agencies including the National Science Foundation (NSF), the National Security Agency (NSA), NOAA, US Environmental Protection Agency, the Defense Logistics Agency (DLA), the NJ Meadowlands Commission, and NASA.

Nick Adams is a Research Fellow and has been at the International Teledemocracy Centre, Napier University, for over 4 years. Prior to this he completed a PhD in Artificial Intelligence at Edinburgh University in 2001. Since 2004 he's been running the Centre's e-Petitioner projects; re-writing the software from an experimental pilot to a full-featured commercial application; has subsequently deployed e-Petitioner with a number of English local authorities and the German

Bundestag; and now manages the e-Petitioner software for the Scottish Parliament and all of these other clients. Additionally he retains active research interests in the e-Government and e-Democracy spheres.

Dr. Peggy Agouris is Professor of Remote Sensing at George Mason University and the Associate Director of GMU's Center for Earth Observing and Space Research. Before joining GMU in January 2007, Dr. Agouris was Associate Professor of Spatial Information Engineering at the University of Maine and a senior researcher with the National Center for Geographic Information and Analysis (NCGIA). She has received her Dipl. Eng. from the National Technical University of Athens (Greece), her M.S. and Ph.D. degrees from the The Ohio State University (in 1988 and 1992 respectively). Upon graduation from The Ohio State University she joined the Swiss Federal Institute of Technology (ETH) in Zurich, Switzerland as Senior Scientific Associate (until 1995), and then joined the University of Maine and the Department of Spatial Information Science and Engineering as Assistant Professor in the fall of 1995. At UMaine, Dr. Agouris headed the Digital Image Processing and Analysis Laboratory. Her expertise and current research activities are focused in the area of digital image processing and analysis for extraction, intelligent retrieval, and management of spatiotemporal information, geo-spatial information systems, digital photogrammetry, and remote sensing. She has authored or co-authored more than 100 articles in journals, books and conference proceedings, and has co-edited three books in her field of expertise.

Dr. Vijay Atluri is a Professor of Computer Information Systems and research director for the CIMIC Center at Rutgers University. Her research interests include Information Systems Security, Databases, Workflow Management and Multimedia. She serves as a member of the Steering Committee for ACMSIG on Security Audit and Control and for the ACM Symposium on Access Control Models and Architectures. She was a recipient of the NSF CAREER Award in 1996, and the Rutgers University Research Award for untenured faculty for outstanding research contributions in 1999.

Dr. S. Ann Becker is a research professor of computer science and management information systems and the director of the National Center for Small Business Information at Florida Institute of Technology. She has a Master of Business Administration from St. Cloud State University, and a Master of Science and Ph.D. in Information Systems from University of Maryland, College Park. Dr. Becker has published over 100 articles in Web usability and accessibility, gerotechnology, database management, and software engineering. Dr. Becker has received research funding from Texas Instruments, IBM, the National Science Foundation, the Jet Propulsion Laboratory, the Alzheimer's Association, and the Agency for Healthcare Research and Quality. Dr. Becker is an associate editor for the *Journal of Database Management, Journal of Electronic Commerce in Organizations,* and *International Journal of Cases on Electronic Commerce.* She is the recipient of the 2005 Joan Bixby Women's History Award at Florida Institute of Technology and 2002-2004 Northern Arizona University Mark Layton Award for Research Excellence.

Benjamin B. Bederson is an Associate Professor of Computer Science and the Human-Computer Interaction Lab at the Institute for Advanced Computer Studies at the University of Maryland, College Park. His work is on mobile device interfaces, information visualization, interaction strategies, digital libraries, and accessibility issues including voting system usability. He completed his Ph.D. in 1992 and his M.S. in 1989 at New York University in the Courant Institute of Mathematical Sciences in Computer Science. He graduated with a B.S. from Rensselaer Polytechnic Institute in 1986. Dr. Bederson worked as a research scientist at Bellcore in the Computer Graphics and Interactive Media research group, and as a visitor at the New York University Media Research Laboratory in 1993 and 1994. From 1994-1997, he was an Assistant Professor of Computer Science at the University of New Mexico.

Alexander Boer is a senior researcher and computer scientist who has been working for 8 years at the Leibniz Center for Law of the University of Amsterdam. This research institute specializes in computational legal theory and the development of innovative concepts for the application of IT in the field of Law. He has been involved in a number of international research projects involving ontologies, automated legal reasoning, and e-government like CLIME, KDE, eCourt, E-Power, and ESTRELLA.

Christof Bornhövd, Ph.D., is a senior research scientist at the SAP Research Center in Palo Alto focusing on data management, semantics and event-based computing for SAP's next-generation Enterprise Business Applications Architecture. Prior to joining SAP Labs, he worked from 2002 to 2004 as a Research Staff Member at the IBM Almaden Research Center on database caching and replication for e-business applications and the integration of DB2 and WebSphere. From 2000 to 2002 he worked at HP Labs on CRM and Data Warehousing projects. During his time at Darmstadt University of Technology, where he received a Ph.D. in computer science, he was working on semantic data integration and metadata management. His expertise and research interests are in the areas of databases and distributed systems, Web Services technology, and RFID and sensor network technology. Dr. Bornhövd has published in highly recognized conferences and journals like VLDB, SIGMOD, ICDE and JEIM and has filed multiple patent applications in the areas of RFID and sensor technology and database caching.

Alan Borning is Professor in the Department of Computer Science & Engineering at the University of Washington, Adjunct Professor in the Information School, and Co-Director of the Center for Urban Simulation and Policy Analysis. His current research interests are in human-computer interaction and designing for human values, particularly as applied to land use, transportation, and environmental modeling. He has also done work in constraint-based languages and systems, other aspects of human-computer interaction, and in object-oriented programming. He received a Ph.D. from Stanford University in 1979, and is a Fellow of the Association for Computing Machinery.

J. A. Breuker studied cognitive psychology at the University of Amsterdam. He obtained his PhD in 1981 at the same University on a dissertation titled: "Availability of Knowledge". Major areas of research are: experimental cognitive psychology, text understanding, intelligent teaching systems, AI, knowledge acquisition, man-machine interaction. His current work is particularly in: methodology for building knowledge-based systems, intelligent help and tutoring systems, and reasoning in regulation domains (law). Most of the research is performed in collaboration with academic institutes and industries in Europe, in particular within the framework of Esprit. Prof. Breuker holds a chair in Computer Science and Law he was awarded the ECAI-1984 price for expert systems research.

Brian Burke is a senior program associate with the Center for Technology in Government (CTG) at the University at Albany, State University of New York. He manages projects at Center involving government and private sector partners. Prior to CTG, Brian worked for AT&T Government Solutions in the Office of the Secretary of Defense's Program Analysis and Evaluation. Before that, he served as an officer in the United States Air Force. He received the M.A. in International Relations from Creighton University in 2003, and prior to that, the B.A. in History and Political Science from Rutgers College. His recent CTG project involvement has included: Public ROI – Advancing Return on Investment Analysis for Government IT (http://www.ctg.albany.edu/projects/proi), Library of Congress Collaboration for Preservation of State Government Digital Information (http://www.ctg.albany.edu/projects/lc), and Modeling Interorganizational Information Integration (http://www.ctg.albany.edu/projects/miii).

Guoray Cai (Ph.D. University of Pittsburgh, 1999) is an Associate Professor and director of the Spatial Information and Intelligence Laboratory in the College of Information Sciences and Technology at Pennsylvania State University. His research interests include geographical information science, human-computer interactions, and visually-mediated group work. He is a member of ACM, IEEE, and ASPRS.

Chen Chen received his BSc degree from the Department of Computer Science and Technology of Tsinghua University in 2004. Now He is a MSc candidate student Web and Software Technology R&D Center of Research Institute of Information Technology, Tsinghua University. His research interests include Database, Data Mining, Business Intelligence, and so on.

Dr. Soon Ae Chun is an assistant professor of Information Systems at the City University of New York, College of Staten Island. She has received Ph.D. and MBA degrees from Rutgers University, MS and MA degrees from SUNY Buffalo and a BA from Busan National University, Korea. Her areas of expertise are workflow management, database systems, and information security. Her current research interests include context-aware inter-organizational Web

Service composition, security/privacy policy extraction and modeling, and semantic annotation of Deep Web Services. Her past research activities include projects funded by NSF, NOAA and New Jersey Meadowland Commission, focusing on regulatory ontology-based multi-organizational business and environmental service integration and customization, geospatial-temporal authorization models and conflict-of-interest issues in decentralized workflow execution. Her research has been published in journals, and in many conference proceedings. Her professional activities include serving as editorial board member and review board member of journals, and organizational member and program committee member for many conferences.

Stephen Coleman is Professor of Political Communication at the Institute of Communications Studies, University of Leeds. He has written extensively about e-governance and e-democracy. Before taking his position at Leeds, Stephen Coleman was Cisco Professor in e-Democracy at the Oxford Internet Institute and Senior Research Fellow at Jesus College, Oxford. In recent years he has served as specialist adviser to the House of Commons Information Select Committee inquiry on ICT and public participation in Parliament, policy adviser to the Cabinet Office, a member of the Royal Society committee on public engagement in science, a member of the Puttnam Commission on parliamentary communication with the public and chair of the Electoral Reform Society's Independent Commission on Alternative Voting Methods.

Frederick G. Conrad is Research Associate Professor at the Institute for Social Research at the University of Michigan. His research interests lie at the intersection of human-computer interaction and social measurement including surveys and voting. Conrad's training is in cognitive psychology and much of his work involves applying ideas and methods from cognitive psychology to improving measurement processes. He serves on the Editorial Board of Public Opinion Quarterly and is an Associate Editor of the Journal of Official Statistics.

James F. Cooper is a General Manager with the Port Authority of New York and New Jersey in the Public Safety Department, Office of Emergency Management. Mr. Cooper is responsible for the oversight of the Port Authority of NY & NJ Office of Emergency Management technologies and systems integration. Mr. Cooper has over twenty-five years of operational experience in security, sensors and information systems. Current efforts include the development of a enterprise wide collaborative environment to provide real-time information and sensor fusion to support real-time decision-making during events. This program connects the legacy sensors and critical incident management systems for the airports, ports, tunnels, bridges and rail system to provide for the sharing of real-time geospatial ands sensor information between first responders, command staff and decision makers. Mr. Cooper is the lead architect for the Regional Information Joint Awareness Network (RIJAN). RIJAN expands the Port Authority of NY & NJ information-sharing environment to both regional and Federal entities in the Department of Homeland Security and Department of Defense.

Dr. Arie Croitoru received his B.Sc. from the Technion – Israel Institute of Technology, Department of Transportation and Geo-Information Engineering in 1992. Between 1992 and 1999 he was involved research and development, mainly in photogrammetry, image processing, and 3D spatial data analysis. He received his M.Sc. (1997) and Ph.D. (2002) in Geodetic Engineering, also from the Technion. Between 2002 and 2003 Dr. Croitoru has been a research fellow at the Geospatial Information and Communication Technology (GeoICT) laboratory at York University (Canada). Currently, he is Assistant Professor at the University of Alberta (Canada). His main research interests are in digital image processing and analysis, automated geospatial feature extraction, photogrammetry, and spatio-temporal data analysis.

Rowena Cullen is Associate Professor in the School of Information Management at Victoria University of Wellington, and teaches in the Master of Information Management and Master of Library and Information Studies programmes. She has a PhD from Victoria University of Wellington, and an MLitt from the University Edinburgh, along with MAs from Canterbury and Otago. Her current research work focuses on e-government, health informatics, and the evaluation of information services. She is co-editor and co-author of the recently published *Comparative Perspectives on E-Government: Serving Today and*

Building for Tomorrow (Scarecrow Press, 2006) and author of *Health Information on the Internet* (Greenwood Press, 2006), as well as a number of other articles on e-government. She is a senior editor of the *Journal of E-Government*, and on the editorial boards of *Performance Measurement and Metrics, Health Information and Libraries Journal, Journal of Academic Librarianship, Education for Information,* and *LibRes.* She has been a keynote speaker at several international conferences, and has published over 100 articles, book chapters and conference papers.

Dr. Lois Delcambre is a Professor of Computer Science at Portland State University (PSU). She works in the database field of computer science with a particular interest in database data models as well as other models for structured information including thesaurus models, knowledge representation models, semi-structured models such as XML and RDF, and ontology models. Dr. Delcambre received her PhD in Computer Science from the University of Louisiana, Lafayette (formerly the University of Southwestern Louisiana) in 1982, her MS in Mathematics from Clemson University in 1974, and her BS in Mathematics with a minor in Computer Science from the University of Louisiana, Lafayette in 1972. From 1974 to 1979, she was a Systems Design and Software Development Manger at the Division of Information Systems Development at Clemson University.

Walter Díaz is an Associate Professor of Political Science at the University of Puerto Rico-Mayagüez. He obtained his Ph.D. from the University of Michigan in 1998. His current research interests include political participation, the social implications of technological innovation and disaster research.

Fabio Fioravanti received his Laurea degree in computer science from the University of L'Aquila (Italy) in 1997. In 2001, he has been a visiting research scientist at the University of Southampton (UK). In 2002 he earned his Research Doctorate (PhD) degree in computer science at the University of Rome – La Sapienza (Italy), defending a thesis about transformation of constraint logic programs for software specialization and verification. From 2005 he is an assistant professor at the Department of Sciences – University "G. d'Annunzio" of Chieti – Pescara (Italy). His research interests include security and certification of network services provision in business and government inter-organizational contexts, constraints in security, verification of concurrent systems and bioinformatics.

Ruth D. Förster is a PhD student in the Institute for Spatial and Landscape Planning at the Swiss Federal Institute of Technology in Zurich (ETH Zurich), and currently staying as research scholar at the Center for Urban Simulation and Policy Analysis at the University of Washington. Her research topic is the application of quantitative, integrative computer models for decision making in regional planning, particularly regarding how the interaction between model developers and potential users affects the application. She received her diploma degree in mechanical engineering from RWTH Aachen, Germany 1990 and her postgraduate qualification in didactics from ETH Zurich 1999.

José Fortes received his BS degree in Electrical Engineering from the Universidade de Angola in 1978, his MS degree in Electrical Engineering from the Colorado State University, Fort Collins in 1981 and his PhD degree in Electrical Engineering from the University of Southern California, Los Angeles in 1984. From 1984 to 2001 he was in the faculty of the School of Electrical Engineering of Purdue University at West Lafayette, Indiana. In 2001, he joined both the Department of Electrical and Computer Engineering and the Department of Computer and Information Science and Engineering of the University of Florida as Professor and BellSouth Eminent Scholar. His research interests are in the areas of distributed computing and information processing, digital government and computer architecture. José Fortes is a Fellow of the Institute of Electrical and Electronics Engineers (IEEE) professional society. He was a Distinguished Visitor of the IEEE Computer Society from 1991 to 1995.

Sven Fuhrmann (Ph.D. University of Muenster, 2002) is an Assistant Professor at Texas State University – San Marcos and directs the Geospatial Cognition Laboratory. Fuhrmann has over 15 years of experience in GIScience and Geovisualization, bridging cutting-edge research developments in the United States and Europe. He is an established member in national and international commissions that are concerned with developing geospatial research agendas and novel research strategies. His research interests include GIScience, 3D Geovisualization and Interaction, Human-Centered Design, Emergency Management, Spatial Cognition and Behavior.

Helene Gieber studies Business Administration at the Vienna University of Economics and Business Administration. After being a project assistant at the Institute of Informatics in Business and Government at the Johannes Kepler University Linz, her working focus turned from themes of eGovernment in the Leonardo da Vinci project "eEmployment" to practical experiences in the field of Corporate Identity and Personnel Management in cooperation with the Institute for Applied Knowledge Processing (University Linz). Her research interests include eGovernment, Business Processes, Organizational Learning, and Personnel Management.

J. Ramon Gil-Garcia is a Post-Doctoral Fellow at the Center for Technology in Government and is also on the faculty of the Rockefeller College of Public Affairs and Policy at the University at Albany, State University of New York. At SUNY, he has been an Adjunct Professor at the Department of Management Science and Information Systems of the School of Business and at the School of Information Science and Policy. Before coming to the United States, Dr. Gil-Garcia was Assistant Professor in the Division of Public Administration at the Center for Research and Teaching in Economics (CIDE) in Mexico City. He has lectured on topics such as Public Management, Policy Analysis, Organization Theory, Database Applications, Statistics, Web Development, Quantitative Analysis and Modeling, Research Methods, Public Administration Theory, and Local Government Management. Dr. Gil-Garcia is the author or co-author of articles in academic journals including *The International Public Management Journal*, *Government Information Quarterly*, *European Journal of Information Systems*, *Journal of Government Information*, *Public Finance and Management*, and *Politics Administration and Change*. His research interests include collaborative electronic government, inter-organizational information integration, adoption and implementation of emergent technologies, information technologies in the budgeting process, digital divide policies, education policy, new public management, public policy evaluation, and multi-method research approaches. Dr. Gil-Garcia has a Bachelors Degree in Political Science and Public Administration, a Masters in Public Administration and Policy, and a Ph.D. in Public Administration and Policy. He is also a former Fulbright Scholar.

Amy K. Glasmeier is the E. Willard Miller Professor Economic Geography and the John Whisman Scholar of the Appalachian Regional Commission. She is a professor of geography and regional planning at The Pennsylvania State University. Published fall 2005 by Routledge Press, *An Atlas of Poverty in America: One Nation, Pulling Apart 1960-2003* examines the experience of people and places in poverty since the 1960s, looks across the last four decades at poverty in America and recounts the history of poverty policy since the 1940s. Glasmeier has worked all over the world, including Japan, Hong Kong, Latin America, and Europe. She has worked with the OECD, ERVET Emilia Romagna Regional Planning Agency. She currently is engaged in a retrospective examination of poverty and poverty policy history in the US. The work is leading to new perspectives on the nature and extent of persistent poverty in America and is exploring the theoretical and ideological basis for federal poverty policy since the 1960s.

Åke Grönlund is (full) Professor of Informatics at Örebro University, Örebro (Sweden). Also affiliated to dept of Informatics at Umeå University. Åke's research currently has a strong focus on Electronic Government as part of the more general topic of coordination of organizations and networks using ICT, including electronic service delivery, organizational redesign, electronic information infrastructures, and ICT-enabled coordination of work. Åke is chair of the two large eGovernment researcher communities, one within the US-based Association of Information Systems (sigegov.org) and EGOV Society Europe (www.egov-society.org/). Åke is also Program Chair of the International EGOV conference, consultant to the World Bank e-Government group, member of the Steering Committee of the EU eGovernment "Network of Excellence" DemoNet, scientific leader of the Swedish research programme DemocrIT on ICT in democratic processes, and father of three kids.

Michael J. Hanmer is assistant professor in the Department of Government and Politics at the University of Maryland at College Park. After receiving his Ph.D. in Political Science from the University of Michigan, in 2004, Dr. Hanmer began a position as an assistant professor in the Department of Government at Georgetown University. His research interests are in political participation, electoral reform, public opinion, and political methodology. He has published in the areas of electoral reform and voter turnout.

Wei He received his BSc, MSc, and PhD from Northwestern Polytechnical University in 1999, 2001, and 2004 respectively. Now he is postdoctor in Web and Software Technology R&D Center, RIIT Tsinghua University. His research interests include data mining, bayesian network learning, and data modeling for e-Government.

Paul S. Herrnson is founding director of the Center for American Politics and Citizenship and a professor in the Department of Government and Politics at the University of Maryland. Has published numerous books, including "Congressional Elections: Campaigning at Home and in Washington," "The Financiers of Congressional Elections," and "War Stories from Capitol Hill." He has written more than 100 journal articles and book chapters and is the editor of the Real Politics in America book series with Prentice Hall. The principal investigator of the National Science Foundation and the Carnegie Corporation funded Project to Study Voting Technology and Ballot Design, Herrnson has also directed a U.S. Election Assistance Commission project to recruit, train, and retain election judges, and the Campaign Assessment and Candidate Outreach Project, funded by the Pew Charitable Trusts. His current interests include Congress, political parties and elections, money and politics, and voting technology and ballot design. Dr. Herrnson has served as Vice President of the Southern Political Science Association and an American Political Science Association Congressional Fellow. He has received several teaching awards, including a Distinguished-Scholar Teacher Award from the University of Maryland. He has advised the U.S. Congress, the Maryland General Assembly, the Federal Election Commission, and other governments and commissions on matters pertaining to campaign finance, political parties, and election reform.

Fang-Ming Hsu is an Associate Professor and Chairman of Department of Information Management at the National Dong Hwa University, Taiwan. He is also a member of the committee of evaluation for Gold Archive Award in Taiwan Government. His areas of interest include knowledge management and data mining. He received his B.S. and M.S. degrees in Computer Science and Ph.D. degree in Management Science from National Chiao Tung University. Hsu has published articles covering project management and knowledge sharing in publications such as International Journal of

Technology Management and Journal of Global Business Management. He received a National Science Council (NSC) Research Award in 1999.

Paul J. Hu is an Associate Professor and David Eccles Faculty Fellow at the David Eccles School of Business, the University of Utah. He has a Ph.D. in Management Information Systems from the University of Arizona. His current research interests include digital government, healthcare information systems and management, technology implementation management, electronic commerce, human-computer interaction, and knowledge management. Hu has published papers in *Journal of Management Information Systems*; *Decision Sciences*; *Communications of the ACM*; *IEEE Transactions on Systems, Man and Cybernetics*; *IEEE Transactions on Information Technology in Biomedicine*; *IEEE Transactions on Engineering Management*; *IEEE Intelligent Systems*; *IEEE Software*; *Journal of the American Society for Information Science and Technology*; *Decision Support Systems*; *Social Science Computer Review*; *European Journal of Information Systems*; *Information and Management*, *Journal of Electronic Commerce Research*; and *Journal of Telemedicine and Telecare*.

Vandana P. Janeja is currently in the last semester of her Ph.D. work in Management with Information Technology at Rutgers University. She is a research associate at the Center for Information Management, Integration and Connectivity (CIMIC), Rutgers University. In general, her research interests include Knowledge Discovery and Data Mining. Primarily her work has focused on anomaly detection in heterogeneous datasets.

Dr. Jim Johnston is currently the Clerk to the Public Petitions Committee in the Scottish Parliament having previously been the Clerk to the Communities Committee and Clerk to the Equal Opportunities Committee. He is also Chair of the parliamentary staff e-democracy working group. He has worked in the Scottish Parliament since March 1999. Previously he completed his doctorate on post-war British politics at the University of Birmingham. His published work includes a joint authored book, *Post-war British Politics in Perspective*.

Alan F. Karr is Director of the National Institute of Statistical Sciences (NISS), a position he has held since 2000. He is also Professor of Statistics & Operations Research and Biostatistics at the University of North Carolina at Chapel Hill (since 1993), as well as Associate Director of the Statistical and Applied Mathematical Sciences Institute (SAMSI). Before coming to North Carolina, he was Professor of Mathematical Sciences and Associate Dean of the School of Engineering at Johns Hopkins, where he also chaired both the mathematical sciences and computer science departments. His research activities are cross-disciplinary collaborations involving statistics and such other fields as data confidentiality, data integration, data quality, software engineering, information technology, education statistics, transportation, materials science and E-commerce. He is the author of 3 books and more than 100 scientific papers. Karr is a Fellow of the American Statistical Association and the Institute of Mathematical Statistics, a member of the Board of Governors of the Interface Foundation of North America, an elected member of the International Statistical Institute, and served as a member of the Army Science Board from 1990 to 1996.

Siddharth Kaza is a doctoral student and research associate of the Artificial Intelligence Lab in the Department of Management Information Systems at the University of Arizona. He earned his M.S. in Computer Science from Central Michigan University and his B.Sc. in Mathematical Sciences from University of Delhi. His research interests include data mining, information integration and social network analysis.

Dr. Christine Leitner is Head of the Center for European Public Administration at the Danube University Krems, Austria, where she is responsible for research programmes on public administration and ICT. She hosts expert meetings and conducts lectures at European and international conferences in the field. She is the course director of an executive MPA programme (with a focus on eGovernment and change management). From 1997 she was Senior Lecturer at the European Institute of Pubic Administration (NL) where she et up the eGovernment team and headed the eEurope Awards Project Management Secretariat from 2002-2006. She was a member of the EPAN eGovernment working group from 2002 until 2006, and has been invited as expert in EU programmes and the Speyer Quality Award for eGovernment. She is a Visiting Lecturer at the European Public Affairs Programme,

University of Maastricht and the Programme on Public Administration and Citizenship, University of Roma III. She joined the Ministry of Economic Affairs in Vienna in 1992, where she headed the EU co-ordination unit. In 1995, she was seconded to the European Commission where she worked on ICT standardisation policies. She is author of various publications in the field of eGovernment.

Alan M. MacEachren (Ph.D. University of Kansas, 1979) is 2004-2007 E. Willard and Ruby S. Miller Professor of Geography and Director of the GeoVISTA Center (www.GeoVISTA.psu.edu) at Pennsylvania State University. He also directs the new North-East Regional Visualization & Analytics Center. MacEachren's research foci include: geovisualization, geocollaboration, interfaces to geospatial information technologies, human spatial cognition as it relates to use of those technologies, human-centered systems, and user-centered design. He served as chair of the International Cartographic Association Commission on Visualization and Virtual Environments (1999-2005) and was named honorary fellow of that organization in 2005. He has been a member of the National Research Council Computer Science and Telecommunications Board Committee on the Intersections Between Geospatial Information and Information Technology (2001-2002) and of the National Visualization and Analytics Center R&D Agenda panel (2004-2005). MacEachren is author of *How Maps Work: Representation, Visualization and Design*, Guilford Press, 1995 and *Some Truth with Maps*, Association of American Geographers, 1994 and is co-editor of several additional books (including *Exploring Geovisualization*, Elsevier, 2005) and journal special issues (including a theme issue of *IEEE Computer Graphics and Applications* on Geovisualization, July/Aug, 2006 and a forthcoming special issue of the *International Journal of Geographical Information Science* on Visual analytics & spatial decision support).

Dr. David Maier is Maseeh Professor of Emerging Technologies at Portland State University. He is the author of books on relational databases, logic programming and object-oriented databases, as well as papers in database theory, object-oriented technology and scientific databases. He received the Presidential Young Investigator Award from the National Science Foundation in 1984 and was awarded the 1997 SIGMOD Innovations Award for his contributions in objects and databases. He is also an ACM Fellow. He holds a B.A. in Mathematics and Computer Science from the University of Oregon (Honors College, 1974) and a Ph.D. in Electrical Engineering and Computer Science from Princeton University (1978).

Xiaoning Mao Xiaoling Mao is a Ph.D. candidate in the Antai College of Economics and Management at Shanghai Jiaotong University. He received his BS and MS from Shanghai Jiaotong University. He also serves as a network planning engineer in China Telecom. His current research interests include citizen demand- and service-driven E-government theory and practice. Contact him at philipmao@online.sh.cn.

Andréa Matsunaga received her BS degree in Electrical Engineering from the Polytechnic School of the University of São Paulo (Brazil), in 1998, her MS degree in Electrical Engineering from the Electronic Systems Department (PSI) of the Polytechnic School of the University of São Paulo (Brazil), in 2001; and is currently a graduate student at the Department of Electrical and Computer Engineering of the University of Florida, working with Dr. Fortes. Her research interests are in the areas of distributed computing, information management, computer architecture and distributed shared-memory systems.

Wayne L. Myers is professor of forest biometrics and director of the Office for Remote Sensing and Spatial Information Resources at Penn State University. He holds Bachelor of Science, Master of Forestry and Ph.D. degrees from the University of Michigan. Research specialties are remote sensing, geographic information systems, multivariate analysis and landscape ecology. He has an extensive international experience in quantitative analysis of natural resources, particularly in Asia.

Enrico Nardelli is full professor of Computer Science at University of Roma "Tor Vergata". His research focuses on algorithms and data structures, data models, and tools and environments for inter-organizational information systems. He has been a consultant to the italian Public Administration on security and certification issues in e-Government services, through the NESTOR Laboratory of University of Roma "Tor Vergata". He has authored more than 100 refereed papers in the fields of interest, published in the most reputed international scientific journals and conference proceedings. He is also President of the Italian Association of University Professors in Computer Science.

Dr. Marianne Lykke Nielsen is Associate Professor at the Royal School of Library and Information Science, Denmark. She also consults for several Danish companies and organizations concerning design and evaluation of KOS. Her principal teaching areas are metadata, indexing, and knowledge organization systems (KOS). And her present research activities concentrate on design, construction methodologies, and use of thesauri and taxonomies in digital libraries and other retrieval systems. She received her PhD from Åbo Akademi University, Department of Information Studies, Finland in 2002. She received) a MS in Library and Information Science in 1992 and a first degree in Librarianship in 1983 from the Royal School of Library and Information Science, Denmark. From 1983 and 1994 she worked as information specialist in private and national organizations: FAO (Chile), CPEIP (Chile), APV Pasilac (Denmark), and Aalborg Business College (Denmark), with responsibilities in the area of information retrieval and design of information retrieval systems and domain-specific, in-house thesauri.

Richard G. Niemi is Don Alonzo Watson Professor of Political Science at the University of Rochester, where has taught for 40 years. He has served as Department Chair, Associate Dean for Graduate Studies, and Interim Dean. He earned his Ph.D. from the University of Michigan in 1967. He is co-author or co-editor of *Institutional Change in American Politics: The Case of Term Limits* (University of Michigan Press, forthcoming), *Vital Statistics on American Politics, 2005-2006* (CQ Press, 2005), and other books. He has published more than 100 articles on a variety of subjects, including voting, U.S. ballots, and public opinion.

Mario Núñez is a Professor of Psychology and Associate Dean of Assessment and Learning Technologies at the University of Puerto Rico-Mayagüez. He obtained his Ph.D. from Harvard University in 1997. His current research interests include distance learning, implications of internet technologies for learning and teaching effectiveness.

Gertraud Orthofer studied from 2000 to 2004 Computer Science at the Johannes Kepler University of Linz, Austria. Since October 2004 she is a research assistant at the Institute of Informatics in Business and Government (University Linz). She is a PhD student and her research interests are in the field of eGovernment, Knowledge Management, Business Processes, Portal Development, and Semantic Modelling.

John Paczkowski is the Director of the Office of Emergency Management (OEM), where he is responsible for oversight of all enterprise-wide security and emergency readiness programs for the Authority's aviation, transit, tunnel and bridge, and maritime cargo facilities. He holds a BS in Industrial Engineering and MS in Management Engineering from the New Jersey Institute of Technology, along with an MA in Organizational Psychology from Columbia University. He is currently attending the Naval Postgraduate School pursuing advanced studies in Homeland Defense and Security. A graduate of the Marine Corps Command and Staff College, his military awards include the Legion of Merit Medal and three Naval Commendation Medals. John has supervised comprehensive security assessments of all PA facilities, implemented new security and emergency management practices, prepared WMD consequence management plans for the Authority's aviation, port, transit and highway businesses, and has spearheaded several national Homeland Security incubation projects with various DHS agencies. These include a comprehensive Risk and Needs Assessment program, a WMD Countermeasures Test Bed program, a Regional Radiological Detection and Interdiction pilot project, and a Regional Information Sharing and Collaboration effort. In September of 2005 he led a Port Authority emergency management team that assisted the City of New Orleans in reestablishing incident command. In 2005, John retired as a Colonel with 33 years of active and reserve time in the US Marine Corps. He was the initiator for the Marine Corps Emergency Preparedness Liaison Program, part of a joint-service effort to coordinate DoD support to civil authorities during national emergencies. His last assignment was with the National Guard Bureau as Chief of the Civil Support Division where his staff coordinated employment of National Guard forces during several natural disasters and Homeland Security contingencies.

Aabhas V. Paliwal is currently in the last semester of his Ph.D. work in Management with Information Technology at Rutgers University. He is a research associate at the Center for Information Management, Integration and Connectivity (CIMIC), Rutgers University. In general, his research interests include Business Services, E-commerce, Service Oriented Architecture and Semantic Web. Primarily his work has focused on semantic based discovery and orchestration of web services.

Theresa A. Pardo is Deputy Director of the Center for Technology in Government located at the University at Albany, State University of New York. Dr. Pardo is a member of the faculty of Public Administration and Policy as well as Informatics at the University. She has written articles, research reports, book chapters and case studies focusing on IT innovation in the public sector, inter-organizational information integration, trust and knowledge sharing, preservation of government digital records, multi-method research and XML as a content management technology. Dr. Pardo is one of the developers of the highly ranked Government Information Strategy and Management curriculum at Albany. This program focuses on the policy, management and technology dimensions of information and technology use in the design and delivery of government programs. She is also an investigator in a number of ongoing funded research projects including two U.S. National Science Foundation funded projects – the first, on behalf of the U.S. Library of Congress, is focused on building capability for the preservation of government information in digital form, and the second is focused on the development of models of the social and technical processes of interorganizational information integration. Her most recent grant funded effort is in serving as a co-chair for an international digital government working group focused on transnational and multi-jurisdictional information integration. Dr. Pardo is conference co-chair for the 2007 International Digital Government Research Conference and mini-track co-chair for Emerging Topics in Electronic Government for the 2007 Hawaiian International Conference on System Sciences. Dr. Pardo holds a Ph.D. in Information Science from the Rockefeller College of Public Affairs and Policy at the University at Albany, State University of New York.

G.P. Patil. For everyone, Professor Patil is GP. He is Distinguished Professor of Mathematical and Environmental Statistics in the Department of Statistics at the Pennsylvania State University, and is a former Visiting Professor of Biostatistics at Harvard University in the Harvard School of Public Health. He has a Ph.D. in Mathematics, D.Sc. in Statistics, one Honorary Degree in Biological Sciences, and another in Letters. GP is a Fellow of American Statistical Association, Fellow of American Association of Advancement of Science, Fellow of Institute of Mathematical Statistics, Elected Member of the International Statistical Institute, Founder Fellow of the National Institute of Ecology and the Society for Medical Statistics in India. GP has been a founder of Statistical Ecology Section of International Association for Ecology and Ecological Society of America, a founder of Statistics and Environment Section of American Statistical Association, and a founder of the International Society for Risk Analysis. He is founding editor-in-chief of the international journal, *Environmental and Ecological Statistics* and founding director of the Penn State Center for Statistical Ecology and Environmental Statistics. He has published thirty volumes and three hundred research papers. GP has received several distinguished awards which include: Distinguished Statistical Ecologist Award of the International Association for Ecology, Distinguished Achievement Medal for Statistics and the Environment of the American Statistical Association, Distinguished Twentieth Century Service Award for Statistical Ecology and Environmental Statistics of the Ninth Lukacs Symsosium, Best Paper Award of the American Fisheries Society, and lately, the Best Paper Award of the American Water Resources Association, among others. Currently, GP is principal investigator of a multi-year NSF grant for surveillance geoinformatics for hotspot detection and prioritization across geographic regions and networks for digital government in the 21st Century. The project has a dual disciplinary and cross-disciplinary thrust. You are invited.

Dr. Shashi Phoha's research interests are in computational sciences that enable dependable distributed automation of multiple interacting devices over ad hoc and long haul networks. She has held senior technical and management positions in academia, government, and industry. During 2004 and 2005, she was the Director of a premier national laboratory, the Information Technology Laboratory (ITL) of the National Institute of Standards and Technology (NIST), which conducts research in Mathematical and Computational Sciences, Computer Security, Software, Advanced Networking, Information Access, and Statistical Engineering. Since 1991, she has been a Professor of Electrical and Computer Engineering at the Pennsylvania State University and the Director of the Division of Information Sciences and Technology at its Applied Research Laboratory. Prior to that, she was the Director of C4I and Systems Analysis Division of the Computer Sciences Corporation where she led the development of the Global Transportation Network for DoD. She worked in Command, Control, Communications and Intelligence Systems at ITT and at the MITRE Corporation. She was awarded the 2004 Technical Achievement Award by the IEEE Computer Society. She has authored over 200 research papers, three books, and has two patents in her name. She has held leadership positions in many national and international organizations and given over a dozen invited keynote addresses at conferences and symposia. She was the Guest Editor of Special Issues of IEEE Transactions (TMC) on Mission-oriented Sensor Networks, an associate editor of the IEEE Transactions on Systems, Man, and Cybernetics for five years and is editor of the International Journal of Distributed Sensor Networks. She received her M.S. in Operations Research from Cornell University (1973) and Ph.D. from Michigan State University (1976).

Susan L. Price is a Ph.D. student in computer science at Portland State University. She received an MD from the University of Virginia, Charlottesville, Virginia and practiced anesthesiology prior to receiving an MS in medical informatics at Oregon Health & Science University (OHSU), Portland Oregon. From 1999 to 2002 she was an Assistant Professor of Medical Informatics at OHSU before beginning her computer science graduate studies.

Stephen L. Rathbun is associate professor of biostatistics at the University of Georgia. He holds Bachelor of Science and Master of Science degrees in Biology from Florida State University, and Master of Science and Ph.D. degrees in Statistics from Iowa State University. Research interests include spatial statistics, environmental statistics, event history data, and spatial epidemiology. He is currently involved in building a biostatistics program in the new College of Public Health at the University of Georgia.

Priscilla M. Regan is one of two Program Directors in Science and Society with responsibility for proposals in ethics and values of SET (science, engineering and technology) and in studies of policy, science, engineering and technology. She is on leave from George Mason University where she is a Professor of Government and

Politics. Prior to joining the GMU faculty in 1989, she was a Senior Analyst at the Congressional Office of Technology Assessment. Her research involves analyses of the social and legal implications of new communications and information technologies, with particular attention to their privacy implications. She is also doing research on e-government initiatives, especially how they affect congressional-executive relations. She has a PhD in Government from Cornell University.

Pedro I. Rivera-Vega is a Professor of Computer Science at the University of Puerto Rico Mayaguez. He obtained a Ph.D. in Computer Science from the University of Florida on 1990 and currently conducts research in the areas of Digital Government and Distributed Systems.

Dr. Joachim Schaper completed his Ph.D. in computer science at the Technical University of Karlsruhe working for DEC in the area of computer assisted learning, taking the director position of CEC Karlsruhe in 1997. Since 1999 director of SAP's research group, CEC Karlsruhe as part of SAP AG's corporate research. Joachim held the position as Vice President of Americas from 2003 – 2005 to develop the SAP Research group in Palo Alto. Since 2005 he is Vice President of EMEA for SAP Research in Sophia Antipolis, Pretoria, developing new groups in Darmstadt, Dresden, Belfast and St. Gallen and guiding the strategic technology research in the EMEA region.

Dr. Manuel Rodriguez-Martinez received the Ph.D. degree in Computer Science from the University of Maryland, College Park (2001). He also holds a M.S. degree in Computer Science from the University of Maryland, College Park (1996) and a B.S. degree in Mathematics from the University of Puerto Rico, Rio Piedras. His research interests focus on Database Middleware Systems, Peer-to-Peer Database Architectures, Web-based Information Systems, and applications for Mobile Environments. He serves as Co-Principal Investigator for project "Intelligent Power Routers for Distributed Coordination in Electric Energy Processing Networks", an NSF/ONR funded initiative. He has published papers on prestigious international forums such as ACM SIGMOD, EDBT and IASTED. He has served as reviewer for research papers for several international conferences such as VLDB, ACM SIGMOD and IEEE ICDE. In addition, he has served as panelist for reviewing NSF SBIR proposals. He is a member of the ACM society and the SIGMOD special interest group.

Jochen Scholl is an assistant professor in the University of Washington's Information School. He teaches and conducts research on information management, process change, and organizational transformation in government and other organizations. He employs both quantitative computer simulation techniques and qualitative research designs. Jochen has studied the strategies, motives, and focal areas of business and process change in digital government projects as well as the current practices employed in such projects. His special interests include integration, interoperability, organizational transformation, and the strategic choices in mobile technology diffusion in digital government. He is the PI of the NSF-funded Fully Mobile City Government research project (2005 to 2008). Jochen is involved in the organization of the three major conferences on electronic or digital government. He chairs the Electronic Government Track at the Hawaii International Conference on System Sciences (HICSS). He also serves as a member of the organizing committees of dgo2006 and the DEXA/EGOV conferences. He has been engaged in the formation of the Digital Government Society of North America and was elected to the board of officers by public vote. He has also been appointed to serve on the European E-Government Society's board as liaison to the North American Society. Jochen facilitated the worldwide discussion and voting processes on both the Society's Mission Statement and its constitutions. He has also been an active member of the Society's journal committee.

Dr. Anthony Stefanidis is Associate Professor with the Department of Earth Systems and Geoinformation Sciences at George Mason University. Before joining GMU in January 2007, he was Associate Professor with the Department of Spatial Information Science and Engineering and the National Center for Geographic Information and Analysis (NCGIA) at the University of Maine. He holds Ph.D. and M.S. degrees in this field from The Ohio State University (1993 and 1988 respectively), and a Dipl. Eng. Degree from the National Technical University of Athens (1986). His expertise and research activities are focused in the area of digital image processing for geospatial information extraction, video analysis, geosensor networks, spatiotemporal knowledge modeling and management, and digital photogrammetry, and they are supported by grants from various sources including NSF, NASA, BAE Systems, NGA (NIMA), NRO, and others. His past research activities include projects funded by NSF, NASA, the USGS, and the European Union. His teaching activities include courses in digital video analysis, motion imagery analysis, and statistics for information engineering. Dr. Stefanidis has co-edited three books, two on geosensor networks, and another on image analysis for GIS applications. He has also authored or co-authored numerous articles in journals and fully refereed conference proceedings. His work has been featured in various international professional publications.

Dr. Timothy Tolle is recently retired from the USDA Forest Service where he served as the Pacific Northwest regional ecosystem management officer. There, his work focused on adaptive management, monitoring and evaluation, and collaborative stewardship. He also worked as a Planning Team Leader and was involved with Forest Planning. He received an interdisciplinary Ph.D. in water resources from Oregon State University. He formerly worked as forest hydrologist in Montana and water resource analyst in Oregon for Water Resources Board. And he served as Associate Supervisor for two Conservation Districts: Lincoln Co., Montana and Okanogan Co., Washington.

Michael W. Traugott is Professor of Communication Studies and Political Science and Senior Research Scientist in the Center for Political Studies at the Institute for Social Research at the University of Michigan. His research interests include campaigns and elections, the mass media and their impact on American politics and political communication during campaigns. He primarily examines media coverage of political campaigns and the impact they have on voter behavior, use of the media by political candidates, and the use of political surveys and polls to cover campaigns and elections.

Maurício Tsugawa received his BS degree in Electrical Engineering from the Polytechnic School of the University of São Paulo (Brazil), in 1998, his MS degree in Electrical Engineering from the Electronic Systems Department (PSI) of the Polytechnic School of the University of São Paulo (Brazil), in 2001; and is currently a graduate student at the Department of Electrical and Computer Engineering of the University of Florida, working with Dr. José Fortes. His research interests are in the areas of distributed computing, virtual networking, parallel processing, computer architecture and configurable logic design.

Andrè Valente received a doctorate (PhD) degree from the University of Amsterdam (1995) with a thesis on artificial intelligence and law. He also received a bachelor degree in mechanical-aeronautics engineering (1986) and a master degree in computer science (1990) from the Technological Institute of Aeronautics (ITA, Su Josh dos Campos, Brazil). He published about 30 articles in the field of Artificial Intelligence. Between 1986 and 1991 he has worked for major brazilian corporations, doing applied research and development on the fields of knowledge engineering (particularly knowledge acquisition), systems connectivity and software engineering. Presently, he is a researcher at the Information Sciences Institute of the University of Southern California, where he develops research on the Expect Project (a knowledge acquisition architecture with explanation facilities) and the ARPA-Rome Planning Initiative.

Tom M. van Engers studied Cognitive Artificial Intelligence at the Utrecht University and received his PhD at the faculty Mathematics and Information Sciences at the Free University in Amsterdam. He has worked at the Ministry of Finance in different functions amongst them as research manager. Van Engers is professor in Legal Knowledge Management and Managing Director of the Leibniz Center for Lawat the University of Amsterdam. Furthermore Van Engers is CEO of the Regulatory Knowledge Foundation. Van Engers is coordinator of several international research projects such as E-Power, Trias Telematica, Estrella and SEAL (see for more information the Leibniz Center for Law website, at http://www. LeibnizCenter.org).

Bienvenido Vélez-Rivera is an assistant professor in the Department of Electrical and Computer Engineering, University of Puerto Rico, Mayaguez campus. He obtained his Ph.D. in Computer Science from the Massachusetts Institute of Technology (1999), his M.S. in Computer Science from the University of California Berkeley (1988) and his B.A. in Computer Science from Cornell University (1986). During his doctoral work, he designed algorithms for assisting users of information retrieval systems fulfill their information needs effectively. Hi continues to conduct research in Multi-lingual Information Retrieval Systems as well as in Distributed Computing and Digital Government. Dr. Vélez-Rivera is a member of the ACM and the IEEE Computer Society.

Paul A. Waddell is Professor in the Daniel J. Evans School of Public Affairs and the Department of Urban Design and Planning at the University of Washington, and Director of the Center for Urban Simulation and Policy Analysis. His current research interests are in developing simulation models to support land use, transportation and environmental policy analysis. He received his Ph.D. from the University of Texas at Dallas in 1989.

Mathew Jon Weaver is the Chief Technical Officer for EarthSoft, Inc., a manufacturer of environmental data management software. His research interests include a variety of aspects of database technology, conceptual models, metadata, and digital libraries. His professional activities include membership in the ACM and the IEEE Computer Society, and he is a Microsoft Certified Professional. He received a BS degree in Computer Science from Brigham Young University in 1999 and an MS and PhD degree in Computer Science and Engineering from the OGI School of Science and Technology at Oregon Health and Science University in 2003 and 2005, respectively.

Dr. Angus Whyte is a Senior Research Fellow in the International Teledemocracy Centre at Napier University in Scotland. He joined the Centre in 2000 and has played a leading role in many of its projects with government, industry and civil society partners in Europe. His work has focused on evaluation, combining interests in sociotechnical theory with methodologies drawn from the Information Systems and Computer Supported Cooperative Work fields. Angus gained his doctorate in Information Science from Strathclyde University in 1998, and has worked previously in the software, medical and voluntary sectors.

Dr. Radboud G.F. Winkels (1959) is associate professor in Computer Science and Law at the "Leibniz Center for Law (http://www.lri.jur.uva.nl/) (LCL) of the Faculty of Law (http://www.jur.uva.nl/) of the University of Amsterdam (http://www.uva.nl/), the Netherlands. His research deals with Intelligent Learning Environments, and Artificial Intelligence and Law. In 1992 he received his PhD for a thesis entitled "Explorations in Intelligent Tutoring and Help (http://www.lri.jur.uva.nl/~winkels/bibreferences.html#Winkels-92a) (IOS Press), that describes the results of five years of R&D, mainly on a shell for building Intelligent Help

Systems (EUROHELP, at http://www.lri.jur.uva.nl/~winkels/eurohelp.html), and an Intelligent Coaching System for Physiotherapy (FYSIODISC, at http://www.lri.jur.uva.nl/~winkels/fysio-eng.html). In the field of AI and Law his main research interests are legal ontologies, computational models of legal reasoning, intelligent access to legal databases and (standardisation efforts for) the legal semantic web. Since 1998 Winkels is a member of the executive committee of the Dutch Society for Legal Knowledge Systems (JURIX, at http://www.jurix.nl/), first as the scientific coordinator and since 2002 as the president. He is also a member of the executive board of the International Association of AI and Law (http://weblog.iaail.org/).

Chun-Xiao Xing received the BSc degree from the Beijing University of Aeronautic and Astronics (now BeiHang University) in 1990. He received PhD. degree from Northwestern Polytechnical University in 1999, and finished his postdoctor from the Department of Computer Science and Technology of Tsinghua University in 2001. Now he is professor and director of Web and Software Technology R&D Center of Research Institute of Information Technology, Tsinghua University. He also is director of Digital Government Research Center of Tsinghua University. His research interests include database/data warehouse, software engineering, Web service, distributed multimedia systems, Digital library, and e-Government. He is a member of the IEEE.

Ping Yan is currently pursuing the Ph.D. degree in the Department of Management Information Systems at the Eller College of Management of the University of Arizona. She received the B.S. degree in computer science from the University of Science and Technology of China, Hefei, China, and the M.S. degree in computer science from the University of Hong Kong. Yan's research interests include public health informatics, systems architectures for public health systems, and data mining for health-related applications. She is an active member of the BioPortal project led by Chen and Zeng. Her recent papers examine syndromic surveillance systems.

Ji-Jiang Yang received his BSc and MSc degree from Tsinghua university in 1990 and 1995, and his PhD from National University of Ireland (Galway) in 2004. He is the vice director of Web and Software Research Center of RIIT (Research Institute of Information and Technology), Tsinghua University. He is also an associate professor of Tsinghua University. During working in CIMS/ERC of

Tsinghua university, he had joined or been in charge of different projects funded by the State Hi-Tech program (863 program), NSFC(China), and European Union. His interested research areas are involved in ERP, SCM, Business process collaboration, e-Government related technologies.

Daniel Zeng is an Associate Professor and the Director of the Intelligent Systems and Decisions Laboratory in the Department of Management Information Systems at the University of Arizona's Eller College of Management. He is also an affiliated professor at the Institute of Automation, the Chinese Academy of Sciences. He received his BS in operations research/economics from the University of Science and Technology of China, and his MS and PhD in industrial administration from Carnegie Mellon University. His research interests include software agents and multi-agent systems, spatio-temporal data analysis, security informatics, infectious disease informatics, complex systems analysis, recommender systems, digital economic institutions, and automated negotiation and auction. He has directed a number of National Science Foundation-funded research projects as PI or co-PI. He has co-edited seven books and published more than 80 peer-reviewed articles in Management Information Systems and Computer Science journals, edited books, and conference proceedings. He serves on editorial boards of eight Information Technology-related journals and has co-edited special topic issues for four leading journals. He's also the chair of the INFORMS College on Artificial Intelligence and the Vice President for Technical Activities of the IEEE Intelligent Transportation Systems Society. He is a Senior Member of the IEEE. Contact him at zeng@email.arizona.edu; www.u.arizona.edu/~zeng.

Pengzhu Zhang is Chair Professor in MIS & E-Commerce, Director of Center for Management Information Systems, Antai School of Management, Shanghai Jiaotong University. His articles have appeared in Decision Support Systems, Information Systems Engineering and many journals in Chinese. His research interests include group decision/team support systems, financial management information systems, E-government & E-commerce. He received his Ph.D. in 1993 from the Department of Information and Control Engineering, Xi'an Jiaotong University.

Yong Zhang received his BSc and PhD degrees from the Department of Computer Science and Technology of Tsinghua University in 1997 and 2002 respectively. From 2002 to 2005, he worked as postdoctor at the Unilever Centre for Molecular Informatics, Cambridge University, UK. He is currently working as a faculty of Research Institute of Information Technology in Tsinghua University. His main research interests are in Database, XML, e-Science and GIS.

UNIT 1

Foundations of Digital Government and Public Policy

Chapter 1

FOUNDATIONS OF DIGITAL GOVERNMENT

Stephen Coleman

Institute of Communications Studies, University of Leeds, Leeds, U.K, (s.coleman@leeds.ac.uk)

CHAPTER OVERVIEW

This chapter provides a critical introduction to the idea of digital government. It argues that governance is itself a technological project. The main barriers to e-governance are considered and the concept of governmentality – and the governed e-public – are explored.

1. GOVERNANCE AND/AS TECHNOLOGY

To govern is to shape and regulate social order. This is not a task that is carried out by a single body – *the* government or state -, but is shared by a variety of agencies, often acting with little or no knowledge of what the others are doing. The term 'governance' describes this messy, multi-levelled, reticular exercise of power, whereas 'government' describes a more centralized, linear notion of rule which fails to capture the complexity of the contemporary polity. The space of governance is 'the historically constituted matrix within which are articulated all those dreams, schemes, strategies and manoeuvres of authorities that seek to shape the beliefs and conduct of others in desired directions by acting upon their will, their circumstances or their environment' (Rose and Miller 1992). This amounts to more than merely collecting taxes, setting speed limits and declaring occasional wars. Governance embraces a range of social projects, from the construction of 'the good citizen' to the daily disciplining of behaviours deemed to be undesirable. In short, governance is implicated in diverse aspects of taste, moral choice and personal regulation; it is an inescapable regime.

Governance has always been dependent upon technology, in the broadest sense of knowledge, skills, techniques and epistemological strategies, as well as devices, hardware, software and power circuits. As the reach of governance has spread – into new areas of the globe as well as new aspects of hitherto personal relationships -, it has come to rely upon more complex assemblages of technically stored and disseminated knowledge. Information and communication technologies (ICT), from the invention of the alphabet to the ubiquitous presence of close-circuit television (CCTV) cameras, have been employed in the service of governance.

Technologies are constitutive tools: they do not simply support predetermined courses of action, but open up new spaces of action. For example, the emergence of the printing press in Europe generated a space in which publics could come together as cohabitants of imagined communities; centralised states could disseminate their propaganda to mass populations; and vernacular idioms and dialects could be systematised into official languages. As Benedict Anderson argued in his magisterial study of the rise of nationhood, 'the convergence of capitalism and print technology on the fatal diversity of human language created the possibility of a new form of imagined community, which in its basic morphology set the stage for the modern nation' (Anderson 1983). Similarly, the invention of the telegraph gave rise to hugely optimistic political predictions about its capacity to assemble 'all mankind upon one great plane, where they can see everything that is done, and hear everything that is said, and judge of every policy that is pursued at the very moment those events take place' (Salisbury 1889, quoted in Rhys Morus 2000). Predating some of the more sanguine claims for the Internet as a democratically consultative medium, some mid-nineteenth-century commentators expected the telegraph to give rise to 'a series of conversations carried out … between the metropolis and the world, and every capital of northern and central Europe, as intimately as though the speakers were bending their heads over the dinner table and talking confidentially to the host' (Wilson 1855, quoted in Rhys Morus, 459). In reality, telegraphic communication had more to do with transmitting the dominant values of Empire to the furthest corners of the world than initiating a global dinner party.

Not only hard technologies, but modes of technical thought, have had profound effects upon governmental strategies. For example, the emergence of cybernetics in the 1940s led governments to think of 'feedback' mechanisms as being integral to the liberal democratic process (Wiener 1948; Beniger 1986). As Agar has shown in his study of the British civil service, the mechanisation of bureaucratic routines, from the use of punch-cards to computers, served to shift authority and expertise from individual powerbrokers to institutionalised channels. The image of democracies as self-regulating mechanisms which function best when thcy are responding to public demand underlies the contemporary rhetoric of e-government, which tends to combine the consumerist norms of new public management (Osborne and Gabler 1992) with the cybernetic principles of liberal technocracy (Mayr 1976).

Because technologies are not simply *used by* governments, but are a constitutive element of governance, it makes sense to think of the rules, routines, structures, language, skills and networks of governance as *a political technology.* At the end of the Seventeenth Century Trenchard argued that 'a government is a mere piece of clockwork, and having such springs and wheels, must act after such a manner: and there the art is to constitute it so that it must move to the public advantage' (Trenchard 1698). To speak metaphorically of the *machinery* of government, political *leaks* and *re-engineering* government is to tacitly acknowledge that governance is best understood as a technology. An anecdote might illustrate the point. At a recent meeting in Brussels, organised by the European Commission, a group of technologists sat down with a group of legislators and political scientists to work out ways of using digital technologies to support the legislative work of elected Members of the European Parliament. The technologists, who were very aware of the complexity surrounding their technical language, went to great lengths to explain their 'solutions.' The legislators and political scientists were impressed, but had to point out that the European Parliament operates in a number of unique ways - for example, that most legislation is initiated by the Commission and that legislative revision has more to do with negotiation outside the Parliament than what takes place in the chamber. What we were witnessing in this meeting was a process of mutual translation between two technical systems. Wiring the two together required a recognition of potential synergies, but also technical incompatibilities.

2. DIGITISING GOVERNANCE

E-governance entails the digitised coding, processing, storage and distribution of data relating to three key aspects of governing societies: the representation and regulation of social actors; the delivery of public services; and the generation and circulation of official information. Digitally-encoded governance is particularly appropriate to processes in which power relationships are steered and shared between diverse state and non-state agencies, rather than being centralised within traditionally linear hierarchies.

Four distinct features characterise digital governance. Firstly, digitised organisations tend to undergo a morphological transition from revolving *around* fixed centres to operating *between* dispersed information nodes. Nobody has described this political process with greater clarity than Manuel Castells:

> Historically, power was embedded in organizations and institutions, organized around a hierarchy of centres. Networks dissolve centres, they disorganize hierarchy, and make materially impossible the exercise of hierarchical power without processing instructions in the network, according to the network's morphological rule. …
>
> The fundamental dilemma in the network society is that political institutions are not the site of power any longer. The real power is the power of instrumental flows, and cultural codes, embedded in networks.
>
> … The state reacts to its bypassing by information networks, by transforming itself into a network state. So doing, its former centres fade away as centres becoming nodes of power-sharing, and forming institutional networks. (Castells 1996)

Secondly, digitised governance moves from a condition in which information is scarce, and its value determined by its exclusivity, to a condition of information abundance, in which the most successful networks are those which collectively generate, share and borrow information. As Bimber has argued in relation to collective action,

> New means for elites to distribute and acquire information, new possibilities for citizens to identify and communicate with one another, changes in the ways that citizens interact with the news system, and the historical preservation of information, among other developments, contribute toward a state of information abundance in the political system. (Bimber 2003)

Thirdly, digital governance is inherently interactive. When governments constructed around analogue technologies sought to interact with the public, the will to communicate tended to be frustrated by their capacity to transmit rather than receive messages. As I have argued elsewhere,

> The megaphone is the metaphorical medium of demagogic politics. Megaphones transmit, but do not receive; they amplify the voices of the leaders above those of the led; they are territorial, reaching a geographically-defined public in a specific space; they are authoritarian: it is hard to heckle a speaker with a megaphone. (Coleman 2005)

By contrast, digitised communication resists the logic of what Postman has called 'the one-way conversation' (Postman 1986). A government website which said to its users, 'This is what we want you to know. Read it and then leave us alone' would be regarded as breaching the implicit protocol of digital communication. The potential for feedback is central to the promise of digital communication. (That is why political parties and politicians have had such great difficulty adapting to digital media: they want to talk to their public, but do not yet know how to cope with the public speaking back.)

Fourthly, the digitisation of governance impacts upon organisational behaviour, both at the level of institutional purpose and capacity (structure) and human action and reflexivity (agency.) This is what is meant when digitisation is sometimes referred to as a 'transformative' process. The characteristics of technologies both shape and are shaped by the routine generation of meaning, power and norms which define structures. Zuboff's theory of automation and informatization refers to 'the dual potential of information technology to *automate* and to *informate'*:

> The same systems that make it possible to automate office transactions also create a vast overview of an organization's operations, with many levels of data coordinated and accessible for a variety of analytical efforts. ... Information technology ... introduces an additional dimension of reflexivity: it makes its contribution to the product, but it also reflects back on its activities and on the system of activities to which it is related. Information technology not only produces action but also produces a

> voice that symbolically renders events, objects, and processes so that they become visible, knowable, and shareable in a new way. (Zuboff 1985)

At the same time, as the structural logic of the organisations in which they are working are rendered more visible by the process of digitisation, users find themselves in a more reflexive relationship with their environment, becoming more aware of hitherto tacit sources of power, relations with external actors and unintended consequences of what had once seemed like parochial activities. In the context of e-governance, the effects of informatization and greater user reflexivity could either strengthen or destabi lise existing cultures of order and efficiency. For example, street-level bureaucrats, such as local housing officials, might find that the decisions they are compelled to make within an e-governance regime are increasingly systematised and non-negotiable; become more aware of the shortcomings of the system logic by which they are bound; make greater efforts to penetrate areas of governance networks that would have been traditionally inaccessible to them; and even form alliances with co-workers from whom they would once have been spatially disconnected. That, of course, is only one conceivable narrative of e-governance, but it serves to illustrate the ways in which digitisation both disrupts and opens new avenues for techniques of governing.

In outlining these characteristics of digital technologies and their potential effects upon governance, there is an inevitable risk of this being read as technological determinism: the assumption that cultures and structures cannot resist effects produced by the properties of technologies. Instead, I want to argue for a more sophisticated understanding of this relationship, which owes much to Giddens' theory of structuration and Orlikowski's application of that theory to the study of technological change. As Orlikowski argues, 'The theory of structuration recognizes that human actions are enabled and constrained by structures, yet that these structures are the result of previous actions.' (Orlikowski 1992, p.404) There is a constantly reciprocal interplay between structural logic and human reflexivity. Orlikowski summarises this well when she states that

> technology is physically constructed by actors working within a given social context, and technology is socially constructed by actors through the different meanings they attach to it and the various features they emphasise and use. However, it is also the case that once developed and deployed, technology tends to become reified and institutionalized, losing its connection with the human agents that constructed it or gave it meaning, and it appears to be part of the objective, structural properties of the organization. (Orlikowski 1992, p.406)

From this perspective, one should not be too quick to speak about e-governance as a single configuration of meaning, power and norms. The digitisation of governance is as much cultural and interpretive as technical and objective.

3. BARRIERS TO E-GOVERNANCE

While there would seem to be a conceptual fit between governance and digitisation, theoretical expectations and empirical realities are rarely consistent. In the descriptive and evaluative literature on e-governance, four major barriers to success have been repeatedly identified. Firstly, large-scale government projects which utilise emerging and uncertain technologies face the risk of not knowing where technical orthodoxy will eventually settle. As a result, such projects are often blighted by an absence of defined technical standards. Governments can find themselves encumbered by legacy systems which tie them in to commercial and technical arrangements that, even if they ever provided short-term benefits, constrain opportunities for future flexibility. At the same time, government, and various local, national and supranational bodies, which are supposed to be 'joined up' through e-governance, often find themselves more disconnected than ever because ICT purchased by different agencies at different times turn out not to be interoperable.

Secondly, there is much evidence to suggest that citizens do not trust governments to collect, store and act upon their personal data. There is a widespread public fear that all interactions with governments are monitored; that governments are unwilling to share information they gather, and will find ways of evading Freedom of Information laws; that data is transferred between agencies without citizens' consent; that stored data will be used to construct negative and unaccountable profiles of particular citizens; and that government data is inherently vulnerable to unscrupulous hackers. As customers in the marketplace, most people are more willing to exchange secure data with supermarkets or travel agencies than they are in their role of voters, tax-payers, service-users or community residents. Public anxieties about the political motives of government actors has led Warkentin et al. to propose that for e-government to be regarded as legitimate 'it must be removed from the political arena in the minds of the citizens' (Warkentin et al. 2002) – by, for example, the use of dedicated intermediaries, such as GovWorks in the USA and DirectGov in the UK acting as information and transaction brokers. Public distrust is not helped by the failure of legislators to enact similar rules for digital as for analogue environments. For most citizens, it remains much easier to authenticate their identity in face-to-face encounters – or even on the telephone – than when they are online.

Thirdly, despite the pervasive talk of 'joined-up' governance and the seamless communication flows enabled by ICT, most governments are highly bureaucratically fragmented and internally fiercely resistant to change. Ironically, the devolutionary benefits of e-governance have often been most successfully implemented by centralised, top-down policy drives which have reengineered processes by overwhelming the oppugnancy of conservative bureaucrats. In their study of the UK Government's web presence, Margetts and Dunleavy (2002) noted that government officials have 'a tendency to find reasons for inaction and for exaggerated risk-averse behaviour on Internet or Web issues' and exhibit 'an unwillingness to divert resources from established ways of doing things' when developing Internet communications or transactions. In the face of this, politically-conceived e-governance strategies often look very different on paper than in practice.

Fourthly, access to computers and skills are unevenly distributed throughout the population, with those who are most excluded from the political process and most in need of government services most likely to be digitally excluded. A number of studies have shown that Internet users and non-users are distinguished by socio-economic status, age and ethnicity. (Thomas and Streib 2003; Carter and Belanger 2005) Furthermore, those accessing e-government are drawn from an even more exclusive range than Internet users in general. (Thomas and Streib 2003) Carter and Belanger argue that

> E-government represents yet another technical innovation that certain members of society are excluded from. Benefits such as increased convenience and responsiveness could mobilize the technically savvy while disenfranchising those who are less efficacious regarding computer use. (Carter and Belanger 2005, p.5)

A technology which improves system efficiency at the expense of exacerbating social exclusion is open to serious normative criticism. Indeed, it is precisely in this normative context that most evaluations of e-governance fall down. There has been a utilitarian tendency to assess e-governance projects either in term of cost benefits (are they cheaper than other methods?) or whether they provide technocratically convincing 'solutions' (do they 'work'?). The more important evaluative questions, that are rarely asked, concern the normative purpose of e-governance. Are the digitally governed freer, happier, more empowered? What are the relationships between e-governance and social justice? Are citizens entitled to 'digital rights?' How easily might citizens who feel oppressed or disillusioned by new networks of virtual power escape from the clutches of e-governance? These are the thorny questions that we must now address.

4. GOVERNING THE E-PUBLIC

Amidst the heady rhetoric of modernised, rationalistic e-governance, it is easy to lose sight of those who are being governed. The public, which is always an amorphous spectre within models of democratic politics, is the absent body which can only become present through representation. Political representation is necessary when citizens are removed - physically, cognitively or otherwise - from the locus of public decision-making and their interests, preferences and values have to be expressed via an aggregating medium. To govern democratically is to both acknowledge the absence of the *demos* from day-to-day decision-making and to conjure it into existence through the ventriloquised voice of representative governance.

In contradistinction to the institutional-bureaucratic conception of 'the virtual state' as 'a government that is organised increasingly in terms of virtual agencies, cross-agency and public-private networks whose structure and capacity depend on the Internet and the web' (Fountain 2001, p.4) is the notion of the virtual public which must be imagined, cultivated, defined and regulated before it can be governed. If the primary objective of e-governance is to produce subjects who are fit to be governed, rather than simply to provide neutral information and functional services in response to objectively discernible public demand, there is a need to understand the specific ways in which public behaviour, knowledge and attitudes are being shaped by technologies of digital governance. This entails an investigation of ways in which governance has moved from being a process of coercive subjection to one of moral subjectification.

Foucault's concept of *governmentality,* particularly as developed by contemporary social theorists such as Rose and Barry, is useful in helping to illuminate the ways in which e-governance acts upon human conduct with a view to stimulating habits of self-discipline and moralised responsibility which diminish the need for involuntary regulation (Foucault 1982). Rose has argued that 'Liberal strategies of government ... become dependent upon devices (schooling, the domesticated family, the lunatic asylum, the reformatory prison) that promise to create individuals who do not need to be governed by others, but will govern themselves, master themselves, care for themselves' (Barry et al. 1996, p.45). E-governance, which is a form of what Rose has called 'governing at a distance' (Rose and Miller 1992, p.49) can be understood as precisely such a mode of power in which norms of self-governing conduct are cultivated and disseminated via informal communicative networks rather than centralised command structures. To what extent is it the case that the behaviour, knowledge and attitudes of citizens are moulded by the subtle regime of e-governance?

5. REGULATING THE BEHAVIOUR OF E-CITIZENS

E-citizens are presented with a rhetoric of freedom and an environment of circumscription. In this sense, e-governance accords with the contemporary liberal discourse in which free choice is blithely offered and then constrained by an abundant array of techniques to manage, persuade, incentivise and cajole 'customers' along paths consistent with economic efficiency and moral responsibility. Citizens wanting to contact government agencies are increasingly faced with the experience of being at the other end of the line to a call centre, in which all questions will be answered and needs provided for, as long as they are specified questions and legitimate needs. Template rationality is not good at acknowledging or responding to desire, curiosity or dissent, but seeks to promote forms of behaviour consistent with a particular conception of orderly social conduct. In his study of *Information Politics on the Web,* Rogers has argued that citizen feedback to e-government is restricted by what he calls 'the politics of information formatting.' Citing the example of the UK Government's *Citizenspace* portal, in which citizens were invited to debate aspects of Government policy, Rogers notes that, firstly, the rules of the site disallowed external hyperlinks to the debate unless permission is given, and secondly, that debate topics followed 'the lines of ministerial responsibility instead of gleaning or grabbing them from society …' (Rogers 2004, p.11) In short, to participate in this particular e-governance exercise, citizens were expected to cut themselves off from the network potentiality of the web and conform to an imposed structure and agenda of debate.

Failure to conform to programmed rationalities can result in a loss of time and money for frustrated citizens, as well as the omnipresent threat that their recalcitrance has been registered by the surveillant gaze of the state. Lyon (2002) has shown how monitorial government technologies are designed to discriminate between fields of action deemed anti-social – and even to identify types of actor expected to manifest nuisance value. As Howard has argued, online interactions with political websites are never inconsequential:

> We often cast a data shadow when we complete an electronic purchase, browse websites or agree to participate in a survey. The data shadow follows us almost everywhere. It represents us by profile, but with little

> color. We are not always aware of its appearance, but others can note the silhouette. It is the silhouette created by our daily activities, and it is one of the parties to the new digitized social contract. Some people have more crisply defined data shadows, depending on how many political hypermedia they interact with. Credit card purchases, voter registration records, polling data, and magazine subscriptions all help create the data shadow. Increasingly, the data shadow represents us in political discourse. The data shadow has become an important political actor. Data shadows not only follow citizens, but political candidates, and institutions cast them as well. Few people can effectively op-out of their digital shadow. (Howard 2003)

Digital ICT are not unique in their capacity to regulate the behaviour of users. All social communication entails some involuntary accommodation between individuals wishing to finds things out, contact others or be heard and the cultural-technical logic of mediation. The problem of e-governance technologies is not that they are designed with a view to promoting certain forms of behaviour and discouraging others, but the absence of transparency or accountability for these strategies. Governing is a social practice – as is being governed. Such practices do not lend themselves to the discourse of rational functionalism, but should be understood as specific socio-technical choices.

6. CULTIVATING THE SKILLS OF E-CITIZENSHIP

Historically, citizenship has been regarded as a birthright, the entitlements of which have been the subject of contestation and negotiation over the past three centuries. The free citizen is characterised by autonomous moral agency which is most potently exercised within the public sphere. In this sense, it is the liberal freedom *from* interference, especially by the state, which makes civic action so precious to effective democracy.

More recently, however, a number of cultural and political trends have precipitated a shift towards what Garland has called 'the responsibilization of citizenship' (Garland 2000). These trends include the weakening of strong welfare structures, which leave more people, in more areas of life, having to fend for themselves; the decline of political deference and rise of volatile political consumerism, which leaves citizens feeling rather like shoppers who can buy whatever they want, as long as they can afford it and predict the uncertain consequences; and the adoption of a strong ideological commitment by both conservatives and social democratics towards a belief that social rights must be balanced by communitarian duties. The need to produce citizens who are prepared for these new conditions has given rise to an expanded field of pedagogy which includes citizenship education in schools; risk communication; the training of expert patients; offender rehabilitation schemes; lifestyle courses and various projects to promote 'sensible' interactions with the media. Citizenship becomes something more like an apprenticeship. One is no longer simply governed; one is educated through a variety of practices, discourses and technologies to become a responsible collaborator in governance. In this context, the Committee of Ministers of the Council of Europe, in their Recommendation No. 19/2001, has urged member states to pay attention to

> improving citizenship education and incorporating into school curricula and training syllabuses the objective of promoting awareness of the responsibilities that are incumbent on each individual in a democratic society, in particular within the local community …

E-governance projects are well-suited to such normative shaping of skills and knowledge. Learning to be an e-citizen entails becoming familiar with techniques of online information-searching, protocols for digitally interacting and the legal regulation of software use. The cultivation of these skills – often referred to as digital literacy - not only point citizens towards a particular view of governance, but govern the process of being governed. What has been called 'digital literacy' is a regulatory project intended to cultivate a citizenry capable of responsible digital interaction. In the context of e-governance, this includes knowing which level of governance one should address in relation to particular problems; being able to navigate through the bureaucratic divisions of departmental and agency remits; behaving in a civilised way; and having appropriate (i.e., well managed) expectations about outcomes. From the perspective of governmentality, none of these skills are politically neutral. A good example of this is the way in which most e-government websites seek to draw an artificial distinction between governance and politics. (For example, few local authority websites in the UK explain the partisan composition of council committees; and councillors are not allowed to use official web spaces to promote their 'political' views.) This online illusion reinforces an implicit view that governments are there to get things done efficiently and politics is there to cause arguments and get in the way. Similarly, government websites tend to be dull and solemn, designed in ways that impress upon users the 'seriousness' of their purpose and their distance from fun or frivolity. None of these messages are inevitable. The politics of governance could be made more explicit. The democratic process could be made to feel more like pleasure. The emphases and absences to which I have pointed reflect decisions that have been made about how to govern the civic relationship and what citizens need to know to be governed effectively. But who is accountable for these decisions? What if the public would prefer to be communicated with in different ways?

7. MANAGING INTERACTIVITY

The most famous characteristic of digital ICT is the capacity for two-way communication. Instead of the monological discourse of transmissive mass media, the rigid dichotomy between message producers and receivers collapses in an environment of digital interactivity. This has had profound effects upon ways in which shoppers interact with the marketplace, students with educational resources and networks of friends with one another. There are two senses in which e-governance has been an exception to this trend. Firstly, as many studies have found, governmental and political institutions have been slow to incorporate interactive features into their web sites. They still regard the web as a means of one-way narrowcasting. Secondly, even where governments have encouraged a degree of interactivity, this has tended to be vertical (G2C) rather than horizontal (C2C). Governing elites have failed to connect in their everyday policy-making with the numerous networks of grass-roots discourse which could, if properly harnessed, give substance to contemporary aspirations towards co-governance (Ostrom 1996).

E-governance has tended to be risk aversive, acknowledging (sometimes reluctantly) the functional efficiencies of delivering services or conducting transactions online, but refusing to engage with the opportunities for more dialogically and directly representing the public's interests, preferences and values. For example, there have been many strategies, some more successful than others, for the online collection of payments from citizens, ranging from local taxes to parking fines. There is no technical reason why payment for services could not be combined with e-consultations about policies for spending the money being collected, i.e., making a direct connection between taxation and representation. The choice not to do so is a political one. Indeed, it may well be the right policy, but, like much else in the sphere of e-administration, it is presented, in the absence of any debate, as a *fait accompli.*

There is a need for a political debate about digital interactivity and its consequences rather than a bureaucratic strategy to 'manage' the over-talkative public. A strategy for e-governance which integrated horizontal networks with the vertical channels of institutional power, and then attended to the thorny problems of how best to respond respectfully to a newly-empowered public, would look very different from the forms of e-governance that we have come to expect. Its main effect would be to encourage a democratic attitude amongst citizens, which we might define as a perspective based upon the assumptions that power belongs to the *demos,* rather than to politically or economically privileged elites; that policies and social affairs can be influenced by collective action; that no aspect of policy formation or decision-making is off limits for the public; and that neither age, gender or ethnicity, nor vernacular and idiomatic ways of speaking, are barriers to being acknowledged and respected. At the moment, most e-governance projects do little to promote such a democratic attitude, and often create implicit or intentional obstacles to the political efficacy of 'ordinary' people.

8. WHAT CAN BE EXPECTED FROM E-GOVERNANCE?

The first question to be asked about any technological arrangement is, What is it supposed to do? The answer to this question is far from clear in the case of e-governance. There is no shortage of simplistic and inadequate answers: that e-governance is intended to make government more efficient or less expensive or of a higher quality or simply less conspicuous. But none of these responses refer to the wider question of what governance itself is for. As with debates around e-learning, which have had to engage with theoretical, empirical and normative accounts of why, how and to what ends people acquire knowledge, e-governance cannot be discussed intelligently in purely functionalist terms. Before scrutinising technologies of e-governance as potential 'solutions,' the original problematics of democratic governance need to be identified and debated. This entails political contestation – a process that has tended to be conspicuously absent from both studies and policy statements about e-governance.

For most citizens, relationships with governmental power are opaque and uncomfortable. They do not trust governments to tell them the truth. They regard the political language of governance as remote and tricky. They see bureaucracies as labyrinthine and unfeeling. They sense that power is unjustly distributed and their capacity to influence government decisions rather limited. From a functionalist perspective, none of this matters. The key questions revolve around whether e-governance technologies 'get things done.' By contrast, a social justice perspective seeks to raise questions about the extent to which technological arrangements weaken or empower the governed. Such a perspective calls for research in three specific areas of e-governance, which have hitherto been somewhat neglected. Firstly, there is a need to consider the extent to which e-citizens possess – or should possess - digital rights. What kinds of guarantees should e-citizens expect when they are interacting with governments online? As well as concerning the obvious questions of data protection, information transparency and security from malignant third parties, there are broader questions to be considered concerning the terms of interactive relationships and opportunities to find and form lateral networks. Secondly, the e-governance agenda need to connect with the important ongoing debate about governance of the Internet as a social space. How far should the Internet be accountable to its users? What protection should the public expect from state or corporate control of cyberspace? To what extent are the codes embedded within commonly-used software a means of manipulating public action and debilitating democratic energies? Thirdly, as with any aspect of social existence, there is a debate to be had about the extent to which e-governance is exacerbating or diminishing traditional social inequalities and the potentiality of redistributing social power by strengthening the communicative resources of those who are traditionally the least powerful members of society.

This chapter has not contributed substantially to the analysis of e-governance from the perspective of social justice, but has attempted to prepare the intellectual ground so that some of these questions can be addressed in subsequent chapters and volumes, hopefully disrupting some of the more unreflective certainties about the nature of e-governance and setting the scene for some critical analyses of why, how and to what ends society is both governed and e-governed.

REFERENCES

Anderson, B. (1983) Imagined Communities: Reflections on the Origin and Spread of Nationalism. Verso, London

Barry, A., Osborne and Rose, N. (eds.) (1996) Foucault and Political Reason: Liberalism, Neo-Liberalism and Rationalities of Government. UCL Press, London

Beniger, J. (1986) The Control Revolution: technological and economic origins of the information society. Harvard University Press, Cambridge, MA

Bimber, B. (2003) Information and American Democracy: Technology in the Evolution of Political Power. State University of New York Press, NY, p.92

Carter, L. and Belanger, F. (2005) The utilization of e-government services: citizen trust, innovation and acceptance factors. Information Systems Journal 15

Castells, M. (1996) The Information Age: Economy, Society, and Culture: The Rise of the Network Society. Blackwell, Oxford, (Vol I)

Coleman, S. (2005) New Mediation and Direct Representation: reconceptualizing representation in the digital age. New Media & Society 7:2

Foucault, M. (1982) The Subject and Power. Critical Inquiry 8:4

Fountain, J. (2001) Building the Virtual State: information technology and institutional change. The Brookings Institution, Washington DC

Garland, D. (2000) The culture of high crime societies. British Journal of Criminology 40: 347–75

Howard, P. (2003) Digitizing the Social Contract: Producing American Political Culture in the Age of New Media. The Communication Review 6

Lyon, D. (2002) Surveillance as Social Sorting: Privacy, Risk and Digital Discrimination. Routledge, London
Margetts, H. and Dunleavy, P. (2002) Cultural Barriers to e-Government National Audit Office, London
Mayr, O. (1976) The Science-Technology Relationship as a Historiographic Problem. Technology and Culture 17:4
Orlikowski, W. (1992) The Duality of Technology: Rethinking the Concept of Technology in Organizations. Organization Science 3:3
Osborne, D. and Gabler, T. (1992) Reinventing Government: How the Entrepreneurial Spirit is Transforming the Public Sector Reading. Addison-Wesley, MA
Ostrom, E. (1996) Crossing the great divide: coproduction, synergy, and development. World Development 24 (6)
Postman, N. (1986) Amusing Ourselves to Death: Public Discourse in the Age of Show Business. Penguin Books, NY
Rhys Morus (2000) The nervous system of Britain: space, time and the electric telegraph in the Victorian age. British Journal for the History of Science 33: 254
Rogers, R. (2004) Information Politics on the Web. MIT Press, MA
Rose, N. and Miller, P. (1992) Political Power Beyond the State: Problematics of Government. British Journal of Sociology 43 (2): 175
Thomas, J. and Streib, G. (2003) The New Face of Government: Citizen-Initiated Contacts in the Era of e-Government. Journal of Public Administration Research and Theory 13
Trenchard, (1698) Short History of Standing Armies
Warkentin, M., Gefen, D., Pavlou, P. and Rose, G. (2002) Encouraging Citizen Adoption of E-Government by Building Trust. Electronic Markets 12:3
Wiener, N. (1948) Cybernetics. Wiley, NY
Zuboff, S. (1985) Automate/Informate: The Two Faces of Intelligent Technology In: Organizational Dynamics. Autumn, p.9

SUGGESTED READINGS

- Barry, A. (2001) Political Machines: Governing a Technological Society. Athlone Press, London.
- Ellul, J. (1954) The Technological Society. Vintage Books, NY.
- Blumler, J.G. and Coleman, S. (2001) Realising Democracy Online: A Civic Commons in Cyberspace. IPPR/Citizens Online, London.

ONLINE RESOURCES

- Coleman, S. and Gotze, J., Bowling Together: Online Public Engagement in Policy Deliberation: http://www.bowlingtogether.net

QUESTIONS FOR DISCUSSION

1. Is there a meaningful distinction between governance and government? What are the main characteristics of e-governance?
2. What is meant by saying that we live in a network society?
3. Why is interactivity so essential to the effectiveness of e-governance?
4. Can you think of good examples, from your own experience, of automation and informatization?
5. How does the concept of *governmentality* help us to understand e-governance?
6. How might e-governance be scrutinised from the perspective of social justice?

Chapter 2

DISCIPLINE OR INTERDISCIPLINARY STUDY DOMAIN?

Challenges and Promises in Electronic Government Research

Hans J. (Jochen) Scholl

The Information School, University of Washington, Seattle, WA, USA (jscholl@u.washington.edu)

CHAPTER OVERVIEW

Digital or Electronic Government Research (EGR) finds itself at a crossroads. While the body of electronic-Government-related knowledge is rapidly growing, questions have been raised about whether EGR qualifies as a legitimate discipline, and what the accepted methods and procedures of inquiry should be. This chapter proposes that EGR will be fortunate not to develop into a traditional discipline and not to restrict itself to a narrow set of procedures. Rather, EGR should keep drawing upon multiple disciplines spanning the whole spectrum of hard-pure, hard-applied, soft-pure, and soft-applied sciences. In so doing, EGR might best thrive as a multi-, inter-, or transdiscipline with the prospect of becoming an academic role model for integrative knowing capable of coping with the complexity of problems and phenomena without unduly simplifying them.

1. INTRODUCTION

Like its siblings "e-Business" and "e-Commerce" the once "electrifying" acronym "e-Government" is seemingly losing its magic. Despite (or, perhaps because of) the initial absence of a clear definition, the term's primary appeal in the late 1990s must probably be ascribed to the notion of doing something radically new and far apart from traditional business models and likewise something very different from traditional information systems (IS) and information technology (IT). On the surface and for the most part, those perceived differences between traditional and "new" referred to the enabling roles of Internet and Web technologies. From an end-of-the-20th-century perspective, those technologies facilitated an unprecedented universality and immediacy of information access or transaction, elegant and easy bridging of boundaries and barriers as well as new business models developed as a consequence. During those years, "e-xcitement" spiraled out of proportion and the list of ever-new e-words grew long with hilarious "e-xaggerations."

Academia ineffectually adopted the three classical terms of "e-Business," "e-Commerce," and "e-Government" providing an after-the-fact definition (AACSB, 2000; Scholl, 2003) and justification, and also guidance for research. Yet others like the US National Science Foundation (NSF) coined their own term of "Digital Government" for the same phenomenon (Anonymous, 2006). Regardless of the labels "digital" or "electronic" in combination with the term "government," today governments heavily invest in e-Government projects; specific legislation has been introduced, practitioner congresses on the subject matter abound; graduate degree programs evolve; academic conference and journal coverage has substantially grown, new academic journals have emerged, and two regional Digital/E-Government Societies (North America and Europe) have been formed. On the one hand, those developments seem to clearly indicate a growing recognition and importance of the subject matter. E-Government it appears has become mainstream. On the other hand, for quite some time, scholars have criticized the definitional weakness and potential faddishness of both terms "Digital Government" and "e-Government" and challenged the adequacy and long-term sustainability of those labels for academic research and governmental practice. The growing importance and influence of e-Government research (EGR) seemingly coincides with the fading twinkle of the terms and the growing academic discontent with them presenting us with a paradox. However, why should we care?

This chapter asserts that the fading appeal of the terms "e-Government" and "digital government" is not coincidental but may rather indicate a certain intellectual weakness in EGR concepts and a growing need for reassessing the EGR agenda. More importantly, EGR's scientific foundations, shared perspectives, and expectable prospects need clarification. This chapter is intended to contribute to and advance a recently launched discussion on the subject (Grönlund, 2004; Cushing & Pardo, 2005; Delcambre & Giuliano, 2005; Grönlund, 2005).

EGR studies "the use of information and technology to support and improve public policies and government operations, engage citizens, and provide comprehensive and timely government services" (Anonymous, 2005b). This widely accepted academic definition of e-Government and EGR, however, defines a field or a domain of study, which spans across the boundaries of quite a number of existing disciplines including public administration, political sciences, organizational sciences, information science, computer science, information systems research, sociology, library science, statistics, law and ethics, and a host of other disciplinary sciences. According to Grönlund, a common study object alone does not establish a discipline or a field; rather a set of distinguishing theories and accepted methodologies are needed for defining a "classical" discipline in its own right (Grönlund, 2004, 2005). Hence, the question arises what, if any, is the disciplinary home turf of EGR in terms of theory, method, study object, and research community? Or, if EGR systematically goes beyond the scope of any one discipline, what are the characteristics and acceptable standards of this multi-, inter-, or transdisciplinary science?

The chapter is organized as follows: First, it discusses whether EGR is (or, at least, can be expected to become) a discipline. Then, it exemplarily looks at traditional disciplines involved with aspects of EGR including public administration, information systems research, and computer science. Third, the chapter discusses the challenges and opportunities of cross-disciplinary EGR. Finally, the chapter ponders the idea of defining and establishing EGR as a multi-, inter-, or transdiscipline rather than a discipline.

2. WOULD EGR PASS AS A "LEGITIMATE" DISCIPLINE?

To information scientists the discussion of "discipline versus field versus domain versus interdisciplinary science" provides the experience of déja-vu, since information science (InfSci), although some half century old (Bush, 1945; Shannon & Weaver, 1962) with well-established and fully-fledged colleges, schools, departments, journals, conferences, societies, and research methods, has only recently gone through that debate (again). For the purpose of our discussion on the foundations of EGR it is insightful to draw upon that InfSci debate, which was rather charged at times. It shows that even more mature sciences than EGR might occasionally find themselves in the midst of an identity crisis. However, the InfSci-related discussion provided that researcher community with meaning and orientation and was productive.

It surfaced several important indicators and dimensions of what defines a discipline: (1) a formal definition of the discipline/field, (2) a common base of knowledge, (3) a unique cluster of research problems, (4) unifying theories, (5) an accepted set of procedures and methods of inquiry, and (6) a shared vision of the discipline/field's impact.

Collateral indicators may include (7) structural elements on university level (departments, schools, colleges), (8) graduate programs and students (9) a worldwide researcher community, (10) both academic and professional associations, (11) journals and recurring conferences, (12) researcher self-identification with the discipline, (13) icons, that is, leading and visible scholars, (14) textbooks, (15) expressed allegiance to the discipline via artifacts and accepted rules (of, for example, promotion), (16) discipline-specific terminology, and (17) strong interaction between the academic discipline and its field of practice (Kuhn, 1970; Heilprin, 1991; Saracevic, 1999; Becher & Trowler, 2001; Webber, 2003; Grönlund, 2004, 2005). These indicators, although not exhaustive, provide a basis for an initial assessment of the disciplinary nature of EGR and show that EGR satisfies a number of these criteria, while it falls short on several others:

Formal Definition. As shown above, a widely accepted formal definition of EGR exists.

Knowledge Base. Also, the accumulated knowledge on the subjects of EGR is rapidly growing. A recent survey of published peer-reviewed academic work shows a growing swell of literature in established and new journals and conferences. The current worldwide English-language literature base is estimated at 19 monographs, 83 articles in established journals, 35 articles in new journals, and over 400 articles at conferences. NSF has funded some 150 major EGR projects between 1999 and 2006. The European Union has likewise sponsored several dozens of EGR projects. With an estimated current annual going rate of some 120 peer-reviewed publications based on the number of recurring conferences, journal issues, and monographs, the knowledge base of EGR is rapidly expanding.

Unique Cluster of Research Problems. EGR uniquely intersects advanced IS- and IT- and government-related research problems, which have gone widely unattended and unaddressed in, for example, both the academic public-administration and information-systems literatures. Papers dedicated to and based on EGR were found 16 times in the top-five journals of Public Administration between 1999 and early 2006, while no single EGR-based publication was found in the top-two IS journals in the US for the same period of time. In contrast, the topical breakdown of EGR problems includes among other themes the uniqueness of (a) IS/IT-based services and tools, (b) IS/IT-related managerial and organizational issues, (c) infrastructure, integration, and interoperation, (d) knowledge and information management, (e) information security, (f) inclusion, participation, and voting, and (g) mobility of services and operations, (h) archiving, electronic record keeping, and document life management, and (i) policy, law, and governance issues with a growing body of knowledge in each cluster.

Unifying Theories. Grönlund (2004, 2005) empirically analyzes the academic contributions at three major conferences and finds EGR immature and under-theorized. Delcambre & Giuliano (2005) identify two main clusters of EGR, one centering on developing IT tools in response to practical government problems and the other one revolving around government processes researched from a socio technical perspective. Certain EGR theory development, for example, has been dedicated to the integration, change, and transformational impacts of e-Government (Layne & Lee, 2001; Kubicek *et al.*, 2003; Scholl, 2003; Klischewski, 2004; Scholl, 2004a, 2005a, 2005b, 2005c). However, those theoretical contributions certainly have neither created a grand or unifying theory, nor a set of major competing theories (for example, like transaction-cost theory versus resource-based theory in economics).

Procedures and Methods of Inquiry. EGR has been found using almost the full spectrum of methodological and procedural approaches ranging from anecdotal accounts (Grönlund, 2004, 2005) over action research (Scholl, 2004b) and traditional survey-based research (Moon, 2002; Moon *et al.*, 2005) to computational modeling (Hovy, 2003; Pantel *et al.*, 2005) and simulation (Cresswell *et al.*, 2002; Black *et al.*, 2003). Such large range of procedures and methods representing very different fields and epistemic paradigms makes it difficult to assess the nature and quality of contribution (Delcambre & Giuliano, 2005), that is, neither an accepted set of methodologies and procedures nor a shared definition of rigor in EGR exists reminiscent of Feyerabend's provocative ideal of "anything goes" (Feyerabend, 1975).

Shared Vision of Impact. The long-range vision and impact of EGR has moved onto center stage of the discussion among members of the researcher/practitioner community only recently. It is fostered by the formation of a global Digital Government Society and also sponsored via research projects both in the EU and the US (Anonymous, 2005a, 2005b, 2006). A shared vision of the impact still needs to emerge.

When briefly analyzing the collateral indicators, the results remain mixed: *Structural elements* on university level (departments, etc.) are still rare except for a few research centers (in the US, examples include centers at

Harvard/U Massachusetts, SUNY/Albany, and the University of Southern California). At *graduate study* level, a few EGR-based curricula have been established (for example, at Örebro University, Sweden, University at Koblenz, Germany, and the Rockefeller College of Public Affairs and Policy, USA). An EGR-oriented doctoral program is under development by Örebro University in cooperation with the Copenhagen School of Business. The *worldwide EGR community* has substantially grown over the years. If the number of authors with at least three EGR publications at peer-reviewed conferences and journals is taken as an indicator, the hard core of researchers invested in EGR can be estimated at approximately two hundred researchers worldwide. With over 1,500 peer-reviewed contributions to-date, the larger EGR researcher community presumably numbers between six and seven hundred scholars in early 2006. The Digital Government Society has been formed as a global *professional association*. Furthermore, recurring *conferences and journals* focusing on EGR have been established. *Self-identification* of scholars with EGR is detectable both at conferences and in publications. *Icons* and figureheads with a von Neumann-, Turing-, Simon-, or Dewey-level standing do not exist in EGR at this point in time. At least one EGR *textbook* project is underway. Several monographs have been dedicated to special topics (for example, (Fountain, 2001; Huang *et al.*, 2004)). In absence of established rules, procedures, or promotional pathways, no disciplinary *allegiance* has been found. Likewise absent is EGR-specific *terminology*, most prominently evident in the lack of an accepted term for the area of study itself (Digital Government, e-Government, e-Government, e-Gov, etc.). However, compared with other areas of study, the *interaction between practitioners and scholars* seems to be relatively strong in EGR (Grönlund, 2001, 2004, 2005).

In summary, while EGR passes on the first three primary indicators of what constitutes a "classical," "legitimate" discipline, it fails the test on the other three primary indicators: There is no unifying theory or competing theories; no accepted standards of methods and procedures of inquiry have been established, and no shared vision of EGR's long-term impact has emerged. Also, when referring to collateral indicators, EGR would not fully qualify as a discipline, either, and fail the test for at least four indicators. So, in the classical and narrow sense EGR does not pass as a "legitimate:" discipline in its own right.

Hence, three questions arise (cf., also (Delcambre & Giuliano, 2005)): (1) what are the prospects for EGR to ultimately develop into a fully-fledged "legitimate" discipline? (2) Does it matter if EGR never assumes the status of a "legitimate" discipline in academia? And, (3) what are the alternatives, if any? The remainder of the article discusses these three questions from various angles.

3. NEIGHBORING "INCUMBENT" DISCIPLINES: PUB ADMIN AND ISR/CS

In part and at the very least, EGR shares study objects with two neighboring disciplines, Public Administration (Pub Admin) as well as Information Systems Research (ISR) and Computer Science (CS). Pub Admin research itself would have trouble with satisfying all seventeen disciplinary indicators presented above. Unlike EGR, Pub Admin is solidly established on university level with colleges and departments, and it has developed a century-long tradition of scholarship and teaching. Like Business Administration it heavily draws upon other disciplines, for example, from administrative theory and organization science including human resource management research and also finance theory. Some authors label it an interdisciplinary applied science emphasizing its close relationship to the practice of government and not-for-profit organizations (Golembiewski, 1977; Rabin *et al.*, 1998). In Woodrow Wilson's classical definition, Pub Admin studies "first, what government can properly and successfully do, and, secondly, how it can do these proper things with the utmost possible efficiency and at the least possible cost either of money or of energy" (Wilson, 1886). Although the study of IT and IT-based information in government undoubtedly falls within and not outside its realm, Pub Admin has hardly directed its efforts towards this increasingly important area. For example, unlike business schools, Pub Admin schools rarely have the equivalent to MIS departments, if any, let alone EGR units, that is, IS/IT topics are hardly researched nor taught at Pub Admin departments. This surfaces also in the top-five (Forrester & Watson, 1994) academic research outlets in Pub Admin research ("Public Administration Review (PAR)," "Administration & Society (A&S)," "American Review of Public Administration (ARPA)," "Journal of Public Administration Research and Theory (JPART)," "Public Administration Quarterly, (PAQ)"). Those journals combined a total of 1,252 research articles between 1999 and early 2006, only 41 of which were dedicated to information technology in the widest possible definition, including16 articles on EGR, representing just 1.3 percent of all articles published. Traditional Pub Admin journals, although not entirely insensitive to the academic relevancy of EGR, allot publishing space to EGR topics occasionally at best. EGR-related papers published in the top-five journals remain distanced from the IT artifact and are mainly concerned with organizational ramifications and technology acceptance in the wake of IT diffusion on an rather high and aggregate level, as it appears to best accommodate the survey method of inquiry widely used in Pub Admin research (cf., (Moon, 2002; Moon *et al.*, 2005)). Greatly missing, for example, are micro- and mezzo-level studies on immediate organizational outcomes of IT implementation, the IT artifact in its specific Pub Admin context, and the respective informational challenges and opportunities. EGR as it has been advanced via Pub Admin scholarship resembles traditional public management information systems research (cf., (Bozeman & Bretschneider, 1986; Bretschneider, 1990; Donald F. Norris & Kraemer, 1996)) in its remoteness from technology and practice and its unvarnished skepticism towards the concepts and efficacy of e-Government (for two examples, see (Bretschneider, 2003; D. F. Norris, 2003)). To the established Pub Admin departments and the scholarly publishing outlets IT-related research is peripheral. Hence, they grossly under-represent the rapidly growing importance and quantity of EGR. Due to long-term scholarly commitments and emphases directed elsewhere, this under-representation of EGR is unlikely to end any time soon.

EGR also shares study objects with ISR and CS. While ISR widely overlaps with CS in research and teaching of IS foundations, programming, analysis and design, data management, data communications, it also extends into the analysis of IS policy and strategy as well as enterprise-level interoperation. CS, on the other hand, besides a focus on engineering and practical tool development also aims at the algorithmic formalization of problem solutions (Delcambre & Giuliano, 2005). ISR has its home in the IS departments of business schools, while CS research is conducted in departments and schools of its own. By disciplinary boundary definition, CS research is unambiguous about its orientation towards the technical engineering and computational side of a problem. In contrast in ISR, this boundary is not as sharply drawn. ISR deliberately considers task, structure, and context parameters of the organizational environment when researching the IS artifact (Benbasat & Zmud, 2003). However, it stops short of inquiring the rippling effects and impacts of the IS artifact in the formal and informal organization (ibid). Neither in CS departments nor in B-school IS departments, EGR occupies central focus. To CS researchers, EGR is another area for the application of computational tools with some potential for theoretical generalization and formalization. The application area itself is of no particular concern or interest. Also, to IS scholars, EGR is mostly beyond the scope of the B-school agenda. Likewise, CS scholars are interested in providing the CS tools for tackling a government problem, however, the implementation, use, and usefulness of the tool in its context is beyond the scope of CS (Delcambre & Giuliano, 2005) leaving open a critical feedback loop. More importantly, the specifics of the government task, structure, and context only occur as an input to research around the IT artifact but certainly not as a worthwhile study focus in its own right, in which the unique embeddedness of the IT artifact would be of central interest. Needless to say that a search on EGR literature in, for example, the leading ISR journals *MIS Quarterly* and *Information Systems Research* yielded no result. Hence, like in the traditional Pub Admin sphere, so in the ISR and CS disciplinary areas, EGR is unable to establish a home for itself as, for example, a recognized or "legitimate" sub-discipline.

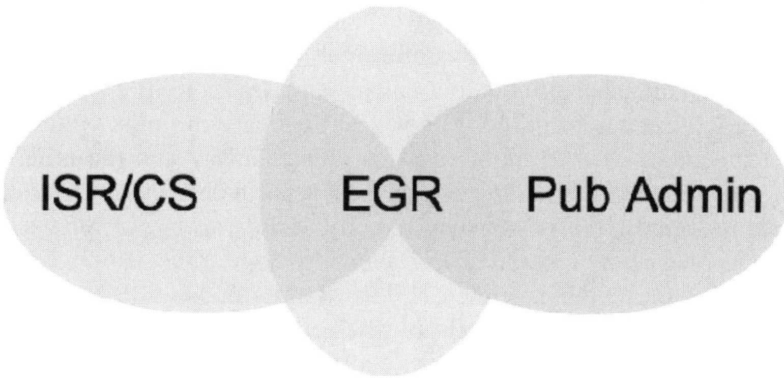

Figure 2-1. Disciplinary Overlap between EGR, ISR/CS, Pub Admin

This discussion also delivers partial answers to the first and the third question posed above: EGR draws upon both Pub Admin and ISR/CS connecting the objects of study as well as using procedures and methods of inquiry also found in both fields. However, like Bioscience with the natural sciences, EGR spans across disciplines by studying unique clusters of research problems, which tend to fall outside the boundaries of a single discipline. Further, EGR is not limited in its reach to Pub Admin and ISR/CS but rather includes relevant study objects, procedures and methods of inquiry as well as research questions shared with other disciplines such as information science, statistics, sociology, political science, geography, and the natural sciences among quite a few others. EGR, hence, appears to belong to the class of integrative interdisciplinary sciences addressing evolving clusters of research problems systematically underserved and understudied within the boundaries of established disciplines.

4. CHALLENGES AND OPPORTUNITIES FOR CROSS-DISCIPLINARY EGR

Whether disciplinary or non-disciplinary, among the foremost challenges for any new endeavor in academia ranks gaining peer recognition and the status of legitimacy. Particularly for any non-single-disciplinary science, this has always proven an arduous undertaking, since disciplinary structures along with ruling paradigms have deeply shaped and pervaded the administrative, financial, and promotional framework of academia powerfully reinforcing its disciplinary and paradigmatic composition (Kuhn, 1970; Lattuca, 2001; Mervis, 2004; Bailey, 2005; Lélé & Norgaard, 2005; National Academies (U.S.). Committee on Facilitating Interdisciplinary Research. *et al.*, 2005). One coping mechanism when dealing with such peer and system pressure has been to defensively draw the boundaries of an emerging new (sub-)discipline rather narrow and design it after the image of an existing legitimate discipline. ISR would be a case in point, which in its phase of inception defined its boundaries rather narrow and the criteria of rigor in a way acceptable to the established departments in B-schools (cf., (Benbasat & Zmud, 2003)), however, greatly at the expense of relevance to practice (Applegate & King, 1999; Davenport & Markus, 1999; Klein & Myers, 1999; Lee, 1999; Lyytinen, 1999; Markus & Lee, 1999). In other words, the initial fit into the system has helped send the sub-discipline into maintaining self-defeating standards leading to a serious identity crisis (Benbasat & Zmud, 2003) and a fight for survival (Dennis *et al.*, 2006) at a later stage. EGR might want to avoid that trap.

Besides structural and self-imposed impediments, when crossing intra- and interdisciplinary boundaries other profound obstacles have confronted EGR and will continue to thwart it (Delcambre & Giuliano, 2005). When using Biglan's classification system of academic disciplines, four distinct categories emerge (Biglan, 1973): (1) hard science (that is, an epistemic stance, which relies on measurable facts, quantification, repeatability, generalizability, closely coupled concepts and principles, which are hierarchically arranged representing the world "as it really is"); (2) soft science (that is, an epistemic stance, which incorporates inter-subjective concepts of reality with open and loosely coupled concepts and principles, including qualitative accounts, with no claim regarding an objective reality); (3) pure science (examples include theoretical physics, mathematics, etc; applicability is circumstantial at best); and (4) applied science (examples include mechanical and electrical engineering, psychotherapy, pedagogy, etc; applicability is the mainstay).

The four pairs of hard-pure, hard-applied, soft-pure, and soft-applied help distinguish disciplines further: Examples for hard-pure can be found in the natural and computer sciences, for hard-applied in engineering and medicine, for soft-pure in history, sociology, and geography, and for soft-applied in law, education, and fine arts.

EGR as depicted in figure 2-2, covers the entire Biglan spectrum. In CS, formal models and generic tools have been developed, which were transferred into practical e-Government Information Systems (EGIS) and other computer-/ network-aided tools, that is, the pure-applied boundary crossing can be observed, at least on the hard science side. When mapping the HICSS40 topical orientations into the grid, it also becomes obvious that EGR is all over the place. However, epistemic boundary crossing (hard/soft) has not been observed and might become the real challenge ahead for EGR (Delcambre & Giuliano, 2005).

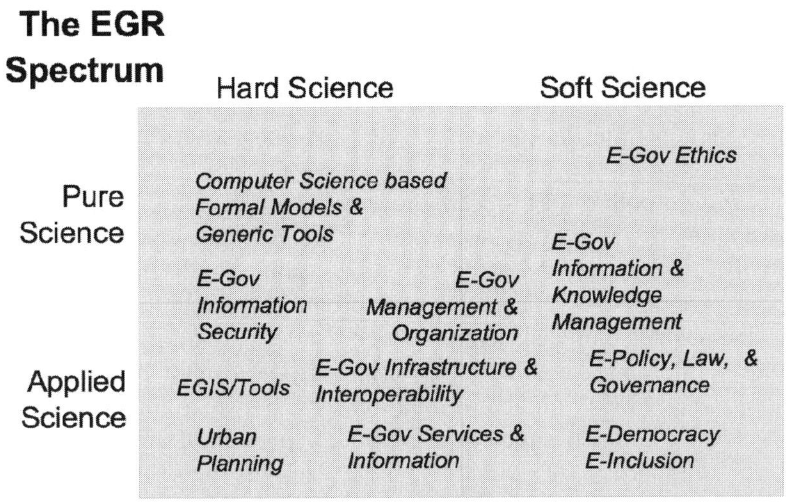

Figure 2-2. Exemplary Research Orientations

Finally, traditional PMIS or MIS scholars both in Pub Admin and ISR might denounce EGR as a home turf intruder, or as overrated and a fad soon to disappear (Bretschneider, 2003). However, the first wave of EGR contributions has already outnumbered traditional PMIS research manifold and has most probably had a far higher impact on government practice than PMIS over the past two decades, although that claim might need further empirical demonstration. With the growing roles of information, IT, and IS in every aspect of government, it is unlikely that EGR will vanish any time soon.

Despite the many obstacles, any new research endeavor, small or large, including EGR has a few natural allies, which it can count on and which begin to counterbalance the disciplinary-departmental power structure:

Fragmentation of a discipline. The explosive growth of disciplinary knowledge (Lattuca, 2001) brings about increasing degrees of specialization, which is also in part the result of reduction in the process of inquiry; however, in its wake the body of knowledge within a discipline begins to scatter (Despres *et al.*, 2004). Such fragmentation has empirically been documented to most frequently occur in applied disciplines such as engineering- and technology-related research (Morillo *et al.*, 2003). Thus, with the increasing complexity resulting from growth, reduction, and fragmentation, a need and a tendency to re-integrate the pieces emerge, which do not necessarily halt at disciplinary boundaries (Despres *et al.*, 2004).

Practical application and relevance. A strong driver for integration has traditionally been found in applied research and in practice itself (Epton *et al.*, 1983), which for all practical purposes (for example, the military) defies disciplinary straitjackets. ISR, as seen before, has perceived itself in a dichotomist tradeoff between rigor and relevance and opted in favor of the former with detrimental consequences (it will remain the task of a future paper to demonstrate that the perceived rigor-versus-relevance tradeoff is a flawed conception).

Funding. In both the European Union and the US, funding agencies (see, for example, www.esf.org, www.europa.eu.int, or www.nsf.gov) have repeatedly emphasized the need for cross- and interdisciplinary research (IDR) in program announcements and proposal solicitations. While some critics dismiss this emphasis as lip service (Bailey, 2005), the problem might be more subtle, since evaluation criteria for IDR cannot be preconfigured (Epton *et al.*, 1983), predetermined bridges between inter-working disciplines (particularly, if situated in antipodal epistemic frames) do not exist (Lélé & Norgaard, 2005), and, for the lack of personnel alternatives, proposal reviews are performed by disciplinary-oriented referees (Bailey, 2005). Despite those potential shortcomings, funding agencies have supported EGR touching all four quadrants of the Biglan spectrum.

In summary, while the challenges to cross-disciplinary EGR are formidable, it has already established itself as a multi-discipline endeavor spanning the full spectrum of hard and soft as well as pure and applied sciences. The three strong drivers, complexity, relevance, and external funding, favor cross- and interdisciplinary EGR, which has already produced a sizeable body of knowledge. This again partially answers the first and second question above. While EGR might remain a co-hosted or spread-across-discipline science for some time, its legitimacy will rise the more it demonstrably copes with the complexity inherent in EGR producing high impact and relevant results in practice (cf., (Saracevic, 1999)).

5. EGR ON THE CONTINUUM BETWEEN DISCIPLINE AND TRANSDISCIPLINE

Truly interdisciplinary studies have not yet emerged in EGR, at least, when analyzing NSF-funded projects, which cluster around tool-development studies in a CS sense and socio-technical systems research with a social science orientation (Delcambre & Giuliano, 2005). If multiple disciplines are involved in a project, the research designs are of multi-disciplinary nature at best (ibid). At this point, it seems appropriate to recall the differences between disciplinary, multi-disciplinary, inter-disciplinary, and trans-disciplinary research (see figure 2-3).

While a disciplinary community researches a problem or phenomenon based on its particular worldview (Bruce *et al.*, 2004) including accepted methods and procedures of inquiry, multi-disciplinary efforts obviously involve multiple disciplinary communities, and hence realities, and attempt to approach the phenomenon from the perspectives of the each discipline. However, each contribution remains within its disciplinary boundaries. Cross-discipline interaction, if any, is minimal (ibid). Results of such parallel studies are either not integrated or merely synoptically presented (Ramadier, 2004). However, this approach "highlights the different dimensions of the studied object and respects the plurality of points of view" (p. 433).

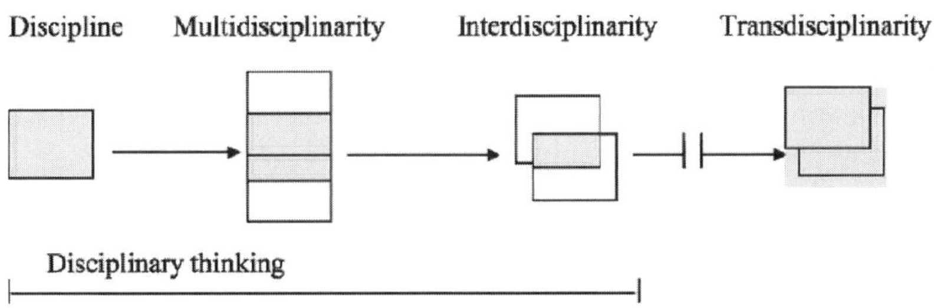

Figure 2-3. Ramadier's Disciplinarity/Transdisciplinarity Continuum (2004)

In contrast, interdisciplinary research strives to develop a shared model of understanding of a given problem/phenomenon by engaging the participating disciplinary scholars in a dialog with the goal of reaching synthesis (Gibbons, 1994; Lattuca, 2001; Bruce *et al.*, 2004; Ramadier, 2004). Two approaches towards that end have been observed in practice, a hierarchical integration via models and tools, where participating researchers agree that one discipline takes the lead and specifies rules and procedures, to which the other disciplines adhere and submit (Lattuca, 2001; Bruce *et al.*, 2004; Ramadier, 2004). In the other approach, a non-hierarchical relationship between the participating disciplines is negotiated and established through adopting and translating each discipline' s concepts into the other disciplines (Balsiger, 2004; Ramadier, 2004). Disciplinary perspectives are fully maintained also in interdisciplinary integration (see figure 2-3), even though it requires each participating discipline to reinterpret the knowledge of another discipline within its own boundaries. It appears intuitively evident that interdisciplinary research, which involves antipodal epistemic stances, is unlikely to incorporate the hierarchical model.

As Ramadier points out, both interdisciplinary and multi-disciplinary research approaches avoid "paradoxes and having to solve them," and as a consequence neither approach ultimately overcomes the problem of fragmentation and reduction (Ramadier, 2004).

Transdisciplinary research has been suggested as an alternative to disciplinary approaches including multi- and interdisciplinary arrangements. It challenges fragmentation in science by emphasizing the hybrid nature of all knowledge, its inter-subjectivity, reflexivity, and context-dependency as well as its dependence on and grounding in practice (Balsiger, 2004; Bruce *et al.*, 2004; Despres *et al.*, 2004; Horlick-Jones & Sime, 2004; Ramadier, 2004; Thompson Klein, 2004).

Essentially, transdisciplinarity combines multidisciplinarity and interdisciplinarity to the extent that, while different levels of reality are explicitly accounted for (as in multi-disciplinary approaches), "it has adopted the effort to reinterpret knowledge in order to readjust the different levels of reality" (Ramadier, 2004) from interdisciplinary approaches. Transdisciplinary research attempts to integrate those levels of reality by assessing "the impact of one level on the relationship" (ibid) between other levels involved without suppressing paradoxes and ambiguities.

As discussed before, EGR already spans the full Biglan classification spectrum of sciences, however, predominantly in a single-discipline fashion. Given the acknowledged complex nature of e-Government phenomena, multi-, inter-, and transdisciplinary research approaches, albeit initially more difficult to receive funding for and to practice under current administrative and paradigmatic constraints, holds the promise of richer results, deeper understanding, and greater impact and relevance to practice. If such outcomes materialize, EGR will gain a profile and academic recognition as a multi-, inter-, or transdiscipline (see figure 2-4, next page), which could greatly take care of discipline-oriented worries of legitimacy. On the contrary, EGR might not want to enter into the confines and subsequent torpidity of a discipline but rather maintain a standing of a new knowledge enterprise in line with Gibbons's mode-2 characteristics (Gibbons, 1994).

The efforts for turning such ambitious goals into reality should not be underestimated. For example, Delcambre and Giuliano assume the epistemic divide in EGR to mainly fall along the lines of hard (CS) and soft (Social Sciences) (Delcambre & Giuliano, 2005); however, Social Sciences are anything but "epistemologically homogenous" (Horlick-Jones & Sime, 2004). Some social sciences hold strong positivist[1] stances, which may

---

[1] Although it has developed several flavors, by and large, positivism holds that "the world" and "reality" are governed by a set of universal laws and patterns, which can be discovered, unambiguously explained, and completely understood by human observers through employing the scientific method. Examples of positivist social sciences are the

alleviate collaboration between hard sciences with similar epistemic stances. Other social sciences, or even strands and sub-disciplines within a social science, may embrace a non-positivist stance, which can easily cause friction when collaborating with an antipodal stance.

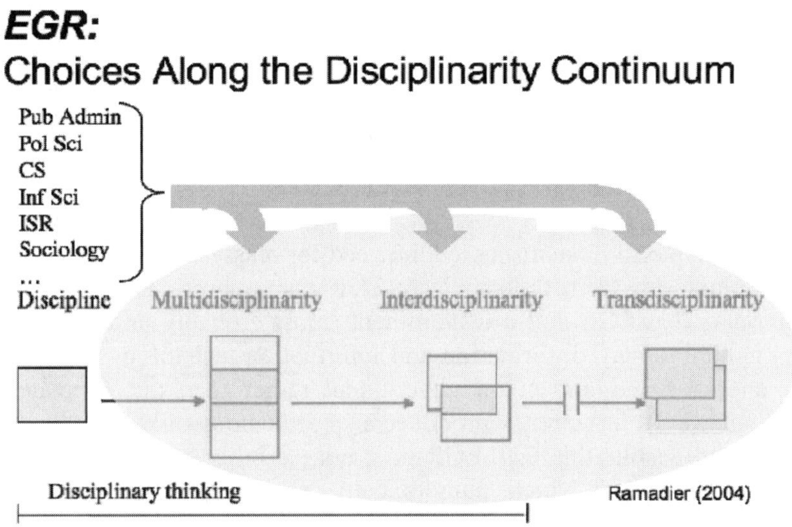

Figure 2-4. EGR-from disciplines to transdisciplinarity

Just cross-training participant researchers will be important but may prove insufficient when crossing the borderline between multidisciplinary to interdisciplinary thinking, let alone when crossing the gap that separates all kinds of disciplinary thinking and truly transdisciplinary approaches. Still, any EGR endeavor, which ventures beyond a single discipline, will add to the understanding of the requirements when moving along the continuum towards transdisciplinarity.

In summary, from what has been discussed in this and the previous sections and in answering the three questions posed before it appears that (1) EGR is unlikely to become a traditional "legitimate" discipline; (2) however, this outcome is unlikely to stop or even slow down EGR in the future; and (3) the prospects for EGR's sustained impact and success might lie in developing into an integrative science with multi-, inter-, and transdisciplinary characteristics. If EGR produces successful exemplars of multi-, inter-, and transdisciplinary projects, it may have the capacity to serve as

dominant strands in Economics, Psychology, Sociology, and Public Administration, even though non-positivist and constructivist strands are also increasingly found in those sciences.

role model for other scientific endeavors of that nature. Such a development would fulfill Polanyi's vision of science as chains and networks of knowing:

> Each link in these chains and networks will establish agreement between the valuations made by scientists overlooking the same overlapping fields, and so, from one overlapping neighborhood to another, agreement will be established on the valuation of scientific merit throughout all the domains of science (Polanyi & Grene, 1969, 55–56).

6. CONCLUDING REMARKS

In this chapter, I have discussed the need for reassessing the EGR agenda and for reassuring both the scholarly EGR community and e-Government practitioners that EGR and e-Government (most probably under a different name) is here to stay. Information and information technology will grow in importance for and impact on government rather than the opposite. Not surprisingly, EGR has already produced a sizeable body of knowledge.

However, despite this fact, EGR does not pass the test of a fully-fledged academic discipline, which paradoxically might be advantageous. The chapter has analyzed how the neighboring "incumbent" disciplines of Pub Admin and ISR have approached e-Government. For different reasons, the two disciplines have proven little receptive and hardly attentive to e-Government-related problems and phenomena. One reason for this restraint may lie in the complexity of e-Government-related problems and phenomena themselves, which greatly exceeds the scope of any single academic discipline, and in particular, the two disciplines of Public Admin and ISR. EGR intersects the two disciplines but also goes way beyond their scope.

EGR problems have been researched from fairly different disciplinary perspectives. In addition, EGR covers the entire spectrum of hard-pure, hard-applied, soft-pure, and soft-applied sciences making it unlikely to ever develop into a traditional "legitimate" discipline. However, little cross-pollination between those single-discipline approaches has been found. Yet the current intra- and interdisciplinary fragmentation prevents both EGR and e-Government practice from tapping its full potential of understanding and impact. EGR, this chapter suggests, might be most effective when established as a multi-, inter-, and transdiscipline representing a more integrative understanding of knowing.

By assuming such an integrative and transdisciplinary understanding and through extending Wilson's definition (Wilson, 1886), one could characterize EGR's "aboutness" (Hjorland, 2001) as "first, what government can properly and successfully do *with information and information technology*, and, secondly, how it can do these proper things with the utmost possible efficiency and at the least possible cost either of money or of energy."

ACKNOWLEDGEMENTS

The author is the PI of a grant from the National Science Foundation, which studies the effects and impacts of fully mobile wirelessly connected information technology in local City government.

REFERENCES

AACSB. (2000). E-business. Education. Retrieved 10/4, 2000, from http://aacsb.edu/e-business/definitions.html

Anonymous. (2005a). Calls on e-Government. Retrieved 1/27, 2006, from http://europa.eu.int/information_society/activities/e-Government_research/calls/index_en.htm

Anonymous. (2005b, 1/26). Digital government society mission statement. Retrieved 1/27, 2006, from http://faculty.washington.edu/jscholl/DGS/DGS_Mission_Final.html

Anonymous. (2006). The National Science Foundation Digital Government Research Program: Linking it research with government mission and studying its impact on democracy and governance. Retrieved 1/27, 2006, from http://www.diggov.org/

Applegate, L. M., & King, J. L. (1999). Rigor and relevance: Careers on the line. *MIS Quarterly, 23*(1), 17-18.

Bailey, K. D. (2005). Fifty years of systems science: Further reflections. *Systems Research and Behavioral Science, 22*(5), 355-361.

Balsiger, P. W. (2004). Supradisciplinary research practices: History, objectives and rationale. *Futures, 36*(4), 407-421.

Becher, T., & Trowler, P. (2001). *Academic tribes and territories: Intellectual enquiry and the culture of disciplines* (2nd ed.). Philadelphia, PA: Open University Press.

Benbasat, I., & Zmud, R. W. (2003). The identity crisis within the is discipline: Defining and communicating the discipline's core properties1. *MIS Quarterly, 27*(2), 183-194.

Biglan, A. (1973). The characteristics of subject matter in different academic fields. *Journal of Applied Psychology, 57*(3), 195-203.

Black, L. J., Cresswell, A. M., Luna, L. F., Pardo, T. A., Martinez, I. J., Thompson, F., et al. (2003). *A dynamic theory of collaboration: A structural approach to facilitating intergovernmental use of information technology*.

Bozeman, B., & Bretschneider, S. (1986). Public management information systems: Theory and prescriptions. *Public Administration Review, 46* (November (special issue)), 475-489.

Bretschneider, S. (1990). Management information systems in public and private organization: An empirical test. *Public Administration Review, 50*(September/October), 536-545.

Bretschneider, S. (2003). Information technology, e-government, and institutional change. *Public Administration Review, 63*(6), 738-741.

Bruce, A., Lyall, C., Tait, J., & Williams, R. (2004). Interdisciplinary integration in Europe: The case of the fifth framework programme. *Futures, 36*(4), 457-470.

Bush, V. (1945). As we may think. *Atlantic Monthly, 176*(July), 101-108.

Cresswell, A. M., Pardo, T. A., Thompson, F., Canestraro, D. S., Cook, M., Black, L. J., et al. (2002). *Modeling intergovernmental collaboration: A system dynamics approach.*

Cushing, J., & Pardo, T. (2005). Guest editors' introduction: Research in the digital government realm. *Computer, 38*(12), 26-32.

Davenport, T. H., & Markus, M. L. (1999). Rigor vs. Relevance revisited: Response to benbasat and zmud. *MIS Quarterly, 23*(1), 19-23.

Delcambre, L., & Giuliano, G. (2005). Digital government research in academia. *Computer, 38*(12), 33-39.

Dennis, A. R., Valacich, J. S., Fuller, M. A., & Schneider, C. (2006). Research standards for promotion and tenure in information systems. *MIS Quarterly, 30*(1), 1-12.

Despres, C., Brais, N., & Avellan, S. (2004). Collaborative planning for retrofitting suburbs: Transdisciplinarity and intersubjectivity in action. *Futures, 36*(4), 471-486.

Epton, S. R., Payne, R., & Pearson, A. W. (1983). *Managing interdisciplinary research.* Chichester [West Sussex]; New York: Wiley.

Feyerabend, P. K. (1975). *Against method: Outline of an anarchistic theory of knowledge.* Atlantic Highlands, N.J.: Humanities Press.

Forrester, J. P., & Watson, S. S. (1994). An assessment of public administration journals: The perspective of editors and editorial board members. *Public Administration Review, 54*(5), 474-482.

Fountain, J. E. (2001). *Building the virtual state: Information technology and institutional change.* Washington, D.C.: Brookings Institution Press.

Gibbons, M. (1994). *The new production of knowledge: The dynamics of science and research in contemporary societies.* London; Thousand Oaks, Calif.: Sage Publications.

Golembiewski, R. T. (1977). *Public administration as a developing discipline.* New York: M. Dekker.

Grönlund, A. (2001, January). Democracy in an it-framed society. *Communications of the ACM, 44,* 23-26.

Grönlund, A. (2004, Aug 30 to Sep 3). *State of the art in e-Gov research: A survey.* Paper presented at the Third International Conference, E-GOV 2004, Zaragoza, Spain.

Grönlund, A. (2005). State of the art in e-Gov research: Surveying conference publications. *International Journal of Electronic Government Research, 1*(4), 1-25.

Heilprin, L. B. (1991). The library community at a technological and philosophical crossroads: Necessary and sufficient conditions for survival. *Journal of the American Society for Information Science (1986-1998), 42*(8), 566.

Hjorland, B. (2001). Towards a theory of aboutness, subject, topicality, theme, domain,field, content. And relevance. *Journal of the American Society for Information Science and Technology, 52*(9), 774-778.

Horlick-Jones, T., & Sime, J. (2004). Living on the border: Knowledge, risk and transdisciplinarity. *Futures, 36*(4), 441-456.

Hovy, E. (2003). Using an ontology to simplify data access. *Communications of the Acm, 46*(1), 47-49.

Huang, W., Siau, K., & Wei, K. K. (2004). *Electronic government strategies and implementation.* Hershey PA.: Idea Group Pub.

Klein, H. K., & Myers, M. D. (1999). A set of principles for conducting and evaluating interpretive field studies in information systems. *MIS Quarterly, 23*(1), 67-88.

Klischewski, R. (2004). Information integration or process integration? How to achieve interoperability in administration. In R. Traunmüller (Ed.), *Electronic government: Third International Conference, e-gov 2004, Zaragoza, Spain, August 30-September 3, 2004. Proceedings* (Vol. 3183, Lecture notes in computer science, pp. 57-65). New York, NY: Springer.

Kubicek, H., Millard, J., & Westholm, H. (2003). Methodology for analysing the relationship between the reorganisation of the back office and better electronic public services. In R. Traunmüller (Ed.), *Electronic government: Second international conference, e-gov 2003, Prague, Czech Republic, September 2003: Proceedings* (Vol. 2739, Lecture notes in computer science, pp. 199-206). New York, N.Y.: Springer.

Kuhn, T. S. (1970). *The structure of scientific revolutions* (2d, enl. ed.). Chicago: University of Chicago Press.

Lattuca, L. R. (2001). *Creating interdisciplinarity: Interdisciplinary research and teaching among college and university faculty* (1st ed.). Nashville: Vanderbilt University Press.

Layne, K., & Lee, J. (2001). Developing fully functional e-government: A four stage model. *Government Information Quarterly, 18*(2), 122-136.

Lee, A. S. (1999). Rigor and relevance in mis research: Beyond the approach of positivism alone. *MIS Quarterly, 23*(1), 29-27.

Lyytinen, K. (1999). Empirical research in information systems: On the relevance of practice in thinking of is research. *MIS Quarterly, 23*(1), 25-27.

Lélé, S., & Norgaard, R. B. (2005). Practicing interdisciplinarity. *Bioscience, 55*(11), 967.

Markus, M. L., & Lee, A. S. (1999). Special issue on intensive research in information systems: Using qualitative, interpretive, and case methods to study information technology–foreward. *MIS Quarterly, 23*(1), 35-38.

Mervis, J. (2004). Risky business. *Science, 306*(5694), 220-221.

Moon, M. J. (2002). The evolution of e-government among municipalities: Rhetoric or reality? *Public Administration Review, 62*(4), 424-433.

Moon, M. J., Welch, E. W., & Wong, W. (2005). *What drives global e-governance? An exploratory study at a macro level.*

Morillo, F., Bordons, M., & Gomez, I. (2003). Interdisciplinarity in science: A tentative typology of disciplines and research areas. *Journal of the American Society for Information Science and Technology, 54*(13), 1237-1249.

National Academies (U.S.). Committee on Facilitating Interdisciplinary Research., Committee on Science Engineering and Public Policy (U.S.), National Academy of Sciences (U.S.), National Academy of Engineering., & Institute of Medicine (U.S.). (2005). *Facilitating interdisciplinary research.* Washington, D.C.: National Academies Press.

Norris, D. F. (2003). Building the virtual state. Or not? A critical appraisal. *Social Science Computer Review, 21*(4), 417-424.

Norris, D. F., & Kraemer, K. L. (1996). Mainframe and pc computing in American cities: Myths and realities. *Public Administration Review, 56*(6), 568-576.

Pantel, P., Philpot, A., & Hovy, E. (2005). Data alignment and integration [US government]. *Computer, 38*(12), 43-50.

Polanyi, M., & Grene, M. G. (1969). *Knowing and being; essays.* [Chicago]: University of Chicago Press.

Rabin, J., Hildreth, W. B., & Miller, G. (1998). *Handbook of public administration* (2nd ed.). New York: Marcel Dekker.

Ramadier, T. (2004). Transdisciplinarity and its challenges: The case of urban studies. *Futures, 36*(4), 423-439.

Saracevic, T. (1999). Information Science. *Journal of the American Society for Information Science, 50*(12), 1051-1063.

Scholl, H. J. (2003, 1/6 to 1/10). *E-Government: A special case of business process change.* Paper presented at the 36th Hawaiian International Conference on System Sciences (HICSS36), Waikoloa, HI.

Scholl, H. J. (2004a). The dimensions of business process change in electronic government. In W. Huang, K. Siau & K. K. Wei (Eds.), *Electronic government strategies and implementation* (pp. 44-67). Hershey PA.: Idea Group Pub.

Scholl, H. J. (2004b). Involving salient stakeholders: Beyond the technocratic view on change. *Action Research, 2*(3), 281-308.

Scholl, H. J. (2005a). E-government-induced business process change (BPC): An empirical study of current practices. *International Journal of Electronic Government Research, 1*(2), 25-47.

Scholl, H. J. (2005b). Motives, strategic approach, objectives & focal areas in e-Gov-induced change. *International Journal of Electronic Government Research, 1*(1), 58-77.

Scholl, H. J. (2005c, August 22 to 26). *Organizational transformation through e-Government: Myth or reality?* Paper presented at the 4th International Conference E-GOV05, Copenhagen, Denmark.

Shannon, C. E., & Weaver, W. (1962). *The mathematical theory of communication*. Urbana: University of Illinois Press.

Thompson Klein, J. (2004). Prospects for transdisciplinarity. *Futures, 36*(4), 515-526.

Webber, S. (2003). Information Science in 2003: A critique. *Journal of Information Science, 29*(4), 311-330.

Wilson, W. (1886). The study of administration. Retrieved 2/14, 2006, from http://teachingamericanhistory.org/library/index.asp?document=465

SUGGESTED READINGS

- Kuhn, T. S. (1996). The structure of scientific revolutions (3rd ed.). Chicago, IL: University of Chicago Press. Kuhn's famous book paved the way for a new understanding of the nature of scientific advances. Although not a light read, this book is an indispensable prerequisite for understanding the choices, which the study domain of digital government might face on its path to the new frontier of a transdiscipline.
- Orlikowski, W. J. (1992). The duality of technology: Rethinking the concept of technology in organizations. Organization Science, 3(3), 398-427. Using Giddens' structuration theory, Orlikowski argues that technology enacts organizational structure, however, that in turn the structure and the human actors shape the technology through emergent and situated use. For E-Government researchers, the interaction of human actors, information technology, formal and informal organization poses a unique challenge, which is hard to grasp from a single discipline's perspective. Orlikowski's article is foundational for understanding this interaction.
- Burrell, G., & Morgan, G. (1979). Sociological paradigms and organisational analysis: Elements of the sociology of corporate life. London: Heinemann. The various schools of thought in social sciences employ distinct worldviews and assumptions about reality. The two authors identify those assumptions and demonstrate how they determine

the diverging interests, directions, and conclusions of research, for example, in organizational analysis. For E-Government researchers, an understanding of these underpinnings is essential when engaging in interdisciplinary collaboration.

ONLINE RESOURCES

- Aurora Online: Gareth Morgan: http://aurora.icaap.org/archive/morgan.html
- Wikipedia: http://en.wikipedia.org/wiki/Interdisciplinarity

QUESTIONS FOR DISCUSSION

1. What makes it difficult to study the phenomena of digital government from a single discipline's perspective?
2. What are some of the challenges a computer scientist and a public administration scholar may face, when they want to study a certain phenomenon in digital government together?
3. What are the choices those two researchers may have in their research design(s)?
4. What would be the likely differences in the results and in the depth of understanding regarding the various research options?
5. What would be some of the challenges, if a researcher who favors "hard" and "applied" science and a researcher who favors "soft" and "pure" science come to work together on a digital government research project?
6. Why would it be easier for researchers from either the "hard" or the "soft" side of the research spectrum to work together as opposed to working across the "hard/soft" divide?
7. What would be some of the promises of truly interdisciplinary research over disciplinary or multidisciplinary research in digital government?
8. To what extent does the current structure of universities support interdisciplinary research?

Chapter 3

AN OUTLINE FOR THE FOUNDATIONS OF DIGITAL GOVERNMENT RESEARCH

Eduard Hovy

Digital Government Research Center (DGRC) and Information Sciences Institute, University of Southern California, Marina del Rey, CA US (hovy@isi.edu , http://www.isi.edu/~hovy)

CHAPTER OVERVIEW

This chapter asks: Is Digital (or electronic) Government (DG) a legitimate new field of research? If so, what aspects of government should be studied, and why? Since DG is obviously an interdisciplinary endeavor, which disciplines can or should play a role, and why? How can they interact? Is it likely that a single integrated language, research methodology, project style, and structure of research paper will evolve, and if so, what might this hybrid look like? The chapter presents a model in which government is viewed from three perspectives. First, the technological. As a processor of information, government uses the results of ICT research and development, as performed by computer scientists and human factors specialists. This begs the question: which new technologies should be designed and built, and why? Second, therefore, the normative. The idealized (or at least improved) functioning of government, which tends to be the purview of political scientists, ethicists, and legal scholars, must furnish models toward which new ICT and its deployment can strive. In turn, this begs the question: how well does newly-enabled ICT-enriched government actually do? Third, therefore, the evaluative. This involves the challenges of studying the effects of using technology on society and government itself, enterprises that tend to be the domain of some sociologists and public administration researchers, and, within government, of organization management and information systems specialists. The chapter suggests that good research in DG, and good DG research papers, should combine these three perspectives, thereby including in each study all three aspects: technological, normative, and evaluative.

1. INTRODUCTION: A NEW FIELD OF RESEARCH

Digital (electronic) Government concerns the use of digital technology to support and enhance government[1]. While its value for society has always been apparent, Digital Government has recently emerged as a distinguishable topic of research for government officials, academics such as computer scientists, political scientists, and others, and commercial vendors of information and communications technology. If it is indeed to become a new research field, some rather interesting questions arise: What areas does it cover, exactly? Why? Which different disciplines does it draw from? What questions do its different researchers (tend to) study? How can they interact? What format(s) and methodologies should researchers adopt?

The process of forming a new multidisciplinary research area requires the development, early on, of a common mode of discourse, which includes at least the following: (somewhat) standardized terminology; commonly agreed-upon criteria for judging the value of research; and effective transfer of results and products across the gaps that divide its component disciplines. Scholl, in his chapter in this volume (Scholl, 2007), provides and excellent discussion of these issues. If this development does not occur, the area remains simply a meeting place where friends talk past one another, and eventually it dissolves.

To date, there have been few attempts to study Digital Government (DG) as a new field of research (for notable exceptions, see (Fountain, 2001; Grønlund, 2004; Cushing and Pardo, 2005), and none that fully describes the emergent field (if indeed it is one) in its own, new, multidisciplinary terms and perspectives. As a field, DG is simply too young.

In order to think about a framework for the new field, this chapter addresses some of the very basic issues that have arisen in the DG community over the past years, taking as approximate starting point the first national DG conference in the USA (dg.o), held in Los Angeles in 1999. The chapter is organized around six basic questions.

First question: What is Digital Government, and, more specifically, what is DG research? Clearly, it involves the use of computers (more broadly, information and communication technology or ICT) in government. Does this mean that every time a government official writes email, or searches the web, he or she is conducting digital government? Somehow, these actions do not seem like DG, nor appropriate as objects of DG research. Perhaps they are simply too mundane. But if so, where does one draw the line? What actions *do* constitute DG, and what topics are legitimate for DG research, and why?

---

[1] I use the terms *Digital Government* (current in the USA) and *eGovernment* (current in Europe and Asia) interchangeably in this chapter.

Second question: At first glance, it seems clear that DG should involve some computational technology, as well as, obviously, some government agency or service. But what precise role(s) should computer scientists play in DG? Since ICT by no means covers the full extent of DG, how should social scientists and others contribute? Here especially one thinks of the work of political scientists, legal scholars, public administration specialists, organization management theorists, and information systems specialists. Which social sciences form a natural part of the DG research picture? And which other disciplines? Given all these parties, in what ways do they interact? Why? How else can or should they interact?

Third question: What are the basic assumptions behind DG research? What conditions should obtain before one should be willing to devote resources to DG research? Why?

Fourth question: How does DG differ from apparently similar enterprises such as eHealth, eEduction, or eBusiness? What special characteristics does it have (for example, in situations such as crisis response, international (cross-border) problems, and universal access)?

Fifth question: What are the differences between the conception of e-Government R&D in the EU and Digital Government R&D in the US? Are these differences important? Why did they come about, and what are their effects?

Sixth question: How should DG researchers communicate their research? What is the ideal form and content of a DG rcscarch project? Since the various disciplines involved have such different styles of communication, is it possible to define a single general structure for DG research papers?

This chapter provides some observations on these questions, in the hope that this may help clarify the nascent field (if indeed it will become a field), and possibly assist in the development of the 'theory' of DG (should this eventually come about).

2. A TRIPARTITE MODEL OF ICT IN GOVERNMENT

One way to address these questions is to elaborate the general process of R&D in Digital Government. For this, three complementary perspectives are helpful: government as an *information processor*; government as a *function*; and government as an *organization*. Each perspective highlights different kinds of questions:

- Use ICT how? Here we search for elucidations of manner and processing

- Why use ICT? Here we search for definitions and descriptions of purpose
- Use ICT how well? Here we search for measures of effectiveness

We discuss each perspective in turn, and then assemble them into a tripartite model of R&D in DG.

Government as information processor. This part of the model is the most apparent in current DG research. From the perspective of Computer Science, a government is just another processor of information, with government officials and/or citizens as users. Therefore we can ask: How does government *function as an information processor*? What information collection, storage, transformation, and dissemination needs exist in the business of government? In what ways can existing ICT be deployed? What new ICT can be developed to assist with the government's information processing needs? These questions are, obviously, of primary interest to computer scientists and human factors psychologists and ergonomists. The answers involve 'hard-core' ICT research in algorithms, data structures, systems, and human-computer interfaces, as well as software and hardware construction and testing.

Government as function. This part of the model is normative. Here we ask: How should government *function in the ideal case*, and how can existing and new ICT be used to help achieve these ideals? What kinds of processes, data, and decisions would improve government? Fundamentally, these questions are based on ethical and legal principles, and on the controls to be exercised in government. This is because government occupies a unique position in society, one that requires the citizen's trust, simultaneously, in the arenas of force (policing, security, and the military), universality (contrary to business, the government has to serve all people equally, even ones in inaccessible places or with debilitating conditions), and privacy (the government has access to sensitive information such as personal finances and perhaps health conditions). These concerns manifest themselves as guidelines for the invention, development, and deployment of ICT for government. The questions in this dimension are of primary interest to practical ethicists, political scientists, and legal scholars. The answers involve studies that can be interpreted normatively to produce desiderata, guidelines, and suggestions for new ICT solutions for better government.

Government as organization. This part of the model is evaluative. Here we ask: How well does or can government *function in practice*, using ICT? Can one find better methods of employing existing or new ICT? Can one improve government effectiveness with new ICT? In this dimension as well, the government occupies a unique position vis à vis the roles of business, health care, education, and other social functions: in the business of governance, government has no competitor! The citizen, as consumer of government services, has to pay taxes, but has no choices for alternative service providers. Worse, the citizen is not in a position easily to demand any direct accountability. Without such capitalist-like forces to keep them in line, governments have a notorious tendency to become inefficient, bloated, and authoritarian. To counter this, researchers and developers of ICT for government should be especially alert to the potential for inefficiency and waste. The questions in this dimension are of primary interest to the organization and management scholar, the information systems researcher, and the sociologist and social anthropologist interested in government's practical effect on society. The answers involve measurements that quantify the utility and effectiveness of ICT in government, and that should be of central importance to the developers of such ICT.

Clearly, this tripartite model is a strong simplification. Please note explicitly that the claim is not that normative studies are the exclusive domain of political scientists, legal scholars, and applied ethicists, or that evaluative studies can be performed only by organization and management scholars, etc. Of course each discipline can, and should, have its own view of all aspects of government. But taken on average, the government-as-function disciplines tend to focus on the normative issues and frame their arguments in terms of theories dealing with the good of society, while the government-as-organization disciplines tend to focus on measurements and frame their arguments in terms of improving the here-and-now of government.

Assembling the three parts of the model, the possible types of interaction between the various research areas become apparent. As illustrated in Figure 3-1, normative studies can be interpreted by ICT developers as desiderata for new ICT systems to be designed and developed in pursuit of ideal (or at least better) government, while evaluative studies can be used by ICT developers as measures for how well their systems are being used in practice.

Conversely, providers of normative studies can investigate the potential for ICT to be useful in realizing the ideal function of government, and providers of evaluative studies can measure the use of ICT for more efficient performance of government. To the extent all these researchers do this work, they are performing Digital Government research.

Researchers may choose to close the grand loop, involving in a single study normative, computational, and evaluative work all together. But most studies are more focused. In the past each discipline tended to study government and ICT independently, with in most cases no cross-discipline feedback, but this situation is rapidly changing, as seen for example in (Gil-Garcia and Pardo, 2006).

This model highlights the limitations of any single-discipline approach. No ICT can be developed without some rudimentary consideration of the kinds of government functioning it is aiming at, and no ICT product can be said to have been completed successfully without at least minimal evaluation of its effectiveness. Similarly, normative studies of the potential of ICT for better functioning of government can never be realistic without some dialogue with ICT specialists about what new technology and processes are truly feasible, and no evaluative studies of the actual use of ICT can be complete if they are not based on an accurate picture, obtained from the ICT developers, of what the technology is capable of doing and was designed to do.

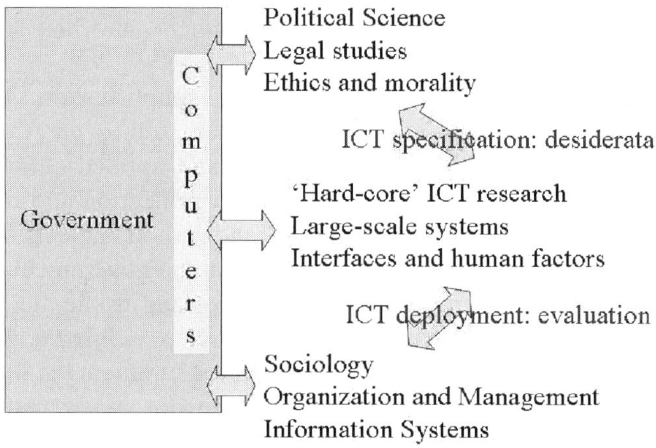

Figure 3-1. Interactions between DG research areas.

This argument suggests that truly 'complete' DG research should involve not only the government partner, but researchers from each major dimension—typically, a team of at least four people, and possibly more. If performed well, the results would represent a model project. But the tripartite model of Digital Government also suggests two smaller R&D collaboration loops:

- Normative+ICT: studies of this kind focus either on how DG practice falls short of society's needs, or on what new ICT-supported government functioning is desirable and technically feasible, given hypothesized ICT solutions, or even ICT prototypes, without much concern for the efficiency of the procedures in place.
- Evaluative+ICT: studies of this kind focus either on what technology and processes are in use, or on how to improve existing DG practice, without trying to invent fundamentally new ones and new technology.

3. RELATED WORK

Given the very recent emergence of Digital Government and its development into a potentially separate field of study, there is little relevant research on its nature as a field. The principal work available is without doubt (Fountain, 2001), in which some foundational notions implicit in the interaction between government and digital technology are developed. Fountain identifies two views on ICT: as conceived and built for the general case (which she calls *objective technology*) and as designed for a specific situation and deployed (which she calls *enacted technology*). "My framework separates objective technology—Internet, other telecommunications, hardware and software—from enacted technology, the particular designs, applications, programs, and systems developed through negotiation among political and institutional actors" (p. 5). Fountain studies how different organizations within the US government (including the International Trade Data System, a government-wide system for processing international trade; the U.S. Business Advisor, the nation's first federal government web portal; and the Ninth Infantry Division, the high technology testbed for the tactical Army) select components of objective technology and 'enact' them to suit their needs. She continues: "Institutions and organizations shape the enactment of information technology. Technology, in turn, may reshape organizations and institutions to better conform to its logic or systems of rules. New information technologies are enacted—made sense of, designed, and used (when they are used)—through the mediation of existing organizational and institutional arrangements with their own internal logics or tendencies. These multiple logics are embedded in operating routines, performance programs, bureaucratic politics, norms, cultural beliefs, and social networks" (p. 7). In terms of the tripartite model of this chapter, objective technology more closely fits the technology perspective, while enacted technology is the driver of the evaluative perspective. This model complements Fountain's framework by highlighting the kinds of concerns that arise around the enactment of ICT in government and listing the research disciplines typically associated with them.

Grønlund (2005) presents a theory for e-gov information systems drawn from a model of governance derived from a general model of society. He focuses on the effectiveness of government operations, with the intent of providing a general framework within which the evolution of the utility of using ICT in government can be assessed. This work is an excellent example of the evaluative perspective.

Scholl (2007; this volume) discusses the characteristics that provide DG the potential to persist as a research field, and not merely pass in a few years. These include a growing body of data and publications, a unique cluster of research problems, the emergence of a shared vision, and a slowly growing body of well-known and respected researchers. However, for DG to grow established, he identifies the ways in which the style and topics of DG researchers must adapt. Also in the chapter, Scholl outlines the overlap of DG research with research in Public Administration and Information Systems. But he points out the remoteness of Public Administration research to technology—a point that stands in stark contrast to the tripartite model outlined in this chapter—and the point at which Information Systems research tends to decouple from inquiring about the effects of ICT on the formal and informal organization of government. His conclusion meshes well with the model presented here: no extant discipline covers enough of the concerns of DG to do an adequate job, but DG must stretch in several very different directions to cover all the bases.

More remote areas of study with some relevance for the normative DG disciplines address the semiotics of political systems (especially work in Eastern Europe) and the socio-political effects of technology; see for example part IV of (MacKenzie and Wajcman, 1985), which contains chapters focusing on the military effects of ICT. Echoing Fountain's enacted technology, several authors discuss the political effects of technology, including ICT, when situated within culture and nature; see for example (Michael, 2000). Bijker (1995) provides an excellent overview of studies of technology from socio-historical perspectives. On the technology-oriented front of human factors and ergonomics, the volume edited by Nardi (2006) provides a cognitive model of human-computer interaction that may inform especially the evaluative DG disciplines.

4. ASSUMPTIONS BEHIND DG RESEARCH IN LIGHT OF THE MODEL

One cannot walk into any government office and expect that DG research will be welcomed, will be possible, or will make a difference, no matter how well it has been executed. The following assumptions, published by Delcambre and Giuliano (2005) and used here with their permission, express the preconditions for successful DG research:

1. A substantial number of problems facing government workers are technical enough in nature to be addressed by ICT;
2. There is something unique about government problems that researchers would not come across otherwise;
3. These problems are of sufficient interest and complexity to engage researchers;

4. Government partners can define the problem in terms that researchers can understand;
5. Researchers are willing and able to do the research and (to some degree) the technology transfer;
6. Government partners are willing to adopt and use the R&D results.

The tripartite model frames these preconditions, helping to differentiate those that are more axiomatic from those that do not necessarily always hold, or hold directly. It is not, for example, obvious a priori why Precondition 2 must hold. But in context of the model, one sees that government problems include an ethical/moral dimension within the normative cluster that may be absent, or much less prominent, in other areas of application, such as eEducation or eAgriculture. One could therefore reformulate Precondition 2 as follows:

2'. Government problems suitable for DG research involve some normative aspect, such as the need for privacy, universal service, or accountability, that researchers would not normally encounter in other problems.

Precondition 2 can obviously also be broadened to include the evaluative dimension, though it seems less strong here, since efficiency is also important to other enterprises. But Precondition 3 does speak more directly to the evaluative, for two reasons: (1) the lack of accountability in government offices (relative to commercial enterprises) makes highly desirable that ICT be almost incapable of being used inefficiently (to the extent this is possible), and (2) the requirement of government universality means that even the least computer-literate citizen should be able to use properly the ICT provided for him or her. One could therefore reformulate Precondition 3 as follows:

3'. These problems are of sufficient interest and complexity to engage researchers; specifically, the challenge is to develop ICT solutions that are crafted to minimize user misunderstanding, misuse, and inefficiency.

Precondition 6 has proven to be rather optimistic, after nearly a decade of DG research. But it is almost certainly the case that well-crafted DG research that represents all three the model's dimensions has a much higher chance of being adopted by government employees. One might reformulate Precondition 6 as follows:

6'. Government partners are more willing to adopt and use R&D results that have been carefully designed under the goals of good governance, that have been well crafted, and that have been deployed and tested in situ to ensure maximal efficiency, than they are to adopt R&D results that exhibit only some of none of these characteristics.

5. THE CHARACTER OF DG AND SIMILAR RESEARCH IN DIFFERENT APPLICATIONS

This section addresses the basic question of how DG differs from apparently similar enterprises such as eHealth, eEduction, or eBusiness, and what special nature it adopts in specific instances of government such as Crisis Response. Since a great deal of literature compares them, this section simply highlights some differences as they pertain to the tripartite model.

ICT-enhanced **government** requires ICT solutions for the following areas primarily: technology to support policy creation; the recording and retrieval of ethical and legal questions; tools for policy enforcement and legal issues; public-government communications; technology for security and privacy; and tools to improve general government data processing efficiency. Its special roles as trusted controller of force and as holder of private personal information make government a primary consumer of normative DG research and ICT developments.

eHealth highlights the areas of data capture, storage, and management; privacy and security; and health-related communications and broadcasting. As for government, eHealth workers are in possession of private personal information and also need normative research.

eBusiness has especial need for technology that facilitates communication; handling of legal issues; and efficient data management. Given how efficiency equates to profit, business has a special need for the evaluative dimension of DG research, but the ethical dimension should not be overlooked.

ICT-enabled **crisis response and management** has the need for ICT solutions in organization structure and management, communication, legal issues, and security and privacy. The time pressure and chaos often present with crises makes efficiency (hence the evaluative dimension of DG research) of prime concern, though the normative aspects of ethics and legality, which become more critical in the long run, also mandate normative studies and solutions.

6. DIGITAL GOVERNMENT RESEARCH IN THE USA AND EU

The two continents' governments have pursued different goals in funding DG research. A brief look at the differences, and their effects, is instructive for understanding the nature of DG research.

The EU's e-Government R&D program, in its past several frameworks, required that projects involve cooperation between government partners (as users), researchers (mostly in ICT), and companies (typically software companies); for example, for information about FP6 visit (http://europa.eu.int/information_society/activities/e-Government_research/index_en.htm). The program emphasized companies, who were expected to deliver working technology; relatively little effort was devoted to core research in ICT and other disciplines. The results are relatively mature technology at the expense of innovation.

In contrast, in the USA, the National Science Foundation's Digital Government research program (http://www.digitalgovernment.org/) required that projects involve cooperation between government partners (as users) and researchers, and (after the first round of funding) that the government partners provide some input in funds or in time. Although the initial cycle of funding focused almost exclusively on ICT research, increasingly social science researchers have been funded as well, notably political scientists. Unfortunately, the absence of funding for companies meant that very little of the research has been transformed into commercial products to date.

With respect to the tripartite model, the EU's model emphasizes the technological and evaluative dimensions, while the DG's model pays somewhat more attention to the normative.

7. WHAT MAKES A GOOD DG RESEARCH PAPER?

It has been a perennial problem in DG-related conferences and journals to specify exactly what structure a good DG research paper should have[2]. Obviously, it should reflect the essence of Digital Government, it should be clear to most scholars in the field, regardless of their specialty/ies, and it should report on innovative and well-executed work. Clearly, the paper should describe the setting: the principal research question being addressed and its contextualization in some government application(s). Also, following standard scholarship practice, it should contain a section on related work, which may appear early or late in the paper, as appropriate.

But that said, what guidelines exist for authors? At what point do they include too much detail from their own specialty? How much detail is required from other specialties?

---

[2] The author was program or conference chair for the National Digital Government conferences (dg.o) in the USA for several of the early years, and has first-hand experience of this problem!

Here we can employ the tripartite model as a guide. Following the model, the best DG paper (like the best kind of DG research project) should include some effort from all three dimensions: normative, technological, and evaluative. The normative should express the goals and desiderata; the technical should discuss the ICT; the evaluative should provide effectiveness measures and improvements. It is unlikely, however, that a typical eight-page paper will be able to do all this and still provide enough details in any specific discipline to make a true contribution and not simply be a general summary. Thus the relative amounts of space and levels of detail for the three sections should differ. Exactly what minimal relative percentages are acceptable is up to the personal tastes of the author and the reviewer, and rather depends on the amount of space available and the professional sophistication of the expected readers. One can however imagine some rule such as

- Introduction + problem: 15%
- Related work: 5%
- Principal research dimension: not more than 40%
- Secondary research dimensions: not less than 15% each for each discipline represented
- Conclusion: not more than 5%, typically

This rule is pretty generic, and allocates a reasonable amount of space for each secondary discipline. A project with partners in only two disciplines (say, computer science as the primary discipline and political science as the secondary one) would quite naturally fall short in the evaluative dimension, and the act of writing a paper according to this rule would highlight the need to pay more attention to the missing part. Naturally, this work could be performed by one of the existing partners, but would have to be conducted in accord with the accepted standards and norms of one of the disciplines in the evaluative dimension and be presented in the appropriate style and form.

While enforcing this kind of rule as a strict policy for journals and conferences would, at this time, place quite a burden on DG researchers—they might feel they suddenly have to become experts in at least two other disciplines, or else find the appropriate partners—its gentle introduction, increasingly enforced over time, would prompt DG researchers to learn from one another and would work toward forging a new breed of researcher, skilled in just the relevant aspects of several disparate disciplines. At the same time, it would help bring about a new genre, the Digital Government research paper.

A few example papers are shown graphically in Figure 3-2. Acceptable relative amounts are shown in medium gray, unacceptable ones in darkest gray, and borderline ones in lightest gray.

A very interesting survey (Grønlund, 2004) of some 170 research papers published at three major e-gov conferences finds that "theory generation and theory testing are not frequent while case stories (no theory, no structured data collection) and product descriptions (no analysis or test) are". These papers clearly do not adequately represent the various dimensions required for a 'true' DG paper. As such, it is hardly surprising that "only a few of the cases where theories are either tested or generated concern the role and nature of government, most concern general organizational issues which could well find a place within traditional Information Systems conferences". Grønlund concludes that e-gov conferences have to begin developing criteria for quality, for both rigor and relevance, for DG (or e-Government) to develop into a distinct research field.

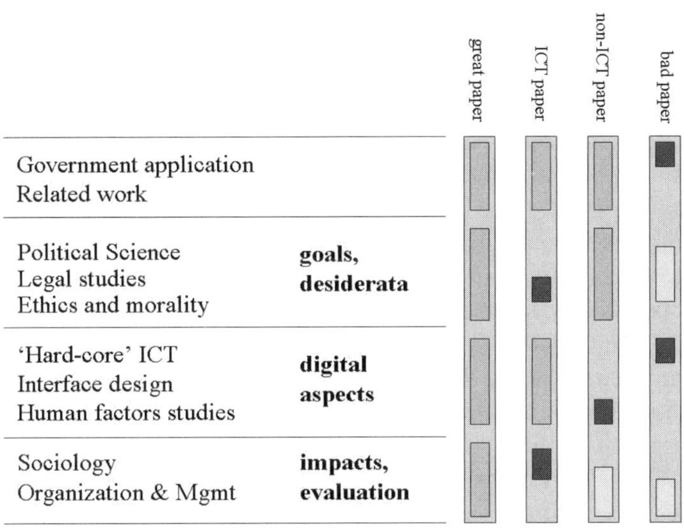

Figure 3-2. Examples of relative amounts of types of material in various genres of DG paper.

8. DG EDUCATION

Many universities today offer DG or e-Government degree or diploma programs, usually spanning one or two semesters. Most of them are aimed at training government employees who want to learn (a) what's available in ICT, (b) how to conceptualize a new system for their problem; and (c) how to estimate or measure the likely political, economic, and social impact.

Despite a certain amount of search, however, the author has nowhere yet found a program that reflects in equal depth all three principal dimensions of the tripartite model of DG presented in this chapter. It is perhaps too much to ask of students to become experts in areas as diverse as ICT, political science, law, public administration, information systems, and organization management, to name the principal ones. Is it too much to ask of university staff to create such groupings and offer a really widely multidisciplinary program? Perhaps not, in the near future. A major obstacle is creating a coherent intellectual vision and experience for the students. Hopefully, the model presented in this chapter can help. One way to focus the program is to train students on imaginary case studies involving hypothesized new ICT capabilities, and explore all their various ramifications across the disciplines (see question 2 at the end of this chapter).

9. CONCLUSION

This chapter describes a very simple model of DG that approaches research in DG from three complementary perspectives: *normative* (comprising such disciplines as political science, legal scholarship, and applied ethics), *technological* (comprising ICT and human factors design in its various forms), and *evaluative* (comprising such disciplines as information systems, organizational behavior and management, public administration, and even aspects of sociology). This model is then used to support the argument that fully-rounded DG research should include some aspect(s) of all three dimensions, and that a well-written DG paper should include specified minimal amounts of each dimension, expressed in the style and form of the selected discipline in each case.

An approach such as the one outlined here may assist the DG research community to develop its own methodology, style, and criteria for good work. Such developments may enable the emergence of an eventual theory of Digital Government.

ACKNOWLEDGEMENTS

The ideas in this chapter were developed over several years, and benefited greatly from discussions with Yigal Arens, Larry Brandt, Sharon Dawes, Lois Delcambre, Jane Fountain, Gen Giuliano, and Valerie Gregg; from discussions with Jamie Callan, Hans Jochen Scholl, Stuart Shulman, and René Wagenaar; from DG project collaborations with government partners; and finally from comments by participants at the EU-NSF Digital

Government workshop in Seattle in May 2004, the EU-NSF e-Government workshop in Delft in November 2004, the NSF-OAS DG planning meeting in Washington in November 2004, the International DG workshop in Atlanta in May 2005, participants at the E-GOV conference in Kraków in September 2006, and the e-gov seminar at ISI by Prof. Soung Hie Kim and Prof. Byungchun Kim and their group from the KAIST e-Government Research Center in Korea. My thanks go to all of them.

Funding for the research and meetings that prompted all this thinking about Digital Government was generously provided, over the course of six years and several different projects, by the National Science Foundation's Digital Government program. My grateful acknowledgment to the NSF for this support.

REFERENCES

Bijker, W.E. 1995. Of' Bicycles, Bakelites, and Bulbs: Toward a Theory of' Sociotechnical Change. Cambridge, MA: MIT Press.

Cushing, J. and T. Pardo. 2005. Guest Editor Introduction: Research in the Digital Government Realm. IEEE Computer Magazine (Special issue on Digital Government) 38(12), 26–32.

Delcambre, L. and G. Giuliano, 2005. Digital Government Research in Academia. IEEE Computer Magazine (Special issue on Digital Government) 38(12), 33–39.

Fountain, J.E. 2001. Building the Virtual State: Information Technology and Institutional Change.Brookings Institution Press.

Gil-Garcia and T. Pardo. 2006. Multi-Method Approaches to Digital Government Research: Value Lessons and Implementation Challenges. System Sciences, 2006. Proceedings of the 39th Annual Hawaii International Conference (HICSS-39).

Grønlund, Å. 2004. State of the Art in e-Gov Research—A Survey. In R. Traunmüller (ed), Electronic Government: Proceedings of the Third International Conference (E-GOV), pp. 178–186. Heidelberg: Springer Verlag.

Grønlund, Å. 2005. What's in a Field—Exploring the e-goverment Domain. Proceedings of the 38th Annual Hawaii International Conference on System Sciences (HICSS), pp. 125–131.

Grønlund, Å. 2006. e-Gov Research Quality Improvements since 2003: More Rigor, but Research (Perhaps) Redefined. Electronic Government: Proceedings of the 5th International Conference (E-GOV), pp. 1–12. Heidelberg: Springer Verlag.

MacKenzie, D. and J. Wajcman (eds). 1985. The Social Shaping of Technology. Open University Press.

Michael, M. 2000. Reconnecting Culture, Technology, and Nature, pp. 18–26. London: Routledge.

Nardi, B. (ed). 1996. Context and Consciousness: Activity Theory and Human-Computer Interaction. Cambrdige, MA: MIT Press.

Scholl, H.J. 2007. "Discipline or Interdisciplinary Study Domain? Challenges and Promises in Electronic Government Research." In this volume.

SUGGESTED READINGS

The books, chapters and papers listed in the *References* section above are recommended reading for anyone endeavoring to understand the foundations of digital government.

ONLINE RESOURCES

- The Digital Government Society of North America (DGSNA) and the European E-Government Society (E-GOV-S) are multi-disciplinary societies intended to foster progress in digital government research and e-government initiatives. Among other interesting items, their websites list upcoming conferences at which current research in digital government and issues and progress in e-government initiatives will be presented.
  DGS: http://www.dgsociety.org/
  E-GOV-S: http://www.uni-koblenz.de/FB4/Institutes/IWVI/AGVInf/community/e-gov-s
- A number of centers have been created to study issues related to digital government. Their websites feature not only upcoming conferences and other events, but also research in current topics. Some of the centers are:
  - The Digital Government Research Center (DGRC), headquartered in the University of Southern California's Information Sciences Institute. DGRC has a focus on information technology research as well as community building: http://www.dgrc.org/
  - The National Center for Digital Government, located at the University of Massachusetts, Amherst. The center intends to serve as a clearinghouse for digital government research: http://www.umass.edu/digitalcenter/index.php
  - The Center for Technology in Government (CTG), based at SUNY-Albany. CTG works to develop information strategies for government: http://www.ctg.albany.edu/

QUESTIONS FOR DISCUSSION

1. Read four papers from any recent dg.o or E-GOV conference. Identify regions that can be classified into the research paper sections listed in Section 7 above. (It is ok to assign a region to more than one section.) Measure the relative lengths of each section (counting words, or lines),

and also the unclassifiable regions, and create a bar chart that compares the four papers. On the bar chart, draw lines representing minimum acceptable lengths. Rate each paper, and outline the kinds of suggestions you would make to their authors for rounding out their work and improving the balance of their papers. Also analyze the content of the unclassifiable regions. Are these parts necessary for the paper? Should additional sections be added to the list of Section 7, or should the authors perhaps focus their efforts more? Discuss this.

2. Imagine a completely new ICT capability, such as being able to track your application for a dog license as it wends its way through government. Work out its ramifications, within e-government, from all three dimensions of the tripartite model. What would a lawyer, an ethicist, and a politician recommend? What would an organization management researcher, a public administration specialist, and a sociologist investigate? What would a computer scientist build? And don't forget: what would the government officials in question prefer? Where do these perspectives fit together well, and where do they disconnect? Now change the capability just a little, from tracking a dog license to tracking a letter to your elected official requesting action on an issue such as global warming or gun control. How do the work and commentary of each researcher change?

Chapter 4

LOST IN COMPETITION?

The State of the Art in E-Government Research

Åke Grönlund

Informatics, Örebro University, Örebro, Sweden (ake.gronlund@esi.oru.se)

CHAPTER OVERVIEW

Electronic Government (e-gov) research is mainly applied research serving a rapidly growing field of practice. Hence it is torn between academic analysis and practice demands for solutions to immediate problems. The research field has grown rapidly and now features several journals and a huge amount of conferences. Research quality is important to positively influence practice, but it takes time for a research field to settle with focus, borders, and quality standards. This paper follows up on an earlier study (Grönlund, 2004), which found quality lacking, by assessing 117 papers from two e-gov conferences, E-GOV 2005 and HICSS 2006, using rigor and relevance criteria derived from a straightforward maturity model. We find that since the last measurement, e-gov research papers on average are increasingly technically rigorous, increasingly descriptive (as opposed to analytical), increasingly product descriptions, and increasingly focus on IT rather than government, society, or individuals/citizens. Some potential explanations to the findings are discussed, and the paper concludes by discussing the issue of the nature of e-Government research – are we headed towards academic maturity or rather towards production of technical artefacts to support industry in a short-term perspective?

1. INTRODUCTION

Electronic Government (e-gov) is a rapidly growing field, and as it is young it needs to establish focus, borders, and quality standards. The period 2003–2005 may be seen as consolidating in e-gov research. After a period of rapid growth quality discussions had started and led to quality measures being taken. Grönlund (2004) surveyed 170 papers at three main (2003) e-gov conferences for the purpose of measuring the maturity of the field as a research area as indicated by the quality of papers. The study, perhaps not surprisingly, found the e-gov field quite immature. Regarding rigor, theory generation and theory testing were not frequent, whereas case stories (no theory, no data) and product descriptions (no analysis or test) were very frequent. Dubious claims (beyond what is reasonable given the method used) were also frequent, appearing in 29% of the papers. Regarding relevance, only a few of the cases in which theories were either tested or generated concerned the role and nature of government. Most instead concerned general organizational issues which could as well find a place within traditional Information Systems (IS) conferences.

This article investigates if and how the situation has changed since 2003 by examining a total of 117 papers from 2005 and 2006 conferences using the same method as the 2004 study. We discuss some of the findings from comparing the two studies, which can be summarized as:

- e-gov research is becoming increasingly descriptive (as opposed to analytical)
- e-gov research is increasingly product descriptions
- e-gov research is increasingly focusing on IT (as opposed to society, organization, individuals/citizens, and methods for change)
- e-gov research papers are technically increasingly rigorous
- Financing of research is often not clearly stated, which raises concerns about independence

The paper proceeds as follows. After a brief discussion of the problem, the relations between research and practice, and the issue of research quality, we present the research model. The bulk of the article is then spent on displaying data and discussing interpretations and possible explanations. We conclude by discussing the role of e-gov research.

2. RESEARCH AND PRACTICE

What is the relation between research and practice? How can they best complement each other for the benefit of both? This long-standing issue often needs to be revoked in view of new phenomena. Here we contrast two views currently struggling for hegemony as a background to the ensuing review of e-gov research quality.

Research is the process of looking for the unknown—creating *new* knowledge. Research is (ideally) looking with open eyes, that is, not being biased by having a stake in what is being researched. This way, knowledge stemming from research will be trusted to be as good—true, credible— as possible. A researcher will be happy to try out new methods for the purpose of being able to observe, interpret, and measure the world from some new angle in order to achieve more complete knowledge. We have measured the universe for long time without necessarily seeing any direct economic outcome. We want to know, that's it, and/or we believe that eventually we will make better decisions the more we know. It is a matter of degree, of course. In researching, in particular of social phenomena, no-one is completely objective. But it is not impossible to avoid many dangers. Independent financing, adherence to proper method, and critical review are good measures to take.

Development, in contrast, is the process of using existing knowledge to create new things. In that process, new knowledge may be found, but development projects try to avoid the unknown and stick to tools and methods that are *not new*. An engineer may want to build a longer bridge than anyone before has built, or one innovatively designed, but s/he will not abandon proven calculation and measurement methods. Further, even more than researchers, all developers have a stake in the successful outcome of their work. Either they are paid to develop something and have a schedule and or defined success criteria to meet, or they hope to make future gain from their developed artifact. Either way, they will not have time to look around for possibly better solutions than the one planned. Moreover, they have already sold a particular solution to some investor—private or public— and coming back six months later to say "well, maybe this wasn't such a good idea after all" is indeed not a good idea (Table 4-1).

Table 4-1. Characteristics differentiating research and development.

Research	Development
Looks for new knowledge	Uses proven knowledge as far as possible to minimize risk
Independent of object of study—researcher must not be stakeholder	Highly involved with object in focus—developer is stakeholder
Uncertainty about findings is motivation	Minimizes uncertainty, ideally to zero
Rejected hypotheses can be a positive result as knowledge increases.	Initial idea must not fail as investment is made for later return.
Great adaptability	Little adaptability

e-gov is a field that has emerged in practice but gradually has become popular also at research conferences. We find many such conferences today. e-gov researchers usually pride themselves on being in close contact with practitioners, and often report findings from development projects. And in fact, not only in e-gov research, but in research in general, the current trend in research funding is research-practitioner cooperation. This means that increasingly researchers must join up with business to do research at all; just observing and analyzing is not enough to obtain research grants. As the only Swedish e-gov research funding agency, Vinnova, puts it in their 2005 call, "Researcher(s) in the project shall take part in developing the e-service, not just evaluating it" (Vinnova, 2005, p 4; author's translation). There is no question that this means researchers will have a stake in the development project. Further, in response to this call, despite being called research, universities were not even allowed to apply, only companies were. Researcher participation was mandatory, however. This reveals the view that researchers are only assistants in development projects, a view that today is common among many research funding institutions.

Any applied research works in the field between science and practice. This always poses the tension between becoming too practical or too "theoretical" (too oriented towards general problems). Being too practical has the consequence that research does not contribute anything beyond what practitioners can achieve themselves. Being too oriented towards general problems has the consequence that the immediate concerns of practice will not easily find solutions as there will be a "communication gap", since researchers generally do not rest with studying only the immediate problems.

Today, we see a great and growing number of e-gov research conferences, and quite a few journals publishing e-gov research. This means that the volume of e-gov research available has grown considerably over just a few years. But the current thinking in research funding is that this is not enough. Researchers should participate in person in development projects, not to examine, assess, and measure, but also to produce. There are some good arguments behind this thinking, and some bad. Let us examine a few of them.

One argument is an intellectual one: research literature is hard to interpret, and in general practitioners do not have time to read it. Hence, having researchers themselves on board in development projects will ensure that findings are used, and are used in a proper way, not misunderstood.

Generally, it is of course a good idea that researchers understand practice so as to understand what problems can and should be researched. It is also good to have open channels of communication between researchers and practitioners, and personal contacts are no doubt an efficient way.

A second argument is basically economic but posed in an intellectual disguise. It says that research is too expensive and takes too long from idea to utilization. To increase the rate, researchers should only deal with things industry can make use of in ongoing projects, not things that may or may not be useful for 5 to10 years, or even later. This argument is concealed by phrases such as "research should be more relevant to practice", "no ivory tower research", "research should produce useful knowledge", etc. The main argument, however, is that research funds should be used to subsidize industry directly, as the increasingly competitive environment requires shorter lead times for new products. Sometimes this argument appears with no disguise, as when (in 2004) General Motors threatened to close the Swedish car manufacturer SAAB, which GM had bought a couple of years earlier, and concentrate production in a German plant. In response, the Swedish government immediately promised huge economic support, including research in "telematics", IT use in cars. There was already such research in Sweden, but it was paid mainly by industry. The sales threat made government promise to pay a (much) larger share of that research.

Arguments against researcher participation in development have been weakly voiced, but generally focus on traditional views of research quality, as quoted above. Research should be independent and critical. Its quality is distinct from its economic value, and should be reviewed for stringency of argument and methodological rigor. Beyond this non-stakeholder argument there is one of thinking out of the box; there is often a need for researchers to be free of traditional development methods so that radically new ones can be invented and perfected.

In summary, there are some good arguments for researchers and practitioners to work in parallel rather than in a sequence. There has over several years been an increased interest in Action Research, and methods have been developed to as best possible avoid the risks that are involved. The main risk is that researchers will become too keen stakeholders in development projects and hence less independent. Intellectually, this is of course a disaster, but even from an economic practitioner perspective it is highly problematic. Researchers will then produce less analytical and critical research, and as a consequence research findings will become increasingly uninteresting and ultimately less useful for industry. Industry will probably understand this quickly, and become less interested in support from government financed researchers. In this way, government devalues its own potential to infuse government support into industry. This is a risk scenario that should be guarded against.

Next, let us consider the development of the field—which direction is it taking? The evidence is limited, and we concentrate on the research quality side. The question is, *has e-gov research matured over the years?* We investigate the current status of e-gov research in view of two hypotheses, or perhaps better named propositions (since measurements cannot be that exact), based on the two above thought models:

1. e-gov research is maturing as a research field towards better alignment between empirical data and theories (tested as well as developed ones).
2. e-gov research is increasingly becoming an engineering activity developing tools based on already established knowledge (often found in other fields).

To address these propositions, this study examines research papers from 2003 and 2005/6, enabling us to measure changes over time. As a basis for the study we use a maturity model (presented below). If P1 is true, we will find more theory testing and generating. If P2 is true, we will find more product descriptions and less analysis.

Before presenting our findings we introduce a research maturity model used as the research model.

3. A RESEARCH MATURITY MODEL

A scientific field is characterized not just by a common object of study, but also by a set of theories which can be used to understand the objects and processes of study in the field, and a set of preferred methods and/or general methodological practices and understandings of what to investigate and how. While these are usually not undisputed, they serve as ingredients of a culture of the field, if not homogenous so at least to a large extent shared (King & Lyytinen, 2004).

Taking a rigorous perspective, a mature research field e-gov would include a critical amount of methodologically sound examination of relevant issues, be they related to technological quality, user understanding, extent and qualities of use, or other. As with any research, e-gov research must draw on earlier work. For e-gov, there are several long traditions to draw on. A literature on "IT in government", goes back at least to the 1970s [Kraemer, et al., 1978, Danziger and Andersen, 2002]. This literature concerns IT use within government, while the recent e-Gov literature more often concerns external use, such as services to the citizens. While some earlier e-Gov computer issues, such as office automation, may not be highly relevant to research today, many issues are, for example decision making, service processes, and values. More generally, the field of "Information systems", dating back to the 1950s but defined in the 1960s (Langefors, 1973) and expanding mainly from the 1970s onward, studies the role of information technology in organizations (Hirschheim, et al., 1995). Not to mention political science with really long traditions. From a relevance perspective, the e-gov field must relate to both ICT and government, at least. e-gov must create theories specific to e-gov practice, which means understanding the relations and dependencies *between* people, government, and IT, not each separately. e-gov must integrate political science/public administration and IT-related disciplines to understand the role of IT in government and governance processes.

Most research fields undergo a maturation process along the lines of the following model, in which new, unknown phenomena are studied first as explorations and later in increasingly structured ways. The following stages roughly delineate the different phases of maturity.

Philosophical When new phenomena are observed, people start wondering about them. As there are no or few theories in the field and empirical data is scarce or uncertain since the object of study is changing rapidly, studies will at this stage be mainly speculation based on philosophy, properties of technology, world view, etc. A striking example of this stage is the geocentric world view that prevailed before actual measurements of planetary movements proved the idea wrong. In the e-gov context an example would be when in the mid 1990s government web pages appeared but there was little integration with back-office systems and little knowledge about users. Hence, both production and use were open to speculation regarding future user skill and preferences as well as regarding how production processes could economically benefit from IT-enabled reengineering.

Anecdotal case stories At this stage there is an increasing amount of data, but there is still no clear focus in the field so studies focus on "emerging" features, usually grounded in the researchers' field of origin, personal interests, and/or commercial focus (in the case of e-gov, of relevant IT developments). The focus remains on exploration, finding new exciting traits of the development. The researcher is a Vasco da Gama or a Christopher Columbus exploring new territory. In the e-gov field there are numerous such stories telling about early developments that have been successful in some way, sometimes only by actually doing something before others, as measurements of success in societal endeavors are inconclusive. Hence we have for ten years seen stories about how Canada, Australia, Korea and some other countries lead the way. We have also seen a lot of benchmarking, which basically substitutes for evaluation by doing as the (perceived) leader(s) rather than evaluating performance against goals. Another consequence is that the typical measurements of e-gov development have through the early years mainly been amount of information and services online.

Clustering At this stage cases abound and people start looking for similarities to be able to group findings according to similarities among cases. Based on these, they identify the most salient general properties (and also the properties that are less foundational and hence can be ignored) and use them to hypothesize clusters, which give rise to an initial inventory of the types that eventually form the principal elements of the theory. In the case of e-gov, at this stage people identify, for example, effects of centralized and de-centralized strategies respectively. Stakeholders are identified, and the various views of these are investigated to see, for example, whether there are choices that have to, or should, be made.

Theory creating Once enough similarities are found, people start looking for more stable relationships among the similarities, and with them create models and theories about the generalizations so as to more credibly inform further research, product development, and organizational remodeling. Theories can also be used for making predictions about future development, subsequently driving measurement for verification?] This is where we start figuring out reasons for the apple to fall to the ground.

Theory testing (using theories found by inductive methods or borrowed from other fields pertinent to government and/or IT). This stage generally appears slightly after the previous one, as theory creating is usually qualitative and builds on smaller but richer data sets than theory testing and hence is more suitable to earlier stages of development where radical changes are about, but thereafter they continue in parallel. At this stage we start dropping not just apples but also other things, heavier and lighter and differently shaped to test the theories we have conceived.

This model should not be interpreted strictly. For one thing, the nature of the objects of study will influence the development, as do traditions and cultures in different research communities. Even if predictions about future development mature, any field studying a moving target, a changing reality, has to contain at least some component of each of the above stages, although as the field matures there will be a progression. Generally, a new, immature, field will contain more of the early stages while a mature field will contain more of the later ones.

In the following, P1 is taken to mean a development along the lines of this model. The view inherent in P2 often implies there is less need for the latter two stages, primarily because they often cannot deliver results quickly enough in a highly competitive world where time to market often is crucial.

For the purposes of our investigation we associated the variables Method and Research type with the stages in the model, as shown in Table 4-2.

Table 4-3 explains the definitions of the Method types.

Table 4-2. Categorization and characterization of Method.

Maturity stage	Research type	Description	Method
Philosophical	Philosophical	Reflects upon a phenomenon without data or reference to any theory	Argument
	Theoretical	Reflects upon a phenomenon based on some theory but without empirical data or with only anecdotal and particular examples	
Anecdotal case studies	Descriptive	Describes a phenomenon in its appearance without any use of theory	Case story Product description
Clustering	Descriptive	Describes a phenomenon in its appearance without any use of theory	Literature study Case story
Theory generation	Theory generation	Attempts to analyze/interpret quantitative or qualitative data in a systematic manner for the purpose of model building and prediction generation	Ethnography Grounded theory Literature study Experimentation Interpretative studies
Theory testing	Theory testing	Attempts to test a theory using quantitative or qualitative data in a systematic manner, i.e. not just strict theory testing	Experimentation Interpretative studies Literature studies

Table 4-3. Index to categories used for "Method" in Table 4-2.

Category	Description
Argument	Logical argument but not based on any particular theory or relating explicitly or by clear implication to any theory
Case story	Tells about a case but as opposed to a case study there is no strict data collection method. Usually own experiences or anecdotal evidence
Ethnography	Any attempt to understand actions by systematic observation and interpretation
Experiment	Both laboratory and field experiments are included
GT	Grounded theory
Interpretative	Any kind of more strictly performed data collection than "case story" but not necessarily strictly explained or spelled-out method for interpretation. A case study belongs here, but also more limited studies where qualitative or quantitative data is analyzed. Multi-method studies are also included here
Literature study	Only documents used, be they scientific, policy documents or other. Not necessarily strict method or even explicitly labeled as literature study
Product description	IT product, method, or similar, described by the manufacturer. This category was added from experience – many papers were just this and did not meet the requirements of any other category. They were not research papers, still we needed a category for them.
Survey	This covers also qualitative overviews of several documents or cases
Unclear	Used when even the widely defined categories above fail to capture the method of an article

3.1 Research Design

The design of the research model started from similar studies previously conducted. As for rigor, Dubé & Paré (2003) list attributes used to assess IS positivist case studies (p 606) based on earlier work by Benbasat et al (1989), Eisenhart (1989), Lee (1989) and Yin (1994). These criteria fall into the categories of Research design, Data collection, and Data analysis. While the Dubé & Paré study concerns just one type of research – positivist case studies – most of the criteria could be used also for other research methods. For example "clear research question", and "multiple data collection methods" are qualities honored in most methods. But as e-gov research includes all kinds of methods and it is very hard to directly compare quality across methods – for example comparing qualitative and quantitative methods on how, in detail, a research question should be formulated – the strive was to use criteria that assessed rigor and relevance in a more general way. Some effort was also put into as far as possible avoiding interpreting articles by trying to find objectively measurable criteria. Also, as e-gov is currently moving from practice to research, a primary concern was to distinguish between papers that at all met academic standards and those which were merely practitioner-oriented case stories. This resulted in using the following rigor categories: Research type, Method, Claim, and Number of references. The investigation also included relevance criteria, including Focus unit, Target audience, Discipline, Collaborative, and Country. Of these, only Focus unit is discussed in this article.

Research type. This category uses broad labels to distinguish between descriptive and theoretical studies, and between those applying theory to data in one way or another and those who do not. (Table 4-2)

Method (Table 4-3). The categories used here are a mix of the whish to keep the number of categories as low as possible while still including any quantitative and qualitative method and also being specific enough to not hide the fact that sometimes very specific methods are used. The latter is the reason for including Grounded Theory as a separate item (which otherwise could have been included under "interpretative"). The first criterion is the reason for including both quantitative and qualitative methods under the category "interpretative", which is then used in a non-standard way. The category "product description" was not preconceived but emerged (during the first measurement in 2003) as a necessary item to describe some papers that clearly were just that and could not fit in with any other category. This method of going about the category definitions revealed, for one thing, that there were not that many uses of specific methods in the sample studied (because then this list would have been longer including, for example, names on specific ethnographic methods).

Sometimes papers were based on some earlier study, for example a survey, but this new research only used that study as a background to, for example, a case description. The categorization would then be based on the most salient study. If the case was used to test a framework created by the survey, the classification would be theory testing, provided there was indeed a test. If the paper only used the survey as a general reference and did not refer the case studied in any clear way to the survey it would be a case story. As many papers were very brief and not clear on how previous material was used, sometimes an ounce of judgement was applied to make the categorization. A generous approach was applied – any evidence of actually using previous research in any systematic way was actively searched for and appreciated in the classification. The reason was that when you watch things grow you need patience, and sorting out the weed at an early stage is a subtle task that should be handled with care. There was also a reason of validity; to make sure tiny plants were not done away with, and perhaps leaving some weeds when in doubt meant that *at least* this was not done.

Focus unit (Table 4-4). Here, the categories used were largely those used to define other fields, such as HCI, CSCW, and IS. The category "Society" was added because the literature study clearly showed the importance of governance factors in e-gov: to reflect practice, the e-gov research field should consider not just internal efficiency but also the societal role of IT use.

Table 4-4. Focus unit.

Unit	Description
Group	Focus on work group – the work, not the technology used
Individual	e.g. HCI, workplace design, tasks, but in this case also individuals as customers.
IT	Either technical details or application of systems, such as workflow management system, where the products or technology are in focus rather than aspects of their use. Focus can be on different aspects including performance, technical integration, security, implementation etc.
Method	Either methods of practice such as "a methodology for e-government assessment" or methods of research
Organization	Anything that has to do with how organizations are designed and operate, such as "back office reorganization", MIS, workflow management, etc.
Society	The phenomenon under study applies neither to one single organization, nor to organizations in cooperation but to society. Examples are "access" as in "bridging digital divides, and "democracy". It also include government agencies when they act as counterparts to citizens, for instance in consultations. Consequently, this category also includes individuals when they are dealt with in their role as citizens (which defines a societal role, not properties of an individual).

Claim. This category concerns what validity authors claim for their results. *Normative* means the paper claims generality beyond the case studied. *Descriptive* papers claim validity but not generality. The authors claim to have described the situation correctly and/or credibly. *Lessons* only claim anecdotal value, e.g. "we learned that we need a champion and we weren't prepared for that". *Ongoing* means research is not completed and although insights or experiences may be reported the paper does not make any claim as to the validity or generality of the findings, not even in principle.

When the claim was not explicitly stated, it was often very clearly implied by the way findings were formulated. When claims were not possible to discern, the paper was classified as ongoing.

3.2 Validity

As is clear from the above method and research model description, some interpretations had to be made. There are intersections between criteria where a line has to be drawn. How much empirical data, and how much analytical structure are needed to distinguish between a "case story" and an "interpretation", for example? In the clear-cut cases there should be no problem, but as (1) many papers are very short and descriptions of method brief, and (2), many papers are limited both in terms of amount of data and stringency in data collection and interpretations, there were many cases where a choice had to be made. One general choice could have been to discard everything that was not clearly stated. This method was deemed to be too harsh and would throw out some babies along with the bathing water. One reason is that at least two of the conferences explicitly target practitioners and invite project reports, and with that follows less strict demands for academic rigor for at least those sections of the conferences. Another reason is that not only rigor but also relevance was looked for, and given the assumption that e-gov is a nascent field in development towards becoming a research field with the more rigorous demands that follow, it might be unwise to unduly disrepute highly relevant projects, topics and developments on basis of them being not yet rigorously described. Third, as even a strict research model would involve interpretations, it is important to avoid unnecessarily imposing the reviewers' views of what is good research. Therefore a "generous" interpretation of the criteria was chosen. This meant that whenever in doubt, a more "positive" category was chosen. For example, when in doubt whether a report from a case would be a "case story" or an "interpretative" analysis, the latter would be chosen whenever some evidence of analysis could be found, even if not clearly structured or that well exemplified by reference to empirical findings. This is a difference from for example Dubé and Paré (2003) who (implicitly) claim to know exactly what a "clearly formulated" research question is.

For these reasons it was decided not to apply a too strict model, but rather look for interesting developments that might turn into more rigorous research over time. This means that the end result is an account on the positive side, as positive interpretations were made wherever there was uncertainty. The advantage of this approach is that it makes the conclusions more credible. As one conclusion is that the e-gov field is indeed quite immature, the use of positive interpretations means that it can claimed that there are *at least* this large number of case stories, *at the most* this very limited amount of theory testing and creating, and *at least* this high number of dubious claims.

Some checks were made to ensure that the above reasoning was supported by our data analysis method. Papers were read in the order they were published in the proceedings. The first 50 papers were coded independently on the criteria that involved interpretation, Research type, Method, Focus Unit, and Claim, by both authors, in chunks of 10. After each chunk, coding was compared and differences discussed. By the 5th chunk, coding was close to identical. There were differences only in 4 cases (10%), and the differences could be explained by papers being at the border between two categories. The remaining papers were then coded by the first author only, using the "positive interpretation" method in cases of uncertainty as explained above. In some cases there is no more positive value. For example, for "Focus unit", sometimes a distinction had to be made between several topics involved, such as "Organization" and "Method", which sometimes is a subtle matter of choice – when developing a new method for systems development, what is more in focus, the organizational issues which are dealt with by the method or the method itself ?. These differences are not important for the discussions of rigor. They are of importance, though, for the discussion of the focus of the field, so in that respect the findings must be treated with caution.

4. FINDINGS

In the following, we compare data from the E-GOV 2003 and HICSS 2003 conferences, reported in (Grönlund, 2004), with a new survey covering E-GOV 2005 and HICSS 2006 (Sprague, 2006). For comparison with the field more generally, we also display 2003 results from ECEG. In the Figures, "EGC" refers to the conference itself, as reported in the proceedings (Wimmer et al, 2005), "EGW" refers to the workshop proceedings (Andersen et al, 2005). The findings, summarized here, are discussed one by one below.

- e-gov research is becoming increasingly descriptive (as opposed to analytical);
- e-gov research is increasingly product descriptions;
- e-gov research is increasingly focusing on IT (as opposed to society, organization, individuals/citizens, and methods for change).
- e-gov research papers are technically increasingly rigorous.
- Financing of research is often not clearly stated, which raises concerns about independence.

4.1 E-gov Research Is Becoming Increasingly Descriptive

As shown in Figure 4-1, the share of descriptive research has increased both at HICSS and E-GOV. The difference is greatest at HICSS, from 24% to 38%. Theory generation increased at E-GOV 2005 compared to E-GOV 2003, but decreased by 7% at HICSS. On the whole there is not much difference and no trend to be clearly spotted. Theory testing has increased slightly over the two E-GOV conferences and considerably in the HICSS conference papers, but the numbers are still very small. Theoretical research has decreased to the point of extinction—only 3 papers in 2005 as compared to 17 in 2003. Philosophical research has decreased, but from a low level.

To support our maturity model, and hence P1, philosophical and theoretical research has largely disappeared. A more mature field would also include more theory testing and creation, and indeed theory generation and theory testing research have both increased, but not much. Finally, we predicted less of description, but this category has instead increased at all conferences. This finding rather provides support for P2.

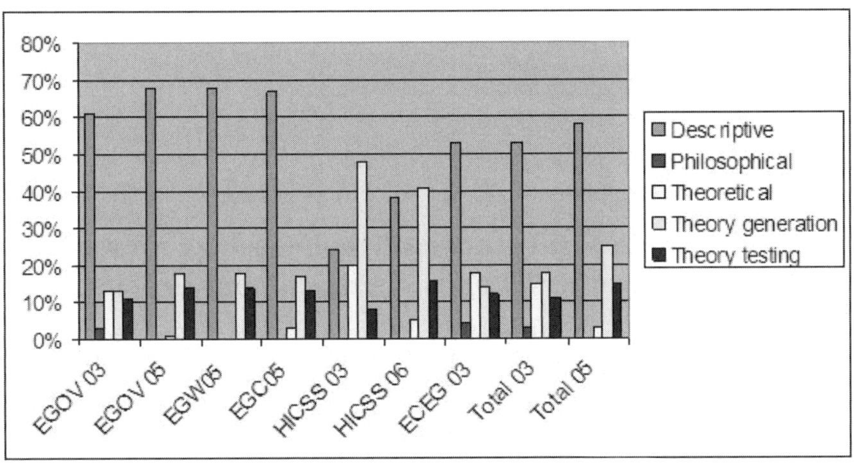

Figure 4-1. Research type

4.2 E-gov Research Is Increasingly Product Descriptions

As shown in Figure 4-2, "Argument" has in 2005 become almost extinct. Case stories are down from 34% to 10% at E-GOV, most so at the conference. This time we find more rigorous descriptions and less of stories, which is a quality improvement. Interpretative research has increased considerably, from 14% to 35% at E-GOV and from 32% to 57% at HICSS, which can be seen as supporting P1. Contradicting P1, "Product descriptions" have increased from 14% to 31% at E-GOV. At HICSS the figures for 2006 are similar to those of 2003, hence the changes for this category at E-GOV seem most of all to reflect the design changes made at the E-GOV conference.

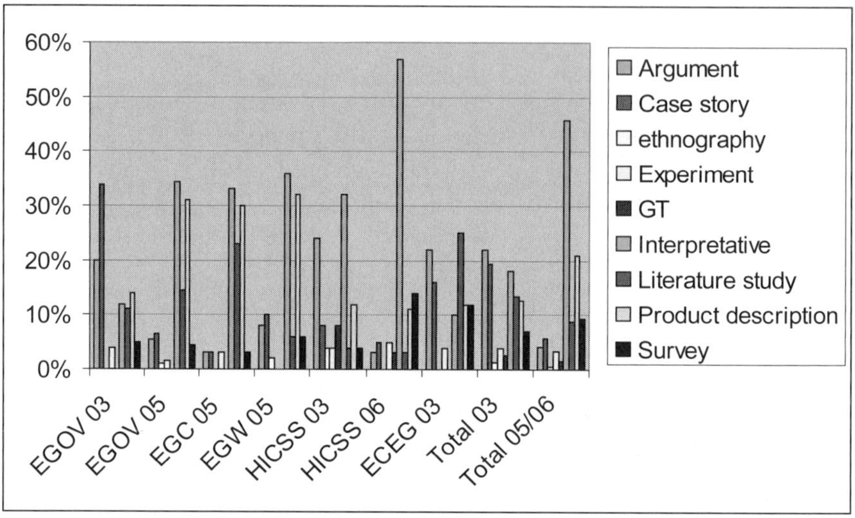

Figure 4-2. Method

4.3 E-gov Research Is Increasingly Focusing on Traditional IS Areas Rather Than Government and Society

As shown in Figure 4-3, the already strong focus on IT has increased at E-GOV, from 33% in 2003 to no less than 60% in 2005 (70 at the workshop, 43 at the conference). "Society" scores marginally higher, counting all conferences. "Individual" is dropping, but from a low number. At HICSS, focus on IT is down and is in 2006 is almost exclusively on organization and method.

This finding is only partially in line with our maturity model and P1. If the field were about to mature in the sense of creating a distinct set of theories, we should see more focus on the criteria that have to do with the relation between government and citizen, that is, "individual" and "society". While the increasing focus on Method and Organization at HICSS seems reasonable from the perspective of putting IT in context, which is also a sign of maturity, it does not signal a new field, rather an extension the traditional Information Systems field's domain to encompass government as well.

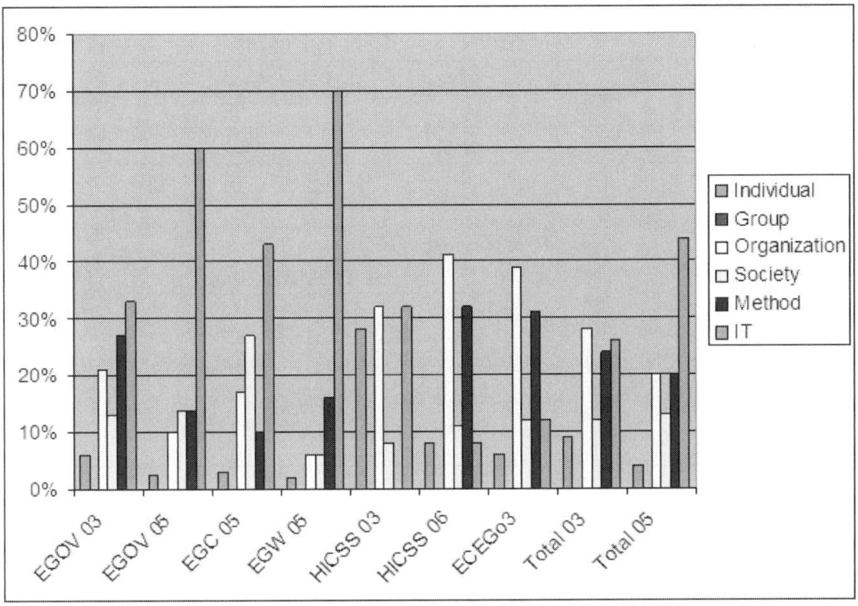

Figure 4-3. Focus unit

4.4 E-gov Research Papers Are Technically Increasingly Rigorous

In 2005/6, there are more signs of awareness of the scientific literature, and the claims are more reasonable. In 2003 we measured the connection with the scientific community by counting the number of references. A low number would indicate a practitioner focus, while a high one would indicate more focus on research (Tables 4-5a and 4-5b). While in 2003, 62% of the E-GOV papers contained fewer than 9 references, in 2005 93% at the conference and 90% at the workshop contain 9 or more (97% at HICSS). Forth-three percent of the conference papers include more than 20 references (70% at HICSS). It should also be mentioned that the references at E-GOV 2006 are much more academic than those of 2003 (as assessed by the authors at a glance without counting). In 2003, the reference list included many company and government websites, mainly promotional. These may still be there, but now there are also academic references to relevant literature discussing the issues under investigation. In this sense, academic quality has improved. For HICSS, there is not much difference between 2003 and 2006, simply because the number of references was already quite high in 2003.

Table 4-5a. Number of references 2003.

No of refs	E-GOV 03		HICSS-03		ECEG-03	
0-5	33	35%	1	4%	5	10%
6-8	25	27%	2	8%	5	10%
9+	36	38%	22	88%	41	80%

Table 4-5b. Number of references 2005/6.

No of refs	E-GOV 05		E-GOV workshop 05		HICSS 06	
<=5	1	3%	3	6%	0	0
6 to 8	1	3%	5	10%	1	3%
>=9	28	93%	45	90%	36	97%
(>=20)	13	43%	10	20%	26	70%
(>=30)	2	7%	3	6%	15	41%
(>=40)	2	7%	1	2%	7	19%

Another factor indicating rigor is the credibility of the claims. To investigate this, we matched the categories "research type", "method", and "claim". A reasonable combination would be, e.g., that a "descriptive" type implemented by an "argument" would result in modest claims. In 2003, we found no fewer that 49 dubious claims, equivalent to 29% of the papers. "Dubious" is here related to the combination, not to the propositions themselves. A case story, for example, can by definition not lead to normative conclusions; yet the conclusions stated may be reasonable in themselves. There were several combinations, the largest group being a descriptive case story resulting in normative claims (11 cases) and theoretical argument ending by normative claims. In 2005 we found a completely different picture. At E-GOV, the number of dubious claims was now only 5 (6%), 2 at the conference and 3 at the workshop. At HICSS, we found 2 papers (5%) This seems to be a huge improvement.

4.5 The Role of Researchers Is Obscure

Research origin and funding is important for research independence. As for research origin, the affiliation of the first author is overwhelmingly a university at all conferences. In 2003, the figure for all conferences was 83%, while in 2005 the figure for E-GOV conference is 97%, for the workshop 94%, and for HICSS 86%. For only 5 papers in total the first author came from a company, and 4 from government. This seems to indicate independence. However, research can be collaborative (Tables 4-6a and 4-6b); indeed, in 2003, around 1/5 of the papers were collaborative (involving more than one institution). Still, most of these involved no practitioners, but only researchers from more than one university or more than one discipline within the same university. Only 11 papers involved at least one practitioner and one researcher (6 at E-GOV, 2 at ECEG, and 3 at HICSS). In 2005, collaboration has increased at E-GOV, both the conference and the workshop, to 39% in total, with a slightly higher figure for the workshop. Still, collaboration with practice is low, indeed lower than in 2003, only 7 papers (as one is double-counted). At HICSS, in 2003 7 out of 25 papers were collaborative, in 2006 10, meaning there is no increase in percentage.

Table 4-6a. Collaborations, E-GOV 2003 and 2005.

	E-GOV 05		E-GOV Workshop 05		Total	
Non-collab	20	67%	29	58%	49	61%
uni-gov	1	3%	4*	8%	5	6%
uni-biz		0%	4*	8%	4	5%
uni-uni	9	30%	14	28%	23	29%
Total papers	30		50		80	

*One paper included gov-biz-uni and is here counted in both categories

Table 4-6b. Collaborations, HICSS 2003 and 2006.

	HICSS 03		HICSS 06	
Non-collab	18	72%	27	73%
uni-gov	(no data)		1	3%
uni-biz	(no data)		2	5%
uni-uni	(no data)		7	19%

These figures seem to indicate low collaboration, but they should be questioned. Today, research funding is increasingly hard to find without joining up with business and some development project. Some would say it is impossible in a field such as ICT. The papers presented in the examined conferences are to a large extent reports from EU funded projects. Since the EU funding for e-gov projects makes explicit that only partnerships of researchers and companies would be funded, and that the bulk of the funding went to companies, the relative absence of practitioner-researcher papers may seem rather surprising, and may suggest that researchers tend not to write with their practitioner counterparts. We tried to trace just what was the relation between the researcher and the practice/some project, but that proved impossible. One explanation is given by the findings on "method" above; product descriptions indicate the researcher delivered an artifact such as a model, an architecture, or a system, to the project, and this indicates some close relation. We tried to count the number of papers that described some such close relation with a development project, but found nothing definite. Only in few cases were the funding sources explicitly mentioned, and as funding in projects often derives from many sources, including the university itself, it is often not clear exactly which euro went to a project report and which to a research conference paper based on that report. In many cases we could recognize ingredients from projects we know of, but no direct references to that project were made.

In conclusion we find that the funding underlying the research is not easy to trace, and hence the independence of the researchers is not clearly established. This is in itself a problem.

5. CONCLUSIONS AND DISCUSSION

This article compares the nature and quality of a total of 250 research articles published at e-gov conferences in 2003 and 2005. We have showed that:

1. e-gov research is becoming increasingly descriptive (as opposed to analytical);
2. e-gov research is increasingly product descriptions;
3. e-gov research is increasingly focusing on IT and information systems organization and methods, as opposed to government, governance society, individuals/citizens, and methods for change;
4. e-gov research papers are technically increasingly rigorous;
5. The role of researchers is obscure.

Considering these findings in view of the two propositions P1 and P2, we find mixed results. In support of P1 we find more rigorous research, and less philosophical and theoretical writing. But we do not see a change towards more theory testing and theory building. Rather, in support of P2 we find considerable increase in product descriptions. Items 1,2 and 3 above rather support P2. Item 4 is not decisive, it is positive for both P1 and P2. P5 is mainly negative for P1. Clearly, findings are inconclusive. Measurements are only made at two points in time and hence may reflect fluctuations rather than trends. As e-gov is a young field such fluctuations may be stronger than they would be at a more mature stage. Also the sample of two conferences may not accurately reflect the whole field, even though the two ones chosen are generally seen as important in the domain, and are among the largest.

The principal contributions of this paper are:

- It suggests some trends, which require further, and more detailed, study
- It provides a methodology for a meta-study of the evolution of e-gov as a research field (and by implication, other emerging fields as well)

We might speculate about the reasons for these results. One is the already mentioned fact that the basis of research—the funding principles—has changed so dramatically that our model, P1, which was pertinent to traditional academic discipline development, does not fit any longer, mainly because the field has changed in nature. The principle underlying the current e-gov funding is not to support the study and analysis of better ways of conducting government, but to provide government support to industry in development projects decided by other mechanisms. This view is sometimes explicit, as in the above quote from VINNOVA, and sometimes implicit, but in practice it means that researchers are constrained to contribute to developing methods, software, architectures etc., rather than to critically examine them and discuss alternatives.

A second reason for the lack of strong support for P1 might be the "publish or perish" demand on researchers, which is increasingly a reality everywhere (as it has long been in the US). The huge and increasing number of conferences supports this argument. A third reason could be the increasing volume and de-academization of higher education, parts of which include research being increasingly project funded and competitive, and education—including Ph.D. studies—becoming increasingly instrumental as job preparation and less as academically intellectual enterprises.

Clearly this study does not provide evidence to the reasons for the quite dramatic change in research output. It only displays the result. Further research to discover the reasons would be useful. Independent science is historically a highly valued force in society, similar to the idea of an independent press, and if the current development is detrimental to this independence it should at least be discussed. Of course we can learn also from practice. But research is supposed to help us avoid learning only by trial and error. It is supposed to create general knowledge that can be applied as input to development projects to prevent repeated invention of the wheel. In this respect, the findings presented here should trigger some discussion about e-gov as a research field. Our production has become more technically rigorous since last measure two years ago. But are we doing good research? Do we have anything to transfer to practitioners that they do not already know? If the current trend of dependent funding continues, we are likely to see a continuation to the development we have shown in this paper.

REFERENCES

Andersen, K.V., Grönlund, Å., Traunmüller, R., Wimmer, M.A. (2005) Electronic Government. Workshop and Poster Proceedings of the Fourth International E-GOV Conference. 2005, Denmark. Linz: Trauner

Bannister, F., Remenyi, D. (2003) 3rd European Conference on e-Government. Trinity College, Dublin, Ireland, 3-4 July, 2003. ISBN 0-9544577-1-4

Benbasat, I., Goldstein, D.K., Mead, M. (1987) The Case Research Strategy in Studies of Information Systems. MIS Quarterly, 11, 3, pp 369-385

Danziger, J. N. and K. V. Andersen (2002). "The Impacts of Information Technology in

Public Administration: An Analysis of Empirical Research from the "Golden Age" of Transformation." *International Journal of Public Administration* (25)5, pp.591-627

De, R. (2004) E-Government Systems in Developing Countries: Some Research Issues. ICIS workshop on e-Government, Washington, December 2004. In Press.

Dubé, L. Paré, G. (2003) Rigor in Information Systems Positivist Case Research: Current Practices, Trends and Recommendations. MIS Quarterly, 27,4, pp 597-635

Eisenhart, K.M. (1989) Building Theories from Case Study Research. Academy of Management Review, 4,4, pp 532-550

EU (2004) e-Government Research in Europe. European Commission. http://europa.eu.int/information_society/programmes/e-gov_rd/text_en.htm

EU (2004b) IST e-Government Research in FP6 (2003-2006). Introduction (http://europa.eu.int/information_society/programmes/e-gov_rd/fp6/text_en.htm, visited Nov 15, 2004)

Grönlund, Å. (2004) State of the art in e-Gov research – a survey. In R. Traunmüller (ed) Proceedings of Electronic Government Third International Conference E-GOV 2004, pp 178-185. LNCS 3183. Berlin: Springer.

Hirschheim, R., Klein, H. K. & Lyytinen, Varu, N. K. *Information systems development and data modeling: Conceptual and philosophical foundations*. Cambridge & Aston University Press, 1995. IEEE (2003) Proceedings of the 36th Hawaii International Conference on System Sciences 2003. IEEE

King, J.L., Lyytinen, K. (2004) Reach and Grasp. MISQ 28, 4, December 2004.

Kraemer, K. L., et al. (1978). *Local Government and Information Technology in the United States*. Paris: OECD Informatics Studies #12.

Langefors, B. (1973) Theoretical analysis of information systems. Lund: Studentlitteratur; Philadelphia, Auerbach, 1973 (4th edition).

Lee, A. (1989) A Scientific Methodology for MIS Case Studies. MIS Quarterly, 13,1, pp 33-52

Sprague, Ralph H. (Ed.). (2006). Proceedings of the 39th Hawaiian International Conference on System Sciences; Kauai, HI, USA, January 4-7. Los Alamitos, CA: IEEE Computer Scoiety. 492 p.

Traunmüller, R. (2003) Electronic government. Second International Conference, E-GOV 2003, Prague, Czech Republic, September 2003. Springer Lecture Notes in Computer Science.

Vinnova (2005) Cross-departmental public e-services for businesses (Gränsöverskridande offentliga e-tjänster för företag). Call 2 within the programme E-services in public sector. Stockholm: Vinnova, 2005-02189

Wimmer, M.A., Traunmüller, R., Grönlund, Å., Andersen, K.V. (2005) Electronic Government. Proceedings of 4th International Conference, E-GOV 2005. Copenhagen, Denmark, August 2005. Heidelberg: Springer, Lecture Notes in Computer Science, LNCS 3591

SUGGESTED READINGS

The discussion of rigor and relevance in Information Systems research has yielded many publications. Often these have been part of a struggle between proponent of quantitative and qualitative methods respectively. Some interesting readings out of that history include:

- Benbasat, Izak, and Zmud, Robert W. 1999. Empirical Research in Information Systems: The Practice of Relevance. *MIS Quarterly,* 23(1), pp. 3-16. [T58.6 ISR SC, ISSN 1047-7047], March.
- Myers, Michael D., & Avison, David (Eds.) (2002). *Qualitative Research in Information Systems*. Sage Publications
- Lee, Allen (1989) A Scientific Methodology for MIS Case Studies. MIS Quarterly, March 1989, pp 33-50
- Galliers, R.D., Land, F.F. (1987) Choosing Appropriate Information Systems Research Methodologies. Communications of the ACM, November 1987, Vol 30, No 11, pp 900-902

ONLINE RESOURCES

- The most comprehensive library of resources and debate on research methods, quality and relevance is the AIS (Association for Information Systems) resource web AIS-net <http://www.isworld.org/#research>

QUESTIONS FOR DISCUSSION

1. Is the development described in this article generalizable beyond the conferences studied?
2. Is the methodology generalizable to other emerging fields of study? What, if anything, should be changed, and why?
3. Is the time span 2003-5/6 enough to spot a trend, or is this just a fluctuation? What would be the reasons of suspecting the latter?
4. Is the development described here positive or negative—which direction should e-gov research take?
5. If we accept the "serve-industry" paradigm for research, what quality measures should be taken to ensure research quality, impartiality being one such criterion?

Chapter 5

E-DEMOCRACY AND E-PARTICIPATION RESEARCH IN EUROPE

Ann Macintosh

International Tele-democracy Research Centre, Napier University, Edinburgh, UK

CHAPTER OVERVIEW

This chapter considers e-democracy and e-Participation research across Europe. This is a relatively new and emerging area of research when compared with other physical and social science disciplines. The range of contrasting and, in some instances, conflicting definitions of the terms emphasize the 'newness' of the domain. For this chapter, e-democracy and e-Participation can be considered as the use of information and communication technologies to broaden and deepen political participation by enabling citizens to connect with one another and with their elected representatives. The chapter begins by discussing the critical need for such research given that a large proportion of western society is drifting away from political activities such as voting in elections and joining political parties. Having discussed the growing apathy to formal political processes, the chapter then proceeds to discuss the current status of research and practice. e-democracy and e-Participation, by their very nature, are multi-disciplinary research activities with research based in democratic theory, political science, communication studies, information management, computer science and more. As such, researchers need to understand how to harmonize and align concepts and methods from this range of academic disciplines to ensure that an inter-disciplinary approach is adopted.

1. INTRODUCTION

Local, regional and national governments throughout Europe are striving to broaden democracy by providing an effective channel between themselves and civil society using innovative information and communication technologies (ICT) to deliver more open and transparent democratic decision-making processes. But why are they doing this and what digital government research is needed to support this?

A large proportion of western society is drifting away from political activity – activities such as voting in elections and joining political parties. This growing apathy to formal political processes does nothing to change current political policies but risks undermining our current model of representative democracy. As noted by Held (1996):

Democracy has been championed as a mechanism that bestows legitimacy on political decisions when they adhere to proper principles, rules and mechanisms of participation, representation and accountability. (p297)

However, when that representation is through elected representatives elected by a minority of the electorate, this brings into question the legitimacy of decision-making. In a number of European countries where voting is not obligatory, there has been a growing decline in the number of people willing to turn out and vote in local, national and European level elections. The European Parliament was directly elected for the first time in 1979 and at each election since then the voter turnout has fallen on average across Europe by about 2-3% every five years. The turnout in the 2004 elections followed a similar downward trend with the average turnout in Portugal approximately 38.6%, while in Slovakia it was even lower at 16.96%.[1] At national level, in the UK 2001 Parliamentary general election, voter turnout fell to 59.4%, its lowest level since the election of 1918 and down from 71.6% in 1997. The situation is similar in other liberal democratic countries.[2] Turnout at elections is not the only indicator of apathy and dissatisfaction. A survey on political engagement undertaken in the UK (The Electoral Commission and the Hansard Society, 2006) indicated that most adults do not feel they know much about politics, with only 14% saying that they are politically active. It is clear from the increasingly low turnout at elections and similar indicators that traditional democratic processes do not effectively engage people. The situation has reached such levels that there is a serious democratic deficit across Europe. The core

---

1 See:http://www.europarl.europa.eu/elections2004/ep-election/sites/en/results1306/ turnout_ep/ index.html, accessed 19 January 2007.

2 See: http://www.electoralcommission.org.uk/templates/search/document.cfm/7299, accessed 19 January 2007

principle of representative democracy is the participation of citizens as demonstrated by their voting in elections. The most common reason quoted for not voting is that politicians do not listen. This is leading to a situation where citizens are feeling a loss of ownership in the democratic process and where the 'representativeness' of elected assemblies is put into question.

In the US, the decline in civic participation has been explored in the influential work of Putman (2000). Putman argues the need for citizens to come face to face to discuss issues and that such meetings enable individuals to gain necessary negotiation skills and appreciate the viewpoints of others; skills which are essential for a thriving democracy. However with the introduction of home-based technologies such as the television, the public are staying at home and not going out to join civil societies and, therefore, social capital is decreasing. However, Putman's paper falls short of examining in-depth the potential role of ICTs.

The potential for technology to enhance democracy by increasing political participation has been the subject of academic debate for a number of years (e.g. Dutton, 1992). The arrival of more sophisticated ICTs has produced a growing community of research and practice that is investigating the use of such technology to re-engage people with the democratic process, aiming at making decision-making more transparent, inclusive and accessible. ICT provides the potential for citizens to be involved in political processes, offering opportunities for more participatory democracy (Held, 1996). Held's participatory model of democracy reflects the need to engage both citizens and civil society organizations in open debate, therefore there is a need to consider:

> how an adequate space might be created, and procedures established, for debate and decision-making around issues to which citizens brought divergent views and interests. (p312)

However, in order for citizens to participate, he and others recognize the need for citizens to become informed. Fishkin (1995) argues the need for 'mass' deliberation by citizens instead of 'elite' deliberation by elected representatives. Instant reactions to telephone surveys and television call-ins do not allow time to think-through issues and hear the competing arguments of others:

> A major part of the problem of democratic reform is how to promote mass deliberation – how to bring people into the process under conditions where they can be engaged to think seriously and fully about public issues. (p41)

On the other hand it has also been recognized that not everyone will actually participate. Some of those that choose not to participate do so because they feel their interests are already being accounted for by their elected representative. Therefore there is a need to retain representatives and there is a need to consider participatory representative models of democracy that allow civil society to do more than just vote for their representative every four to five years (Coleman, 2005a). While democratic outcomes are not always certain, there is little doubt that new technology offers possibilities to strengthen participatory discussion through virtual meetings not dependent on time, location or physical presence. On the other hand, Barber (1984) whilst presenting the concept of strong democracy, warns that the use of technology could diminish the sense of face-to-face confrontation and increase the dangers of elite manipulation. Similarly, Van Dijk (2000), in addressing the role of technology to inform and activate the public, warns of the consequences of bad designs of technology:

> Computerized information campaigns and mass public information systems have to be designed and supported in such a way that they help to narrow the gap between the 'information rich' and 'information poor' otherwise the spontaneous development of ICT will widen it. (p44)

The history of politics over the last 500 years documents the fragile nature of democracy and how difficult it can be to sustain it. In applying ICT to the democratic process, care has to be taken not to make democracy a more vulnerable concept. Issues such as the digital divide, political equality, privacy of personal data and trust in the democratic process are all potential danger areas.

The motivation to re-engage the public in order to address the democratic deficit discussed above and the arguments over the potential or otherwise of ICT to support democracy usefully set the scene to discuss e-Participation and e-democracy research in the remainder of this chapter. The following section discusses concepts underpinning e-democracy and the current research and practice. This is followed by an appraisal of the research landscape across Europe based on work undertaken in the Demo-Net project, a Network of Excellence on e-Participation research funded by the European Commission. Finally, conclusions are drawn for future research direction.

2. CURRENT RESEARCH AND PRACTICE

e-democracy is a term that is used widely but also has widely different interpretations. It can be described as the use of ICT to support the democratic decision-making processes. However, this definition is too abstract and needs further elaboration. In some countries and in some government circles e-democracy has become synonymous with e-voting, however, voting is not the only mechanism whereby citizens can influence democratic decision making. In August 2002 the UK government issued a consultation paper on a policy for electronic democracy (HM Government, 2002). This consultation document usefully argues that e-democracy can be divided into two distinct areas – one addressing e-participation and the other addressing e-voting. In the case of latter the paper argues that e-voting should be viewed as a technological problem. In the case of the former, the document sets out the possibilities for greater opportunity for consultation and dialogue between government and citizens. Hacker and van Dijk (2000), using the term 'digital democracy' as opposed to e-democracy, discuss the emergence of the concept and how technology is shaping democratic practices. They define digital democracy as:

> a collection of attempts to practice democracy without the limits of time, space and other physical conditions, using ICT or CMC[3] instead, as an addition, not a replacement for traditional 'analogue' political practices. (p1)

Previous work (Macintosh 2004) gave a definition of e-democracy as:

> concerned with the use of information and communication technologies to engage citizens, support the democratic decision-making processes and strengthen representative democracy. The principal ICT mechanism is the internet accessed through an increasing variety of channels, including PCs, both in the home and in pubic locations, mobile phones, and interactive digital TV. The democratic decision making processes can be divided into two main categories: one addressing the electoral process, including e-voting, and the other addressing citizen e-participation in democratic decision-making.

This chapter builds on these baseline definitions and uses a working definition of e-Participation, as the use of ICTs to support information provision, top-down engagement which is concerned with support for government-led initiatives, and ground-up empowerment which is mainly concerned with the support to enable citizens, civil society organizations and other democratically constituted groups to engage with their elected representatives and officials. Effective information provision is clearly seen as a prerequisite for both engagement and empowerment (see Figure 5-1).

These three types of participation supported by ICT are based on previous work undertaken by the OECD (2001: p23) which defines information provision, consultation, and active participation. The latter is described as a relation based on partnership with government, in which citizens actively engage in the policy-making process. It acknowledges a role

---

[3] These terms were expanded earlier in the reference as Information and Communication Technology and Computer-Mediated Communication

for citizens in proposing policy options and shaping the policy dialogue – although the responsibility for the final decision or policy formulation rests with government.

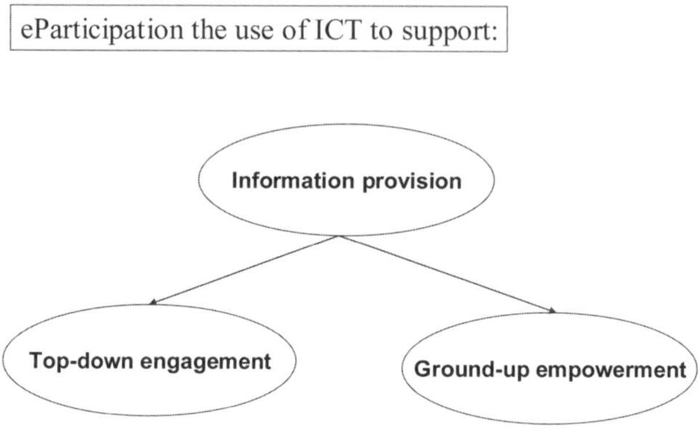

Figure 5-1. e-Participation

Much of the literature tends to focus on the ground-up empowerment perspective of e-Participation. For example, Tsagarousianou, Tambini and Bryan (1998), give descriptions of a number of projects involved with e-democracy and civic networking. These authors suggest government-led top-down initiatives will clearly differ from ground-up community developments, but argue also that "*civic networking will not realise its objective unless it becomes more realistic in its goals and methods*" (p13). The authors examine a range of community networks in the USA and Europe, and come to the conclusion that there was a low level of take-up and relative inactivity even when some of the structures were set up specifically to support democratic practices and feed into public authority decision-making. Perhaps, given the year of their work, this could be explained by inequality of access and fewer sophisticated tools available for use. Becker and Slaton (2000) explore initiatives that are specifically designed to move towards direct democracy, while the work of Rheingold (2000) on virtual communities assesses the potential impact of community networks, questioning the relationship between virtual communities and the revitalisation of democracy. From the ground-up perspective, citizens appear to be emerging as producers, rather than just consumers, of policy (Macintosh *et al.,* 2002). This recognizes the need to allow citizens to influence and participate in policy formulation instead of reacting to an agenda set by government - ground-up perspective which allows civil society to set the agenda. Chadwick (2006: p98) describes a number of community-based networks bounded by geographical location aiming at enhancing social capital and also a number of virtual communities which he claims have been inspired by the need for increasing citizen deliberation.

From a top-down perspective, governments are addressing issues such as how to provide easier and wider access to government information and how to ensure that citizens have the ability to give their views on a range of policy related matters. This perspective is characterised in terms of user access to information and reaction to government-led initiatives. An OECD publication (Macintosh, 2003) considers how ICT can be applied to enhance citizen participation in policy-making. The report provides an initial analytical framework to characterize e-participation which has since been used by a number of other authors. The report suggests four overarching objectives for applying ICT to the democratic decision making processes. These are:

- reaching a wider audience to enable broader participation
- supporting participation through a range of technologies to cater for the diverse technical and communicative skills of citizens
- providing relevant information in a format that is both more accessible and more understandable to the target audience to enable more informed contributions
- engaging with a wider audience to enable deeper contributions and support deliberation.

Once again this emphasizes that political participation must involve both the means to be informed and the mechanisms to take part in the decision-making. Previous top-down initiatives have used e-Participation tools based on discussion boards. For example, Macintosh and Smith (2002) describe an online participation study to consult citizens on environmental policy issues and Luhrs, et al (2003) describe a large scale participation exercise in the City of Hamburg. Coleman and Gøtze (2001) describe a number of projects some of which use other technologies for online engagement, ranging from email to chat rooms. It is important to note that most authors recognize that the top-down approach alone is inadequate for strengthening democracy, as Sclove (1995) states:

> Numerous political theorists agree that decision-making processes are democratically inadequate, even spurious, unless they are combined with relatively equal and extensive opportunities for citizens, communities, and groups to help shape decision-making agendas. (p39)

Nowadays a large range of tools are available to form the basis for e-Participation applications. For both top-down and ground-up perspectives their functionality needs to support users to access factual information provided by a stakeholder, whether that stakeholder is an individual citizen, civil society organization or government agency; formulate opinions based on the views of others; contribute their own opinion either privately or publicly to a specific stakeholder; initiate their own issue and become a stakeholder for that issue. These four functions are not so dissimilar from those discussed by Jankowski and van Selm (2000) in their analysis of the cyberdemocracy typology put forward by Tsagarousianou who considers: obtaining information; engaging in deliberation; and participating in decision making both formally through top-down initiatives and through bottom up community actions. The authors go on to state:

> this typology constitutes, in our opinion, the essence of activities related to the democratic process (p152)

It is also now well accepted that a technical, social and political factors need to be considered when developing e-Participation applications and using any type of ICT to enhance democracy is a challenging task (Mambrey, 2004). Similarly authors have argued that it is insufficient to consider technology in isolation and that the technology should be viewed as an enabler in specific 'democratic contexts'. In order to make more explicit these democratic contexts a framework to characterize e-Participation initiatives has been developed based on previous OECD work (Macintosh, 2003). This framework, developed around ten key dimensions for government-led initiatives and in particular for citizen participation in policy-making, enables tools and projects to be described in different democratic contexts. But what technology, other than discussion boards which have been discussed earlier, is relevant to e-Participation?

During 2004 to 2005 the UK government funded the national project on local e-democracy as part of a £80 million National Project Program aiming to help drive the modernization of local government services The e-democracy project had the following five high-level objectives:

1. to encourage all local authorities to consider the ways in which they can use e-democracy tools to enhance local democracy and to develop locally appropriate strategies for implementing such tools where relevant.
2. to ensure that the knowledge and experience of e-democracy that already exists is systematically exposed and shared across local government to the benefit of all.
3. to develop new tools that support or enhance local democratic practice both within local government and beyond.
4. to provide a focal point for democratic innovation and the dissemination of best practice.

5. to begin a sustainable process of electronically enabled participation and engagement that complements existing democratic structures and processes.

This resulted in two main e-Participation strands based on top-down government-led e-Participation initiatives and ground-up citizen-led e-Participation initiatives. Both these strands underwent in-depth evaluations (Whyte et al 2005 and Coleman, 2005).

As part of the overall UK initiative, Macintosh, Coleman and Lalljee (2005) developed an eMethods Guide for public authorities. The report, directed at councilors and officers in local government, discusses e-Participation tools in specific democratic contexts. It usefully describes thirteen types of tools which have been used for e-Participation. To different degrees they support the four participation functions described earlier, i.e. they allow users to: access factual information provided by a stakeholder; formulate opinions based on the views of others; contribute their own opinion either privately or publicly to a specific stakeholder; initiate their own issue and become a stakeholder for that issue. A sample of the tools is presented in Figure 5-2 along with the type of functionality that can be expected from it in an e-Participation sense.

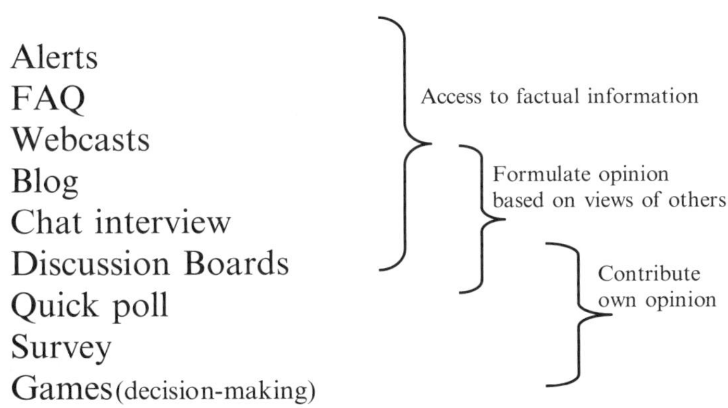

Figure 5-2. Tools and their e-Participation functionality

The full details and a number of working papers from the UK national project on local e-democracy can be found on the website for the International Centre of Excellence for Local Democracy (ICELE).[4]

[4] See the ICELE website at: http://www.icele.org/site/index.php, accessed 19 January 2007.

3. THE RESEARCH LANDSCAPE

This section examines who is conducting research into e-Participation and the tools, methods and techniques they are using for this research. The section is based on work undertaken as part of the Demo-Net project. This is a network of excellence funded by the European Commission, with the objective of connecting together the leading European research organizations in the field of e-Participation. Research in e-democracy and e-Participation in Europe has suffered from being fragmented, disparate and unfocused, with researchers often unaware of developments in different disciplines. Therefore the aim is to bring together key researchers from a variety of countries and academic disciplines in order to consolidate and build upon existing technical and socio-technical research in e-Participation. Full details of the European initiative can be found at http://www.demo-net.org (accessed 22 December 2006). The project started in January 2006 and is funded for four years.

During 2006, under the Demo-Net initiative, Macintosh and Coleman (2006) conducted an online survey on "who was doing what" research across Europe. They found that the geographical spread of research groups was considerable with 76 research groups from 20 European countries responding to their survey.

Figure 5-3 gives an indication of the spread of e-Participation research in Europe. There is a relatively large number of research centres, 53, based in northern Europe, 17 based in southern Europe and only 6 from eastern Europe.

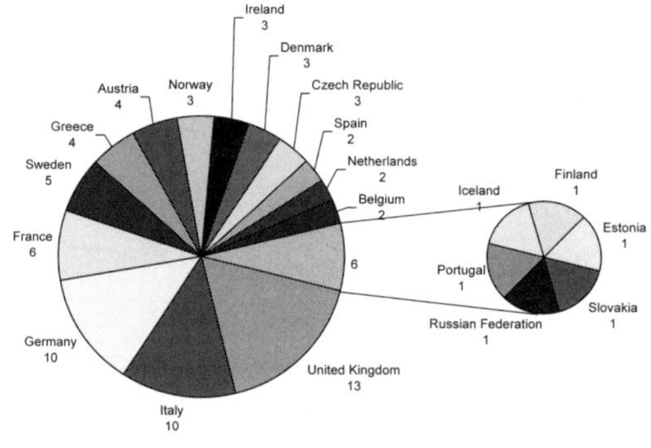

Figure 5-3. The European research landscape

The survey identified 23 specific e-Participation research activities ranging from campaigning to referenda/voting. These are reproduced in Table 5-1. Apart from Finland, Russian Federation and Slovakia, all countries tended to show a strong research base in online deliberation.

Research into consultation, evaluation and policy processes was also strongly represented.

Table 5-1. e-Participation research activities

e-Participation Research Activities
1. Campaigning - examining the use of ICT in lobbying, protest, lobbying, petitioning and other forms of collective action
2. Collaborative Environments - supporting collaborative group working, e.g. developing and/or using groupware and CSCW, to progress shared agendas
3. Community Informatics - understanding how and why individuals come together to form communities and how tools support and shape such communities.
4. Consultation - official initiatives by a public or private agencies to allow stakeholders to contribute their opinion, either privately or publicly, on a specific issue
5. Cultural Politics - understanding new online spaces and practices which touch on power, but are not traditionally political
6. Deliberation - understanding why, when and how citizens participate in formal and informal talk; design of tools to support virtual, small and large-group discussions; assessing the quality of messages and interactions in structured and unstructured online dialogue
7. Discourse - supporting the understanding, analysis and representation of discourse, including discourse analysis, argumentation, issues of scalability with large corpora
8. Electioneering – studying the use of ICT by politicians, political parties and lobbyists in the context of election campaigns
9. Evaluation - understanding what and how to assess e-participation projects and practices
10. ICT Design Issues - understanding how to design and implement systems, development of systems, issues include design methods, HCI and accessibility
11. Inclusion/Exclusion - understanding digital, social and cultural exclusion based upon such divisions as gender, ethnicity, linguistic identity, socio-economic status and disability
12. Information Provision - understanding how to structure, represent and manage information, includes information architectures, content design and content management
13. Journalism - examining ways in which the mass media and traditional journalistic practices are changing, for example, the emergence of news blogs, user-generated content and online versions of press content
14. Knowledge Management - understanding how to identify, acquire, represent and apply relevant knowledge
15. Mediation – studying the use of techniques intended to resolve disputes or conflicts in an online context
16. Mobile Communication – design and use of mobile channels of communication and issues of location-based services/initiatives
17. Policy Processes - studying changes to the policy process in an online world and the effects of networked governance
18. Polling - the use of ICT to measure public opinion and sentiment
19. Security - understanding why and when secure processes are required, design and

(Continued)

Tab le 5-1. (Continued)

e-Participation Research Activities
implementation of secure systems, includes privacy issues, authentication and identity management
20. Service Delivery - examining the design and implementation of e-services and exploring interfaces between the delivery of services and opportunities for e-participation
21. Spatial planning - understanding design and application of systems for use in urban planning and environmental assessment
22. Visualization - the design, development and use of visualization technologies such as GIS, Virtual Reality and 3D environments
23. Voting - examining the use of online tools in the context of public voting in elections, referenda or local plebiscites

For each of these activities the survey asked whether the group's research was concerned with *conducting* e-Participation or whether they were *observing/studying* the area. The reason for this was that there was a need to distinguish those research centers focusing their research into the design and application of e-Participation tools, i.e. the technology-based centers as opposed to those research centers focusing on study of e-Participation. In each case they were then asked to provide details of the tools, techniques and methods they were employing.

For *conducting* e-Participation, the tools, techniques and methods were grouped under five main categories: those to support and provide underpinning infrastructures; those providing platforms/tools; those addressing design techniques; those supporting content management; and those to support interaction and comprehension. Table 5-2 summarizes the categories with examples of the various methods, tools and techniques on the survey.

The survey indicated lack of research in supporting *interaction and comprehension, content management* and *underlying infrastructures*. The first two are critical in supporting the diverse range of e-Participation stakeholders to access and understand information. The large amount of information associated with e-Participation requires structuring and representing in such a way as to aid user navigation through it. Closely associated with this is the need to support users to understand complex information through research on interaction and comprehension.

For *observing/studying* e-Participation, the tools, techniques and methods were grouped under six main categories: those to support contextualizing the e-Participation activity; those providing understanding of the political and cultural outcomes, giving impact assessment; those to support understanding of how people interact and what they do during an e-Participation activity; those to support understanding what people think during e-Participation activities; those that examine the content and text of e-Participation; and finally those that help us to understand what the system does, leading to technology assessment. Table 5-3 summarizes the categories with examples of the various methods, tools and techniques on the survey.

Table 5-2. Tools, methods and techniques for conducting e-Participation

Underpinning infrastructures / techniques	Platforms/tools	Design	Content management tools	Supporting interaction & comprehension
Open architectures	Discussion forums	Participatory design	KM tools	Argument visualisation tools
Standards	Weblogs	Requirements analysis	Ontological engineering tools & techniques	Natural language interfaces
Semantic web technology	Petitions	Systems analysis		Discourse analysis
Semantic web languages	GIS	Holistic design		Meta & domain ontologies
Semantic web tools	Web portals	Modeling		Dialogical research
Agent technology	newsletter	Interviews		Content analysis tools
	Question-time via email	Soft systems methods		Term extraction
	Collaborative environments	Socio-technical systems analysis		
	Consultation platforms	Organisational analysis		
	Deliberative surveys	Political systems analysis		

Table 5-3. Tools, methods and techniques for observing e-Participation

Political & Cultural Framing	Understandin g Political & Cultural Outcomes	Understand-ing What People Do & How They Interact	Understand-ing What People Think	Examining Content / Text	Understand-ing What Systems Do: Technology Assessment
Social theory	Cost benefit analysis	Social network analysis	Interviews	Data mining	Systems analysis
Cultural theory	Comparative analysis of practice	Statistics of demography & usage	Surveys	Data analysis	

(Continued)

Table 5-3. (Continued)

Political & Cultural Framing	Understanding Political & Cultural Outcomes	Understanding What People Do & How They Interact	Understanding What People Think	Examining Content / Text	Understanding What Systems Do: Technology Assessment
Political theory		Grounded theory	Polling	Argument visualization	
		Ethnography	Focus workshops	Discourse analysis	
		Observation	Scenario based workshops	Qualitative text analysis	
		Case studies	Deliberative survey tools	Cognitive maps	
				Content analysis	
				Document analysis	

The survey indicated a lack of research on *technology assessment* and *impact assessment*. An understanding of technological systems is a clearly needed for informed and rigorous research in this area. Similarly, an understanding of political and cultural outcomes of e-Participation is critical.

The full report from the 2006 survey can be found on the Demo-Net website. The e-Participation research investigation is on-going. The final deliverable, the Multidisciplinary Roadmap and Report on e-Participation Research, considers the e-Participation research landscape in Europe and the rest of the world. Early analysis indicates a strong research base that spans social science, socio-technical, information science and computer science disciplines. However in the past these different academic disciplines have tended to conduct their research in isolation and only recently have inter-disciplinary groupings been formed to enable a richer base of research methods and techniques to be used in order to understand better the design, deployment and evaluation of e-Participation systems.

4. CONCLUSION AND FUTURE RESEARCH DIRECTION

This chapter discussed the research and practice in e-Participation and in doing so described the type of research and research methods being used across Europe. But where should future research be directed and what are the main challenges still facing e-Participation?

During 2004-2005 a major study funded by the European Commission into e-Government was conducted. This was the IST PRISMA project. One aspect of this study was to consider scenarios on the future use of e-Participation tools (Kubicek and Westholm, 2005). The study developed a contingency model for e-democracy tools and assessed this against three possible scenarios for the future of democratic participation based on: a prosperous and more just Europe; a turbulent world; and recession and reorientation. The resulting paper highlighted a number of issues with regard to technology design and development. Firstly, the increasing amount of information available over the internet implies a need for knowledge and information management systems. Secondly the range of stakeholders involved requires personalized communication integrated with the delivery of relevant information. Thirdly, it highlighted the need for information systems design to move towards a more collaborative working environment to support government and civil society to work in partnership. The need for a rigorous evaluation framework was stressed.

A similar future research direction is reported by Macintosh (2006) who arrives at five key issues for future information systems research to support e-Participation. The first concerns moving from experimentation and pilots to large-scale usage of e-Participation applications. 'Scale' is addressed from both the point of view of the increasing number of stakeholders that need to be reflected in the design of the technology and the need to address navigation and analysis of large volumes of information. The second challenge is concerned with understanding how to design tools to facilitate online deliberation and support collaborative working environments. The third challenge addresses the need for an underpinning representation of the information and analysis of contributions made by civil society. Fourthly, the author stresses the need to embed the technology into political processes rather than as isolated e-Participation exercises. The final challenge, like Kubicek and Westholm, is concerned with evaluation, so as to understand what has and has not been achieved.

e-Participation raises many research challenges from both political and computer science perspectives. There is a need for these two disparate domains to work closely together to appreciate better how to design, deploy and evaluate e-Participation systems from technical, cultural and organizational perspectives that take account of the social and political complexity of the domain.

REFERENCES

Barber, B. (1984). *Strong democracy: Participatory politics for a new age.* Berkeley: University of California Press.

Becker, T. & Slaton, C. (2000). *The Future of Tele-democracy.* Westport, Conn. 2000. LC .

Chadwick, A. (2006) *Internet Politics.* Oxford University Press 2006.

Coleman, S. and Gøtze, (2001) J. Bowling Together: Online Public Engagement in Policy Deliberation. London: Hansard Society, 2001, available at http://bowlingtogether.net/ bowlingtogether.pdf;

Coleman, S. (2005a) *Direct Representation: Towards a conversational democracy.* Publised by IPPR, London

Coleman, S. (2005) *e-democracy from the Ground up Down: An Evaluation of community-focused approaches to e-democracy* Bristol City Council. Published by Bristol City Council for The Local e-democracy National Project.

Dutton, W. H., (1992) "Political Science Research on Tele-democracy" *Social Science Computer Review,* 10(4), pp.505-22.

van Dijk, J. (2000), "Models of Democracy and Concepts of Communication", in K.L. Hacker and Jan van Dijk., (eds) *Digital Democracy issues of theory and practice.* Sage Publications.

Fishkin, J. S. (1995), *The Voice of the People. Public Opinion and Democracy,* Yale University Press.

Hacker and van Dijk (2000) 'What is Digital Democracy?'. In Hacker, K.L and Jan van Dijk., (eds) *Digital Democracy issues of theory and practice.* Sage Publications.

Held, A,. (1996). *Models of democracy.* Cambridge: Blackwell Publishers.

HM Government. (2002) In the Service of Democracy – a consultation paper on a policy for electronic democracy. Published by the Office of the e-Envoy, Cabinet Office, London.

JanKowski, N. and van Selm, M. (2000) 'The Promise and Practice of Public Debate in Cyberspace'. In Hacker, K.L and Jan van Dijk., (eds) *Digital Democracy issues of theory and practice.* Sage Publications.

Kubicek, H., and Westholm, H. (2005) Scenarios for Future Use of e-democracy Tools in Europe, *International Journal of Electronic Government Research,* 1(3), p33-50, July-September 2005.

Luhrs, R., Albrecht, S., Lubcke, M and Hohberg, B. (2003) How to Grow? Online Consultation about Growth in the City of Hamburg: Methods, Techniques, Success Factors; in: R. Traunmuller (Ed); Electronic Government, Second International Conference, E-GOV 2003, Prague, Czech Republic, September 1-5, 2003 Proceedings. Springer (Lecture Notes in Computer Science; Vol. 2739)

Macintosh, A. (2003); "Using information and communication technologies to enhance citizen engagement in the policy process"; in *Promises and Problems of E-Democracy: Challenges of online citizen engagement,* pp20-141. Paris: OECD. ISBN 92-64-01948-0. Available at: http://www1.oecd.org/publications/e-book/4204011E.PDF

Macintosh, A. (2004) 'Characterizing E-Participation in Policy-Making'. In the Proceedings of the Thirty-Seventh Annual Hawaii International Conference on System Sciences (HICSS-37), January 5 – 8, 2004, Big Island, Hawaii.

Macintosh, A. (2006) e-Participation and Policy-Making: the Research and the Challenges. In P. Cunningham & M. Cunningham (Eds.) Exploiting the Knowledge Economy: Issues, Applications and Case Studies; IOS press, ISBN 1-58603-682-3, pp.364-369.

Macintosh, A., Coleman, S., and Lalljee, M. (2005) *E-Methods for Public Engagement: Helping Local Authorities communicate with citizens.* Published by Bristol City Council for The Local e-democracy National Project.

Macintosh, A. and Coleman, S. (2006). *Demo-Net: Deliverable 4.2 Multidisciplinary roadmap and report on e-Participation research.* Winter 2006. Available at www.demo-net.org.

Macintosh, A., E. Davenport, A. Malina and A. Whyte "Technology to Support Participatory Democracy" In Å. Grönlund (2002), (ed.). *Electronic Government: Design, Applications, and Management.* Umeå University, Sweden: Idea Group Publishing.

Macintosh, A. and Smith, E.; Citizen Participation in Public Affairs; In: R.Traunmuller and K.Lenk (Eds); Electronic Government, First International Conference; proceedings / E-GOVS 2002, Aix-en-Provence, France, September 2002. Springer (Lecture Notes in Computer Science; Vol. 2456), pp. 256-264

Mambrey, P. (2004) Networked ICT to foster e-democracy; in: R.Traunmuller (Ed); Electronic Government, Third International Conference, E-GOV 2004, Spain, 2004 Proceedings. Springer (Lecture Notes in Computer Science; Vol. 2739)

OECD (2001). *Citizens as Partners: Information, consultation and public participation in policy-making:* OECD, Paris.

Putman, R. D. (1995) "Bowling Alone: America's Declining Social Capital" *Journal of Democracy* 6 (1).

Rheingold, H. (2000), *The Virtual Community,* The MIT Press, Mass., US.

Sclove, R. (1995), *Democracy & Technology.* NY: Guildford Press.

The Electoral Commission and The Hansard Society (2006); *An audit of political engagement 3.* Research Report March 2006. ISBN: 1-904363-78-4.

Tsagarousianou, Rosa. Tambini, Damian. & Bryan Cathy. (1998). (eds). Cyberdemocracy: Technology, cities and civic networks. London & New York: Routledge.

Whyte, A., Renton, A. and Macintosh, A. (2005) *e-democracy from the Top Down: An Evaluation of e-democracy Activities Initiated by Councils and Government* Bristol City Council. Published by Bristol City Council for The Local e-democracy National Project.

SUGGESTED READINGS AND ONLINE RESOURCES

For models of democracy, Held, 1996 gives a good overview, with advantages and disadvantages of each. The OECD 2001 report provides useful background to citizen participation in policy-making providing a number of guiding principles for off-line engagement. The follow-on OECD report (Macintosh 2003) provides the technology enabled approach to citizen participation with a number of case studies from OECD member countries and with five grand challenges for the research. The "Bowling Together Report" by Coleman and Gotz gives valuable insight into e-Participation practice. Finally, the 2005 report by Macintosh, Coleman and Lalljee is a useful guide to what technologies have been used and how. For citations to these and other works, see section "References," above.

See www.demo-net.org for what is intended to be an archive of state-of-the-art research reports on e-Participation. The website http://www.icele.org/site/index.php is the repository for the reports resulting from the UK National project on Local e-democracy. The website http://itc.napier.ac.uk/ provides useful links to a number of on-going initiatives and up-to-date list of conferences and workshops. Finally the various Do-Wire Groups provided by Steven Clift provide invaluable news and comment on current initiatives, see: http://www.publicus.net/

QUESTIONS FOR DISCUSSION

1. Can e-Participation address the democratic deficit and re-engage the public in activities such as voting?
2. Can e-Participation change the power relationship between government and civil society, is it leading to direct democracy?
3. Is there any relevance to ground-up e-Participation initiatives without the direct support of government; whose listening?
4. To what extent can current technology facilitate deliberation; is this a technology challenge or societal challenge for active citizenship?

Chapter 6

INTRODUCTION TO DIGITAL GOVERNMENT RESEARCH IN PUBLIC POLICY AND MANAGEMENT

Sharon S. Dawes

Center for Technology in Government, University at Albany/SUNY, New York, U.S.A. (sdawes@ctg.albany.edu)

CHAPTER OVERVIEW

Digital government research aims not only to generate new knowledge but also to make useful connections between research and practice. To achieve both ends, digital government research ideally derives research problems from practical challenges, and translates research findings into both new knowledge and usable results. Ubiquitous problems related to data availability, quality, and usability; information value; technology choices; and organizational and cross-boundary information-enabled processes are all of interest to both scholars and managers. These challenges take specific forms in different organizational and policy settings, but they also have common characteristics that can be usefully approached using analytical lenses that focus on some combination of strategy, policy, data, skills, costs, and technology. This chapter uses a public management perspective, represented by a set of real-life case studies, to explore how these considerations interact to produce both desirable and undesirable results. These interdependencies present researchers and managers with special challenges to overcome as well as unique opportunities to collaborate.

1. INTRODUCTION

Most conceptualizations of digital government center on government's use of the internet and World Wide Web to communicate with and provide information and services to citizens. While this view is extremely important (and is the focus of much political, economic, and managerial attention) it actually represents only a small portion of the information-driven activities of government. Most information-intensive work actually takes place behind the scenes of public web sites, in the "back offices" of government agencies. Here is where the necessary policies and strategies are developed and the associated processes, systems, and data resources are devised, managed, and used. In this work, information technology is intertwined with public policy and management concerns. Since the mid-1990s, a rich and varied research agenda has emerged around this combination of concerns.

An agenda-building workshop sponsored by the National Science Foundation Digital Government Research Program focused attention on these organizational, managerial, and policy components of digital government. Participants identified topics that presented serious challenges to government managers and important questions for both social science and computer science researchers. These challenges included secure and trusted systems that are integrated with both business processes and other systems, new service delivery models that take full advantage of emerging information technologies, networked forms of organization, decision support tools for policy makers and leaders, electronic records management and preservation tools, and better methods of IT management (Dawes, et al., 1999b). While each of these topics is important in its own right, the workshop report emphasized that the most important impacts and opportunities probably lay in the way these topics interact. A major conclusion stated that because "policy guidelines, organizational forms, and technology tools constantly interact with one another" they generate "many questions and conflicts about what is technically possible, organizationally feasible, and socially desirable (p. iii)." A variety of NSF-funded digital government research projects (NSF, 2004) have responded to these issues including studies on knowledge networking in the public sector, the social and technical processes of information integration, development of information-based tools for policing, application of natural language technologies to the rulemaking process, and the development of digital libraries to support the management of national forests.

Digital government research can be valuable to government leaders and managers who are responsible for IT adoption and deployment. It can help them appreciate the strategic possibilities that technology presents for creating, improving, or streamlining government processes, functions, and programs (Scholl, 2005, Kim and Layne, 2001; Huxham and Vangen, 2000; Andersen, et al., 1994). Some studies suggest that IT adoption and government reform are interacting processes (Scavo and Shi, 2000) and that IT implementation visibly affects performance, at least at the agency level (Heintze and Bretschneider, 2000). Conversely, research shows a common fallacy exists that technology can solve problems that actually demand managerial, organizational, or policy solutions (Klein, 2000). Indeed, information technology may not only fail to solve many problems, it can generate new policy problems and unintended consequences (e.g., Roberts, 2000). In addition, traditional principles of public administration have apparently had little effect on government IT strategies and decisions (Holden, 2004). In fact, IT adoption prompts expectations of administrative reform, but these are seldom, and only partly, realized (Kraemer and King, 2006). This lack of strong effect appears to be due to the mitigating influence of institutional structures (Fountain, 2001) and existing political power relations (Kraemer and King, 2006).

Increasingly, important public problems, such as health care, public safety, and environmental quality, require that agencies share information. In these situations, managers and policy makers need to understand both benefits and risks (Dawes, 1996) and the mechanisms and limits of coordination (Dawes, et al., 2004). In response, they need to create and control integrated systems that cross the boundaries of agencies, levels of government, and sectors of the economy (Landsbergen & Wolken, 2000). In addition, increasing reliance on the private sector to perform many aspects of public service (Milward and Provan, 2000) makes the management of public-private and public-nonprofit relationships more prevalent and more important (Dawes and Prefontaine, 2003; Globerman and Vining, 1996). Moreover, some important IT developments involve the public directly in expressing needs and making design decisions. One example is in systems that help determine urban growth and transportation patterns (e.g., Waddell and Borning, 2004).

This suite of public policy and management challenges crosses all levels and domains of government. Each one is worthy of research attention, and together they represent an interconnected, dynamic set of problems that can also be investigated in concert. A three-year research program in New York State explored these challenges holistically by working with eight agency-based initiatives that all depended on effective information use inside government. A needs assessment at the beginning of the effort involved nearly 100 public managers from 34 state agencies and local governments plus private sector and university representatives. The participants identified many specific issues associated with using information to do their jobs. They noted the absence of a value proposition for information, explaining that executives and policy makers have only a limited appreciation for the value of information for program planning, monitoring, and evaluation. Participants expressed concern that agency executives often lack an appreciation for the extent to which information issues pervade their programs. Accordingly, few fully understand the nature and level of financial, technical, and human investments necessary to use information well. As a result, participants reported their organizations made inadequate use of existing information, and lost opportunities to create shared information resources that would benefit the public sector more widely.

The needs analysis also described a general lack of incentives, policy coordination mechanisms, and practical tools for intra- and inter-agency information sharing. The participants considered this a significant barrier to program coordination efforts. In addition, laws that prohibit (or that are interpreted to prohibit) certain activities like data integration across service areas were seen to further limit the application of government information resources to narrowly defined uses.

Another key problem was simply knowing what information exists, and then locating what is needed from among myriad databases and organizational sources. The lack of useable, up-to-date metadata that accurately describes data holdings or documents data definitions was also noted. As a result, when managers identify seemingly relevant data, they must sort out non-standard, undocumented definitions, or make risky assumptions about what the data actually mean. In addition, much information is duplicated in multiple files and locations, requiring considerable effort to assess and identify which source is most correct or current. Often managers are faced with contradictory information and must invest resources to resolve data conflicts and locate missing information. This is compounded by the lack of metadata, which might make it quite feasible to select information that is suitable for a particular use from among different sources or versions. For example, it might be the case that less timely data is easily available and perfectly useful, but without metadata to confirm its status, users are reluctant to use it and often either do without or collect new information for their needs. Other problems included concern about handling sensitive, personal, and confidential information; or drawing incorrect conclusions from inaccurate, out-of-date, incompatible, or poorly defined data.

Data ownership, stewardship, and related organizational issues were also prominent, including difficulties in identifying who has the authority to release information or to make data sharing or technology transfer decisions. Many participants noted that agency-wide information management, access, and use policies (which would help resolve these common problems) were missing, as were government-wide policies on the same subjects.

Inadequate, inappropriate, and stand-alone technologies and systems were also common problems. Participants agreed that agencies tend to acquire equipment and software on an opportunistic and ad-hoc basis, leading to incompatible systems, little or widely varying capability for data analysis, and a patchwork of high-, low-, and no-tech work units. Major information systems and their related databases tend to be built-in isolation from one another so that merging, comparing, and integrating data for analysis, evaluation, and decision making was inordinately difficult and expensive, and therefore seldom attempted.

Workforce issues were another concern, including difficulty in attracting and retaining IT managers and professionals in government service. Many participants thought that across the entire public service, information handling and analytical skills received too little attention. Communication, negotiation, and collaboration skills needed to succeed at cross-boundary activities that involve interagency, intergovernmental, and public-private interactions were also scarce. Necessary collaboration skills that are crucial to good working relationships between IT and program staff were also lacking. These kinds of problems make both professional communities less effective than they could be. For example, software developers may not pay enough attention to the actual information needs of users, or the information products desired from an application, because they believe that the users can easily get what they need from the application. On the other hand, program staff may not understand or appreciate the tools that are at their disposal for queries, analysis, and reports.

2. CASE STUDIES

The issues described above became the framework for a three year applied research program. Eight partnership projects focused directly on government's ability to manage and use information. These projects represented the full range of issues that emerged from the needs assessment and collectively they provided a real-life test bed for exploring and experimenting with ways to overcome them.

The cases, briefly summarized in Table 6-1, provided a rich and detailed body of qualitative data for assessing the causes of and some solutions to the problems described above. The case analyses resulted in a set of six complementary considerations that can guide public agencies in designing future information-intensive initiatives.

Table 6-1. Case Studies

		Issues Addressed					
Focus	Summary	Strategy	Information Policies	Data Quality & Management	Cost Factors	Skill Gaps	Technology Choices
Homeless Information Management System	The New York State Bureau of Shelter Services developed a prototype system to track and evaluate services for homeless adults and families. The shared repository involved state and local governments and nonprofit service providers.	✓	✓	✓	✓	✓	✓
Agency IT Investment Decisions	The State Department of Transportation (DOT) created a new process for evaluating and approving information technology investments and linking them to business, management, and budget processes.	✓	✓	✓		✓	
An IT Knowledge Bank in New York City Government	New York City's technology management agency sponsored a knowledge bank to help IT professionals share data about system planning and budgeting, procurement, staffing, and data management across all agencies	✓		✓			✓
Comprehensive Childhood Indicators Data	The New York State Council on Children and Families developed Web-based "Kids Well-being Indicators Clearinghouse" of statistical indicators that draws its data from the service programs of 13 state agencies.	✓	✓	✓	✓	✓	✓
Annual Reassessment Program (Lavigne, et al., 2000; CTG, 2001e)	The State Office of Real Property Services (ORPS) launched a new property tax reassessment program which gives municipalities incentives to base property values on annual statistical adjustments rather than physical property valuations.	✓		✓	✓	✓	✓

(Continued)

Table 6-1. (Continued)

Focus	Summary	Issues Addressed					
		Strategy	Information Policies	Data Quality & Management	Cost Factors	Skill Gaps	Technology Choices
Revitalizing the State Central Accounting System	The Office of the State Comptroller launched a redsign of the State's 18-year-old Central Accounting System, the state's financial backbone. It serves accounting, reporting, planning, and control functions for every state agency, all municipalities, and hundreds of private organizations.	✓			✓	✓	✓
Transition From Regulation to Service in Municipal Affairs	The State Comptroller's Division of Municipal Affairs deals with the financial health of 3000 local governments. The diversity of data sources, uses, and users spread among six field offices made information management difficult and service delivery inconsistent.	✓		✓		✓	✓
Managing a Dynamic Distributed Workforce	Central New York Psychiatric Center managers make frequent staff deployment decisions to deal with the dynamic pattern of admissions, discharges, and turnover in geographically dispersed mental health units. Delays in data gathering caused decisions to be made with incomplete or out-of-date information.			✓			✓

3. DISCUSSION: SIX PUBLIC POLICY AND MANAGEMENT CONSIDERATIONS FOR DIGITAL GOVERNMENT

Six themes, illustrated in Figure 6-1, emerged from an analysis of these cases. These themes held true regardless of the purpose, technical framework, size, focus, or length of the project, or the number and type of organizations involved. They represent a set of management and policy concerns that must be understood in an integrated way in order to avoid or overcome the many problems cited in the workshop.

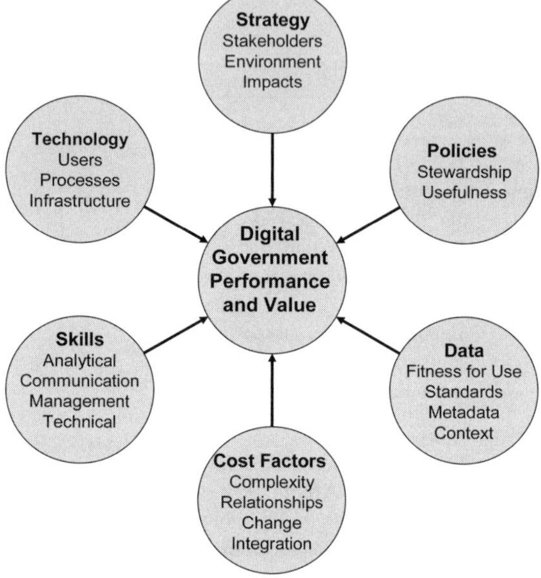

Figure 6-1. Public policy and management considerations in digital government initiatives

Strategy—Effective strategies emerge from a clear value proposition concerning the costs and benefits of any IT initiative. This proposition rests on an understanding of the mission-oriented need to be served, the larger social and political environment, and existing infrastructure and culture.

Policy—Information policies are needed to guide decisions about information and technology use. These policies materially affect the quality, availability and usability of information.

Data—Data quality, content, and context all affect information value, which in turn affects the performance of a system and those who must use it. Data considerations are usually deeply embedded in practices.

Costs—The costs of tangible resources such as staff, hardware, software, and consultants are easiest to estimate and track. However, other costs that are intangible, but substantial, are often overlooked. These are the costs of establishing and managing relationships, changing cultures and practices, and integrating both information and tasks into new processes.

Skills—Data analysis, project management, technical, and communi cation skills are all necessary to effective design, management, and implementation. These go beyond the skills of designers and managers and must include users in a variety of settings.

Technology—Technology choices represent long-term investments that strongly affect performance and limit future options. Early exploration of options and their likely effects is much more effective than trying to make changes after decisions have been made.

3.1 Strategy

Whether in business or in government, strategic thinking is concerned with mission-critical objectives, with an emphasis on customers and stakeholders. Strategies place a high value on human, organizational, and technological resources and seek maximum return on those investments, rather than minimized costs.

The cases underscore one very common reason why IT initiatives fail: failure to fully understand the underlying problem or need that a new or revised system must address. The first element of strategy, then, is a clear and agreed upon description of the business, policy, or program need that is the reason for the effort. This is often very difficult to achieve because different people see different symptoms of the problem, but seldom see the problem as a whole. The underlying problem is usually embedded in at least one business process and most individuals are able to see only the elements that are connected to their own part of the process. Consequently, the analysis necessary to uncover and define the full problem cannot be a solitary effort, but one that includes all relevant perspectives.

All governmental programs and initiatives have multiple stakeholders, that is people or organizations who care about the idea and how it affects them or other things they care about. The users or customers of services are key stakeholders and most efforts to use information on their behalf take them into account. But stakeholder considerations go far beyond this group to include (1) those who are directly involved in the process of designing, delivering, and paying for the system or service and (2) those who are indirectly affected, either by the outcome of the initiative or by the competition for resources that could have gone to a different effort that they value. Stakeholder analysis needs to identify both positive and negative impacts on all these groups. While it is important to understand how certain stakeholders can benefit, it is equally important to know who must contribute and who can be hurt and how.

Sound strategies also address existing reality. Every new information system goes into some pre-existing situation. That situation probably includes other, older information systems, business processes that channel work and information flow, and standard operating practices that have grown up over time to accommodate past problems and changing needs. The existing situation also reflects political relationships that strongly influence the distribution of power and resources. In addition, institutional imperatives and organizational culture reflect long-standing, generally-accepted ways of doing things. Institutional factors are usually powerful forces for inertia while cultures are more variable. Some cultures value analysis; others value action. Some prefer stability and avoid risk while others favor dynamic environments and encourage and embrace new ideas. Organizational culture usually reflects past experience, so understanding the history of relationships and activities is a prerequisite to changing them. Often multiple cultures exist, even inside a single organization, and they can conflict with each other.

A strategy should have a reasonably long life so it can guide action into the foreseeable future. Technology is the one component of information-based strategies that is likely to change quickly. Consequently, technologies that can be integrated into or readily replace existing infrastructures create the fewest undesirable dependencies, conflicts, and costs. The future is also a political realm. For many projects, upcoming legislative or budget decisions provide the authority or resources to proceed. In those arenas, competing initiatives will be proposed by others. While these can be difficult politically, they may also represent potential opportunities for partnerships or synergies.

At the strategic level, communication needs to be clear, consistent, focused on the essentials, and delivered in plain language. Strategy is not conveyed in a detailed work plan, but rather a high level statement that tells stakeholders and observers what kind of project to expect. It answers key questions such as: What is the goal? Will the approach be incremental or more radical? How long will it take? Who will do the work? Who is the leader? What roles do users and other stakeholders play? Who pays for what? What kind of technology will be used? What are the major phases or milestones?

Example from the cases

State Central Accounting System (CAS): The overhaul of a backbone system like the CAS inevitably raises concerns about project size and scope, technical feasibility, stakeholder involvement and support, and cost. The project team sponsored an extensive stakeholder needs analysis to address these concerns. Thirteen stakeholder workshops, involving hundreds of users, produced a strategy for an incremental course of action that adds more information at each step to guide both decisions and cost estimates. For the first phase of work, the focus centered on detailed process analysis. Later project phases would redesign and test simplifications in core processes and then add extended functionality. All along, the existing system would be maintained in full operation while current and potential users are kept informed and educated. This approach reduced uncertainty and provided decision points for each major phase of work. By following this incremental strategy, the lead agency postponed costly system decisions to later project phases when other vital information, such as the potential for business process simplification, would become available. This phased strategy offered more control over costs, better information for each decision point, less reliance on assumptions, and more options for action than would be the case if the entire project were laid out in detail from the outset.

3.2 Policies

Information policies in the form of laws, regulations, executive orders, and other official statements guide actions and decisions about why, how, when, and who uses information. Public information policies rest on fundamental democratic principles and include freedom of expression, the free flow of information in society, right to privacy in personal affairs, right of public access to government records, and right to profit from invention or ideas.

Information policies are also instruments of public management. In this case, policies generally fall into two main categories: policies that promote information *stewardship* and policies that promote information *use*. These two kinds of policies are complementary. Policies of stewardship help produce better quality, more reliable, more useable information and tested rules for using it in different situations. Good stewardship thus leads to more information use and more reliance on policies that promote use. Increasing use then increases the demand for stewardship in the form of better information and clear, consistent rules.

Stewardship is a conservative principle that recognizes government information is a public "good" like clean air and safe streets. It is concerned with accuracy, integrity, preservation, and protection of information. The stewardship principle does not necessarily imply "ownership," but rather it emphasizes a trusted relationship in which information is handled with care regardless of its original source or collector. Policies that promote stewardship address such topics as data definitions, data and system security, records management, personal privacy, confidential treatment of sensitive information, and long term preservation of information with enduring social, legal, or historical value. These policies become doubly important when information is used for important decisions, shared across organizational boundaries or re-used for purposed beyond its original one.

The usefulness principle recognizes that government information is a valuable government-wide or public asset that can generate real benefits through active use and innovation. These policies promote the use of information to improve the quality or lower the cost of services. They encourage agencies to use information to create new services or to devise better ways of doing business. Policies that promote usefulness often address interagency and intergovernmental information sharing, public access rights, public-private information partnerships, reuse of information for new purposes, and accessibility of information for all users.

Example from the cases

IT Investment Decisions: The Department of Transportation (DOT) replaced an ineffective IT investment decision making process by combining new information requirements with fundamental changes in IT governance. New standards for investment information addressed the need for more business-oriented proposals, higher quality analysis, and comparability from one unit of the agency to another. The new information standard called for a well-defined and detailed self-assessment of risks as well as business benefits and technology approaches. The information was communicated to and used by both IT and business unit evaluators, as well as senior executives. By adopting standards for content and format, the agency established a consistent information framework for proposals that helped them evaluate and compare them more objectively. Associated changes in governance structures assured that these decisions reflected agency-wide priorities and linked IT investment decisions to subsequent budget decisions and strategic plans.

3.3 Skills

Organizations, like people, must be adept information users. Every information-intensive government project needs a variety of skills.

Analysis and interpretation skills are necessary at every stage of an information project. They start with problem definition, the process by which an organization describes current symptoms and uncovers the processes, policies, and practices that are contributing factors. At this stage, process analysis, system audits, stakeholder analysis, customer satisfaction surveys, performance reviews, statistical trending, or similar activities are needed. In later stages, analysis of user needs, business process alternatives, work flow, and information flow become more important. Research into what other people and organizations are doing to solve similar problems is also critical. These analyses contribute to the design of the system and associated processes. When a new system is prototyped, tested, and implemented, the analytical skills of system users increase in importance.

People skilled in information management know how to treat information as a valuable organizational or societal resource. They know that content, quality, format, storage, transmission, accessibility, usability, security, and preservation all contribute to value. With so many factors to consider, information management skills show up in many job types. Program managers and staff are likely to have the skills and knowledge that ensure valid content, clear data definitions, solid metadata, and many kinds of data quality. IT professionals have to be counted on to create the formats, files, and databases that represent and organize information. They also handle the interfaces and security features that assure both usability and integrity. Archivists and librarians have specialized skills in classification, searching, and preservation. Researchers often work with program specialists to construct data definitions, design data collection processes, and institute quality control measures. Finally, many kinds of staff can be involved in developing and implementing mechanisms for information sharing among agency staff and with other organizations.

Depending on the type of problem to be solved, higher order technical skills will probably be required. These can include managing databases and the individual, program, service, and other data they contain; designing and implementing systems that are compatible with the existing technical infrastructure; and developing user interfaces that make it easier for users to find and use information. Technical skills are also needed to transform data from one system or format to another so that it can be "fit for use" in new ways and to create data repositories that integrate information from various sources for easy retrieval and wider use. Some projects also require skills in designing and administering networks of computer systems. This highly technical skill set is the one agencies often "buy" from private contractors. As a consequence, agencies also need contract and contractor management skills.

The technical skills of users are also critical, but often overlooked. These include the ability to operate a computer, use e-mail and a Web browser, manipulate word processing and spreadsheet software programs, manage electronic files, and understand basic security policies and procedures. These are all in addition to their ability to use and understand a particular application in order to do their work.

Communication skills comprise the ability to distill complex information into both written and oral forms that are useful for a particular audience. These skills are needed to convey important facts without oversimplifying. Throughout a project, managers need to communicate goals, progress, issues, and results. Presentations may include meetings with legislative or executive leaders to obtain initial and continuing funding and support.

Meetings with a variety of stakeholders are needed to explain how they will be affected and to encourage their buy-in and participation.

Project management skills include the ability to plan, organize, estimate and allocate resources, negotiate, track progress, measure results, troubleshoot and, most importantly, to communicate. These skills determine how and how well a project or program handles scope, time, cost, quality, complexity, and risk.

Example from the cases

Municipal Affairs (MACROS): The project team envisioned a system that would support geographically dispersed, relatively independent professionals serving a very diverse customer population. Not only would the system assist regional offices in their efforts to serve municipalities, it would also support the central office's efforts to increase consistency of service, improve data collection, and encourage information use statewide. The project team applied both analytical and communication skills to involve key players in the effort to elaborate this vision into an implementable plan. The primary vehicle for engaging them was a business case which contained the analysis and became the cornerstone of a communications plan. This case systematically analyzed the Division's information management problem from many stakeholder perspectives. It included a clear and widely endorsed definition of the business problem and clear statements of the outcomes the team expected to achieve. The case then presented the results of a series of analyses about the stakeholders, the resources required, and related best practices in the field, ending with specific policy, management, and technical recommendations for moving forward. The success of the business case rested not only on rigorous analysis, but also on the team's ability to communicate the case analysis in terms of the business needs of the agency. The case not only built interest in and support for the MACROS project; it also became a tool for opening discussions about similar information management challenges in other parts of the agency.

3.4 Data Challenges

Public managers must bridge the gap between business needs (i.e. program initiatives and work practices) and the relevant data available to support them. Data is the raw material for decision making and planning—the foundation for actions taken by the agency. Turning data into usable information requires an understanding of what work must be accomplished as well as the data available to help. Determining the heritage of the data, and assessing its timeliness and quality, are all critical and complex parts of this process. The activities usually involve significant work to identify relevant data, determine its usability, address inaccurate or incomplete data, deal with the inability to solve certain data problems, and manage confidence and expectations. Consequently, all organizations face four fundamental data challenges: quality, standards, metadata, and context.

The quality of data comprises its accuracy, completeness, timeliness, relevance, and interpretability in the context of its "fitness for use." In other words, data quality must be "good enough" for its intended purpose. In practice, good data quality management demands both analytical and organizational perspectives. From the analyst's perspective data quality management requires a sound understanding of the nature of data, identifying the factors that determine its quality, and defining the costs associated with obtaining and maintaining "good enough" data. From an organizational perspective, data quality management means insuring quality commensurate with the use of the data by specifying policies, identifying techniques, and establishing quality control procedures. Improving data quality is costly and time consuming; each degree of improvement costs time, money, and opportunity. These costs need to be considered in the context of intended use to determine when they are warranted.

Standards increase the value and usability of government information. Many thousands of files, databases, and data warehouses have been developed by government, but they are seldom compatible. Consequently, they limit ability to share and integrate information. The lack of common data standards across these various systems creates a significant barrier to information use. The challenge of creating and implementing unified data standards is compounded when the effort to use information spans organizational boundaries. Creating data standards within this environment requires sustained effort and compromise. The involved organizations need to identify the data models each is using and the extent to which they are compatible. They also need to describe specific data elements and how they are used in various contexts. Sometimes a "meta-standard" can be developed to guide integration of multiple data sources from multiple organizations.

Information about the data—or metadata—often contains a data set's history, information on how it has changed over time, and what specific rationale guided those changes. Unfortunately, this information is seldom fully documented so that users can readily know why a data set was created, what rules governed the creation, who the intended users were, and what it should and should not be used for. The information required to guide fitness for use decisions, to determine standards used in data collection, and many other questions about the potential value of a data resource is often unavailable. This can often result in unused, or unknowingly misused, data resources.

Like metadata, contextual knowledge is important to avoid misuse of data. Government data are usually derived from something else—perhaps a program, a service, a person, or a process. Anyone who uses the information needs to know about its context in order to use it well. But this knowledge is not always available in the form of explicit metadata, because metadata standards generally do not require this type of information. Contextual knowledge is usually embedded in the working knowledge gained through years of experience of working in programs and services. For this reason, program staff and managers need to be involved in both initial and ongoing discussions regarding the functional design of a system and the way in which it uses information.

Example from the cases

Kids Well-Being Indicator Clearinghouse (KWIC): The transition from a printed book consisting of prepared tables to a dynamic Web-based resource consisting of actual data sets required a new understanding of the differences among data sources and ways to manage them. One of the primary advantages of the Clearinghouse for users is data manipulation capability. But this feature required the project team to review many aspects of the data that had not been important before. For example, differences in data collection cycles and geographic coverage needed to be considered. The Education Department collects its data on the basis of the school year, by school district; the Health Department on the basis of calendar year, by county. The KWIC designers therefore needed to understand the limitations of cross-indicator comparisons. Accordingly, each data set was reviewed in the context of every other potentially related set to identify characteristics that might result in validity problems. The developers and data providers then determined when the differences were sufficiently important to formally block comparisons across indicators, when they warranted a warning to the user, or when they could be addressed by a simple statement in the "How to use the data" section of the Clearinghouse. A critical resource in this process was knowledge about the history and creation of each data set. In some cases the necessary knowledge came from metadata. In other cases, the formal metadata was insufficient, and experts in the agencies needed to develop these descriptions and rules before the data could be added to KWIC.

3.5 Cost Factors

Failure to identify all cost categories and to estimate true costs is a growing concern in both public and private sector IT projects. The costs of information technology initiatives are almost always underestimated for two reasons. First, planners tend to under-appreciate the costs of complexity and, second, they lack good models or guides for identifying all cost factors, especially soft ones. Common cost estimation models usually capture the cost of dedicated staff and purchases such as hardware, software, and consulting services, but these fall far short of full costs. Accommodating complexity, managing relationships, adapting to change, and achieving integration all generate substantial costs that are seldom estimated up front.

Complexity and interdependencies influence total costs as much or more than any direct expense. The more data sources and the greater their differences, the more it will cost to make use of them. The more interdependent the tasks in the work plan, the costlier the work will be—and the higher the risk of failure. Separating tasks and managing them as independent and potentially parallel efforts can help limit these costs, but doing so depends on the ability of the management team to clearly see the tasks that must be attended to and the extent to which they are truly independent of one another.

Three kinds of relationships must be considered in estimating the relationship costs in a project. The first is managing the relationships inside the day-to-day working environment of the project. The second has to do with maintaining relationships with immediate project sponsors, who may be in different parts of the government. The third is managing relationships in the larger environment. Identifying external stakeholders, securing strategic partnerships with them, and maintaining those relationships all require more time and money than most organizations recognize. The network of relationships that is necessary for a simple information initiative conducted by a single organization is likely to be small and stable. As projects become more complex, involving multiple units and crossing organizations, levels of government and program domains, these networks become larger and much more dynamic. Understanding the character of an initiative, assessing and securing the necessary relationships, and managing those relationships to a successful outcome are often overlooked as tasks that incur heavy costs.

The more familiar the strategy and tasks involved, and the more the new process or program resembles the old one, the more likely accurate cost estimates can be developed. When assumptions, methods or technologies change, the costs go well beyond the cost of training in new tools. They also extend to the opportunity costs incurred in the post-training productivity dip while staff work to assimilate new skills or tools. The greater the difference between current practices and tools and new ones, the greater the effort and time required to adapt and become proficient. In addition, differences among data resources in terms of form and format, definitions and standards, or accepted development practices are significant cost factors. When data resources are highly dissimilar or unfamiliar, the level of effort associated with using them increases.

"Integration" is often used to mean systems that "talk" to one another, or data that is merged from several sources to create a new repository designed for uses that are different from those supported by the source data sets. Integration can also mean integrated business processes, organizational structures, and policy frameworks. For example, several benefit programs could be highly integrated by combining eligibility assessments and service delivery, or they could be loosely integrated by co-locating offices and coordinating information dissemination. The tighter the integration of formerly separate things, the higher the cost. A good understanding of the degree of integration in areas such as program goals, funding, staff, infrastructure, and data will improve the accuracy of project cost estimates.

Example from the cases

Annual Reassessment Program: Part of the problem of implementing annual reassessment is that it can have major impacts on the staffing and operations of local government assessors, who must follow state laws but are funded by local appropriations. To understand these impacts the project team commissioned a model to analyze the feasibility and cost implications of the reassessment program. To obtain the data for the model, managers mapped the processes for conducting a reassessment and identified 25 categories of tasks. A simulation model was built to analyze the staffing, process, and cost implications. Each of the tasks was analyzed for its impact on state regional offices, county staff, and municipal assessors. Detailed time estimates for accomplishing each task were taken from benchmarking those local and county governments where continuous reassessments were already being conducted, supplemented by expert judgment where appropriate. The estimated costs were considerably higher than either the state or the municipalities had expected. As a result, the implementation strategy was simplified and extended over a number of options and a longer time period, and proposals for a special implementation fund were prepared for the state legislature.

3.6 Technology

Technology choices have powerful immediate and long-term implications. These choices influence many aspects of an organization, including skills and staffing patterns, work processes, and the choice and operation of other technologies. New technology usually comes with new business rules, practices, and processes that become resistant to change after implementation. Thus, once implemented, a particular technology becomes embedded in the way people work and influences the way they perceive and understand what they do.

Business processes analysis is very useful for understanding how current work is done and how existing technologies will affect the work. By breaking work processes into their component parts and associating steps with business rules and information flows, analysts can see and communicate the current situation and better understand the changes that will be needed to move to a new (and presumably better) way of working. These changes can affect roles and responsibilities, work flow, information flow, decision points, business rules, and standard practices. For example, moving from 9-to-5 to 24-by-7 service availability requires much more than having a system online 24 hours a day. It also demands substantial adjustments in staffing, security, records management, and maintenance that also need to be built into the way work is done. For these reasons, regardless of the size or complexity of an IT initiative, users must be an integral part of problem definition activities, planning, decision-making, and testing. The user's perspective is essential if a system is to be well integrated with organizational factors and operational needs.

The status of the existing technology infrastructure is another critical factor in decisions about which technology to choose and how to deploy it. Changes in the type and number of users, responsiveness, capacity, level of security, types of connection, and interfaces with legacy systems will all need to be considered in both acquisition and implementation. In addition, enormous diversity may exist in organizational environments and infrastructures, especially when a system connects different agencies or different levels of government where technology resources and expertise can vary widely.

Example from the cases

Homeless Management Information System (HIMS): One key aspect of the system was that the application, housed in the state capital, would be accessed by the homeless service providers via the Internet. By allowing this type of access, the project team initially believed the user platform and training requirements could be minimized. However, in many instances shelter providers either lacked the technology or the knowledge of how to work within this environment. Some had never had access to a PC let alone the Internet. Those who did have PC capabilities often had either no access to the Internet or had organizational policies that limited their access. Overall, the majority had limited funds, staff, and knowledge of how to access and use such a system. Consequently, the project team adopted a developmental strategy. They started by working with the larger nonprofits and the participating local governments. At the same time, those not yet able to adopt the system were encouraged to adopt the new data definitions so they would be ready when technology could be put in place. The state project leaders also helped these providers find and encourage software developers to listen to their needs and develop low-cost, easy-to-use, service management systems that could eventually improve their technological capacities and data resources. The costs of developing these capabilities were also added to the legitimate costs that shelters could build into their rates for determining state funding.

4. CONCLUSION

Digital government research aims not only to generate new knowledge but also to make useful connections between research and practice. To achieve both ends, digital government research derives research problems from practical challenges, and translates research findings into both new knowledge and usable results. Each of the problems described in the needs analysis summarized in the introduction to this chapter is worthy of continuing investigation by both scholars and managers. Similarly, each of the wider considerations described in the foregoing section (strategy, policy, data, skills, costs, and technology) represents a broad area ripe for further research, learning, and improvement. The public management perspective represented by the cases enhances the possibilities for digital government research because of its practical need to understand better how these considerations interact to produce both desirable and undesirable results. These interdependencies present researchers and managers with special challenges to overcome as well as unique opportunities to collaborate.

ACKNOWLEDGEMENTS

I am grateful to the State of New York for sponsoring the Using Information in Government Program at the Center for Technology in Government, University at Albany and to the Digital Government Research Program at the National Science Foundation for a subsequent grant that supported a longitudinal study of the UIG cases under the Knowledge and Distributed Intelligence (KDI) program.

REFERENCES

Andersen, David F, Salvatore Belardo, and Sharon Dawes. (1994). Strategic information management: conceptual frameworks for the public sector, *Public Productivity and Management Review* 17(4): 335–353.

Cats-Baril, William and Ronald Thompson. (1995). Managing information technology projects in the public sector. *Public Administration Review* 55(5): 445-462, September/October.

Center for Technology in Government. (2000). The Insider's Guide to Using Information in Governemnt. On line at: http://www.ctg.albany.edu/publications/online/insider_guide?sub=online

Dawes, Sharon S. (1996) Interagency information sharing: achievable benefits, manageable risks, *Journal of Policy Analysis and Management* 15(3), Summer.

Dawes, Sharon S., Peter A. Bloniarz, Kristine Kelly, and Patricia Diamond Fletcher. (1999b). *Some Assembly Required: Building a Digital Government for the 21st Century*. Albany, NY: Center for Technology in Government, University at Albany/SUNY. Online at http://www.ctg.albany.edu/research/workshop/dgfinalreport.pdf

Dawes, Sharon S., Cresswell, Anthony, and Cahan Bruce. (2004). "Learning from Crisis: Lessons in Human and Information Infrastructure from the World Trade Center Response," *Social Science Computer Review* 22(1).

Dawes, Sharon S. and Lise Prefontaine. (2003). "Understanding New Models of Collaboration for Delivering Government Services," *Communications of the ACM*, January.

Fountain, Jane E. (2001). *Building the Virtual State: Information Technology and Institutional Change*. Brookings Institution Press.

Globerman, Steven and Aidan R. Vining. (1996). A framework for evaluating the government contracting-out decision with an application to information technology. *Public Administration Review* 56(6): 577-586, November/December.

Heintz, Theresa and Stuart Bretschneider. (2000). Information technology and restructuring in pubic organizations: does adoption of information technology affect organizational structures, communications, and decision making? *Journal of Public Administration Research and Theory* 10(4): 801-830.

Holden, Stephen H. (2003). The evolution of information technology management at the federal level: implications for public administration, pp. 53-73, Garson, G.D., ed. *Public Information Technology: Policy and Management Issues*. Hershey, PA: Idea Group.

Huxham, C. and Vangen, S. (2000). Leadership in the shaping and implementation of collaboration agendas: how things happen in a (not quite) joined-up world. *Academy of Management Journal*, 43(8): 1159-1175.

Kim, Soon Hee and Karen Layne. (2001). Making the connection: E-government and public administration education. *Journal of Public Affairs Education*, 7(4): 229-240.

Klein, Hans. K. (2000). System development in the federal government: how technology influences outcomes, *Policy Studies Journal* 28(2) 313-328.

Kraemer, K.; King, J. L, (2006). Information Technology and Administrative Reform: Will E-Government Be Different? *International Journal of Electronic Government Research*, Vol. 2, No. 1, 1-20.

Landsbergen, David and George Wolken. (2000). Realizing the promise: government information systems and the fourth generation of information technology, *Public Administration Review*; Mar/Apr 61(2): 206-220.

Milward, H. B., & Provan, K. G. (2000). Governing the Hollow State. *Journal of Public Administration Research & Theory*, 10(2): 359-379.

Roberts, Alasdair S. (2000). Less government, more secrecy: reinvention and the weakening of Freedom of Information Law, *Public Administration Review* 60(4):308-320, July/August.

Scavo, Carmine and Yuhang Shi. (2000). Public administration: the role of information technology in the reinventing government paradigm—normative predicates and practical challenges, *Social Science Computer Review* 18(2): 166-178.

Scholl, Hans J.(2005). Motives, Strategic Approach, Objectives & Focal Areas in e-Gov-Induced Change: *International Journal of Electronic Government Research*, Vol. 1, No. 1, 59-78.

US National Science Foundation. (2004). *Digital Government Program Solicitation*, NSF 04-521, http://www.nsf.gov/pubs/2004/nsf04521/nsf04521.htm

Waddell, Paul and Borning Alan. (2004). A case study in digital government: developing and applying UrbanSim, a system for simulating urban land use, transportation, and environmental impacts. *Social Science Computer Review*, 22(1) 37-51.

SUGGESTED READINGS

- Choose any of the e-government research papers sponsored by the IBM Endowment for the Business of Government to understand more about the interdependencies that are embedded in digital government initiatives. These publications can be downloaded from: http://www.businessofgovernment.org/main/publications/grant_reports/grant_area/index.asp#2
- Choose any of the case studies that are the basis for this chapter. All can be found in Center for Technology in Government's Insider's Guide to Using Information in Government: http://www.ctg.albany.edu/static/usinginfo/Cases/cases.htm

ONLINE RESOURCES

- Center for Technology in Government, The Insider's Guide to Using Information in Government: http://www.ctg.albany.edu/publications/online/insider_guide?sub=online
- Center for Technology in Government, Making Smart IT Choices: http://www.ctg.albany.edu/publications/guides/smartit2
- Council for Excellence in Government, E-Government Program: http://www.excelgov.org/index.php?keyword=a43292b81accf2
- Federal Enterprise Architecture: http://www.whitehouse.gov/omb/e-gov/a-1-fea.html
- European Commission, E-Government Observatory: http://ec.europa.eu/idabc/en/chapter/140

QUESTIONS FOR DISCUSSION

1. Digital government research assumes a mutually beneficial connection between research and practice. What would be the characteristics of a research project that both generates new knowledge and helps to solve a practical problem? Who would participate and how? What difficulties might be encountered and how could they be addressed?
2. Choose a digital government initiative from recent news. Who are the stakeholders? What are their interests? Where do these interests coincide and where do they conflict?
3. Review the same digital government initiative from the six perspectives discussed in this chapter. Formulate at least one question that a policy maker might ask about its strategy, policy considerations, data challenges, skills needs, cost factors, and technology choices.

Chapter 7

PRIVACY IN AN ELECTRONIC GOVERNMENT CONTEXT

Priscilla M. Regan

Department of Public and International Affairs, George Mason University, Fairfax, Virginia, U.S.A. (pregan@gmu.edu)

CHAPTER OVERVIEW

Protecting information privacy in the context of e-government is critical to achieve the potential benefits promised by e-government. If individuals do not believe that their privacy will be protected, they will not use available e-government features. In order to identify and analyze relevant privacy issues, this chapter uses Layne and Lee's (2001) four-stage e-government model: 1) cataloguing; 2) transaction; 3) vertical integration; and 4) horizontal integration. The chapter also evaluates the privacy protecting solutions that are available and necessary at each of the four stages. The analysis demonstrates that privacy protections are most effective when they are formulated as part of the early design of e-government initiatives, not when they are added on after complaints and concerns have been registered.

1. INTRODUCTION

As governments move their information and activities into the online world, many of the same policy issues that faced e-commerce organizations are similarly raised for government organizations. Prominent among these issues are those associated with information privacy – the ability for individuals who are the subjects of information to exercise some control over what information is collected, how it is used, with whom it is shared, and to whom it is disclosed. (Regan, 1995) Over the more than forty years of policymaking about information privacy, the policy template continues to most prominently feature "fair information principles," first developed in 1973 by an advisory committee in the Department of Health, Education and Welfare. (HEW, 1973) These principles emphasize individual knowledge, consent and correction, as well as the responsibility of organizations to publicize the existence of record system, to ensure the reliability of data and to prevent misuse of data. In general, ensuring that such principles are respected can be achieved through a variety of regulatory, legal and technical mechanisms including government regulation and oversight, organizational self-regulation, individual redress of grievances through administrative or court processes, and privacy enhancing technologies for those with the requisite technical knowledge.

Protecting information privacy in the context of e-government is critical to achieve the potential benefits promised by e-government. If individuals do not believe that their privacy will be protected, they will not use available e-government features. In the US, this was illustrated early in the evolution of e-government when the Social Security Administration piloted an online system allowing individuals to make requests at SSA's website for their Personal Earnings and Benefit Estimate Statements (PEBES) and receive an online version of their statement. The initial pilots were well-received and raised no privacy concerns in part because SSA had consulted organizations with experience in online banking to develop additional privacy protections. National online access to PEBES became operational in early March 1997 but in early April press reports of privacy concerns about the availability of this information over the Internet precipitated both public and congressional reaction and SSA suspended the online system. The press stories emphasized the possibilities that people might be able to request access to information other than their own, or that the SSA might in error disclose personal information to someone other than the relevant individual, or that the entire PEBES website could be compromised. (Mahler and Regan, 2002, 331-3)

Since the SSA incident, government agencies have recognized the critical importance of being able to ensure potential users of e-government that their information privacy will be protected. Current popular and policy concerns about identity theft underscore the importance of protecting personally identifiable information. As in the e-commerce world, trust is of critical importance to individual users. Public opinion polls confirm this with 45% of Americans agreeing that government will be able to provide better services if they submit personal information to government websites but also agreeing that by submitting such information they may risk their privacy. (Council for Excellence in Government, 2003) In a carefully conducted analysis of citizens' attitudes towards e-government, Moon and Welch concluded that high levels of concern about security and privacy are also associated with a desire to slow the implementation of e-government initiatives. (2005, 258) Thus protecting privacy is key to the realization of the full potential of e-government.

2. OVERVIEW

When considering privacy in the context of electronic government, the clearest way to identify the privacy issues is to use Layne and Lee's (2001) four-stage e-government model: 1) cataloguing; 2) transaction; 3) vertical integration; and 4) horizontal integration. At each of these stages different information privacy issues occur and different privacy protecting solutions are available and necessary.

2.1 Cataloguing

At this initial stage, governments use internet web sites to post information that is likely to be of interest to citizens, businesses, beneficiaries of programs, individuals from other countries, and other governments. The range of information is enormous spanning every activity of government and the potential number of users is equally enormous. Two privacy issues occur at this stage: tracking of individual users and compromising the privacy of data subjects.

There are a number of ways of tracking the activities of online users. First, each site that a user visits obtains the user's Internet Protocol (IP) address. The IP address is the unique address that a user has when connected to the Internet. It locates that computer on the Internet. Although the IP address may not yield personally identifiable information, it does allow tracking of Internet movements from a particular computer. Second, "cookies" can be placed on the user's hard drive so that a website can determine a user's prior activities at that website when the user returns. (Camp 1999) This information reveals not only what pages the user viewed but also how the user arrived at the website and where the user went on departure. A user can set up her browser to warn her every time a cookie is about to be stored in her computer. This enables a user to see the contents of a cookie before the computer accepts it. A user also can read the cookie file on the hard drive and can delete the cookies that are stored there. Some sites require users to accept cookies, so if a user has deleted a cookie file a new file will be created on the next visit to the site. Another online tracking device, known as "web bugs," is being used by Internet marketing companies and others. A Web bug is a graphics embedded in a Web page or email message that monitors who is reading the page or message.

In general, the policy response to such online tracking has been to require, or recommend, that websites post information about whether and how online activities are tracked, how one might disable the tracking and what the consequences of doing so might be. Since 1999 US federal agencies have been required by OMB to post clear privacy policies on their websites informing visitors about the collection of information, the purposes of that collection, and uses of that information. In 2000 OMB strengthened its guidance to say that cookies should not be used unless there was "clear and conspicuous notice" as well as a compelling need for their use. (Relyea, 2002, 20) The E-Government Act of 2002 further emphasized the importance of privacy notices and moved agencies in the direction of posting machine readable privacy policies that can be readable by a browser that can automatically inform a user whether or not the privacy policy matches the user's privacy preferences. The Act also underscored the restrictions on persistent tracking technologies, such as cookies. Finally the Act required agencies to begin to develop uniform standards for web content including with respect to privacy notices. Having followed the experiences of online commercial websites, federal agency e-government personnel recognize the importance of clear and comprehensive privacy notices. In response to an informal survey of several agencies conducted by Mahler and Regan (2006), respondents reported that among the OMB Policies for Federal Public Websites, the "commons sense" requirements were easiest to implement. Among these were the requirements for protecting privacy.

The second privacy issue that occurs with cataloguing of information is that posting of public record information may compromise the privacy of data subjects. This has tended to occur most often with respect to court information. As the judiciary moves into the era of e-government, the ability to provide public access to electronic court records enhances the accountability of the judicial system to the public. But this also provides 24-7, worldwide access to what is oftentimes considered private or sensitive information. The practical constraints of going to the courthouse, waiting, and copying information are removed making it more difficult to maintain the "practical obscurity" that in the past has provided protection for privacy in public records. (Davis, 2005)

For example Megan's Law requires states to make information available when a violent sex offender moves to a neighborhood in order to inform parents and schools, and to provide them a way to protect children against predators. Prior to the Internet, this was accomplished through registries maintained in local police stations and flyers distributed in schools and neighborhoods. But now most states have online registries of information about convicted sexual offenders, allowing individuals to search, generally by zip code, to determine if there are any convicted sex offenders in a certain neighborhood. The online sites, usually managed by the state police, generally reveal names, addresses, and criminal records. In several states there have been challenges to these laws and their constitutionality was challenged but upheld by the US Supreme Court. (*Smith v. Doe,* 2003) Also the posting of court records, such as divorce and bankruptcy proceedings, may compromise privacy interests and these concerns have prompted state court administrators to develop model guidelines balancing interests in privacy and public access. (Conference of Chief Justices and Conference of State Court Administrators, 2002) Issues about privacy and online access to public record information have also occurred with county property assessment data, state voter registration records, autopsy records and birth records. (Solove, 2002) In general the question of how "public" public records should be in an era of e-government remains one of increasing policy debate as people recognize the need to balance competing interests, such as that of public safety and the value of what Blanchette and Johnson (2002) call "social forgetfulness."

2.2 Transaction

At this stage of e-government, governments create online interfaces that enable individuals or businesses to directly interact with the government and communicate information that enables them to accomplish a task. These transactions may be as simple as requesting that information be sent to a mailing address but may be as complex as paying taxes or renewing a drivers' license. In these latter functions, some form of financial payment is usually involved. Interactions may also reveal substantive policy preferences of individuals as citizens may comment on a pending rule promulgated by a federal agency or may participate in an online discussion of county government. At this transaction stage, new and more complex information privacy issues are raised while the privacy issues from the first stage continue to be important and solutions such as notice of collection, use and disclosure of personally identifiable information continue to be operative.

The critical privacy issue with respect to transactions is that government websites need to be able to confirm that they are dealing with the person with whom they think they are dealing. Generally this will require the individual to reveal some personally identifiable information in order to prevent unauthorized or accidental disclosure of information and to ensure the trustworthiness of the transaction. (National Research Council, 2002a) This issue of online "authentication" is one that has been subject to much scrutiny and analysis, and poses unique questions in the e-government context because many such transactions are mandatory, the user population is so heterogeneous, and the relationship is often long-term but marked by intermittent contacts. (National Research Council, 2003)

The NRC's 2003 report, *Who Goes There? Authentication through the Lens of Privacy,* points out that authentication is both more simple and more complex than most people believe. In many cases, authentication, for example to permit a person access to a building or a database, does not require that the individual be identified but only requires that the system verify that the individual is authorized for that access. In other cases, for example release of a payment or access to a system wherein an individual could see or change his or her own personally identifiable information, authentication does require that an individual be identified. In developing online authentication systems for e-government, it is important that the system be designed so that the minimum amount of personally identifiable information is collected and retained. The three common approaches in authentication systems are: "something you know" (a password, date of birth or mother's maiden name); "something you have" (a token); or "something you are" (biometric identifier). In many instances, simple passwords or tokens suffice and exchanges of personally identifiable information are not necessary. Adhering to a minimum exchange and collection of personally identifiable information is important both to protect against identify theft and to curtail the overuse of identity documents. As the NRC report points out, state issued driver's licenses, birth certificates, Social Security cards and passports are considered "foundational documents" for numerous authentication systems but their reliability and validity are far from ideal. Although these are often issued by government entities, they are not uniquely tied to a specific individual and thus can be easily forged or a replacement issued to a person other than the original holder. Driver's licenses provide a good example of a document that can be forged and for which a replacement can be sought by another individual. Additionally the issuing agency does not always retain an interest in the documents' validity and reliability; this is especially true for birth certificates.

At the stage of online transactions, many organizations and government agencies begin to develop systems that use and accept electronic signatures.

In the US, the Government Paperwork Elimination Act of 1999 (GPEA) requires OMB to provide direction and oversight for the development of electronic signatures. (Fletcher, 2002) OMB has been working with the National Telecommunications and Information Administration (NTIA) on a variety of pilot projects and system developments. (Relyea, 2002, 19) Many of these involve cryptographic digital signatures using some form of public key infrastructures (PKI). Most of these have been implemented for business and organizational, rather than for individual, transactions with government. But in the future a system of electronic signatures will be a standard component of many e-government transactions.

Online transactions that the individual participates in as a citizen, such as commenting on proposed federal rules, raise particularly important privacy concerns. In such cases, the individual may wish to be anonymous in posting comments and consistent with First Amendment protections websites should be designed to allow for anonymity. The challenges of designing online voting systems illustrate a number of vexing privacy issues. (Internet Policy Institute, 2001) In this instance, not only does the citizen need to be authenticated but the ballot and the individual need to be delinked in order to ensure a secret ballot – but the system would also need to be designed to allow for the relinking of the individual and his/her ballot under some conditions, such as legal challenges to the election outcome.

Much of the discussion about e-government has focused on executive agencies and their activities and functions. But legislative branches have also moved into the e-government environment and individual legislators see great potential for improving their communications with constituents through e-government applications. An analysis done by the Congressional Management Foundation (2005) found that postal and email communications to the US Congress have increased almost 300% since the Internet was first used on Capitol Hill. In a survey of congressional websites, Mahler and Regan found that virtually all members' websites had posted a privacy policy, the substance of which followed the fairly standard template used elsewhere in the federal government. Interestingly, however, they also found that in all but a few instances when a constituent wished to contact a member of Congress about a casework issue, the member required that the constituent sign a form permitting the federal agency to disclose information to the member's office as required by the Privacy Act of 1974 and then mail that form back to the congressional office prior to action on the casework request. (2005) Congressional and executive offices have not yet developed an electronic method of conveying a constituent's permission for disclosure.

2.3 Vertical Integration

At this stage, governments at different levels – in the US federal, state, and local – communicate with each other so that when an individual or business conducts a transaction with one level of government any necessary changes or related activities with other levels of government would be directly communicated and transacted. This type of integration brings great efficiencies for the individuals and government bureaucracies involved. It also improves the accuracy and timeliness of the information that government agencies use to make decisions about individuals. At the same time, such vertical integration needs to be done in such a way to ensure: that the information that is communicated from one part of government to another is only communicated to agencies that need that information; that the transaction itself is secure; that the receiving agency retains, uses, and communicates the information under similar privacy protections as the original agency; and that the individual knows that the transfer is taking place.

At this stage of e-government, notices of privacy policies and reliable identification and authentication of personally identifiable information both continue to be important means of protecting information privacy. However, additional protections are also necessary because the exchanges of information are not transparent to the individual. At this stage, some controls beyond that of individual monitoring are necessary. Technical safeguards, bureaucratic procedures, and government oversight also become critical components for protecting information privacy. In order to implement this stage, governments may need to overcome public perceptions of previous misuses or security breaches of government electronic systems. For example, the US Government Accountability Office (GAO) reported in 2000 that 23 of 70 agencies surveyed had disclosed personal information they had collected at their websites to third parties, including private sector organizations such as retailers. (GAO, 2000) Media coverage of such misuses and security breaches raise public concerns and mistrust. Effective privacy protections, and oversight and accountability of those protections, is necessary to ensure the success of the third stage of vertical integration.

In the US, the E-Government Act of 2002 requires agencies to conduct a privacy impact analysis (PIA) for new information systems and for the conversion of partially electronic systems to fully electronic. The Office of Management and Budget issued guidelines in 2003 that require agencies to address a series of questions including: the nature of the information collected: the purpose for the collection; the uses and sharing of information; the opportunities for individuals to decline to provide or to consent to uses; and, the technical and administrative means for protecting security of information. (OMB, 2003) OMB describes these PIAs as "a description of business processes, data flows and technologies in the context of applicable privacy principles." (OMB, 2004) Holden and Millet suggest that in order to maximize the effectiveness of PIAs they should be done early in the development of the information system and the primary authors of the PIA should be the system owner and technical staff designing the system and not the privacy staff. (2005, 373)

How well privacy impact statements, and similar mechanisms, will work to protect information privacy during vertical integration will depend largely on how much oversight is exercised and whether privacy impact statements are carefully evaluated and enforced. Most previous information privacy policies have become largely bureaucratic requirements, focused on records management or information processing, that have become somewhat boilerplate and uninspired. This was certainly the case with the establishment and practices of the US Data Integrity Boards that agencies were required to establish under the Computer Matching and Privacy Protection Act. (Regan, 1993) And in many cases there are either exceptions to the more stringent protections or there is little active enforcement. Instead agencies wait for complaints and then make incremental changes to their policies and practices.

2.4 Horizontal Integration

At this fourth stage of e-government, government bureaucracies, and their concomitant information silos, become transparent to citizens and other users as users can go to one portal site to conduct all necessary transactions with government. This makes it much easier for individuals to interact with governments because they no longer first need to determine which government agency or which level of government has jurisdiction over a particular area. This stage involves a fairly large transformation of traditional government bureaucracies. As Layne and Lee note "with the support of the Internet, the government processes defined by specialization may not be efficient, effective, or citizen friendly...Functional specialization may not be suitable as a governing structure in e-government." (2001, 133)

Most governments are only just entering this fourth stage. For example, two "Access America" sites, one designed for senior citizens and one for students, exist in the US. Because this stage involves a fundamental re-engineering of government and challenges not only traditional bureaucratic routines and structures but also bureaucratic staffing and funding, this stage is most likely to evolve slowly and in response to the needs of particular and discrete populations. Senior citizens and students both have fairly defined interactions with governments. Businesses, especially small businesses, likewise have defined interactions. But horizontal integration to provide one-stop access to all government services will not be likely in the near term. The barriers will be primarily bureaucratic and technical but the design and functioning of this fourth stage will raise new privacy challenges as well.

Most individuals occupy many different roles and identities in their daily lives as social, political and economic actors. And they prefer, especially in the United States, to keep those identities distinct and separate. Fragmented identities protect privacy. People do not want their employers to know the details of their income taxes, property holdings, library borrowings, educational experiences, travel destinations, and medical histories. All of these are found in a variety of government record systems maintained by various government bureaucracies at different levels of government. With horizontal integration, these systems become somewhat fungible and may well be perceived as undermining the ability of individuals to maintain distinct identities and thus protect their privacy. Debates in a variety of countries, the United States and Australia for example, about a national identification card and the national identity system that would accompany such a card well illustrate some of the issues and concerns that are likely to occur as more instances of horizontal integration of government go online. (NRC, 2002b)

3. CONCLUSIONS

Privacy should not be seen as a barrier to e-government any more than it is viewed as a barrier to government generally. Protection of privacy is of fundamental importance in terms of ensuring citizens' trust in government and providing for accountability of government. Privacy protections need to be integrated into each of the stages of e-government. Otherwise the advantages offered by e-government, those of convenience, efficiency, and effectiveness for example, will not be fully realized. Privacy protections are most effective when they are formulated as part of the early design of e-government initiatives, not when they are added on after complaints and concerns have been registered.

REFERENCES

Blanchette, Jean-Francois and Deborah G. Johnson. 2002. "Data Retention and the Panoptic Society: The Social Benefits of Forgetfulness," *The Information Society* 18: 33-45.

Camp, L. Jean. 1999. "Web Security and Privacy: An American Perspective," *The Information Society* 15, 249-256.

Conference of Chief Justices and Conference of State Court Administrators. 2002. *Public Access to Court Records: Guidelines for Policy Development by State Courts.* (July 16) www.courtaccess.org/modelpolicy/

Congressional Management Foundation. 2005. *Communicating with Congress: How Capitol Hill is Coping with the Surge in Citizen Advocacy.* (July 11). Available at: http://www.congressonlineproject.org

Council for Excellence in Government. 2003. *The New E-Government Equation: Ease, Engagement, Privacy and Protection.* http:www.excelgov.org/usermedia/images/uploads/PDFs/e-govpoll2003.pdf

Davis, Charles N. 2005. "Reconciling Privacy and Access Interests in E-Government," *The International Journal of Public Administration* 28: 567-580.

Fletcher, Patricia D. 2002. "The Government Paperwork Elimination Act: Operating Instructions for an Electronic Government," *International Journal of Public Administration* 25(5): 723-736.

Government Accountability Office. 2000. *Internet Privacy: Agencies' Efforts to Implement OMB's Privacy Policy* (GAO/GGD-00-191) (Sept.)

Government Accountability Office (GAO), 2000. *Internet Privacy: Agencies' Efforts to Implement OMB's Internet Privacy Policy.* GAO/GGD-00–191. Washington, D.C., September, 2000.

Government Accountability Office (GAO), 2000. *Internet Privacy: Federal Agency Use of Cookies*. Letter GAO-01–147R., DC. Oct. 20, 2000.

Department of Health, Education and Welfare. 1973. *Records, Computers, and the Rights of Citizens.* Washington, DC: Government Printing Office.

Holden, Stephen H. and Millett, Lynette. 2005. "Authentication, Privacy, and the Federal Government," *The Information Society* 21: 367-377.

Internet Policy Institute. 2001. *Report of the National Workshop on Internet Voting: Issues and Research Agenda.* (March). Available at: http://lorrie.cranor.org/voting/ipi-voting-report.pdf

Layne, Karen and Jungwoo Lee. 2001. "Developing fully functional E-government: A four stage model," *Government Information Quarterly* 18, pp. 122-136.

Mahler, Julianne and Priscilla M. Regan. 2002. "Learning to Govern Online: Federal Agency Internet Use," *American Review of Public Administration* 32, #3 (Sept), pp. 326-349.

Mahler, Julianne and Priscilla M. Regan. 2005. "Homestyle Online: Casework over the Internet." Paper presented at the Annual Meetings of the American Political Science Association, Washington, DC (Sept. 1).

Mahler, Julianne and Priscilla M. Regan. 2006. "The Evolution of Web Governance in the Federal Government," *International Journal of Electronic Government Research,* 2(1), 21-35.

National Research Council.2002a. *Information Technology Research, Innovation, and E-Government*. Washington, DC: National Academy Press.

National Research Council. 2002b. *IDs – Not That Easy: Questions about Nationwide Identity Systems*. Washington, DC: National Academy Press.

National Research Council. 2003. *Who Goes There? Authentication Through the Lens of Privacy.* Washington, DC: National Academy Press.

Office of Management and Budget. 2003. *OMB Guidance for Implementing the Privacy Provisions of the E-Government Act of 2002.* http://www.whitehouse.gov/omb/memoranda/m03-22.html

Office of Management and Budget. 2004. *FY 2003 Report to Congress on Implementation of the E-Government Act* (March 8). Available online at: http://www.whitehouse.gov/omb

Regan, Priscilla M. 1993. "Data Integrity Boards: Institutional Innovation and Congressional Oversight," *Government Information Quarterly* 10: 443-459.
Regan, Priscilla M. 1995. *Legislating Privacy: Technology, Social Values, and Public Policy.* Chapel Hill, NC: University of North Carolina Press.
Relyea, Harold C. 2002. "E-gov: Introduction and Overview," *Government Information Quarterly* 19: 9-35.
Smith v. Doe 538 U.S. 84 (2003).

SUGGESTED READINGS

- Davis, Charles N. 2005. "Reconciling Privacy and Access Interests in E-Government," *The International Journal of Public Administration* 28: 567-580. This article presents an extensive analysis of the possible conflicts between providing public access to information and protecting privacy, including relevant legal principles, statutory requirements, and court cases.
- Hiller, Janine S. and France Belanger. 2001. *Privacy Strategies for Electronic Government.* PriceWaterhouseCoopers Endowment for The Business of Government. This was one of the earliest examinations of privacy and e-government and analyses how privacy principles developed for e-commerce might be applied to e-government.
- National Research Council. 2003. *Who Goes There? Authentication Through the Lens of Privacy.* Washington, DC: National Academy Press. This report contains a thorough analysis of the privacy issues raised by authentication. Chapter 6, "Authentication, Privacy and the Roles of Government, will be of particular relevance to those interested in e-government.

ONLINE RESOURCES

- Center for Democracy and Technology, http://www.cdt.org
  CDT provides one of the most extensive websites with analyses of issues, including privacy, related to information technology and democracy. In addition to good overviews of a range of issues, the CDT site contains relevant congressional testimony and bill analyses, as well as links to related reports, articles, and websites.
- Congress Online Project, http://www.congressonlineproject.org
  This web site contains an archive of the reports, data and newsletters from the project conducted by the Congressional Management Foundation from 2001 to 2005.

- Electronic Privacy Information Center, http://www.epic.org
  EPIC provides an wide-ranging amount of information about information privacy generally and with respect to all the privacy issues discussed in this paper.
- Federal Trade Commission. http://www.ftc.gov/privacy/
  The FTC has had a number of workshops and meetings on information privacy issues, including identity theft, and has posted on its website several very important reports including: *Privacy Online: A Report to Congress* (June 1998); *Self-Regulation and Privacy Online: A Report to Congress;* (July 1999); and *Privacy Online: Fair Information Practices in the Electronic Marketplace* (June 2000).
- Privacy Rights Clearinghouse, http://www.privacyrights.org
  This website contains information that is relevant to consumers and citizens. It covers both national and state activities. There is a wealth of information about identity theft on this site.

QUESTIONS FOR DISCUSSION

1. When should governments post personally identifiable information online? What categories of personally identifiable records should be posted? Can public records be "too public"? How should governments balance accountability and the need for the public to know against the information privacy and due process rights of individuals?
2. As a visitor to websites, what authentication schemes are you most comfortable with? How effective do you think they are? What suggestions would you make if you were advising a government agency in designing an authentication system for a new website?
3. What information do you think should be in a privacy notice on a government website? Develop you list. Then visit a number of government, business, and non-profit websites and compare their privacy notices. Do you see differences? Does it seem that one sector has done a better job in crafting clear privacy policies?
4. A large percentage of citizens are critically concerned about identity theft, especially if basic identifying information that can be found on government or non-government websites has been compromised. What do you think the role of government should be in this area? What policy options might you offer?
5. The design of systems and procedures that effectively protect information privacy involves technical experts, program managers, and agency heads.

What should the role of each be? What incentives are there for them to work well together?

6. Some studies of internet users find that in principle individuals value their privacy quite highly but seem ready to compromise that privacy for convenience and ease of use. On government websites, do you think the government has a special responsibility to ensure that convenience does not entail a privacy compromise?

Chapter 8

ACCESSIBILITY OF FEDERAL ELECTRONIC GOVERNMENT

Shirley Ann Becker

Research Professor of MIS and Computer Science, Director of the National Center for Small Business, Florida Institute of Technology, Melbourne, Florida, U.S.A. (abecker@fit.edu)

CHAPTER OVERVIEW

Online access to electronic government does not necessarily guarantee that an individual will be successful in obtaining information and resources sought. Web accessibility barriers must be overcome in order to realize the full capability of electronic government. Federal mandates and statutes have played an integral role in promoting access to electronic government resources by all Americans. However, these have to be enforced over the long run to ensure that Web content and supporting technologies remain accessible to those with and without disabilities. Web accessibility, in this chapter, is discussed as an ongoing concern for federal electronic government.

1. INTRODUCTION

In the U. S. and abroad, the 21st century was heralded as the Dot Gov era due to the proliferation of local, state, and federal, electronic government (e-government). By 2003, e-government as a whole ranked fourth in overall traffic with only AOL Time Warner, MSN, and Yahoo! Web portals surpassing it (Mark, 2003). During this time period, it was estimated that the number of e-government Web pages ranged between 20,000 and 30,000 with the federal government in the U.S. being the largest single content provider of Web information (Ellison, 2004). It was also reported that 77% of all Internet users in the U.S. utilized e-government in the search for information or to communicate with agencies (Horrigan, 2004).

The proliferation of e-government can be attributed to the delivery capability of government information, resources, and services through 24 hours per day, seven days per week Web access[1]. The overall objective is the utilization of information and communication technologies in providing efficient, timely, and accessible means of linking U.S. citizens to federal agencies. E-government offers a virtual bridge to all Americans including those who in the past had difficulty gaining access to federal government through traditional channels.

Unfortunately, online access to e-government does not guarantee that an individual will be successful in obtaining information and resources being sought. Web accessibility barriers must be overcome in order to realize the capability of e-government. The individual may already be overwhelmed with having to deal with the government based on past experience or lack of knowledge about how the federal agency works (Stowers, 2002). Compounded with a poorly designed Web site, e-government becomes virtually inaccessible to those who may need it most.

Almost at the onset of the Dot Gov era, federal law was enacted to ensure U.S. government sites provide full access to all Americans regardless of disabilities. Those with disabilities were finding it difficult it not impossible to use basic technology that nondisabled individuals could use freely (McLawhorn, 2001). This disparity of access to electronic data and information was addressed by Congress when it amended the U.S. Rehabilitation Act with the Section 508 statute. Congress recognized that the federal government is the largest technology consumer; and as such, strongly influences the design and manufacture of accessible technologies and supporting products.

Web accessibility is an ongoing concern for federal e-government, as will be explained in this chapter. The types of disabilities that impact universal

---

[1] Holden, Norris, and Fletcher (2002) refer to "24 hours per day, seven days per week" in their definition of e-government.

access of the Web are briefly described. Then, an overview of federal mandates to address the needs of those with disabilities is presented. Web accessibility studies are summarized with a conclusion drawn as to the current state of federal e-government in meeting citizen needs.

2. TYPES OF DISABILITIES

According to the U.S. Census Bureau (1997), approximately one fifth of the U.S. population has some type of disability. The Pew Foundation, in its report on how Americans contact the Government, points out that those with disabilities compose an important sub-population of e-government users (Horrigan, 2004). Fourteen percent of those responding in the Pew Foundation report identified a disability, and more than one-third were over the age of 65 years.

An important aspect of the older adult population, when compared to its younger adult counterpart, is the proportion having some type of disability. Almost 45% of older adults ages 65-69 have a disability and this increases to 73.6% for those 80 years or older (Administration on Aging, 2002; as cited in Becker, 2004a). Chronic disabilities associated with older users include arthritis, hearing impairments, hypertension, heart disease, cataracts, and diabetes, among others. Older adults, as well as others with disabilities, may find themselves homebound or isolated with significant amounts of discretionary time. Internet usage becomes increasingly appealing with the opportunity to access e-government resources and information for health, taxation, Medicaid, and Veteran benefits, among others.

Table 8-1 identifies the different types of disabilities that impact the use of the Web (refer to W3C (2004) for a more comprehensive description). It is widely recognized that Web design features can impose barriers to those with disabilities. For those with aging vision or low vision, font type, font size, foreground and background color combinations, patterned backgrounds, and other design elements may pose as barriers to the use of the Web (Becker, 2004b). Information that is relayed using color alone may be missed by those with color deficient vision (Mates, 2000). For those with cognition disabilities, complex navigational schemas, vertically long pages, and content requiring high reading grade levels may all pose as Web barriers. For users who are blind or deaf, assistive technology provides an alternate means of access only if text equivalent information is comprehensible and audio captions synchronized with video clips. Those with physical disabilities may find the use of the mouse impossible when precise pointing and clicking is needed to navigate a site or to access information through links, buttons, or graphic elements.

Table 8-1. Disabilities and Accessibility Support

Vision disabilities	
Blindness	The user has uncorrectable vision loss in both eyes. Assistive technology (e.g., screen reader) is used to read aloud Web contents.
Low Vision	The user has partial vision in one or both eyes. Tunnel vision is partial in that only the middle of the visual field is seen. Central field loss is partial as only the edges of the visual field are seen (Brewer, 2004). Partial vision may also be the result of poor acuity with blurry or clouded vision. Corrective lenses, Web design features (e.g., font resizing), and assistive technology (e.g., screen reader) may be used to improve readability.
Aging Vision	The older adult user has a reduced ability to focus on close objects due to reduction in lens elasticity. Visual acuity declines with age impacting the ability to see objects clearly. The lens of an aging eye thickens and yellows thus reducing color perception. Sensitivity to light decreases and sensitivity to glare increases. There is also reduced depth perception due to normal aging (American Foundation for the Blind, 2004). Corrective lenses, Web design features, and assistive technology are used to improve readability.
Color Deficiency	The user sees some of the colors in the spectrum but not all of them (Rigden, 1999). The person may not see red, green, or blue color in the visible spectrum of colors. Web design features (e.g., text only pages) may be used to improve readability.
Hearing disabilities	
Deafness	The user has substantial and uncorrectable hearing impairment in both ears. Assistive technology (e.g., captions) is used to transcribe audio files into text descriptions.
Mild Hearing Loss	The use has some uncorrectable hearing loss in one or both ears due to disability or normal aging. Assistive technology may be used to transcribe audio files into text descriptions.
Physical Impairments	
Motor Skills	A user has weak or limited motor control, limited sensation, or joint stiffness due to disability or normal aging. Assistive technology (e.g., special mouse device) or Web design features promote easy navigation, scrolling, data entry, and clicking on Web objects.
Seizures	A user has a type of epilepsy that can be triggered by flickering light or audio at a certain frequency. Web designs do not make use of flickering animation.
Working Memory	Older adult's working and spatial memory task performance declines with age (Holt and Morrell, 2002) making it more difficult to discern details in the presence of distracting information. Web design features promote easy recall and location of information content.

3. GOVERNMENT INVOLVEMENT

The United States government has a strong tradition of providing services, establishing standards for access to public and private services, and enforcing laws that impact those with disabilities (Ellison, 2004). Federal mandates and statutes, as described below, have upheld this tradition by promoting universal access of technology even before the arrival of the Internet.

- *American with Disabilities Act* (ADA) of 1990 – The U.S. American with Disabilities Act is foundational to universal access because it prohibits discrimination and ensures equal opportunity for persons with disabilities in employment, state, and local government services, public accommodations, commercial facilities, and transportation. Several lawsuits have been brought against electronic commerce Web sites citing this act as a basis for Web accessibility of commercial sites.
- *Section 255 of the Telecommunications Act of 1996* - Section 255 of the U.S. Telecommunications Act is foundational to Web accessibility in that it requires manufacturers of telecommunications equipment and providers of telecommunications services to ensure equipment and services are accessible to persons with disabilities, if readily achievable. As such, it establishes standards in telecommunications that later could be applied to the Internet.
- *Assistive Technology Act of 1998* - The U.S. Assistive Technology Act establishes a grant program, administered by the U.S. Department of Education, to provide federal funds to support state programs addressing assistive technology needs of individuals with disabilities. Some interpret this law as a mandate for state and local governments to ensure Web accessibility (Nobel, 2002).
- *Sections 501 and 504 of the Rehabilitation Act of 1973* - Section 501 of the U.S. Rehabilitation Act prohibits discrimination on the basis of disability in federal employment and requires federal agencies to establish affirmative action plans for the hiring, placement and advancement of people with disabilities in federal employment. Section 504 of the U.S. Rehabilitation Act prohibits discrimination based on disability in federally funded and federally conducted programs or activities including employment programs.
- *Section 505 of the Rehabilitation Act of 1973* - Section 505 of the U.S. Rehabilitation Act establishes enforcement procedures for title V of the Rehabilitation Act. Section 505 (a) (1) specifies that procedures and rights set forth in Section 717 of the Civil Rights Act of 1964 shall be available with respect to any complaint under Section 501. Section 505 (a)(2) specifies that remedies, rights and procedures set

forth in title VI of the Civil Rights Act of 1964 shall be available to any person alleging a violation of Section 504. Section 508 is enforced through the procedures established in Section 505 (a)(2).

- *Section 508 of the Rehabilitation Act* - In 1998, Congress amended the 1973 U.S. Rehabilitation Act[2] with Section 508 to require federal agencies to make electronic and information technology accessible to people with disabilities. Section 508 was enacted to eliminate barriers in electronic and information technology, make available new opportunities for people with disabilities, and encourage the development of technologies that will help achieve these goals. The law applies to all federal agencies when they develop, procure, maintain, or use electronic and information technology. Under Section 508, agencies must give disabled federal government employees and citizens access to information that is comparable to the access available to others without disabilities.

All of these mandates and statutes have played an integral role in promoting universal accessibility regardless of disabilities. Section 508 is perhaps most commonly known by the public as the Web accessibility standard put forth by the U.S. government. In fact, much of the public perceives Section 508 as being synonymous with Web accessibility, though it has a much broader application in the technology realm. Section 508 is further described in terms of its technology standards, implementation, and e-government outcomes.

4. SECTION 508 ACCESSIBILITY STANDARDS

Section 508, which went into effect in June 2001, requires all federal agencies to comply with accessibility standards administered by the Architectural and Transportation Barriers Compliance Board commonly referred to as the Access Board.[3] These standards ensure that electronic and information technology is accessible to disabled persons to the extent it does not pose an undue burden on an agency. When Section 508 went into effect, federal agencies could no longer procure noncompliant electronic and information technology (Charles, 2001). This meant that vendors, who supply hardware, software, Web, telecommunications, and other information technologies, must ensure compliance with Section 508 accessibility in order to obtain government contracts.

---

[2] Rehabilitation Act of 1973, as amended by § 508, 29 U.S.C. § 794(d) (1998).

[3] Architectural and Transportation Barriers Compliance Board is an independent federal agency, established by Section 502 of the 1973 Rehabilitation Act. Its primary function is to promote accessibility for individuals with disabilities.

The Access Board defines electronic and information technology as, "information technology and any equipment or interconnected system or subsystem of equipment used in the creation, conversion, or duplication of data or information" (www.access-board.gov). This definition encapsulates telecommunications, information kiosks, transaction machines, Web sites, copiers, faxes, and other multimedia office equipment. It does not include embedded information technology; back office equipment used only by service personnel for maintenance, repair, or similar purposes; or computer hardware and software, equipment, services, and other resources that automatically manipulate, acquire, store, manage, move, control, display, switch, interchange or transmit data or information (McLawhorn, 2001).

Table 8-2 identifies each section of the technology standards put forth by the board. The technical categories in the table focus on the functional capabilities covered under Section 508. These standards address assistive technologies (e.g., screen reader devices) and alternative technologies (e.g., keyboard navigation instead of mouse navigation) allowing access to federal employees and those with disabilities. Though not described in the table, each standard outlines the technical and information dissemination requirements for the use of electronic and information technologies (full descriptions can be obtained at www.section508.gov).

Table 8-2. Section 508 Technology Standards

Technical Categories	Subsection
Software applications and operating systems	1194.21
Web-based information or applications	1194.22
Telecommunications products	1194.23
Video or multimedia products	1194.24
Self-contained, closed products	1194.25
Personal computers and portable computers	1194.26

This chapter focuses on the Web accessibility component of Section 508 subsection 1194.22, as it is the mandate for accessibility compliance by federal e-government. Though subsection 1194.22 doesn't apply specifically to local and state e-government or commercial Web sites, many have utilized its standards in promoting Web accessibility for local and state constituencies.

5. WEB ASSESSMENT GUIDELINES

The World Wide Web Consortium (W3C) formed the Web Accessibility Initiative (WAI) in order to develop the Web Accessibility Initiative

Guidelines (WCAG) 1.0 for accessible Web designs (Chisolm, Vanderheiden, and Jacobs, 2001). WCAG 1.0 was organized into a set of checkpoints each of which was assigned a priority level. A priority rating of "1" was to ensure universal accessibility, "2" was to address potential barriers making it difficult to access Web content, and "3" was to make the Web site more usable.

There is a close mapping between the WCAG 1.0 checkpoints and Section 508 1194.22 standards, as shown in Table 8-3. Only one of the Section 508 standards is not directly supported by a checkpoint and only four checkpoints (1.3, 4.1, 6.2, and 14.1) are not specifically mapped to a Section 508 standard (Thatcher, 2005). Many accessibility studies have been conducted over the years using WCAG not only because of the mapping to Section 508 standards; as well as, automated tools utilizing WCAG in identifying errors in Web designs.

Since these early studies, most federal sites have made great strides in complying with Section 508 Web accessibility standards through support of automated tools, such as provided by Watchfire Bobby™ 5.0, W3C HTML Validation tool, Microsoft FrontPage®, University of Toronto's Adaptive Technology Resource Center's A-Prompt, and Macromedia's Dreamweaver®. These tools provide feedback on noncompliance errors associated with WCAG and Section 508 standards.

Table 8-3. WCAG Checkpoint and Section 508 Standard Mappings (Thatcher, 2005)

WCAG 1.0 Checkpoints	Section 508 Standard	Section 508 Standard Description
1.1	1194.22 (a)	A text equivalent for every non-text element shall be provided.
1.4	1194.22 (b)	Equivalent alternatives (e.g., captions) for any multimedia presentation shall be synchronized with the presentation.
2.1	1194.22 (c)	Web pages shall be designed so that all information conveyed with color is also available without color.
6.1	1194.22 (d)	Documents shall be organized so they are readable without requiring an associated style sheet.
1.2	1194.22 (e)	Redundant text links shall be provided for each active region of a server-side image map.
9.1	1194.22 (f)	Client-side image maps shall be provided instead of server-side image maps except where the regions cannot be defined with an available geometric shape.
5.1	1194.22 (g)	Row and column headers shall be identified for data tables.

(Continued)

Table 8-3. (Continued)

WCAG 1.0 Checkpoints	Section 508 Standard	Section 508 Standard Description
5.2	1194.22 (h)	Markup shall be used to associate data cells and header cells for data tables that have two or more logical levels of row or column headers.
12.1	1194.22 (i)	Frames shall be titled with text that facilitates frame identification and navigation.
7.1	1194.22 (j)	Pages shall be designed to avoid causing the screen to flicker with a frequency greater than 2 Hz and lower than 55 Hz.
11.4	1194.22 (k)	A text-only page, with equivalent information or functionality, shall be provided to make a Web site comply with the provisions of this part, when compliance cannot be accomplished in any other way. The content of the text-only page shall be updated whenever the primary page changes.
6.3	1194.22 (l)	When pages utilize scripting languages to display content, or to create interface elements, the information provided by the script shall be identified with functional text that can be read by assistive technology.
6.3, 6.4, 8.1	1194.22(m)	When a web page requires that an applet, plug-in or other application be present on the client system to interpret page content, the page must provide a link to a plug-in or applet that complies with §1194.21(a) through (l).
10.2, 12.4, 9.3	1194.22 (n)	When electronic forms are designed to be completed on-line, the form shall allow people using assistive technology to access the information, field elements, and functionality required for completion and submission of the form, including all directions and cues.
13.5, 13.6	1194.22 (o)	A method shall be provided that permits users to skip repetitive navigation links.
No Match	1194.22 (p)	When a timed response is required, the user shall be alerted and given sufficient time to indicate more time is required.

Bobby, owned by Watchfire Corporation (www.watchfire.com), remains perhaps the most popular automated tool for checking the Web accessibility of a site. Bobby was developed by the Center for Applied Special Technology (CAST) in 1996. CAST worked closely with W3C's WAI in developing the technology to check for compliance with WCAG. By the end of 2001, Bobby also provided automated testing for Section 508 Web accessibility standards.

6. E-GOVERNMENT COMPLIANCE

Early studies identified noncompliance issues that would have to be corrected for federal e-government accessibility to become a reality. A study performed by Jackson-Sanborn, Odess-Harnish, and Warren (2002) utilized the Bobby tool to assess homepage accessibility of 100 federal e-government sites. The results found that 60% of federal homepages had no WCAG priority level 1 errors. The study also found that the government sites had a higher compliance rate than commercial and education sites. Stowers (2002) conducted a study on the accessibility of 148 federal websites. It was found that only 13.5% had zero accessibility problems as reported by the Bobby tool. An additional 56% had between one and three errors; many of which were missing alternate (alt) text (description of nontext objects) or had missing text labels on frames. West (2002) conducted a study on 59 federal websites and found 28% to have some form of disability access using one of four measures. In order for the site to be considered accessible to a disabled user, it could display a TTY (text telephone) or TDD (telephonic device for the deaf) phone number, be approved by the Bobby tool, have Web accessibility features consistent with Section 508 standards, or provide a text version of the site. The study identified 18% of the federal sites having a text version or text labels on graphics, 8% utilizing TTY/TDD phone lines, 5% Bobby approved, and 5% compliant with W3C or Section 508 standards.

More recently, Ellison (2004) conducted an accessibility study on 50 federal e-government homepages using Bobby. This study differs slightly than the previous ones, as the newer version of Bobby allows for Section 508 standards to be used specifically in the assessment results. Twenty-two percent of the federal homepages passed given there were no violations of Section 508 standards. Of the homepages that did not pass, approximately 62% had missing alt text associated with images on the homepage. Becker (2005) conducted a manual assessment of 50 federal e-government sites in terms of nondescript or cryptic alt text associated with navigational links. Sixty percent had poorly designed alt text that could pose as barriers to comprehending the navigational schema of the e-government site.

All of these studies identified federal noncompliance with Section 508 standards, especially in terms of providing alt text for images, graphics, frames, and other Web elements. There are significant methodological differences, however, making it difficult to draw additional conclusions. Jaeger (2003) points out that these studies provide limited information for whom the sampled sites are accessible, the types of accessibility options made available, and the types of Web pages that are accessible.

Previous studies have not accounted for normal aging factors, though the older adult population is growing at a rapid pace. In a study conducted by Becker (2004b), 25 federal e-government sites were assessed utilizing the U.S. National Institute of Aging guidelines on senior-friendly Web sites. It was found that 46% used patterned backgrounds with the potential to impact readability of overlaying text. Ninety-six percent used a 10 point or smaller font size, and 16% used a serif font size both of which could impact readability for older adults or those with low vision.

7. CONCLUSION

Accessibility of e-government resources and information by those with disabilities and aging adults is a social necessity in the U.S. Universal access of federal e-government embodies the idea that all Americans have the right to be included in society regardless of disabilities, age, geographic location, literacy, or other factors (Thatcher, Bohman, Burks, Henry, Regan, Swierenga, Urban, and Waddell, 2002; cited in Sierkowski, 2002). Though progress has been made through the collaborative efforts of researchers and practitioners, there is room for improvement to ensure universal access of federal e-government.

A significant number of e-government sites have alternative texts ("alt text") that are cryptic, incomplete, or incorrect. A missing alt text that fails to identify a link, for example, may pose as an accessibility barrier in successfully navigating a site. An alt text that mislabels a link may also be a barrier in terms of providing insufficient navigational information. These simple design flaws are easily fixed by updating the markup language associated with a page. Unfortunately, there is little automated support in identifying these potential barriers to accessing a federal Web page.

Web developers may feel compelled to provide alt text for all images including those used to improve the visual presentation of a Web page. By doing so, the Web developer has fully complied with Section 508 standards, and automated tools would generate zero errors associated with missing alt text. However, these alt text descriptions actually impede accessibility for a disabled user relying on assistive technology. When read aloud to a disabled user, alt text associated with design images (e.g., spacer gif) add "noise" to the Web page and may significantly slow down the processing of the page. Simple Web design solutions, not presented here, can produce a visually appealing Web page while promoting accessibility for all users. Asakawa (2005) discusses these and provides insight into accessible designs for a blind user.

There are several areas of Web accessibility that are typically overlooked. The use of color on a Web site often is not included in accessibility studies except from the perspective of color deficiency (e.g., do not use color to relay information as mandated by Section 508 1194.22 (c)). For older adults or those with low vision, the use of pastel foreground and background color combinations can render a Web site virtually unreadable. The use of saturated foreground and background color combinations (e.g., blue text overlaying a red background) may cause eye fatigue particularly for those with vision problems (Becker, 2004b).

Another area for improvement is literacy and the comprehension of e-government content. When reading comprehension requirements of a Web site are misaligned with the reading comprehension skills of a targeted user, the results could be severe (Becker, 2004a). Though not in violation of Section 508 standards, incomprehensible Web content can result in accessibility barriers to a large part of the U.S. population. E-government and literacy requirements should be studied to identify guidelines for universally accessible information content on e-government sites.

Web accessibility is a long-term commitment due to constant changes to Web content and the introduction of new technologies. A Web page that is compliant today may be inaccessible tomorrow when changes do not adhere to Section 508 standards. To handle these changes, it is important that developers and their managers have expertise in Web design as well as Section 508 standards, accessibility guidelines put forth by W3C, and automated support for ongoing assessments.

ACKNOWLEDGEMENT

The National Science Foundation, under Grant No. 0203409 supported this work. Any opinions, findings and conclusions or recommendations expressed in this content are those of the author and do not necessarily reflect the views of the National Science Foundation.

REFERENCES

Administration on Aging. (2002). A profile of older Americans: 2002. Administration on Aging, U.S. Department of Health and Human Services. http://www.aoa.gov/prof/Statistics/profile/2002profile.pdf.

American Foundation for the Blind. (2004). Normal changes in the aging eye. Retrieved May 20, 2006, from http://www.afb.org/Section.asp?SectionID=35&TopicID=212&SubTopicID=39.

Asakawa, C. (2005). What's the Web like if you can't see it? Proceedings of the 2005 International Cross-Disciplinary Workshop on Web Accessibility (W4A), Chiba, Japan, 1-8.

Becker, S. A. (2004a). A study of Web usability for older adults seeking online health resources. *ACM Transactions on Human-Computer Interaction, 11*(4), 387-406.

Becker, S. A. (2004b). E-government visual accessibility for older adult users. *Social Science Computer Review, 22*(1), 11-23.

Becker, S. A. (2005). Technical Opinion: E-government Usability for Older Adults. *Communications of the ACM, 48*(2).

Brewer, J. (2004). Web accessibility highlights and trends. *Proceedings of the 2004 International Cross-disciplinary Workshop on Web Accessibility (W4A),* New York, New York, 51-55.

Charles, S. (2001). Section 508 compliance – not a simple yes or no. Immix Group. Retrieved May 21, 2006, from http://www.immixgroup.com/pslibrary/eu_display.cfm?ID=91.

Chisolm, W., Vanderheiden, G., and Jacobs, I. (2001). Web content accessibility guidelines. *Interactions of the ACM, 8*(4), 35-54.

Ellison, J. (2004). Assessing the accessibility of fifty United States government Web pages: Using Bobby to check on Uncle Sam. *First Monday, 9,* 7. Retrieved May 13, 2006, from http://firstmonday.org/issues/issue9_7/ellison/index.html.

Holt, B. J., and Morrell, R. W. (2002). Guidelines for Web site design for older adults: The ultimate influence of cognitive factors. In R. W. Morrell (Ed.), *Older Adults, Health Information, and the World Wide Web,* (109-129). Mahwah, NJ: Lawrence Erlbaum Associates, Inc.

Holden, S. H., Norris, D. F., and Fletcher, P. D. (2002). Electronic government at the grass roots: Contemporary evidence and future trends. *Proceedings of the 36th Hawaii International Conference on System Sciences,* Hawaii. IEEE Society.

Horrigan, J. B. (2004). *How Americans Get in Touch with Government.* Pew Internet & American Life Project, Washington D.C.

Jackson-Sanborn, E., Odess-Harnish, K. and Warren, N. (2002). Web site accessibility: A study of six genres. *Library Hi Tech, 20*(3), 308-317.

Jaeger, P. T. (2003). The importance of accurately measuring the accessibility of the federal electronic government: Developing the research agenda. *Information and Technology and Disabilities E-Journal, IX*(2). Retrieved May 21, 2006, from_http://www.rit.edu/~easi/itd/itdv09n1/jaeger.htm.

Mark, B. (2003). Government sites surge in popularity. *Boston.Internet.Com.* Retrieved May 20, 2006, from http://boston.internet.com/news/article.php/2120061.

Mates, B. T. (2000). *Adaptive Technology for the Internet: Making Electronic Resources Accessible to All.* Chicago, IL: American Library Association.

McLawhorn, L. (2001). Recent development: Leveling the accessibility playing field Section 508 of the Rehabilitation Act. *North Carolina Journal of Law & Technology, 3*(1), 63-100.

Nobel, S. (2002). Web access and the law: A public policy framework. *Library Hi Tech, 20,* 4, 399-405.

Rigden, C. (1999). The eye of the beholder – Designing for colour-blind users. *British Telecommunications Engineering, 17,* 2-6.

Sierkowski, B. (2002). Achieving Web accessibility. *The 30th Annual ACM SIGUCCS Conference on User Services*, Providence, Rhode Island, 288-291.

Stowers, G. N. L. (2002). The state of federal websites: The pursuit of excellence. PricewaterhouseCooper Endowment for the Business of Government report.

Thatcher, J. W. (2005). Side by side, WCAG 1.0 versus 508. Retrieved May 13, 2006, from http://www.jimthatcher.com/508wcag2.htm#508towcag2.

Thatcher, J., Bohman, P., Burks, M., Henry, S. L., Regan, B., Swierenga, S., Urban, M., and Waddell, C. (2002). *Accessible Web Sites.,* Birmingham, UK: Glaushaus.

U.S. Census Bureau. (1997). Disabilities affect one-fifth of all Americans. Census Brief. Washington D.C., U.S. Department of Commerce, CENBR/97-5.

West, D. M. (2002). State and federal e-government in the United States. Center for Public Policy, Brown University, Providence, Rhode Island. Retrieved May 21, 2006, from http://www.insidepolitics.org/E-govt02us.html.

W3C. (2004). How people with disabilities use the Web. W3C working draft, December 10. World Wide Web Consortium (W3C) Web Accessibility Initiative. Retrieved May 12, 2006, from http://www.w3c.org/WAI/EO/Drafts/PWD-Use-Web/20041210.

SUGGESTED READINGS

- Reading: Asakawa, C. (2005). What's the Web like if you can't see it? Proceedings of the 2005 International Cross-Disciplinary Workshop on Web Accessibility (W4A), Chiba, Japan, 1-8. Description: The real world experience of a blind user is discussed in terms of full Web accessibility.

- Reading: Becker, S. A. (2004). E-government visual accessibility for older adult users. Social Science Computer Review, 22(1), 11-23. Description: This research describes aging vision and its impact on the accessibility of government web sites.

- Reading: Jaeger, P.T. (2003). The importance of accurately measuring the accessibility of the federal electronic government: Developing the research agenda. Information and Technology and Disabilities E-Journal, IX(2),http://www.rit.edu/~easi/itd/itdv09n1/jaeger.htm. Description: The article analyzes major studies of e-government in terms of the treatment of accessibility, including methodological problems and issues of accessibility that are not addressed.

- Reading: Stowers, G. N. L. (2002). The state of Federal Websites: The pursuit of excellence. PricewaterhouseCooper Endowment for the Business of Government report.
  Description: Federal websites are rated in terms of online services, quality of user help features, quality of navigation, site legitimacy, and accessibility.

ONLINE RESOURCES

- Core Techniques for Web Content Accessibility Guidelines 1.0, http://www.w3.org/TR/2000/NOTE-WCAG10-CORE-TECHS-20000920/ This document describes techniques for authoring accessible content that apply across technologies.
- Department of Justice Section 508 Home Page. http://www.usdoj.gov/crt/508/ Federal e-government site providing background information on enforcement and links to Section 508 resources.
- Section 508, http://www.section508.gov/ Federal e-government site providing information and resources on Section 508 standards.
- Side by Side WCAG vs. 508, http://www.jimthatcher.com/sidebyside.html Web content accessibility checkpoints are mapped to Section 508 Web accessibility standards.
- Trace Center Collation of Access Board's 508 Final Rule and Guides. http://trace.wisc.edu/docs/508-collation/06092004v1.1.pdf
  A compilation and collation of Section 508 standards and guides released by the Access Board.
- Usability.gov, U.S. Department of Health and Human Resources, http://www.usability.gov/Online resources for designing usable, useful, and accessible Web sites and interfaces.

QUESTIONS FOR DISCUSSION

1. Should standards and guidelines include literacy as part of Web accessibility to federal e-government?
2. What measures should be taken to ensure that federal e-government continues to be compliant with Section 508 Web accessibility standards?
3. Should Section 508 Web accessibility standards be enforced at state and local levels of e-government to promote universal access in the U.S.?
4. Why is it important to address the accessibility needs of the aging population in the U.S. from an e-government perspective?
5. What role should the U.S. federal government play in the development of assistive technologies?
6. What are the relationships between personal privacy, security, and accessibility in promoting universal access to federal e-government?

Chapter 9

THE CURRENT STATE OF ELECTRONIC VOTING IN THE UNITED STATES

Paul S. Herrnson[1], Richard G. Niemi[2], Michael J. Hanmer[3], Benjamin B. Bederson[4], Frederick G. Conrad[5], and Michael W. Traugott[6]

[1]Center for American Politics and Citizenship, Department of Government and Politics, University of Maryland, College Park, Maryland, U.S.A. (pherrnson@capc.umd.edu); [2]Department of Political Science, University of Rochester, Rochester, New York, U.S.A. (niemi@rochester.edu); [3]Department of Government and Politics, University of Maryland, College Park, Maryland, U.S.A. (mhanmer@gvpt.umd.edu); [4]Human-Computer Interaction Lab, Computer Science Department ,Institute for Advanced Computer Studies, University of Maryland, College Park, Maryland, U.S.A. (bederson@cs.umd.edu); [5]Survey Research Center, University of Michigan, Ann Arbor, Michigan, U.S.A. (fconrad@umich.edu); [6]Center for Political Studies, Department of Communication Studies,University of Michigan, Ann Arbor, Michigan, U.S.A. (mtrau@umich.edu)

CHAPTER OVERVIEW

The 2000 election called attention to the need for assessing the usability of voting systems and accelerated the introduction of electronic voting systems across the United States. An expert review, usability laboratory study, and field study were conducted to assess six electronic voting systems and four vote-verification/election audit systems. Though most of the systems were evaluated favorably, there were significant differences among them in the difficulty of correcting mistakes, casting a write-in vote, or changing a vote. The differences could be traced to characteristics of the systems, such as the use of automatic advancing, mechanical navigation, and a full-face ballot. It required more time and movements to cast a ballot on some systems; the more time and movement required, the lower the satisfaction ratings. Systems also differed in the frequency with which help was needed. Most voters succeeded in casting their votes as intended, but several types of errors were found, including voting for an opposing candidate. Ballot type greatly affected performance. In addition, certain voter characteristics related to the digital divide had an impact on their voting experiences. There were noteworthy differences in voters' assessments of the verification systems; these were related to ease of use, extent of distraction, and the need for help.

1. INTRODUCTION

The 2000 presidential election in the United States was the first of a number of recent events calling attention to the need for assessing the usability of voting systems. Antiquated technology, poorly designed ballots, and an extremely close election combined to produce an outcome some believe was decided by the courts, not the voters. The election left some American citizens, as well as foreigners, questioning the ability of the United States to conduct a fair election. Many voters in minority and poor communities felt especially aggrieved. Elections in the U.S. since then have been subject to intense scrutiny, and while there have been no problems rivaling those in 2000, stories of registration difficulties, voting machines that failed to work properly, and votes that were not counted have kept the spotlight on the matter of how we conduct our elections.

Many of the difficulties observed in recent elections have been due to shortcomings in voting system usability. Nonetheless, little research has been undertaken to address citizens' abilities to interact successfully with electronic voting systems. Much speculation and some isolated facts about the usability (and security) of voting systems have been reported by the mass media and presented as testimony to various groups of legislators and election officials in Washington, D.C. and many state capitals, but there has been little systematic study of these systems.

After a review of the literatures on voting systems and public policy related to them, this chapter presents the findings of a series of usability studies. These studies evaluated six electronic voting systems and four vote-verification election-audit systems (VVEASs) designed to be retrofitted to current voting systems.[1] Most of the voting systems and some of the VVEASs are commercially available; others were prototypes at different stages of development. The voting systems incorporate an assortment of design principles: a paper ballot/optical scanner system, computerized touch screens, a printed paper record, a dial and push button system, and a full-face system in which the entire ballot is visible at once. The VVEASs include a printed paper record, an independent computer and monitor, an analog tape recorder with headphones, and an independent computer that uses a cryptographic-based technique of voter verification. The final section discusses some of the challenges facing election officials when attempting to select and implement new voting systems or VVEASs.

---

[1] We use VVEAS over the more frequently used voter-verifiable paper-audit trail (VVPAT) or voter verifiable paper trail (VVPT) because, as noted, several verification systems do not rely on paper records.

2. LITERATURE REVIEW

States and localities in the United States traditionally have used a variety of voting systems, ranging from paper ballots to mechanical lever machines to computer-readable punch cards and an array of direct recording electronic systems (DREs). Since the passage of the Help America Vote Act of 2002, a large shift has occurred away from punch cards, lever machines, and paper ballots to optical scan equipment and, especially, to electronic systems (Election Data Services, 2006).

A wide range of ballots also has been employed in U.S. elections (Niemi and Herrnson 2003). Different forms of ballots are routinely used during the same election but in different locations. The most common ballot forms are office bloc ballots (the candidates for one office are situated in a group) and party-row or party column ballots (all of the candidates affiliated with one party are listed one after the other across or down the ballot. (Examples of these ballots are provided in Figure 9-1, at the end of section 2.) Some of these ballots have a straight-party option, which offers voters the option of using one action (filling in a circle or completing an arrow, moving a lever, or pushing a button) to vote for every candidate affiliated with a party.

Voting systems and ballot designs can affect how individuals perform in the voting booth. Voting systems, ballots, and combinations thereof should meet at least five minimal requirements. First, they should enable voters to register their voting intentions accurately. Second, they should accurately record votes. Third, they should accurately count votes. Fourth, they should prevent coercion or vote tampering. And fifth, they should instill confidence in elections and the political system among voters. Not every voting system used before or after the 2000 election meets these criteria.

Most of the research that touches on usability consists of statistical studies. Wand et al. (2001) analyzed voting on the butterfly ballot, finding solid statistical evidence that many voters using the butterfly ballot in the 2000 presidential election in Palm Beach Co., Florida likely intended to vote for Democratic nominee Al Gore but ended up voting for Reform candidate Patrick Buchanan. Clearly, the butterfly ballot did not meet the first and did little to advance the fifth one.

Studying the same election, the Caltech/MIT Voting Project estimated that about 2 percent of all those who went to the polls did not have a vote counted for president. In making this calculation, they created a single aggregate measure, referred to as the residual vote, which combines "overvotes" (where a voter selects more candidates for an office than is allowed), "undervotes" (where a voter has not selected a candidate for a given office), and uncounted ballots into a single measure (Caltech/MIT 2001). Other studies have continued to rely on the residual vote (Tomz and

Van Houweling 2003, Stewart 2005; Traugott et al. 2005). They report that voters appear to vote with greater accuracy on some voting systems than others, and some systems are more effective at counting votes and instilling voter confidence. For example, Ansolabehere and Stewart (2005) report that individuals who voted on punch cards in 2000 (about one-third of all voters) cast 50 percent more residual votes than those using other methods.

More recent research has included the possibility of intentional undervoting, the impact of different ballot formats, and the effects of specific voting arrangements, such as precinct-based versus centralized optical scan systems (Bullock and Hood 2000; Kimball and Kropf 2005, 2006). These studies report that differences in voting technology and ballot design can influence the number of residual votes. However, their findings are far from conclusive. Some studies report that due to their familiar, straightforward character, paper ballots lead to the fewest mistakes (Caltech/MIT 2001; Bullock and Hood 2002), but others dispute this expectation (Brady, Buchler, Jarvis, and McNulty 2001). It may be that review screens on DREs encourage individuals to check their votes more carefully. Other design features that could influence the accuracy with which people vote are the number of contests presented to the voter at one time, whether the system uses a touch screen or mechanical input devices like dials and buttons, and whether the system automatically advances the voter through the ballot or ballot navigation is left under the control of the voter.

Moreover, the nature of the tasks voters are asked to perform also can affect voter accuracy. The probability of mistakes increases when citizens are given the opportunity to vote for more than one candidate for a given office or when they attempt to change their initial selection of one candidate to another. Certain ballot types can complicate the voting process (Walker 1966; Wattenberg, McAllister, and Salvanto 2000; Jewett 2001; Herron and Sekhon 2003). Lengthy ballots with many offices can cause voter fatigue. Ballots that include a straight-party feature that enables voters to push a button, fill in an oval, or push a lever, etc., to select all of a party's candidates for every partisan office can make voting more difficult, in part because it is not clear how to avoid voting entirely for that party's candidates and also because voters sometimes forget to vote for the nonpartisan offices and ballot questions that follow the partisan elections (Niemi and Herrnson 2003). The same is true of ballots that list the candidates for a single office on more than one page. Each of these features can result in significant declines in voter accuracy.

Additional research demonstrates that voter characteristics can influence how well they interact with voting systems. Those who have never voted before probably face more challenges in the voting booth than those who turnout regularly. Similarly, voters who have limited experience with computers, including touch screen automatic teller machines (ATMs) and gasoline pumps, may have less success using computerized voting systems than those who fall on the other side of the "digital divide." Research utilizing aggregate data generally conclude that election precincts with many low income and less educated citizens report higher levels of voter errors. The findings for race are much less consistent, with some reporting that minorities are more likely than whites to perform more poorly at the polls and others finding no significant difference (see Vanderleeuw and Engstrom 1987; Darcy and Schneider 1989; Vanderleeuw and Utter 1993; Nichols and Strizek 1995; Nichols 1998; Wattenberg et al. 2000; GAO 2001; HCGR 2001; Brady et al. 2001; Bullock and Hood 2002; Knack and Kropf 2003; Tomz and Van Houweling 2003; Herron and Sekhon 2003, 2005; Kropf and Knack 2004; Alvarez, Sinclair, and Wilson 2004; Kimball and Kropf 2006). Studies investigating the impact of previous voting experience report minor differences among precincts with many and fewer newly-registered voters (Bullock and Hood 2002).

Social scientists have not been the only group to respond to the difficulties associated with the 2000 elections. As states and localities began to consider and then adopt electronic equipment, computer scientists and others began to discuss the technology on which these systems were based, especially with an eye toward their security from hackers and others with malicious intent. Many fear that massive, undetectable vote fraud could occur. They have written numerous position papers, editorials, and some scholarly articles. These researchers have faced significant challenges in substantiating some of their claims because virtually every voting system manufacturer considers its voting system proprietary and is generally unwilling to release its software for research or other purposes. Nevertheless, a team of researchers was able to analyze a version of the Diebold AccuVote-TS's source code they found on the Internet. Their report raised concerns about the system's ability to withstand tampering and concluded the system has "significant security flaws: voters can trivially cast multiple ballots with no built-in traceability, administrative functions can be performed by regular voters, and the threats posed by insiders, such as poll workers, software developers, and janitors is even greater" (Kohno, Stubblefield, Rubin, and Wallach 2004). While the conclusions apply to only one voting system and include some hyperbole—the voters, poll workers, and janitors would need substantial knowledge of computer programming and easy access to the voting systems—several have been supported by the research of others (SAIC 2003; RABA 2004) and have caused alarm in a various quarters. Although most of the writing on security does not deal with usability issues (e.g., Fischer 2003), some of the research on proposed solutions—especially about the use of various types of paper trails and other

VVAESs—raises questions about how voters interact with voting systems (e.g., Shamos 2004).

Political activists, politicians, and governments also responded to the 2000 elections, pressuring for change in many facets of election administration, ranging from the maintenance of voter registration rolls to imposing requirements for the certification of voting systems. The U.S. Congress responded by passing the Help America Vote Act of 2002 (HAVA), which provides mandates, guidelines, and some funding to assist states with their own reform efforts. Some states conducted studies, usurped the power to purchase voting equipment from counties that previously possessed it, bought new equipment, and revamped their election procedures; others did virtually nothing. Florida, Georgia, and Maryland quickly enacted major changes in their election systems; Idaho, Virginia, California, Pennsylvania, and Missouri took more incremental approaches; and Arizona, Illinois, and New York lagged behind these other states in their reform efforts (Palazzolo and Ceaser 2005). Some of the states that moved early are reconsidering their decisions. Activist groups in Maryland, for example, are waging a well publicized campaign to require the state to modify its touch screen voting systems to include a voter-verifiable paper receipt or switch to paper ballot/optical scan voting systems.

At the time of this writing no systematic studies have been published comparing the 2000 and 2004 presidential elections. However, there is abundant anecdotal evidence to suggest that 2004 was considerably less problematic than its predecessor. Most obviously, the winner was announced without significant delay. There also were no large scale protests over the results or the way the election was conducted in any of the 50 states. Moreover, fewer problems were reported at the polls. Nevertheless, there were enough reports of poll workers having difficulties operating various e-voting systems and voters finding that their names did not appear on the voter rolls to conclude that further improvements are needed in the way U.S. elections are conducted. Likewise, reports on elections in 2006 point to a wide variety of problems related to voting per se and to the overall conduct of elections.[2]

---

[2] See especially Election Science Institute (2006).

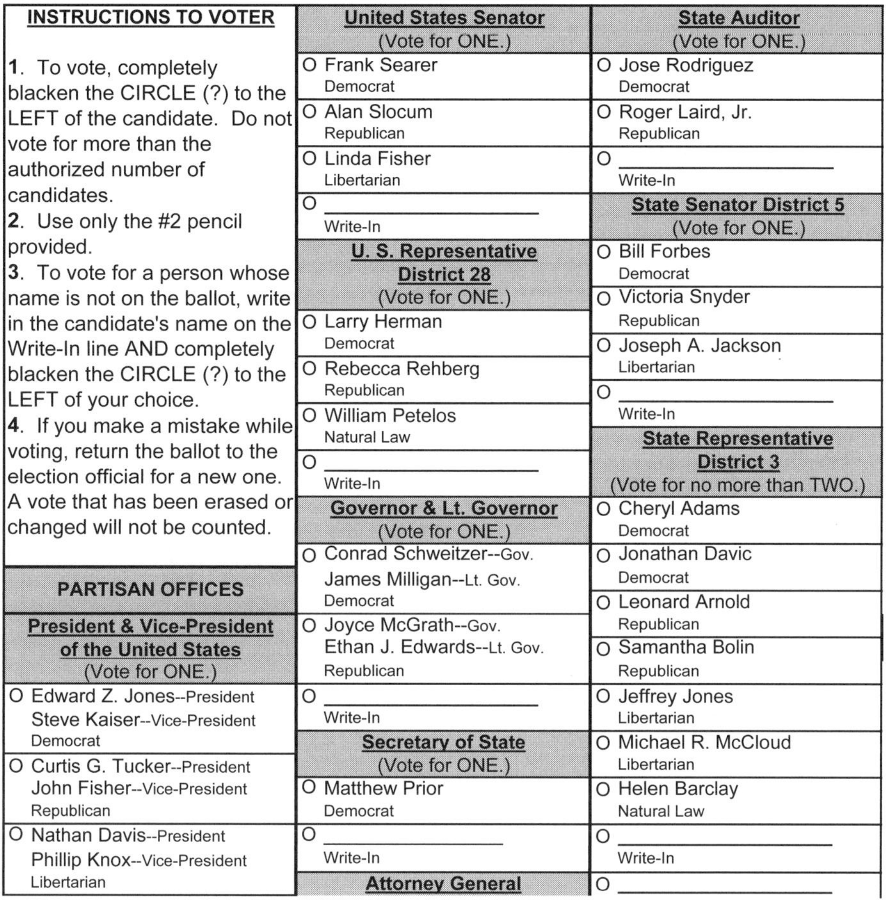

INSTRUCTIONS TO VOTER

1. To vote, completely blacken the CIRCLE (?) to the LEFT of the candidate. Do not vote for more than the authorized number of candidates.
2. Use only the #2 pencil provided.
3. To vote for a person whose name is not on the ballot, write in the candidate's name on the Write-In line AND completely blacken the CIRCLE (?) to the LEFT of your choice.
4. If you make a mistake while voting, return the ballot to the election official for a new one. A vote that has been erased or changed will not be counted.

PARTISAN OFFICES

President & Vice-President of the United States
(Vote for ONE.)
O Edward Z. Jones--President
Steve Kaiser--Vice-President
Democrat
O Curtis G. Tucker--President
John Fisher--Vice-President
Republican
O Nathan Davis--President
Phillip Knox--Vice-President
Libertarian

United States Senator
(Vote for ONE.)
O Frank Searer
Democrat
O Alan Slocum
Republican
O Linda Fisher
Libertarian
O ________________
Write-In

U. S. Representative District 28
(Vote for ONE.)
O Larry Herman
Democrat
O Rebecca Rehberg
Republican
O William Petelos
Natural Law
O ________________
Write-In

Governor & Lt. Governor
(Vote for ONE.)
O Conrad Schweitzer--Gov.
James Milligan--Lt. Gov.
Democrat
O Joyce McGrath--Gov.
Ethan J. Edwards--Lt. Gov.
Republican
O ________________
Write-In

Secretary of State
(Vote for ONE.)
O Matthew Prior
Democrat
O ________________
Write-In

Attorney General

State Auditor
(Vote for ONE.)
O Jose Rodriguez
Democrat
O Roger Laird, Jr.
Republican
O ________________
Write-In

State Senator District 5
(Vote for ONE.)
O Bill Forbes
Democrat
O Victoria Snyder
Republican
O Joseph A. Jackson
Libertarian
O ________________
Write-In

State Representative District 3
(Vote for no more than TWO.)
O Cheryl Adams
Democrat
O Jonathan Davic
Democrat
O Leonard Arnold
Republican
O Samantha Bolin
Republican
O Jeffrey Jones
Libertarian
O Michael R. McCloud
Libertarian
O Helen Barclay
Natural Law
O ________________
Write-In
O ________________

*Figure 9-1*a. Example of an Office Bloc ballot

INSTRUCTIONS TO VOTER

1. To vote, completely blacken the CIRCLE (•) to the LEFT of the candidate. Do not vote for more than the authorized number of candidates.
2. Use only the #2 pencil provided.
3. To vote for a person whose name is not on the ballot, write in the candidate's name on the Write-In line AND completely blacken the CIRCLE (•) to the LEFT of your choice.
4. If you make a mistake while voting, return the ballot to the election official for a new one. A vote that has been erased or changed will not be counted.
5. To vote for every candidate of one party, blacken the CIRCLE (•) to the LEFT of the name of the party for which you wish to vote. To vote for non-partisan offices, blacken the CIRCLE (•) to the LEFT of the candidate for whom you wish to vote.

STRAIGHT PARTY VOTING

O Democratic Party
O Republican Party
O Libertarian Party
O Green Party
O Natural Law Party

PARTISAN OFFICES

President & Vice-President of the United States
(Vote for ONE.)

O Edward Z. Jones--President
Steve Kaiser--Vice-President
Democrat

O Curtis G. Tucker--President
John Fisher--Vice-President
Republican

O Nathan Davis--President
Phillip Knox--Vice-President
Libertarian

United States Senator
(Vote for ONE.)

O Frank Searer
Democrat

O Alan Slocum
Republican

O Linda Fisher
Libertarian

O ____________
Write-In

U. S. Representative District 28
(Vote for ONE.)

O Larry Herman
Democrat

O Rebecca Rehberg
Republican

O William Petelos
Natural Law

O ____________
Write-In

Governor & Lt. Governor
(Vote for ONE.)

O Conrad Schweitzer--Gov.
James Milligan--Lt. Gov.
Democrat

O Joyce McGrath--Gov.
Ethan J. Edwards--Lt. Gov.
Republican

O ____________
Write-In

Secretary of State
(Vote for ONE.)

O Matthew Prior
Democrat

O ____________
Write-In

Attorney General

State Auditor
(Vote for ONE.)

O Jose Rodriguez
Democrat

O Roger Laird, Jr.
Republican

O ____________
Write-In

State Senator District 5
(Vote for ONE.)

O Bill Forbes
Democrat

O Victoria Snyder
Republican

O Joseph A. Jackson
Libertarian

O ____________
Write-In

State Representative District 3
(Vote for no more than TWO.)

O Cheryl Adams
Democrat

O Jonathan Davic
Democrat

O Leonard Arnold
Republican

O Samantha Bolin
Republican

O Jeffrey Jones
Libertarian

O Michael R. McCloud
Libertarian

O Helen Barclay
Natural Law

O ____________
Write-In

O ____________

Figure 9-1b. Example of an Office Bloc Ballot with Straight-Party Option

INSTRUCTIONS TO VOTER

1. To vote, completely blacken the CIRCLE (•) to the LEFT of the candidate.
Do not vote for more than the authorized number of candidates.
2. Use only the #2 pencil provided.
3. To vote for a person whose name is not on the ballot,
write in the candidate's name on the Write-In line
AND completely blacken the CIRCLE (•) to the LEFT of your choice.
4. If you make a mistake while voting, return the ballot
to the election official for a new one.
A vote that has been erased or changed will not be counted.

PARTISAN OFFICES

President & Vice-President of The United States (Vote for ONE.)		
O Edward Z. Jones -- President Steve Kaiser -- Vice-President Democrat	O Curtis G. Tucker -- President John Fisher -- Vice-President Republican	O Nathan Davis -- President Phillip Knox -- Vice-President Libertarian
United States Senator (Vote for ONE.)		
O Frank Searer Democrat	O Alan Slocum Republican	O Linda Fisher Libertarian
United States Representative District 28 (Vote for ONE.)		
O Larry Herman Democrat	O Rebecca Rehberg Republican	

Figure 9-1c. Example of a Party Column Ballot

3. USABILITY STUDIES

3.1 Expert Reviews, Field Experiments, Laboratory Studies

The most recent approaches to studying voting systems have moved beyond aggregate-level data analyses of voting systems and ballots that group different systems together by system type (touch screen, paper ballot/optical scan, punch card, etc,) to include individual-level assessments involving comparisons of specific voting systems and VVEASs. These studies—often referred to as usability studies—have several advantages over aggregate analysis. First, they enable researchers to learn how individuals respond to the systems, that is, whether they rate them highly on such criteria as ease of use, perceived accuracy, trustworthiness, and their overall satisfaction using them. Second, they report the types of challenges individuals encounter when using the systems and whether individuals needed help. Third, they allow researchers to record the amount of time and the number of physical movements it takes to cast a completed ballot. Fourth and perhaps most important, researchers can determine the degree to which voters are able to cast their votes as intended and the types of voting errors they frequently make. Such studies can be conducted using a variety of techniques, including review by human-computer interaction researchers who have expertise in voting systems and similar computer interfaces, laboratory experiments, and field studies. Taken together, the findings from these studies put researchers in a position to assess different types of voting systems and ballots and to observe how diverse groups of voters perform on them. This knowledge can serve as a foundation for voting system manufacturers, ballot designers, and election officials who wish to improve their products, purchase products that are best suited to local voters, or more efficiently allocate voting systems or election personnel.

Although of obvious value, this research has both limitations and shortcomings. Among the limitations is the need to obtain participation of voting system manufacturers; as noted above, some manufacturers are hesitant to make their products available for study. A second limitation is that individuals—whether experts or ordinary voters—must be recruited to participate and can reasonably be expected to vote on and assess only a relatively small number of systems. A third limitation is that the research only assesses the front end of the voting process, e.g., voters' opinions about the performance of the systems. Thus, while it enables one to draw conclusions about voters' perceptions of the security of voting systems, it does not permit assessment of the internal operations or security of the systems.

3.2 NSF-Funded Study of Six Voting Systems[3]

An expert review, usability laboratory study, and field study were conducted to assess five commercially available voting systems and a sixth system designed specifically for this project. Each of the systems represents an array of design principles. The most important differences concern the user interface. Three—the Diebold AccuVote-TS, Avante Vote-Trakker, and Zoomable Prototype—use a touch screen similar to those found on the automatic teller machines (ATMs). A fourth—the Hart InterCivic eSlate—uses a mechanical interface requiring a voter to turn a dial and physically press buttons. "Membrane buttons," smooth buttons located behind the ballot that must be depressed in order to vote, are the major feature of the Nedap LibertyVote system. The final system—the ES&S Model 100—combines a paper ballot and an electronic optical scanner that checks the ballot before it is cast. Another major difference among the systems is whether they include what is frequently referred to as a voter-verifiable paper trail. The Avante system incorporated this, and, of course, it is inherent in the ES&S's paper ballot. Other differences among the systems include how much of the ballot is displayed at any one time, and whether the voter is automatically advanced through the ballot after each vote is recorded. (Pictures of the systems are provided in Figure 9-2, starting on the next page.)

The expert review relied on twelve nationally-renowned human-computer interaction specialists, including some who were familiar with the workings of voting interfaces. Overall, they found that while the systems were likely to work well for a majority of voters, there was a range of usability problems in every system they examined, and they were generally surprised by the lack of design maturity in these systems. For example, they found basic problems such as unclear fonts, colors, and language. Some systems had interfaces that made it difficult to navigate within a complex ballot or to obtain on-line help when the voter did have difficulty. Some made it overly difficult to modify a selection once a candidate was selected. Most of these problems were considered easily correctable and unlikely to result in inaccurate vote selection for most voters. However, they could cause a problem for less experienced or physically disabled voters, and they would be likely to decrease overall confidence in the voting process.

---

[3] This study is reported in Bederson, Herrnson, Conrad, Traugott, and Niemi (2005); Conrad, Peytcheva, Traugott, Herrnson, Bederson, Hanmer, and Niemi (2005); Traugott, Hanmer, Park, Herrnson, Niemi, Bederson, and Conrad (2005); Herrnson, Niemi, Hanmer, Francia, Bederson, Conrad, and Traugott. (2005); Herrnson, Niemi, Hanmer, Bederson, Conrad, and Traugott (2006); and Niemi, Herrnson, Hanmer, Bederson, Conrad, and Traugott (2006).

(a)

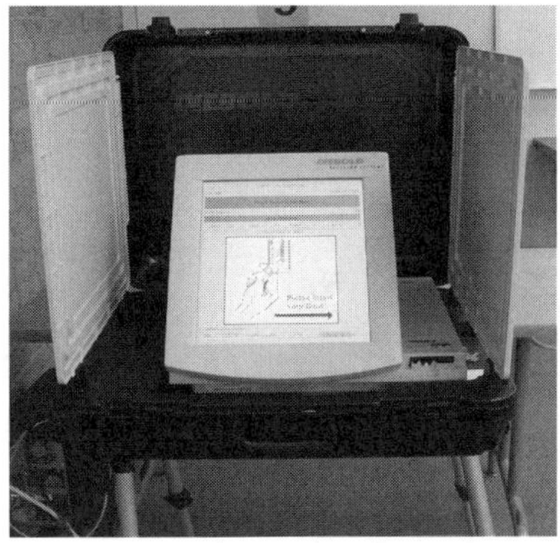

(b)

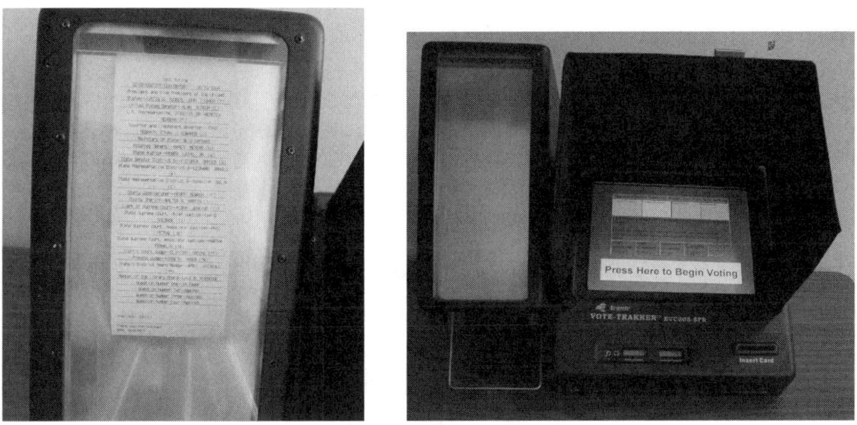

(c)

Figure 9-2. (a) ES&S Model 100. (b) Diebold AccuVote-TS. (c) Avante Volte-Trakker. (d) Zoomable Voting Proto-type. (e) HArt InterCivic eSlate. (f) Nedap Liberty Vote.

Figure 9-2. (Continued)

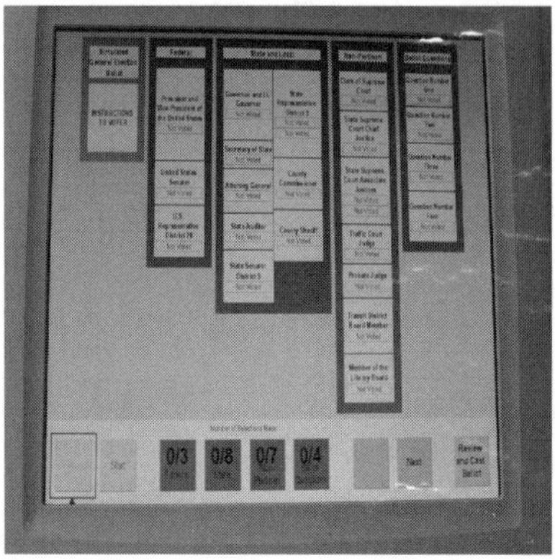

(d)

(e)

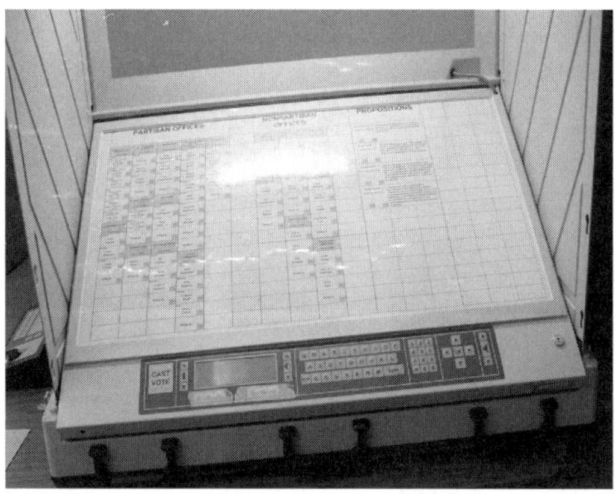

(f)

There also was a usability laboratory experiment in which forty-two individuals participated, including several who had no previous computer or voting experiences. Subjects entered their voting intentions in a voter information booklet and then began voting, in random order, on the six systems. After voting on each system, they filled out a questionnaire that asked them to record from 1 (lowest) to 7 (highest) their reactions to the system: confidence their vote was accurately recorded, the system's ease of use, comfort, the readability of the characters, the ease with which they could understand the ballot, the ability to correct mistakes, to cast a write-in vote, and to change a vote. Another question asked them about their need for help. Finally, the subjects' background characteristics, voting history, and computer usage patterns were collected when they completed the experiment.

Most of the systems were given favorable evaluations, but the Avante, Hart, and Nedap systems were rated somewhat lower on a variety of measures than the others. Subjects were somewhat less comfortable using these systems, and found it harder to correct mistakes, cast a write-in vote, or change a vote on them. The Avante's automatic advance system, the Hart InterCivic's system of mechanical navigation, and the Nedap's full-face ballot, which displayed the names of all of the candidates and election issues at once, appeared to have produced these lower evaluations. The ES&S system, which was evaluated fairly well overall, also was not rated highly when it came to correcting mistakes or changing a vote—no doubt because this required participants to repeat the voting process on a new ballot (if they followed the manufacturer's instructions) or erase the circle they had first filled in and fill in another (which might have raised questions about whether they had succeeded in voting for the intended candidate). This usability laboratory experiment also demonstrated that it required more time and physical movements to cast a ballot on some systems than others and that the more time and movement required the lower the satisfaction ratings. In addition, many individuals did not bother to review their ballots before casting them.

Finally, a field study was conducted that included the participation of 1,540 individuals at multiple voting sites located in Maryland, Michigan, and New York. Subjects followed the same set of procedures as in the laboratory but in more realistic settings designed to ensure a more diverse set of participants. This research tested a variety of hypotheses on the impact of voter characteristics and ballot formats on their evaluations of the voting systems, need for help, and abilities to cast their votes as intended.

Subjects' responses to the eight questions that evaluated systems (i.e., ease of use, comfort, confidence their vote was accurately recorded, and the like) were sufficiently correlated to warrant creating an index of overall voter satisfaction. All six systems scored highly on the index. Each received an average rating above 5, with two of them garnering ratings of close to 6 on a continuous scale from 1 to 7. Nevertheless, several noteworthy differences were recorded. First, subjects had more confidence that their votes would be accurately recorded on the three touch screen systems than the other systems, including the paper ballot/optical scan system. This suggests that critics of these systems may have been overly harsh or premature in their judgments. Second, the fact that the Hart and the Nedap systems were not evaluated as favorably as were the touch screen systems indicates that voters are more comfortable with interfaces that have high levels of visible computerization than systems that rely on mechanical interfaces. This may be due to the increased feedback that touch screen systems offer or voters' familiarity with using ATM devices. Third, the Avante did not perform as well as the other touch screen systems in terms of correcting mistakes and changing votes, implying that voters probably were challenged by its automatic advancing mechanism and preferred systems that allowed them to exercise more control over the voting process.

These findings were reinforced by the portion of the study that investigated whether individuals felt the need for help when using the voting systems. This is an important issue because it raises privacy concerns, and it has implications for the amount of time it takes to cast a ballot and the amount of assistance that voters may require from poll workers. Two touch screen systems—the Diebold and the Zoomable prototype—performed quite well in this regard, as did the ES&S paper ballot/optical scan system. Somewhat more participants (almost 30 percent) needed help on the Avante system, presumably because of the difficulties they encountered using its automatic advance navigation. Significantly more voters reported needing help with the Hart system (36 percent) and the Nedap system (44 percent). Many voters found the dial and buttons on the former system somewhat unwieldy to use. Even more appeared to be overwhelmed by the amount of information presented at one time by the latter system and had difficulty locating the points on the ballot that needed to be pressed to trigger its membrane buttons.

The third set of results involved individuals' abilities to cast their ballots as intended. While most voters succeeded in casting their votes as intended, several types of errors were found: 1) failing to vote for a candidate when a vote was expected; 2) voting for the candidate immediately before or after the intended candidate (a "proximity error"; and 3) voting for some other candidate other than the intended candidate.[4] The proximity error is by far the most costly in that not only does the intended candidate fail to receive a vote, but the recorded vote often goes to a candidate's major opponent. Proximity errors also are the most frequently committed mistake, accounting for as many as 3 percent of the votes cast on the paper ballot system and as few as 1.4 percent on the Zoomable prototype. Voters committed as few, if not fewer, of these errors and errors overall, on the touch screen systems as the other systems.

The importance of the ballot design as a conditioning element for voter satisfaction and performance constitutes the fourth set of findings. Regardless of the voting system on which they were programmed, simple office bloc ballots performed better than ballots featuring a straight-party option (or party row ballots, in the case of the Nedap system). Individuals using voting systems programmed with the office bloc ballot expressed

---

[4] Overvoting can constitute a fourth error, but it is only possible on the paper ballot system.

higher levels of voter satisfaction, less need for help, and made significantly fewer errors casting their ballots than did those who voted on systems programmed with the other ballots.

Finally, certain voter characteristics related to the digital divide had an impact on their voting experiences. Younger voters, native English speakers, men, and voters with higher levels of computer usage and more education typically reported needing the least assistance while voting. Previous voting experience had a less consistent impact on voters' need for help, and partisanship had no impact at all. Furthermore, frequent computer users, more educated, and younger individuals made the fewest voting errors. Voters who spoke some language other than English, and African Americans consistently made more errors. Although the results are not as consistent, men and Hispanics made somewhat more mistakes on a few of the systems.

The findings of this study demonstrate that voting system and ballot design features can contribute to or detract from voters' experiences at the polls, including their abilities to cast their votes as intended. They identify areas for improvement in the design of voting systems, including hardware and software, and have important implications for those creating the ballots to be used on them. They also show that certain voters are likely to need extra assistance casting their ballots, which can help election officials anticipate which precincts might need additional poll workers. Finally, the importance of the findings and the limited number of voting systems and sites included in the project suggest the need for more research in this area.

3.3 Maryland Study of Vote Verification Election Audit Systems[5]

An expert review and a field study were conducted on the usability of four vote verification systems and a voting system with no verification system: 1) The Diebold_AccuVote-TSx with AccuView Printer Module combines a paper printout that lists the candidates' names with a touchscreen voting system. After voters submit their votes, they are given the opportunity to review their selections. 2) The VoteHere Sentinel uses a mathematical cryptographic-based technique for voter verification that includes an independent computer and a stand-alone printer. The verification system records individuals' votes on an independent computer, which can be used for election auditing and recounts.[6] 3) The Scytl Pnyx system has an independent computer and monitor connected to the voting system. After verifying their selections on the small monitor, race by race, voters have the

---

[5] This study is reported in Herrnson, Bederson, Niemi, and Hanmer (2006).

[6] In this study, voters could not actually check their votes, though they were told how they could in a real election.

opportunity to cast their ballot or change it. 4) The MIT Audio system has a set of headphones attached to a voice-activated analog cassette tape recorder and a small computer unit that attaches to the voting system. Voters hear a computerized voice that repeats their candidate selection immediately after each selection is made. (Pictures of the systems are provided in Figure 9-3, next page.)

The part of the study that involved an expert review by nine nationally-known user interface and voting system experts reached a number of conclusions. First, and perhaps most important, there was a trade-off between usability and security. In all cases, the verification system appeared to reduce the usability of the voting process compared to the Diebold AccuVote-TS, which had no verification system. Second, there was a trade-off in actual security as opposed to perceived security. The experts knew that the cryptographic solutions were likely to be more secure in practice, but they felt that many voters would only truly trust the system if they could understand it themselves (i.e., a paper system). Finally, some real or perceived privacy concerns also were raised about each of the four vote verification systems.

A diverse sample of 815 Marylanders participated in the field study of the VVAESs, including people with little-to-no experience using computers. Participants voted, in random order, on the five systems.

After voting on each system, they filled out a questionnaire about the verification system before proceeding to the next system, addressing such issues as the system's ease of use, perceived accuracy, and trustworthiness. At the end, they were asked whether they needed help in using any of the systems. In general, all of the systems were viewed favorably, including the system with no verification feature. However, there were noteworthy differences in voters' assessments of some aspects of the systems. For example, the MIT audio and Scytl systems were rated somewhat lower on privacy concerns, presumably because voters were concerned that these verification systems would allow others to hear or see how their votes were cast. Also, the AccuView Printer was evaluated more highly than the other two VVEASs in terms of verifying a write-in vote. The AccuView prints out the name of the write-in candidate, whereas on the MIT system the sound quality made it difficult to understand the name of the write-in candidate and the Scytl system merely produced the word "write-in" when a person wrote in the name of the candidate.[7]

---

[7] The VoteHere system was not included in this comparison because it did not provide voters with a written or verbal record of their vote.

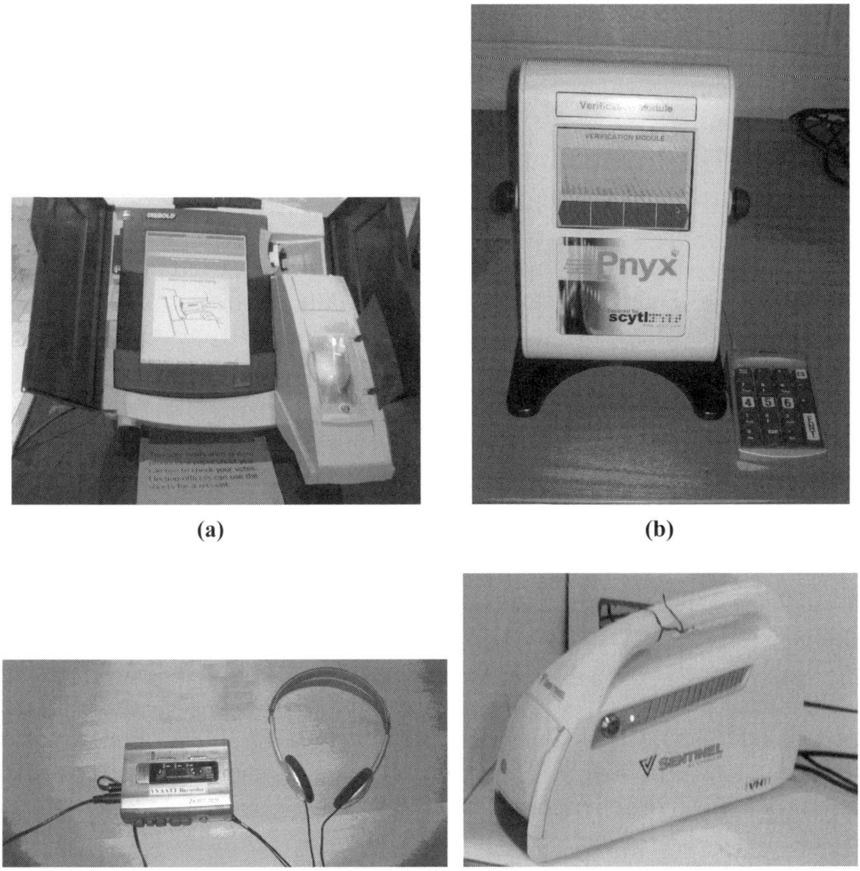

(a) (b)

(c) (d)

Figure 9-3. (a) Diebold AccuVote-TSx Printer Module. (b) Scytl Pnyx. (c) MIT Audio System. (d) VoteHere Sentinel.

Other findings were that voters considered the MIT audio system distracting. It failed to generate as much confidence as other systems and was criticized by some users because of sanitary concerns related to the repeated use of the same headset. Participants needed the least amount of help when using the Diebold AccuVote-TS system (with no VVEAS). The Diebold with AccuView Printer system came next. Voters received more help using the VoteHere (cryptographic), MIT (audio), and Scytl (monitor) systems.

The study also produced a number of findings relevant to election administration. Chiefly, adding any of the four verification systems greatly increased the complexity of administering an election. Among other things, the paper spool in the Diebold AccuView Printer had to be changed frequently, and changing it was fairly complex. Also, it was difficult and time consuming to set up the Scytl system.

3.4 MIT Laboratory Study of Vote Verification Election Audit Systems

In a study conducted by Cohen (2005), thirty-six subjects, who were mostly young, highly educated, and technically proficient, completed four elections on a voting machine with a paper trail and four elections on the same MIT audio system tested in the Maryland study of VVEASs. An experimental touch screen system was modified for each type of audit trail. Subjects were variously instructed to vote for a specific candidate, to vote for a candidate of their choice, or to skip an office. Subjects were randomly assigned to vote first on the machine with the paper trail or on the machine with the audio trail. Several types of voting errors were purposefully (and randomly) introduced into the exercise, including having the wrong candidate listed/played back, no candidate listed/played back, and an office skipped.

Both systems were rated quite favorably on usability, and few problems were noted (perhaps not so surprising given the technical background of the experimental subjects). However, the subjects were able to find almost 10 times as many errors with the audio feedback as in the paper trail. The types of errors noticed or reported differed sharply between the two kinds of trails; changed names were noticed with the audio trail but evidently not with the paper trail. Subjects perceived that it generally took longer to vote on the audio system, even though this was not always the case.

Participants' behaviors towards the paper audit were apathetic. They spent little time reviewing the paper record, sometimes casting their vote while the record was printing. At the same time, subjects expressed considerable confidence in the paper records but less confidence in the audio trail. When asked which type of system they would prefer for their own county elections, almost all subjects preferred the paper trail.

4. CONCLUSION

The 2000 U.S. presidential election raised significant concerns about how Americans vote. Policymakers reacted by commissioning studies, purchasing equipment, and revamping some aspects of how elections are administered. Researchers responded first by developing new methods to assess the impact of voting technology on aggregate measures of the vote. Next, they investigated the usability of different voting systems, ballot designs, and combinations thereof on the voting experience. More recently, usability techniques have been used to study vote-verification election audit systems.

The results of these studies demonstrate that how people vote can influence their overall satisfaction with the voting process, need for assistance at the polls, and ability to cast their ballots as intended. They also show that individuals' experiences with voting systems vary according to their background characteristics. While all of the tested systems performed fairly well, the results demonstrate that, with some modifications, individuals' voting intentions could be registered and recorded with greater accuracy and their confidence in the electoral process could be improved. Perhaps most important, the findings suggest that issues pertaining to voting are too important to ignore.

Some voting manufacturers have responded to the scientific studies, as well as to public pressure. This has led to changes in the voting systems available for purchase. For example, Diebold has incorporated suggestions from the NSF-funded research (particularly the expert review) when modifying the voter interface for its most recent generation of the AccuVote-TS, according to a company representative. That company, along with Hart InterCivic and some other firms, has manufactured versions of their voting systems that have VVEASs in response to the pressure of pro-paper trail groups.

Regardless, the fact that some citizens and election officials are challenged by the voting systems currently on the market strongly suggests that further improvement is in order. If citizens do not understand how to use their voting system and are unable to vote on it with near-complete accuracy, if they become frustrated in the polling booth, if they believe voting systems and ballots are biased for or against a party or its candidates, or if they have little faith in election outcomes for whatever reason, democracy may be in danger.

ACKNOWLEDGMENTS

This work was supported in part by National Science Foundation grant number 0306698, Carnegie Corporation grant number D05008, and the Maryland State Board of Elections. We wish to thank Mario Stylianou, Jr. for assistance.

REFERENCES

Alvarez, R. Michael, D. E. "Betsy" Sinclair, and Catherine Wilson. 2004. "Counting Ballots and the 2000 Election: What Went Wrong?" In *Rethinking the Vote*, ed. Ann Crigler, Marion Just, and Edward McCaffery. New York: Oxford University Press.

Ansolabehere, Stephen, and Charles Stewart III. 2005. "Residual Votes Attributable to Technology." *Journal of Politics* 67:366-89.

Bederson, Benjamin B., Paul S. Herrnson, Frederick Conrad, Michael Traugott, and Richard Niemi. 2005. "Designing Interfaces for Voting Machines." Presentation at the American Association for the Advancement of Science, Washington, DC, Feb. 17.

Brady, Henry E., Justin Buchler, Matt Jarvis, and John McNulty. 2001. "Counting All the Votes: The Performance of Voting Technology in the United States." Survey Research Center and Institute of Governmental Studies, University of California, Berkeley. http://ucdata.berkeley.edu/ new_web/countingallthevotes.pdf (accessed September 20, 2006).

Buchler, Justin, Mattew Jarvis, and John E. McNulty. "Punch Card Technology and the Racial Gap in Residual Votes." *Perspectives on Politics* 2:517-24.

Bullock, Charles S. III, and R. E. Dunn. 1996. "Election Roll-Off: A Test of Three Explanations." *Urban Affairs Review* 32:71-86.

Bullock, Charles S. III, and M. V. Hood III. 2002. "One Person–No Vote; One Vote; Two Votes: Voting Methods, Ballot Types, and Undervote Frequency in the 2000 Presidential Election." *Social Science Quarterly* 83:981-93.

Caltech/MIT. 2001. Caltech/MIT Voting Technology Project. 2001. Residual Votes Attributable to Voting Technology: An Assessment of the Reliability of Existing Voting Equipment. http://www.hss.caltech.edu/~voting/CalTech_MIT_Report_Version2.pdf. Accessed September 20, 2006.

Cohen, Sharon B. 2005. "Auditing Technology for Electronic Voting Machines" Undergraduate thesis, Department of Electrical Engineering and Computer Science, Massachusetts Institute of Technology.

Conrad, Frederick, Emilia Peytcheva, Michael Traugott, Paul Herrnson, Benjamin Bederson, Michael Hanmer, and Richard Niemi. 2005. "An Evaluation of Six Electronic Voting Machines." Paper presented at the annual meeting of the Usability Professionals' Association Conference, Montreal, QB, June 27.

Darcy, Robert, and Anne Schneider. 1989. "Confusing Ballots, Roll-off, and the Black Vote." *Western Political Quarterly* 42:347-64.

Election Science Institute. 2006. DRE Analysis for May 2006 Primary Cuyahoga County, Ohio.

Fischer, Eric A. 2003. "Election Reform and Electronic Voting System (DREs): Analysis of Security Issues." Congressional Research Service, Order Code RL32139. Nov. 4.

Herrnson, Paul S., Benjamin B. Bederson, Richard G. Niemi, and Michael J. Hanmer. 2006. The Usability of Four Vote Verification Systems: A Study Conducted for the Maryland State Board of Elections Center for American Politics and Citizenship and Human-Computer Interaction Lab, University of Maryland, College Park, MD.

Herrnson, Paul S., Richard G. Niemi, Michael J. Hanmer, Peter L. Francia, Benjamin B. Bederson, Frederick G. Conrad, Michael Traugott. 2005. "How Voters React to Electronic Voting Systems: Results from a Usability Field Test." Revised version of a paper presented at the annual meeting of the Midwest Political Science Association, Chicago, IL, April 7-10.

Herrnson, Paul S., Richard G. Niemi, Michael J. Hanmer, Benjamin B. Bederson, Frederick G. Conrad, Michael Traugott. 2006. "The Not so Simple Act of Voting: An Examination of Voter Errors with Electronic Voting." Paper presented at the annual meeting of the Midwest Political Science Association, Chicago, IL, April 20-23.

Herron, Michael C., and Jasjeet S. Sekhon. 2003. "Overvoting and Representation: An Examination of Overvoted Presidential Ballots in Broward and Miami-Dade Counties." *Electoral Studies* 22:21-47. 2003.

Herron, Michael C., and Jasjeet S. Sekhon. 2005. "Black Candidates and Black Voters: Assessing the Impact of Candidate Race on Uncounted Vote Rates." *Journal of Politics* 67:154-77.

Jewett, Aubrey. 2001. "Explaining Variation in Ballot Invalidation among Florida Counties in the 2000 Election." Paper presented at the annual meeting of the American Political Science Association, San Francisco, August.

Kimball, David C., and Martha Kropf. 2005. "Ballot Design and Unrecorded Votes on Paper-Based Ballots." *Public Opinion Quarterly* 69:1-22.

Kimball, David C., and Martha Kropf. 2006. "Ballot Initiatives and Residual Ballots in the 2004 Presidential Election." Paper presented at the annual meeting of the Southern Political Science Association. Atlanta, January 7.

Kimball, David C., Chris T. Owens, and Katherine M. Keeney. 2004. "Unrecorded Votes and Political Representation." In *Counting Votes: Lessons from the 2000 Presidential Election in Florida*, Robert P. Watson, ed. Gainesville: University Press of Florida.

Knack, Stephen, and Martha Kropf. 2003. "Voided Ballots in the 1996 Presidential Election: A County Level Analysis." *Journal of Politics* 65:881-98.

Kohno, Tadayoshi, Adam Stubblefield, Aviel D. Rubin, and Dan S. Wallach. 2004. "An Evaluation of an Electronic Voting System," *IEEE Symposium on Security and Privacy 2004*. IEEE Computer Society Press, May. http://avirubin.com/vote.pdf.

Nichols, Stephen M. 1998. "State Referendum Voting, Ballot Roll-off, and the Effect of New Electoral Technology." *State and Local Government Review* 30:106-17.

Nichols, Stephen M., and Gregory A. Strizek. 1995. "Electronic Voting Machines and the Ballot Roll-off." *American Politics Quarterly* 23:300-18.

Niemi, Richard G., Paul S. Herrnson, Michael J. Hanmer, Benjamin B. Bederson, Frederick G. Conrad, Michael Traugott. 2006. "Voters' Abilities to Cast a Write-in Vote Using Electronic Voting Systems." Paper presented at the annual meeting of the Midwest Political Science Association, Chicago, IL, April 20-23.

Palazzolo, Daniel J., and James W. Ceaser. 2005. *Election Reform: Politics and Policy*. Lanham, MD: Lexington.

RABA Technologies. 2004. Trusted Agent Report: Diebold AccuVote-TS Voting System.

Saltman, Roy G. 2006. *The History and Politics of Voting Technology*. New York: Palgrave Macmillan.

Science Applications International Corporation. 2003. Risk Assessments Report: Diebold AccuVote-TS System and Processes. September 2. http://www.dbm.maryland.gov/dbm_publishing/public_content/dbm_search/technology/toc_voting_system_report/voting systemreportfinal.pdf

Stewart, Charles III. 2005. "Residual Vote in the 2004 Election." Caltech/MIT Voting Technology Project Working Paper 2.3.

Tomz, Michael, and Robert P. Van Houweling. 2003. "How Does Voting Equipment Affect the Racial Gap in Voided Ballots?" *American Journal of Political Science* 47:46-60.

Traugott, Michael W., Michael J. Hanmer, Won-ho Park, Paul S. Herrnson, Richard G. Niemi, Ben B. Bederson, and Fred G. Conrad. 2005. "The Impact of Voting Systems on Residual Votes, Incomplete Ballots, and Other Measures of Voting Behavior." Presented at the annual meeting of the Midwest Political Science Association. Chicago, April.

Vanderleeuw, James M., and Richard L. Engstrom. 1987. "Race, Referendums, and Roll-Off." *Journal of Politics* 49:1081-92.

Vanderleeuw, James M., and Glenn H. Utter. 1993. "Voter Roll-Off and the Electoral Context: A Test of Two Theses." *Social Science Quarterly* 74:664-73.

Walker, Jack L. 1966. "Ballot Forms and Voter Fatigue: An Analysis of the Office Block and Party Column Ballots." *Midwest Journal of Political Science* 10:448-63.

Wand, Jonathan N., Kenneth W. Shotts, Jasjeet S. Sekhon, Walter R. Mebane, Jr., Michael C. Herron, and Henry E. Brady. 2001. "The Butterfly Did It: The Aberrant Vote for Buchanan in Palm Beach County, Florida." *American Political Sci Review* 95:793-810.

Wattenberg, Martin P., Ian McAllister, and Anthony Salvanto. 2000. "How Voting is Like Taking an SAT Test: An Analysis of American Voter Rolloff." *American Politics Quarterly* 28:234-50.

SUGGESTED READINGS

- Herrnson, Paul S., Richard G. Niemi, Michael J. Hanmer, Benjamin B. Bederson, Frederick G. Conrad, Michael W. Traugott. 2007._*Voting Technology: The Not-So-Simple Act of Casting a Ballot.*_Washington, D.C.: Brookings Institution Press.
- Niemi, Richard G., and Paul S. Herrnson. 2003. "Beyond the Butterfly: The Complexity of U.S. Ballots." *Perspectives on Politics* 1:317-26. The length, complexity, and variability of U.S. ballots create problems for voters and voting technology. This paper illustrates some of the quirks, major and minor, in ballots across the states.
- Saltman, Roy G. 2006. *The History and Politics of Voting Technology.* New York: Palgrave Macmillan. A readable history of voting technology, with an emphasis on developments since 2000.
- Shamos, Michael Ian. 2004. "Paper vs Electronic Voting Records – An Assessment." http://euro.ecom.cmu.edu/people/faculty/mshamos/paper.htm#_edn34 A thoughtful, vigorous, argument in support of electronic systems over paper records.

ONLINE RESOURCES

- Brady, Henry E., Justin Buchler, Matt Jarvis, and John McNulty. 2001. "Counting All the Votes: The Performance of Voting Technology in the United States." Survey Research Center and Institute of Governmental Studies, University of California, Berkeley. http://ucdata.berkeley.edu/new_web/countingallthevotes.pdf (accessed September 20, 2006). This paper studies which voting systems do the best job of recording and tabulating votes by minimizing the residual vote percentage.
- Caltech-MIT Voting Technology Project - This site contains reports on voting technologies and projects dating back to 2001. Publications also include the effect of various voting machines on previous elections. http://vote.caltech.edu/

- Center for American Politics and Citizenship - This site has a page that lists a usability project of six voting systems and four vote verification/election audit systems, as well as publications of previous public policy recommendations. http://www.capc.umd.edu/

- Cohen, Sharon B. 2005. "Auditing Technology for Electronic Voting Machines." Undergraduate thesis, Department of Electrical Engineering and Computer Science, Massachusetts Institute of Technology.
  A controlled experiment comparing the use of paper and audio paper trails by 36 subjects. Voters found more errors using an audio auditing system but preferred a paper system.
  http://www.vote.caltech.edu/media/documents/draft%20a.pdf

- Election Data Services, Inc. 2006. "2006 Voting Equipment Study." Shows numbers and percentages of counties, precincts, and people using various kinds of voting equipment, along with changes since 2000. http://electiondataservices.com.

- Electionline Weekly - A new report finds that while 25 states will require the use of paper trails in time for the 2008 presidential election, so far only 15 states currently plan to use them as the official record in a recount of votes. How or if they would be used in recounts - and how difficult that process might be - are questions many states still need to answer.
  http://www.electionline.org/Portals/1/Publications/ERIPBrief12.SB370updated.pdf

- National Association of Secretaries of State - Lists election reform resources, a project to engage young voters in the electoral process, and publications of surveys. http://www.nass.org/

- National Conference of State Legislatures - *The States Tackle Election Reform*. Describes changes since 2000 in equipment for casting and counting votes, voter education programs, recount procedures, voter registration systems, and absentee voting procedures. Management of elections has changed dramatically since November 2000. For a detailed listing of states with new laws in the following areas, see the table on page three.
  http://www.ncsl.org/programs/legman/elect/taskfc/TackleElectRef.htm

- U.S. Commission on Civil Rights - *Voting Irregularities in Florida during the 2000 Presidential Election*. There was no conspiracy to disenfranchise voters, but the state's highest officials responsible for ensuring efficiency, uniformity, and fairness in the election failed to fulfill their responsibilities and were subsequently unwilling to take responsibility. http://www.usccr.gov/

- United States Election Assistance Commission (EAC) - The EAC, an independent bipartisan agency, is authorized by the Help America Vote Act (HAVA) to serve as "...a national clearinghouse and resource for the comparison of information" on various matters involving the administration of Federal elections. http://www.eac.gov/

QUESTIONS FOR DISCUSSION

1. Should states adopt a single voting system for all to use throughout the state?
2. Should all of the states be encouraged to adopt a single voting system?
3. Should states be encouraged to simplify their ballots—e.g., by eliminating straight-party voting, by eliminating write-in voting (at least for some offices), by staggering certain elections?
4. Overall, are optical scan systems or DREs preferable?
5. Can voter verifiable paper trails be designed that voters will in fact pay attention to?
6. Jurisdictions that use paper ballots have been reported to have higher "roll-off" rates (i.e., lower rates of voting for offices further down the ballot) than those using electronic systems. Why? Is this a reason to support the use of DREs?
7. Should voting be held in large, centralized locations such as shopping malls, downtown office buildings, city halls, and so on, so each can provide well-trained staff, voting systems for the disabled, back-up systems, and the like?

Chapter 10

E-ENABLING THE MOBILE LEGISLATOR

Democratizing E-Government?

Angus Whyte

ITC, Napier University, Edinburgh, UK (A.whyte@napier.ac.uk)

CHAPTER OVERVIEW

This chapter considers the importance of 'e-enabling' elected representatives to support their *legislative* role, and relates that firstly to their roles as representatives of constituents and civil society groups, and secondly as actors in political parties. The Introduction considers legislators ICT support as a gap in e-governance development, and outlines a current project, eRepresentative, which is addressing European assemblies' needs to provide web-based mobile services to support their elected members. Recent literature portrays an increasing pace of change in European assemblies, but with parliamentarians mostly adopting new ICT tools of their own accord rather through strategic development by political parties or parliamentary administrations. The chapter describes the rationale for the eRepresentative project goals and requirements; to enable legislators to get personalized, specific, filtered data 'anywhere, any place and anytime'; to collaborate with each other and appropriate stakeholders, securely and conveniently, and influence the legislative process in a timely and convenient manner. Interim conclusions focus on the research questions emerging from the organisational change issues likely to affect usage of a pilot service in the five participating assemblies.

1. INTRODUCTION

The apocryphal complaint of disaffected electors is that they only ever see their elected representatives during election campaigns. Recent innovations in mobile and security technologies in principle offer elected representatives an opportunity to connect with the people they represent and other actors involved in policy making, at mutually convenient places and times and with relevant information to hand.

Yet considering the long standing concerns about public disengagement with the political process, a student of the e-government literature might be forgiven for objecting that 'you only see politicians around here at election times'. The e-government and e-democracy field has a growing literature on e-enabled public services, e-voting, online policy consultation and e-rulemaking, and an ever-expanding number of cases to draw on. Similarly the use of the Internet for electoral campaigns has seen a surge of interest in the last decade, much of it drawing on U.S. examples. However elected representatives are mainly considered as beneficiaries of such tools rather than as users of them or as actors in other aspects of the legislative process.

This chapter considers the importance of 'e-enabling' elected representatives to support their *legislative* role, and relates that firstly to their roles as representatives of constituents and civil society groups, and secondly as actors in political parties. The literature review following this introduction first considers definitions of e-government, e-democracy, e-enabling and e-governance – and frames the need for ICT support in terms of the latter.

A critical awareness of how such terms are used is important for our topic, as can be seen from the following:

> "ICTs provide new opportunities for government to receive feedback from, and consult with, individual citizens directly during policy-making - *without the mediation of elected politicians or civil society organizations*" ('Citizens as Partners: Information, consultation and public participation in policy-making' OECD, 2001, p.56 emphasis added)

This definition could be taken to mean that elected politicians' roles as intermediaries between people and state should be re-engineered away, in favor of more direct exchanges between online officials and interest groups. Whether or not it does, it draws into sharp relief the need to consider whether and how elected representatives' roles actually benefit from ICT 'support' for policy-making.

Despite much recent work by parliaments to e-enable the legislative process, support for elected representatives appears to lag behind government-led initiatives in e-voting, e-participation and e-government.

Evaluations or case studies of the latter are rare (Whyte and Macintosh, 2003), and studies of representatives' use of ICT are even thinner on the ground. Alongside the need to close that gap, the literature review considers:

- Recent studies of parliaments' work to e-enable the legislative process, elected representatives' roles in relation to it, and their attitudes to and usage of web-based technologies meant to support those roles.
- The importance of XML and related standards for data exchange, as an enabler of information sharing between elected assemblies and government, public or civil society actors in policy-making.
- Recent experiments in public consultation by European parliaments.

The eRepresentative project is introduced in the third section, as a case of ICT development to support the work of elected representatives at national, regional and local level by making legislative services more effective and more tailored to meet their individual requirements[1].

eRepresentative explores the extent to which a novel combination of information management, mobile technologies and security systems can be designed to enable information sharing and access to large-scale information repositories to provide elected representatives with a mobile, personalised working environment. The eRepresentative desktop application is conceived in terms of support for the elected representative to:

- Get an overview of facts and opinion relevant to current political issues
- Form an opinion together with party colleagues and other stakeholders in the committee decision-making process
- Make decisions on the appropriate legislative action

Currently eRepresentative has established a more detailed rationale and high-level requirements with the elected assemblies. The section briefly reviews the systems they currently provide to support the legislative process, and describes the high-level requirements alongside the assemblies' goals for eRepresentative.

In the concluding section we consider the research questions that will frame the assessment of eRepresentative pilots planned for early 2007, and relate these to the question in the title. The overall conclusions are that

---

[1] Assemblies participating in eRepresentative are the Catalonian Parliament, Dutch Parliament, Hungarian National Assembly, Lithuanian Parliament, Westmeath County Council. eRepresentative software is developed by HP, Gov2U and Scytl in collaboration with the assemblies and Napier University.

elected representatives and e-governance researchers alike require 'e-tools' designed for their needs, and the support and political will to ensure 'good e-governance'.

2. EUROPEAN ELECTED ASSEMBLIES AND E-GOVERNANCE

The term 'governance' has become associated with the coordination of and interaction between public, private and civil society actors. It signifies a change in focus to accommodate both inter- and intra-organisational aspects of public administration (Jann, 2001). Thus e-governance is "about the use of information and communications technology to improve the quality and efficiency of all phases of the life cycle of legislation" (Gordon, 2004). Some commentators place a specific emphasis on the use of ICT to provide "citizens" opportunities to influence and participate in policy-making and related processes" (Anttiroiko, 2004).

Thus for the purposes of this chapter e-governance spans all aspects of e-Government relevant to elected representatives' roles, including engaging in dialogue with the public. Before reviewing these roles and examples of how ICT supports them in European assemblies, we consider the types of system provided by assembly administrations in relation to more general e-governance categories.

ICT support for policy-making, implementation and review is described by Snellen (2002), using seven broad categories summarised below. Alongside those, Table 10-1 below includes more recent and specific types of system used by elected assemblies in Europe, drawn from recent studies by the European Parliaments Research Initiative (EPRI, 2005) and by Hoff and colleagues (Hoff, 2004).

Table 10-1. e-governance systems and applications for members of elected assemblies

Systems used in e-governance generally (Snellen, 2002)	Applications provided by elected assemblies or used by members
Networking technologies: internet-supported file-sharing, email, websites, navigating, chatting, message targeting, video-conferencing etc.; specialised intranets and extranets.	• Parliamentary websites, intranets and extranets; • Email and CRM ('citizen relationship management'); • Party websites, newsgroups • Members' personal web pages or blogs
Personal identification, tracking, tracing and monitoring technologies including personal identification numbers, smart cards, and other tracing or tracking devices for identification purposes, used by public services to monitor mobility or track usage according to profiles.	• Secure access and authentication technologies for intranet and extranets; • Smart cards securing members' physical access to assembly premises.

(Continued)

Table 10-1. (Continued)

Systems used in e-governance generally (Snellen, 2002)	Applications provided by elected assemblies or used by members
Object registration databases providing general registration data on populations, legal entities such as institutions, enterprises etc. Make legally reliable societal exchanges possible, but do not perform concrete transactions.	• Legislative databases recording bills, amendments or other motions registered with assembly secretariats.
Office automation and multimedia technologies support information generation, handling, rearrangement and retrieval. Includes calendaring, text and audio-visual records, serving all types of audits to which public administration is subjected including legal, political, democratic, managerial and historical auditing.	• Parliamentary workflow systems; • Agenda management systems; • Members' personal diaries. • Meeting webcasts, transcripts and verbatim minutes; • Word processing/ office tools;
Decision support technologies ranging from simple processing (case-handling) systems to complex knowledge-based systems, including abstracts from databases linked across government departments or domains.	• Online press/media extracts • Bibliographic legal databases e.g. of comparative law • Group-working tools; • Consultation tools/ results • Petitioning tools; • Electronic voting in assembly chambers or remotely.
Sectoral databases support basic transactions in a specific sector of public administration such as social security, health care, police, traffic and transport.	• Interfaces to government databases.
Control databases perform and monitor the expenditure of financial, human and physical resources within public organisations… providing transparency and accountability to partners in civic society through performance indicators and benchmarking.	• Parliamentary administrations' accounting systems.

Table 10-1 excludes tools that, while not used directly by elected representatives, are part of the technical infrastructure they depend on. These include open standards for information storage and interchange, particularly those based on the generic XML standard. More specific standards for legislative information, serve in turn as the basis for integrating disparate government and non-government systems, and providing tools that are interoperable between them (Chadwick, 2003)[2].

The *uses* of the systems and applications to support elected representatives' various roles are also excluded from Table 10-1. Three main roles are characterised by Coleman and Nathanson (2005, p. 7), together with three main purposes of ICT for elected representatives' use:

---

2 See also the various European initiatives listed at the end of the chapter under Online Resources.

- Legislator: a tool to improve performance, i.e. efficiency
- Party actor: a tool for communication and marketing, i.e. publicity
- Representative: a tool to establish democratic connections, i.e. democracy

ICT is regarded as having the greatest impact on the *legislative* role, according to a survey of 41 parliamentarians from 24 European countries (EPRI, 2005). The online publication of legislation, and access to databases of pre-legislative drafts and procedural information was considered to better inform parliamentarians themselves and to lead to more inputs from citizens and interest groups. However security risks, incompatibilities between services and information overload were cited as problems, compounded by lack of attention by parliamentary administrations to the planning and procedural changes needed for effective use of ICT investments (ibid.). Deploying document management or workflow systems in legal domains entails serious organisational challenges since efficiency gains may not be achievable if regulations surrounding the maintenance of public archives and associated issues of authorization, security and privacy are not addressed (van Kralingen et al., 2001).

In their roles as *party actors* email is predominantly used by representatives, with increasing interest in web-based forums and chat (Coleman, 2005) These are regarded as supplements to face-to-face contact with party members and officials, and as tools for more efficient communication at the cost (from the individual representatives' view) of greater pressure to stay informed about their party's positions and conform to them (ibid.).

Elected politicians' role as *representative* of their electors' interests has involved growing use of ICT in communication with citizens according to the EPRI study, again with email cited as the main tool. These parliamentarians felt ease of communication had increased the volume of citizen participation, but had not increased either the level of interest or their own understanding of citizens' views and interests (ibid.).

Although it is the norm for European assemblies to refer legislative proposals to committees, who may consult experts and others affected, the EPRI study, like earlier ones (Caldow, 1999, Treschel et al., 2003) reported little use of structured consultation tools. The UK parliament is an important exception. Over the last decade, standing committees have piloted a variety of online consultations. An important rationale has been to use the opportunity afforded by pre-legislative scrutiny to enable the public to give "direct and relevant evidence of their own experience" (Hansard Society, 2006 p.3). However a variety of approaches have been successfully tested including 'closed' consultations, i.e. where particular individuals deemed to have in-depth knowledge or experience are invited to take part in a password-protected discussion.

Overall the picture that emerges from the studies cited here is of an increasing pace of change, with parliamentarians mostly adopting new ICT tools of their own accord rather through strategic development by political parties or parliamentary administrations. The patchy uptake of ICT by parliaments compared with government departments has led some to query whether elected representatives role in governance will become increasingly marginalized (Chadwick, 2003). Others draw comparisons with NGO and activist movements' use of the Internet to organize in new ways. Elvebakk (2004) for example concludes that "...the limited knowledge of the Internet displayed [by MPs surveyed in seven European countries] can also indicate a lack of political competence in a society that is in the process of being transformed by networking technologies…" (p.52).

Representatives' legislative role appears better served by parliamentary administrations' efforts than other roles, and recent studies suggest better support for mobility, security and inter-operability of systems are key to improving that provision (Coleman and Nathanson, 2004). Meanwhile there is a clear need for further and more detailed study of elected representatives' use of ICT in its (inter) organizational context (Jann, 2001, Chadwick, 2004).

3. EREPRESENTATIVE: MOBILISING THE LEGISLATOR?

The literature reviewed above identifies concerns over security and data incompatibilties as barriers to the mobile legislator. Just as significantly, various studies remark on the marginalisation of elected politicians, relative to public servants, and the need for studies of the organizational contexts that shape and are shaped by e-governance systems.

eRepresentative aims to contribute to knowledge and practice in the area; its main premise being that legislators may perform their role more effectively if provided with a novel combination of information management, mobile technologies and security systems, designed for information sharing and access to large-scale information repositories, using a mobile, personalised working environment.

The results discussed here are of the first 4 months of this 2 year project, and refer to the requirements definition phase, which paralleled work to model the legislative process in 5 elected assemblies across Europe, and at national regional and local (municipal) level.

The research methodology combines action research and qualitative socio-technical evaluation, which in the former case involves collaboration with the assembly and technical partners on defining user requirements, and in the latter case collaboration on the evaluation of pilots in each assembly. The prototype eRepresentative desktop therefore serves both as a potentially useful tool for elected representatives, and as a research instrument to explore how and why it is 'fit for purpose' or not, in the context of use (Whyte and Macintosh, 2003).

The requirements gathering approach used questionnaires and semi-structured interviews to identify the legislative information management activities to be supported; the scope of current legislative systems, actors and stakeholders involved and their rationale for change. At time of writing these have been articulated in a requirements specification and legislative process model, using use cases and UML (Unified Modelling Language) notation (Cockburn, 2001).

Currently the requirements for security and mobile device support are being elaborated and implemented using a rapid application development approach, and leveraging technical partners capabilities in open-source digital repository technologies, particularly Dspace (see 'online resources'), and in remote e-voting and software agent design. Then the eRepresentative prototype will be piloted and evaluated, both against pre-defined criteria and indicators and to qualitatively analyse field observations of how, when and where politicians, public servants and others accomplish their tasks using the technology or are constrained by it.

3.1 Representatives' Requirements and Their Rationale

Figure 10-1 illustrates the high-level functional requirements established for the eRepresentative prototype. The requirements are defined in relation to drivers, i.e. problems or areas where improvements are sought and which the eRepresentative desktop is expected to address, together with the goals, i.e. how the desktop is expected to address them. These overall goals are to provide support for representatives to do the following:

- Obtain personalized, specific, filtered data 'anywhere, any place and anytime'
- Collaborate with each other and appropriate stakeholders, securely and conveniently
- Influence the legislative process in a timely and convenient manner

Following each of the sub-heading below, in italics, the goals are related to each of the four drivers:

1. Improved access to legislative documents
2. Better reporting of time-sensitive developments
3. Improved and more transparent collaboration and consultation
4. Remote participation in legislative decision-making

In each case the reasons for change are given below. These were articulated in discussion with user panels, comprising senior staff of assembly secretariats, IT staff and representatives. The concluding section discusses research questions identified for each area.

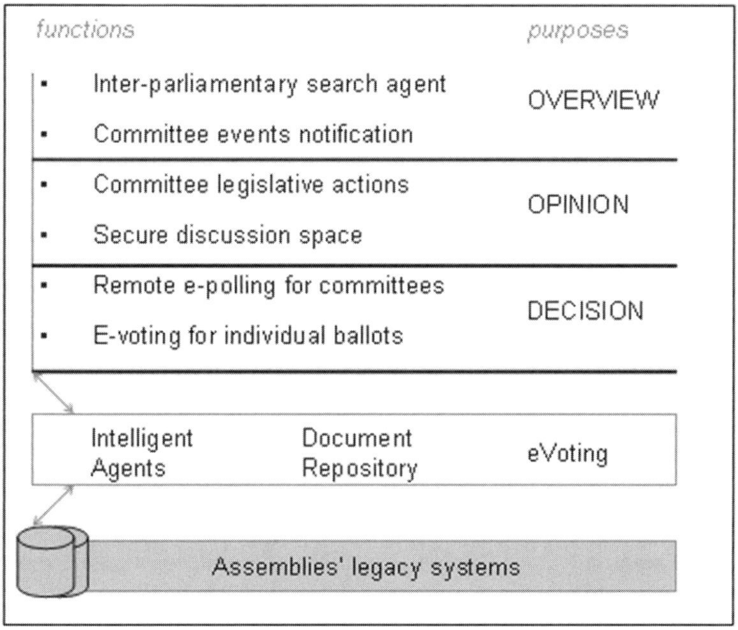

Figure 10-1. Functional requirements established for the eRepresentative prototype

3.1.1 Improved Access to Legislative Documents

Improve representatives' access to legislative documents by providing personalized, specific, and filtered information in a timely manner

There are two aspects to the need for improved access; firstly relating to the legislative work of the representatives' own assembly and secondly relating to other assemblies.

Firstly, the need for improved access to legislative documents in representatives' own assembly is partly convenience. While most of the assemblies are well served by intranet access to databases of legislative documents, these are either not available remotely (intranet/extranet) or, if they are, they are not designed to provide convenient access on mobile devices.

For representatives, improved access from mobile devices comes with risks of information overload. The Hungarian National Assembly provided a pertinent example: having emailed weekly personalized dossiers of forthcoming legislative activity to MPs every week on a trial basis. MPs reportedly felt overloaded, with the conclusion that the 'push/pull' balance should shift towards 'pull'.

A broader rationale can be found in the policy-making environment. Hungary, in common with other EU member states, has recently introduced Freedom of Information legislation (applicable to the same assemblies that passed the legislation). It has become common for assemblies to publish on their web portals all legislative proposals, amendments and voting results. Plenary and committee meeting proceedings are routinely made available both in webcast form and as verbatim transcripts. Committee minutes in particular are nevertheless considered difficult to digest. According to our participants, representatives would benefit from the availability of summary 'action minutes' of the meetings, linked to the documents discussed on the agenda, and with the positions of party members shown explicitly.

The latter can be regarded as a negotiating position for subsequent meetings, and as a representation of the officially recorded (by the committee chair) current status of amendments. These are not made public in all assemblies, nor are they always currently recorded in legislative databases. Providing them in a form easily accessible on mobile devices, to authorized committee member potentially enables them to act as they see fit more effectively.

Secondly, inter-assembly document exchange can be considered from several angles:

- *Horizontally*: i.e. access by local, regional and national assembly members to legislative documents of others at the same 'level'.
- *Vertically:* i.e. access to legislative documents of assemblies at a different level.

In each case the main rationale is for representatives to learn from the legislative activity of their colleagues who have or are addressing similar issues. Horizontal exchange faces language barriers, at least among national assemblies. Vertical exchange is seen as offering benefits when linked to horizontal exchanges between assemblies at the regional or local levels.

Existing European measures to promote information exchange include the *Eurovoc* multi-lingual thesaurus, and the IPEX initiative for online exchange of legislative responses to EU law. eRepresentative complements these by providing shared repositories of reports from committees that have similar remits, and collaborative search tools.

3.1.2 Better reporting of time-sensitive developments

Improve access to time-sensitive legislative information by providing personalized, specific, and filtered data 'any place, at any time'.

Representatives involved in pre-legislative scrutiny need to keep track of a variety of events, particularly if they may want to contribute to the deliberations of committees they are not members of, through party colleagues who are.

The assemblies' current internet and intranet services provide access to both personal and legislative agenda details, but our user panels looked for better integration of these with information on the status of amendments, and improved design for access and notification on mobile devices, particularly where there are fixed periods for committee members to register amendments (e.g. the Catalonian Parliament).

3.1.3 Improved and more transparent collaboration and consultation

Improve representatives' access to views of colleagues and experts, by providing a convenient remote and secure capability for them to collaborate, and for others to influence the legislative process in a timely manner.

The need to enable committee members and others to share comments online has three main drivers:

1. To increase the opportunities to share positions on matters raised (or to be raised) in their in-person meetings;
2. Improve support for party groups to form views on the need for proposals (or amendments) before registering them;
3. Improve structured interaction between committees and interest groups they wish to consult, including groups in *other* assemblies where relevant.

Some committees meet relatively infrequently, e.g. in municipal level assemblies like Westmeath County Council, with a need to maintain continuity between meetings. The need was also thought important by user panels in Hungary and Lithuania, to help MPs make more productive use of their time between meetings. That time naturally includes informal discussions in assembly buildings, by email and on the phone. However as these have no formal relation to committee business they are not transparent, in that they are not accessible to all members or anyone else other than their direct participants. Also for members with constituencies located far from the assembly buildings, informal meetings can be inconvenient to arrange.

Provision for political parties to discuss matters online varies markedly between assemblies but is typically highly secured. By contrast, security requirements for legislative documents concern their integrity rather than accessibility since public access is assumed in the interests of transparency.

The need extends to online dialogue with groups that committees wish to consult. Here our participants will learn from the experiences of online consultation in the UK Parliament (e.g. Hansard Society, 2006). Flexibility in the degree of openness is desirable; committees commonly include non-representatives in a different category of membership or have the power to invite them to give expert testimony.

3.1.4 Remote participation in legislative decision-making

Enable representatives to participate in decision-making while away from their assembly location, by providing a convenient remote and secure capability for them to express preferences or record their vote.

Representatives and assembly civil servants are interested in remote voting or (non binding) polling on legislative decisions. Three of the five assemblies participating in eRepresentative currently use electronic voting systems in plenary sessions. What most do not do, and now wish to explore, is electronically record the votes of members who are not present in the normal place of voting, whether that is the assembly chambers or a committee room.

Representatives talked of e-voting as a way of easing pressures on them to attend committee votes. Committees do have formal or informal arrangements for proxies to act for absent members. However very close election results have been a feature of recent European elections, placing pressure on such arrangements that make online (remote) working more attractive. The acceptability of remote working to committees is likely to depend largely on the flexibility provided, given their widely working practices.

Decision-making in some assemblies (e.g. the Dutch Parliament) involves committees acting largely by consensus to approve committee reports. In these, remote participation may best take the form of online polling, enabling views on non-binding decisions to be gauged until a consensus is achieved or voting initiated. Secret ballots are relatively rare in our participating assemblies, but include elections of representatives to official posts, where benefits are sought in the efficiency of the process.

4. CONCLUSIONS

Our interim conclusions are formed by relating the themes emerging from the eRepresentative requirements analysis to the recent studies of other European assemblies summarised earlier in the chapter. It is too early for the project to offer conclusions on the factors underlining the acceptability or otherwise of its prototype. However for each of the goals described in the preceding section, we discuss below the research questions to be asked in the investigation of eRepresentative's impact. These will be answered through qualitative analysis of interviews, field observations and systems usage (Whyte and Macintosh, 2002).

4.1 Improved Access: Actors' Roles and Document Interchange Issues

Senior civil servants among our participating assemblies are aware of the need to pay careful attention to possible conflicts between the facilitating roles of the civil servants who administer assembly business, and the political roles of the politicians they serve. Disparities in the uptake of ICT between them are commonly remarked upon. According to Snellen (2002) for example, "Document information systems and calendaring systems may facilitate the work of politicians as well as public servants and the public at large. Nevertheless, the impression from research is that public servants profit most, even from facilities that were especially created for politicians" (p.187).

Tangible benefit to public servants is a pre-requisite for acceptance. A well established factor in collaborative systems take-up is sufficient versatility and ease of use for administrative workers to use systems through choice rather than managerial mandate (Grudin and Palen, 1995) However current research lacks detailed assessments of the pros and cons traded-off when collaborative systems are implemented by parliamentary administrations.

Standardized ways to report committee deliberations, and provide access to such reports, and the documents discussed, may provide advantages in terms of efficiency, effectiveness and transparency that are apparent to public servants, yet seen by committee chairs and members as unwarranted intrusion into their working practices.

The research questions on this theme therefore focus on the pros and cons of standardizing how committees present their deliberations and associated documents, and on whether remote access to these documents allows representatives to realistically make use of them.

Q1. What characteristics of online document and delivery formats do committee members consider helpful to accessing legislative documents between meetings, and how do those characteristics fit with varying committee practices regarding confidentiality and accountability?

Q2. To what extent do eRepresentative desktop attempts to standardise the representation of committee actions affect the facilitating role of assembly staff?

4.2 Translation and Retrieval Issues

Terms used to describe legislative proposals by the information specialists in each assembly need to be translatable across their boundaries. This is partly addressed by the availability of common descriptors, implemented in the Eurovoc thesaurus (used in the national and regional assemblies).

Eurovoc descriptors support multi-language retrieval. However the effectiveness of any controlled vocabulary in giving precise search results is limited by issues of synonymy (different terms with similar meanings) and homonymy (similar terms with different meanings), which are likely to be exacerbated by differences in working practice between assemblies e.g. in the number of terms typically used to describe documents.

Effectiveness may also be impaired if descriptors are used to refer to legislative issues that have particular meanings within different nations' legal systems. For example van Laer (1998) mentions the term "family provision" as one with different meanings in English and continental European legal systems.

Language translation issues are of course significant and an additional issue. Assemblies have limited resources for human translation, and eRepresentative cannot add to them. However representatives themselves have language skills and often have contacts in other assemblies. One possibility to be explored then is the extent to which eRepresentative can help representatives to overcome language barriers by drawing on the language skills of their colleagues contacts, in their own and other assemblies.

These factors give rise to the following questions:

Q3. What characteristics of document descriptors most affect the elected representatives' ability to retrieve documents from other assemblies' collections that meet their relevance criteria?

Q4. What characteristics of search functionality and the terms used to express legislative issues relevant to elected representatives in one assembly help them to find documents from another assembly that are considered relevant to the same issue by its elected representatives?

4.3 The Politics of Reporting Time-Sensitive Developments

The need to address email overload is clear from studies cited earlier (Coleman and Nathanson, 2005, Cardoso et al., 2004). It is clearly vital therefore to appropriately balance 'push' and 'pull' aspects. In other words, emailing detailed information that apparently matches a representative's committee roles or interest profile will be counterproductive if the representative feels that the information is not specific enough or there is simply too much of it.

An effective notification service for committee events presupposes that representatives are provided with a consistent menu of possibilities across all relevant committees, and that the choices are to a level of detail that suits their needs. That may be difficult to achieve when committees vary in their working styles and their chair's ICT skills.

Effectiveness will depend also on whether it is *practical* for the representative to act on the information received when he or she gets it. As well as the more obvious concern that documents are readable on the device to hand, timing is likely to be crucial. In the legislative context, the meaning of 'timely' is seen as highly political. For example legislators notified that an opposing party has introduced a bill may choose to do nothing until the last possible moment, before introducing an amendment. Understanding how a notification service benefits them therefore calls for attention to their observed behavior as well as their reported views.

Q5. What characteristics of notification content, device form and location of use do committee members think help them receive and act upon timely information on their committee work, and which act as barriers?

Q6. What trade-offs are required between individual effort and perceived benefits from improved coordination, on the part of:

- committee chairs, clerks and support staff, to define generic notification events and provide the information to trigger notifications?
- representatives, to define a personal profile of events and topics that interest them?

4.4 Improved and More Transparent Collaboration and Consultation

Provision of a discussion facility for (secure) communication between *members of the same party* raises organizational- and party-political issues; an increase in the assembly administration's facilitative role may imply crossing into territory regarded as party political.

The value for other participants is also a key issue. Previous online parliamentary consultations in the UK have, for some, had unmet expectations of vigorous debate between elected representatives and members of the public. Other participants have felt the experience worthwhile as a way to appreciate unfamiliar views or life experiences (Hansard Society, 2006). The criteria for 'valuable online discussion' are likely to vary between assemblies, e.g. where MPs are regarded mainly as delegates of their party rather than as representatives of constituents.

Q7. How do issues of secure access affect participation in online discussion between members of the same political party, and the role of assembly staff in facilitating the legislative process?

Q8. What factors affect the value to committee members of online discussion on issues of common interest to their colleagues and other consulted stakeholders in their own or other assemblies?

4.5 Remote Participation in Legislative Decision-Making

Elected assemblies governing statutes commonly require members to attend committees *in person*. Moreover there is strong public pressure on representatives to be seen to be present in plenary sessions. As assembly proceedings are commonly televised and/or streamed live on the assembly's web portal, representatives are conscious that the public only consider them to be performing their role when they are visibly present in the chambers.

These are significant barriers to e-voting or any other form of remote participation in meetings. A convincing case would be required for assembly's to change their statutes to permit remote participation. The Catalonian Parliament offers a precedent for this, since its standing orders were changed following a previous pilot of Scytl's Pnyx.parliament e-voting platform. A pilot of e-polling and/or e-voting therefore needs to gather detailed evidence for and against deploying this technology.

Q9. What factors affect the ability of committee members to participate remotely in their committee's decision-making?

Q10. What evidence do representatives and other stakeholders consider relevant to the case for amending assembly statutes that currently require in-person attendance by committee members?

4.6 Overall Conclusions

The literature review and discussion of eRepresentative points to the need for elected representatives to effectively deploy:

- Tools to conduct, intervene in and analyze online dialogue with citizens and interest groups.
- Tools to assemble, access and comprehend a large and diverse range of texts and audio-visual material, in order to appreciate the breadth

and depth of knowledge and opinion represented online on issues of current concern.

Assemblies and their members also require the political will to marshal resources for the research, development and training needed to ensure elected representatives can use online tools effectively. Moreover 'good e-governance' requires a better appreciation of what can be accomplished if politicians begin to scrutinize information from online sources provided by government and parliamentary administrations as effectively as they would other forms of executive action, and start to lead and re-present online dialogue with the public as effectively as other forms of civic action.

ACKNOWLEDGEMENTS

The eRepresentative project (FP6-2004-26985) is part-funded by the European Commission. The author thanks colleagues in project partners the Catalonian Parliament, Dutch Parliament, Hungarian National Assembly, Lithuanian Parliament, Westmeath County Council, Gov2U, HP and Scytl.

REFERENCES

Anttiroiko, A-V (2004) Introduction to democratic e-governance. In: Mälkiä, M. and Savolainen, R. (eds.) eTransformation in governance. Idea Group Publishing, Hershey, PA. USA. pp. 22 - 49

Caldow, J. (1999) The Virtual Ballot Box: A Survey of Digital Democracy in Europe. Institute for Electronic Government, IBM Corporation

Cardoso, G., Cunha, C., and Nascimento, S. (2004) Ministers of parliament and information and communication technologies as a means of horizontal and vertical communication in Western Europe. Information Polity. 9: 29-40

Chadwick, A. (2003) Bringing E-Democracy Back In: Why it Matters for Future Research on E-Governance. Social Science Computer Review 21: 443 – 455

Cockburn, A. (2001) Writing Effective Use Cases. London: Addison Wesley

Coleman, S. and Nathanson, B. (2005) Learning to Live with the Internet: How European parliamentarians are adapting to the digital age. European Parliaments' research Initiative. Available at: http://www.epri.org/epriknowledge/contents/Home.php (May 2006).

Elvebakk, B. (2004) Virtually competent? Competence and experience with Internet-based technologies among European parliamentarians. Information Polity 9: 41-53.

EPRI (2005) Parliamentarians & ICTs: Awareness, understanding and activity levels of European Parliamentarians. European Parliamentary Research Association EPRI knowledge project D101 available at:
http://www.epri.org/epriknowledge/contents/Home.php (May 2006)

Gordon, T. (2004) e-governance and its Value for Public Administration. In: Malerba, D. (ed.) KDNet Symposium on Knowledge-Based Services for the Public Sector. Bonn, June 3 - 4, 2004

Grudin, J and L. Palen, L. (1995) Why groupware succeeds: Discretion or mandate? In Proceedings of the ECSCW'95, Kluwer Dordrecht, Netherlands, pp. 263-278

Hansard Society (2006) 'TellParliament.net Interim Evaluation Report' available at: http://www.hansardsociety.org.uk/programmes/e-democracy/tellparliament

Hoff, J. (2004) Members of parliaments' use of ICT in a comparative European perspective. Information Polity 9, pp. 5-16.

Jann, W. (2001) Managing Parliaments in the 21st Century: From Policy-Making and Public Management to Governance. In: Falconer, P., Smith, C. and Webster, C.W.R. Managing Parliaments in the 21st Century. IOS Press, Amsterdam.

Macintosh, A. (2004) Characterizing E-Participation in Policy-Making. System Sciences, 2004. Proceedings of the 37th Annual Hawaii International Conference (HICSS-37) 5-8 Jan. 2004 pp.117 – 126. ISBN: 0-7695-2056-1

OECD (2001) Citizens as Partners: Information, consultation and public participation in policy-making: Organization for Economic Cooperation and Development, Paris.

Snellen, I. (2002) Electronic Governance: implications for citizens, politicians and public servants. International Review of Administrative Sciences 68, pp. 183-198.

Trechsel, A. Kies, R, Mendez F. et al. (2003) Evaluation of the use of new technologies in order to facilitate democracy in Europe, University of Geneva. Available at: c2d.unige.ch/int/OverviewInstits/ Main_Report_final%201.pdf (May 2006)

van Laer, C.J.P. (1999) The impact of the internet on legal bibliography. In: Hondius, E. (ed.) Netherlands Reports to the Fifteenth Annual Congress on Comparative Law, Bristol, 1998 Oxford: Hart Publishing

Ward, S. and Lusoli, W. (2005) From Weird to Wired: MPs, the Internet and Representative Politics in the UK. Journal of Legislative Studies. 11: 57-81

Whyte, A. and Macintosh, A. (2002) Analysis and Evaluation of e-consultations; e-Service Journal. 2: pp.9-34

SUGGESTED READINGS

- Coleman, S. and Nathanson, B. (2005) Learning to Live with the Internet: How European parliamentarians are adapting to the digital age. European Parliaments' research Initiative. Available at: http://www.epri.org/epriknowledge/contents/Home.php (May 2006).
- Comprehensive review of current possibilities for ICT support to elected members of European assemblies, drawing on a survey of 'early adopters' among them.
- Falconer, P., Smith, C. and Webster, C.W.R. Eds. (2001) Managing Parliaments in the 21st Century. IOS Press, Amsterdam.
- Important collection describing problems and possibilities for assemblies to introduce management approaches from other public administration fields without encroaching on the powers of their elected members.
- Latour, B. and Weibel Eds. (2005) Making Things Public: Atmospheres of Democracy MIT Press: Boston, Mass. USA.

- Stimulating edited collection, including broader deliberations on the nature of parliaments, representation and the 'politics of things' (e.g. parliamentary architecture).

ONLINE RESOURCES

- eRepresentative project: http://www.erepresentative.org
- EPRI Knowledge project: http://www.epri.org/epriknowledge/contents/Home.php
- Eurovoc thesaurus: http://eurovoc.europa.eu/
- IPEX Interparliamentary EU Exchange: http://www.ecprd.org/ipex/
- Metalex project: http://www.metalex.nl/

QUESTIONS FOR DISCUSSION

1. From what political and theoretical perspectives would direct communication between public servants and citizens without involvement of elected politicians be considered desirable? From those perspectives, in what circumstances would their involvement be desirable?
2. What approaches should e-Government systems developers use to ensure that systems used primarily by public servants and citizens meet demands from elected politicians for effective scrutiny of their development and deployment?
3. How would you expect elected representatives to be involved in parliamentary and government online consultations, and how should the planning and design of each cater for their needs?

UNIT 2

Information Technology Research

Chapter 11

HISTORY OF DIGITAL GOVERNMENT RESEARCH IN THE UNITED STATES

Lawrence E. Brandt[1] and Valerie J. Gregg[2]

[1]Consultant, Arlington, Virginia, U.S.A. (lbrandt@nsf.gov), and [2]Assistant Director for Development, Digital Government Research Center, Information Sciences Institute, University of Southern California, Marina Del Rey, California, U.S.A. (vgregg@isi.edu)

CHAPTER OVERVIEW

In beginning to understand the phenomenon of electronic government, it will be useful to look at the history of the World Wide Web (WWW) as it swept through U.S. government agencies. At first, the Web was used by agencies for making public paper documents available online. Quickly it became apparent that Internet technologies could be used to improve the efficiency and effectiveness of government service delivery to citizens and other government agencies, yet many technological and public policy challenges would need to be solved when working in the electronic or digital government domain – e-Government faces different challenges than eBusiness. The U.S. National Science Foundation understood the need for identifying these challenges and in response to the research community and government practitioners established a digital government research program in 1997. This chapter provides context, background, case studies, references and the history of the digital government research program in the United States.

1. INTRODUCTION

Years before the Web sprang from the head of Tim Berners-Lee, the National Science Foundation (NSF) and the Defense Advanced Projects Agency supported the computer and network research that underpins the Web. In beginning to understand the phenomenon of electronic government, it will be useful to look at the history of the World Wide Web (WWW) as it swept through government agencies. Initially the Web began to be deployed primarily by scientific-oriented Federal agencies with high technical skills – NASA, the intelligence community, the Department of Energy's national laboratories – as early as 1993, with the release of the Mosaic browser and Apache server. At first, the Web was used by agencies for making public paper documents available online. The multimedia capabilities of Mosaic made the goal of duplicating paper attainable. This was a one to many broadcasting model. Next, agencies began to realize that their Web sites could contain agency internal information such as manuals and that these could be indexed and made searchable; a completely different model. One unexpected benefit was the re-examination of the approval process for release of information outside the agencies – many unnecessary steps were deleted and antiquated language improved, bringing the agency staff closer to the consumer of the information. Then came the direct release of public data in native form with the elimination of the middleman; in particular the Federal Statistical agencies pushed the envelope here (see FedStats discussion below). At state and local government levels, even more innovation could be found, as a result of the greater agility of smaller agencies and a better understanding of day-to-day needs of the citizen.

Before the Web, agencies were trying to use the Electronic Data Interface (EDI) to speed their business processes, but EDI was complex and the time and cost for implementing an EDI solution was high; a critical mass of agencies and vendors was not reached. The desire for electronic business remained, however, and the Web's capabilities were easily turned in this direction by agencies; at the same time the private sector was coming to a similar conclusion. Now the use of the Web in supporting agency business processes is commonplace and essential.

Uptake of the Web within an agency could usually be traced to a technical individual; often an independent sort who was highly enthused by the Web vision, the ease and availability of Web tools across all common operating systems, the open-source nature of Web software and the sense of community which arose. Senior agency staff was not only less enthused about the uncontrolled release of agency material being released, but often were unaware of the existence of those servers. Enlightened managers were willing to "let a thousand flowers bloom" for a while, but eventually control of an agency's Web presence would be re-established as new policy was established. In many cases, this control was implemented via required style templates that required all pages for a given agency to include common graphics, contact information, and naming schemes.

NSF was also one of the earliest agencies with a Web presence and quickly became a strong embracer of Web technologies to support its own key business processes (see award-winning fastlane.nsf.gov). The uptake of the Web in NSF's science and engineering research community in general was extraordinary (broad, deep, and fast) and many innovative applications were developed in the late 1990s to the benefit of government agencies in general. It became natural for Federal agencies to turn to NSF and the NSF research community for leadership, innovation, and strategic understanding.

NSF did not disappoint; it created the Federal World-Wide Web Consortium, and as described in the following sections of this chapter, NSF established a digital government research program. NSF understood that the emergence of the Internet and related applications fundamentally altered the environment in which government agencies conduct their missions and deliver services. The changes in underlying mechanisms of democracy and civic discourse are also pivotal. Concurrently, expectations of the public for government are being driven by their experience of the private sector's rapid uptake and use of information technologies in business-critical applications. Government requirements may inform the needs of large enterprises in the private sector. However, business models for IT uptake and usage are not necessarily or easily transferable to government, which is unique in a number of ways including: 1) Distributing activities, data, and services across multiple agencies at local, regional, tribal, state, Federal, and international levels of government; 2) collecting, interpreting, and maintaining large and societally-important public data and government records; 3) Delivering services to citizens, regardless of location, income level, or capability; 4) Maintaining a compact of trust, privacy, and reliability with citizens; 5) Preserving and archiving important governmental digital objects in perpetuity; and, 6) Implementing societal mores, expressed in law, regulation, and administrative procedures.

Responding to these unique aspects, DG grants are expected to develop new scientific understanding of the application and impact of information technologies (IT) on both government missions and on democracy. Digital Government proposals should focus on: 1) Research that advances information technologies applied in support of governmental missions; and/or 2) Research that enhances understanding of the impact of IT on the structures, processes, impact and outcomes within government, both from the perspective of government agencies and from the viewpoint of the citizenry at large. Multidisciplinary projects that simultaneously advance IT in governmental applications and that provide new knowledge of the impact of this work on society are strongly encouraged. The projects draw upon the expertise of researchers in computer and information science and in the social sciences as well as other sciences, and in many cases require a partnership with stakeholders—government practitioners.

2. LITERATURE REVIEW AND OVERVIEW OF THE FIELD

For three years, starting in 1994, a dozen Federal agencies (the Federal Web Consortium) combined resources to support the software development group of the University of Illinois' National Center for Supercomputing Applications. The software of interest was known as Mosaic (see below). This "experiment" proved that government agencies with varying missions could benefit from collaboration with researchers on IT development of joint interest at the same time as academics learned by working with real world problems and data. The agencies moved beyond the Mosaic technologies once the marketplace produced Web browsers and agreed to explore other technologies that would be useful to the agencies, such as firewalls, universal access technologies, the Java programming language and data mining and integration. The collaborating agencies called themselves the Federal World Wide Web Consortium.

It is common practice for the academic research community to bring to NSF's attention new areas of intellectual curiosity. Typically, the agency then will convene a workshop to more fully explore the domain. This was the case for digital government research as well and the initial digital government research program solicitation can be traced from this first workshop.

The 1997 NSF-sponsored workshop[1] organized by Herbert Schorr (ISI/USC) and Salvatore Stolfo (Columbia) brought computer and information science researchers and government practitioners together to define a compelling research agenda. Research topics with a special focus on the unique characteristics of the Federal information services domain include storing and archiving information, finding and accessing information, integrating information from multiple sources, mining and knowledge discovery, universal access to information, validating and visualizing

---

[1] The workshop report Towards the Digital Government of the 21st Century; A Report from the Workshop on Research and Development Opportunities in Federal Information Services can be found at: http://www.dgsociety.org/library/workshops.php

information, security, privacy and electronic commerce. The report identified some of the unique attributes the digital government domain provided researchers including i) the scale, breadth and complexity of government systems, applications and services, and ii) the requirement that government serve all citizens fairly, equally and in a trustworthy manner. The workshop participants were enthused about academic/government collaborations, and strongly recommended that the NSF establish a research program in Digital Government and encouraged NSF to work with other agencies to fund such a program.

While the initial workshop and call for proposals from NSF focused on computer and information sciences, it soon became evident that the digital government research domain was ripe with social science-related challenges. NSF-sponsored two important workshops that helped to broaden the program beyond the Federal government by defining a social science research agenda for digital government.

The first of these workshops, organized by Dr. Sharon Dawes (SUNY Albany), focused on understanding the interrelationships between multiple levels of government and other segments of society including citizens, businesses and non-governmental organizations. This 1998 workshop identified research ideas that had the potential to be of use in government. The report[2] describes eight specific needs: 1) Interoperable systems that are trusted and secure, 2) Methods and measures of citizen participation in democratic practices, 3) Models of electronic public service transactions and delivery systems, 4) New models for public-private partnership and other networked organization forms, 5) Intuitive decision-support tools for public officials, 6) Archiving and electronic records management, 7) Better methods for IT management, and 8) Matching research resources to government needs.

The second workshop[3], organized by Dr. Jane Fountain and held in 2002, advanced a basic social science research program for digital government. The workshop report states:

> "The purpose of the workshop was to broaden and deepen the research base for digital government by drawing more extensively and strategically on the social and policy sciences to expand the range of theories and conceptual frameworks that might be leveraged in this domain. A powerful research base is intended to foster a stronger

---

[2] The workshop report *Some Assembly Required: Building a Digital Government for the 21st Century* can be found at http://www.ctg.albany.edu/publications/reports/some_assembly

[3] The workshop report *Information, Institutions and Governance: Advancing a Basic Social Science Research Program for Digital Government* is Working Paper Number: RWP03-004 and can be found at: http://www.umass.edu/digitalcenter/Research/working_papers/rwp03_004_fountain.pdf

democratic society; to build capacity for policymaking, government operations, and service delivery; and to maintain the ability of the United States to lead digital government research and practice internationally."

The research agenda outlined could lead to 1) a knowledge base that could provide greater understanding of the interdependence among IT, organizations, governance for researchers, decision-makers and IT developers, 2) Research results and understanding to build more effective government that is responsive to citizens in terms of accuracy, speed, convenience, cost and access; democratic in its structures and processes; and secure and reliable, and 3) Insights, tools and frameworks for government decision-makers and those charged with building and managing digital government.

In response to these workshop recommendations, beginning in 1998 NSF released an annual series of calls for research proposals in the Digital Government area, initially soliciting technical proposals with Federal government and academic research collaborations. By 2003, NSF had opened the Digital Government research program to all levels of government, from international to local and had broadened its interest to include social science, with a strong interest in proposals featuring social and computer science research.

It is clear that this decision to create a program in digital government was the right one, for in the course of eight years, NSF received over 600 Digital Government proposals for research, made over 170 grants, and committed over $70 million from NSF and from over 50 government partner agencies. Of these awards, 27 were for relatively small planning or start-up grants, and 25 were for workshops. This is indicative of the need for a proactive program management style. Throughout the Digital Government program, but especially in its early years, the Program Managers recognized that it would take some time for agencies to connect with academic researchers and vice versa. Workshops to develop research agendas in such government domains as e –rulemaking, crisis management and response, e-voting and on-line citizen identity offered an arena in which the different sectors could meet and begin to "speak each other's language". Planning grants offered a similar, but a more in-depth, opportunity to understand each other's interests.

3. CASE STUDIES

3.1 Mosaic and the Federal WWW Consortium - An Existence Proof for Digital Government Research

In 1992, the software development group of the National Center for Supercomputing Applications (NCSA) at the U. of Illinois discovered the work of Tim Berners-Lee of the European high-energy research center CERN. Dr. Berners-Lee had developed the initial vision and protocols for the World Wide Web. NCSA immediately began to develop their own browser and Web server, adding many features to increase the Web's capabilities and attractiveness; primary the ability to display multi-media information. NCSA's software was christened Mosaic, and it was first released in early 1993, running on Unix.

Mosaic was a sensation and NCSA was soon inundated by demands for greater stability, features, licensing, etc. In late 1993, Mosaic for Windows and the Macintosh was released, adding to the tidal wave. NSF agreed to accept a proposal from NCSA that requested $1M annually for 3 years. The merit review of the proposal was positive though it was clear that the proposal was not basic research, but rather what might now be called CyberInfrastructure (see below).

Word of Mosaic spread quickly through Federal agencies, other NSF research programs, and the broad NSF academic community. Agencies with traditional research interests, such as NASA, NSF, and the National Library of Medicine were the first. The software was demonstrated to various government organizations; one of these was Vice President Gore's National Performance Review team. Two NPR staffers from the Nuclear Regulatory Commission (Neil Thompson and Janet Thot-Thompson) collaborated with NSF to develop a model for involving agencies and deriving funds for NCSA's proposal; it was decided to raise the funding in $100,000 chunks from interested NSF programs, NRC, and other Federal agencies. Soon the NSF/NCSA Federal World-Wide Web Consortium was born. By 1994, the Consortium was in place, and during the next three years a dozen agencies participated.

The Consortium served as part of NSF's oversight process for NCSA's work; the agencies provided interesting data, user experience, and other drivers for the Mosaic software development, adding such things as public/private key security elements and HTML protocol additions (tables in particular) to support access by disabled persons. In addition to software development, NCSA staff provided training for agencies while learning more about the agencies' missions and interests.

As the Consortium entered its second year, some of the technical agencies lost interest, but by that time other agencies not IT research-oriented had joined, such as the Dept. of Housing and Urban Development, the Bureau of the Census, the Bureau of Labor Statistics, the Defense Technical Information Center, and others. In 1995, to respond to the need for Federal training and education, the Consortium created the first annual Federal Webmasters Workshop, with an attendance of about 800 on the NIH campus. By 1999 Web software had become well commercialized, and the

Consortium handed off the workshop to a set of agencies without IT research missions, headed by the General Services Administration. Over the next year the research-based Federal Web Consortium faded away.

Commercialization was on the horizon quickly. Marc Andreesen, the leader of the undergraduate developers of Mosaic, started Netscape in partnership with Jim Clark, a successful commercial technologist. Andreesen moved to Silicon Valley and recruited many of the Mosaic development team to join him; an especially high-bandwidth form of technology transfer. Mosaic was licensed non-exclusively to a small number of companies, and finally a master license was signed with Spyglass, Inc., a small Illinois company, which in turn licensed the software to Microsoft. Finally, and perhaps of greatest impact, the NCSA Web server software was turned over to a group of software developers around the world. Features were added and changes made, and the software was released as no-cost open-source, under the new name of Apache. The Apache server software is still free, still being enhanced, and has remained the most commonly used Web server software on the Internet. Mosaic was named the product which has most shaped today's networking industry by Network Computing magazine; the Apache server was rated number six (see the full article at http://www.network computing.com/ 1119/1119f1products_intro.html).

The success of the Mosaic experience was not lost on NSF, as NSF created a more general opportunity to encourage and fund proposals in digital government broadly speaking (see above).

3.2 The Federal Statistics Agencies

The Federal Statistical community (over 100 agencies and offices of the Federal Government have a statistical function) has had a successful collaboration with NSF digital government researchers on how to improve the Federal Statistical community's data and information dissemination programs. The NSF's DG program funded more than a dozen "FedStats"[4] research projects that examined such topics as privacy and confidentiality issues in microdata files, new ways to display information contained in statistical tables, tools and methods for automatically building metadata, distributed architectures for data integration, and data collection technologies such as those involved in the use of handheld devices and wireless data transmission.

---

[4] The Interagency Council on Statistical Policy, headed by Katherine Wallman, Chief Statistician of the United States, established and directs the award winning "one-stop shopping for Federal statistics" web portal known as "FedStats". See: http://www. fedstats.gov.

As one of the first set of Federal agency partners with the NSF in its Digital Government program, the statistical agencies improved upon their historical tradition of being in the forefront in exploring new and novel ways to better handle the ever-increasing volume of data that flow from the varied statistical programs of the U.S. government. In turn, the NSF and the research community came to recognize that the Federal Statistical agencies have a unique challenge in ensuring that statistical information is collected and provided to the public in as robust and reliable manner as possible, while ensuring that cost-efficiencies are achieved. The individuals who made this exemplary collaboration are listed in the Acknowledgment section below.

4. CONCLUSIONS AND DISCUSSION

A few of the many lessons learned as the NSF digital government research program has progressed include:

Managing expectations of researchers and government practitioners

It must be kept in mind that most research is not successful in accomplishing what was originally proposed. Consistent success is, in NSF's eyes, an indicator that the original work was not sufficiently innovative. NSF-style research must be cutting edge. Further, government agencies' mental models of useful systems are based on commercial software. In the formation of a government-academic research partnership, care must be taken to set expectations correctly, i.e. the academic vs. the government reward systems must both be accounted for.

Academics need to publish results of cutting edge research; commonplace research conclusions are not interesting nor do they support the progress of an academic's career path. On the other hand, Government agencies are inherently risk-averse; often it is more important that one avoid failures than to have success. It is quite challenging for agencies to work collaboratively with each other let alone introducing researchers to the equation.

There are a few Federal government agencies whose needs press against the cutting edge of research, but most agency missions can be accomplished through procurement of commercial software. A related truth is that academic researchers will not be successful in developing and supporting software that is hardened and suitable for operational environments. Even so, agencies in a successful partnership with academic researchers can have confidence that the partnership will help inform their strategic planning over a 3-7 year timeframe.

Technology and knowledge transfer[5]

With a very successful product as a result of a Digital Government project, there may be a desire to transition the software to some organization with an interest in supporting it and making it more "bullet-proof". This is made somewhat easier since NSF gives the intellectual property to the grantee (the university receiving the grant) and because most universities understand the potential profit of innovative software. There are several possible paths to transition technology: 1) Launch or collaborate with a start-up company to develop and market a commercial product, 2) Release the software under an open source licensing agreement, 3) Release the software directly to the government agency where it could be (perhaps completely) re-implemented within the context of existing software systems, and, 4) Hire a team of software consultants to develop the production version of the system, tailored to the needs of the government agency.

Whatever path is chosen, it is more likely to be successful if it is put in place as early as possible.

International Digital Government

Over the past decade, growing evidence demonstrates the emergence of a global field of inquiry at the intersection of government, society, and information and communication technologies. This domain is often characterized by "e-government," "e-governance," "information society," and other related terms. The United States uses the term "digital government" to encompass this collection of research ideas. In the US, the NSF's Digital Government Research Program has provided leadership and support for this relatively new domain of research. In Europe, the European Commission, as part of its Information Society Technologies (IST) program [http://europa.eu.int/information_society/activities/e-Government_research/index_en.htm], sponsors an ambitious e-government research program. At the same time, the research councils of individual European states support comparable research programs within their borders. Similar efforts are established or emerging in Canada, Australia, India, the Pacific Rim, Latin America, and Africa. International organizations such as the United Nations and World Bank support e-government development and are also becoming interested in associated research.

Because of the relative newness of the DG field, there is insufficient interaction among researchers in different countries compared to what one finds in more established scientific disciplines. As this is a relatively new domain of inquiry, it involves multiple disciplines (a challenge within a single country, let alone internationally) and there are very few support mechanisms and forums to engage DG researchers with their peers working

---

[5] This example is courtesy of Dr. Lois Delcambre, Portland State University.

in this domain around the globe. Furthermore, once a potential collaboration starts that could lead to joint research efforts, it is logistically and financially difficult to sustain it to the point of joint research proposals and reliably funded projects. Consequently, comparative and transnational issues in DG, which are of growing importance in an increasingly networked world, are not receiving the attention they deserve.

The NSF's DG research program has awarded a four-year effort (2005 – 2009) to create a framework for a sustainable global community of practice among digital government researchers and research sponsors. The project will support an international reconnaissance study describing the current status of digital government research, an annual research institute, a framework for several international working groups, and travel support for US investigators and doctoral students to participate actively in international conferences and workshops. Project results will be disseminated widely using a variety of publication and communication channels (for more information, see: http://www.ctg.albany.edu/projects/dgi).

DG and CyberInfrastructure (CI)

Looking a bit to the future for Digital Government research, one important new possibility is the NSF initiative in CyberInfrastructure (see http://www.nsf.gov/dir/index.jsp?org=OCI). CI is intended to provide reliable IT services in support of research; at present CI is exemplified by NSF's national advanced computing centers and a variety of networking activities, including the development of middleware such as the Teragrid. Very soon there will be working examples of CI in support of data services such as distributed repositories and long-term archiving. As holders of societally important data, government will have a strong role. In fact, the notion of 'infrastructure' is implicitly governmental and the use of cyber-infrastructure to label a large-scale development effort must also be strongly tied to government support for the common good. Following over the next several years will be services such as identity management, privacy, and other foundational technologies that are more useful the more they are used. As these capabilities are developed in the research community, they will naturally be of interest to government and the citizenry on topics such as ubiquitous and reliable service, universal access, confidentiality, privacy, and information collection, sharing and evaluation[6].

---

[6] See 2003 whitepaper entitled "*Digital Government and Cyberinfrastructure*" by Yigal Arens, Jamie Callan, Sharon Dawes, Eduard Hovy, Jane Fountain and Gary Marchionini. http://www.dgsociety.org/library/library/pdf/dg_cyberinfrastructure.pdf

ACKNOWLEDGEMENTS

Without the strategic vision of the National Science Foundation, digital government research in the United States would not have advanced so far. In particular, the authors wish to acknowledge the guidance and support over the past nine years by Drs. Peter Freeman, Ruzena Bajcsy, Michael Pazzani, Rick Adrion, Suzi Iacono, and Melvyn Ciment. Under the able leadership of Janet Thot-Thompson and Neil Thompson, the Federal World Wide Web Consortium of Federal Government agencies, a precursor to the digital government research program, proved that agencies could and would collaborate with academic researchers trying to solve common technology and policy challenges. The U.S. Bureau of the Census committed early in the digital government program's history by enabling Valerie Gregg to work with Larry Brandt at NSF to build the digital government program. Special thanks go to Arnold Jackson and Richard Swartz (Associate Directors for Information Technology) for their willingness to let Valerie pursue the digital government vision. The Federal Statistical Community under the leadership of Katherine Wallman (Chief Statistician of the United States) and Cathryn Dippo (Bureau of Labor Statistics--retired), committed time, energy, and resources by collaborating with digital government researchers on a breadth of projects. USC's Digital Government Research Center at the Information Sciences Institute, under the untiring leadership of Dr. Yigal Arens, organized the annual research conferences that helped to build this multi-disciplinary, cross-sector, and now, international community. The authors also wish to acknowledge the organizers of over twenty-five research workshops in the digital government domain funded by NSF. Finally, without the imagination and dedication of each principle investigator and their government practitioner partners, the digital government research program would have never been possible.

REFERENCES

The most complete source of digital government references can be found in over twenty research workshop reports, the proceedings from seven annual digital government research conferences, and in several special issue magazines and journals.

Digital government research workshops cover a wide range of topics including electronic voting, biodiversity and ecosystem informatics, long-term preservation of digital information, crisis response and management, electronic rulemaking, sustainable development, and identity management. These workshop reports and many others can be found at:
http://www.dgsociety.org/library/workshops.php

The electronic proceedings from the seven (dgo2000 – dgo2006) annual digital government research conferences can be found at http://www.dgsociety.org/library

Three special issue magazines feature digital government research articles. These include:

- *Computer*; December 2005, Volume 38, Number 12, IEEE Computer Society.[7]
- *Communications of the Association for Computing Machinery*, January 2003, Volume 46, Number 1.[8]
- *Computer*; February 2001, Volume 34, Number 2, IEEE Computer Society.[9]

One special issue of *Social Science Computer Review*; Spring 2004, Volume 22, Number 1, Sage Publications.[10]

SUGGESTED READINGS

In the previous sections, we've identified many of the key works that encapsulate the essence of why digital government research is intellectually challenging for academics while at the same time providing government practitioners an opportunity to glimpse the future, both in terms of new technologies and the effect technologies could have on public policies. There are several further readings that provide additional intellectual insights into the digital government research domain.

The National Research Council's Computer Science and Telecommunications Board received an award from the NSF's digital government to undertake an independent study of the digital government domain. The four-year study resulted in the seminal work entitled *Information Technology Research, Innovation and E-Government* published in 2002. The report was based in part on two CSTB workshops (*Information Technology Research in Crisis Management* and *Information Technology Research in Federal Statistics*) held in 1998 and 1999 respectively [11].

---

7 http://csdl2.computer.org/persagen/DLAbsToc.jsp?resourcePath=/dl/mags/co/&toc= comp/mags/co/2005/12/rztoc.xml

8 http://portal.acm.org/toc.cfm?id=602421&coll=ACM&dl=ACM&type=issue&idx=J79&part=periodical&WantType=periodical&title=Communications of the ACM&CFID=78420671&CFTOKEN=93420686

9 http://csdl2.computer.org/persagen/DLAbsToc.jsp?resourcePath=/dl/mags/co/&toc=comp/mags/co/2001/02/r2toc.xml

10 http://hcl.chass.ncsu.edu/sscore/toc22n1.htm

11 The three NRC/CSTB reports can be found at: http://www.dgsociety.org/library/workshops.php

The most important finding of this report in developing an NSF digital government research program was the following:

> "Finding 3.2. A cooperative alliance between researchers and agency end users in defining requirements for new IT-based capabilities has benefits for both groups. Researchers gain a better understanding of the real challenges and obstacles, along with access to data and artifacts that can inform or validate design. Agency users, especially those that lack in-house research capability gain understanding of emerging and future technologies. By collaborating directly, the two groups can converge more rapidly on requirements that meet real needs and that are technologically achievable - and that may not have been expected by either party in advance of the collaboration."

Other recommendations and findings of this report include: 1) Realizing the potential of digital government will require technical progress, but this will not succeed unless progress is made on other fronts; i.e., organization, policy, technology transition, systems architecture and engineering practice. 2) Government should follow the commercial trend toward integrated services, moving from program or agency-centered services to user-center services that aggregate services from multiple agencies and private-sector third parties. 3) Government can leverage its dual roles as a user of IT and as an investor in IT research, thus increasing its awareness of IT advances at the cutting edge and influencing commercial products. 4) Government needs to improve its program management practices in transition of new technology to the commercial marketplace. and, 5) Federal government should provide a centrally-managed cross-agency technology innovation fund to encourage risk-taking[12].

ON LINE RESOURCES

There are several key sources of on line information relevant to better understanding digital government-related research. These sources include:

- The Digital Government Society of North American (DGSNA) website provides information of particular interest including various digital government research workshop reports and the annual research conference proceedings (http://www.dgsociety.org). For over five years, the National Science Foundation sponsored a digital government

---

[12] Recommendation 5 was never implemented despite several years of effort by Mark Forman, the US Office of Management and Budget's director for E-government.

research website, http://www.digitalgovernment.org, which is no longer in use; its content is maintained on the DGSNA website.

- The official E-Government website of the United States: http://www.whitehouse.gov/OMB/e-gov/
- The Digital Government Research Center website: http://www.dgrc.org
- The Center for Technology in Government website at Albany, State University of New York: http://www.ctg.albany.edu
- The National Center for Digital Government website the University of Massachusetts in collaboration with Harvard University's John F. Kennedy School of Government: http://www.umass.edu/digitalcenter/index.php?id=Links&page=index
- The National Science Foundation website as a whole, with special emphasis on two particular subordinate pages: the Division of Information and Intelligent Systems (home of digital government research activity) and the Office of Cyberinfrastructure: http://www.nsf.gov; http://www.nsf.gov/div/index.jsp?div=IIS; and, http://www.nsf.gov/dir/index.jsp?org=OCI
- The European Commission's E-Government Program: http://europa.eu.int/information_society/activities/eGovernment_research/index_en.htm
- The European E-Government Society: http://www.uni-koblenz.de/FB4 Institutes/IWVI/AGVInf/community/eogov-s

QUESTIONS FOR DISCUSSION

1. What lessons can be drawn from the Federal Web Consortium as a model for introducing IT research into government agencies. What barriers were encountered? Are there other examples of consortia that jump-started innovations and then stepped aside as innovations matured into practice?
2. What value do you see in doing DG research from a researcher perspective? From a practitioner's perspective? In both cases, what are the challenges to this kind of research?
3. What are the incentives to engage in DG research from the private sector perspective? How do these mesh with the incentives of academics and civil servants?
4. Can you think of examples of dg-type multidisciplinary research projects?

5. Can you think of global challenges that should be studied through a digital government lens?
6. Can you think of ways to evaluate the progress and success of DG initiatives?

Chapter 12

DATA AND KNOWLEDGE INTEGRATION FOR E-GOVERNMENT

Eduard Hovy

Information Sciences Institute, University of Southern California, Marina del Rey, California, U.S.A. (hovy@isi.edu)

CHAPTER OVERVIEW

Data integration is one of the most significant IT problems facing government today. Using information technology, government agencies have collected vastly more data than was ever possible to collect before. Unfortunately, for lack of standardization, most government data today exists in thousands of different formats and resides in hundreds of systems and versions, spread across dozens of agencies. This situation makes the data almost impossible to find, re-use, and build upon after further data collection. A considerable amount of research has been performed over the past decades to overcome this problem. Within Digital Government, several projects have focused on government data collections. Three principal approaches have been followed: (1) direct access, using information retrieval techniques; (2) metadata reconciliation, using ontology alignment techniques; and (3) data mapping, using information theoretic techniques. This chapter discusses each approach, and provides specific examples of the last two.

1. INTRODUCTION

Government is, in principle, a data-intensive enterprise: in the ideal case, the more data available about some issue, organization, or individual, the better decisions government agencies can make. Information technology has enabled government agencies to collect vastly more data than was ever possible before. But this ability comes at a cost: in order to be useful, the data must be properly organized, standardized, and maintained. Unfortunately the situation most characteristic of present-day government in almost all its branches is that much data has been collected, and stored, but has not been stored in a uniform way, in a common representation, or using a standardized system. That is, the data may reside in hundreds of different formats, systems, and versions. While the information might be somewhere, the user often doesn't know where to find it, how to access it, or how to convert all variations of it to a single useful format.

It is therefore no surprise that one of the most significant problems experienced by government agencies is data and knowledge integration. Reconciling the differences across data collections is not a trivial matter. Data and information integration involves several aspects: recognizing that two data sets describe the 'same' topic; understanding their differences (in numerous ways, including specificity, accuracy, and coverage); creating a common description or framework of metadata for them; establishing equivalences by performing data mapping across the data collections; and possibly converting the actual data from one or more data sources into a common form.

One of the principal problems facing efforts to integrate nonhomogeneous data sets is terminology standardization: what one agency calls *salary* another might call *income*, and a third might call *wages* (even while it may have something else entirely that it calls *salary*). Defining *exactly* what data has been obtained, and making sure that the actual method of data capture employed did in fact accurately observe the specifications, is a task for specialists, and may require some very sophisticated analysis and description. It is not uncommon for specialists in different government agencies to spend weeks or even months understanding precisely what differences exist between their respective data collections, even when to the untrained eye the collections seem essentially identical. For example, it makes a difference when you want to record gasoline prices in a given area not only in which locations you measure the prices, but also whether you measure the prices every Tuesday or once a month, for example. Determining how significant the differences in measurement are, and deciding how to reconcile them (simple numerical average? Average weighted by volume sold?) into a single number, is a matter of interpretation, and may easily have unexpected policy consequences—after all, the results will presumably used by some lawmaker or reported in some publication, or by the press. Not only technically difficult, the data integration process is fraught with potential unexpected legal and social ramifications.

Several IT researchers have performed research on data and information integration with e-Government data collections. As can be expected, most of them have avoided the definitive final integration, mostly by providing tools and/or methods that government specialists can use to make their own integration decisions. Three principal approaches exist:

- Direct access, using information retrieval techniques
- Metadata reconciliation, using ontology alignment techniques
- Data mapping, using information theoretic techniques

We discuss these in the next section, and provide specific examples of the last two in Section 3.

2. OVERVIEW OF THE FIELD

2.1 Direct Access using Information Retrieval

Direct access methods do not aim to provide a single uniform perspective over the data sources. Rather, along the lines of web search technology like Google, the IT tools return to the user all data pertinent to his or her request, after which the user must decide what to do. As one might expect, this approach works best for textual, not numerical, data. Typically, the technology inspects metadata and the text accompanying the metadata, such as documentation, commentary, or footnotes (Gravano et al., 1994; Lewis and Hayes, 1994; Pyreddy and Croft, 1997; Xu and Callan, 1998)

Experience with traditional forms of metadata such as controlled vocabularies shows that it is expensive and time-consuming to produce, that authors often resist creating it, and that information consumers often have difficulty relating their information need to pre-specified ontologies or controlled vocabularies. Controlled vocabularies and relatively static metadata ontologies are difficult to update and hence not really suitable to support the rapid integration of new information that must be easy for the general population to use and that must be maintained at moderate expense.

To address this problem, one approach is to try to generate metadata automatically, using language models (lists of basic vocabulary, phrases, names, etc., with frequency information) instead of ontologies or controlled vocabularies. These language models are extracted by counting the words and phrases appearing in the texts accompanying the data collections. Most retrieval systems use term frequency, document frequency, and document length statistics.

This approach has been adopted by information retrieval researchers (Callan et al., 1995; Ponte and Croft, 1998). It is based on older work on the automatic categorization of information relative to a controlled vocabulary or classification hierarchy (Lewis and Hayes, 1994; Larkey, 1999). Ponte and Croft (1998) infer a language model for each document and to estimate the probability of generating the query according to each of these models. Documents are then ranked according to these probabilities. Research by Callan et al. (1999) shows that language models enable relatively accurate database selection. More details of this approach, and a comparison with the following one, appear in (Callan et al., 2001).

2.2 Metadata Reconciliation

Almost all data collections are accompanied by metadata that provides some definitional information (at the very least, provides the names and types of data collected). Given several data collections in a domain, people often attempt to enforce (or at least enable) standardization of nomenclature, and facilitate interoperability of IT across data sources, by creating centralized metadata descriptions that provide the overarching data 'framework' for the whole domain. When the metadata for a specific data resource is integrated with this centralized framework, the data becomes interpretable in the larger context, and can therefore be compared to, and used in tandem with, data from other data collections similarly connected.

In the US, the government has funded several metadata initiatives, including the Government Information Locator Service (GILS) (http://www.gils.net/) and the Advanced Search Facility (ASF) (http://asf.gils.net/). These initiatives seek to establish a structure of cooperation and standards between agencies, including defining structural information (formats, encodings, and links). However, they do not focus on the actual creation of metadata, and do not define the algorithms needed to generate metadata.

A large amount of research has been devoted to the problem of creating general metadata frameworks for a domain, linking individual data collections' metadata to a central framework, and providing user access to the most appropriate data source, given a query (Baru et al., 1999; Doan et al., 2001; Ambite and Knoblock, 2000; French et al., 1999; Arens et al., 1996). Two major approaches have been studied. In the first, called the *global-as view,* the global model is defined and used as a view on the various data sources. This model first appeared in Multibase and later in TSIMMIS (Chawathe et al., 1994). In the second, called the *local-as view* or sometimes *view rewriting*, the sources are used as views on the global model (Levy,

1998). The disadvantage of the first approach is that the user must reengineer the definitions of the global model whenever any of the sources change or when new sources are added. The view rewriting approach does not suffer from this problem, but instead must face the problem of rewriting queries into data access plans for all the other sources using views, a problem that is NP-hard or worse.

Below we describe an example of a hybrid approach that defines the data sources in terms of the global model and then compiles the source descriptions into axioms that define the global model in terms of the individual sources. These axioms can be efficiently instantiated at run-time to determine the most appropriate rewriting to answer a query automatically. This approach combines the flexibility of the view rewriting with the efficiency of the query processing in Multibase and TSIMMIS.

To date, the general approach of integration by using metadata to find similarities between entities within or across heterogeneous data sources always requires some manual effort. Despite some promising recent work, the automated creation of such mappings at high accuracy and high coverage is still in its infancy, since equivalences and differences manifest themselves at all levels, from individual data values through metadata to the explanatory text surrounding the data collection as a whole.

2.3 Data Mapping

Formally defined metadata may provide a great deal of useful information about a data source, and thereby greatly facilitate the work of the IT specialist required to integrate it with another data source. But all too often, the metadata is sketchy, and sometimes even such basic information as data column headings are some kind of abbreviated code. In addition, such auxiliary data can be outdated, irrelevant, overly domain specific, or simply non-existent. A general-purpose solution to this problem cannot therefore rely on such auxiliary data. All one can count on is the data itself: a set of observations describing the entities.

A very recent approach to data integration skirts metadata altogether, and focuses directly on the data itself. Necessarily, this data-driven paradigm requires some method to determine which individual data differences are significant and which are merely typical data value variations. To date, the approach focuses on numerical data only. The general paradigm is to employ statistical / information theoretic techniques to calculate average or characteristic values for data (sub)sets, to then determine which values are unusual with respect to their (sub)set, and to compare the occurrences of unusual values across comparable data collections in order to find corresponding patterns. From such patterns, likely data alignments are then proposed for manual validation. Davis et al. (2005) proposed a supervised learning algorithm for discovering aliases in multi-relational domains. Their method uses two stages. High recall is obtained by first learning a set of rules, using Inductive Logic Programming (ILP), and then these rules are used as the features of a Bayesian Network classifier. In many domains, however, training data is unavailable.

A different approach uses Mutual Information, an information theoretic measure of the degree to which one data value predicts another. Kang and Naughton (2003) begin with a known alignment to match unaligned columns after schema- and instance-based matching fails. Given two columns *A.x* and *B.x* in databases *A* and *B* that are known to be aligned, they use Mutual Information to compute the association strength between column *A.x* with each other column in *A* and column *B.x* and each other column in *B*. The assumption is that highly associated columns from *A* and *B* are the best candidates for alignment. Also using Mutual Information, the work of Pantel et al. (2005), which we describe in more detail below, appears to be very promising.

3. TWO EXAMPLES

In order to provide some detail, we describe EDC, an example database access planning system based on metadata reconciliation, and SIFT-Guspin, an example of the data mapping approach.

3.1 The EDC System[1]

The Energy Data Collection (EDC) project (Ambite et al., 2001; 2002) focused on providing access to a large amount of data about gasoline prices and weekly volumes of sale, collected in several quite different databases by government researchers at the US Energy Information Administration (EIA), the Bureau of Labor Statistics (BLS), the Census Bureau, and the California Energy Commission. In all, over 50,000 data tables were materialized and used in the final EDC system. The system could be accessed via various interfaces, including cascaded menus, a natural language question analyzer for English and Spanish (Philpot et al., 2004), and an ontology (metadata) browser. Other research in this project focused on data aggregation to integrate data collected at various granularities (Bruno et al., 2002), query and result caching for rapid access to very large data collections (Ross,

[1] Parts of this section were written by Jose Luis Ambite and Andrew Philpot.

2002), and the automated extraction of ontology terms from data glossary definitions (Klavans et al., 2002).

The principal problem was to develop a system that could present a single unified view of all the disparate, heterogeneous, data, in such as way as to support the needs both of experts and of users relatively unfamiliar with the data, such as journalists or educators, while also being formally specified so as to be used by an automated data access planner. This planner, inherited from the SIMS project (Ambite and Knoblock, 2000; Arens et al., 1996), used Artificial Intelligence techniques to decompose the user's query into a set of subqueries, each addressed to a specific database, and to recompose the results obtained from the various sources into a single response.

This research took the following approach. Rather than building domain models from scratch, the researchers adopted USC/ISI's 70,000-node terminology taxonomy (a very simple ontology) called SENSUS as overarching meta-model and extended it to incorporate new energy-related domain models. To speed up this process, they developed automated concept-to-ontology alignment algorithms (Hovy et al., 2001), and developed algorithms that extracted terms from data sources and clustered them in order to jump-start model building (Klavans et al., 2002; Hovy et al., 2003).

In order to connect SENSUS terms with the individual metadata models of each source database, a domain model of approximately 500 nodes was created manually to represent the concepts present in the EDC gasoline domain, and manually connected to the various metadata models. This model was then semi-automatically linked into SENSUS using a new type of ontology link called *generally-associated-with* (GAW) that held between concepts in the ontology and domain model concepts. GAW links enabled the user while browsing to rapidly proceed from high-level (quite general and perhaps inaccurate) concepts to the (very specific and precise) domain model concepts associated with real data in the databases. In contrast to the links between data sources and domain model concepts, which were logical equivalences as required to ensure the correctness of SIMS reasoning, the semantics of GAW links was purposely vague. Such vagueness allowed a domain model concept (such as *Price*) to be connected to several very disparate SENSUS concepts (such as *Price, Cost, Money, Charge, Dollar, Amount, Fee, Payment, Paying,* etc.). Clearly, while these links cannot support automated inference, they can support the non-expert user, allowing him or her to start browsing or query formation with whatever terms are most familiar. In addition, the vague semantics had a fortunate side effect, in that it facilitated automated alignment of concepts from domain model to SENSUS.

A considerable amount of effort was devoted to developing semi-automated term-to-term alignment discovery algorithms (Hovy et al., 2001). These algorithms fell into three classes: name matches, with various heuristics on decomposing term names; definition matches, that considered term definitions and definitional descriptions from associated documents; and dispersal matches, that considered the relative locations in SENSUS of groups of candidate matches. A fairly extensive series of experiments focused on determining the optimal parameter settings for these algorithms, using three sets of data: the abovementioned EDC gasoline data, the NHANES collection of 20,000 rows of 1238 fields from a survey by the National Center for Health Statistics, and (for control purposes) a set of 60 concepts in 3 clusters extracted from SENSUS. Although the alignment techniques were never very accurate, they did significantly shorten the time required to connect SENSUS to the domain model, compared to manual insertion. For GAW links, they were quite well suited. Research in (semi-) automated ontology alignment is an ongoing and popular endeavor; see http://www.atl.lmco.com/projects/ontology/.

3.2 The SIFT-Guspin System[2]

Not all data is equally useful for comparison—some observations are much more informative and important than others. This work uses Pointwise Mutual Information to calculate the information content (approximately, the unpredictability) of individual data items in various data collections, and then compares groupings of unusual (i.e., unpredictable in surprising ways) ones across collections. In simple terms, the hypothesis of this work is that correspondences of unusual values are much more indicative of likely data alignments than correspondences that arise due to 'random' variation.

When assessing the similarity between entities, important observations should be weighed higher than less important ones. Shannon's theory of information (Shannon, 1948) provides a metric, called Pointwise Mutual measuring to what degree one event predicts the other. More precisely, the formula measures the amount of information one event x gives about another event y, where $P(x)$ denotes the probability that x occurs, and $P(x,y)$ the probability that they both occur:

$$mi(x,y) = \log \frac{P(x,y)}{P(x)P(y)}$$

Given a method of ranking observations according to their relative importance, one also needs a comparison metric for determining the

[2] Parts of this section were written by Patrick Pantel and Andrew Philpot.

similarity between two entities. An important requirement is that the metric be not too sensitive to *unseen* observations. That is, the absence of a matching observation does not as strongly indicate dissimilarity as the presence of one indicates similarity. Since not all distance metrics make this distinction (Euclidean distance, for example, does not), a good choice is the cosine coefficient, a common metric in which the similarity between each pair of entities e_i and e_j is given by:

$$sim(e_i, e_j) = \frac{\sum_o mi(e_i, o) \times mi(e_j, o)}{\sqrt{\sum_o mi(e_i, o)^2 \times \sum_o mi(e_j, o)^2}}$$

where o ranges through all possible observations. This formula measures the cosine of the angle between two pointwise mutual information vectors: a similarity of 0 indicates orthogonal (unrelated) vectors whereas a similarity of 1 indicates identical vectors.

Pantel et al. (2005; 2006) use individual data sets from various Environmental Protection Agency (EPA) offices in California and the US. In one experiment, they align data measuring air (pollution) quality collected by several of California's Air Quality Management Districts with corresponding data compiled by the central California Air Resources Board (CARB). The process of aligning all 26 districts' data with CARB's database, currently performed manually, takes about one year. The SIFT system, developed by Pantel and colleagues, used Pointwise Mutual Information to align the 2001 data collections (which cover facilities, devices, processes, permitting history, criteria, and toxic emissions) of the air pollution control districts of Santa Barbara County, Ventura County, and San Diego County, with that of CARB, over the period of a few weeks in total, once the system was set up and the data downloaded.

The Santa Barbara County data contained about 300 columns, and the corresponding CARB data collection approximately the same amount; a completely naïve algorithm would thus have to consider approximately 90,000 alignment decisions in the worst case. Using Pointwise Mutual Information, SIFT suggested 295 alignments, of which 75% were correct. In fact, there were 306 true alignments, of which SIFT identified 221 (or 72%). Whenever the system managed to find a correct alignment for a given column, the alignment was found within the topmost two ranked candidate alignments. Considering only two candidate alignments for each possible column obviously greatly reduces the number of possible validation decisions required of a human expert. Assuming that each of the 90,000 candidate alignments must be considered (in practice, many alignments are easily rejected by human experts) and that for each column the system were to output at most k alignments, then a human expert would have to inspect only $k \times 300$ alignments. For $k = 2$, only 0.67% of the possible alignment decisions must be inspected, representing an enormous saving in time.

The Guspin system, also developed at ISI, has been used to identify duplicates within several databases of air quality measurements compiled by the US EPA, including the CARB and AQMDs emissions inventories as well as EPA's Facilities Registry System (FRS). In summary, Guspin's performance on the CARB and Santa Barbara County Air Pollution Control District 2001 emissions inventories was:

- with 100% accuracy, Guspin extracted 50% of the matching facilities;
- with 90% accuracy, Guspin extracted 75% of the matching facilities;
- for a given facility and the top-5 mappings returned by Guspin, with 92% accuracy, Guspin extracted 89% of the matching facilities.

4. CONCLUSION

The problem of data and information integration is widespread in government and industry, and it is getting worse as legacy systems continue to appear. The absence of efficient large-scale practical solutions to the problem, and the promise of especially the information theoretic techniques on comparing sets of data values, make this an extremely rewarding and potentially high-payoff area for future research. Direct access and metadata alignment approaches appear to be rather inaccurate and/or still require considerable human effort. In contrast, the approach of finding possible alignments across data collections by statistical measures on the actual data itself holds great promise for the future.

ACKNOWLEDGEMENTS

The author wishes to thank Bruce Croft and Jamie Callan for help with Section 2.1, Jose Luis Ambite and Andrew Philpot for help with Section 3.1, and Patrick Pantel and Andrew Philpot for help with Section 3.2.

Writing this paper was funded in part by NSF grant no. EIA-0306899, dated 08/12/2003, awarded to the author under the NSF's Digital Government program.

REFERENCES

Ambite J.L. and C.A. Knoblock. 2000. Flexible and Scalable Cost-Based Query Planning in Mediators: A Transformational Approach. *Artificial Intelligence Journal*, 118(1–2).

Ambite, J.L., Y. Arens, E.H. Hovy, A. Philpot, L. Gravano, V. Hatzivassiloglou, and J.L. Klavans. 2001. Simplifying Data Access: The Energy Data Collection Project. *IEEE Computer* 34(2), February.

Ambite, J.L., Y. Arens, L. Gravano, V. Hatzivassiloglou, E.H. Hovy, J.L. Klavans, A. Philpot, U. Ramachandran, K. Ross, J. Sandhaus, D. Sarioz, A. Singla, and B. Whitman. 2002. Data Integration and Access: The Digital Government Research Center's Energy Data Collection (EDC) Project. In W. McIver and A.K. Elmagarmid (eds.), *Advances in Digital Government*, pp. 85–106. Dordrecht: Kluwer.

Arens, Y., C.A. Knoblock and C.-N. Hsu. 1996. Query Processing in the SIMS Information Mediator. In A. Tate (ed.), *Advanced Planning Technology*. Menlo Park: AAAI Press.

Baru, C., A. Gupta, B. Ludaescher, R. Marciano, Y. Papakonstantinou, and P. Velikhov. 1999. XML-Based Information Mediation with MIX. *Proceedings of Exhibitions Program of ACM SIGMOD International Conference on Management of Data.*

Bruno, N., S. Chaudhuri, and L. Gravano. 2002. Top-k Selection Queries over Relational Databases: Mapping Strategies and Performance Evaluation. *ACM Transactions on Database Systems*, 27(2), June 2002.

Callan, J., M. Connell, and A. Du. 1999. Automatic Discovery of Language Models for Text Databases. *Proceedings of the 1999 ACM-SIGMOD International Conference on Management of Data*, pp. 479–490.

Callan, J., Z. Lu, and W.B. Croft. 1995. Searching distributed collections with inference networks. *Proceedings of the Eighteenth Annual International ACM SIGIR Conference on Research and Development in Information Retrieval*, pp. 21–28.

Callan, J., W.B. Croft, and E.H. Hovy. 2001. Two Approaches toward Solving the Problem of Access to Distributed and Heterogeneous Data. In *DGnOnline*, online magazine for Digital Government. http://www.dgrc.org/dg-online/.

Chawathe, S., H. Garcia-Molina, J. Hammer, K. Ireland, Y. Papakonstantinou, J. Ullman, and J. Widom. 1994. The TSIMMIS Project: Integration of Heterogeneous Information Sources. *Proceedings of IPSJ Conference*, pp. 7–18.

Davis, J., I. Dutra, D. Page, and V.S. Costa. 2005. Establishing Identity Equivalence in Multi-Relational Domains. *Proceedings of the International Conference on Intelligence Analysis.*

Doan, A., P. Domingos, and A.Y. Halevy. 2001. Reconciling Schemas of Disparate Data Sources: A Machine-learning Approach. *Proceedings of SIGMOD-2001*, pp. 509–520.

French, J.C., A.L. Powell, J. Callan, C.L. Viles, T. Emmitt, and K.J. Prey. 1999. Comparing the performance of database selection algorithms. *Proceedings of the 22nd Annual International ACM SIGIR Conference on Research and Development in Information Retrieval.*

Gravano, L., H. García-Molina, and A. Tomasic. 1994. The effectiveness of GLOSS for the text database discovery problem. *Proceedings of SIGMOD 94*, pp. 126–137.

Hovy, E.H., A. Philpot, J.L. Klavans, U. Germann, P.T. Davis, and S.D. Popper. 2003. Extending Metadata Definitions by Automatically Extracting and Organizing Glossary Definitions. *Proceedings of the dg.o 2003 conference.* Boston, MA.

Hovy, E.H., A. Philpot, J.-L. Ambite, Y. Arens, J.L. Klavans, W. Bourne, and D. Sarioz. 2001. Data Acquisition and Integration in the DGRC's Energy Data Collection Project. *Proceedings of the NSF's National Conference on Digital Government dg.o 2001.*

Kang, J. and J.F. Naughton. 2003. On Schema Matching with Opaque Column Names and Data Values. *Proceedings of SIGMOD-2003.*

Klavans, J.L., P.T. Davis, and S. Popper. 2002. Building Large Ontologies using Web-Crawling and Glossary Analysis Techniques. *Proceedings of the NSF's National Conference on Digital Government dg.o 2002.*

Larkey, L. 1999. A Patent Search and Classification System. *Proceedings of Digital Libraries (DL 99).*

Levy, A.Y. 1998. The Information Manifold Approach to Data Integration. *IEEE Intelligent Systems* (September/October), pp. 11–16.

Lewis, D. and P. Hayes (eds.). 1999. Special issue on Text Categorization, *ACM Transactions on Information Systems*, 12(3).

Pantel, P., A. Philpot, and E.H. Hovy. 2005. An Information Theoretic Model for Database Alignment. *Proceedings of Conference on Scientific and Statistical Database Management (SSDBM-05)*, pp. 14–23.

Philpot, A., E.H. Hovy, and L. Ding. 2004. Multilingual DGRC AskCal: Querying Energy Time Series in English, Spanish, and Mandarin Chinese. System demo and description in *Proceedings of the NSF's National Conference on Digital Government dg.o 2004.*

Ponte, J. and W.B. Croft. 1998. A Language Modeling Approach to Information Retrieval. *Proceedings of the 21st International Conference on Research and Development in Information Retrieval*, pp. 275–281.

Pyreddy, P. and W.B. Croft. 1997. TINTIN: A System for Retrieval in Text Tables. *Proceedings of the ACM Conference on Digital Libraries*, pp. 193–200.

Ross, K.A. 2002. Conjunctive Selection Conditions in Main Memory. *Proceedings of the 2002 PODS Conference.*

Shannon, C.E. 1948. A Mathematical Theory of Communication. *Bell System Technical Journal*, 20, pp. 50–64.

Xu, J. and J. Callan. 1998. Effective retrieval of distributed collections. *Proceedings of the 21st Annual International ACM SIGIR Conference on Research and Development in Information Retrieval*, pp. 112–120.

SUGGESTED READINGS

- Access to textual data using Information Retrieval methods. A general overview appears in Turtle, H.R. and W.B. Croft, 1992. A comparison of text retrieval models. *Computer Journal*, 35(3), pp. 279–290. An early work on language models for IR is Ponte, J. 1998. *A Language Modeling Approach to Information Retrieval.* Ph.D. thesis, Computer Science Department, University of Massachusetts.

- Automated database access using an Artificial Intelligence planner to decompose user queries into database queries from individual databases and recompose them, within the approach of a central integrating metadata model. See Ambite J.L. and C.A. Knoblock. 2000. Flexible and Scalable Cost-Based Query Planning in Mediators: A Transformational Approach. *Artificial Intelligence Journal*, 118(1–2).

- General method of applying Pointwise Mutual Information to discover mappings across individual columns or rows of numerical data. See Pantel, P., A. Philpot, & E.H. Hovy. 2005. Data Alignment and Integration. *IEEE Computer* 38(12), pp. 43–51. For more details, see Pantel, P., A. Philpot, and E.H. Hovy. 2005. An Information Theoretic

Model for Database Alignment. *Proceedings of Conference on Scientific and Statistical Database Management (SSDBM-05)*, pp. 14–23.

QUESTIONS FOR DISCUSSION

1. Which of the three methods for data and information integration is most suitable for the following kinds of data?
   - Collections of workplace safety regulations and associated backup documents (studies, etc.)
   - Daily numerical readings of traffic density and flow in a city
   - Databases about crop characteristics (text) and annual growth (numbers)

   Why, in each case?

2. Let each student create a hierarchical (ontology-like) metadata model of foods (fruits, vegetables, meats, dairy products, baked foods, etc.), where each type contains between 1 and 4 defining characteristics. Include at least 20 different individual foods, and group them into types. Compare the various models for both content and organization. Are some models better than others? If so, why? If not, why not?

3. How would you use a search engine like Google to locate the most appropriate data table from a collection that contains only numerical information?

4. Build a system to compare numerical databases. First try simple column-by-column comparisons such as summing cells with data equality; then implement Pointwise Mutual Information and the cosine distance metric and use that. Download data from the EIA's site http://www.eia.gov that contains pages in which data from various states has been combined. Also download some of the sources and evaluate your system's results against the combinations produced by the EIA.

Chapter 13

ONTOLOGIES IN THE LEGAL DOMAIN

Tom Van Engers, Alexander Boer, Joost Breuker, André Valente, and Radboud Winkels

Leibniz Center for Law, Faculty of Law, University of Amsterdam, The Netherlands (vanEngers@uva.nl)

CHAPTER OVERVIEW

Since the emergence of the Semantic Web building ontologies have become quite popular and almost every conference on information science including artificial intelligence and e-Government have tracks that cover (legal) ontologies. Ontologies are the vocabularies that can be used to describe a universe of discourse. In this chapter we want to explain the roles (legal) ontologies play in the field of legal information systems and (juridical) knowledge management. We emphasize the fact that these ontologies are social constructs that can be used to express shared meaning within a community of practice and also have a normative character. Many different ontologies have been created for similar and different purposes and two of them, both core ontologies of law that specify knowledge that is common to all domains of law, will be explained in more detail. The first one, is a Functional Ontology for Law (FOLaw). This ontology describes and explains dependencies between types of knowledge in legal reasoning. FOLaw is rather an epistemological framework than an ontology, since it is concerned with the roles knowledge plays in legal reasoning rather than with legal knowledge itself. Nevertheless FOLaw has shown some practical value in various applied European ICT projects, but its reuse is rather limited. We will also explain some aspects of the LRI-Core ontology which captures the main concepts in legal information processing. LRI-Core is particularly inspired by research on abstract commonsense concepts. Legal knowledge is based upon these commonsense concepts. Since legal knowledge always refers to the 'real world', although in abstract terms, the main categories of LRI-Core are physical, mental and abstract concepts. Roles cover in particular social worlds. Another special category is occurrences; terms that denote events and situations. In this chapter we illustrate the use of LRI-Core with an ontology for Dutch criminal law, developed in the e-Court European project and an ontology for Dutch administrative law developed in a project for the Dutch State Council.

1. INTRODUCTION

Almost every conference or book on legal information systems covers ontologies. This is largely due to the attention that is paid to the development of the so-called Semantic Web in which ontologies play a pivotal role. There the intended use for ontologies is to provide a means to describe the content of the overwhelming amount of information on the internet. Generally speaking ontologies are the vocabularies that can be used to describe a universe of discourse. An ontology describes a domain by the collection of the terms involved and specifically by the way these terms are structured and defined. This structure tells us ''what a domain is about''.

Ontologies are intended to provide the semantics for the Semantic Web, i.e. the definitions of terms that constitute a particular domain. These semantics are cast in a knowledge representation formalism called Web Ontology Language (OWL[1]) which allows machine based inference and reasoning. The Semantic Web was designed to allow machine understanding of (annotated) web pages. As the *web-agents* that incorporate these competences are to be intermediaries (brokers) for web-services, the definitions of the terms used should coincide with human understanding. In other words: the definitions of terms as represented in ontologies should be **shared** by (virtual or real) communities of users.

Ontologies are not only used as support for the semantic web. Their role ranges from specifications of knowledge bases for knowledge systems to concept based indexes for managing large repositories of documents (knowledge management and information retrieval). In the next section we present an overview of roles of ontologies.

1.1 Applications of Ontologies

Typically ontologies are used for five types of purposes:

1. organizing and structuring information;
2. reasoning and problem solving;
3. semantic indexing and search;
4. semantics integration and interoperation;
5. understanding the domain.

1.2 Organize and Structure Information

Ontologies are used to describe things or phenomena in the domain of interest. In this role ontologies organize and structure information in the

[1] See: www.w3c.org

domain. The ontology thus plays the role of vocabulary. It serves as the lexicon describing the domain expressing which terms can be used. It also describes the semantics and describes which valid sentences can be expressed. In AI & Law various ontologies have been developed to define legal vocabularies. Although many of them are not really ontologies in the sense that they describe the universe of discourse of the world or domain the law is working on, e.g. taxes, crime, traffic, immigration, etc. rather than the typical legal vocabulary. Two examples of such ontologies are the Jur-Wordnet ontology (Gangemi et al. 2005) and CRIME.NL, an ontology of Dutch criminal law that was constructed with the specific aim to be re-used and adapted for Italian and Polish criminal law in the European eCourt project (Breuker & Winkels, 2003) and the ontology for Dutch administrative law developed in a project for the Council of State of the Netherlands.

1.3 Reasoning and Problem Solving

Ontologies can be used as the terminological part of a knowledge base enabling the understanding of assertions about the problem situation to be solved. The basic role of ontologies in this case is to represent the knowledge of the domain so that an automated reasoner can represent problems and generate solutions for these problems. The purpose of using ontologies here is to enable reuse of generic knowledge. Already in the eighties and nineties of the previous century knowledge engineers aimed at improving the cost-effectiveness of their design methods. By broadening the scope of the domain to be modelled and grasping the more generic knowledge, knowledge bases can be created that not only solve the problem at hand but are also better maintainable, easier to extend, etc. Ontologies used this way, i.e. as an engineering tool, are however not perspective neutral. Ontological choices are strongly influenced by the purpose of the ontology. How the knowledge expressed in the ontology will be structured or formalized depends on how it will be used by the reasoner in reaching the desired conclusions. This reasoning context consequently limits an ontology's reusability. This phenomenon is also called 'inference bias'. Striving for reusability however remains a good idea, but it can never be accomplished completely.

1.4 Semantic Indexing and Search

Ontologies are most frequently used as the semantic index of information that enables semantic search for content. The role of ontologies in this case is to represent the contents of documents or other ''soft'' information sources (picture, movies, etc.). Within the legal domain, practitioners and scientist have to work with and produce vast amounts of knowledge in the form of documents, charts, schemas, etc. Ontologies can help to organize them and enable retrieving these documents in a more effective way compared to keyword search. The traditional example that shows the need for this use of ontologies is the existence of multiple meaning of words. Ontologies can also be used in a more intentional way, as a mechanism for creating annotations i.e., allowing a person to semantically mark content so it can be found later.

1.5 Semantic Integration/Interoperation

Ontologies can serve as the interlingua between communicating information systems. The ontology in that case defines the specific vocabulary to be used to interchange information. Within e-Government applications ontologies will be needed to allow federative, cooperative systems, e.g. within public administrations. Ontologies enable governmental information systems to interoperate. In a sense these ontologies function as a semantic information schema and these ontologies usually reuse parts of ontologies created for other uses.

1.6 Understand a Domain

The most basic role of ontologies is to provide a view of what a domain is about. The ontology can be viewed as a map that specifies what kinds of knowledge can be identified in the domain and thus may help when making sense of that domain and acquiring relevant knowledge. This type of ontology can be used as a basis for designing more specialized representations. These types of ontologies are also called *core* ontologies (Valente et al. 1999), because they represent the nature of the domain. Frequently these ontologies are drawn from theories of the domain. In this chapter we will discuss an example of this type of ontology; the Functional Ontology of Law.

2. ONTOLOGIES AND MEANING

Ontologies are supposed to capture the meaning of terms. However, the problem is whether meaning can be specified independent of the context of its use. For instance, the term ‘car’ may mean a commodity (for a car salesman), a device (for the mechanic), a means of transport (for me), a motorized vehicle (for the traffic code), etc. In each of these cases the properties that define a car are different ones. Despite these differences, we all do understand these variations in "meaning". In fact, one may say that given a context, the meaning of a concept becomes restricted to a particular **sense**. The different senses do not just add up to a meaning. More specifically: selective attention to the concept of car does not merely result in a subset of the relevant properties of a car, but in radically different expectations of the car. If a route planner application allows you to select a mode of transport, and you specify that you take a car, the route planner will (reasonably) assume that the car works. The route planner does not know about the distinction between working and broken cars, and it doesn't need to: the only behaviour it knows of cars is driving people to locations at a speed allowed by the roads, and this may indeed be the necessary and sufficient criterion for classifying something as a car. The car mechanic will however not expect that cars work, and know of a broad spectrum of behaviours of cars, each explained by one or more of its parts not working. However, it does not make sense to specify all we know about a car when constructing an ontology for the community of car dealers. The particular sense of car as a commodity will do the job and we need the consensus of all car dealers in the world to model this sense so that it will not give rise to misunderstandings among these car dealers. Of course, we would wish a similar attitude when it comes to terms used in legislation, but that is more difficult as it is difficult to assign the community of practice except for the communities of professional lawyers and policy makers. It is far from reality to propose the ones who addressed by law (say: the citizen) to be involved in this construction of common understanding.

The more abstract terms (concepts) are, the less properties they have and therefore the less difference there is between "sense" and meaning. Highly abstract ontologies that capture universal notions like time, space, causality, object, process, etc., are part of **top-ontologies**. Terms in a top ontology are supposed to be invariant over domains. The invariant concepts in a field of practice are collected in a **core-ontology**, which can be subsumed by a top ontology. For instance, a core ontology of law will have typical concepts like obligation, right, liability etc., which can be specializations of notions of desirability, expectation, respectively causation and intention.

3. LEGAL KNOWLEDGE

Ontologies play an important role in knowledge representation in general and are essential to the design of legal knowledge systems. Before we explain specific knowledge representation aspects of legal ontologies and the function of building of such ontologies in the social process within the legal domain in more detail we will discuss some characteristic features of the legal domain.

First of all the law is a social construct and in modern democracies it is based upon a dialectical process where the outcome has to fit the different preferences of the stakeholders involved. Usually the law is expressed in natural language which introduces ambiguity and interpretation problems due to open evaluative terms and vagueness (not to mention inconsistencies). The law is furthermore not something static as it reflects the already mentioned preferences. Both the law and case decisions reflect changes in those preferences.

Developing theories about these characteristics can be done at two abstraction levels:

1. When one studies the effects, coherence, practical implications of applying the law on cases etc., we call this legal theory jurisprudence.
2. When one studies the mechanisms of designing, laws, legal reasoning, argumentation etc., we can abstract from specific cases and so we call this meta-juridica.

The law is revealed by different legal sources, for example legislation, case decisions etc. The existence of various legal sources has caused a specific scope problem when studying law. This problem referred to in previous work and is also called the 'individuation problem' (Breuker and Winkels 2003), i.e. the problem that although a difference exist between 'the law' and 'laws', there is an ongoing debate between legal-philosophers about what counts as the unit of law.

There are two extreme views. The first one takes all legally valid statements in legal sources (legislation, precedence law, etc.) as a whole: the law. The assumption to that view is that in principle the individual statements constitute a coherent whole. Although this is the predominant view in jurisprudence and legal philosophy as conducted by people with legal backgrounds people that have a background in AI usually doubt that such coherence exists and they consequently argue that the legal system should be the object of proper knowledge management. So the assumption that such coherence is 'genetically' built-in by the constraints provided by fundamental, 'natural' legal principles is not uncontroversial.

The other extreme takes all legally valid statements as being individual, independent laws. In extremis this view is incorrect, if only because one needs at least one other legal (meta-)statement about the validity of other legal statements: we need law about law, and this dependency is a serious issue for legal scholars (Kelsen 1991). Legal theory is in the first place concerned with justifying law, so legal scholars will not easily take validity statements in law as a side issue.

The coherence of law in a legal system, as postulated by many legal scholars, should prevent the occurrence of contradictory outcomes in assessing legal cases: the law should not contain serious contradictions. That is, no unintended contradictions, since most prima facie contradictions are in fact valid exceptions. In many studies we conducted for different ministries we found however that even recently written new laws contained such contradictions. From experience we also know that it doesn't get any better when a law has been enacted for some time and changes are made to it while case decisions introduce new interpretations.

By coherence we usually mean more than 'not contradictory': there should also be no conceptual 'gaps'. An example of such a gap are the statements "every house has an owner" and "cars have wheels". These two unrelated statements may not contradict one another but they do not form a coherent text, they have no (obvious) relationship and consequently form an incoherent text. This lack of 'semantic coherence' (Van der Velden 1992) is a major and typical problem in modelling legislation. The normative statements that make up the bulk of legislation refer to some domain of social activity, but do not describe this domain in a coherent way (probably because the legislative drafter expects that the addressees can fill in the gaps from their 'world knowledge'). That "drivers of vehicles should keep to the right" and that "pedestrians should cross driving lanes in a perpendicular way" are incoherent, even if both refer to trajectories of participants in traffic. A legal source is therefore incomplete and this means that a knowledge engineer has to reconstruct and reverse engineer the social domain that a legal source is about.

4. ONTOLOGIES AS KNOWLEDGE MANAGEMENT TOOL

Within Knowledge Management ontologies are primarily used for establishing a common vocabulary (and consequently a common understanding) of a certain knowledge domain. In other words the primary function of the ontology is to serve as a shared conceptual model. In the process of shared conceptual modelling a group discussion is organized in which the members are invited to express their ideas, beliefs and knowledge about a system is held. An external representation of these ideas, beliefs and knowledge is then created. Such an external representation is called a (shared) conceptual model. This representation allows the members of the group to easily adapt their ideas, beliefs and knowledge together.

Different methods exist to create a shared conceptual model within communities of practice (see e.g. Van Engers et al. 2000, Checkland 1989, Vennix 1995).

Applied ontologies within Knowledge Management are built with the aims of:

1. Establishing the mental models of the participating individuals;
2. Creating a representation or conceptual model;
3. Creating a situation in which information about the mental models of participating individuals can be exchanged (i.e. creating a shared conceptual model);
4. Creating a shared mental model between participating individuals (i.e. every individual internalizes the shared conceptual model thus creating a shared mental model, i.e. a mental model that is similar for the relevant aspects with the other group members).

An example of such application is the ontology for Administrative Law (in Dutch AWB) created for the Dutch State Council. This organisation uses many different information systems that provide access to varying legal content such as case decisions, legislation and 'legis-prudence' (judgements about draft legislation). The problem for the users of those systems (and the systems designers that want to create an integrated search function) is that even within one legal (sub)domain the terms that should be specified for text search differ from source to source. In order to enable (future) improvement of the State Councils search and retrieval software one needs to align the terms that are currently used (some 4000) for indexing these resources. This is a labour intensive job that is done without much automated support.

The users of the search and retrieval software were very unhappy with the existing indexing system, because of the huge number of search terms, the lack of relationships between them, the unclear labels of some terms and the fact that some terms are too specific for their purposes. Due to both the labour intensive and error prone indexing process and the technical implementation the software is not able to provide a satisfactory recall/ precision ratio.

We created the ontology by using the core concepts in the Administrative Law as a starting point (e.g. Administration, Stakeholder, Decision, Objection, Request) and describing their relationships, features etc.

The ontology we created consists of about 300 classes and 170 properties (both features and relationships with other classes). The top classes of our ontology are classes such as *Agent*, *Role*, *Act* and *Legal mental concept*. These concepts are generic concepts that also are part of LRI-core which will be explained later. This helps to incorporate the ontology for Administrative Law within the top ontology LRI-core.

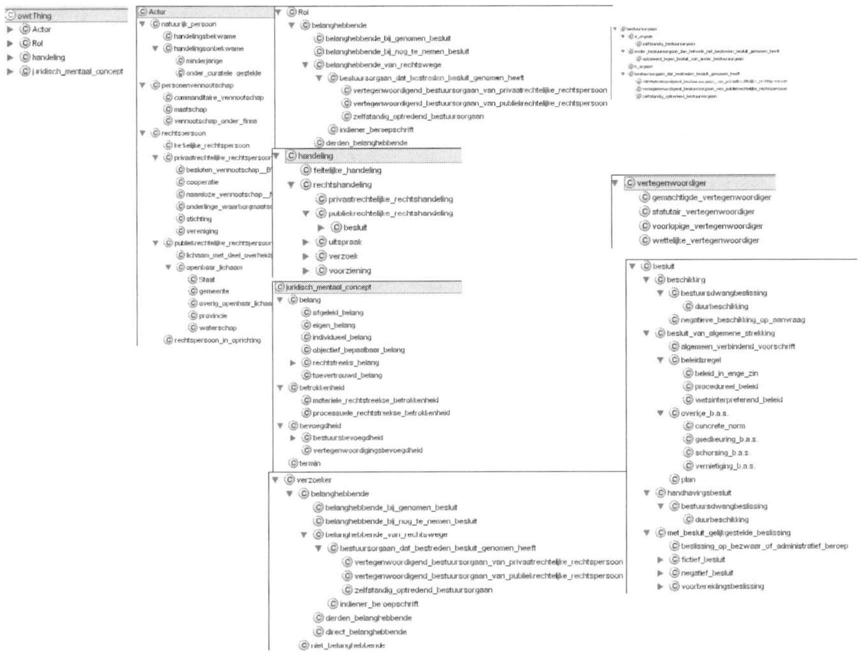

Figure 13-1. An ontology describing the concepts in the Dutch Administrative Law

The class *Agent* is super class of the concepts natural person, legal body, Limited *Natural Person, Legal Body, Limited Company* etc. One of the properties of agents is *Identity* which is not only an ontological feature but also a legal one (according to Dutch Administrative Law it is necessary that the identity of persons that do a request can be established). Agents can play different roles which are described by the subclasses of class Role. Roles are not independent concepts but determine the behaviour of an agent. A specific individual is an instance of the class Agent (or one of its subclasses). The class Act describes the activities that agents perform (in a certain role).

The property *performed-by* uses the class Role as range. A Role can never act independently from an agent. We decided to leave out factual acts and limit the ontology to legal acts (being subclasses of Act). Private Law Acts were also not included since we limit this ontology to those concepts relevant for Administrative Law.

The class *Legal Mental Concept* contains concepts that can't be reduced to acts or roles. The classes Interest, Competence and Involvement are sub classes of *Legal Mental Concept*.

The ontology was used to prune the terms that were used for indexing the documents, but the search and retrieval software based on it has not been developed yet. Building the ontology helped us to better understand the concepts within Dutch Administrative Law and to create a common vocabulary that's now in use by the experts working at the Dutch State Council responsible for tagging the documents within their content management system.

5. ONTOLOGIES VERSUS EPISTEMOLOGICAL FRAMEWORKS

Ontologies always go hand-in hand with epistemological frameworks. Epistemological frameworks describe the role knowledge plays in reasoning in a certain domain, while the concepts and concept relations are described in an ontology. Therefore, it is no surprise to see that most 'legal ontologies' are rather epistemic frameworks (Valente, 1995; Van Kralingen, 1999; Hage and Verheij, 1999).

We will explain the difference between ontologies and epistemological frameworks using FOlaw, being an epistemological framework rather than an ontology, despite its misleading name (Functional Ontology of Law) and LRI-core being a legal core-ontology.

5.1 FOlaw

FOlaw was designed in the mid-90s, originally as a core ontology distinguishing types of knowledge (Valente 1995; Valente et al., 1999). FOLaw served a number of purposes. The first one was to distinguish the various types of knowledge in legal reasoning, and in particular those types that are typical for legal reasoning. Related to this role it also explained the dependencies between these types of knowledge in legal reasoning. This typing and its dependencies could easily be translated into an architecture for legal reasoning: ON-LINE.

The second role is the typical core-ontology role: to organize and index libraries of domain ontologies and to support knowledge acquisition to construct new ontologies.

FOlaw was designed as a functional ontology. This means that the roles the legal system plays in society are taken as point of departure. A legal-sociological view was taken, rather than a perspective from the law itself, as in most legal theoretical studies. FOLaw furthermore identifies the dependencies between the types of knowledge, which indicate the roles that types of knowledge play in the reasoning. This is the reason that FOlaw is strictly speaking not an ontology, since it contains both ontological and epistemological elements. We will give here a summary description of FOLaw. 13-2 provides the comprehensive picture of dependencies of the various types of knowledge in legal reasoning. At the same time it also

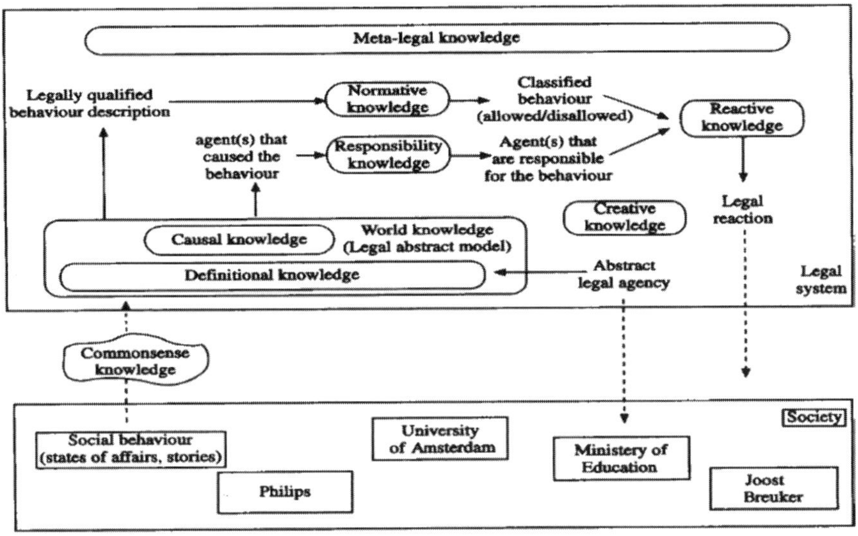

Figure 13-2. FOLaw, a functional ontology on law (Valente 1995)

expresses the role of the legal system as controlling the actual social behaviour of individuals and organisations in society.

The major types of knowledge that are distinguished in FOlaw are normative knowledge, world knowledge, responsibility knowledge, reactive knowledge, creative knowledge and meta-legal knowledge

5.1.1 Normative knowledge

Normative knowledge is the most typical category of legal knowledge, to such an extent that to many authors 'normative' and 'legal' are practically the same thing. The basic conception of norm used in the ontology is largely derived from (Kelsen, 1991). A norm expresses an idealization: what ought to be the case (or to happen), according to the will of the agent that created the norm. This view on norms is a generally accepted one, but it should be noted that this view does not make norms different from any abstraction. A model is also an idealisation with respect to reality, and modelling decisions are motivated by modelling preferences; not by the match between model and reality. A more obvious example is the notion of role. A role is also an idealisation: a behavioural model of how to act. One can play the role in accordance with these 'prescriptions' or fail, similar to the fact that one may violate a norm. Social roles contain the 'social contracts' that build complex societies in which members can predict and rely on the behaviour of others.

Norms limit possible behaviours and the assumption is that this subset of possible behaviours results in better choices (from the perspective of politics at least). This only works if the norms are based on a good model of the domain of action and only refer to agent based activities that are intentional and this requires making assumptions about physical and intentional processes.

5.1.2 Meta-legal knowledge

In FOlaw the perspective was taken that the law is defined on the basis of individual norms: e.g. individual articles in a regulation. The difference between the standard defined by the normative system on the one hand and the standards defined by the norms on the other hand is fundamental to understanding the role of normative knowledge in law, and it is accounted for by knowledge about individual norms. This distinction is captured by defining the categories of primary norms and meta-legal knowledge or secondary norms.

Primary norms are entities that refer to agent caused, human behaviour, and give it a normative status. This normative status is, in principle, either allowed (legal, desirable, permitted) or disallowed (illegal, undesirable, prohibited). Each norm refers to specific types of behaviour, i.e. norms can only be applied to certain types of situations (cases, or a productive characterisation of norms), or to a specific action in specific circumstances (a behavioural characterisation of norms). For the remaining types of cases, or remaining actions in specific circumstances, the norm is said to be silent.

Individual norms may conflict: if that is intended then some norm may be an exception to another norm. In order to solve these normative conflicts, meta-legal knowledge is applied. Typical conflict resolution is provided by meta-legal rules that state for instance that the more specific rule should be applied rather than a more general one: ''lex specialis derogat legi generali'' expresses this age old wisdom in law. Because of this kind of meta-norms there may be a difference between the normative status given by a single norm and the one ultimately given by the normative system as a whole. Meta-legal knowledge is not only used for solving conflicts between norms. Another function is to specify which legal knowledge is valid. Validity is a concept which can be used both for specifying the dynamics of the legal system and its limits. A valid norm is one that belongs to the legal system (Winkels et al., 1999).

5.1.3 World knowledge

Law deals with agent-caused behaviour and consequently contains some description of this behaviour. Norms are descriptions of how the world should be and therefore norms also describe how things can be. Laws are underspecified in the sense that the norms in law provide only a partial and incidental description of this possible world. This world is assumed to be known by the agents who are addressed by legal sources (in general by their social roles). If we want a machine to understand a domain of legislation and related legal cases, we have to represent this world. In the first place by the terminological knowledge involved – i.e. the ontology of the domain –, and further by all generic relationships that explain behaviours. This knowledge may be abstract and selective as it should represent the legislators view on the domain. For instance, in the traffic code, actions of drivers of vehicles consist of simple changes of positions, like turn taking, parking etc, on parts of road. From the traffic code perspective the physics of road and car constructions do not play a role. This legal view on a domain is called 'legal abstract model' (LAM). The LAM is an interface between the real world and the legal world. It allows, for instance, to interpret an informal case description – e.g. some traffic accident – to be translated and viewed in legal terms, in particular those terms that are used to express norms. Therefore, the LAM consists of definitions of concepts that represent entities and relations in the world, i.e. it is to be viewed as an ontology.

Apart from describing the world, we should represent the behavioural reasoning that is used in law. The concept Cause is central to possible and relevant behaviours and the relationships between causes and behaviour are determining for the assignment of responsibility of an agent for a certain case. Causal knowledge, however, refers or uses a static description of the world (e.g. to model world states). The world model should be composed of two related types of knowledge: terminological or definitional knowledge and causal knowledge. The definitional knowledge (ontology) is used by the normative knowledge to describe the ideal world defined as a subset of the possible world covered by the LAM. The causal knowledge is used by the responsibility knowledge to describe who or what have caused a given state of affairs, and is a source for the attribution of responsibility and guilt, besides the legal constraints imposed by liabilities.

5.1.4 Responsibility knowledge

Responsibility is the intermediary concept between normative and reactive knowledge, since a reaction can only occur if the agent is held responsible for a certain norm violation. Responsibility knowledge plays the role of linking causal connections with a responsibility connection – i.e. that connection which makes an agent accountable for a norm violation and possibly subject to legal reactions. As Hart and Honoré (1985) point out, however, responsibility does not have "any implication as to the type of factual connection between the person held responsible and the harm" – that is, causal connections are only a "non-tautologous ground or reason for saying that [an agent] is responsible" (Hart and Honoré 1985, p. 66). There are two basic mechanisms which are used in responsibility knowledge. First, the law may establish a responsibility connection independent of a causal connection – i.e. a responsibility assignment often by way of explicit liabilities. This can be seen in a rule used in many legal systems, by which parents are held responsible for the damage done by their children even if there is no specific causal link between their attitudes or actions and the damage. Second, the law may limit the responsibility of an agent under certain circumstances, disregarding some possible causal connections – i.e. a responsibility restriction. For instance, in England a man is not guilty of murder if the victim dies more than one year after the attack, even if the death was a consequence of this attack. Other well-known factors that may influence the establishment of responsibility connections in law are knowledge and intention.

We refer here to the work in which these notions are further specified in ontologies, and in an experimental system that identifies causal relations between and in event descriptions (Lehmann 2003, Breuker and Hoekstra 2004).

5.1.5 Reactive knowledge

To reach the conclusion that a specific situation is illegal (based on normative knowledge), and that there is some agent to blame for it (responsibility knowledge), would be probably useless if the legal system could not react toward this agent. Knowledge that specifies which reaction should be taken we call reactive knowledge. Usually this reaction is a sanction, but in some situations it may be a reward. The penal codes, which are usually a fundamental part of legal systems of the Romano-Germanic tradition, are for instance more concerned with responsibility and reactive knowledge than with a rigorous definition of crime.

Reaction occurs after a violation of the law takes place. Reactive concepts like seeking remedy in court, a fine, or a prison sentence, are usually introduced in normative statements addressed, often implicitly, to the party that is directed, or merely permitted, to react to the violation of the law. In private law this is usually the beneficiary whose interests are protected by the existence of the violated law who is allowed to react with the assistance of the legal system. In public and criminal law it is (a part of) the legal system itself that is instructed to react.

5.1.6 Creative knowledge

Legislation may enable the creation of new or fictive legal entities – usually some institution or other legal person –, using what we call creative knowledge. This creative function has a somewhat exceptional status if compared to the other ones.

5.2 LRICore

As stated before FOLaw is rather an epistemological framework. Besides that, it is not sufficiently detailed. FOLaw, based upon notions of Kelsen, Hohfeld and Hart, has shown us two distinctive sets of concepts that are typical for law:

1. normative terms (and their definitions and axioms), and
2. responsibility terms (liability, guilt, causation, etc.), which confirms what we have found in legal theory.

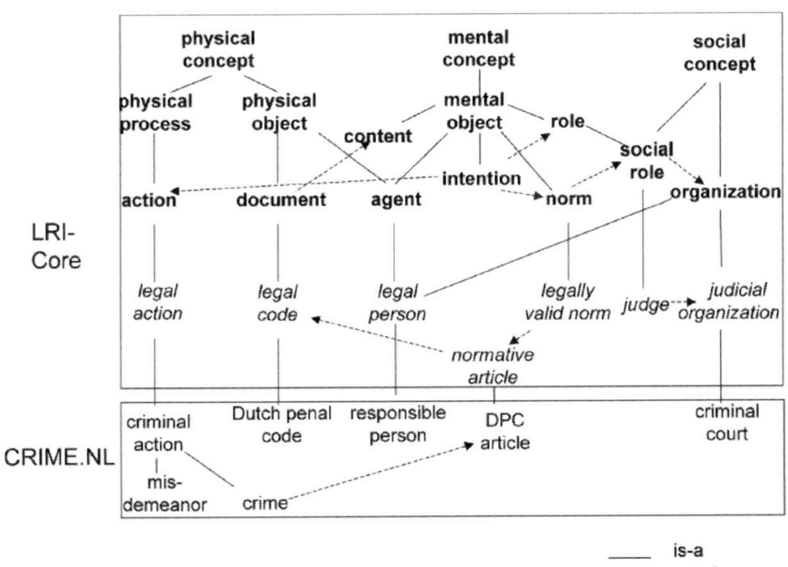

Figure 13-3. LRI-core, a top ontology for law

The LRI-Core legal core ontology was developed in order to provide a super-structure that would carry the meaning of recurring, abstract concepts, to facilitate knowledge acquisition of legal domain ontologies. Figure 13-3 depicts how LRI-Core is a legal specialization of some highly abstract common-sense concepts.

Existing foundational or ‘‘upper’’ ontologies e.g. Sowa’s (Sowa 2000), or SUMO, the IEEE-Standard Upper Ontology weren’t suited because their focus is rather on describing the physical and formal-mathematical world; social, mental and communicative concepts are distributed over physical and abstract categories and do not provide a coherent view of these worlds.

Another reason for not starting from already available foundational ontologies is that these do not very well cover the concepts typical for law such as roles, mental objects and processes, documents, social and communicative actions, etc. Extensions of DOLCE do, (Gangemi et al., 2005), but DOLCE was not available yet when the development of LRI-Core started. Also, DOLCE rather defines what (meta-)features should be used in an ontology that is aimed at the existence of objects and events rather than of classes that can be specialized. DOLCE has a strong philosophical flavour, where ontology is more concerned with existence and reality than with terminology.

The foundational layer of LRI-Core is not meant to be a fully worked out stand-alone foundational ontology. It contains relatively few concepts, no more than about 300. Only those concepts that have a legal significance are fully worked out (the ‘anchors’ in Figure 13-3). The other concepts are intended as a coherent coverage. LRI-Core is currently still under active development. It is expressed in OWL-DL. A first version of LRI-Core has been developed and used to support knowledge acquisition in the e-Court project (Breuker et al., 2002).

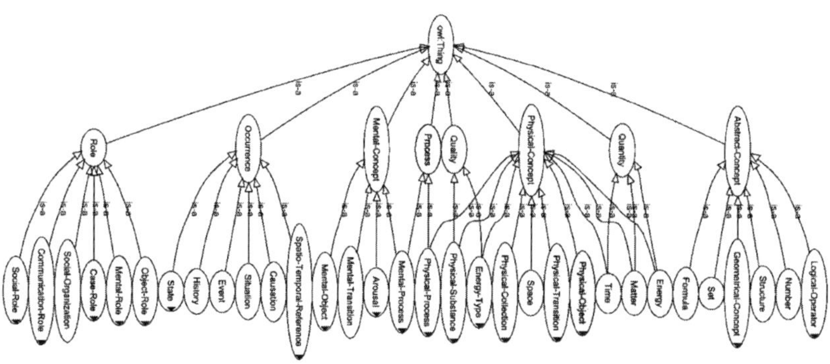

Figure 13-4. The top two layers of LRI-core

The top of LRI-Core consists at the moment of five major categories: each referring to a ‘world’. These five are: physical and mental concepts, roles, abstract concepts and terms for occurrences.

5.2.1 Occurrences

The concepts defined in an ontology enable us to recognize entities and their relations as they occur in the (or better in any possible) world. The basic assumption behind LRI-core is that all entities in situations are 'temporal' (perdurants) and all concepts are 'eternal' (endurants). The distinction between a concept and its occurrence is particularly relevant where mental concepts get executed. For instance, plans, norms and roles and their execution (respectively, their observation) may show divergences that can be marked as 'bad' or even illegal. A divergence can only be identified if a mental plan, norm or role still exists so that it can be compared with actual behaviour (or its memory or recording). The category of occurrences in LRI-Core captures those strictly temporal aspects related to the execution of scenarios involving objects and processes. This means that events are occurrences, but processes are not. Where processes contain the explanation of the changes they cause, events only describe a discrete difference between the situation before and after the event took place. All this does not reduce the need for terms to talk about occurrences in general. Therefore, LRI has a category of 'occurrences'. The distinction between real occurrences and ontology is reflected in a major distinction in human memory. Psychological research has identified two types of 'declarative' memories. The distinction between semantic memory and episodic memory is well established. Semantic memory corresponds with our knowledge about the world, i.e. ontology; episodic memory contains memories of events (occurrences). Semantic memory emerges in child development earlier than episodic memory: we have to know before we can understand events and situations.

5.2.2 Physical entities

The physical world evolves around two main classes: physical objects and processes. Objects are bits of matter, which in turn is typed by its substance. Objects have mass, extension, viz. form and aggregation state (limiting form). The existence of objects expresses the notion that matter (in particular solid matter) is what renders the physical world relatively stable and observable. Physical situations are usually described by the arrangement of individuals of physical objects. This intuition does not exist for the second major class that governs the physical world: process. Processes consume energy to change objects, or parts of objects. Processes are described by the changes they bring about. Change is an inherently temporal concept, belonging to the realm of occurrences. Through interaction, processes can cause one another, leading to series of events that only stop at some equilibrium: in general conceived as that there are no interactions at all.

The concept of process is often used as synonymous to action and activity. LRI-Core defines actions as processes that are initiated by an agent acting as actor. The mental perspective implied by agent-causation is that actions are intended: they are preceded by some kind of intentional decision to act.

5.2.3 Mental entities

Conceptions of the mental world have a strong analogy to the physical world. We conceive the mind as consisting of (mental) objects, like concepts and memories, which are processed by mental processes that transform or transfer these objects. Memories are retrieved; concepts are formed.

There is however, an important difference between the mental and the physical world. Where physical processes are governed by causation, mental processes are controlled by intention. For processes governed by intention (free will) we rather use the term ‘action’. Thinking is an action, as we assume that we have full control over our thoughts and can decide about what we are thinking. However, where our mind escapes our conscious intentions, as e.g. in getting in uncontrollable emotional states, or in forgetting an appointment, we rather take a physical than an intentional stance. Despite this subtle difference, we keep the term mental process to cover both, as we want to reserve the term action for agent-caused processes. Note that actions may affect the mental or the physical world. Special types of actions are speech acts: actions that have physical effects (speaking/writing) but are intended to affect the mind of a hearer/reader.

5.2.4 Roles

Roles cover functional views on physical objects (devices), on agent behaviour or on mental processes. In particular, social behaviour and social organizations are explained as (consisting of) roles. Typical mental roles are epistemological ones. For instance conclusion, evidence and hypothesis are roles in problem solving processes and can therefore also be categorized under mental classes (Breuker, 1994). From a role perspective, functions are roles of physical objects, e.g. we may use objects for non-intended functions.

Roles are behavioural requirements on role execution and on qualifications of role taking. These requirements are prescriptions, i.e. they are normative. In modern society many roles have formal requirements enforced by law. Legislation addresses actors by the roles they play. If actual behaviour deviates from the norms attached to these roles we violate the law. Violations are based upon the distinction between the prescription (role) and role performance. Therefore, in court, it is the actor of the role who is made responsible: as a person; not as a role. Even the fictitious concept of legal-person for social organizations turns into concrete responsibilities of the liable persons who have mis-performed their roles.

5.2.5 Abstract entities

As all concepts are abstractions, one may argue that a separate abstract world is difficult to see. However, common-sense knows about a (small) number of proto-mathematical concepts, such as collections, sequences and count-numbers (positive integers). We know about geometric simplifications such as line, circle, square, cube, etc. Nonetheless, these kind of semi-formal abstractions do not play a very central role in law, and therefore LRI-Core is thinly populated with abstract classes.

The role of the concepts defined in LRI-Core can be illustrated by explaining fragments of an ontology of Dutch criminal law, as developed in the e-Court project. This was aimed at the semi-automated information management of documents produced during a criminal trial: in particular the transcriptions of hearings. The structure of this type of document is determined by the debate/dialog nature of these hearings, but also by specific, local court procedures. Besides tagging its structure, it is also important to identify (annotate) content topics of a document. These vary from case descriptions (e.g., in oral testifying) to topics from criminal law (e.g., in the indictment). The case descriptions have a strong common-sense flavour, but the legal professionals who are the main intended users are primarily interested in the (criminal) legal aspects of a case. We developed an ontology that covers Dutch criminal law, whose major structure we will discuss below.

We will illustrate the use of 'anchors' in the LRI-Core ontology with parts of the ontology for Dutch criminal law (CRIME.NL).

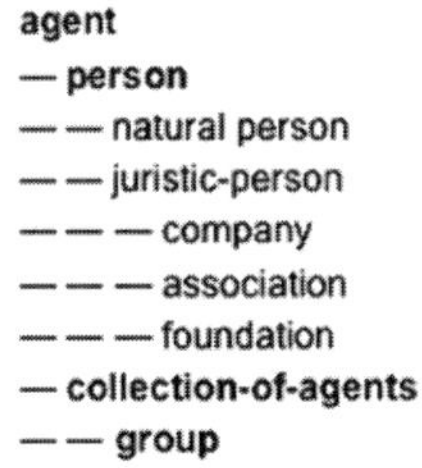

Figure 13-5. Agents in Dutch criminal law (CRIME.NL) (excerpt)

In Figure 13-5 the boldface terms are terms from LRI-Core. LRI-Core makes a distinction between a person with a lifetime identity and the roles that a person may perform. Roles are taken by persons who are agents.

role
— **social-role**
—— **legal-role**
———juridical-role
————judicial-role
—————judge
——————judge-presiding
—————prosecution-role
——————public-prosecutor
—————defense-role
——————defense-counselor
—————defendant
——————principal-defendant
——————accessory-defendant
——————offender
—————witness
————clerk-of-court
————lawyer
————the-State
———public-servant
———owner-of-goods
———owner-of-rights/duties
————creditor/debtor

social-organization
—— **legal-organization**
———public organization
————Ministry-of-Justice
————courts-by-jurisdiction
—————criminal-court
—————administrative-court
————courts-by-level
—————cantonal-court
—————court-of-appeal
—————Supreme-court
— **social-function**
——public-social-function
———jurisdiction
————public-prosecution
———criminal-investigation
————forensic-investigation

Figure 13-6. Roles and functions in Dutch criminal law (CRIME.NL) (excerpt)

In Figure 13-6 a selection of typical legal roles in criminal (procedural) law is presented. In LRI-Core we distinguish between social roles and social functions. Social functions are external roles of organizations. Social roles make up the functional internal structure of an organization. In these figures we cannot show multiple classification, nor other relations between classes than subsumption. For instance, an organization has social functions and 'has-as-parts' social roles. This is not the only view on the composition of an organization. The hierarchy of authority is another one, but this hierarchy maps onto the roles: authority is a mental entity: to be precise a 'deontic legal-role-attribute' Figure 13-7 presents some of the major categories of the mental world.

In this representation of the mental world we have skipped some views. Some mental legal objects, such as 'accusation' are in fact (illocutionary) acts. In legal discourse an accusation is really treated as an object, i.e. it is the (content; sometimes the literal surface structure) text that is referred to. However, its meaning is indeed the act of accusation, so it should inherit properties of mental objects and those of (illocutionary) mental actions. Legal procedures may objectify or 'reify' these actions. Many objects of the mental world are reifications of epistemological roles. Terms like 'reason', 'evidence', 'explanation', 'problem', 'dispute', etc. come from the vocabulary of reasoning methods and are concerned with assessing (trust in) the truth of (new) beliefs. As stated in the Introduction, law is particularly concerned with justifying legal decisions, so roles in argumentation and reasoning play an important role in legal discourse in general. Note that these terms are not part of Dutch criminal law, except some global terms like 'evidence' and 'doubt'. We have added some because they occur frequently in court discourse.

The hard core of the CRIME.NL consists of actions. There are two major types. First the criminal actions themselves (called 'offences'). These are of course the actions executed by the person who is successively acting as suspect, defendant, and eventually convict (if true and proven). On the other side, the convict may be at the receiving end of the 'punishment' actions that are declared by the legal system etc. Crime and punishment are the keys to criminal law that is synonym to penal law.

mental-object
— juridical-mental-object
— — legal-norm
— — judicial-mental-object
— — complaint
— — accusation
— — judicial-decision
— — — verdict
— — — — conviction
— — — — acquit
— — — — final-verdict
— — juridical-qualification
— — — deontic-qualification
— — — — deontic-legal-role-attribute
— — — — — right
— — — — — duty
— — — — — authority
— — — — deontic-modalities-of-norms
— — — — — permission
— — — — — obligation
— — — — — prohibition
— reasoning-role
— — evidence
— — — testimony
— — — — eye-witness-testimony
— — — forensic-evidence
— — problem-solving-role
— — — solution
— — — problem
— — — problem-solving-method
— — argumentation-roles
— — — debate-argument-role
— — — — accusation-position
— — — — defense-position
mental-process/action
— internal-mental-processes
— — reasoning
— — communicative-mental-action
— — testifying
— — interrogating
— — argument
— — dialog
— — — dialogical argument
— — — — dispute
— — — — — judicial-dispute

Figure 13-7. Mental objects, processes and states in Dutch Criminal Law (CRIME.NL) (excerpt)

6. QUALITY OF ONTOLOGIES

In the previous sections we explained some ontologies we have created and their purposes, and we explained some of our theoretical considerations. However, (legal) ontologies should first and foremost do what they are designed for. This brings us to the aspect of quality.

We already explained that 'neutral' ontologies do not exist. But given a certain epistemological framework (i.e. a specific intended use for that ontology) is there a way to establish the best ontology, in other words are there quality criteria that help us to select between different ontologies with the same intended use?

If we use ontologies as the representation of shared conceptualisations (i.e. as shared conceptual models) we might want to evaluate if the ontology really represents a shared conceptualisation. If different knowledge engineers have created ontologies of the same domain we might want to establish the similarity between their ontologies or the inter-coder dependency of a procedure that is used to produce those ontologies. Currently no complete set of convincing measures exists that expresses either the intrinsic quality of an ontology or the similarity between different ontologies or the inter-coder dependency of ontology production. Nevertheless some measures have been developed and in this section we give a brief overview of such measures that can help to inspect the quality of ontologies.

If we want to measure whether a conceptualisation is shared, we can use measures originally developed for comparing graphs. Goldsmith and Davenport (1990) for example discuss two ways to measure the similarity of two graphs:

1. *Based on path lengths.* If the distances between concepts are the same in two graphs then the graphs are equal.
2. *Based on neighbourhood similarities.* If in one graph the same concepts are linked as in the other graph, then the two graphs are equal.

These two types of measurements may have different results. Research indicates that for empirical derived networks the second option is the most suitable.

Some other measures that can be used to inspect specific characteristics of conceptual networks representing the knowledge structures can also be applied to ontologies:

1. Node centrality.
   Node centrality is measured by dividing the amount of emanating links of each node by the total amount of links of that network. This measure indicates the importance of each concept in the network.
2. Internal coherence.
   This measure indicates the relatedness of different parts of the concept network.

Some measures are used in the comparison of different concept networks or groups of concept networks:

3. Netsim.
   Netsim is computed by counting the amount of common links. Netsim is an indication for the overall similarity of networks.
4. Assigned weights of the links.
   The assignment of weights reveals characteristics of the relationships between concepts. The weights are derived from the proximity matrix data. This method allows detailed inspection in structural differences.

Some important qualities like understandability and modifiability are much harder to measure and should typically be measured empirically. With respect to the latter it should be remarked that for ontologies modification refers to extension and specialisation rather than restructuring, since ontologies should reflect unchangeable concepts in the domain of discourse.

In their OntoQA, a metric-based ontology quality analysis method, Tartir et al. (2005) assess the quality of ontologies using different perspectives:

1. The external perspective, i.e. they measure in how far a schema represents a real-world domain.
2. The internal quality in which they measure the depth, breadth, and height balance of the schema inheritance tree.

Their description however makes a distinction between two other 'qualities' when they state that "the quality of a populated ontology (i.e., KB) can be measured to check whether it is a rich and accurate representative of real world entities and relations…" and "finally, the quality of KB can be measured to see if the instances and relations agree with the schema" since these qualities correspond respectively with the first and second perspective.

As stated before this is just a small subset of different measures that are suggested but no general accepted framework about measuring ontologies' quality currently exists. The growing number of ontologies and the fact that these ontologies are aimed to be reused unavoidably must lead to increased demands for objective quality measures. We would then be able to use these measures when selecting similar ontologies and making decisions on reusing them or create new ones ourselves.

OntoClean (Guarino & Welty, 2004) is typical of another approach to validation of ontologies. This method consists of validating an ontology against a selected set of desirable meta-properties like identity, unity, essence – design principles for good ontologies. A good ontology reflects the design decisions selected by the validation method. This approach is basically the same thing as using a top ontology based on these same meta-properties to categorise concepts in the domain of interest. While it is possible to first design an ontology, and then test whether there is a natural mapping from the ontology to one or more top ontologies, it is more obvious to use a top ontology of high quality and to learn why it is structured as it is in the first place when designing a domain ontology. The same message obviously applies to core ontologies and epistemological frameworks, which are mentioned less often in relation to the quality of ontologies.

7. CONCLUSIONS

We report in this chapter about more than 15 years of research and some of this material has been published before. We learned a lot from our attempts to represent legal knowledge using ontologies and other formal representations. We now better understand how difficult it is to keep ontologies clean and preserve them for describing the concepts in the domain of discourse. Due to the expressive power of description logics underlying OWL DL one is often tempted to express epistemological frameworks in OWL and this easily contaminates the ontological conceptualisation.

We have used ontologies both as a means to express domain knowledge and as an instrument for knowledge discovery. By the latter we refer to the experiences we had when we modelled concepts from legal theory and discovered subtle differences between legal experts, or between legal experts and the layman's intuitive conceptualisation. The precision needed to create an ontology combined with the expressive power of description logic (underlying OWL DL), OWL modelling tools (such as Protégé) and the availability of reasoners (such as Pellet) help the knowledge engineer to validate his or her intuition by examining how cases are classified in an ontology. Although we didn't address the issue in this paper we found during our pursuit that the expressive power of OWL DL is somewhat limited for describing legal ontologies. In a current European project, called Estrella[2], we hope to find solutions for these problems.

Our experiences in actually building ontologies gave us confirmation that what is the case in many domains also holds in the legal domain, i.e. the majority of legal terms refers to the common-sense terms that in their turn are referring to the physical world. This is due to the fact that the power of law is limited: it cannot command the physical world (so what is desirable in law is always a subset of what is possible). Therefore, only those concepts and relations are object of law that can be affected by human conscious (and individual) intervention.

The division that is universally conceived and taught at law school, that between private and public law doesn't help very much when we want to construct legal ontologies. Each of these domains of law can be described using concepts that may have evolved from common-sense, but which have

[2] See: www.estrellaproject.org

received a typical and exclusive meaning in these sub domains of law. Like in all domains of professional practice, within law new concepts have been developed. Understanding and use of the current state of these legal-domain specific concepts is what legal education is about.

We observed that although the legal domain is founded upon common sense concepts these concepts are transformed over time into concepts only understandable and usable for legal professionals. Nevertheless the legal system is part of reality. Without a close correspondence between the legal conceptualisation and the common sense view of the world and its terminology no one besides lawyers would be able to understand the law or interpret legal cases. This limits the free expression of legislative drafters and other legal professionals. Cases are accounts of what has happened and they are cast in narrative discourse: events that are connected by causes and intentions (reasons). Therefore, a mapping between legal and common-sense concepts has to be maintained. All this is to say that a core ontology for law in general has problems in covering this large area of world knowledge and has to resort in a first approach to common-sense foundational ontologies.

We have also identified terms which are not exclusive, but still very typical and well elaborated for law: document, document-structure, role, etc. are central terms in law and may be grounded in a core ontology that imports these notions from a still high level and simple foundational (common-sense) ontology.

Ontologies are essential for knowledge representation. Consequently within knowledge based systems design and knowledge management the need for establishing the quality of ontologies is increasingly important. Evaluating ontologies is not only important if we create one ourselves, but especially if we want to reuse existing ones or have to chose between rather similar ones. Connection to high quality top or core ontologies increases the expressive power of an ontology and its extensibility.

In the sixties of the previous century knowledge engineers created generic reasoners that helped us to productively create knowledge based systems. In the mid-eighties of that century generic task frames and problem solving methods further improved reuse and increased productivity (we called them epistemological frameworks in this paper).

Ontologies are used to represent domain knowledge. By representing this domain knowledge in formal languages such as OWL DL we can apply automated reasoning to make derivations about cases. This will not only help us to improve efficiency when we design automated support (in the form of knowledge based systems) for legal practice, but also provides us with a powerful tool to examine legal reasoning as it is done by legal practitioners.

Depending to their explanatory power ontologies may get a more normative effect on legal practice itself.

REFERENCES

Breuker, J. 1994. Components of Problem Solving. In: L. Steels, G. Schreiber, and W. van de Velde (eds.): A Future for Knowledge Acquisition: proceedings of the EKAW-94, European Knowledge Acquisition Workshop. Berlin, pp. 118–136, Springer Verlag.

Breuker, J. and Hoekstra, R. 2004. Core concepts of law: taking common-sense seriously. In Proceedings of Formal Ontologies in Information Systems FOIS-2004, pages 210-221. IOS-Press, 2004.

Breuker, J., Elhag, L., Petkov, E., and Winkels, R. (2002). Ontologies for legal information serving and knowledge management. In: T. Bench-Capon, A. Daskalopulu and R. Winkels (eds.), Legal Knowledge and Information Systems. Jurix 2002: The Fifteenth Annual Conference. Amsterdam: IOS Press, 2002, pp. 73-82

Breuker, J., Winkels, R., 2003, Use and reuse of legal ontologies in knowledge engineering and information management, in ICAIL 2003 proceedings Workshop on Legal Ontologies & Web Based Legal Information Management.

Checkland, P. (1989), Soft Systems Methodology, In: Introduction: old and new paradigms of analysis, in Rational Analysis for a Problematic World: Problem Structuring Methods for Complexity, Uncertainty and Conflict, John Wiley & Sons, Chichester, ISBN 0 471 92285 4.

Van Engers, T.M., Vork, L., Puerta Melguizo, M.C., (2000). Kennis productiviteit in groepen. In: Opleiding & Ontwikkeling, Elsevier Bedrijfsinformatie, ISSN 0922-0895.

Gangemi, A., Sagri, M., and Tiscornia, D. (2005). A Constructive Framework for Legal Ontologies. In Benjamins, V., Casanovas, P., Breuker, J., and Gangemi, A. (eds.), Law and the Semantic Web, 97–124, Springer Verlag.

Goldsmith, T. E., & Davenport, D. M., 1990, Assessing structural similarity of graphs. In: R. W. Schvaneveldt (Ed.), Pathfinder Associative Networks: Studies in Knowledge Organization. Norwood, New Jersey: Ablex Publishing Corporation.

Guarino, N. and Welty, Ch. 2004. An Overview of OntoClean. In Steffen Staab and Rudi Studer, eds., The Handbook on Ontologies. pp. 151-172. Berlin: Springer-Verlag.

Hage, J. and Verheij, B. (1999). The Law as a Dynamic Interconnected System of States of Affairs: A Legal Top Ontology, International Journal of Human Computer Studies 51: 1034–1077.

Hart, H. and Honoré, T. 1985. Causation in the Law. Oxford University Press, New York, second edition, 1985.

Hohfeld, W. 1919. Fundamental Legal Conceptions as Applied in Legal Reasoning. Yale University Press. Edited by W.W. Cook, fourth printing, 1966.

Kelsen, H. 1991. General Theory of Norms. Clarendon Press, Oxford, 1991.

Kralingen, R. W. V. 1995. Frame-based Conceptual Models of Statute Law. Ph.D. thesis, University of Leiden, The Hague, The Netherlands.

Lehmann, J. (2003). Causation in Artificial Intelligence and Law: A Modelling Approach. Ph.D. thesis, University of Amsterdam.

Sowa, J.F. 2000. Knowledge Representation: Logical Philosophical and Computational Foundations. Brooks Cole Publishing Co, Pacific Grove, CA, 2000.

Tartir, S., Arpinar, I. B., Moore, M., Sheth, A., Aleman-Meza, B., 2005, OntoQA: Metric-Based Ontology Quality Analysis, IEEE ICDM 2005 Workshop on Knowledge Acquisition from Distributed, Autonomous, Semantically Heterogeneous Data and Knowledge Sources. Houston, Texas, November 27, 2005.

Valente, A. 1995. Legal knowledge engineering: A modelling approach. IOS Press, Amsterdam, The Netherlands, 1995.

Valente, A., Breuker, J., and Brouwer, P. (1999). Legal Modelling and automated reasoning with ON-LINE, International Journal of Human Computer Studies 51: 1079–1126.

Van der Velden, W. 1992. Coherence in Law: A Semantic and Deductive Explanation. In Brouwer, B., Hol, T., Soeteman, A., Van Der Velden, W., and De Wild, A. (eds.), Coherence and Conflict in Law. Deventer, Boston/Zwolle, 257–287. Kluwer Law and Taxation Publishers/W.E.J. Tjeenk Willink. Proceedings of the Third Benelux-Scandinavian Symposium in Legal Theory, January 3–5-1991, Amsterdam.

Vennix, J.A.M. (1995). Building Consensus in Strategic Decision Making: System Dynamics as a Group Support System, in Group Decision and Negotiation, 4, 335-355, Kluwer Academic Publishers.

Winkels, R.G.F., Bosscher, D., Boer, A. and Breuker, J.A.. Generating exception structures for legal information serving. In Th.F. Gordon, editor, Proceedings of the Seventh International Conference on Artificial Intelligence and Law (ICAIL-99), pages 182–195. ACM, New York, 1999.

SUGGESTED READINGS

Ontologies (general)

- S, Staab & R. Studer, *Handbook on Ontologies*, Springer, 2004
- Dieter Fensel, *Ontologies: A Silver Bullet for Knowledge Management and Electronic Commerce.* Springer
- Journal: Applied Ontology (IOS-Press)

Ontologies (legal)

- AI and Law Journal, 2 Special Issues on Legal Ontologies
  - Joost Breuker, Daniella Tiscornia, Radboud Winkels & Aldo Gangemi (eds.) Ontologies in Law, Vol 12, nr 4, Dec. 2004
  - Jos Lehmann, Maria Angela Biasiotti, Enrico Francesconi, Maria Teresa Sagri (eds) Legal Ontologies and Artificial Intelligence Techniques, vol 13, nr 2
- V.R. Benjamins and P. Casanovas and J. Breuker and A. Gangemi (Eds*) Law and the Semantic Web*, Springer, 2005

Semantic Web/OWL:

- T. Berners-Lee, J. Hendler, and O. Lassila. The Semantic Web. *Scientific American* 284 (May 2001): 34-43.
- Grigoris Antoniou & Frank Van Harmelen *A Semantic Web Primer* MIT-Press, 2005
- OWL Web Ontology Language: http://www.w3.org/TR/2004/REC-owl-guide-20040210/

Knowledge Representation

- Randall Davis, Howard Shrobe, and Peter Szolovitz. What is a knowledge representation. *AI Magazine*, Spring: 17 – 33, 1993.

- D. Nardi and R. J. Brachman. An introduction to description logics. In F. Baader, D. Calvanese, D.L. McGuinness, D. Nardi, and P.F. Patel-Schneider, editors, Description Logic Handbook, pages 5–44. Cambridge University Press, 2002.

ONLINE RESOURCES

General Ontologies

- AI topics at AAAI: http://www.aaai.org/AITopics/html/ontol.html
- Protégé wiki: http://protege.cim3.net/cgi-bin/wiki.pl/
- Semantic Web Search : http://swoogle.umbc.edu/

Legal Ontologies

- LRI Core: http://wiki.leibnizcenter.org/index.php/LRI_Core
- The successor of LRI Core: http://www.estrellaproject.org/lkif-core/
- LOIS (/Lexical Ontologies for legal Information Sharing)/: http://search.elois.biz/clir/searchmclir?type=search&term_query=&gui_avanzata=1&eprecision=1&dd_topic=legal&language=en
- LoaWiki: http://wiki.loa-cnr.it/index.php/LoaWiki:CLO

QUESTIONS FOR DISCUSSION

1. Why do ontologies play a pivotal role on the Semantic Web? Is a Semantic Web without ontologies possible? Explain.
2. Ontologies are used for very different purposes. Is it conceivable that the chosen conceptualization for a top ontology depends on its purpose? And for a core ontology? And for an ontology in general? Explain.
3. What method(s) would you use to validate your ontology? Motivate your choice.
4. Administrative law defines the concept of public body. In which category of FOLaw does this definition belong? Explain.
5. Criminal law uses the rule of *ne bis in idem* (meaning that no legal action can be instituted twice for the same cause). In which category of FOLaw does this rule belong? Explain.
6. Are there analogies to the so-called individuation problem (discussed in relation with FOLaw) in other domains of knowledge?

7. The notion of common sense plays a central role in legal theory. To attribute responsibility it is imperative to know what knowledge can be ascribed to someone. Is the category of world knowledge in FOLaw similar to this sense of common sense? Explain.
8. What is the difference between mental entities and abstract entities in LRICore?
9. Is LRICore a legal ontology in your view? Explain.
10. Concepts like *norm* and *hypothesis* are epistemological roles, and it is of course possible to make an ontology of epistemological roles. Why does the chapter stress that ontology and epistemological framework should be distinguished? In what way does the epistemological framework differ from an ontology of epistemological concepts?

Chapter 14

PUBLIC SAFETY INFORMATION SHARING

An Ontological Perspective

Siddharth Kaza and Hsinchun Chen

Department of Management Information Systems, Eller College of Management, University of Arizona, Tucson, AZ U.S.A. (sidd@email.arizona.edu; hchen@eller.arizona.edu)

CHAPTER OVERVIEW

In recent years there has been a thrust on public safety related information-sharing efforts. However, many public safety information systems are incapable of efficient data sharing due to their heterogeneous nature. Digital government research has focused on the use of ontologies as they might play a key role in achieving seamless connectivity between heterogeneous systems. In this chapter we conduct a survey of public safety information sharing initiatives and discuss the ontological implications of the systems and standards. We also include a comprehensive review on ontologies and ontology-based information sharing and integration approaches in the digital government and other domains. We discuss the importance of ontology mapping for the public safety domain and present a survey of the state-of-the-art in ontology mapping. To showcase ontology-based sharing efforts we present two case studies: the first on evaluating mapping tools with law enforcement data and the second on using ontologies for sharing and analysis of extremist data.

1. INTRODUCTION

Information sharing and analysis are a growing focus in digital government research [5, 16, 36]. This is especially true for the public-safety community in the United States which comprises of several thousand state and local police agencies, hundreds of federal agencies ranging from the FBI to the Government Printing Office police, and thousands of courts, prosecutor's offices, and probation departments. Each of these agencies has one or more internal information systems as well as links to national information systems. In the past few years there has been a thrust on information sharing between systems in agencies responsible for local law enforcement and national security. However, majority of these agencies have records management systems that are technologically incapable of sharing information with each other in an efficient manner because they are not interoperable.

The interoperability problem exists because there is a need to connect information systems that are heterogeneous and incompatible. The problem has been a major focus of the research and practitioner communities alike. There is a large body of work in the database and information integration fields that ranges from matching database schemas to answering queries from multiple systems. Recently research has focused on the use of ontologies as they might play a key role in achieving seamless connectivity between systems [3]. However, there has not been much ontology related research in the public-safety domain due to the lack of standard ontologies and the sensitive nature of information.

In this chapter we conduct a survey of public safety information sharing initiatives and discuss the ontological implications of the systems and standards. We also include a comprehensive review on ontologies and ontology-based information sharing and integration approaches in the digital government and other domains. We discuss the importance of ontology mapping for the public safety domain and present a survey of the state-of-the-art in ontology mapping. To showcase ontology-based sharing efforts in this domain we present two case studies: the first on evaluating mapping tools with law enforcement data and the second on using ontologies for sharing and analysis of extremist data. Finally we conclude and provide the reader with some interesting readings and online resources.

2. LITERATURE REVIEW

2.1 Challenges in Information Sharing and Interoperability

The problem of bringing together heterogeneous and distributed computer systems is known as the interoperability problem [42]. Data and database heterogeneity is classified into structural (data is in different structures) and semantic (data in different sources has different meaning) heterogeneity. Even though structural conflicts pose major problems in information integration, they have been addressed to a great extent in the schema matching literature, see Rahm et al. [38] for a comprehensive survey. Semantic heterogeneity and conflicts have been identified as one of the most important and pressing challenges in information sharing [25]. The conflicts have been categorized into many different taxonomies by previous studies including data level and schema level conflicts [37]; confounding, scaling, and naming conflicts [12]; and data entry and representation conflicts [21]. Semantic conflicts in the public safety information domain include:

- Data representation/expression conflicts: Data are recorded in different formats, e.g., different representations of date ('050798' vs. '7-May-98').
- Data precision conflicts: The domain of data values differ, e.g., five levels of security alerts (DHS advisory system) vs. four level systems (many police agency alert systems).
- Data unit conflicts: the units of data differ, e.g., measurement of height in inches vs. in feet.
- Naming conflicts: The labels of elements differ, e.g., an element might be called 'Person' in one data source whereas it might be called 'Individual' in another.
- Aggregation conflicts: An aggregation is used in one data source to identify a set of entities in another source, e.g., date is represented as month, date, and year as separate attributes in one source and as combined attributes in another source.

Ontologies can be used to communicate a shared and common understanding of a domain in formal and explicit terms. This can help alleviate the interoperability problem.

Another important challenge in sharing public safety related data is addressing privacy, security, and policy concerns. Federal, state, and local regulations require that agreements between agencies within their respective jurisdictions receive advanced approval from their governing hierarchy. This precludes informal information sharing agreements between those agencies. The requirements vary from agency to agency according to the statutes by which they were governed. Sharing information among these agencies requires many months of negotiation along with formal agreements. Though extremely important, these concerns are not the primary focus of this chapter. We refer the reader to the suggested readings at the end of the chapter for a through discussion on privacy, security, and policy issues.

2.2 Public Safety Information Sharing

The domain of public safety information sharing has not been adequately explored in the research community. This stems from the sensitivity and policy issues associated with obtaining this information for research purposes. However, there have been some successful national, state, and local efforts to share data among public safety agencies. Table 14-1 (next page) lists the major public safety information sharing efforts along with their potential ontological contributions. Selected initiatives are also discussed in detail in the following sub-sections.

2.2.1 National level sharing initiatives

Most national level initiatives are championed by the Government. Perhaps the most important recent one is a data model standardization effort by the U.S. Department of Justice called the Global Justice XML Data Model (GJXDM, http://it.ojp.gov/jxdm). The GJXDM is an XML based standard intended to be a data reference model for the exchange of information within the justice and public safety communities. It defines the semantics and the structure of common data elements that are used in the community. The data elements are based on approximately thirty-five different data dictionaries, XML schema documents, and data models used in the justice and public safety communities. The purpose of the GJXDM is to provide a consistent, extensible, maintainable XML schema reference specification for data elements and types that represent the data requirements for a majority of the community. It is intended to allow database schema developers to base the components and structures of the schema elements on a universally accepted standard. From the ontological perspective, the GJXDM is an important step in the right direction. It provides a comprehensive collection of data classes in addition to a taxonomy outlining relationships among them. This will allow future public-safety ontology engineers to base their ontology on a commonly used standard thus enabling easy interoperability.

An established national level data sharing initiative is the Regional Information Sharing Systems (RISS, http://www.iir.com/riss/) program that links law enforcement agencies throughout the nation, providing secure communications, information sharing resources, and investigative support. Existing information systems in agencies connect as nodes to the RISS network and use standardized XML data exchange specifications to exchange information on individuals, vehicles, and incident reports.

Table 14-1. National and regional public safety information sharing efforts

		Type	**Agency Participation**	**Ontological contributions**
NATIONAL	GJXDM (DOJ)	Data standard	40 justice related federal, state, and local agencies (April 2005), but likely to expand soon	Classes (objects), properties, and comprehensive taxonomy for the justice community
NATIONAL	NIEM (DHS, DOJ) www.niem.gov	Data standard	13 federal, state, and local agencies (May 2006)	Classes and properties for homeland and border security agencies
NATIONAL	RISS (BJA)	Data standards and communication network	485 state agencies and 920 federal agencies (May 2006)	Message exchange ontologies and classes for law-enforcement data
NATIONAL	N-Dex (FBI)	Data warehouse	20 pilot federal, state, and local agencies (March 2006)	Classes for incident reports
NATIONAL	NLETS (multiple agencies)	Comm. network	Several hundred federal, state, local, and some international agencies	Message exchange ontologies
NATIONAL	NCIC (FBI)	Data warehouse and comm. network	Several hundred federal, state, and local agencies	Primarily individual and vehicle related classes
REGIONAL	COPLINK® (multiple regions including AZ and CA)	Data warehouse and analysis suite	Over three hundred state and local agencies and a few federal agencies	Comprehensive classes and properties for law enforcement data and analysis results
REGIONAL	ARJIS (San Diego, CA region)	Distributed query and communication network	50 state and local agencies and a few federal agencies	Law enforcement message exchange ontologies
REGIONAL	CAPWIN (Washington, D.C.)	Distributed query and communication network	40 state and local agencies and 10 federal agencies	First responder (police, fire, EMS) data and message exchange ontologies
REGIONAL	FINDER (Florida) finder.ucf.edu	Distributed query and communication network	121 local agencies	Message exchange ontologies for individual, vehicle, and pawn records
REGIONAL	LINX (VA and others) www.hrlinx.com	Data warehouse	27 state and local agencies	Incident report classes

In addition to data standardization efforts, other national level information sharing efforts include the National Law Enforcement Telecommunications System (NLETS) and the FBI's National Crime Information Center (NCIC) network. Both of these systems are telecommunications networks that enable agencies to submit and access public safety information. Most information in these systems is entered manually, and all local and state law enforcement information is not available through them. Even though the systems are in wide use, their narrow scope and the lack of efficient methods of mapping information to them limit their use.

2.2.2 Regional level sharing initiatives

The initiatives described in this sub-section have attempted to address the problem of interoperability at a smaller scale among the state and local public safety agencies. Many of these systems are capable of scaling up to the national level and adapting to larger scale public safety related applications. One of the most successful efforts in regional data sharing is the COPLINK® [6] system. COPLINK® is based on mapping multiple database schemas into one standard schema. It allows diverse police departments to share data seamlessly through an easy-to-use interface that integrates different data sources including legacy records management systems. The system is being used by over three hundred law enforcement agencies in more than twenty states.

Another regional sharing effort is the Automated Regional Justice Information System (ARJIS, www.arjis.org) in the San Diego, C.A. region. The ARJIS system uses a query translation approach to send distributed queries to various agencies on the network. A third notable regional sharing effort is Capital Wireless Integrated Network (CapWIN, www.capwin.org) in the Washington, D.C. region. Each of these widely deployed systems defines its own schema to represent law-enforcement information, intensifying the need to define mappings to share information.

2.3 The Role of Ontologies

The term 'Ontology' originated in philosophy (meaning subject of existence) and acquired a different meaning in the context of information sharing. In the artificial intelligence and information integration literature, ontology is "a formal, explicit specification of a shared conceptualization [14]." In simpler terms an ontology is a formal description of concepts (known as classes) and relationships (known as properties) that exist between them. An ontology differs from a taxonomy in that it describes an entire domain in a formal description language instead of specifying just class/sub-class relationships. An ontology can also be queried and provides methods to describe properties for classes and relationships between them.

There are several languages to represent ontologies, the most prominent ones include: OWL (Web Ontology Language, www.w3.org) based on description logic, DAML (DARPA Agent Markup Language, www. daml.org) based on frame-logic, and RDF (Resource Description Language. www.w3.org) based on class hierarchy definitions. Four roles of ontologies can be identified in the information integration literature [41, 42]:

- Neutral authoring: Modeling all the data in an enterprise to enhance maintainability and long term knowledge retention.
- Interoperability: Explicating content to allow multiple systems to interoperate.
- Ontology-based specification: Building software systems based on predefined ontologies.
- Ontology-based query models: Using ontologies as a global query schema, sub-queries are reformulated based on a global ontology.

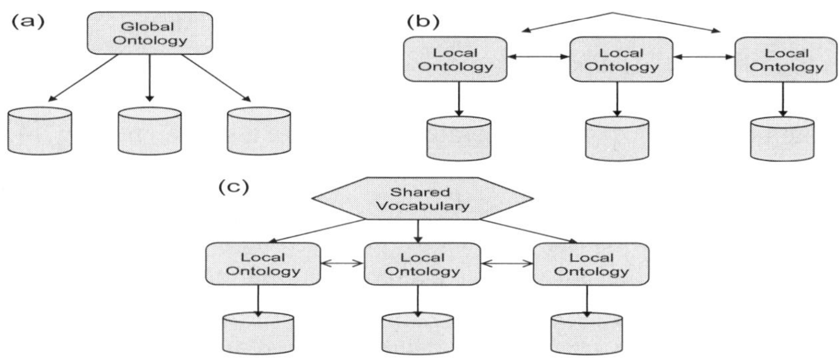

Figure 14-1. Information integration approaches - (a) single, (b) multiple, and (c) hybrid ontology approach

In this review we concentrate on the role of ontologies for interoperability and information integration. Three approaches have been used for information sharing using ontologies [42].

- Single ontology approach (a): In this approach all the information sources are related to one global ontology. It assumes that each data source has nearly the same view of the domain and committed to the ontology before development. An advantage of this approach is that local sources can be mapped to each other easily. Examples of systems using this approach include SIMS [2] and the EDC project [17].

- Multiple ontology approach (b): Each source is described by its own ontology. The sources are mapped to each other for interoperability. An advantage of this approach is that new sources can be added without modifying any existing local ontologies. A disadvantage of this approach is that each ontology needs to be mapped to others, which is a difficult and time consuming task. An example of a system using this approach is OBSERVER [27].
- Hybrid approach (c): Each source is described by its own ontology, but they share a common vocabulary. The vocabulary contains the lexicon used in a specific domain. An advantage of this approach is that new sources can be added without modifying any existing local ontologies. A disadvantage is that any existing local ontologies (not based on the shared lexicon) cannot be used. An example system using this approach is COIN [12].

Ontology-based information sharing techniques have been used in many domains including e-commerce [10, 35], health [4], finance [9], electronics [8], bioinformatics [39] and manufacturing [15]. Some of these studies have used the multiple ontology approach [4, 9, 10, 35] while others have preferred the hybrid approach [8, 15, 39]. Many times the selection of an approach depends upon the availability of standard vocabularies [30]. This is an important challenge in ontology-based approaches since most communities that need to interoperate do not share a single ontology [41] or have source-specific disparate ontologies already defined for them [34]. This is especially true in the public-safety information domain where different sources use different representations of information (some of which may be proprietary). From the ontological perspective, sharing data between such sources requires mapping between the disparate ontologies. Ontology mapping is a difficult and time consuming task and has been extensively studied in the literature.

2.4 Ontology Mapping

Identifying semantic correspondences (mappings) between ontologies and database schemas has been the focus of many works from diverse communities [19, 38]. There are two major approaches for discovering mappings between ontologies [30]. If the ontologies share the same upper model then this common grounding is used to establish mappings. There are several upper ontologies that include SUMO [29], DOLCE [11], SENSUS [1], and Cyc [22]. The second set of approaches use heuristics-based or machine learning techniques that that use characteristics of ontologies like structure, names and definitions of classes, and instances of classes to establish mappings. Some techniques also use other external reference ontologies to establish mappings. These are similar to schema matching techniques but sometimes use automated reasoning to identify hierarchies. The second approach is more suitable in the public safety domain as there is still a lack of consensus on middle and upper level ontologies. Table 14-2 presents a representative set of these techniques and their main characteristics.

Table 14-2. Representative set of ontology mapping techniques. The techniques include Prompt [32], Anchor-Prompt [31], Prompt-Diff [33], Chimaera [26], FCA-Merge [40], Glue [7], OMEN [28], IF-Map [18], and LOM [23].

		Mapping Methods	Input Type - Output Type	Use Data Instances	Level of Automation	Availability
Primarily NLP Based	Prompt, Anchor-Prompt, PromptDiff	NLP Methods. Heuristics based on structure.	*Input*: OWL, RDF Output: *Merged* ontology with suggestions of similar concepts to guide the user.	Yes. Not necessary for func-tioning.	Semi-Automated. Guides users through merging steps.	Available as parts of the Protégé ontology developm ent environm ent.
	Chi-maera	NLP Methods Structural heuristics (only within the Ontolingua environment	*Input*: Ontologies in multiple representations *Output*: Merged ontology with suggestions of similar concepts.	No.	Semi-automated. Guides users through merging steps.	Available as part of the Ontoling ua environm ent and as a stand-alone online tool.
	FCA-Merge	NLP Methods	*Input*: Documents containing domain concepts. *Output*: Mappings between concepts	Yes. Necessary for func-tioning.	Relies on human expert to construct ontology from similar concepts.	Not available for public use.
Structure Based	GLUE	Probabilistic definitions of several similarity measures. Uses relation labeling to incorporate domain constraints.	*Input*: Taxonomies (not ontologies) *Output*: Mapping between concepts.	Yes. Necessary for func-tioning	Automated. No human necessary. Probably will need experts to verify and correct mappings.	Not Available .

(Continued)

Table 14-2. (Continued)

		Mapping Methods	Input Type - Output Type	Use Data Instances	Level of Automation	Availability
External Sources	OMEN	Probabilistic definitions of several similarity measures. Different from GLUE in that this uses the semantics of ontology relations.	*Input*: RDF *Output*: Mappings between similar concepts.	No.	Automated. No human necessary. Probably will need experts to verify and correct mappings.	Not Available.
	IF-MAP	Logic Isomorphism – Generates subclass relationships between local ontologies and reference ontology.	*Input*: Multiple – Ontology libraries, editors, Web, ontology representations *Output*: Merged ontology	Yes. Necessary for functioning.	Semi-automated. Needs Expert.	Not Available.
	LOM	NLP Methods. In addition, uses Wordnet Synsets and SUMO types to match concepts.	*Input*: DAML/RDF *Output*: Mappings between similar concepts.	No.	Automated. Gives a probability for each match.	Prolog demo implementation available for download.

In the following section we present a case-study that uses some of the listed mapping techniques in the public safety information domain.

3. CASE STUDIES

3.1 Case Study 1: Evaluating Ontology Mapping Tools in the Public Safety Information Domain

This study [20] evaluated various types of ontology mapping tools with real-world data representations from the public safety information domain. As mentioned earlier, since there are many representations of data in this domain, mapping between ontologies is important for effective sharing of information.

3.1.1 Study design and testbed

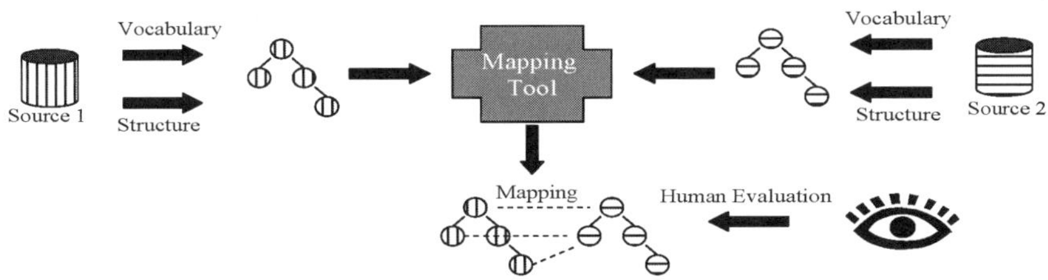

Figure 14-2. Research design for evaluating ontology mapping tools

The research design was based on the multiple ontology approach where ontologies are defined for individual sources that provided the structure and vocabulary for the ontology (Figure 14-2). A mapping tool was used to suggest the mappings between two source ontologies and these were compared to a benchmark. The benchmark mappings were provided by a domain expert who had intricate knowledge of the structure and semantics of the data sources. Precision (# of correct mappings suggested/total # of mappings suggested) and recall (# of correct mappings suggested/total # of correct mappings) metrics as used by previous evaluative studies of mapping tools were used for evaluation. The F-measure represented as

$$F(\beta) = \frac{(\beta^2 + 1) * P * R}{\beta^2 * P + R}$$

was used to combine precision (P) and recall (R). The parameter β adjusts the relative weight of precision and recall. In this study β was set at 0.5 to make recall half as important as precision to suit the sensitive domain. The study evaluated the performance of three mapping tools: Chimaera [26] (uses NLP techniques to find mappings), PROMPT [32] (uses NLP and structure), and LOM [23] (uses external sources).

3.1.2 Data sources

Three data sources were used to create three ontologies for the study. The first two data sources were database schemas used by many police agencies in the U.S. The first data source (hereafter referred to as PD1) contained 3 million police incident records with information on 1.8 million individuals recorded over 10 years. The second data source (PD2) contained 2.1 million police incident records with information on 1.3 million individuals recorded over 10 years. The third data source was the GJXDM (JX) by the U.S. Department of Justice. Schema elements from these data sources were used to make person ontologies (using OWL and RDF) for each of the data sources. The person ontologies from PD1, PD2, and JX contained 33, 17, and 73 classes respectively.

3.1.3 Results

Table 14-3 lists the precision and recall values achieved by the three matching tools in matching person ontologies. Figure 14-3(a) is a histogram of the precision achieved by the three tools.

Table 14-3. Precision and recall in matching person ontologies

	PROMPT		Chimaera		LOM	
	Precision	Recall	Precision	Recall	Precision	Recall
PD1 – PD2	0.6	0.46	1	0.3	0.8	0.3
PD1 – JX	1	0.05	1	0.05	0.6	0.5
PD2 – JX	1	0.13	1	0.13	0.7	0.5

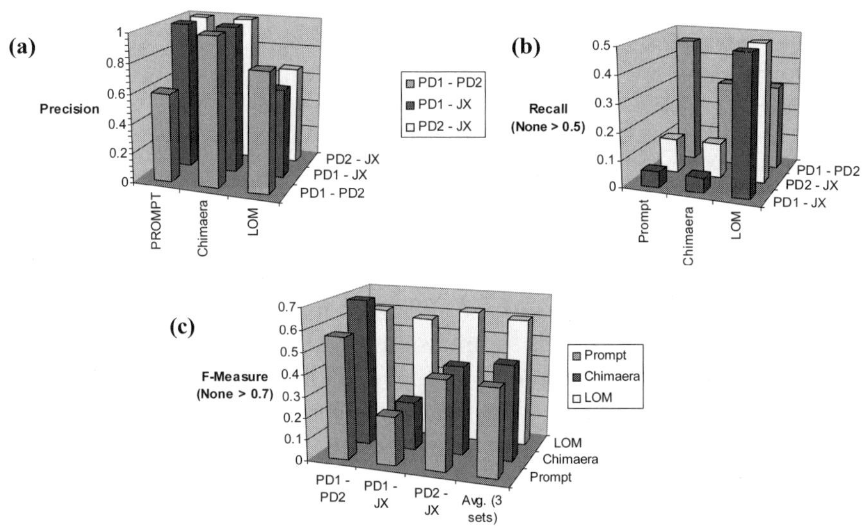

Figure 14-3. (a) Precision, (b) Recall, (c) F-measure - in matching person ontologies

The three tools are represented on the X-axis, the precision values are shown on the Y-axis, and on the Z-axis are the pairs of ontologies being matched. It can be seen that Chimaera consistently identified the most accurate matches across all three pairs of ontologies.

LOM was generally lower in accuracy then the other two techniques; however this statement is qualified by the recall metrics in Figure 14-3(b).

As can be seen from the figure, none of the tools had a recall greater than 50%. LOM had a higher recall in matching both PD1 and PD2 to JX. The advantage of referring to secondary sources like WordNet was clear as LOM suggested matches like 'gender' to 'sex.' It appeared that the NLP techniques of the tools suffered due to GJXDM's use of the ISO standard naming system for data elements (e.g., 'PersonGivenName' instead of 'GivenName'). This may have prevented exact and partial matches on class names. LOM had a higher average F-score (0.66) as compared to Chimaera (0.44) and PROMPT (0.40) as shown in Figure 14-3(c). Please note that the values on the X-axis and Z-axis in Figure 14-3(c) have been swapped for clarity.

3.1.4 Study conclusions

The study concluded that the three mapping tools PROMPT, Chimaera, and LOM achieved a high average precision of 85% when matching three ontologies with the number of classes ranging from 17 to 73. However, the tools suffered in recall (average of 27%) probably because of the lack of common terminology between the ontologies. Since the U.S. Department of Justice is encouraging the use of GJXDM as a standard for information interchange it would be beneficial to use GJXDM as a vocabulary to define public safety ontologies so current mapping tools can achieve better accuracy and recall.

3.2 Case Study 2: Using Ontologies for Sharing and Analysis of Extremist Data

This study [13] done at University of Maryland College Park explored the use of semantic web technologies for consolidating, analyzing, and sharing of terrorist related data using a web portal[1]. The web portal provides any user the ability to submit RDF or a Uniform Resource Indicators (URIs) of documents with data pertaining to the identity properties, activities, relationships, and other details of an extremist individual. Using ontologies, the portal can combine statements (facts) from various files into a single model [13]. This is done by mapping between concepts to connect items that are related or equivalent.

After a major crime or in this case, a terrorist attack, investigators in multiple agencies investigate and collect data on possible perpetrators. This frequently involves various ranks of investigators in multiple agencies from

---

[1]The demo of the Semantic Web Terrorism Knowledge Base is available at http://profilesinterror.mindswap.org/

all tiers of government. Usually it is found that the suspects have contacts with multiple public safety agencies in many jurisdictions. This information is commonly stored in agency specific data sources that may be ad-hoc databases or even link-charts and other details on paper. Many times the structure of these data sources is only understandable to the individual or team that created them.

The Semantic Web Terrorism Knowledge Base facilitates the construction and use of these sorts of informal databases [13]. It also allows the sharing of data electronically and shows the process of the investigation – the quality of information, the false leads, and even hunches [13] to all parties involved in the investigation using a uniform and standard platform.

The portal is powered by a terrorism ontology[2] that has been written in OWL DL (Description Logic). It contains seventy classes and 173 properties for topics including events, relationships, resources, locations, and the relationships among them [24].The ontology is used to annotate these topics (classes) among news stories (and possibly other sources). Once the classes are annotated, the ontology can be used to derive relationships to help users analyze the data. Figure 14-4, next page, shows an example of a semantic web page for a terrorist event. It can be seen that the ontology can not only be used to annotate important properties about the event but can also visualize the relationships between them.

Even though this study showcases the use of a terrorism ontology; such ontologies can make a big impact in the sharing and analysis of data in all spheres of public safety.

Study conclusions

The study concluded that semantic web technologies hold great promise for efforts towards counter-terrorism and public safety. Ontologies allow information to be encoded so that the processing abilities of the computer can be employed to sift through data. This capability is likely to help analysts quickly obtain relevant information and can effectively multiply their capabilities by using automated techniques and bringing more analysts into the process [13].

4. CONCLUSION

Sharing information between public safety agencies is a task fraught with policy issues in addition to technical challenges. Ontologies provide a

[2] www.mindswap.org/dav/ontologies/terrorism.owl

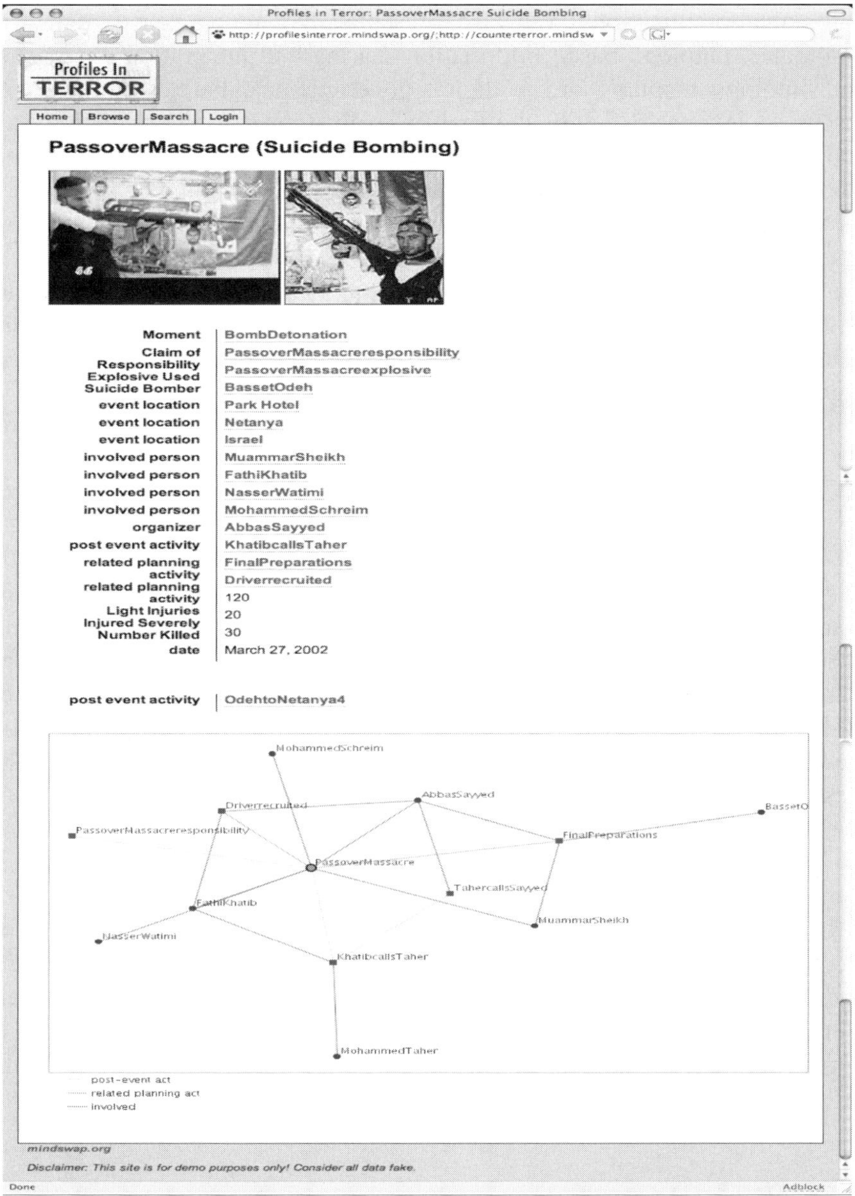

Figure 14-4. An example semantic web page from the Semantic Web Terrorism Knowledge Base (From [13])

promising solution to address the information sharing and interoperability problems in this domain.

In this chapter we conducted a survey of public safety information sharing initiatives and found that the major initiatives had many important ontological implications. We also presented a comprehensive review on ontologies, ontology-based information sharing and integration approaches, and ontology mapping in the digital government and other domains. We discussed two case studies, the first on evaluating ontology mapping tools and the second on using ontologies for sharing and analysis of extremist data. The mapping study concluded that ontology mapping tools suffer in recall when the data sources do not share a common vocabulary. The second case study showed that the use of ontologies provides an opportunity for analysts at multiple public safety agencies to share and analyze information with relative ease. Future research in ontology-based public safety information sharing can make significant contributions to the discipline of digital government.

ACKNOWLEDGEMENTS

This research (including Case Study 1) was supported in part by the NSF Digital Government (DG) program: "COPLINK Center: Information and Knowledge Management for Law Enforcement" #9983304, NSF Knowledge Discovery and Dissemination (KDD) program: "COPLINK Border Safe Research and Testbed" #9983304, NSF Information Technology Research (ITR) program: "COPLINK Center for Intelligence and Security Informatics Research - A Crime Data Mining Approach to Developing Border Safe Research" #0326348, and Department of Homeland Security (DHS) through the "BorderSafe" initiative #2030002.

We thank our BorderSafe project partners: Tucson Police Department, Pima County Sheriff's Department, Tucson Customs and Border Protection, ARJIS (Automated Regional Justice Information Systems), San Diego Super Computer Center (SDSC), SPAWAR, Department of Homeland Security, and Corporation for National Research Initiatives (CNRI). We also thank Homa Atabakhsh of the AI Lab at the University of Arizona and Tim Petersen of the Tucson Police Department for their contributions to this research.

REFERENCES

1. J. L. Ambite, Y. Arens, E. Hovy, A. Philpot, L. Gravano, V. Hatzivassiloglou, and J. Klavans (2001) Simplifying Data Access: The Energy data Collection Project. IEEE Computer 18 47-54
2. Y. Arens, C.-N. Hsu, and C. A. Knoblock (1996) Query Processing in the SIMS Information Mediator. AAAI Press, California, USA
3. T. Berners-Lee, J. Hendler, and O. Lassila (2001) The Semantic Web. Scientific American

4. A. Bouguettaya, M. Ouzzami, B. Medjahed, and J. Cameron (2001) Managing government databases. Computer 34 56-64
5. H. Chen (2002) Digital Government: Technologies and Practices. Decision Support Systems 34 223-227
6. H. Chen, D. Zeng, H. Atabakhsh, W. Wyzga, and J. Schroeder (2003) COPLINK Managing Law Enforcement Data and Knowledge. Communications of the ACM 46
7. A. Doan, J. Madhavan, P. Domingos, and A. Y. Halevy (2002) Learning to Map between Ontologies on the Semantic Web. In: Proc. of 11th International World Wide Web Conference (WWW 2002)
8. T. Edgington, B. Choi, K. Henson, T. S. Raghu, and A. Vinze (2004) Adopting ontology to facilitate knowledge sharing Commun. ACM 47 85-90
9. A. Firat and S. Madnick (2001) Knowledge Integration to Ontological Heterogeneity: Challenges from Financial Information Systems. In: Proc. of Twenty-Third International Conference on Information Systems (ICIS), Barcelona, Spain
10. A. Gal, G. Modica, H. Jamil, and A. Eyal (2005) Automatic Ontology Matching Using Application Semantics, in *AI Magazine*.
11. A. Gangemi, N. Guarino, C. Masolo, and A. Oltramari (2003) Sweetening Wordnet with DOLCE, in *AI Magazine*. vol. 24, pp. 13-24.
12. C. H. Goh (1997) Representing and Reasoning about Semantic Conflicts in Heterogeneous Information Sources: MIT.
13. J. Golbeck, A. Mannes, and J. Hendler (2005) Semantic Web Technologies for Terrorist Network Analysis in *Emergent Technologies and Enabling Policies for Counter Terrorism* IEEE Press.
14. T. R. Gruber (1993) A Translation Approach to Portable Ontologies. Knowledge Acquisition 5 199-220
15. M. Gruninger and J. B. Kopena (2005) Semantic Integration through Invariants, in *AI Magazine*.
16. R. V. Hauck, H. Atabakhsh, P. Ongvasith, H. Gupta, and H. Chen (2002) Using Coplink to Analyze Criminal-Justice Data. Computer 35 30-37
17. E. Hovy, A. Philpot, J. L. Ambite, Y. Arens, J. Klavans, W. Bourne, and D. Saroz (2001) Data Acquisition and Integration in the DGRC's Energy Data Collect Project. In: Proc. of First National Conference on Digital Government (dg. o 2001), Los Angeles, California
18. Y. Kalfoglou and M. Schorlemmer (2002) Information-flow-based Ontology Mapping. On the Move to Meaningful Internet Systems 2002: CoopIS, DOA, and ODBASE - Lecture Notes in Computer Science, Springer,
19. Y. Kalfoglou and M. Schorlemmer (2003) Ontology Mapping: the State of the Art. The Knowledge Engineering Review 18 1-31
20. S. Kaza and H. Chen (2005) Evaluating Ontology Mapping Techniques: An Experiment in Public Safety Information Sharing. In: Proc. of Workshop on Information Technologies and Systems (WITS 05), Las Vegas, NV
21. W. Kim and J. Seo (1991) Classifying Schematic and Data Heterogeneity in Multidatabase Systems. IEEE Computer 24 12-18
22. D. B. Lenat (1995) Cyc: A Large-Scale Investment in Knowledge Infrastructure. Commun. ACM 38 33-38
23. J. Li (2004) LOM: A Lexicon-based Ontology Mapping Tool. In: Proc. of Information Interpretation and Integration Conference (I3CON)
24. A. Mannes and J. Golbeck (2006) Building a Terrorism Ontology. http://profilesinterror.mindswap.org/2005/TerrorOntologyfinal.pdf, Accessed: May 5 2006.

25. S. March, A. Hevner, and S. Ram (2000) Research Commentary: An Agenda for Information Technology Research in Heterogeneous and Distributed Environments. Information Systems Research 11 327-341
26. D. McGuinness, R. Fikes, J. Rice, and S. Wilder (2000) An Environment for Merging and Testing Large Ontologies. In: Proc. of 17th International Conference on Principles of Knowledge Representation and Reasoning (KR 00)
27. E. Mena, V. Kashyap, A. Sheth, and A. Illarramendi (1996) OBSERVER: A Approach for Query Processing in Global Information Systems Based on Interoperability Between Pre-existing Ontologies. In: Proc. of 1st IFCIS International Conference on Cooperative Information Systems (CooPIS '96), Brussels
28. P. Mitra, N. F. Noy, and A. R. Jaiswal (2004) OMEN: A Probabilistic Ontology Mapping Tool. In: Proc. of 3rd International Conference on the Semantic Web, Hiroshima, Japan
29. I. Niles and A. Pease (2001) Towards a Standard Upper Ontology. In: Proc. of The Second International Conference on Formal Ontology in Information Systems, Ogunquit, Maine
30. N. F. Noy, A. Doan, and A. Y. Halevy (2005) Semantic Integration, in *AI Magazine*.
31. N. F. Noy and M. A. Musen (2001) Anchor-PROMPT: Using Non-Local Context for Semantic Matching. In: Proc. of Workshop on Ontologies and Information Sharing at the International Joint Conference on Artificial Intelligence (IJCAI)
32. N. F. Noy and M. A. Musen (2000) PROMPT: Algorithm and Tool for Automated Ontology Merging and Alignment. In: Proc. of 17th national Conference on Artificial Intelligence (AAAI'00)
33. N. F. Noy and M. A. Musen (2002) PROMTDIFF: A Fixed-point Algorithm for Comparing Ontology Versions. In: Proc. of 18th national Conference on Artificial Intelligence (AAAI '02)
34. D. E. O'Leary (2000) Different firms, different ontologies, and no one best ontology. Intelligent Systems and Their Applications, IEEE [see also IEEE Intelligent Systems] 15 72-78
35. B. Omelayenko (2001) Integration of product ontologies for B2B marketplaces: a preview SIGecom Exch. 2 19-25
36. P. Pantel, A. Philpot, and E. Hovy (2005) Aligning Database Columns using Mutual Information. In: Proc. of The 6th National Conference on Digital Government Research (dg.o), Atlanta, GA
37. J. Park and S. Ram (2004) Information Systems Interoperability: What Lies Beneath? ACM Transactions on Information Systems 22
38. E. Rahm and P. A. Bernstein (2001) A Survey of Approaches to Automatic Schema Matching. VLDB Journal 10
39. R. Stevens, P. Baker, S. Bechhofer, G. Ng, A. Jacoby, N. W. Paton, C. A. Goble, and A. Brass (2000) TAMBIS: Transparent Access to Multiple Bioinformatics Information Sources. Bioinformatics 16 184-185
40. G. Stumme and A. Maedche (2001) Ontology Merging for Federated Ontologies on the Semantic Web. In: Proc. of International Workshop for Foundations of Models for Information Integration (FMII 2001)
41. M. Uschold and M. Gruninger (2004) Ontologies and Semantics for Seamless Connectivity. SIGMOD Record 33
42. H. Wache, T. Vogele, U. Visser, H. Stuckenschmidt, G. Schuster, H. Neumann, and S. Hubner (2001) Ontology-Based Integration of Information - A Survey of Existing Approaches. In: Proc. of IJCAI Workshop: Ontologies and Information Sharing, Seattle, WA

SUGGESTED READINGS

- H. Chen (2006) Intelligence and Security Informatics for International Security: Information Sharing and Data Mining. Springer, Berlin. This book has a comprehensive coverage of various aspects of information sharing and data mining techniques in the public safety domain.
- D. Fensel (2001) Ontologies: A Silver Bullet for Knowledge Management and Electronic Commerce. Springer, Berlin. Systematically introduces the notion of ontologies to the non-expert and gives practical examples on the use of ontologies for knowledge management.
- J. W. Seifert (2006) Data Mining and Homeland Security: An Overview. Congressional Research Service. Washington, D.C. This report to the congress discusses privacy concerns with the sharing of data among various government and private agencies. It includes several information sharing systems developed by the government and private companies.
- H. Atabakhsh, C. Larson, T. Petersen, C. Violette, and H. Chen (2004) Information Sharing and Collaboration Policies within Government Agencies. In: Proc. of Intelligence and Security Informatics (ISI 2004), Tucson, AZ. This paper discusses the security, privacy, and policy issues of sharing information between public safety and health related agencies. Detailed case studies are also presented.

ONLINE RESOURCES

- Global Justice XML Data Model
  http://it.ojp.gov/jxdm/
  The official site of the GJXDM. Contains links to the standard and sample data structures based on it.
- National Information Exchange Model
  http://www.niem.gov/
- The Protégé Ontology Editor and Knowledge Acquisition System
  http://protege.stanford.edu/
- Presidential Executive Order 13356
  http://www.fas.org/irp/offdocs/eo/eo-13356.htm
  The executive order of the U.S. president requiring the sharing of information among public safety agencies.
- University of Arizona Artificial Intelligence Lab, Public safety research
  http://ai.eller.arizona.edu/

QUESTIONS FOR DISCUSSION

1. Why is it important for government and especially public safety agencies to share information with each other?
2. What are the challenges in sharing information among public safety agencies? Are these challenges purely technical in nature?
3. What are the recent initiatives for national level information sharing? Why do you think most of the new initiatives concentrate on defining global data standards?
4. Discuss the various approaches to ontology-based information integration. Is any one of these approaches especially suited to the public safety domain?
5. Do you think ontologies can truly provide no-hassle, seamless connectivity between disparate sources in the digital government and other domains?

Chapter 15

COLLABORATIVE CYBERINFRASTRUCTURE FOR TRANSNATIONAL DIGITAL GOVERNMENT

Maurício Tsugawa, Andréa Matsunaga, and José A. B. Fortes

Department of Electrical and Computer Engineering, University of Florida, Gainesville, Forida, U.S.A. (fortes@ufl.edu)

CHAPTER OVERVIEW

This chapter discusses issues faced when both the IT infrastructure of the government agencies of different countries and existing software applications must be reused without modification to develop a cyberinfrastructure for transnational digital government. The sources of heterogeneity across IT infrastructures and software applications are identified and the impact of these sources on interoperability and compatibility of hardware, software, communication, data and security mechanisms are analyzed. Virtualization technologies are introduced as a means for coping with infrastructure heterogeneity and enabling the deployment of unmodified applications on existing infrastructures. A concrete case of digital government that entails the sharing of immigration information between Belize and the Dominican Republic is described. This example is also used to validate and evaluate the benefits of virtualization technologies in developing and deploying the cyberinfrastructure needed to implement a transnational information system for border control.

1. INTRODUCTION

Transnational digital government (TDG) entails collaboration among organizations of different countries towards solving problems whose nature transcends geopolitical borders and boundaries. Primary means of collaboration include services for the exchange of data and information, and processes that make it possible for knowledge to be extracted from data and for informed actions to take place. These forms of collaboration are precursors and enablers of other types of collaboration such as the sharing of human expertise, health assistance, financial support, disaster relief, and successful solutions to common problems.

This chapter discusses a general approach for developing cyber-infrastructure for collaborative digital government based on experiences and lessons learned from a concrete TDG system implementation. The TDG project, involving three countries, required the integration of existing applications into the information systems of immigration agencies in Belize and the Dominican Republic. The applications include conversational user-interfaces, automatic translation tools and a distributed query system. In this context, the key problem to be addressed (and the focus of this chapter) can be stated as follows: what methods and technologies should be used to build and deploy transnational DG systems that aggregate several independently developed applications with different resource requirements, without modifying either the IT infrastructure of the government agencies or the software of the applications.

The implementation of TDG is complicated by several interrelated problems which include:

- Sociopolitical issues: these result from differences in cultural, governmental and strategic goals and practices among participating entities of different countries; these differences often result into conflicting requirements for the design, implementation and operation of TDG systems; examples of similar challenges and how they can be addressed are the subjects of Chapters 21 through 30 of this text.
- Scalability and sustainability issues: these result from the need to integrate a potentially large number of participants and the common expectation of effective participation by all of them (possibly over long periods of time); in regional and global efforts the numbers of participants can be in the hundreds or even thousands and the overall system may be compromised by the weakest link (i.e. any participating entity that fails to fulfill its part in the collaborative effort).
- Cyberinfrastructure issues: these result from the ever-present, often extreme, differences in hardware, software and data schemes used by

information technology (IT) infrastructures of participating entities from distinct countries; unless mitigated by proper system design and technologies, these differences exacerbate the sociopolitical, scalability and sustainability issues. They can prevent the deployment of essential IT services for TDG and/or their interoperability.

Broadly speaking, the cyberinfrastructure issues can be divided into two categories. The first, associated with the physical infrastructure and services layers of every system, includes the challenges of creation and interoperation of information processing environments – programs, tools, databases and libraries – for the deployment and operation of cyberinfrastructure needed for digital government activities. The second, associated with the data and semantics layers, includes the need to integrate data and extract information and knowledge from distributed sources, and implement processes enabled by the services layer. Information on data integration issues can be found in chapters 11 and 12 of this text. The focus of this chapter is on the first category of cyberinfrastructure issues, i.e. those faced in enabling each participating entity to implement the necessary services for it to play an effective role in a distributed IT system capable of supporting collaborative processes for TDG. The ensuing text discusses the issues in detail and describes applicable solutions, with particular emphasis on the use of virtualization technologies which are also briefly reviewed and explained. Subsequently a case study of a system for transnational collaboration in border control is presented. Conclusions and topics for further reading are included at the end of the chapter.

2. OVERVIEW AND REVIEW OF RELEVANT APPROACHES

The first and most obvious obstacles faced when integrating resources from different countries into a collaborative cyberinfrastructure are those that result from heterogeneity across IT systems. In general, heterogeneity is inevitable as it results from differences in economical and technical capabilities of the countries, as well as from conceptual mismatches due to differences in agency missions and their regulatory context (which may, for example, specify what kind of software must be used) and inequalities of human IT resources. In general, integration may require the use of new and/or existing hardware and/or software at different locations, processing and accessing data located in distinct government agencies, and communication among many IT entities. In this context, heterogeneity can lead to several types of incompatibilities among infrastructures, as shown in Table 15-1.

The heterogeneity that causes the problems listed in Table 15-1 can be easily eliminated when entirely new systems are created by a single software developer (often a major IT provider who can create integrated solutions). This developer can create (and typically sell) entire distributed systems whose software and hardware components are either homogeneous or interoperable. This approach is unrealistic in the many instances of TDG that are either transient, incremental to local government, responsive to unpredictable events, or intended to allow participating countries to join as needed and as possible. Two general scenarios arise in these instances. One is the case when all the necessary software for TDG is to be developed anew. The other occurs when the countries decide to use components previously developed by different sources (possibly by members of the transnational partnership, open sources, etc.).

Table 15-1. Incompatibilities due to system heterogeneity

Incompatibility	Description
Hardware	When machines do not have the architecture or capabilities needed to run machine-dependent software.
Software	When TDG software components require additional software that is either unavailable or conflicts with software used for local government functions. The extreme case is that of software that runs on operating systems that are different in type/version from the ones needed by local applications.
Communication	When TDG software components lack (1) interfaces for communication or (2) commonly understood protocols for communication. Both are often absent in components originally intended for stand-alone machines, legacy software and in-house software developed for local government.
Data	When data maintained by TDG software components use different organization, structure, semantics and natural language, making the direct integration and interoperation of these components impossible.
Security and accessibility	When TDG software components that need to be integrated either lack or have distinct non-interoperable mechanisms for network security and access control.

In the first case it is possible to adopt common interfaces and protocols for communication among all software components (using, for example, a Web Service architecture [21]) and use a machine-independent language (such as Java [37] and C# [9]) to develop the software. Unfortunately the second case is more common as there are significant opportunities for increased functionality and lower cost when reusing existing software and only developing middleware to glue, or add to, existing components. This suits government agencies because (1) they typically have their own established IT infrastructure, which cannot easily be replaced or modified, and (2) time and resource constraints preclude the rewriting of existing software. Previously-developed software can in some cases be "wrapped" or converted into standards-complying solutions (e.g., turned into Web Services). This approach is not sufficient or universally applicable and, as exemplified by the case study of this chapter and in [36], it should be viewed as only an important part of a general solution.

A problem that is related to that of deploying software on heterogeneous IT infrastructures is that of integrating heterogeneous information systems. Several approaches have been put forward to address this problem in the context of enterprises. For example, the Enterprise Application Integration (EAI) approach [47, 29, 31, 18] advocates the use of a common communication framework for directly coupling applications. This framework prescribes the use of not only the standard ISO/OSI protocols but also common syntax, semantics and pragmatics as needed to enable the understanding of data, associating data with real-world objects and conveying actions among objects, respectively. Existing and emerging Web Service technologies exemplify some of the standards needed to implement EAI, particularly for distributed enterprises and cross-organizational business processes. As already mentioned, digital government can reuse similar concepts and technologies to hide process-level heterogeneities.

However, both EAI and Web Service approaches assume that (1) the underlying information systems are already operational or no obstacles exist for them to be deployed, and (2) any needed additional IT modules can be integrated and deployed into these existing information systems. As such, EAI and Web Services are insufficient for the rapid integration of previously-developed software into existing information systems that lack the kinds of resources needed for execution of that software. They are also insufficient for the deployment of information systems that are to be built out of existing subsystems with different resource requirements. These situations are common in transnational government where resources are disparate and hard to acquire, replace or update due to economical, administrative and socio-political constraints of the participating countries. In such cases resource virtualization, as explained in the remainder of this chapter, is a must.

This chapter advocates the use of virtualization technologies to mask away heterogeneity of hardware and software execution environments (the first two items in Table 15-1), as a necessary complement to the use of other higher-level forms of virtualization (e.g., Web Services [21] and Enterprise Application Integration [18]) to address interoperation incompatibilities (the last three items in Table 15-1). The following paragraphs briefly introduce machine virtualization technologies and their benefits in the context of the first three incompatibilities identified in Table 15-1 - hardware, software and communication. Also briefly discussed is the use of Web Services and related technologies to help address the other three types of incompatibilities – communication, data and security.

2.1 Hardware Incompatibility

Any widely-applicable sustainable IT-based approach to transnational digital government must assume that resources are heterogeneous. Heterogeneity manifests itself in more ways than the architectural differences among the machines being used. Differences in processor speed, memory and storage size, operating system type and version, network connectivity, and installed software all contribute to heterogeneity. Even if it was possible to create a homogeneous infrastructure distributed across several agencies, such infrastructure would, over time, become heterogeneous as machines, operating systems and other software get maintained and upgraded (or not) at different points in time by different government agencies.

The need to deal with hardware architecture mismatches and the associated inabilities to run certain codes (e.g., binaries for which source codes are not available) has long been recognized by industry. A variety of approaches have been proposed, all of which can be viewed from the perspective of machine virtualization. Smith and Nair's taxonomy and introduction to virtual machines (VMs) [33] puts extant approaches into a clear perspective which is briefly summarized here. Virtualization denotes the use of software that emulates the desired architecture on a different architecture by translating instructions for the former into instructions for the latter. When translations are done only for the application binary interface (i.e. the processor and operating system instructions accessible by application binaries) then the resulting VMs are called process-VMs (in this context, the term "process" has a different meaning - associated with running a program - from the same term used in the context of enterprise applications where it is associated with operational procedures of an enterprise). When translations are also done for system instructions the VMs are called system-VMs. This apparently small distinction leads to VMs with significantly different capabilities. Informally, and to provide some intuition on the differences, process-VMs preserve the host system view and translate both the (process) code and state into what the system expects from a native process, whereas system-VMs translate between the entire host system and an entirely new guest system where the computer process runs as if it was running on the system for which it was originally programmed.

Examples of process-VMs include popular software used to run Windows applications on SUN Sparc [15] and on Linux platforms [4]. Other examples are the so-called High Level Language (HLL) VMs which include the JAVA-VM architecture [37] and the Microsoft Common Language Infrastructure [9] where the translation occurs via a software-defined machine specially developed for each type of architecture. Examples of system-VMs include both commercial and public-domain products. Commercial offerings include VMware [44], VirtualPC [16] and z/VM [17] whereas public domain examples are Bochs [23], Xen [5], QEMU [6] and PearPC [7]. To expand on the differences between process-VMs and system-VMs, the former allow many computer processes designed for different OSes to run on a given platform (a platform denotes the combination of a machine with a given Instruction Set Architecture (ISA) and the installed operating system). On the other hand, system-VMs allow many different systems to coexist in the physical host, each system possibly being a platform of different type. For example, the process-VM Darwine [46] allows a Macintosh machine to execute a Windows application, and the Java-VM allows it to execute any Java application, but there is only one operating system (OS) environment which is the MacOS running on the physical machine. In contrast a system-VM VMware Workstation can be used to create several VMs on a Linux machine, where each machine could be either a distinctly configured Windows XP/2000/95 machine or another Linux machine.

In the context of TDG, HLL VMs such as the Java-VM offer the possibility of developing code that runs in every physical machine with the HLL VM. However, while this may be an attractive approach for deploying Java code, it can not fully address situations when significant non-Java code also needs to be deployed and interfaced. On the other hand, system-VMs allow the creation of VMs as needed by software and, in principle, can fully eliminate any hardware or OS conflicts. System-VMs can thus remove the need for countries to incur expenses for acquisition of new hardware or changing their existing infrastructures to conform to hardware expectations. Even if economical barriers do not exist, administrative and other barriers (e.g., lack of trained personnel to maintain and operate the new resources) are significant obstacles to the deployment of new hardware. In this sense, system-VMs can be used to circumvent some economic, administrative and logistic barriers to TDG. Moreover, as the ensuing discussion will show, system-VMs also contribute to the elimination of other incompatibilities, and can potentially help mitigate other economical and institutional barriers. For brevity and unless otherwise stated, the term VM is hereon used to mean a system-VM.

Virtualization gets around functional heterogeneity but cannot provide virtual machines of higher performance than that of their physical host. Performance issues can involve processing speed, memory size, storage capacity and network bandwidth. If the physical machines with the required performance are not available in an organization, then remote execution can help by running necessary tasks where computing power is available. In the context of using VMs for TDG, this means that it is possible for an agency to use a VM created at another agency or location. Advances in Grid-computing technology [14], as exemplified by the In-VIGO system [2], and improved networking across countries will make this effective and practical in the near future. Through role-based access control mechanisms [1], Grid resources can be accessed in a secure fashion by users from different agencies. Since VMs are isolated from each other and their host, they naturally support both the secure sharing of the physical resource and the protection of information used by each VM. For all practical purposes, a virtual machine provided by a remote physical machine will appear just as any other local resource.

2.2 Software Incompatibility

Software applications often require other software in order to run properly – this "other'' software and the resources needed to run it define the so-called "execution environment" of the application – it typically includes the operating system, software libraries and possibly other programs. In general, one can say that each application requires an execution environment and that multiple applications can coexist in the same machine only if their execution environments are compatible. This is where VMs can be used to provide separate machines, each with the needed environment for one or more applications. It is possible to envision IT infrastructures with either physical machines or VMs dedicated to local government and locally-managed environments for local applications, along with VMs dedicated to TDG and separately-managed environments for the associated applications. Many different VMs can run on the same physical resources, thus allowing the consolidation of several machines needed by several distinct execution environments into a single machine. This eliminates the need to acquire or install additional resources thus further removing potential economical or logistic barriers to TDG deployment.

2.3 Communication Incompatibility

TDG IT systems are inherently distributed and include software components that need to communicate over a network in order to exchange information. If these software components were originally designed to work in isolation or to communicate through the OS of a single machine, it becomes necessary to modify or extend them so that they can use the network. If they are already network-aware, modifications may still be necessary so that communicating peers use mutually-understood protocols to exchange information. This process can involve recompilation (which would be impossible without source code) or reengineering of the components (which would be too slow and expensive). To smooth the initial integration and subsequent management of the components, they should have been designed using loosely-coupled, open standard protocols and cross-technology implementations, (as currently offered by Web Services [21] and Service Oriented Architecture (SOA) solutions). However, this ideal solution is not a realistic expectation, especially for legacy applications. One solution to this problem is to wrap legacy software components into Web Services making them interoperable with each other. This process can, in some cases, be automated. Another solution is to use drivers or bridges that make conversions between protocols, a common approach for accessing data management systems. However, the latter solution scales poorly in the sense that it can require a large amount of code to be developed.

Assuming that one or more of the solutions enable distributed components of a system to communicate with each other within a single administrative domain (e.g., an agency or a country), challenges remain for such communication to occur across domains. Private networks and the presence of firewalls prevent symmetrical connectivity (in the sense that components behind firewalls can initiate communication with other components but a component outside a firewalled domain cannot initiate communication with components behind a firewall). This fact prevents machines in private networks or behind firewalls to run server software components. To address this problem it is necessary to use virtual networks, such as those proposed and studied in [42]. These virtual networks can be thought of as overlays (on the physical network) that use network addresses that are distinct from physical addresses and virtual routers to communicate to/from those addresses using standard protocols.

2.4 Data Incompatibility

In general, information systems manage data in many possible ways. They can use different data models (e.g., data could be stored as flat records in files, hierarchically in directories or XML files, as objects in object-oriented databases, as relations in relational databases). Different query languages can also be used, e.g., LDAP query, XQuery, and different flavors of SQL, along with different communication protocols (usually each database provider defines its own protocol). Also possible are different attribute types, format and precision (e.g., date or timestamp, integers or real numbers with different precision), and schemas (e.g., different table and attribute names). Data granularity can also differ, e.g. a person's name could be stored as a full name or partitioned into first, middle and last names. Other incompatibilities can be due to semantic differences (e.g., a temperature attribute could be stored in Celsius or Fahrenheit), different transaction management (e.g., with or without concurrency control capability), the application of different constraints and the use of distinct natural languages.

The process of integrating components into a system with all the above-mentioned differences is challenging. To hide differences in communication protocol it is possible to find drivers and/or bridges to the majority of systems. For example, drivers for various databases exist following the Java Database Connectivity (JDBC) [38] Application Programming Interface (API), the industry standard for database-independent connectivity between the Java programming language and a wide range of databases; and bridges to create communication between JDBC drivers and Open Database Connectivity (ODBC) drivers or between JDBC drivers and Lightweight Directory Access Protocol (LDAP) servers are available [39, 26]. For the other types of data discrepancies, there are a large number of specific middleware solutions [32, 20, 24, 19], which basically create abstraction layers to mediate the above-listed differences, possibly applying some optimization and preserving the autonomy of the local data management. A typical middleware layer is usually driven by some metadata that can be created either automatically (e.g., assisted by semantic, ontology or linguistic technologies) or manually with system assistance.

2.5 Security Incompatibility

Many software applications do not include security features simply because they were intended to be used locally, possibly by a single user or several users within a government agency or administrative domain. However, once a component is made globally accessible (to other components or users) there is a critical need to add security capabilities such as authentication, authorization, confidentiality, and integrity. At the same time there is a need to enable single-sign on in order to avoid user inconveniences and maintenance overheads. If Web Services are used for software wrapping, existing security standards can often be leveraged to provide the necessary security capabilities.

3. APPLICATION OF MACHINE VIRTUALIZATION TO TDG AND A CASE STUDY

TDG entails both the execution of well-planned long-term inter-government agreements and protocols as well as unanticipated, possibly transient and urgent, multi-government engagements in addressing common problems. While applicable to the former, VMs are particularly well suited for the latter cases. Such cases would require the quick assembly (and possible subsequent disassembly) of collaborating IT systems that must reuse unmodified software components. In such scenarios, it is particularly appealing to create VMs pre-configured with all the software needed for deployment. Services for the efficient automatic creation and deployment of VMs have been shown to be effective in Grid-computing infrastructures such as In-VIGO [2, 22]. Similar approaches could be used for deploying TDG government systems over the Internet.

A generic scenario for TDG, which subsumes many others with fewer requirements, entails the following:

1. The need to deploy several software packages or services at multiple locations in each of several participating countries; each package may require its own type of machine and execution environment. To address this need, as many VMs as necessary are created - on possibly a single physical resource that already exists - at each location. These VMs and the necessary interactions among them can be preconfigured and automatically replicated at each location.

2. The need to enable interactions between (a) the newly deployed software services and (b) these services and pre-existing software and databases.

3. The need for user-interfaces that use languages spoken in each of the countries and intuitive conversational interactions that facilitate the operation of the system in the field. To address this need, machine translation techniques and dialogue engines can be used (as discussed in [36] and in the case study presented in this section).

The ideas discussed so far have been applied in, and partially motivated by, the context of a real-world TDG system [36] intended for border control information sharing, coordination and collaboration among government agencies in two countries: Belize and the Dominican Republic. Typical capabilities enabled by the integrated system include the detection and control of illegal immigration and illicit drug trafficking. Reference [36] describes the overall TDG system and its software components, including technical aspects related to the last two points of the above list. The focus of this chapter is on the first listed item (which is not discussed in [36]) and the interoperability and integration aspects of the last two items. It illustrates the need for a multi-level virtualization approach where machine virtualization is an essential complement of process-level virtualization technologies. As it is likely to happen for most TDG systems, this case study integrates software components developed by several groups in different organizations. Specifically, the following components are used:

1. Distributed Query Processor (DQP) [19]: a distributed component developed at the University of Florida; it allows intra- and inter-government agencies to share information using existing heterogeneous legacy information systems by providing a friendly user-interface to map disparities in schemas exported by each local information component described below.

2. Local Information Subsystem (IS): also developed at the University of Florida, this component manages and contains the actual information that is of interest for each agency and/or country and can potentially be shared. In the TDG project, there is an IS in Belize and another one in the Dominican Republic.

3. Machine Translation component (MT) [8]: a multi-engine translation framework developed at Carnegie Mellon University; it includes an Example-Based Machine Translation (EBMT) engine, a Glossary engine, and a Dictionary engine that translates a sentence from a source language to a target language, in particular English-Spanish and Spanish-English.

4. Conversational System component (CS): a natural language parsing and dialogue management framework; it is based on the following two components from the Communicator Spoken Dialog System [28] developed at the University of Colorado (CU): (1) Phoenix [45], a robust semantic parser designed to extract information from spontaneous speech into domain specific frames; and (2) Dialogue Manager (DM), which maintains a dialogue context and history, and builds database queries (SQL).

5. Event Notification component (EN) [35]: another distributed component developed at the University of Florida; it enables the close communication, coordination, and collaboration of participating countries and their agencies by providing automatic distribution of selected important events to subscribing users; it consists of (1) the Event Server, an event definition, subscription, specification and filtering system, and (2) the Event-Trigger-Rule (ETR) Server, which processes the triggers and the rules defined in each site when an event is received from the Event Server; a small portion of this component is placed on what is called the Host Site, a mutually agreed-upon site by the participating countries where the events are registered.

The relationships among these components are shown in Figure 15-1. Each participant country's agency has, in its local information subsystem, its own information which is fully or partially shared with other participants through the DQP. Since, for example, a query can be issued to the DQP in an English speaking country (Belize) and some desired data may be in a Spanish speaking country (Dominican Republic), the DQP makes requests as necessary to the MT to translate parts of the query or response. The users of this TDG system can use either a web interface provided by the DQP or the CS which accepts queries in natural language and maintains a dialogue context. Finally, the DQP also interacts with the EN when some event of interest occurs in the DQP, sending notifications to subscribers of that event.

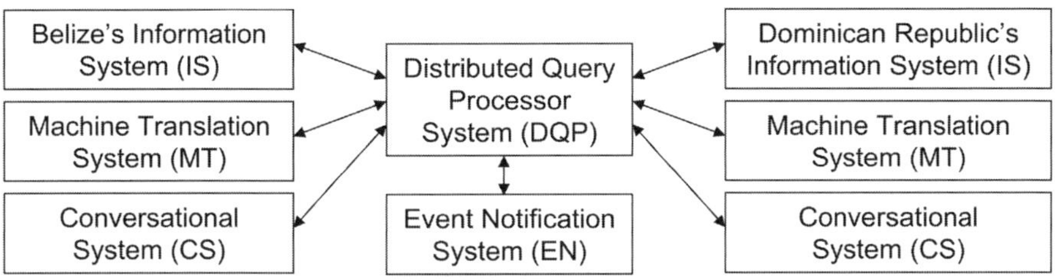

Figure 15-1. Main interacting software components of the TDG system

Table 15-2 shows the different requirements and characteristics of the TDG system components shown in Figure 15-1. An initial decision was made to eliminate hardware incompatibilities by assuming that Windows-machines would be available, since that was deemed to be the case for the prototype system. For cases where the software components required a different OS it was decided to use VMware Workstation version 4.5 to create virtual Windows or Linux machines as needed. The DQP and the EN were partially programmed anew in a platform-independent language (Java) with their main tasks exposed as Web Services. These components were developed in a Windows environment and reused some non-Java components deployed in that environment. Therefore the DQP cannot coexist in the same execution environment as the MT and the CS which run on operating systems other than Windows (Linux). VMware VMs were created for each OS and application in order to enable the DQP, MT and CS to run on the same physical machine. The IS located in Belize and the IS in the Dominican Republic cannot coexist in the same hardware for geographical and political reasons. The MT is network-accessible but, due to its use of a non-standard network protocol, it can not be easily integrated with other components and it lacks security features. The CS does not offer any network capability and is stateful, thus it is not possible to interoperate with this component through the network (only through the OS). It also requires special care in properly wrapping it as a Web Service. Each country's IS uses its own communication protocol, tied to the chosen relational database management system (RDBMS) and has its own structure.

Table 15-2. TDG system components requirements and characteristics

	DQP	EN	MT	CS	ISBE	ISDR
Requirements						
Hardware:						
IBM PC Compatible	✓	✓	✓	✓	✓	✓
Software:						
Windows Operating Sys.	✓	✓			✓	✓
Linux Operating System			✓	✓		
Political:						
Local ownership of local data and their structure					✓	✓
Characteristics						
Source Code Language:						
C			✓	✓		
Java	✓	✓				
Network:						
Distributed System	✓	✓				
Non-Standard Protocol			✓		✓	✓
Standard Protocol	✓	✓				
Interface State:						
Stateless	✓	✓	✓		✓	✓
Stateful				✓		

The integrated system prototype (see Figure 15-2) was successfully deployed by using VMs in a single location with remote access and active-remote display to all university collaborators through In-VIGO. This setup made it possible for different component developers to work independently and collaborate during the integration process despite their geographical distribution and relatively poor network bandwidths for communication with Belize and the Dominican Republic. Another benefit of using VMs during system tests is the possibility of easily changing hardware characteristics (e.g., to find memory leaks or improper network time outs in the software by diminishing the size of memory or the bandwidth of the VM). Furthermore, the system has been easily replicated in Belize and the Dominican Republic since virtualization technology enables whole machines to be cloned [22], thus not requiring software reinstallation in the new set of machines. This feature greatly facilitates field deployment of the system.

Virtualization has more benefits than simply providing many (virtual) machines for the cost of one or a few (physical) machines. Hypothetically, if physical machines became inexpensive enough, one might wonder whether it might be better to use separate physical machines for each distinct environment needed to run different applications instead of using virtualization. However, unlike the use of virtual machines, such solution increases the complexity of management and maintenance of the entire system which could end up having a large number of physical resources with different characteristics (and requiring more people, space and energy). In addition, the use of physical resources does not have the benefits of virtualization which, among others, include the following: (a) virtual machines can be migrated among available physical machines in order to provide load balancing or fault-tolerance (e.g., during host upgrades), (b) identical VM replicas can be created for testing new software or to increase the performance or accessibility of a particular software component, (c) templates of commonly-used VM systems can be created and reused for different purposes, and (d) checkpoints of VM state can be created so that the system can go back to a previous stable state after an unsuccessful system upgrade, reconfiguration or failure.

The legacy components were manually wrapped as Web Services, which required someone with Web Service knowledge to understand the CS and the MT components to create the proper wrappers. It took one person-day to develop the first version. However several iterations were needed involving interactions between the service developer and the CS component developer in order to properly specify the desired service interface. Once these components became network-accessible, it was critical to provide security in this communication by re-using standard Web Services' network security protocols. The communication differences in the local IS were solved by using appropriate JDBC technology-enabled drivers, the data semantic differences (in particular the use of different natural languages) were solved by including procedures that use the MT during the distributed query processing to transform the data. The structural data differences were solved using the DQP [19], which (1) facilitates the manual creation of a global schema with mappings among data entities and attributes based on local schemas exported with some meta-information; and (2) issues distributed retrieval queries mediating the schema differences based on the global schema.

Figure 15-2 depicts the prototype system utilizing the presented solutions.

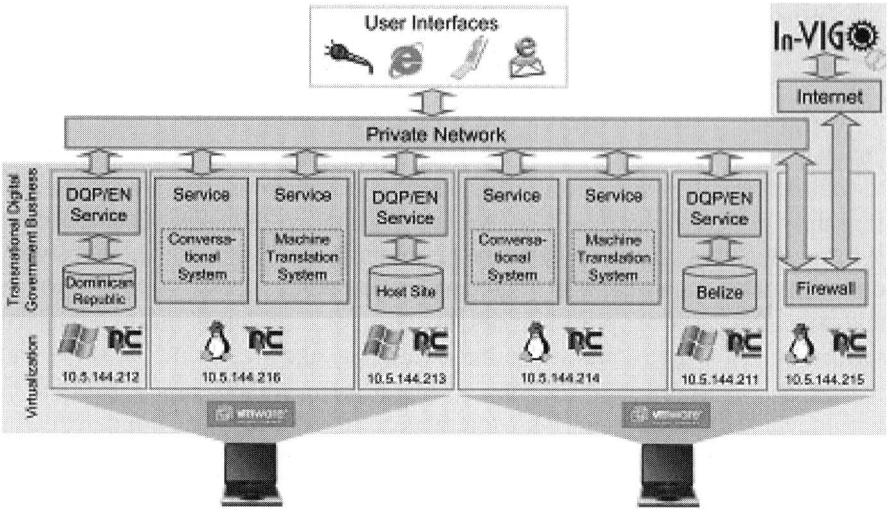

Figure 15-2. Machine virtualization enables the deployment of software components with incompatible operating system requirements on existing hardware and software infrastructures, and Web Services enable the integration and interoperation of deployed applications with incompatible interfaces and communication protocols

While the use of machine virtualization clearly enabled the use of the existing components needed by the TDG system in the available IT resources, the question of whether virtualization overheads would lead to unacceptable software performance had to be considered. The overhead of using VMs depends on the physical host system and characteristics of the workloads of both the physical and virtual machines [10]. For classic VMs, in particular the VMware product used in the TDG project, virtualization overhead is very low for computationally-intensive applications. The overhead is highest when an application requires frequent system and I/O activity. Of the components integrated in the TDG system, IS presents the highest I/O activity. However, this component runs without virtualization, as it is already part of the governments' IT infrastructures. The DQP and EN have moderate I/O activity, mostly from network communication with other components. The CS and MT are both I/O intensive components as they are based on training using samples stored on disk, with the MT having a larger database than the CS. The MT being the worst case scenario when running in VMs, its running times were measured in both a VM and a physical machine where the VM was hosted. The physical machine is a dual Xeon 2.4GHz with hyper-threading enabled, 2.5 GBytes of memory and SCSI U160 disks as storage. The VM is based on VMware Workstation 4.5.2, with the same Xeon processor (but without hyper-threading), 512 MBytes of memory and virtual disk without pre-allocation of storage. By design, in this setup for comparative evaluation, all conditions are favorable to the physical machine: its larger memory supports more file system caching, more physical and logical processors permit OS and application to run simultaneously, and full control of physical disk enables faster disk access. Nevertheless, the observed virtualization overhead (Figure 15-3) was below 8%, which can be considered low and proved not to affect the efficacy of the MT system software. If necessary, the overhead can be further minimized - for example, by using virtual disks with pre-allocation of storage. Furthermore, in the near future, hardware support for virtualization software (e.g., Intel Virtualization Technology [43], and AMD Secure Virtualization Technology [3]) will reduce even further the performance gap between virtual and physical machines.

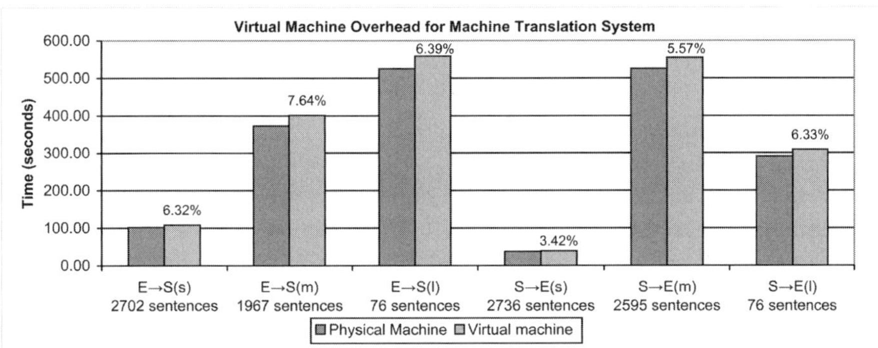

Figure 15-3. VM overheads observed for the Machine Translation System, translating from English (E) to Spanish (S) and vice-versa, with corpora containing small (s), medium (m) and large (l) average sentence lengths

4. CONCLUSIONS

This chapter provides a rationale and a case study for the role of machine virtualization technologies in the creation of collaborative cyberinfrastructures for TDG. The case study demonstrates how virtual machines were used to eliminate heterogeneity barriers to the integration and interoperation of software components of TDG systems. Virtual machine technologies are particularly effective in enabling IT components that need dissimilar machines and execution environments to be used securely and flexibly in existing IT infrastructures. As demonstrated in the case study, they are also beneficial because they (a) support the independent development of software components while allowing them to be tested in an integrated system, (b) enable field-testing without interfering with the remainder of the IT infrastructure, (c) allow rapid development and deployment by facilitating the testing of the system under different conditions, and allowing system-level backups or replicas to be created, and (d) facilitate management and maintenance.

Machine virtualization technologies will be increasingly appealing for TDG. Independently of the reasons discussed in this chapter, they are being widely adopted by IT service providers whenever resource consolidation is needed to achieve savings in delivering IT services that ordinarily require multiple kinds of machines. This fast increasing market for machine virtualization technologies has triggered the introduction of several commercial and public-domain offers of these technologies. Currently, several commercial products are being offered free of charge (e.g., VMware Player, VMware Server and Microsoft VirtualPC). Major processor and computer manufacturers have recently extended or modified their products to support machine virtualization with greater efficiency and lower cost. Public and commercial offerings of these technologies along with emerging hardware support in mainstream architectures will turn virtual machines into pervasive capabilities of commodity computers in the near future [11]. In summary, the initial disadvantages of virtual machines –software licensing costs, performance overheads and programmer's unfamiliarity with the concept – are increasingly negligible due the availability of public-domain virtualization software, hardware-supported virtualization and their wide-spread adoption by major hardware and software suppliers.

Virtualization can also be applied to networks [27, 13], data [48] and applications [25]. The virtualization of data can be accomplished by using virtual file systems and database views that modify the visibility, schema and accessibility of data to different users. Applications and data can also be virtualized by wrapping them as services, as briefly mentioned in this chapter. Recently, several approaches have been proposed for the implementation of virtual networks [42, 40, 30, 41, 34, 12]. They are particularly important for the implementation of distributed cyberinfrastructures for TDG because they can be used to provide isolated separate networks among government entities and, in some cases, can be easily created and quickly disassembled when no longer needed. We thus believe that the use of virtualization technologies, along with other technologies such as Web Services, as put forward and exemplified in this chapter, will continue to be further explored and fully leveraged to address the technical challenges, and mitigate economical and other non-technical barriers, of TDG.

ACKNOWLEDGEMENTS

Research reported in this chapter is funded in part by NSF awards EIA-0107686, EIA-0131886 and EIA-0224442, and the BellSouth Foundation. The authors also acknowledge the members of the TDG project: S. Su, T. R. Kasad, M. Patil (University of Florida) for the DQP system; V. Cavalli-Sforza, J. Carbonell, and P. Jansen (Carnegie Mellon University) for the MT system; W. Ward, R. Cole and J. Brenier (University of Colorado) for the CS; D. Towsley and W. Chen (University of Massachusetts); A. I. Antón and Q. He (North Carolina State University); C. McSweeney, R. Bol, F. Rabbani (University of Belize) for the Belize IS; L. de Brens, J. Ventura, and P. Taveras (Pontificia Universidad Católica Madre y Maestra) for the Dominican Republic IS, R. Connolly, C. Ortega, and B. Piñeres (Organization of American States); O. Brooks (National Drug Abuse Control Council, Belize); and M. Herrera (National Drug Council, Dominican Republic). Any opinions, findings, and conclusions or recommendations expressed in this material are those of the author(s) and do not necessarily reflect the views of the NSF.

REFERENCES

1. Adabala S, Matsunaga A, Tsugawa M, Figueiredo R, Fortes JAB (2004) Single Sign-On in In-VIGO: Role-based Access via Delegation Mechanisms Using Short-lived User Identities. In: 18th International Parallel and Distributed Processing Symposium, pp 26-30
2. Adabala S, Chadha V, Chawla P, Figueiredo R, Fortes J, Krsul I, Matsunaga A, Tsugawa M, Zhang J, Zhao M, Zhu L, Zhu X (2005) From Virtualized Resources to Virtual Computing Grids: The In-VIGO System. J Future Generation Computer Systems, 21(6):896-909
3. Advanced Micro Devices, Inc. (2005) Secure Virtual Machine Architecture Reference Manual. AMD Inc
4. Amstadt B, Johnson MK (1994) Wine. Linux J
5. Barham P, Dragovic B, Fraser K, Hand S, Harris T, Ho A, Neugebauer R, Pratt I, Warfield A Xen and the art of virtualization (2003) In: 19th ACM Symposium on Operating Systems Principles, pp 164-177
6. Bellard F Qemu cpu emulator. http://fabrice.bellard.free.fr/qemu/
7. Biallas S (2004) PearPC - PowerPC Architecture Emulator. http://pearpc.sourceforge.net/
8. Cavalli-Sforza V, Carbonell JG, and Jansen PJJ (2004) Developing Language Resources for Transnational Digital Government Systems: A Case Study. In: 4th International Conference on Language Resources and Evaluation 3:945-948
9. ECMA International (2006) Standard ECMA-335: Common Language Infrastructure (CLI). ECMA International, 4th edn http://www.ecma-international.org/publications/standards/Ecma-335.htm

10. Figueiredo RJ, Dinda P, Fortes JAB (2003) A Case for Grid Computing on Virtual Machines. In: 23rd International Conference on Distributed Computing Systems, pp 550-559
11. Figueiredo R, Dinda PA, Fortes J (2005) Guest Eds' Introduction: Resource Virtualization Renaissance. Computer, 38(5):28-31
12. Ganguly A, Agrawal A, Boykin PO, Figueiredo R (2006) IP over P2P: Enabling Self-configuring Virtual IP Networks for Grid Computing. In: 20th International Parallel and Distributed Processing Symposium
13. Gleeson B, Lin A, Heinanen J, Armitage G, Malis A (2000) A framework for IP-based virtual private networks. RFC2764
14. Global Grid Forum. Global Grid Forum. http://www.ggf.org/
15. Hohensee P, Myszewski M, Reese D (1996) Wabi Cpu Emulation. In: Hot Chips VII
16. Honeycutt H (2003) Microsoft Virtual PC 2004 Technical Overview. http://www.microsoft. com/ windows/virtualpc/evaluation/techoverview.mspx
17. IBM (2004) z/VM General Information Version 5 Release 1. IBM Corporation
18. Janssen M, Cresswell A (2005) Enterprise Architecture Integration in E-Government. In: 38th Annual Hawaii International Conference on System Sciences 2005, pp 118b
19. Kasad TR (2003) Transnational Information Sharing and Event Notification. Master thesis, University of Florida
20. Kossmann D (2000) The state of the art in distributed query processing. ACM Computing Surveys, 32(4):422-469
21. Kreger H (2001) Web Service Conceptual Architecture (WSCA 1.0). IBM Technical White Paper, http://www-306.ibm.com/software/solutions/webservices/pdf/WSCA.pdf
22. Krsul I, Ganguly A, Zhang J, Fortes JAB, Figueiredo RJ (2004) VMPlants: Providing and Managing Virtual Machine Execution Environments for Grid Computing. In: Supercomputing 2004
23. Lawton K, Denney B, Guarneri N, Ruppert V, Bothamy C (2003) Bochs User Manual. http://bochs.sourceforge.net/
24. Litwin W, Mark L, Roussopoulos N (1990) Interoperability of multiple autonomous databases. ACM Computing Surveys (CSUR), 22(3):267-293
25. Matsunaga A, Tsugawa M, Adabala S, Figueiredo RJ, Lam H, Fortes JAB (2006) Science gateways made easy: the In-VIGO approach. Concurrency and Computation: Practice and Experience, Wiley Press
26. OpenLDAP Foundation. JDBC-LDAP Bridge Driver. http://www.openldap.org/jdbcldap/
27. Passmore D, Freeman J (1996) The Virtual LAN Technology Report. White Paper, http://www.3com.com
28. Pellom B, Ward W, Pradhan S (2000) The CU Communicator: An Architecture for Dialogue Systems. In: 6th International Conference on Spoken Language Processing, 2:723-726
29. Puschmann T, Alt R (2004) Enterprise application integration systems and architecture – the case of the Robert Bosch Group. J Enterprise Information Management, 17(2): 105-116
30. Ruth P, Jiang X, Xu D, Goasguen S (2005) Towards Virtual Distributed Environments in a Shared Infrastructure. IEEE Computer, 38(5):63-69
31. Sharif AM, Elliman T, Love PED, Badii A (2004) Integrating the IS with the enterprise: key EAI research challenges. J Enterprise Information Management, 17(2):164-170
32. Sheth AP, Larson JA (1990) Federated database systems for managing distributed, heterogeneous, and autonomous databases. ACM Computing Surveys, 22(3):183-236
33. Smith JE, Nair R (2005) Virtual Machine Versatile Platforms for Systems and Processes. Morgan Kaufmann Publishers

34. Stoica I, Adkins D, Zhuang S, Shenker S, Surana S. Internet Indirection Infrastructure. In: ACM SIGCOMM 2002
35. Su SYW, Lam H (2000) IKnet: Scalable Infrastructure for Achieving Internet-based Knowledge Network. In: International Conference on Advances in Infrastructure for Electronic Business, Science, and Education on the Internet
36. Su S, Fortes J, Kasad TR, Patil M, Matsunaga A, Tsugawa M, Cavalli-Sforza V, Carbonell J, Jansen P, Ward W, Cole R, Towsley D, Chen W, Antón AI, He Q, McSweeney C, de Brens L, Ventura J, Taveras P, Connolly R, Ortega C, Pineres B, Brooks O, Murillo GA, and Herrera M (2005) Transnational Information Sharing, Event Notification, Rule Enforcement and Process Coordination. In International J Electronic Government Research, 1(2):1-26
37. Sun Microsystems, Inc. Java Technology. http://java.sun.com/
38. Sun Microsystems, Inc. JDBC Technology. http://java.sun.com/products/jdbc/
39. Sun Microsystems, Inc. JDBC-ODBC Bridge Driver. http://java.sun.com/j2se/1.4.2/docs/guide/jdbc/getstart/bridge.doc.html
40. Sundararaj A, Dinda P (2004) Towards Virtual Networks for Virtual Machine Grid Computing. In: 3rd USENIX Virtual Machine Research and Technology Symposium
41. Touch J, Hotz S (1998) The X-Bone. In: Global Internet Mini-Conference at Globecom
42. Tsugawa M, Fortes JAB (2006) A Virtual Network (ViNe) Architecture for Grid Computing. In: 20th International Parallel and Distributed Processing
43. Uhlig R, Neiger G, Rodgers D, Santoni AL, Martins FCM, Anderson AV, Bennett SM, Kägi A, Leung FH, Smith L (2005) Intel Virtualization Technology. Computer 38(5): 48-56
44. VMware, Inc. (1999) Introducing VMware Virtual Platform. Technical white paper
45. Ward W (1991) Understanding spontaneous speech: the Phoenix system. In: Int Conference on Acoustics, Speech, and Signal Processing, 1:365-367
46. White J (2002) Darwine Project. http://darwine.opendarwin.org/
47. Zachman JA (1987) A Framework for Information Systems Architecture. IBM Systems J, 26(3):276-292
48. Zhao M, Zhang J, Figueiredo R (2006) Distributed File System Virtualization Techniques Supporting On-Demand Virtual Machine Environments for Grid Computing. Cluster Computing J, 9(1)

SUGGESTED READINGS

- Smith JE, Nair R (2005) Virtual Machine Versatile Platforms for Systems and Processes. Morgan Kaufmann Publishers. Introduces and discusses technical aspects of different forms of machine virtualization and their applications.
- IEEE Computer Magazine, Special Issue on Virtualization technology, Figueiredo R, Dinda PA, Fortes J (2005), 38(5):28-31. Reports on recent developments on virtualization techniques for machines, networks and distributed systems.
- Barry, Douglas K. (2003). Web Services and Service-Oriented Architectures: The Savvy Manager's Guide. San Francisco: Morgan

Kaufmann Publishers. ISBN 1-55860-906-7. Easy-to-read introduction to key aspects of Web Services and how they relate to Service-Oriented Architectures and Enterprise Architectures; also discusses how to create and adapt IT systems to work within a Web Services framework.

ONLINE RESOURCES

- http://www.oasis-open.org/; Web site of OASIS (Organization for the Advancement of Structured Information Standards), a not-for-profit, international consortium that drives the development, convergence, and adoption of e-business standards. Provides information on standardization efforts for Web Services and Service Oriented Architecture.
- http://www.xensource.com/; Web site of open-source virtualization technology Xen.
- http://www.vmware.com/; Web site of commercial vendor of virtualization software; free downloads of most software are possible with some restrictions on usage.

QUESTIONS FOR DISCUSSION

1. Web Services technologies use a standard communication protocol called SOAP and a standard service description language called WSDL to allow different services to interoperate. In a situation when agencies of several countries agree to share data collection and analysis tools for purposes of TDG, such technologies can be particularly useful. Consider the following scenarios and elaborate on the need or sufficiency of Web Service technologies for TDG, particularly with respect for the need or convenience of also using machine and network virtualization technologies:
   - Each agency will reuse its own tools locally and access and run other agencies' tools remotely on their resources.
   - Agencies will have to run both their own tools and tools provided by others on their local resources.
   - Each agency will only be able to access data collected or processed by other agencies but will not be able to use any of their tools (locally or remotely).
2. Emergencies, such as a regional disaster or a major epidemic, often could benefit from the quick establishment of a transnational IT system capable

of tapping into governmental IT resources of different countries. Comment on the viability and desirability of creating a kit of core IT functions needed at each node of the TDG system, and cloning a virtual machine capable of running such functions at existing IT resources. How scalable and sustainable would such an approach be?

3. Comment on the advantages and disadvantages, from a security standpoint, of using the following virtualization technologies to implement collaborative TDG systems:
   - Virtual machines
   - Virtual networks
   - Virtual machines connected by virtual networks
4. Virtual machines and virtual networks can be suspended and have their state saved as files which can later be used to re-instantiate the same machines and networks. Comment on the benefits and possible uses of this feature in the context of TDG and in contrast to alternatives that only use physical resources.

Chapter 16

SEMANTICS-BASED THREAT STRUCTURE MINING FOR HOMELAND SECURITY

Nabil R. Adam[1], Vandana P. Janeja[1], Aabhas V. Paliwal[1], Vijay Atluri[1], Soon Ae Chun[2], Jim Cooper[3], John Paczkowski[3], Christof Bornhövd[4], and Joachim Schaper[4]

[1]RUTGERS University, CIMIC, Newark, New Jersey, U.S.A. (email: adam, vandana, aabhas, atluri@cimic.rutgers.edu); [2]City University of New York, Staten Island, New York, U.S.A. (email: chun@mail.csi.cuny.edu); [3]Operations and Emergency Management, Port Authority of New York and New Jersey, U.S.A. (email: jfcooper, jpaczkow@panynj.gov); [4]SAP Labs, LLC, Palo Alto Research Center, Palo Alto, California, U.S.A. (email: christof.bornhoevd, joachim.schaper@sap.com)

CHAPTER OVERVIEW

Within the Homeland Security domain, it is critical to be able to identify actionable and credible knowledge for the prevention of, response to, and recovery from incidents. This also allows threat and vulnerability assessment. Today's National and Interstate border control agencies are flooded with alerts generated from various monitoring devices. In such an environment, the difficulty of knowledge discovery is compounded by the fact that data is collected by heterogeneous sources having different semantics within various agencies operating in disparate mission spaces. There is an urgent need to uncover potential threats to effectively respond to an event. In this chapter, we present a *Semantics-based Threat Mining* approach that uses the semantic and spatio-temporal contextual relationships among data sources and data flows (events) to identify alerts with potentially dangerous collusion relationships. We use *Semantic Graphs* to represent the potentially dangerous collusion relationships, and further score and prune the edges with semantic weights using a domain specific ontology of known dangerous relationships, resulting in an *Enhanced Semantic Graph* (ESG). The analysis of such an ESG using graph's characteristics of centrality, cliques and isomorphism further enables to mine the global threat patterns that are difficult to see when alerts or clusters of alerts are looked at independently. In the context of shipments crossing the border, which are under the jurisdiction of the respective ports and Port Authorities, we present a Semantic Threat Mining prototype system in the domain of known dangerous combinations of chemicals used in explosives.

1. INTRODUCTION

The Port Authority of New York/New Jersey (PA) manages and maintains bridges, tunnels, bus terminals, airports, PATH commuter trains, and the seaport around New York and New Jersey that are critical to the bi-state region's trade and transportation capabilities. The continuous monitoring of cars, trucks, trains, and passengers is a necessary precaution for preventing major threats to safety. The amount of data and potential alerts generated from these monitoring activities are enormous and heterogeneous in nature due to the different outputs from monitoring devices, ranging from text messages to images, audios and video feeds. The challenge is to mine and identify meaningful potential threats, and minimize false alerts. The ability to infer threats coming from several independent seemingly benign activities is important. Often ignored are the threats implicated when these independent activities are looked at together. We will start by giving a motivating real-world example [13].

Motivating Example: Importers shipping into the United States fill out a manifest form that the U.S. Customs currently gathers in the Automated Manifest System (AMS). Typically, the AMS data for a shipment consists of about 104 attributes, and the profile of each company involved in the shipment consists of about 40 attributes. This data may be gathered by multiple entities, including different ports such as the port of entry, port of departure, point of arrival, or different agencies such as the U.S. Department of transportation (DOT), U.S. Coast Guard, U.S. Customs and Border Protection (CBP), etc. U.S. Customs is currently undergoing modernization of their current systems to produce an integrated trade and border protection system called the automated commercial environment/The International Trade Data System (ACE/ITDS). As a result, additional agencies such as the Bureau of Alcohol, Tobacco, Firearms and Explosives (ATF), CIA, FBI would be tapped for validating shipments in terms of their compliances. Each of these entities collecting data can be treated as a different domain. Let us consider a simple scenario comprising of two shipments.

Shipment 1: A shipment to MerPro, Inc. entering through the eastern border via Newark Port comprising of Liquid Urea, whose destination is Wintersburg, Arizona, which is used as a chemical fertilizer. This shipment will be recorded in the Newark port database (say domain D_1). Assume Liquid Urea is recorded as one of its dimensions, denoted as d_{11}.

Shipment 2: A shipment to a consignee, ChemCo, carrying Ammonium Nitrate, whose destination is Phoenix, Arizona, which is entering through a port at the west coast, e.g., Los Angeles. This shipment will be recorded in the Los Angeles port database (say domain D_2) with Ammonium Nitrate as one of its dimensions (say d_{21}).

While these two shipments are considered in isolation within their own domains, D_1 and D_2, they appear to be benign. However, upon a closer observation of these two shipments, one may discover that the two materials shipped into the country can potentially be used to make an explosive (which in fact can be determined by a chemical expert based on the reactivity of chemicals [25]). Moreover, the fact that the destinations of these two shipments are geographically close increases the likelihood of such a situation materializing. Discovery of such relationships between d_{11} and d_{21} from different domains, D_1 and D_2 may trigger a further analysis on the originating companies' behavior in the financial domain (say D_3) of an unusual financial transaction with respect to the amount of funds transferred. The "amount of funds transferred" could be one of the dimensions in this domain D_3, denoted as d_{31}. In essence, our goal is to identify such potential "threats" based on the entities responsible for these two shipments, so-called the "Threat Structure Mining" problem. Discovering such information can be valuable to a terrorist task force agent.

In our previous work [13] [14], we introduced the concept of Semantic Graphs (SG) to represent the collusion sets (entities or events) and the existence of relationships among these entities. The SG was constructed by using a data mining algorithm to mine the outlier entities and the potential collusion dimensions, called causal dimensions, such as d_{11} and d_{21} in the above example. However, the remaining challenge is not only to identify the co-occurrence of rare collusions but also to establish ranking of the relationships among the collusion entities that distinguishes the strong and "valid" relationships as a real threat from the weak or insignificant relationships.

In this chapter, we present an approach to enhance semantic graphs by discovering collusion relationships existing in spatio-temporal and semantic dimensions among events, using the concept of *Enhanced Semantic Graphs* (ESG). We present an ontology-based semantic matching and filtering technique to prune some of the weak relationships in the semantic graphs, and to assign concrete weights (strengths) of the collusion relationships. This validation of collusion relationships requires knowledge of domain experts (i.e., a corresponding ontology) to confine the analysis to meaningful intervals of time, space and semantic relationships in order to facilitate efficient threat detection and analysis. We modeled this knowledge with a domain ontology to identify semantic relationships and the importance of relationships.

Specifically, the domain ontology represents a domain expert's knowledge on the known dangerous combinations of the chemical elements. The known dangerous combination has certain weights associated to represent the degree of its potential-hazard. The Semantic Graph from the data mining is matched against the known dangerous combination ontology. If the degree/strength of the relationships among collusion entities is below a threshold of a certain known threat combination, then the mined relationships are eliminated from the Semantic Graphs. This semantic pruning results in a more robust and high fidelity semantic graph called Enhanced Semantic Graph (ESG) that can be used to identify genuine threats and threat patterns. The semantic relationships and the weights associated with them in ESG allow the mining of threat structures that are based not only on graph network topologies, such as centrality or cliques but also on the semantic centrality, semantic cliques and semantic isomorphism.

The chapter is organized as follows. Section 2 describes the overall components involved in the semantic data mining approach, section 3 provides the steps to generate a Semantic Graph of potential collusion and threat relationships based on outlier detection. Section 4 presents ESG generation; specifically how to discover the spatio-temporal relationships and semantic relationships to filter potential threats using semantic matching between the Semantic Graph and the known dangerous combination and chemical ontology. Section 5 presents the threat structure mining to identify structures from the ESG based on semantic scores. Section 6 describes the SDM prototype system, followed by related work and conclusions in section 7 and 8, respectively.

2. SEMANTICS DRIVEN DATA MINING

Our approach for semantic threat structure mining consists of the following distinct steps: *i) SG generation by outlier detection:* The nodes in the SG are generated by identifying interesting entities, namely outliers and their causal dimensions [13]. These outliers with their causal dimensions form the nodes of the SG. *ii) ESG Generation:* We next enhance the connectivity between the nodes in SG to generate an Enhanced Semantic Graph (ESG). This is done in a two-step process: a) First we identify spatio temporal relationships between the outliers; b) Second, we identify semantic weights in relationships between the outliers. This is facilitated with the use of ontologies and reasoning. The semantic enhancement includes scoring the relationships between the dimensions using domain ontologies and removing relationships (edges in the SG) that are not supported by the ontology and the reasoner. *iii) Identification of Threat Structures:* Once we have such an ESG with semantic scores, we identify semantics based threat structures using graph properties enhanced to consider semantics such as semantic centrality, semantic cliques and isomorphic paths.

The overall approach is depicted in the first figure. We next describe each step in detail.

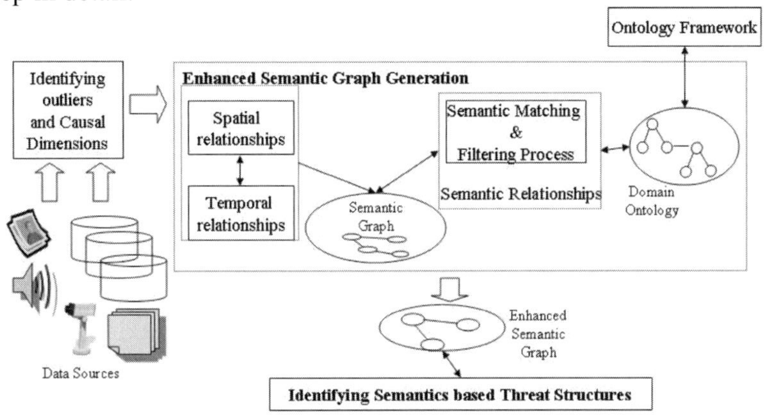

Figure 16-1. Semantic Threat Structure Mining Approach

Outlier detection for semantic graphs

An outlier in a data set is defined as an observation that is very different and inconsistent with the other observations. Different techniques are proposed to detect and subsequently predict such anomalies or outliers. Essentially outliers are defined as those objects that do not have enough neighbors, where neighbors are measured with distance from a given object. However, most distance-based approaches [15, 16, 18] use Euclidean distance in multi-dimensions. This has the following limitations. Firstly, it does not provide intuitive knowledge of the outliers such as which dimension may be causing the extreme behavior. Secondly, it does not scale well for high dimensional data and is not very efficient for large data sets. Most Euclidean distance-based approaches are sensitive to input parameters. In [13], a new distance metric, called *collusion distance metric*, is used for outlier detection to address some of these limitations.

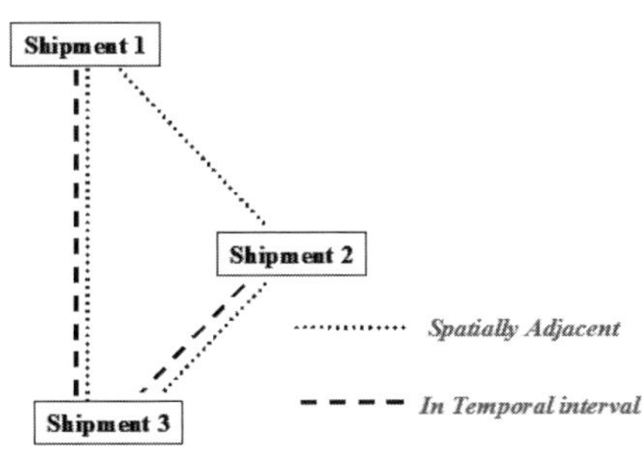

Figure 16-2. Spatial and Temporal Proximities

This distance metric is motivated from the Hausdorff distance metric [19]. It facilitates the identification of the causal dimensions in which an object may be showing extreme behavior. For high dimensional data sets, it can identify outliers better and improves both precision and recall, when compared to the Euclidean distance based outlier detection [15]. The performance results were shown on real data sets (Prognosis Breast Cancer, Diagnostic Breast Cancer, Ionosphere and PIERS) and simulated datasets. However, a collusion distance based method may sometimes miss global outliers. Essentially, given two points X and Y, it computes the maximum of the distances between each of the dimensions of X and Y. This also allows identifying the dimension(s) that causes this maximum difference, hence *causal dimension*. Thus, the *output* from this step is a set of outliers and the causal dimensions for each outlier. These form the nodes of the Semantic Graph. However, at this point there are no linkages (edges) between the nodes. Thus we next identify spatio temporal and semantic relationships to generate an enhanced semantic graph.

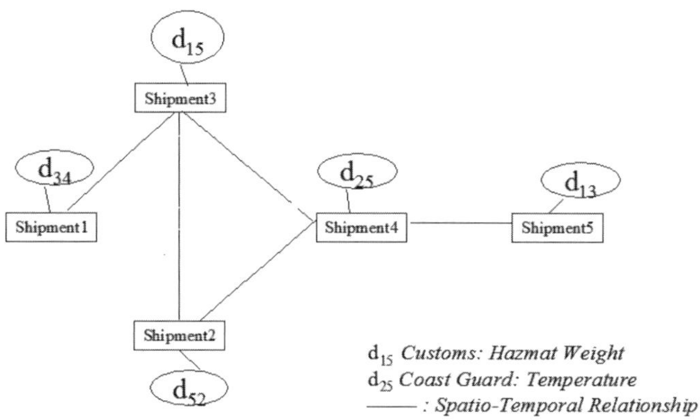

Figure 16-3. Preliminary Semantic Graph Structure

3. ENHANCED SEMANTIC GRAPH

3.1 Spatio Temporal Relationships

Given a set of outliers as nodes in a SG, we identify edges by calculating spatial and temporal proximities (as shown in Figure 16-2) between them. The ***spatial proximity*** is measured by constructing a spatial neighborhood graph, where the nodes correspond to the outlier objects and there exists an edge between the nodes if and only if there exists a neighboring relation between the two nodes identified by spatial relationships. The spatial relations include topological relationships such as *adjacent, inside, disjoint,* etc., direction relationships such as *above, below, north_of*, etc., and distance relationships such as "*distance < 100*".

The *temporal proximity* is identified with relevant temporal relations of time dimension, such as *overlap, before, after, equal-to*, etc. For example, the temporal intervals in our example scenario are the overlapping time periods of shipments or the expiration date of chemicals is being equal to a given date. Further temporal pruning is also performed at the ontological level. The output from this step is a semantic graph, as shown in Figure 16-3, which shows the spatio-temporal relationships between the outliers and associated with each outlier is the meta data namely the causal dimensions. Next step is to identify the *semantic relationships* in casual dimensions between these nodes and to consider its strengths (i.e., the weights of the semantic relationships) to prune unnecessary edges. This step results in an ESG. We next describe in detail our method to identify the semantic relationships among existing edges, using a domain-specific ontology of causal dimensions.

3.2 Semantic Relationships

The identification of semantic relationships first involves locating the relevant ontologies from different domains. The keywords from the causal dimensions in the semantic graph are used as a keyword and if the terms in an ontology match with the keyword, then it is decided that the ontology is relevant. Once the relevant ontology is identified, the combination of concepts in Semantic Graphs are matched against the combination of concepts in the domain ontology to identify the semantic links between nodes in SG with the appropriate weights, and it further prunes the edges in SG if there is no semantic relationships or no significant weights assigned on the edges. This *semantic matching* process will result in the Enhanced Semantic Graph (ESG). In the following sections, we describe the development of the domain ontologies and the semantic matching process.

3.2.1 Domain ontology

An ontology is a graph whose nodes and edges represent concepts and the relationships between those concepts. Ontologies are used for the conceptualization of the application domain in a human understandable and machine-readable form. We use a tiered approach for the development of the ontology framework as illustrated in Figure 16-4.

We have adopted the SUMO[1] (Suggested Upper Merged Ontology) as the top-level description of the domain. The second level of ontologies include

---

[1] http://reliant.teknowledge.com/DAML/SUMO.owl

the concepts described in MILO[2] (Mid Level Ontology) derived from SUMO. The concepts in this level of ontologies also include the predefined Chemical Elements[3] and Chemical Hazard ontology. The chemical hazard ontology is designed to provide information needed for decision making during emergencies that occur when dealing with hazardous chemicals. It serves as a knowledge base to answer questions regarding the boiling point, density or chemical spillage in water.

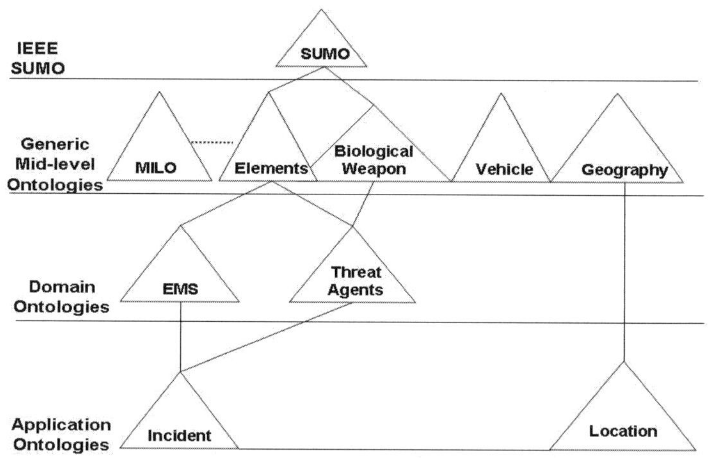

Figure 16-4. Tiered Ontology

Our chemical hazard ontology serves as a starting point to retrieve information regarding the physical, chemical, thermodynamic and response information. This ontology serves as an initial response tool to provide sufficient time to recover more detailed information about the related compounds. Our chemical ontology is based on Coast Guard's CHRIS (Chemical Hazards Response Information System) and NOAA's Chemical Reactivity Worksheet. The next ontology level consists of domain ontologies, such as the Emergency Management System and Threat Agents ontology. Finally, the application level ontology such as the Incident ontology is developed to represent possible incident types. The incidents can have several situational types, such as accidents, natural disaster types or hazardous materials[4]. Each of these subtypes can have finer incident types. For instance, the related incidents can be radiological, chemical or biological incidents, etc.

---

2 http://reliant.teknowledge.com/DAML/Mid-level-ontology.owl

3 http://reliant.teknowledge.com/DAML/Elements.owl

4 http://www.daml.org/2002/10/hazardous/hazardous-cargo-ont

The ontologies are constructed using the Ontology Web Language (OWL) and are restricted to the OWL DL. This allows us to perform the semantic matching using DL reasoning techniques. OWL DL possesses the expressive power of DLs, retains both computational completeness (all conclusions are guaranteed to be computable) and decidability (all computations will finish in finite time).

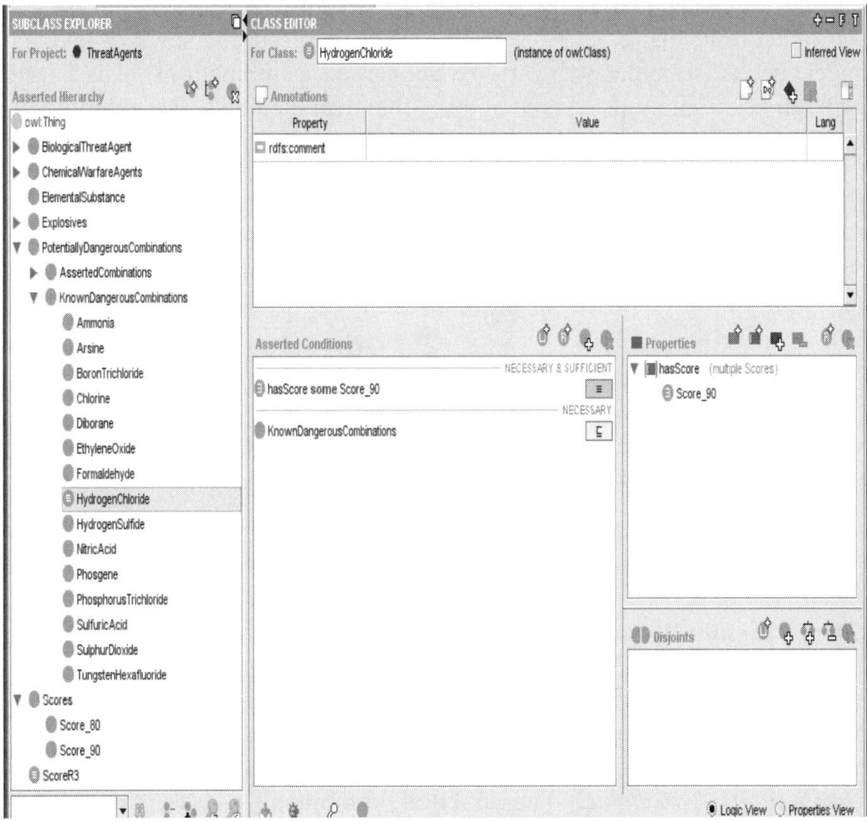

Figure 16-5. Threat Agent Ontology

3.2.2 Threat and potentially dangerous combination ontology

To use domain ontologies to capture the semantics of the domain and to derive the semantic relationships among collusion entities in the semantic graph, we have developed a domain specific ontology on Chemical Threat agents, as shown in Figure 16-5. It includes two major taxonomies: the domain specific concept taxonomy, e.g., types of chemicals, and an operational taxonomy used in the matching process that we refer to as the

Potentially Dangerous Combinations (PDC). The PDC taxonomy is further divided into sub-taxonomies: a taxonomy that represents dangerous combinations of elements that we refer to as *Known Dangerous Combinations (KDC)* and a taxonomy for the information asserted from the semantic graph that we refer to as *Asserted Combinations*.

The KDC is provided by domain experts, and contains basic relationships among chemical agents that are known to be dangerous if they are combined together. The KDC taxonomy, shown in Figure 16-6, has a root concept with a set of score levels (e.g., 90%, 80%, etc) to represent the severity levels of danger in its subtypes of various dangerous combinations. These sub-dangerous combinations consist of a set chemical elements. For example, the concept HCl (Hydrogen Chloride) is defined by domain experts as a subtype of KDC, with the score 90% probabilities of danger, whose elements consist of more specific elements such as chlorine or other halogens.

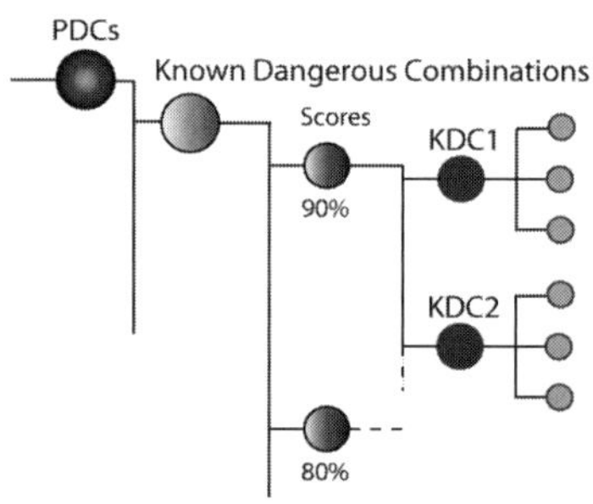

Figure 16-6. Known Dangerous Combinations

3.2.3 Semantic matching

The Semantic Graph constructed from the outlier detection algorithms contains information asserted to be dangerous combinations, e.g., Hydrogen and Fluoride to give HF. Based on this, we construct the *Asserted Combinations Taxonomy*. The asserted combinations taxonomy (Figure 16-7) is created as follows: upon receiving a semantic graph, a set of combinations (C_1, C_2, …C_{n-1}, C_n) is created by extracting the causal dimensions of nodes that are connected with edges in the graph. If a relation includes more than two nodes, multiple combinations are created incrementally starting from two nodes. Therefore, the asserted combinations represent all the possible combinations from the semantic graph.

Given the domain semantics in the KDC ontology and the asserted information (AC) from the semantic graph in concepts, properties, and restrictions, the system enhances the semantic graph and assigns scores on the semantic links by matching the asserted information to some known dangerous sets with the reasoning about them. The following describes specific steps for enhancing the semantic graph with semantic links during the matching process.

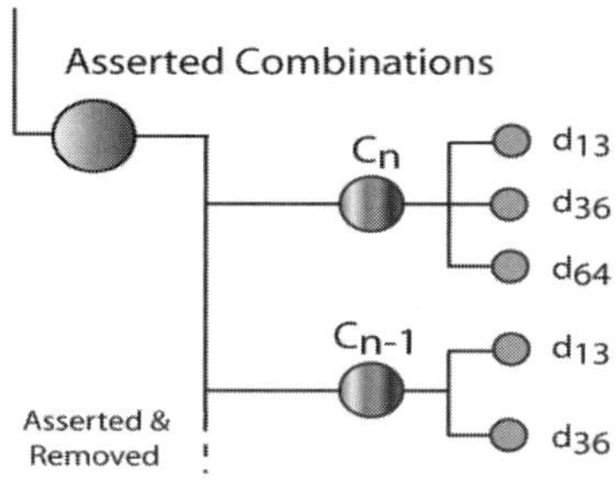

Figure 16-7. Asserted Combinations

The first step of the matching process is to create a parent concept that represents the union of all the nodes in a combination. For instance, in Figure 16-7, the concept C_n is the union of the dimensions d_{13}, d_{36}, and d_{64}. Since DL assumes open world reasoning, we add a *closure axiom* to the definition of this concept and the concepts in the KDC taxonomy as well. The parent concept is then matched to the KDC taxonomy using two reasoning tasks: first, using a class hierarchy reasoning, the parent concept is matched to a combination from the KDC taxonomy where a KDC and a score are identified. If the score is zero, that is, the parent concept does not match any combination in the KDC taxonomy, the second step is skipped.

In the second step, class subsumption reasoning is used to identify the type of matching between the parent concept and the KDC family. The result of the matching is of one of three types: exact match, the parent concept subsumes the KDC combination, or the KDC combination subsumes the parent concept. The latter case is taken to further processing where the score is reduced. The enhanced semantic graph is created by eliminating the links that have scores equal to Zero and by adding the score to the other links in the semantic graph.

4. THREAT STRUCTURE MINING

The enhanced semantic graph constructed identifies the potential dangerous relations among individual shipments. However, the global threat patterns or trends should be identified. To achieve this, we define a *threat structure* to be a subgraph of the ESG, which has a high significance due to strong spatio-temporal and semantic relationships, thus revealing potential threat patterns. We apply graph mining techniques to identify threat structures. Unlike other graph mining techniques where the graph's structural properties are used [23] we employ the semantic properties associated with the ESG. Specifically, we focus on identifying threat structures based on *semantic centrality, semantic cliques* and *semantic isomorphism*. We adapt the concept of semantic centrality and semantic cliques from [14].

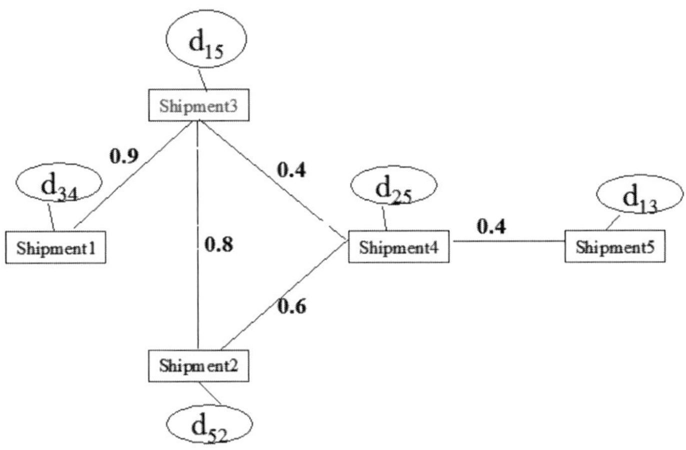

Figure 16-8. Semantic Centrality

Semantic Centrality: Centrality is a concept, which allows us to attach significance to a node as a central node, which can influence other nodes. In a terrorist network this indicates a threat structure and a single node with high centrality may indicate an important member of the network. However we bring into this concept the importance of semantics, thus identifying semantic centrality. Given an enhanced semantic graph E, the semantic centrality of node $a_i \in E$ is a function of the weights of all incident edges on that node, where the function may be sum; max; average.

In Figure 16-8, shipment 3 plays a semantically central role due to the highest semantic weight brought about by the sum of weights of all incident edges. Thus shipment 3 plays a critical role in the formation of a threat structure formed by the combination of shipments 1, 2, and 4 which may potentially be combined to form a dirty bomb, where shipment 3 is a key ingredient and thus must be monitored more carefully. Although Shipment 4, in Figure 16-8, has a high number of edges incident onto it, it is does not have a high semantic centrality due to the lower semantic weight. Essentially, the more the value of the semantic centrality, the more semantically influential is that node in the ESG.

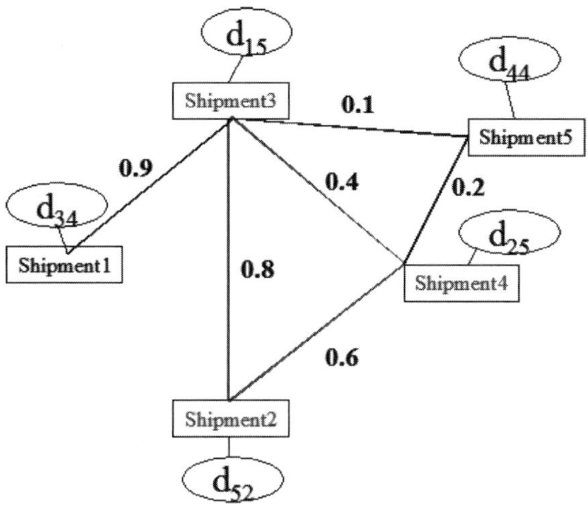

Figure 16-9. Threat Structure Due to Clique Structure and High Scores

Semantic Clique: Clique is defined as a complete sub-graph with total connectivity among the nodes. We use semantic weights to define a semantic clique. The existence of cliques may be indicative of a threat structure in a terrorist network. Given an enhanced semantic graph E, the complete sub-graphs are identified and the semantic weight function (e.g., sum, max, or average) is used to identify semantically significant cliques. An example clique is represented in Figure 16-9, where shipments 2, 3, 4, form a semantic clique. Unlike the clique formed by shipments 3, 4, 5 this clique poses a bigger threat in terms of the spatio-temporal and semantic relationships exhibited by the clique of three shipments 2, 3 and 4, combined. The three shipments, 2, 3, and 4 may be carrying chemicals such as Ammonia, Liquid urea, and ammonium nitrate which may be more dangerous when combined as compared to some other set of chemicals which do not pose as much as threat when combined. The identification of semantically more significant clique with a higher semantic weight will allow focusing resources on the more critical threat structure.

Semantic Isomorphism: Identifying certain shipment paths from the same origination node to the same destination node may reveal some potential threats. We introduce the concept of semantic isomorphism to uncover this kind of threats in an ESG. A path consists of a set of nodes and edges connecting the nodes. Two paths are isomorphic if and only if they have the same length with the same node at the start and at the end. Here path of length n means that the path has n vertices and n-1 edges. This isomorphism can be seen in terms of vertex and edge equivalence. In Figure 16-10, there are three paths A, B, C that are isomorphic, i.e., they are equivalent in terms of number of vertices and edges. Given an enhanced semantic graph E, with a set of paths P={ $p_1,\ldots, p_x$}. Let us say w_i,w_j are the total semantic weights of the paths p_i, p_j. The paths p_i, $p_j \in$ P are semantically isomorphic if the paths p_i, p_j are isomorphic and the difference between the two weights $(w_i - w_j) \leq \delta$, where δ is a user defined threshold.

Thus in Figure 16-10, if we consider δ to be 0.3, then although paths A, B, C are isomorphic, only paths A, C are semantically isomorphic since the difference between the total weights of the two paths is less than δ. Let us say that Shipments 1,5,6,2 in Figure 16-10 are carrying chemicals which are hazardous when combined. There may be other combinations which may pose an equal or greater risk. Isomorphic paths capture such scenarios. However isomorphism is more relevant if the two sets of combinations are semantically more hazardous as compared to other combinations. Thus the two paths may lead to the formation of hazardous chemicals when combined, this essentially means that either one of these paths can be used as a means of forming a dirty bomb and both must be monitored to foil such an event. This will prevent the overlooking of multiple plans terrorist may have in place to achieve their target.

5. SEMANTICS-BASED THREAT STRUCTURE MINING (STM) PROTOTYPE SYSTEM

In this section, we describe the STM prototype system and the experimental setup including the dataset used for evaluation. Here we describe the system in terms of the functionality and process.

5.1 Dataset

We have used the PIERS [26] data, which consists of the U.S. Customs data. It comprises of imports, exports data and U.S. and overseas profiles of companies. The motivation for using the PIERS data for testing gives meaningful results since it comes from multiple ports and agencies. Moreover, some shipments, when observed closely, may lead to suspicious terrorist behavior, which is analogous to the threat structures considered in this approach. We have vertically partitioned the PIERS data into 3 domains such that each domain consists of some part of each record. Inter-relationships between outliers are labeled based on the outliers detected and the semantic weights generated by the ontology framework. The domain experts from the Foreign Operations Division, U.S. Department of Homeland Security helped to identify the semantic relationships within the dimensions of the PIERS data and labeling of the outliers in this data. It was observed that only 50% of the labeled inter-relationships were identified. We believe that this loss is due to the manual partitioning and labeling of the data where, some actual outliers may have been lost.

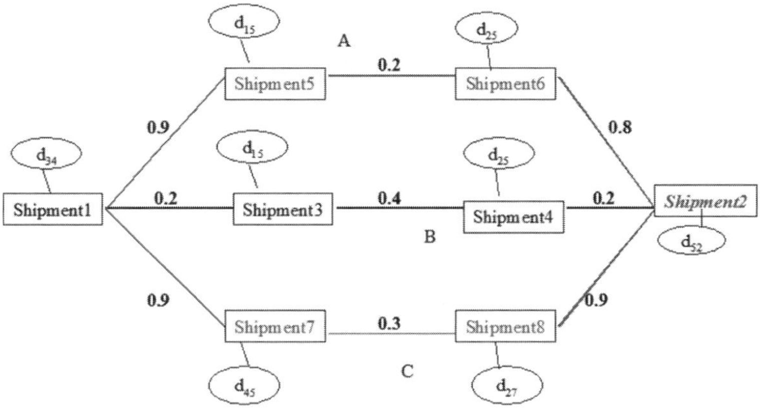

Figure 16-10. Semantic Isomorphism

5.2 Semantic Graph Generation

The semantic graph generation is done based on the distance based outlier detection, where we use the Collusion distance metric [13]. We first describe some results obtained with the Collusion distance metric based (CDB) outlier detection and Euclidean distance based (EDB) outlier detection, as shown in Figure 16-11. For various distance thresholds, it was observed that CDB produces better results by reducing the number of false positives. It was observed that the record, which was split across domains, had been identified as an outlier throughout the domains thus correctly identifying the entire record as an outlier. However, we believe that it may be possible that the manual partitioning and labeling would lead to some loss in outlier detection.

We also observed that the causal dimensions identified by the CDB are indeed the correct dimensions causing outlierness. For this we first take the top q of n dimensions with the most outliers detected in them. Then we performed the CDB outlier detection by considering only these q dimensions to show that that outlier detection in these dimensions is same or better than the case where all dimensions are considered. Since collusion distance uses extreme distances between the dimensions for identifying outliers, the non outlier causing dimensions are eliminated, thus it was observed that the results of the outlier detection is not affected and the performance is indeed equal or better than that observed in the full dimension set [13].

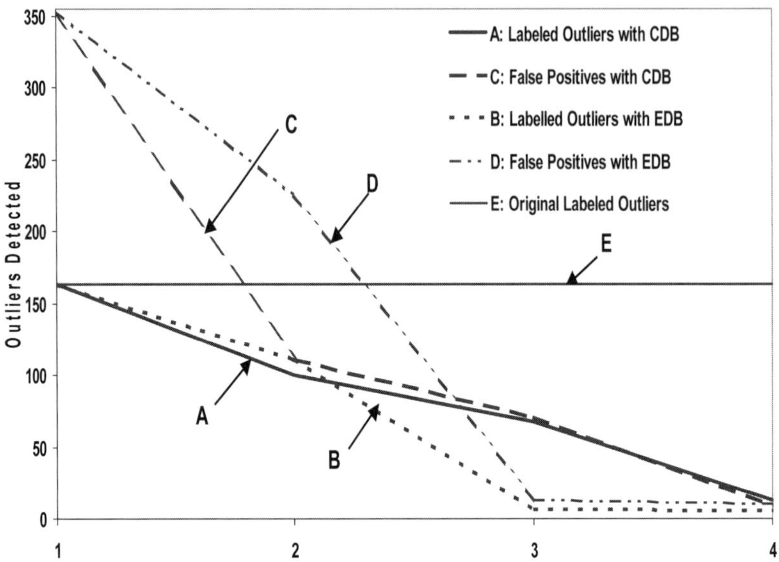

Figure 16-11. Outlier Detection in PIERS Data

CDB essentially produces a set of outliers and the causal dimension for each outlier. We subsequently identify spatial relationships such as adjacency of the spatial dimension of the outliers. The temporal relationships are identified between the outliers by considering temporal constructs such as before, after and equal to in the temporal dimension of the outliers. This essentially prunes away the list of outliers based on their spatial and temporal proximity. Thus at the end of this process we have a semantic graph with outliers and their causal dimensions and spatio-temporal relationships between the outliers.

5.3 Semantic Matching for Semantic Relationship Mining

The matching mechanism (Figure 16-12) is composed of three modules that interact among each other and with the RACER reasoner [9]. The first module is the *ontology loader*, which reads the ontology from an OWL file, converts it to DIG format [5] using the OWL API [21], requests an empty knowledge base from RACER, and submits the converted ontology as a set of *Tells*. DIG is a set of specifications for standardizing the interface to a DL reasoner. The second module, the *query loader*, receives a combination of concepts in the Semantic Graph, creates a parent concept as the union of the combination, asserts the parent concept and the combination, and initiates the third module, the *query processor*. The query processor performs the matching and returns the enhanced semantic graph.

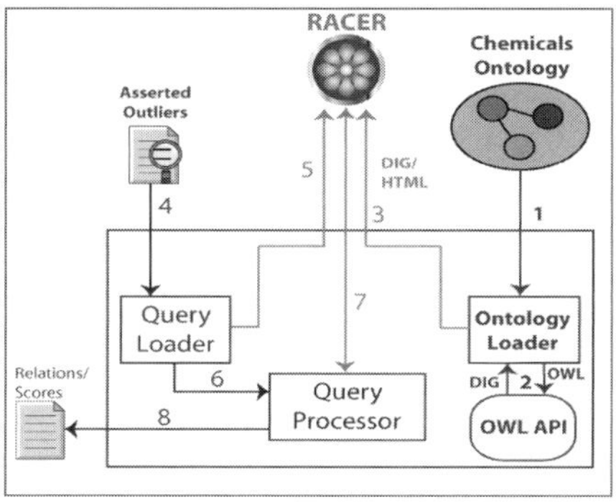

Figure 16-12. Matching Mechanism

While it is possible to create ontology by entering its RDF/XML description in an OWL file, we found that the use of an ontology editor is indispensable. There are several ontology development tools that have been mainly developed by academia including Protégé [21] by Stanford University, Swoop by University of Maryland, and OilEd by University of Manchester. We used Protégé for importing the UNSPSC ontology and for developing the rest of the taxonomies. Protégé provides several wizards and plug-ins that are very useful in saving time and checking correctness of work. Protégé can connect to any reasoner that supports the DIG interface. We used the RACER reasoner to check the consistence of the ontology during the development time. We also used RACER as part of the reasoning mechanism.

5.4 Identification of Threat Structures

Once the system identified the semantic relationships and generated the ESG, it identifies threat structures based on the top weighted semantic relationships, using semantic properties such as semantic cliques, semantic centrality, and semantic isomorphic paths.

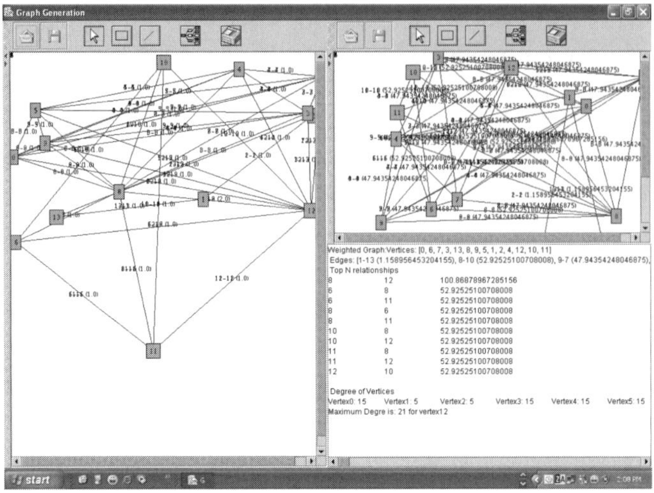

Figure 16-13. PIERS Data

Figure 16-13 shows the results of our system tested on PIERS data. The graph in the left of the window shows the semantic graph, the right top part of the window shows the Enhanced Semantic Graph with the weights in terms of the semantic weights generated by the matching process. The bottom right part shows the discovered top interrelationships and the semantic centrality. Although the system mined all threat structures of the inter-relationships, the figure depicts just top 10 threat structures.

6. RELATED WORK

Outlier detection has been extensively studied in the statistical community [4]. One of the major limitations of these approaches is that the data is made to fit a certain distribution. Thus, in most cases, one does not have enough knowledge of the underlying data distribution. To address this issue, Knorr and Ng [15] have proposed a distance-based outlier detection approach that is both simple and intuitive, which states that a point is said to be an outlier in a dataset 'T' if no more than '*p*%' of points are at or less than a threshold distance from the point.

An extension of this work [16] identifies intensional knowledge for outliers such as, which sets of dimensions explain the uniqueness of the outliers. Ramaswamy et al. [18] have extended the approach based on the distance of a point from its 'k-th' nearest neighbor. After ranking the points by the distance to its 'k-th' nearest neighbor, the top 'k' points are identified as outliers. The concept of local outlier has been introduced in [8], where the outlier rank of a point is determined by taking into account the clustering structure in a bounded neighborhood of the point. However none of these approaches are specially designed to work for high dimensional problems. Other outlier detection approaches OPTICS-OF [7] and LOF [8] also do not address high dimensional outlier discovery. To address the problem of dimensionality curse, Aggrawal and Yu [1] have proposed an approach that considers projections of the data and considers the outlier detection problem in subspace. He et al. [24] proposes a semantics based outlier detection, in which they assign class labels to data based on the semantics, and discover outliers within each group with the same class labels. While there exist a number of proposals for outlier detection, none of these approaches take the semantic relationships among dimensions into account. Moreover, none of these approaches identify the causal dimensions or other causal knowledge of the outliers, which is essential in addressing the problem being tackled in this chapter.

The work in the area of social networks and link analysis is relevant to the problem considered in this chapter. Social network analysis involves the study of prominent patterns within social networks, tracing the flow of information and resources, effect of relationships on various entities, etc [3]. Xu et al. [24] focus on detecting and specifying changes in criminal organizations using descriptive measures from social network analysis. Wang et al. [22] address identification of record linkages using string comparisons to link different deceptive criminal identity records. One key aspect of creating social networks is the formulation of ties. Various methods have been proposed for the sampling of ties such as full network, Snowball, Ego centric, Ego only methods [23]. Snowball method is of specific interest here because it is useful in detecting ties in the more impenetrable social groupings where the entities are few in number and members of such population can be considered deviant. This technique is basically used to identify entities, which are then used to refer to other entities, thus snowballing into a network of connectivities. This technique works well in sampling ties from people; however, this type of information cannot be gleaned from large data sets. Therefore, the results obtained through these approaches can be complimentary to those obtained using data mining approaches.

Kubica et al. [17] propose a graph-based approach for link analysis and collaboration queries. They propose a Bayesian network based technique to identify underlying associations in a social network graph. They account for different types of links, varying in frequency and extent of noise. They also incorporate temporal information pertaining to the link. It learns the underlying graph using weighted counts of co-occurrences to approximate the edge weights, which can be computed from counts gathered during a single scan of the data. The weighting function such as temporal weighting assumes that the recent links will be more indicative of the current graph. However, in many cases the anomalous objects may not co-occur and the only recent links may not provide the most intuitive knowledge. Most importantly, the links may originate from multiple data sources and the weighting functions would need to incorporate such knowledge dynamically, which are not addressed under this approach.

7. CONCLUSION AND DISCUSSION

In this Chapter, we presented an approach to identify semantics-based threat structures by discovering collusion relationships among outliers. Specifically, the Semantic Graph is constructed based on the causal dimensions of outliers as nodes, and the spatio-temporal and semantic relationships among these dimensions as edges. We presented an ontology-based semantic matching and filtering technique to prune the weak relationships in the semantic graphs, and to assign concrete weights (strengths) of the collusion relationships. This semantic pruning resulted in a more robust and high fidelity semantic graph called Enhance Semantic Graph (ESG), which we used to analyze threat patterns, facilitating identification of genuine threats. We have shown a prototype system with domain ontology of Known Dangerous (chemical) Combinations and evaluated our approach with test dataset from US Customs.

As part of our future research, we propose to focus on addressing the general problem of identifying relationships between normal entities without restricting ourselves to simply outliers. We have performed limited set of experiments with real life and simulated datasets, and intend to extend the experiments to labeled social network and link discovery datasets.

Currently the phase of ontology reuse is being executed manually; however, we would have to explore ontological tools for automation the process of ontology selection and reuse. The domain and application ontologies are to be developed as per the requirements of the scenario. The relative difference between attribute values of two concepts is of interest given the different application domains including temporal and spatial features.

Consistency across systems in determining semantic distances and the robustness of such calculations is essential in homeland security domain. We need to investigate determining the relative semantic distance between two concepts through an inspection of the values of selected attributes through a hierarchy of variables ranging from those that most directly related, termed proximate variables, to those most distantly removed, termed ultimate variables. We are also investigating ways of enhancing the proposed semantic search by developing an algorithm for allocation and computation of relevant scores for Known Dangerous Combinations. In particular, we plan to devise measures to compare our search with other existing semantic searches in a quantitative way. We also want to test our approach with larger ontologies to evaluate its scalability.

ACKNOWLEDGMENTS

This work is supported in part by the National Science Foundation under grant IIS-0306838 and SAP Labs, LLC.

REFERENCES

1. Charu C. Aggarwal and Philip S. Yu. Outlier detection for high dimensional data. In Proceedings of the 2001 ACM SIGMOD international conference on Management of data, pages 37{46. ACM Press, 2001.
2. F. Baader, D. Calvanese, D. McGuinness, D. Nardi, and P. Patel-Scneider, "The Description Logics Handbook: Theory, Implementation and Applications", Cambridge University Press, UK, 2003.
3. J.A. Barnes. Social Networks (Addison-Wesley Module in Anthropology, 26). Addison-Wesley, Reading, 1972.
4. Vic Barnett and Toby Lewis. Outliers in Statistical Data. John Wiley and Sons, 3rd edition, 1994.
5. S. Bechhofer, "The DIG Description Logic Interface: DIG/1.1", Available from http://dl-web.man.ac.uk/dig/2003/02/interface.pdf, 2003.
6. S. Bechhofer, P. Lord, R. Volz, "Cooking the Semantic Web with the OWL API", In Proceedings of the 2nd International Semantic Web Conference, ISWC, Sanibel Island, Florida, October 2003.
7. Markus M. Bruenig, Hans-Peter Kriegel, Raymond T. Ng Jorg Sander, OPTICS-OF Identifying Local Outliers, Conference on Principles and Practice of knowledge Discovery in Databases (PKDD'99), Prague, September 1999.
8. Markus M. Breunig, Hans-Peter Kriegel, Raymond T. Ng, and Jorg Sander. Lof: Identifying density-based local outliers. In Proceedings of the ACM SIGMOD, 2000.
9. B. N. Grosof, I. Horrocks, R. Volz, and S. Decker, "Description Logic Programs: Combining Logic Programs with Description Logic", In Proceedings of the Twelfth International World Wide Web Conference, Budapest, Hungary, May 2003.
10. V. Haarslev, R. Moller, "RACER Users's Guide and Reference Manual", Available at http://www.cse.concordia.ca/%7Ehaarslev/racer/racer-manual-1-7-19.pdf, 2000.
11. Zengyou He, Shengchun Deng, and Xiaofei Xu. Outlier detection integrating semantic knowledge. In Proceedings of the International Conference on Advances in Web-Age Information Management, pages 126{131. Springer-Verlag, 2002.
12. I. Horrocks, P. F. Patel-Schneider, and F. Z. van Harmelen, "From SHIQ and RDF to OWL: The Making of a Web Ontology Language", In Journal of Web Semantics, 1(1), December 2003.

13. V.P. Janeja, V. Atluri, J.S. Vaidya, and N. Adam. Collusion set detection through outlier discovery. In IEEE Intelligence and Security Informatics, 2005.
14. V.P. Janeja, V. Atluri, J.S. Vaidya, and N. Adam. "Semantics based discovery of Affiliation Network" Technical report, 2005.
15. Edwin M. Knorr and Raymond T. Ng. Algorithms for mining distance-based outliers in large datasets. In Proceedings of the International Conference on Very Large Data Bases (VLDB 1998), pages 392{403, August 1998.
16. Edwin M. Knorr and Raymond T. Ng. Finding intensional knowledge of distance based outliers. In Proceedings of 25th International Conference on Very Large Data Bases, pages 211-222, 1999.
17. Jeremy Kubica, Andrew Moore, David Cohn, and J. Schneider. Finding underlying connections: A fast graph-based method for link analysis and collaboration queries. In Tom Fawcett and Nina Mishra, editors, Proceedings of the 2003 International Conference on Machine Learning, pages 392{399. AAAI Press, 2003.
18. Sridhar Ramaswamy, Rajeev Rastogi, and Kyuseok Shim. Effcient algorithms for mining outliers from large data sets. In Proceedings of the ACM SIGMOD, pages 427{438, 2000.
19. G. Rote. Computing the minimum hausdorff distance between two point sets on a line under translation. Inf. Process. Lett., 38(3):123-127, 1991.
20. M. K. Smith, C. Welty, and D. L. McGuinness, Editors, "OWL Web Ontology Language Guide" A W3C Recommendation, Latest version available at http://www.w3.org/TR/owl-guide/, February 2004.
21. Stanford University, "The Protege Project", Available from http://protege.stanford.edu, 2005.
22. Gang Wang, Hsinchun Chen, and Homa Atabakhsh. Automatically detecting deceptive criminal identities. Commun. ACM, 47(3):70{76, 2004.
23. S. Wasserman and K. Faust. Social network analysis. Cambridge University Press, 1994.
24. Jennifer Xu and Hsinchun Chen. Untangling criminal networks: A case study. In ISI, pages 232-248, 2003.
25. M.F. Lopez, A. Gomez-Perez, J.P. Sierra, and A.P. Sierra. Building a chemical ontology using methontology and the ontology design environment. "Intelligent Systems", 14: 37–46, 1999.
26. Customs Dataset: http://www.piers.com/default2.asp. Piers global intelligence solutions.

SUGGESTED READING

1. V. P. Janeja, Vijayalakshmi Atluri and Nabil R. Adam, Detecting Anomalous Geospatial Trajectories through Spatial Characterization and Spatio-Semantic Associations, The fifth National Conference on Digital Government (dg.o 2004), Seattle, WA. This work addresses the identification of anomalous geospatial trajectories in the domain of homeland security (for example: a customs agent may want to discover anomalies among cargo routes to identify potentially dangerous shipments even before they cross the border).

2. N.R. Adam, V.P. Janeja, V. Atluri, Neighborhood Based Detection of Anomalies in High Dimensional Spatio-temporal Sensor Datasets ACM

Symposium on Applied Computing, March 2004. This work proposes an approach to identify anomalous sensors for water monitoring efforts in homeland security.

3. V. Janeja, V. Atluri, A. Gomaa, N. Adam, C. Bornhoevd and T. Lin., "DM-AMS: Employing Data Mining Techniques Alert Management", NSF National Conference on Digital Government, 2005. Atlanta, Georgia. This work outlines an alert management system for homeland security.

ONLINE RESOURCES

- Secure Agency Interoperation for Effective Data Mining in Border Control and Homeland Security Applications, Project Home Page: http://cimic.rutgers.edu/~vandana/borderCtrl.htm: The objective of the proposed project was to identify and address, through research and development, some of the challenges encountered in applying information technology to government information services. The Website has links to participants, collaborators, domain experts and links to publications resulting from this project.
- Customs Dataset: http://www.piers.com/default2.asp. Piers global intelligence solutions. Data from PIERS comprises of Imports, exports data and U.S. and overseas profiles of companies.

QUESTIONS FOR DISCUSSION

1. Discuss some examples to contrast the problem of identifying threat structures in outliers vs. the general problem of identifying relationships between normal entities without restricting to outliers.
2. Discuss some applications where threat structure mining in ESGs may benefit from using existing Semantic graphs generated from text data.
3. What are some advantages and disadvantages of using traditional Euclidean distance based outlier detection vs. Collusion distance based outlier detection?

Chapter 17

IDENTITY MANAGEMENT FOR E-GOVERNMENT SERVICES

Fabio Fioravanti[1] and Enrico Nardelli[2]

[1]*Department of Sciences, University of Chieti-Pescara, Italy (fioravanti@sci.unich.it);*
[2]*Department of Mathematics, University of Rome "Tor Vergata," Italy (nardelli@mat.uniroma2.it)*

CHAPTER OVERVIEW

Identity management systems play a critical role in the field of e-Government and e-Business, as they constitute the basic building blocks enabling secure and reliable access to online services. In this chapter, we highlight the main technical and organizational pitfalls of current approaches to identity management which are either based on a centralized architecture or require adoption of common (technological and organizational) standards. We believe that these limitations can only be overcome by designing a common infrastructure which provides applications with transparent access to identity management services, independently of the underlying identity technology. Moreover, we describe the bridging backbone, an interoperability architecture based on a federation of national infrastructures which follows a cooperation-based approach and is fully compatible with and respectful of organizational and technical choices of existing systems.

1. INTRODUCTION

Building secure and effective identity management systems is a critical factor for the successful deployment of e-Government and e-Business services. Indeed, accurate and reliable verification of the electronic identity (e-ID) of the citizen requesting the execution of an online transaction is a prerequisite for customized delivery of high-value e-Services, which have to rely on an environment which provides protection from identity theft and fraud.

An (e-Government) identity management system defines a framework of organizational and technical standards and procedures for creating, storing, validating and using electronic attributes associated with the identity of a physical person. Effective use of an identity management system can help reduce costs and improve quality of delivered services, stimulating the emergence of new integrated services and fostering a service-oriented IT economy. Moreover, preventing illegitimate use of identification and authentication credentials helps States in defending national security, combating illegal immigration, terrorism and other criminal activities.

There exists several technical solutions for identity management employing very different technologies and standards. Many of these solutions are effective in a homogeneous environment, but when inter-operability among different identity management solutions is involved, even the most basic functionalities are not compatible.

However, in the real world economy, the key to success is in interoperability among different systems, not in a centralized approach, as exemplified by the failure of Microsoft's Passport initiative. Additionally, national sovereignty and organizational issues prevent the creation of a single authority for securing the authentication process in its entirety, preserving full autonomy and responsibility of national organizations for citizen authentication. Any centralized solution for addressing secure interoperability issues, although technically feasible and usable in strictly hierarchical environments (e.g. multinational companies), is doomed to fail as it does not satisfy this highly critical organizational constraint.

In order to overcome this limitation, significant standardization efforts for creating commonly agreed upon specifications of interoperable federated e-ID management systems have been made by the Liberty Alliance [10], a consortium of industrial partners including AOL, HP, IBM, Intel, Oracle, RSA and Sun.

However, we believe that these issues can only be overcome by tackling the difficult problem of bottom-up design of an interoperability framework which is based on existing national infrastructures and not by imposing yet another identity management architecture. Indeed, switching to a common standard for e-ID interoperability would require radical changes in existing IT systems and infrastructures which are not acceptable in the short or medium term for several reasons. These include economic arguments (adopting a new technology always requires making large investments on new systems and losing investments on abandoned ones), technical arguments (unexpected difficulties can introduce delays and discontinuity of service provision) and organizational arguments (switching to a third party standard also means losing the possibility of choosing which technologies to use and customizing them according to organizational needs).

European member States have made considerable investments into their national infrastructures and a wide variety of electronic identity management systems have been developed in an independent and uncoordinated way. These systems, which have not been designed for interoperability, use different technologies for hardware tokens (smart-cards, magnetic cards, mobile phones, etc.), biometrics (fingerprint, facial, retinal) and digital signatures. Consequently, member States do not necessarily trust each other's certification service (or other security services) providers. While some bilateral agreements exist between member States, in some scenarios, some of them prohibit – many times, de facto – the usage of authentication, authorization or signature certificates coming from other member States. A further obstacle originates from the fact that different organizational schemes are in use in different States: for example, the responsibility for issuing national e-IDs and validating foreign e-IDs is assigned to a single organization (centralized management of validation) in some member States, and is distributed among different autonomous organizations, even from different public administrations (distributed management of validation) in other States. Moreover, differences in legislation on identification (e.g. use of unique identifiers), data protection and digital signatures, which often reflect socio-cultural differences, hinders deployment of interoperable e-ID management systems.

Therefore a key goal is to research, define and implement an identity management framework that is based on secure and interoperable verification and authentication of identities, thus making the underlying identity technology – be it based on smart-cards or other security devices or biometric attributes – transparent and invisible to the application.

We need to understand which new components are needed, where to allocate them, and how to split tasks between legacy and new components. No ready-made recipe exists for solving such hard interoperability problems of these highly heterogeneous and complex legacy systems.

We propose an interoperability architecture based on a federation of national *citizen e-Authentication infrastructures* (CEIs) following a cooperative approach for trustworthy e-ID verification, which can coexist with any organizational and technical solution used by legacy national CEIs. The rules governing the federation establish roles and responsibilities of involved member States in managing authentication credentials and conditions for their delegation and relaying.

In our approach, security functions are based on a permanent infrastructure layer, since this is the only viable approach for guaranteeing efficiency of e-Service provision and effectiveness of security in open and intrinsically insecure environments like the Internet. Applications should not take care of the management of security functions, which are provided by an independent layer put on top of the layer providing communication services. Applications consider security functions as infrastructural services, analogous to what happens with communication services: details regarding communication protocols used for message delivery are completely transparent at the application level.

Our proposal to address techno-organizational problems in secure interoperability among CEIs is based on defining a permanent infrastructure layer, called *bridging backbone*, providing security services to interactions between national CEIs. Each CEI will continue to operate in the normal way under the national scenario, while it will cooperate with other CEIs under the inter-national scenarios, each working within its responsibility boundaries.

The framework's architecture has provisions for generating proof of evidence for transactions and for clear separation of responsibilities. The cooperative approach is also followed by similar e-Government projects which are currently being deployed in the United States [13], [8], [7].

2. STATUS OF NATIONAL ELECTRONIC IDENTITY IN EUROPE

In this section we report on some of the most prominent architectures, technologies and projects related to electronic identity management which have been developed in Europe. The information we provide is extracted from several sources including the CEN/ISSS WS e-Authentication [1], the European Union IDABC website [11], and presentations given by governmental representatives at meetings of the Porvoo group [9].

2.1 Austria

In 2004, the Austrian Government started issuing electronic cards within the 'Bürgerkarte' project which defines a set of functions and minimum requirements for secure identification and use of digital signatures in e-Government. The reference framework, which is based on open standards and interfaces, supports different ID tokens (e.g. smart-cards and SIM cards). Citizen cards are issued by several private and public sector organizations (including mobile phone operators, banks, civil service, social insurance) and support online access to about one hundred e-Services (which will become 80% of total e-Services by the end of 2007). Cardholder verification mechanisms vary depending on the card issuer (global PIN, application-specific PINs, one time passwords) and usage of biometrics is not envisioned. Authentication and digital signature functions are performed by using two different on-card certificates, and rely on a PKI with three certification authorities: a public one which is managed by the Main Association of the Social Security Institutions, and two private authorities managed by A-Trust (banking) and A1 (cellular phones). Cards and certificates have a validity period which differs from issuer to issuer, with a maximum of five years for qualified certificates. The card is not mandatory and is not a valid official ID document.

E-Government applications using the citizen card for authentication include tax services, request of residence certificates and registered e-mail. However, many more are likely to be developed due to the distribution of MOA (Modules for Online Applications), a set of server-side modules made available by the government for developing applications using the citizen card for authentication and digital signatures.

As of May 1st, 2006, over 10 million e-IDs had been issued, with an expected number of 15 millions e-IDs by the end of 2007. The number of active public sector certificates is 3,200, but they are expected to reach 50,000 by the end of 2006.

The forthcoming e-Health insurance card system ‘e-card’, which should replace paper-based healthcare vouchers (40 million/year), will contain personal and social insurance data and will be ready to include digital signature functionalities. The e-card will be based on the infrastructure provided by the Health Information Network (Gesundheits Informations Netzwerks - GIN) which will connect 14,000 Austrian doctors, social security offices and healthcare service providers.

2.2 Belgium

The official launch of the Belgian personal electronic identity card project (BelPIC) took place in March 2003, involving 11 Belgian pilot municipalities in cooperation with the National Register and the certification authority Belgacom.

The basic functionalities of the system are identification, authentication and digital signature. The Belgian e-ID card is a smart-card with a chip storing cardholder’s personal data (including date of birth, parenthood, civil status, current and past addresses, and military situation, if applicable) and certificates for authentication and digital signature. The card is issued by municipalities, is valid for 5 years, and uses a PIN-based access method. Currently only the photograph is present on the card, but inclusion of other biometric data is envisioned in the long term. The card is also a valid international travel document for the European 'Schengen' countries.

The e-ID card can be used for reliable access to e-Services, e-portal functions, online tax declaration, certified e-mail, e-library services, home banking and other applications that are under construction, including social security, university student services, and access to buildings. Currently, Belgian e-ID cardholders can digitally sign Adobe PDF documents and there are plans to integrate Belgian e-ID technology into Microsoft MSN Messenger for online identification.

In April 2006 a report on technical, legal and deployment requirements for secure and privacy-preserving applications based on the Belgian e-ID card was published by adapID (advanced applications for electronic IDentity cards in Flanders), a project of the Flemish Government (IWT-Vlaanderen) focusing on e-Government, e-Health and trusted archiving applications, and investigating technologies for future enhanced generations of the e-ID card (to be deployed from 2009). In September 2004 the Federal Government started the full national roll-out. In 2005, 1,378,474 citizens had an e-ID card and 8,200,000 citizens were expected to have one by 2009. According to the latest schedule the nationwide distribution will be completed in 2010.

2.3 Estonia

In Estonia national e-ID cards are issued by a public-private partnership under the responsibility of the Citizenship and Migration Board. The card is contact-based, contains a file with personal and card data (including name, national ID code, date and place of birth, sex, card number and validity) and integrates two certificates, and associated private keys, for identification/authentication and non-repudiation purposes. The card is PIN-protected and contains a chip for storing ICAO-compliant facial image and fingerprint biometrics. Certificate validation services are made available by means of certificate revocation lists, an LDAP repository and an OCSP service.

The card is a valid official identity document, a European travel document and supports access to public and private e-Services including tax, migration, citizenship, and e-ticketing services.

The validity of the card is ten years, while digital certificates have a validity of three years. However, there is a proposal for assigning a validity period of five years to cards and certificates. It is worth noting that the Estonian public sector must accept digitally signed documents and process them in the same way as it does with paper signed documents. The card is mandatory for all Estonian citizens and permanent resident foreigners over 15 years of age.

The deployment started in 2002 and, as of May 1st 2006, about 933,662 cards had been issued (over a population of 1,441,780), with an 18% yearly growth rate.

The Finnish Population Register Centre and the Estonian Certification Service Provider have signed a Memorandum of Understanding stating that they "will cooperate to make legally binding digital documents a reality within and between Finland and Estonia." Ongoing relationships with Belgium authorities also exist.

2.4 Finland

The Finnish e-ID card contains the Citizen Certificate, a government-guaranteed 'electronic identity' available to every individual resident in Finland, which is issued by the Population Register Centre (PRC) operating under the responsibility of the Ministry of Interior. The Citizen Certificate, which is based on open standards and secured by a public key infrastructure, can be used for user identification, authentication and confidentiality of the exchanged data, as well as information integrity and non-repudiation of message delivery. The card itself is issued by the police, has a validity of five years, is PIN-protected and contains no biometrics. Optionally, Finnish citizens can have health insurance data included in their electronic ID card.

Several services (over 50) are available to cardholders including social security services, tax services, health insurance, municipal application for employees and payment of meals. Since 2003, it is possible to carry out legally binding transactions using digital signatures.

From 1999 to 2005 about 78,000 chip-cards had been issued with an annual growth rate of 35,000 cards and an expected number of 135,000 cards by the end of 2007. The number of services using e-ID authentication is expected to reach 200 by the end of 2007, with a mid-term goal to provide 1,000 services and to have 35% of the citizens (about 1.8 million people) using the e-ID.

Since 2005, the PRC is storing Citizen Certificates in SIM cards, in cooperation with national telecom operators. This solution allows citizens using mobile devices to access services for address change notification and checking of existing personal details in the Population Information System. A number of additional m-government services are under preparation, including services offered by the Social Insurance Institution, the tax administration, and the Ministry of Labor. Due to the diffusion of mobile phones in Finland, this is expected to become the most inclusive channel for the delivery of electronic public services.

Finland is cooperating with Estonia in a cross-certification project which is developing on two levels: the legislation level and the technical level.

2.5 France

The creation of the French e-ID card was first announced in September 2003 with country-wide deployment scheduled for 2006. However its launch has been postponed until 2008 due to concerns raised by a number of institutions and civil rights associations regarding privacy, security, and use of biometric data in the INES project (Identité Nationale Electronique Sécurisée/National Electronic and Secured Identity), which had provisions for secured information processes for issuing e-ID cards and for a central database storing biometric identifiers.

The French e-ID card will be a multi-application smart-card containing cardholder personal data which will provide citizens with electronic signature facilities and will allow secure execution of both e-Government and e-commerce services and transactions. Integration of facial and finger-print biometrics is envisioned. The e-ID card will be compliant with current international standards, like European Regulation 2252/2004 for travel documents and IASv2 for authentication and signature tools. French citizens are expected to be able to start using e-IDs from 2008. Differently from paper-based identity cards, electronic ID cards will not be mandatory.

In 2004, the French Government started the ADELE e-Government program for modernizing the state infrastructure, for simplifying administrative procedures with the central administration and for developing systems for security identification of citizens. The following services will be made available within the ADELE framework: a call centre service, a one-stop shop service for address change, tenders submission, personalized public services portal, civil registration certificates (birth, marriage, and death certificates), and applications for funding.

The Vitale card is an e-Health insurance card which is issued to all individuals above 16 years of age who are entitled to social security reimbursements. The Vitale card contains administrative and entitlement information and can be used for electronic transmission of reimbursement claims between healthcare professionals and social security institutions. In 2005, a French IT professional managed to create and use a fake e-Health insurance card. For this reason, the Vitale card project will undergo a major security upgrade starting in 2006.

In March 2003, the "Carte de Vie Quotidienne" (daily life card) project was launched, aiming at providing electronic access, and possibly payment functionalities, to local public services through a smart-card-based identification and authentication process.

In April 2006 the French Ministry of Interior announced the imminent introduction of e-Passports. French citizens living abroad will experiment with the use of e-Identification tools in e-Voting during elections on June 18th, 2006.

2.6 Germany

In Germany there exists a plan for switching from the paper-based national ID card, which is mandatory for citizens starting from 16 years of age, to a highly secure smart-card-based ID card which will serve as a travel document and as an authentication token for accessing e-Government (e.g. tax filing, employment and salary certificates) and e-Business applications (e.g. e-Banking, e-Commerce). The card will also include, as an optional add-on, functionalities for qualified signatures which, according to the German Signature Act, are equivalent to handwritten signatures. The card will have a validity of 10 years, will be able to incorporate facial and fingerprint biometric information according to European Union and ICAO specifications and will use contact-less RFID technology. Roll-out is scheduled for 2007.

Following the Council Regulation of the European Union on standards for security features and biometrics in passports and travel documents issued by member States (Council Regulation (EC) No 2252/2004), the German e-Passport, will introduce biometrics in two phases: during the first phase the facial image will be included, while two fingerprints will be added during the second phase (starting in March 2007).

The Digital Health Card contains administrative data, vital patient data, and electronic prescriptions and can optionally be used for qualified signatures. However, the electronic health card and the digital identity card will not be merged and use of the Digital Health Card will not be made mandatory for procedures not related to public health.

The Job card project, which is envisioned to start in 2007, will issue a card for online access to employment services and social benefits systems to economically active citizens.

The Federal Cabinet decision of 9 March 2005 on the e-card strategy for harmonization and consistent usage of smart-cards states that:

- digital signature interoperability should be ensured through adoption of accepted standards, authentication and encryption technologies,
- all German cards must permit inclusion of the qualified digital signature at time of issuance or at a later time, and

- all administrative procedures requiring a qualified signature must support the standards agreed on by the Signature Alliance, a public-private partnership to promote the use of digital signatures.

2.7 Hungary

The Hungarian Government has adopted a national strategy for smart-card usage. This strategy includes the definition of an interoperability framework for smart-card requirements, standards and interfaces and their applications to healthcare and e-ID cards.

The 2005 'act on the general rules of public administration and services' ensures that electronic procedures have the same legal value as paper-based ones. In addition, the Hungarian public administration will be obliged to make information and services available online.

2.8 Italy

The Italian national ID card project CIE (Carta d'Identità Elettronica/ electronic identity card) was launched in 2001 and is aiming to replace the 40 million existing paper-based identity cards.

The first experimental phase ended in June 2003 with about 100,000 cards issued in 83 municipalities. The second experimental phase ended in 2004 with 2 million cards in production and 600,000 cards dispatched to 56 municipalities. Municipal authorities have been distributing 400,000 cards (December 2004) to citizens older than 15. From January 1st, 2007 all municipalities will issue e-ID cards to their citizens. The aim is to issue eight million cards a year for the next 5 years. Cards are manufactured and initialized by the Italian mint (Istituto Poligrafico e Zecca dello Stato), but cardholder's personal information is added by municipalities. The deployment of the infrastructure required to access registry and demographic services and validate data on the card data was completed in Q2 2004, reaching all of the 8,102 Italian municipalities, with 23 million data controls and alignments performed.

The card is a contact smart-card of 32 KB with an optical stripe on the same side of the card with a capacity of 1.8 MB. The card contains holder's personal data, including fiscal code, blood group and a fingerprint template which is embedded in the chip and in the optical stripe. The card carries one digital certificate which can be used for access to e-Services. The certificate itself contains no personal data, which, however, service providers can acquire from the Ministry of the Interior (CNSD-INA) via an online process. Fingerprint and certificate information are only stored in the chip, with no central or local database in accordance with Italian data protection legislation. Currently, the card is PIN-protected and does not support the digital signature for non-repudiation.

The card is a valid national identity document, an official travel document recognized by 32 European and North African countries, and allows an easy and efficient access to public services. Some operational services at the local or national level using the CIE for authentication are: payment of waste collection tax (TARSU), children's school enrolment and school fees payment, city residence and street residence change, payment of fines, age check at cigarette machines, identification check at the polls, check of a citizen's fiscal position, and access to SIM (Mountain Information System). Furthermore, several services are under preparation, including: civil and criminal complaint filing and status control, payment of social charges for house servants, income tax return payment, enrolment to local sport centers, booking of hospital admissions, medical visits, medical tests, welfare requests filing (social support checks, scholarships, ...), house local tax (ICI) variations and payment, economical support to disadvantaged people (elders, orphans, ...).

In Italy there exists another project, named CNS (Carta Nazionale dei Servizi/National Services Card), which aims at becoming an access mechanism for all existing and future Italian e-Government services. The card is equipped with a microprocessor containing holder's personal data, including a personal ID number. As a result of an agreement with the Italian Bankers Association, the card is also being tested for online payments using an existing financial service called Bankpass Web.

The CNS card is not an official identity document and is meant to complement rather than duplicate the national electronic ID card CIE. Indeed, by decree of the Italian Council of Ministers in February 2004 it was laid down that all Italian citizens will be able to access all of the country's e-Government services using a single smart-card. The Decree of the President of the Republic n.117 of 2nd March 2004, containing "Regulations on the diffusion of the National Service Card," states in Art.2, Paragraph 3: At the time of issuing or renovating the national service card, the administration, by means of the telematic services made available through the National Index of Personal Data Registries (INA – Indice Nazionale delle Anagrafi) checks the validity of personal data and verifies the person is not already a holder of the electronic identity card (CIE). If the personal data are valid and if the applicant is not holding an electronic identity card the administration issues the national service card.

So it may be expected that in due time the CNS and CIE cards will merge and only the CIE will remain. Nevertheless, the Italian Government set a target to distribute 10 million CNS cards by Q1 2006. More generally, the new government coming out from the general elections of April 2006 might revise the entire Italian strategy in this area.

2.9 Poland

Poland has plans to introduce an electronic ID and is closely monitoring the solutions and progress in neighboring Hungary. By 2005 the Polish Government plans to replace all old ID booklets with machine readable cards. Smart-cards might be introduced in the future. The Polish Computerization Act is an instrument for the modernization of the public administration which gives citizens and businesses the right to contact public authorities electronically and establishes the Plan for Information Society Development. Additionally, a framework for public sector IT systems was introduced mandating interoperability with other systems, technological neutrality and fulfillment of a set of minimum requirements.

2.10 Slovenia

The Slovenian e-ID project started in 2002, after the definition of the legislative framework and the establishment of the governmental certification authorities, which issue qualified digital certificates to governmental employees (SIGOV-CA, Slovenian Governmental Certification Authority) and to natural and legal persons (SIGEN-CA, Slovenian General Certification Authority).

The identity card contains a chip with holder's personal data and two digital certificates, one for holder authentication and one for digital signature. The card, which is not mandatory, is ready to contain biometric data, in compliance with the EU e-Passport regulation. Adoption of contact-less technology has also been considered.

The Slovenian national e-ID project is divided into three phases. The first phase, which is in progress, is a pilot project. The second phase will follow and will include the tender and the production of a national e-ID. In parallel to the two phases, a third phase, which is already in progress, is focusing on interoperability and e-Services with Slovenian banks and e-ID projects running in EU member States.

E-services considered in the third phase include services which are already available, such as tax return, access to data in state registers (Register of Civil Status, Permanent Population Register, and Vehicle Register), e-forms and e-invoices. In April 2006, the Slovenian Government adopted a Strategy for Electronic Commerce in Public Administration for 2006-2010 which provides for the launching of several additional governmental e-Services including one stop shop for business startup (2006), social transfers, land register and cadastre, e-archiving (2007-2008), with the goal of achieving interoperability with European member States by 2010.

Following recent EU regulations and US demands, Slovenia is introducing new biometric e-Passports which integrate a contact-less chip. Moreover, the health insurance card system, operational since 2000, issues cards both to patients (2 million) and to healthcare professionals (18,000) for identification and data storage. There is a plan to gradually upgrade this system, so as to allow cardholders to use their card for online access to healthcare services.

2.11 Spain

In February 2004 the Spanish Council of Ministers approved the creation and distribution to Spanish citizens of electronic ID cards (DNI Electrónico) which provide secure identification and authentication and digital signature functions for a wide range of online transactions, ranging from e-Government services to e-Commerce and Internet banking.

In order to authenticate themselves or to sign electronically online, cardholders only need their PIN code, a card reader and specific software that will be downloadable from the Internet. The new electronic ID card is meant to become a universal digital signature instrument, valid for all types of transactions.

The electronic ID cards are smart-cards containing the following information stored in the chip: an electronic certificate for authentication purposes, a PIN-protected certified digital signature for signing electronic documents, facial image and fingerprint biometric data, cardholder photograph and handwritten signature in digitized form, in addition to data printed on the card (date of birth, place of residence, etc.).

Cards are manufactured by the Spanish Royal mint (FNMT) and contain several physical security features, enhanced by cryptographic methods and bi-dimensional bar codes. The e-ID cards and electronic certificates therein contained will be issued by the National Spanish Police Department of the Ministry of Interior. The validity of e-ID cards is either five or ten years, depending on the age of the cardholder, while certificates are valid for 30 months.

Services supporting user authentication based on e-ID cards include tax declaration and social security services. As already mentioned, the electronic ID card can also be used for digital signatures which, from a legal perspective, are equivalent to handwritten signatures.

The electronic ID card was officially launched in March 2006 with a high-profile media campaign. There are currently 29 million paper-based ID cardholders in Spain (the card is mandatory starting at 14 years of age), with approximately 6 million cards being renewed each year. It is envisioned to issue 5 million e-ID cards and 10 million certificates by the end of 2007.

According to the government, the Spanish e-ID card will be interoperable and technically compatible with the electronic cards being developed in Germany, France, Italy and the United Kingdom.

2.12 United Kingdom

On March 30th, 2006 the UK Parliament approved the Identity Cards Act after two years of Parliament debates and several readings. This is a major step in the ongoing political debate in the UK on the issue of national ID cards, but there was a strong opposition against introducing such a token on a compulsory basis.

Under this scheme, a National Identity Register will be established containing biometric data (fingerprints, face, irises), which can be accessed by public and private sector organizations to verify a person's identity, with her consent. From 2008 every citizen wanting to apply for or renew a passport will be issued an ID card and her personal data and biometric information will be stored on the National Identity Register database. Until 2010 UK citizens can choose not to be issued a card, but registration will become compulsory for all UK residents by 2013. It will not be compulsory to carry the e-ID card.

According to the government, the scheme will provide citizens with a simple and secure standard for proving their identity in everyday transactions with public and private services and help ensure UK national security. The card will hold basic personal data such as name, age, validity date, entitlement to work, and a unique identification number will appear on the face of the card. The card will feature a secure encrypted chip that will contain a unique personal biometric identifier and will have a 10-year validity period.

The responsibility for managing the National Identity Register and for issuing e-Passports and e-ID cards has been assigned to the Identity and Passport Service, an Executive Agency of the UK Home Office.

A pilot for e-Passports was launched in 2004 for testing recording, recognition and usage of facial, iris and fingerprint biometrics. The roll-out for the introduction of e-Passports should be completed in 2006/07.

3. A COOPERATIVE FEDERATED ARCHITECTURE FOR IDENTITY MANAGEMENT

The model adopted in our approach [15], which is inspired by the CEN's e-Authentication CWA [1], addresses interoperability problems at different architectural layers: the citizen device layer, the infrastructure layer and the application layer.

The physical environment where the device is operating while accessing the infrastructure constitutes the *citizen device layer*. The device can either be a smart-card (as it is common in many member States) or any other device supporting strong authentication (like mobile phones with cryptographic capabilities). Accessing devices must be linkable to personal identity, if needed, but should also be detachable from it in cases where only role identification is performed or where a certain degree of anonymity has to be guaranteed.

The *infrastructure layer* encompasses communication networks and systems which can be found on the path from the physical interface with the citizen device to remote servers, including (i) a *user access point*, that is the local part of the infrastructure used by the citizen device for accessing the system, (ii) an *e-Service access point*, that is the remote part of the infrastructure interfacing with service providers, and (iii) *identity validation services*, supporting e-Authentication procedures.

The *application layer* is composed of the applications which deliver services to authenticated users.

In a federated architecture, organizations cooperating in order to achieve a common goal rely on information provided by other members of the federation. For this reason, it is of fundamental importance that members of the federation agree on the quality of protection they provide when issuing and managing e-IDs and rigorously define reciprocal responsibilities.

Indeed, components at any architectural layer (devices/systems/services) must have a correct understanding of mutual levels of trust during the interaction with other components. For example, an authentication mechanism based on username and password issued during a completely online process cannot share the same level of trust of as an authentication method based on counterfeit-resistant credentials issued after careful physical identification. The definition of various degrees of trust existing in each CEI and a clear mapping between trust levels in various CEIs is therefore needed.

Problems of high technical complexity derive from the need to manage the whole process in an efficient and effective manner while ensuring, at the same time, interoperability of geographically distributed IT-based systems, independently of technical solutions used by participating organizations, and fulfillment of privacy and security constraints in a democratic manner.

Security and performance are, indeed, the most critical functional capabilities of the interoperability architecture.

The first essential functionality is end-to-end security. This refers to the capability of ensuring traditional security requirements (from basic ones:

confidentiality, integrity, authentication, authorization, to derived ones: auditing, non-repudiation, etc.) from the citizen accessing devices all the way down to the point providing the required service.

The second critical functionality is performance experienced by end-users. Due to the cooperative approach that has to be followed in designing the overall interoperability architecture and to the size of federated systems of national CEIs that will result, each service invocation may require establishing and traversing several times geographically long and organizationally complex communication paths. For improved performance, only cross-border interactions, which are important for security and privacy purposes or for documenting interaction between CEIs, will be required to be secured. Moreover, a carefully designed architecture must be able to cache information at usage points and keep it fresh to avoid the well-known attacks based on exploiting stale security information. From a user perspective this is similar to single sign-on, which avoids the need to repeat the process of identification and authentication for a series of transactions.

3.1 Further Interoperability Issues

Interoperability between national electronic identity management systems must be provided at three different levels of functionalities, which are listed below in increasing order of complexity:

- identification and authentication: that is the process of associating a set of attributes or a personal identifier with a citizen (identification) and proving that such association is trustworthy (authentication);
- authorization: that is the process of deciding whether a user is allowed to perform a particular action;
- electronic signature: that is the process of establishing authenticity of data and identity of the signer mainly for the purpose of producing verifiable records of transactions.

Noteworthy semantic problems will have to be solved for enabling interoperability among privilege management systems which handle authorizations and access rights of citizens depending not only on their identity, but also on their role within an organization (e.g. doctor, policeman, CEO). Although this is an important research area to be investigated, role-based privilege management systems [2, 14] must be built on top of effective and reliable authentication systems, and must be kept separate from them.

Interoperability of electronic signatures is another important issue to be solved, which is orthogonal to interoperability of CEIs. In the EU, this is a difficult and very controversial point because some member States have developed very different interpretations of the EU directive containing recommendations for management of electronic signatures. Consequently, using electronic signatures as a basis for performing e-Authentication will lead to potentially never-ending legal and juridical disputes. Additional critical issues are interoperability of security policies, user profiles and certificate validation services.

An additional requirement of an interoperability architecture is support for the specification of privacy preferences, giving the citizen full control over collection, storage and use of personal information, along with support for anonymity schemes and a mechanism for protection against user profiling. An effective system should inform the user every time her electronic identity is used in a transaction and should allow almost immediate revocation by the holder.

3.2 Architectural Interfaces for Interoperability

From an architectural viewpoint it is also important to identify interfaces lying between different components. Indeed, in the case of interoperability of national CEIs, some of them are managed by different national systems, raising the need for establishing a secure and reliable dialog among them. A first interface is between the citizen device used for requesting access to the system and the physical device interacting with it at the user access point. A second interface is between the user access point and the service access point that is between the local terminal application and the access point to the requested service. A third interface, which is highly critical for services requiring user authentication, is between the validation service used to verify the authenticity of user credentials and a user or service access point. The fourth interface is between a service access point and an e-Service.

3.3 Interoperability Scenarios

Depending on whether the citizen device layer, the infrastructure layer and the application layer, are *on-us* (meaning national/domestic) or *not-on-us* (meaning foreign/alien), different scenarios derive, bringing technical and organizational interoperability problems of different dimensions and nature.

If we fix a value for one layer, then all possible interoperability scenarios are clearly identified. For example, the Italian access network (which means that the citizen device is physically in Italy) has to provide access in the five interoperability scenarios listed below:

1. Italian devices accessing Italian services,
2. Italian devices accessing foreign services,
3. foreign devices accessing Italian services, and
4. foreign devices accessing foreign services. This has two sub-cases:

a. foreign devices accessing their national services, and
b. foreign devices accessing services provided by a third foreign country.

As a further example of how this approach to modeling interoperability scenarios works, Table 17-1 shows the possible kinds of interoperability scenarios obtained by choosing the citizen device belonging to the Italian domain.

Table 17-1. Interoperability scenarios

	Italian application	Foreign application	
Italian infrastructure	Italian CEIs	partial operability	
Foreign infrastructure	partial interoperability	same CEIs	partial interoperability
		different CEIs	full interoperability

A synthetic characterization of the different kinds of interoperability scenarios follows:

1. national CEIs: components in all three layers belong to the same domain,
2. partial CEIs interoperability: components in two layers belong to the same domain,
3. full CEIs interoperability: components in each layer belong to different domains.

An example scenario at the widest possible interoperability level is the following: an Estonian citizen wishes to make access to an Italian service while visiting Belgium. In this case, the first interface is physically in Belgium, the second interface spans the three countries, the third interface is physically in Estonia, and the fourth is in Italy.

3.4 The Bridging Backbone Approach

Provision of cross-border services to mobile citizens requires interoperability of national e-ID management systems at different layers. Initially, citizen credentials must be obtained from the citizen device and understood by the access network. Then, the citizen's request is first relayed to the competent CEI for authentication and subsequently to the CEIs which are competent for providing the requested services.

Efficient provision of end-to-end security requires a highly secure and efficient exchange layer among national CEIs, which facilitates quick exchange of all required information to properly authenticate accessing citizens. This exchange layer must be overlaid to and logically distinct from existing CEIs.

We propose an infrastructural solution to security and interoperability issues in provision of cross-border e-Services to mobile citizens: the *bridging backbone*. The bridging backbone provides security services (like confidentiality and integrity services, authentication, authorization and auditing) in an easy and transparent manner, independently from locally deployed network technology and topology. Security services are provided at a layer lying between the application and communication layers, which is in charge of monitoring network connections and securing them according to the cooperation policies of the federation of involved infrastructures (see [5], [4], [6], [3] for details).

A mandatory requirement of the cooperation-based approach is the ability to document transactions that were carried out during interaction between national CEIs. Given the legal value attached to data being managed and exchanged in this process and the fact that many various kinds of mistakes can take place during the interaction, it is necessary to clearly and unequivocally understand who did what. The absence of a super-national organization that can supervise and direct the activity of national CEIs makes these certification functions a mandatory requirement. Moreover, as certification functions in a federation of national infrastructures play a back-office and subordinate role, they are fully acceptable by involved organizations, both from political and organizational viewpoints.

It is important to stress that in the real world of non-electronic services and whenever some kind of contractual responsibility is involved, security functions are always based, to various degrees, on some form of permanent infrastructure. For example, public utilities like power supply, water, and sewage are provided by municipalities to houses on the basis of the house ownership or rental. People interact with banks in buildings and offices clearly and permanently identifiable as bank settings (even ATMs are usually placed in trustable environments). Also e-Banking, the currently most widespread e-Service among the ones where trust is a fundamental aspect, is based on an initial setup phase where a security infrastructure is established: the customer goes physically to branch offices for signing the contract and receives codes and instructions for accessing the service on the Internet.

A further important point regarding security in interaction between institutions (as compared to interaction among people) is that organizations typically do not allow any inside member to unilaterally establish trust with external entities. The reality of institutional cooperation shows that inter-institutional trust is always based on bilateral agreement at the organizational level. The electronic counterpart of this convention is that there must be an infrastructure layer providing security functions, and security functions are provided with reference to and after an agreement is formally in place between the involved organizations.

4. CONCLUSIONS AND DISCUSSION

Our proposal considers an interoperability architecture based on a federation of national infrastructures and follows a cooperation-based approach which is fully compatible with and respectful of organizational and technical choices of existing systems.

In our view security is not an add-on service but is an infrastructural service of inter-organizational communication. By providing applications with security services in a completely transparent, infrastructural way, issues related to security services and business logic are kept separate, thereby reducing the risks of introducing security flaws. This is in contrast with the standard approach, where security services are usually provided at different levels of the protocol stack.

The technological neutrality and the compatibility with legacy systems of our approach do not violate techno-organizational choices of involved organizations. Moreover, since interoperability is not based on country-to-country system interfaces deriving from bilateral agreements, this approach allows the designing and building of a scalable and efficient system. The bilateral agreements approach would be, in fact, viable and effective only when there are very few actors: as soon as the stakeholders are more than three or four its complexity becomes unmanageable.

We solve the organizational pitfall of a naive use of PKIs, where trust can be established unilaterally, by allowing cooperation between members of different organizations only on top of the bridging backbone layer, which is set up only after a bilateral agreement is formally in place at the organizational level.

Additionally, the bridging backbone enables the certification of successful e-Services interaction and composition, identification of culprits of unsuccessful service provision, and monitoring of the actual performance of service provision [5].

REFERENCES

1. CEN/ISSS Workshop on e-Authentication, 2005. http://www.cenorm.be/cenorm/businessdomains/businessdomains/isss/activity/wseaut.asp
2. Gail-Joon Ahn. Specification and Classification of Role-based Authorization Policies. In Twelfth International Workshop on Enabling Technologies: Infrastructure for Collaborative Enterprises June 09 - 11, 2003 Linz, Austria, 2003.
3. Franco Arcieri, Elettra Cappadozzi, Enrico Nardelli, and Maurizio Talamo. SIM: a Working Example of an E-government Service Infrastructure for Mountain Communities. In Workshop Electronic Government (DEXA-e-gov'01), associated to the 2001 Conference on Databases and Expert System Applications (DEXA'01), pages 407–411, Munich, Germany, September 2001. IEEE Computer Society Press.

4. Franco Arcieri, Mario Ciclosi, Fabio Fioravanti, Enrico Nardelli, and Maurizio Talamo. The Italian Electronic Identity Card: a short introduction. In The National Conference on Digital Government Research (dg.o2004), May 24-26, 2004, Seattle, Washington, USA.
5. Franco Arcieri, Fabio Fioravanti, Enrico Nardelli, and Maurizio Talamo. Inter-organizational E-Services Accounting Management. In 3rd IFIP conference on e-Commerce, e-Business, and e-Government (I3E-03) Sao Paolo, Brasil. Kluwer Academic Publishers, September 2003.
6. Franco Arcieri, Fabio Fioravanti, Enrico Nardelli, and Maurizio Talamo. Reliable Peer-to-Peer Access for Italian Citizens to Digital Government Services on the Internet. In Roland Traunmüller, editor, Electronic Government: Third International Conference, (E-GOV'04), Zaragoza, Spain, August 30 – September 3, 2004, volume 3183 of Lecture Notes in Computer Science, pages 250–255. Springer-Verlag, 2004.
7. United States Federal PKI Operational Authority. Federal Public Key Infrastructure (FPKI) Architecture Technical Overview, 2005.
8. United States Federal PKI Policy Authority. X.509 Certificate Policy for the Federal Bridge Certification Authority, 2002.
9. The Porvoo Group website.http://www.vaestorekisterikeskus.fi/vrk/home.nsf/pages/index_eng. Follow the link "Electronic Identity" and then the "Porvoo Group" one.
10. The Liberty Alliance project. http://www.projectliberty.org
11. The Interchange of Data Between Administrations (IDABC) program of the European Union. http://europa.eu.int/idabc/
12. The International Civil Aviation Organization (ICAO) website.http://www.icao.int
13. United States General Accounting Office. Planned e-Authentication Gateway Faces Formidable Development Challenges, 2003. Report to the Committee on Government Reform and the Subcommittee on Technology, Information Policy, Intergovernmental Relations, and the Census, House of Representatives.
14. Ravi S. Sandhu, Edward J. Coyne, Hal L. Feinstein, and Charles E. Youman. Role-Based Access Control Models. IEEE Computer, 29(2):38–47, 1996.
15. Franco Arcieri, Andrea Dimitri, Fabio Fioravanti, Enrico Nardelli, Katia Pallucca, Alberto Postiglione and Maurizio Talamo. An Infrastructural Approach to Secure Interoperability of Electronic IDs: The Bridging Backbone. In Maria Wimmer et al., editors, Electronic Government: Fourth International Conference, (E-GOV'05), Copenhagen, Denmark, August 22-26, 2005, volume 3591 of Lecture Notes in Computer Science, pages 291–299. Springer-Verlag, 2005.

SUGGESTED READINGS AND ONLINE RESOURCES

- The Porvoo Group website:
  http://www.vaestorekisterikeskus.fi/vrk/home.nsf/pages/index_eng
  Follow the link, "Electronic Identity," and then "Porvoo Group." The Porvoo Group is an international cooperative network whose primary goal is to promote a trans-national, interoperable electronic identity, based on PKI technology (Public Key Infrastructure) and electronic ID cards, in order to help ensure secure public and private sector e-transactions in Europe. The Group also promotes the introduction of interoperable certificates and technical specifications, the

mutual, cross-border acceptance of authentication mechanisms, as well as cross-border, online access to administrative services.

- IDABC (Interoperable Delivery of European e-Government Services to public Administrations, Businesses and Citizens):
  http://europa.eu.int/idabc
  IDABC is a European Union project for supporting use of ICT in the delivery of cross-border public sector services to citizens and enterprises in Europe and for improving efficiency and collaboration between European public administrations.
- CEN/ISSS Workshop Agreement on eAuthentication for smart-cards and e-Government applications:
  http://www.cenorm.be/cenorm/businessdomains/businessdomains/isss/activity/wseaut.asp
  A CEN workshop agreement (CWA) is a consensus-based specification, drawn up in an open workshop environment of the European Committee for Standardization (CEN/ISSS).The outcome of the CEN/ISSS Workshop Agreement on eAuthentication is a set of requirements, recommendations and best practices for reliable pan-European interoperable e-ID within an e-Government issued and public-private partnership based multi-application card scheme.
- e-Government Unit of the Directorate General for Information Society of the European Commission: http://europa.eu.int/e-Government_research
  The mission of the e-Government Unit in the DG Information Society is to implement policy, good practice exchange and innovation through the eEurope action plan and the IST program.

QUESTIONS FOR DISCUSSION

1. What are the advantages and disadvantages of adopting a centralized approach to ID management with respect to a federated/cooperative approach?
2. What is the organizational, economic and legal impact of migrating to third party technologies for ID management in a trans-national scenario?
3. How does infrastructural security compare to application-level security?

Chapter 18

FEATURE INTEGRATION FOR GEOSPATIAL INFORMATION

A Review and Outlook

Peggy Agouris[1], Arie Croitoru[2], and Anthony Stefanidis[1]

[1]Department of Earth Systems and Geoinformation Sciences, and the Center for Earth Observing and Space Research (CEOSR), George Mason University, Fairfax, VA, U.S.A; [2]Department of Earth and Atmospheric Sciences, University of Alberta, Edmonton, Canada

CHAPTER OVERVIEW

The global trend of ever increasing volumes of digital data is also evident in spatial and spatiotemporal datasets, as it is estimated that approximately 80 percent of all databases have a spatial component. Furthermore the spatial community is witnessing a diversification in data availability, with complementary datasets available from diverse providers. Thus, government agencies using spatial information are now faced with the challenge of using heterogeneous spatial and spatiotemporal datasets. Consequently, there is an ever-increasing need for reliable and highly automated spatial data integration. The integration may be spatial, whereby two or more datasets depicting complementary information for the same area are brought together to extend their coverage or to aggregate their content; or temporal, whereby two or more similar datasets conveying the same thematic information at different time instances are brought together to analyze the evolution of their content. In this chapter we present some of the dominant approaches for these two types of information integration for geospatial applications, both at the spatial and the spatiotemporal domain. We also present some of the recently developed approaches to spatial and spatiotemporal queries, and discuss their role in spatiotemporal pattern detection and analysis.

1. INTRODUCTION

Recent years have been characterized by a dramatic increase in the volume of digital data. It has been estimated that the amount of data in the world doubles every 20 months, a process that results in an ever-increasing number of databases and clearinghouses. Spatial and spatiotemporal data follow a similar pattern: as it is estimated that approximately 80 percent of all databases have a spatial component, spatial and spatiotemporal databases are likely to follow a similar growth rate. A prominent example to the extent of this growth may be found in the area of remote sensing, where NASA's Terra satellite is capable of generating close to one terabyte of data per day[1], a rate that has doubled NASA's earth data repositories in less than a year. This ability to generate massive amounts of geospatial data (in particular imagery) is likely to further intensify with the introduction of wireless sensor networks (such as video surveillance sensors), as well as by the dissemination of new technologies, such as location aware and GPS-enabled mobile devices, which enable the collection of large amounts of data.

These trends have created an entirely new situation, in which government agencies no longer utilize data from a single source. Instead, such agencies rely on heterogeneous spatial (and spatiotemporal) data from multiple sources, in addition to other spatial and non-spatial data that they may maintain or actively collect. Consequently, there is an ever-increasing need for reliable and highly automated spatial data integration. This integration may be (Fig. 18-1):

- **spatial**, whereby two or more datasets depicting complementary information for the same area (e.g. one depicting road networks, and another depicting criminal activity hotspots) are brought together to extend their coverage (e.g. creating longer mosaics) or to aggregate their content, thus supporting complex analysis (e.g. identifying whether we have increased numbers of criminal activities near exits of major highways), or
- **temporal**, whereby two or more similar datasets conveying the same thematic information at different time instances (e.g. a sequence of satellite images of the same area over a long time period) are brought together to analyze the evolution of their content (e.g. monitoring the spread of a specific crop disease).

In this paper we present some dominant approaches for these two types of information integration for geospatial applications. In Section 2 we discuss approaches for spatial integration, followed by a discussion of

[1]Utilization of Operational Environmental Satellite Data: Ensuring Readiness for 2010 and Beyond. National Research Council publication (2004), p. 50

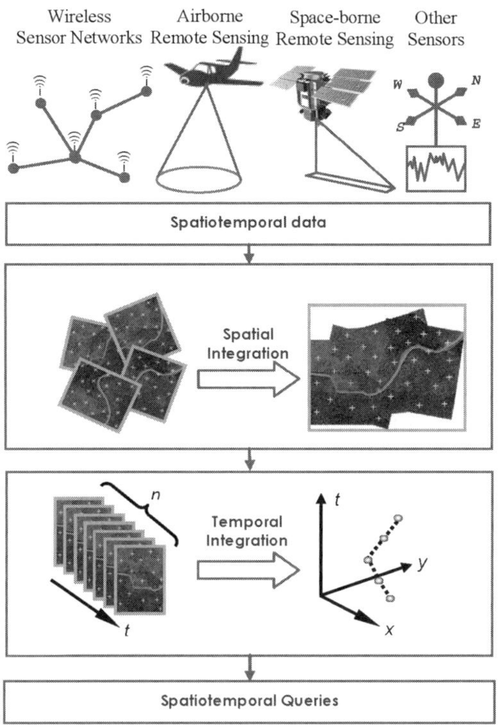

Figure 18-1. An overview of the spatiotemporal data integration framework

spatiotemporal integration in Section 3. We then present some interesting approaches to spatial and spatiotemporal queries in Section 4, followed by concluding remarks and supplementary information and resources.

2. SPATIAL INTEGRATION

The essence of the data integration process is the conflation (fusion) of spatial data from two different sources (Saalfeld 1988), which results in a single data set that incorporates data and attributes from both sources. This is often achieved by first establishing correspondence through a matching process between counterpart features in both data sets, and then integrating the data sets using a local or global geometric transformation. This approach was first suggested by Saalfeld (1988), in which correspondence is first established using a set of anchor points, followed by a Delaunay triangulation-based local piecewise linear transformation (also known as rubber-sheeting) (Saalfeld 1993). This approach was later expanded to line segments (Gabay and Doytsher 1994) and to linear features (Filin and Doytsher 1999; Doytsher et al. 2001).

Despite these efforts fully automated conflation still remains a major challenge, primarily due to the inability of existing matching algorithms to cope with the heterogeneity both in type and characteristics of spatial data. The data sources utilized in the conflation process may vary from data collected in-situ (for example, using a wireless sensor network), through existing vector or raster data, to imagery and video (Jensen et al. 1998). Moreover, such data sets may be of various feature types ranging from point data, to lines, areas, and fields (O'Sullivan and Unwin 2003). As a result, two data sets that should be integrated may not share the same source, feature type, horizontal and vertical reference frames, projection, spatial and temporal resolutions, quality characteristics, attributes, and even coverage (although partial coverage is required). In light of the extent of the possible variability in the data sets, several approaches have been suggested to the feature matching problem, and they may be roughly categorized into three types:

1. **Similarity-based approaches**: in which distance metrics are used as similarity measures between two matching candidates. A common distance metric used in this approach is the Hausdorff distance (Alt et al. 1991; Aichholzer et al. 1997).
2. **Overlay approaches**: in which two datasets are overlaid one on top of the other and correspondence between features (point-point, point-line, and line-line) is discovered using an epsilon-band tolerance region (Gabay and Doytsher 1994). Such approaches assume that the two datasets already share the same reference frame.
3. **Probabilistic approaches**: in which empirical probabilities are iteratively assigned to potentially matching features, while taking into account spatial and topological relations between the features and their neighborhood. One of the most widely known algorithms in this approach is the Relaxation Labeling algorithm (Fekete et al. 1981).

It should be noted that while all three approaches have been applied in the context of spatial data integration, the overlay approach is less preferable due to its reliance on the relative location of features as the primary criterion for establishing correspondence. This may often lead to a situation where only parts of one feature (for example, a linear feature such as road or a shoreline) are matched to parts in its counterpart, thus leading to an ambiguity in the relations between features (Lemarié et al. 1996; Ware and Jones 1998).

Due to the disadvantages of the overlay approach (and the epsilon-band), the similarity-based approach and the probabilistic approach have been recently suggested as a more efficient framework in spatial data integration.

Wang et al. (2006a) have proposed a strategy of achieving correspondence between two data sets based on two sequential processing steps, namely invariant signature generation and signature matching. The purpose of the invariant signature generation step is to eliminate the effect of any shifts, rotations, and scale differences between the two polygonal representations prior to the matching process. This is accomplished by generating an invariant shape signature curve for each polygon using the curvature (κ), a well known geometric invariant (Lipschultz 1969).

Once the invariant signature curves are obtained the matching process then attempts to find the optimal alignment between the two polygonal representations based on their signature curves. To this end, a Modified Smith-Waterman (MSW) sequence matching algorithm has been suggested (Gusfield 1997) for the detection of partial (local) alignments between two given sequences based on a stepwise optimization process that is realized by dynamic programming (Figure 18-2). It should be noted that this approach to the inexact matching of two polygonal representations is close in nature to the longest Common Sub-Sequence (LCSS) based approach that was recently suggested by Vlachos et al. (2002) and Vlachos et al. (2003). Yet unlike the LCSS algorithm the MSW algorithm allows partial matching between linear features, and is therefore applicable in cases where the two data sets are only partially overlapping. Furthermore, the LCSS algorithm does not allow control over the length of gaps, which is important in the case of road matching as it is not expected that the two partially overlapping line segments (left and right) will have long discontinuities or significant differences in their overlapping region.

A probabilistic approach to the spatial data integration problem has been also recently suggested by Wang et al. (2006b). In this approach matching a

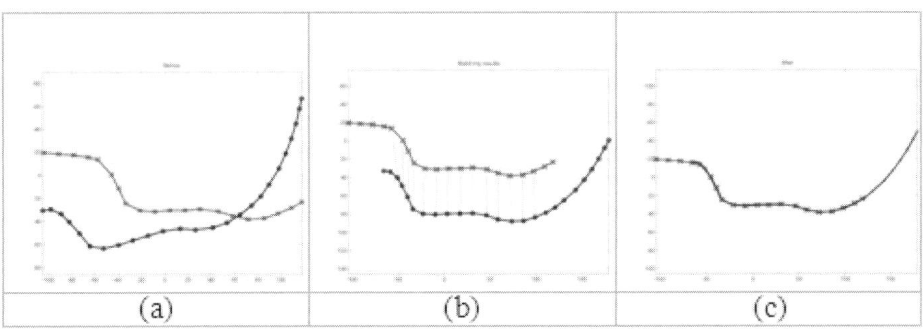

Figure 18-2. Spatial data integration using the Modified Smith-Waterman (MSW) algorithm. (a) A set of overlapping linear features; (b) Matching results of the MSW algorithm; (c) Data integration results

network of linear features (e.g. a road network) is treated as an undirected graph matching problem (Wilson and Hancock 1997; Luo and Hancock 2001; Gautama and Borghgraef 2005), in which the goal is to find an optimal mapping between the nodes of the two graphs (Fig. 18-3). This is achieved by the use of continuous relaxation labeling (Hummel and Zucker 1983). The main advantages of this approach is its invariance to translation, rotation and scale differences (through the use of appropriate attributes), as well as on its use of the network structure (topology) to greatly reduce search space. Furthermore, this approach requires no user-defined thresholds to establish local matches, thus allowing a higher level of automation in the data integration process.

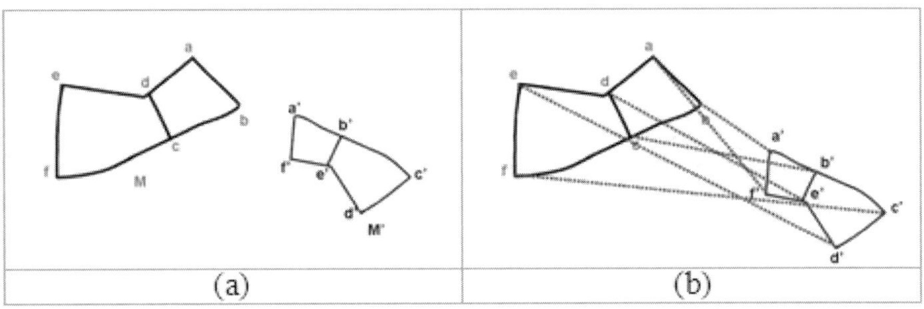

Figure 18-3. Spatial integration by relaxation labeling. (a) Two (corresponding) road networks from different data sets M and M'; (b) Matching results of road intersections by relaxation labeling

It should be noted that some of the difficulties in the data integration problem that are related to the extensive heterogeneity of the data sources could be resolved to some extent through the use of metadata standards such as FGDC-STD-001 (1998), ISO 15046-15, or CEN/TC 287, which can provide well structured data about the characteristics of the data (Jones and Taylor 2003). Metadata can be used during the integration process to allow a more efficient integration processes. One particular aspect of the spatial data integration problem in which the use of metadata has been recently suggested is data quality management: as users are often interested in the quality characteristics of the integrated data set metadata about the quality characteristics of each of the data sources can assist in evaluating the overall quality of the final (fused) data set. Yet, in many application areas the available metadata is not detailed enough, and its implications for a specific usage are unclear (for example, DTM based applications). Consequently, users may still face uncertainty regarding the applicability of the data, even where metadata are available (Croitoru and Doytsher 2002). Furthermore, maintaining and exchanging metadata among organizations is still an unmatched challenge (Jones and Taylor 2003). Nevertheless, as a recent surveys among National Mapping Agencies (NMAs) has shown (Dassonville et al. 2002), with the increased recognition in the importance of metadata along with the evolution of widely accepted metadata standards, the role of metadata in the data integration process is likely to further intensify.

3. SPATIOTEMPORAL INTEGRATION

Spatial data collection tends to be repetitive in nature: satellites for example revisit the same area and capture images of it at regular intervals, while national and regional mapping campaigns are typically repeated at fixed intervals (e.g. every few years). These two examples reflect past tendencies that are still prevalent in classic spatial data collections. This trend is further emphasized by the emergence of novel types of geospatial datasets, especially video, captured e.g. by surveillance cameras ontop of buildings or on-board low-flying sensors like unmanned aerial vehicles (UAVs).

Thus, spatiotemporal analysis is increasingly emerging as a dominant research area, and is expected to have substantial impact on the manner in which geospatial analysis is performed. It should be noted here that the time scale of such applications may vary substantially. Considering collections of multi-temporal imagery as an example, the time interval between successive frames may range from fractions of a second in the case of video, to minutes or even days, when dealing with imagery captured e.g. by a fixed sensor observing a scene, a mobile sensor roaming an area, or even by a satellite revisiting a specific site periodically. Thus, onc often uses the term motion imagery (MI) to refer to such diverse types of multi-temporal image datasets. By their nature, MI datasets capture continuous or near continuous change. However, MI data processing and analysis, and MI database management present well-known inherent challenges, mostly associated with the large storage requirements, and consequently the immense processing time required for their manipulation and analysis, as well as the highly diverse content they may contain.

The efficient modeling of spatiotemporal change as it is depicted in multi-temporal imagery is an important step towards the efficient analysis and management of large MI datasets. Furthermore, the development of concise representation schemes of MI content is essential for the search, retrieval, interchange, query, and visualization of the information included in MI datasets. Towards this goal it is necessary to provide a concise modeling of spatiotemporal change as it is captured in collections of MI data, along with the development of spatiotemporal similarity metrics to compare the evolution of different objects. Within this context *spatiotemporal change* is defined as the variations of the position and/or outline of a geospatial object. Thus ST change may range in temporal scale from slow as it is depicted in satellite imagery (e.g. variations in land use patterns), to rapid as it is captured by a video camera (e.g. the movement of a car). At the same time the corresponding spatial footprint may be highly localized (e.g. the variations of a lake's outline), or it may be constantly changing both location and shape (e.g. a fire front).

Modeling and summarizing spatiotemporal information has been addressed by the image analysis community within the context of video compression. Initial efforts for video summarization tended to focus on shot detection and the selection of few representative frames, thus ignoring semantic content (Rui et al. 1998), or proceeded further with an analysis of visual and speech properties to construct 'skim' video synopses by merging segments of the original video (Smith and Kanade 1995). Video summaries have also been proposed as composites of select key frames from each scene shot (Christel et al. 1998; Pope et al. 1998; Oh and Hua 2000).

In the database community, the well-known models of spatial relations between object MBRs (minimum bounding rectangles) (Papadias et al. 1995) have been extended with the addition of temporal relations to support the spatiotemporal modeling of moving objects contained in video sequences (Pissinou et al. 2001). (Wolfson et al. 1999; Pfoser and Theodoridis, 2000) present an indexing scheme for moving objects, extending established tree structures (see e.g. Sellis et al. 1987). In their work, moving objects are reduced to point data, similar to the approach followed by (Vazirgiannis and Wolfson 2001), while (Sistla et al. 1997; Wolfson et al. 1999) make use of a future temporal logic for spatiotemporal modeling. While these models address geometric trajectories, we also have models of semantic variations like the identity-based approach (Hornsby and Egenhofer 2000), addressing transitions in the state of a geospatial entity, like the initial introduction, or the disappearance of an object. (Vlachos et al. 2002) introduced trajectory similarity metrics through formalizations of the longest common sub-sequence (LCSS).

Spatiotemporal analysis of motion imagery datasets entails identifying an object in successive images and analyzing this information to model the trajectory of this object. Spatiotemporal trajectories can be best visualized by making use of the 3-dimensional (x,y,t) spatiotemporal domain of a scene, comprising two spatial dimensions representing the horizontal plane (x,y), and one temporal dimension (t). The complex trajectory of an object over time is described as the union of its locations over time. It can be visualized by piling the object's recorded positions on top of each other at the corresponding time instances (Figure 18-4). As an example, a circle that

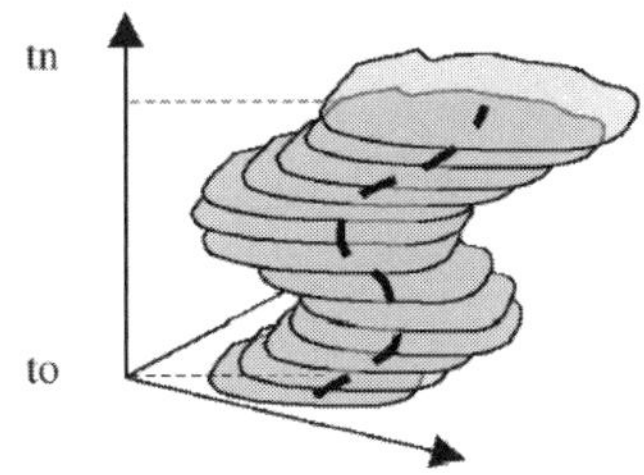

Figure 18-4. Tracing the trajectory of an object in the spatiotemporal domain

remains stable will describe a cylinder in the spatiotemporal domain, while a rectangle shrinking at a constant pace will produce a pyramidal trace.

As an object moves to describe a trace like the one visualized in Figure 18-4, two important types of geospatial information can be identified: movement and deformation. First, the object moves changing its location with respect to an external reference frame. This information is represented by a trajectory describing the movement of the object's center of mass. The second type of spatiotemporal change refers to the object's internal reference frame and describes the variations over time of the object's shape. This change is represented through a set of vectors that pinpoint the placement, direction, and magnitude of the object's change. Depending on the temporal resolution of the MI datasets, the object's spatiotemporal trace may in general have gaps, caused by missing frames in certain instances (it is assumed that an adequate temporal resolution to ensure that change occurs gradually between consecutive MI frames).

The spatiotemporal helix (STH) was introduced as a compact description of an object's spatiotemporal variations. (Agouris and Stefanidis 2003; Stefanidis et al. 2003). A spatiotemporal helix comprises a central spine and annotated prongs. More specifically:

- The central spine models the spatiotemporal trajectory described by the center of the object as it moves during a temporal interval.
- The protruding prongs express deformation (expansion or collapse) of the object's outline at a specific time instance.

Figure 18-5 (left) is a visualization of the concept of the spatiotemporal helix. The spine is the vertical line connecting a sequence of nodes (marked as white circles), and the prongs are shown as arrows protruding from the spine, pointing away from or towards it. The gray blob at the base of the spine is the initial outline of the monitored object. The helix describes object movement whereby the object's center follows the spine, and the outline is

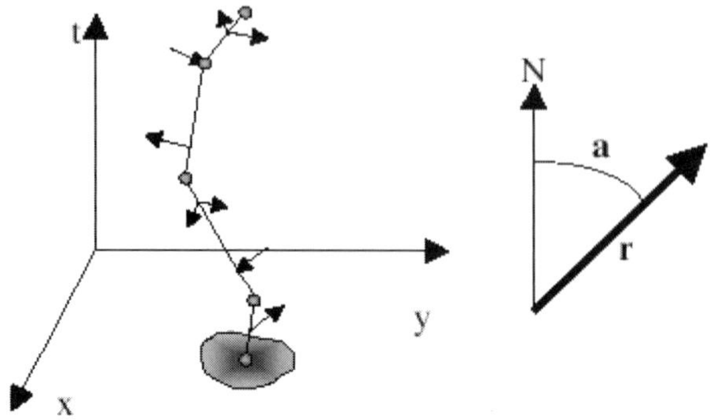

Figure 18-5. A spatiotemporal helix (left) and a detail showing the azimuth of a prong (right)

modified by the amounts indicated by the prongs at the corresponding temporal instances.

As a spatiotemporal trajectory, a spine is a sequence of (x,y,t) coordinates. It is expressed in a concise manner as a sequence of spatiotemporal nodes $S(n_1,\ldots n_n)$. These nodes correspond to breakpoints along this trajectory, namely points where the object accelerated/decelerated and/or changed its orientation. Accordingly, each node n_i is modeled as $n_i(x,y,t,q)$, where:

- (x,y,t) are the node spatiotemporal coordinates, and
- q is a qualifier classifying the node as an acceleration (q_a), deceleration (q_d), or rotation (q_r) node.

The qualifier information q is derived by the local values of spine gradients. High values of the vertical gradient indicate acceleration or deceleration, while high values of the horizontal gradient indicate rotation. While this information can be derived by the other three values it is considered semantically important for describing an object's behavior, and this is the reason we store it separately.

Each prong is a model of the local expansion or collapse of the outline at the specific temporal instance when this event is detected, and is a horizontal arrow pointing away from or towards the spine. It is modeled as $p_i(t,r,a_1,a_2)$ where:

- t is the corresponding temporal instance (intersection of the prong and the spine in Figure 18-5 left),
- r is the magnitude of this outline modification, expressed as a percentage of the distance between the center of the object and the outline, with positive numbers expressing expansion (corresponding arrows pointing away from the spine) and negative numbers indicating collapse (arrows pointing towards the spine),

- a_1, a_2 is the range of azimuths where this modification occurs; with each azimuth measured as a left-handle angle from the North (y) axis (Fig. 18-5 right).

While Fig. 18-5 is a schematic diagram of the helix, its database representation is a sequence of n node and m prong records:

$$Helix^{obj\_id}_{t1,t2} = (node_1,\ldots node_n;\ prong_1,..prong_m), \quad (1)$$

where node and prong records are as described above, obj_id is the corresponding object identifier, and t1, t2 are the start and end instances of the time interval to which the helix refers.

4. SPATIAL AND SPATIOTEMPORAL QUERIES

4.1 Spatial Queries

Metadata provide the easiest and simplest query capabilities for spatial datasets. Through them users can define the specific parameters of the dataset they seek, and the best matches are returned to them. Such approaches typically make use of some standard distance metrics to compare the parameters of a specific dataset to the query request, thus quantifying contextual similarity.

An interesting departure from this standard approach to spatial queries has been based on the use of metric descriptions of abstract relations to describe the content of spatial dataset. The importance of topology, orientation, and distance in assessing spatial similarity of scenes is well-documented (see Egenhofer and Franzosa 1991; Goyal and Egenhofer 2000; Shariff 1996). A combinatorial expression for all these properties has been introduced by (Blaser 2000) to function within a general query-by-sketch environment. This expression can be used to define a function S_{met} that assesses the similarity metric between a query configuration Q and an image I in the database. The function combines different similarity metrics for individual object shapes and relations between them like topolgy, orienttation, and distance. More specifically S_{met} is defined (Blaser 2000; Sefanidis et al. 2002) as:

$$S_{met}(Q,I) = S_{sh}(Q,I)\cdot w_{sh} + S_{top}(Q,I)\cdot w_{top} + S_{or}(Q,I)\cdot w_{or} + S_{dist}(Q,I)\cdot w_{dist}$$

The elements of this formula are as follows:

- S_{sh} is a function measuring the degree/percentage of shape similarity between the objects in *Q* and the corresponding objects in *I*. For example, assuming that $obj_1, \ldots, obj_n$ indicate the n objects in *Q*, then $S_{sh}(Q,I) = [\Sigma match\%(obj_i)]/n$, where $match\%(obj_i)$ is the matching percentage between object in *Q* and the corresponding object in *I*. We can further constrain this formula if we so wish by imposing acceptability constraints. For example we can require that for each i = 1,...,n $match\%(obj_i) > t$, with t a given threshold value. This would make us consider an object obj_i in *Q* as "found" in *I* if and only if the corresponding object in *I* matches to it more than a preset threshold (e.g. 50%).
- S_{top} is a function measuring the degree/percentage of similarity between the set of topological relations characterizing the set of objects in *Q* and the topological relations among the corresponding objects in *I*.
- S_{or} is a function measuring the degree/percentage of similarity between the set of orientation relations characterizing the set of objects in *Q* and the orientation relations among the corresponding objects in *I*.
- S_{dist} is a function measuring the degree/percentage of similarity between the set of distance relations characterizing the set of objects in *Q* and the distance relations among the corresponding objects in *I*.
- w_{sh}, w_{top}, w_{or}, w_{dist} are weight coefficients establishing the relative importance of their corresponding similarity metrics for the overall scene similarity assessment. By minimizing for example the first three coefficients, a search is carried out for configurations resembling the query sketch only in terms of distances between the objects, regardless of their shape, topology, and orientation.

All above similarity metrics are in the range [0,1] with higher values corresponding to higher similarity. By enforcing the following condition:

$$\sum_{j \in J} w_j = 1, \quad J = \{sh, top, or, dist\}$$

we can ensure that the overall scene similarity metric S_{met} will also have a value in the range [0,1].

4.2 Spatiotemporal Pattern Queries

Spatiotemporal patterns have a fundamental role in our perception and understanding of the world as they provide a systematic approach to the evolution of things in space and time. The identification and formalization of such patterns allows us to achieve what is often taken for granted: formalize rules, apply reasoning, and predict future behaviors of spatiotemporal phenomena. Consequently, spatiotemporal patterns have been extensively studied in numerous areas, such as geosciences (Mesrobian et al. 1994), geophysics (Stolorz et al. 1995), ecology (MacKinnon et al. 2001), wildlife (Hays et al. 2001), biogeography (Mielke 1989), and meteorology (Basak et al. 2004). In many of these research and application areas, there is a particular interest in the discovery of spatiotemporal patterns in the trajectories of moving objects. For instance, in wildlife and biogeography research the study of hunting, grazing, or migration patterns of animals has been has long been of interest in an attempt to gain a better understanding of their behavior, while in meteorology the detection of spatiotemporal patterns in the course of tropical storms has a crucial role in emergency response and early warning.

Recently, with the advances and increased availability of mobile computing and location determination technologies (such as GPS enabled devices, Radio Frequency Identification (RFID) devices, cellular, and WiFi (Hazas et al. 2004)), the need to discover and study spatiotemporal patterns in human motion data has also emerged in various applications, such as Locations Based Services (LBS), homeland security, surveillance, and E911 emergency response. The need to detect spatiotemporal patterns is likely to further intensify as mobility becomes an integral part of the modern lifestyle. Now, more than ever, people depend on synchronizing their activities with moving objects such as vehicles, trains, airplanes, and satellites. The planed route and schedule of a bus, the landing maneuver of an airplane, or the daily course of a communication satellite in space are all spatiotemporal patterns that have an essential role in the ability to plan and coordinate activities, and avoid conflicts or hazards.

The study of spatiotemporal patterns in moving objects databases is often based on two complementary techniques, namely data mining and the utilization of query languages. Data mining is commonly applied as a pre-processing step that targets the detection of higher level spatiotemporal objects or formations in a high dimensional database using statistical analysis. This results in well-structured high-level spatiotemporal data upon which spatiotemporal queries can be applied. In general, spatiotemporal queries can be divided into two primary categories (Figure 18-6), namely coordinate based queries and trajectory based queries (Pfoser et al. 2000; Pfoser, 2002; Chakka et al. 2003). Coordinate based queries are of the form $\{r\}\times\{s\}\rightarrow\{s'\}$: given a range $\{r\}$ and a set of trajectory segments $\{s\}$, these queries aim to retrieve all trajectory segments $\{s'\}$ that comply with the specific range. It should be noted that this category includes both time and space ranges, as well as time-slicing and nearest-neighbor queries.

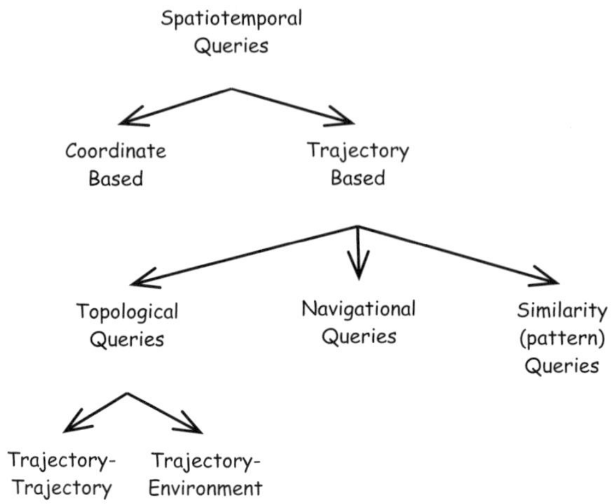

Figure 18-6. A typology of spatiotemporal queries

The second category of trajectory based queries addresses two subclasses of queries, namely topological queries and navigational queries. Topological queries can be further subdivided into two query types based on the entity to which the trajectory relates (Brakatsoulas et al. 2004; Wolfson 2002). The first type is comprised of trajectory-environment queries of the form $\{r\}\times\{s\}\rightarrow\{s'\}$, which address topological relations between a set of trajectories {s} and its environment as it is defined by the range {r} (for example, stay within, bypass, leave, enter, or cross). The second type is comprised of trajectory-trajectory queries of the form $\{s\}\times\{s'\}\rightarrow\{s''\}$, which address topological relations between two sets of trajectories {s} and {s'}, which may involve relationships (for example, intersect, meet, equal, near, or far). Finally, the navigational queries subclass addresses questions such as the traveled distance, the average or extreme speed, or the average or extreme heading.

While it is possible to formalize a range of spatiotemporal queries using these query types, they are mostly inadequate for querying patterns in spatiotemporal data, primarily due to lack of expressiveness, high complexity, and poor usability (Erwig and Schneider 2002). To overcome this a spatiotemporal pattern query framework based on spatiotemporal predicates have recently been suggested (Erwig and Schneider 1999; Erwig and Schneider 2002). A (binary) spatiotemporal predicate P maps a pair of spatiotemporal objects into a binary value, or more formally, P: $\alpha\times\beta\rightarrow$bool where α and β are two spatiotemporal objects (for example a point or a region). The key idea behind spatiotemporal predicates is that they allow aggregating the values of spatial predicates as they evolve through time, thus allowing the modeling of sequences of changes. Similarly, a framework for spatiotemporal pattern queries based on a sequence of distinct spatial predicates (such as range or nearest neighbor) with either an absolute or relative temporal ordering was recently suggested (Hadjieleftheriou et al. 2005).

A key characteristic of the spatiotemporal predicate based pattern detection framework is that it is geared towards describing patterns that are based on topological relations between moving object to regions or between moving objects to other moving objects. While this type of relations is indeed common in patterns it is often difficult to evaluate the similarity between the trajectories of moving objects. To illustrate this consider for example a "smart" video surveillance sensor network for tracking human movement. Such systems are often used for surveillance, control, and analysis (Moeslund and Granum 2001), and can be found in controlling access to restricted facilities, in parking lots, supermarkets and department stores, vending machines, ATMs, and traffic control (Gavrila 1999). One of the primary challenges that have been addressed in such systems is the detection of individuals based on body biometrics. Recently, it has been suggested that this can be accomplished by utilizing the human gait as a biometric feature (Dockstader et al. 2002), (Wang et al. 2004). In the context of human identification gait offers several advantages, among which the most distinctive is its uniqueness: each person seems to have unique gait features, much like a personal signature (Wang et al. 2004). Hence gait features (such as the trajectories of leg-joint angle) is a repeating spatiotemporal pattern that is not necessarily dependent on any topological or geometric relations to other objects (humans tend to have the same gait characteristics regardless of their spatial settings), and therefore can not be expressed using spatiotemporal predicates.

Similarly to the human gait example, other examples of spatiotemporal patterns that are not dependent on topological or geometric relations can be found in other application areas. To illustrate this consider the following scenario. An airport surveillance system captures and stores the movement of passengers as they move through the terminals. Following a terrorist attack it is required to detect passengers that exhibited "suspicious behavior", such as pacing back and forth several times. An example query may therefore be $\boldsymbol{Q_1}$: "Find all passengers that paced back and forth more than three contiguous times during the last 24 hours". Another typical example may be found in a weather analysis system. Consider a weather satellite constellation that tracks hurricanes over time. The system stores the trajectories of the hurricanes and is later used to analyze the weather patterns. During this analysis it is of interest to detect a specific type of motion, which may require a query such as $\boldsymbol{Q_2}$: "Find all hurricanes that moved like hurricane α".

Examples such as these illustrate that some spatiotemporal pattern mining queries cannot be easily formalized using spatiotemporal predicates. Instead, a more natural approach to the formalization of such pattern queries would be the evaluation of the (metric) similarity between two given trajectories. Consequently, the problem of discovering similar trajectories received increasing attention in recent years, and has motivated the development of various algorithms and tools. The focus in this area has been primarily on two complementary sub problems: the development of distance functions between trajectories, and the design of shape signatures for trajectory data.

The problem of developing shape signatures for trajectory data is related to the general problem of shape representation and description (Zhang and Lu 2004). Here, the goal is to develop a set of n shape signatures, each representing one or more dimensions of the data. Different signature schemes can provide different levels of invariance; therefore the choice of the shape signatures utilized determines the number of degrees of freedom (translation, rotation, and scale) that are accounted for between a pair of potentially matching trajectories. A geometric invariant shape signature can be derived using differential invariants, such as the curvature that requires a second derivative and the torsion that requires a third derivative (Lipschultz 1969). Yet, reliable finite difference estimation of these derivatives is difficult in many cases (especially the third derivative) due to their high sensitivity to noise (Kehtarnavaz and deFigueiredo 1988).

As an alternative, (Rodriguez et al. 2004) has suggested approximating the curvature by the angle between consecutive line segments, and the torsion by estimating the angle between the bi-normal vectors of two consecutive planes defined by line segments. Although these approximations provide a more stable estimation of the curvature and torsion, our experiments have shown that they are still largely unstable. This has also been recently reported in (Vlachos et al. 2004a) for 2D trajectories.

Due to the instability of differential invariants, Vlachos et al. (2004a) have recently suggested using the turning angle graph (Cohen and Guibas 1977) as an alternative shape signature. Here, the signature of a 2D trajectory is formed by estimating the angle between a movement vector (V_t) that is defined between two consecutive points (p_{i-1}, p_i) and a reference vector V_{ref} using a signed dot product. Since this signature is not rotation invariant, rotations between trajectories are resolved by an iterative modulo normalization that shifts a turning angle graph according to its mean value. Although this approach is reported to be highly robust, an extension to 3D is not detailed. Furthermore, in the case of a 3D trajectory, normalization of the turning angle graph can not be carried out directly by the iterative modulo normalization due to the different projections of the turning angle.

In order to overcome these difficulties, Croitoru et al. (2005) have recently suggested a non-iterative 3D trajectory matching framework that is translation, rotation, and scale invariant. Invariance is achieved in this framework through the introduction of a pose normalization process that is based on physical principles, which incorporates both spatial and temporal aspects of trajectory data (Figure 18-7). This framework also introduces a new shape signature that utilizes the invariance that is achieved through pose normalization. The reliance on global measures offers improved robustness compared to local measures in the presence of noise.

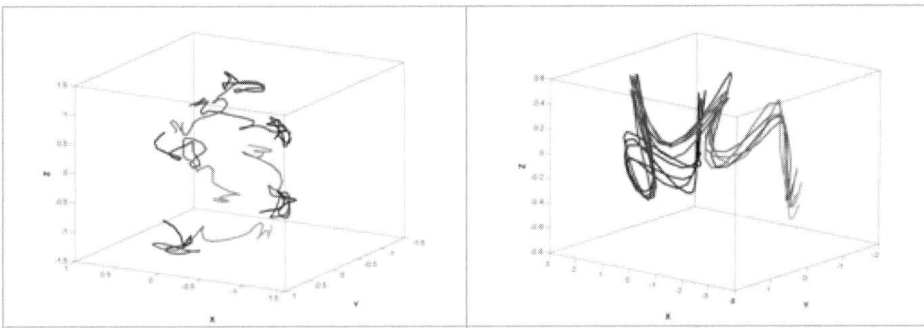

(a) (b)

Figure 18-7. Pose normalization of trajectory data. (a) A set of similar trajectories before pose normalization. (b) The same set of trajectories after pose normalization

In conjunction, Stefanidis et al. (2006) have recently suggested a framework for evaluating the similarity between spatiotemporal helixes, which are based on novel similarity metrics to compare helixes using their node and prong information. To better support the diverse needs of different operations a two-stage comparison process has been suggested: abstract and quantitative. Abstract comparisons aim to support fast queries, identifying as similar helixes that display the same coarse behavior, for example, accelerating or expanding at the same instance, regardless of the actual magnitude of these events. Quantitative comparison aims to support precise geospatial applications, and takes into account actual information on the magnitude of spatiotemporal change when comparing two events. In both cases the objective is to compare nodes and prongs from one helix to the other. Thus the comparison proceeds by selecting node/prong information from a reference helix and comparing it to the corresponding information in the matching candidate helix. For each node/prong under consideration in the reference helix a search is carried out for a matching node/prong in a corresponding time window in the candidate helix. This time window is the temporal tolerance in this framework.

5. CONCLUDING REMARKS

With the availability of a wide range of sensor types and platforms and with the increased accessibility of spatiotemporal data it has become evident in recent years that spatiotemporal data integration is a vital and highly beneficial tool for numerous government agencies in a wide spectrum of applications. Technologies such as high resolution satellites, LIDAR (Light Detection And Ranging), and distributed (wireless) sensor networks have further emphasized the importance of multi-sensor data integration, which is emerging as a powerful paradigm in spatiotemporal data analysis, and serves as a steppingstone for a variety of new applications.

As a result of the wide variety of sensor (and data) types a primary challenge in multi-sensor spatiotemporal data integration is the proper treatment of the resulting heterogeneity. The difficulty in integrating heterogeneous data sources is evident: different data sources do not share the same spatial or temporal resolution, nor do they share the same platform orientation. To address this problem it is necessary to develop novel paradigms that will address the data integration problem both in *space* (spatial conflation) and *time* (temporal conflation). Furthermore, as different sensors have different random and systematic noise characteristics emerging data integration paradigms must be able to take these different characteristics into consideration during the integration process. Last but not least, a higher level of automation in the data integration process is required in order to build the capacity to efficiently process high volumes of spatiotemporal data (including data streams). These are among the challenges we are already required to address today in spatiotemporal data analysis and knowledge discovery.

REFERENCES

Agouris P and Stefanidis A (2003) Efficient summarization of spatiotemporal events, Communications of the ACM, 46(1): 65-66.

Aichholzer O, Alt H, Roth G (1997) Matching shapes with a reference point. International Journal of Computational Geometry and Applications, 7(4): 349-363.

Alt H, Behreneds B, Blomer J (1991) Approximate matching of polygonal shapes. Proceedings 7th Annual Symposium on Computational Geometry, pp. 186-193.

Basak J, Sundarshan A, Trivedi D (2004) Weather data mining using independent component analysis. Journal of Machine Learning Research, 5: 239-253.

Blaser A (2000) Sketching spatial queries. Ph.D. Dissertation Thesis, University of Maine, Orono, Maine.

Brakatsoulas S, Pfoser D, Tryfona N (2004) Modeling, storing and mining moving object databases. Proceedings of Database Engineering and Applications Symposium, Coimbra, Portugal, pp. 68-77.

Christel MG, Smith MA, Taylor CR, Winkler DB (1998) Evolving video skims into useful multimedia abstractions. Proceedings of CHI: 171-178.

Cohen SD, Guibas LJ (1997) Partial matching of planar polylines under similarity transformations, Proceedings ACM-SIAM Symposium on Discrete Algorithms, New Orleans, pp. 777-786.

Croitoru A, Agouris P, Stefanidis A (2005) 3D trajectory matching by pose normalization. Proceedings 13th ACM International Workshop on Geographic Information Systems, Bremen, Germany, pp. 153-162.

Croitoru A, Doytsher Y (2002) A step toward accuracy-based vector-data prioritizing. Proceedings FIG XXII International Congress, Washington DC.

Dassonville L, Vauglin F, Jakobsson A, Luzet C (2002) Quality management, data quality and users, metadata for geographical information. Spatial Data Quality, (W. Shi, P. F. Fisher, and M. F. Goodchild, eds), Taylor and Francis, New York, pp. 202-215.

Dockstader S, Bergkessel K, Tekalp M (2002) Feature extraction for the analysis of gait and human motion. Proceedings 16th International Conference on Pattern Recognition, Quebec City, Quebec, 1: 5-8.

Doytsher Y, Filin S, Ezra E (2001) Transformation of datasets in a linear-based map conflation framework. Surveying and Land Information Systems 61(3): 159-169

Egenhofer M, Franzosa R (1991) Point-set topological spatial relations. International Journal of Geographical Information Systems, 5(2): 161-174.

Erwig M, Schneider M (1999) Developments in spatio-temporal query languages. Proceedings IEEE Int. Workshop on Spatio-Temporal Data Models and Languages, pp. 441-449.

Erwig M, Schneider M (2002) Spatio-temporal queries. IEEE Transactions on Knowledge and Data Engineering, 14(4): 881-901.

Fekete G, Eklundh JO, Rosenfeld A (1981). Relaxation: evaluation and applications. IEEE Transactions on Pattern Analysis and Machine Intelligence (PAMI), 3(4): 459-469.

Filin S, Doytsher Y (1999) Linear approach to map conflation: Matching of polylines. Surveying and Land Information Systems 59(2): 107-114

Gabay Y, Doytsher Y (1994) Automatic adjustment of line maps. Proceedings of LIS/GIS `94 Annual Convention, Phoenix, Arizona, pp. 333-341.

Gautama S, Borgharaef A (2005) Detecting change in road networks using continuous relaxation labeling. ISPRS Workshop 2005, Hannover, Germany.

Gavrila D (1999) The visual analysis of human movement: a survey. Computer Vision and Image Understanding, 73(1): 82-98.

Goyal R, Egenhofer M (2007) Cardinal directions between extended spatial objects. IEEE Transactions on Knowledge and Data Engineering (in press).

Gusfield D (1997) Algorithms on strings trees and sequences. Cambridge University Press. 534 pages.

Hadjieleftheriou M, Kollios G, Bakalov P, Tsotras V (2005) Complex spatio-temporal pattern queries. Proceedings 31st Very Large Data Base (VLDB) Conference, Trondheim, pp. 877-888.

Hays G, Dray M, Quaife T, Smyth T, Mironnet N, Luschi P, Papi F, Barnsley M (2001) Movements of migrating green turtles in relation to AVHRR derived sea surface temperature. International Journal of Remote Sensing, 22(8): 1403-1411.

Hazas M, Scott J, Krumm J (2004) Location aware computing comes of age. IEEE Computer Magazine, 37(2): 95-97.

Hornsby K, Egenhofer M (2000) Identity-based change: A foundation for spatio-temporal knowledge representation, Int. Journal of Geographical Information Science 14 (3): 207-224.

Hummel RA, Zucker SW (1983) On the foundations of relaxation labeling processes. IEEE Transactions on Pattern Analysis and Machine Intelligence (PAMI), 5(3): 267-287.

Jensen J, Saalfeld A, Broome F, Cowen D, Price K, Ramsey D, Lapine L (1998) Spatial data acquisition and integration. UCGIS white paper. http://www.ucgis.org/priorities/research/research_white/1998%20Papers /data.html

Jones M, Taylor G (2003) Metadata: spatial data handling and integration issues. School of Computing, Technical Report CS-03-1, University of Glamorgan, Wales, UK.

Kehtarnavaz N, deFigueiredo JP (1988) A 3-d contour segmentation scheme based on curvature and torsion. IEEE Transactions on Pattern Analysis & Machine Intelligence, (PAMI) 10(5): 707–713.

Lemarie C, Raynal L (1996) Geographic data matching: first investigation of a generic tool. Proceedings of LIS/GIS '96 Annual Convention, Denver, pp. 405-420.

Lipschultz M (1969) Differential Geometry. McGraw-Hill, New York.

Luo B, Hancock ER (2001) Structural graph matching using the EM algorithm and singular value decomposition. IEEE Transactions on Pattern Analysis and Machine Intelligence (PAMI), 23(10): 1120-1136.

MacKinnon J, Petty S, Elston D, Thomas C, Sherratt T, Lambin X (2001) Scale invariant spatio-temporal patterns of field vole density. Journal of Animal Ecology, 70(1): 101–111.

Mesrobian E, Muntz R, Renato J, Mechoso C, Farrara J, Stolorz P (1994) Extracting spatio-temporal patterns from geoscience datasets. Proceedings IEEE Workshop on Visualization and Machine Vision, Seattle, WA. pp. 92-103.

Mielke H (1989) Patterns of life. Unwin Hyman Press. 370 pages.

Moeslund T, Granum E (2001) A survey of computer vision-based human motion capture. Computer Vision and Image Understanding, 81(3): 231-268.

Oh J, Hua KA (2000) An Efficient Technique for Summarizing Videos using Visual Contents. Proceedings IEEE Int. Conference on Multimedia, New York, pp. 1167-1170.

O'Sullivan D, Unwin D (2003) Geographic information analysis. John Wiley and Sons, New York. 436 pages.

Papadias D, Theodoridis Y, Sellis T, Egenhofer M (1995) Topological relations in the world of minimum bounding rectangles: A study with R-trees. SIGMOD '95 (Carey and Schneider eds.), SIGMOD Record 24 (2): 92-103.

Pfoser D, Theodoridis Y (2000) Generating semantics-based trajectories of moving objects, Int. Workshop on Emerging Technology for GeoBased Applications, Ascona.

Pfoser D, Jensen CS, Theodoridis Y (2000) Novel approach to the indexing of moving object trajectories. Proceedings 26th International Conference on Very Large Databases (VLDB), Cairo, pp. 395-406.

Pfoser D (2002) Indexing the trajectories of moving objects. Data Engineering Bulletin, 25(2): 4-10.

Pissinou N, Radev I, Makki K (2001) Spatio-temporal composition of video objects: representation and querying in video database systems, IEEE Trans. on Knowledge and Data Engineering, 13(6): 1033-1040.

Pope A, Kumar R, Sawhney H, Wan C (1998) Video abstraction: summarizing video content for retrieval and visualization. Proc. 32nd Asilomar Conference of Signals, Systems & Computers, pp. 915-919.

Rodriguez W, Last M, Kandel A, Bunke H (2004) 3-dimensional curve similarity using string matching. Robotics and Autonomous Systems, 49(2004):165-172.

Rui Y, Huang TS, Mehrotra S (1998) Exploring video structure beyond the shots. Proceedings IEEE Intl. Conf. on Multimedia Computing and Systems, Austin: 237-240.

Saalfeld A (1988) Conflation: automated map compilation. International Journal of Geographic Information Systems 2(3): 217-228.

Saalfeld A (1993) Conflation: automated map compilation. Computer Vision Laboratory, Center for Automation Research, University of Maryland, Report CS-TR-3066, 80 pages.

Sellis T, Roussopoulos N, Faloutsos C (1987) The R^+ tree: A dynamic index for multi-dimensional objects. Proceedings VLDB '87, Brighton: 507-518.

Shariff AR (1996) Natural Language Spatial Relations: Metric Refinement of Topological Properties, Ph.D. Dissertation, University of Maine, Orono, USA.

Smith M, Kanade T (1995) Video skimming for quick browsing based on audio and image characterization, Tech. Report CMU-CS-95-186, Carnegie Mellon University.

Stefanidis A, Eickhorst K, Agouris P, Partsinevelos P (2003) Modeling and comparing change using spatiotemporal helixes, ACM-GIS'03 (E. Hoel and P. Rigaux eds.), ACM Press, New Orleans, pp. 86-93

Stefanidis A, Agouris P, Bertolotto M, Carswell J, Georgiadis C (2002) Scale and orientation-invariant scene similarity metrics for image queries, International Journal of Geographical Information Science, Vol. 16(8): 749-772

Stefanidis A, Agouris P, Eickhorst K, Croitoru A (2007) Modeling object movements and changes with spatiotemporal helixes. Submitted to the International Journal of Geographical Information Science (IJGIS).

Stolorz PE, Nakamura H, Mesrobian E, Muntz RR, Shek EC, Santos JR, Yi J, Ng, K, Chien SY, Mechoso CR, Farrara JD (1995) Fast spatiotemporal data mining of large geophysical datasets. Proceedings First International Conference on Knowledge Discovery and Data Mining, Montreal, pp. 300-305.

Vazirgiannis M, Wolfson O (2001) A Spatiotemporal Query Language for Moving Point Objects, SSTD'01, Los Angeles, pp. 20-35.

Vlachos M, Hadjieleftheriou M, Gunopulos D, Keogh E (2003) Indexing multi-dimensional time-series with support for multiple distance measures. Proceedings 9th ACM SIGKDD Int. Conference on Knowledge Discovery and Data Mining, San Diego, pp. 216-225.

Vlachos M, Kollios G, Gunopoulos D (2002) Discovering similar multidimensional trajectories. Proceedings 18th Int. Conference on Data Engineering (ICDE'02), San Jose, CA.

Vlachos M, Gunopulos D, Kollios G (2002) Robust similarity measures for mobile object trajectories, 5th DEXA Workshop on Mobility in Databases and Distributed Systems, Aix-en-Provence, France.

Vlachos M, Gunopulos D, Das G (2004) Rotation invariant distance measures for trajectories. Proceedings 10th Int. Conference on Knowledge Discovery & Data Mining (SIGKDD), Seattle, WA.

Wang C, Croitoru A, Stefanidis A, Agouris P (2006b) Image-to-x registration using linear features and networks. Proceedings ISPRS Commission VIII Symposium, Haifa, Israel.

Wang C, Stefanidis A, Croitoru A, Agouris P (2006a) Map registration of image sequences using linear features. Photogrammetric Engineering and Remote Sensing. (in press).

Wang L, Ning H, Tan T, Hu W (2004) Fusion of static and dynamic body biometrics for gait recognition. IEEE Trans. on Circuits and Systems for Video Technology, 14(2): 149–158.

Ware JM, Jones CB (1998) Matching and aligning features in overlaid coverages. Proceedings ACM-GIS '98, pp. 28-32.

Wilson RC, Hancock ER (1997) Structural matching by discrete relaxation. IEEE Transactions on Pattern Analysis and Machine Intelligence (PAMI), 19(6): 634-648.

Wolfson O (2002) Moving object information management: the database challenge. Proceedings 5th Workshop on Next Generation Information Technologies and Systems (WOL02), Lecture Notes in Computer Science Volume 2382, Caesarea, Israel, pp. 75–89.

Zhang D, Lu G (2004) Review of shape representation and description techniques. Pattern Recognition, 37(2004): 1-19.

SUGGESTED READINGS

Due to the increased importance of spatiotemporal data modeling, integration, and analysis there has been an unprecedented number of scientific and other publications in recent years. Readers who may wish to gain some more in-depth insight into spatiotemporal data modeling, integration, and analysis may find the following list of additional sources useful. These resources may also provide readers with additional references to more specific interest areas within this topic area.

- Peuquet DJ (2001) Making space for time: Issues in space-time data representation. Geoinformatica 5(1): 11-32.
- Peuquet DJ (2002) Representations of Space and Time, Guilford Press, New York. 380 pages.
- O'Sullivan D and Unwin DJ (2002) Geographic Information Analysis. Wiley & Sons, New York. 436 pages.
- Saalfeld AJ (1993) Conflation: Automated Map Compilation. PhD Dissertation, University of Maryland, College Park, Publication Number AAT 9327487. 149 pages.
- Galton A (2000) Qualitative Spatial Change. Oxford University Press, Oxford. 424 pages.
- Kang H (2004) Geometrically and Topographically Consistent Map Conflation for Federal and Local Governments. Journal of the Korean Geographical Society, 39(5): 804-818.

ONLINE RESOURCES

Additional online suggested reading:

- Saalfeld AJ (1993) Conflation: Automated map compilation. Bureau of the Census, Statistical Research Division Report Series, Report Number Census/SRD/RR-87/24. 12 pages: http://www.census.gov/srd/papers/pdf/rr87-24.pdf
- Doytsher Y, Filin S, Ezra E (2001) Transformation of Datasets in Linear-based Map Conflation Framework. *Surveying and Land Information Systems,* Vol. 61(3): 159-169: http://cms1.tudelft.nl/live/binaries/7b70630e-4204-4f71-a29b-e3e75d3b11f6/doc/filin_map_conf_transformation.pdf
- Spatiotemporal data servers and datasets:
    - The NOAA Satellite and Information Service: http://www.ssd.noaa.gov/PS/TROP/trop-atl.html

- The UNISYS Weather server:
- http://weather.unisys.com/hurricane/

- Hettich S and Bay SD (1999) The UCI KDD Archive. Irvine, CA: University of California, Department of Information and Computer Science: http://kdd.ics.uci.edu

TOPICS FOR ADDITIONAL DISCUSSION

In addition to the topics outlined in section 5, there are numerous other topics and issues in data integration that should be further discussed and explored. Among these issues various aspects of the data integration problem, such as the ones listed below, should be considered.

- Within the data integration process it is necessary to determine at which levels should the integration be done: while the integration can be done once all the data is obtained, a different approach would be to integrate data as it is made available. Such an on-the-fly approach may lead to a faster and more efficient process, but may also lead to potential integration errors. A deeper understanding of the advantages and disadvantages of each approach as well as their applicability for different scenarios and agencies is therefore required.
- While today the role of metadata is rather limited in the integration process, it is clear that that metadata has a central role in the integration process as it may lead to a faster and more efficient integration process. The collection and management of metadata is largely influenced by the standards and the policies of the different agencies involved in the data collection process. It is therefore necessary to evaluate the applicability and adequacy of current metadata standards, as well as the metadata collection and management process and their impact on the spatial and temporal integration process.
- Data streams, such as video, are emerging in recent years as a powerful and rich data source that can provide in-situ real-time data. While an increasing number of such data streams is being collected the spatial and temporal integration issues of such data are still not fully understood.
- Spatial and temporal integration can be done at different levels. While the previous sections of this chapter have addressed primarily metric aspects of data integration more qualitative aspects, such as topology and shape should be further explored, including a review of

the role of such aspects in the data integration process. Furthermore, other non-metric aspects, such as ontology integration, have should be further developed.

- The data integration process fuses various types of data which may vary considerably in their resolution and quality. Consequently, it is necessary in many cases to evaluate the quality (for example, positional accuracy) of the final integrated data. Although several quality management and error propagation models and schemes have been introduced in recent years, the complexity of the integration operation often necessitates a different approach to data quality management and uncertainty propagation in spatiotemporal data.
- Data collection processes over time may be often interrupted by technical as well as environmental factors. As a result, only partial spatiotemporal data may be available. In contrast, currently employed data integration methods are often based on the implicit assumption that the data sources are complete. It is therefore necessary to develop data integration methodologies and policies for incomplete spatiotemporal data.

Chapter 19

GEOINFORMATICS OF HOTSPOT DETECTION AND PRIORITIZATION FOR DIGITAL GOVERNANCE

G.P. Patil[1], Raj Acharya[2], Amy Glasmeier[3], Wayne Myers[4], Shashi Phoha[5], and Stephen Rathbun[6]

[1]Center for Statistical Ecology and Environmental Statistics, Department of Statistics (gpp@stat.psu.edu); [2]Department of Computer Science and Engineering (acharya@cse.psu.edu); [3]Department of Geography (akg1@psu.edu); [4]School of Forest Resources and Office of Remote Sensing of Earth Resources; Penn State Institutes of Environment (wlm@psu.edu); The Pennsylvania State University, University Park, Pennsylvania, U.S.A.; [5]Division of Information Science and Technology, Applied Research Laboratory, The Pennsylvania State University, University Park, Penn., USA and Information Technology Laboratory, National Institute of Standards and Technology, Gaithersburg, Maryland, U.S.A. (sphoha@nist.gov); [6]Department of Health Administration Biostatistics, and Epidemiology, University of Georgia, Athens, Georgia, U.S.A. (rathbun@uga.edu)

CHAPTER OVERVIEW

A declared purpose of digital governance is to empower public for information access and analysis to enable transparency, accuracy, and efficiency for societal good at large. Hotspot detection and prioritization become natural undertakings as a result of the information access. Hotspot means spot that is hot, that can be of special interest or concern. Hotspot means something unusual—an anomaly, aberration, outbreak, elevated cluster, critical area, etc. The immediate need can be for monitoring, etiology, management, early warning and prioritization. Responsible factors can be natural, accidental, or intentional. Geoinformatic surveillance for spatial and temporal hotspot detection and prioritization is crucial in the 21st century. And so also the need for geoinformatic surveillance decision support system equipped with the next generation of geographic hotspot detection, prioritization, and early warning within emerging hotspots. This chapter describes ongoing cross-disciplinary research and some of the interesting results for geospatial and spatiotemporal hotspot detection and prioritization, driven by a diverse variety of case studies and issues of interest to government agencies, academia, and the private sector.

1. INTRODUCTION

A declared purpose of digital governance is to empower public for information access and analysis to enable transparency, accuracy, and efficiency for societal good at large. Hotspot detection and prioritization become natural undertakings as a result of the information access. Hotspot means spot that is hot, that can be of special interest or concern. Hotspot means something unusual—an anomaly, aberration, outbreak, elevated cluster, critical area, etc. The immediate need can be for monitoring, etiology, management, early warning and prioritization. Responsible factors can be natural, accidental, or intentional. Geoinformatic surveillance for spatial and temporal hotspot detection and prioritization is crucial in the 21st century. And so also the need for geoinformatic surveillance decision support system equipped with the next generation of geographic hotspot detection, prioritization, and early warning within emerging hotspots.

This chapter describes ongoing cross-disciplinary research and some of the interesting results for geospatial and spatiotemporal hotspot detection and prioritization, driven by a diverse variety of case studies and issues of interest to government agencies, academia, and the private sector. The chapter is based on cutting edge statistical research, using a variety of data products and sources across geographic regions and across networks. It deals with national and international applications of societal importance, such as public health, ecohealth, biodiversity, invasive species, watershed management, persistent poverty, sensor networks, homeland security, among others. It has potential to lead to a sophisticated next generation analytical and computational decision support system beyond the present day health area based circular spatial scan system. Our innovation employs the notion of upper level set, and is accordingly called the upper level set scan system. See Patil and Taillie, 2004a and Patil et al., 2006a.

Our prioritization innovation provides capability for prioritization and ranking of detected hotspots and objects based on multiple criteria indicators without integration of indicators into an index. It employs Hasse diagrams for visualization, and partially ordered sets and Markov Chain Monte Carlo methods for analysis. Resulting prioritizations and rankings reflect the contrasting requirements of each application and also of varying stake-holders, while employing a common framework for hotspot detection and prioritization. It is accordingly called the poset prioritization and ranking system. See Patil and Taillie, 2004b and Patil et al., 2006b.

2. LITERATURE REVIEW: FUNDAMENTAL METHODOLOGIES AND COMPUTATIONAL TECHNIQUES

We first present the scan statistic methodology and then the prioritization methodology.

2.1 Scan Statistic Methodology

Although a wide variety of methods have been proposed for modeling and analyzing spatial data, the spatial scan statistic (Kulldorff and Nagarwalla 1995; Kulldorff 1997) has become a popular method for detection and evaluation of disease clusters. In space-time, the scan statistic can provide early warning of disease outbreaks and can monitor their spatial spread. With innovative modifications, scan statistic methods can be used for hotspot analysis in any field.

Spatial Scan Statistic Background. A region R of Euclidian space is tessellated or subdivided into cells that will be labeled by the symbol a. Data is available in the form of a count Y_a (non-negative integer) on each cell a. In addition, a "size" value A_a is associated with each cell a. The cell sizes A_a are regarded as known and fixed, while the cell counts Y_a are random variables. In the disease setting, the response Y_a is the number of diseased individuals within the cell and the size A_a is the total number of individuals in the cell. The disease rate within the cell is the ratio Y_a / A_a. The spatial scan statistic seeks to identify "hotspots" or clusters of cells that have an elevated rate compared with the rest of the region, and to evaluate the statistical significance (*p*-value) of each identified hotspot. These goals are accomplished by setting up a formal hypothesis-testing model for a hotspot. The null hypothesis asserts that there is no hotspot, i.e., that all cells have (statistically) the same rate. The alternative states that there is a cluster Z such that the rate for cells in Z is higher than for cells outside Z. An essential point is that the cluster Z is an unknown parameter that has to be estimated. Likelihood methods are employed for both the estimation and significance testing. Candidate clusters for Z are referred to as zones. Ideally, maximization of the likelihood should search across all possible zones, but their number is generally too large for practical implementation. Various devices (e.g., expanding circles) are employed to reduce the list of candidate zones to manageable proportions. Significance testing for the spatial scan statistic employs the likelihood ratio test. Monte Carlo simulation is used to determine the needed null distributions.

Explication of a likelihood function requires a distributional model (response distribution) for the response Y_a in cell a. This distribution can vary from cell to cell but in a manner that is regulated by the size variable A_a. Thus, A_a enters into the parametric structure of the response distribution. In disease surveillance, response distributions are generally taken as either binomial or Poisson, leading to comparatively simple likelihood functions. The scan statistic that we propose allows continuous response distributions and complex likelihood functions.

2.1.1 Limitations of current scan statistic methodology

Available scan statistic software suffers from several limitations. First, circles have been used for the scanning window, resulting in low power for detection of irregularly shaped clusters (Figure 19-1). Second, the response variable has been defined on the cells of a tessellated geographic region, preventing application to responses defined on a network (stream network, water distribution system, highway system, etc.). Third, response distributions have been taken as discrete (specifically, binomial or Poisson). Finally, the traditional scan statistic returns only a point estimate for the hotspot but does not attempt to assess estimation uncertainty. We address these limitations.

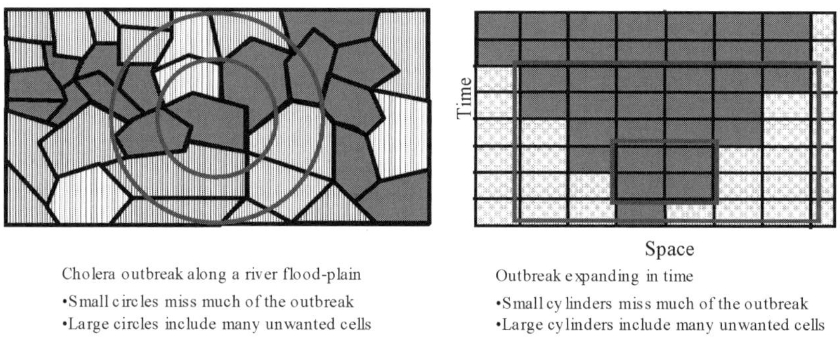

Figure 19-1. Scan statistic zonation for circles (left) and space-time cylinders (right).

2.1.2 Our approach

In our approach to the scan statistic, the geometric structure that carries the numerical information is an abstract graph consisting of (i) a finite collection of vertices and (ii) a finite set of edges that join certain pairs of distinct vertices. A tessellation determines such a graph: vertices are the cells of the tessellation and a pair of vertices is joined by an edge whenever the corresponding cells are adjacent. A network determines such a graph directly. Each vertex in the graph carries three items of information: (i) a size variable that is treated as known and non-random, (ii) a response variable whose value is regarded as a realization of some probability distribution, and (iii) the probability distribution itself, which is called the response distribution. Parameters of the response distribution may vary from vertex to vertex, but the mean response (i.e., expected value of the response distribution) should be proportional to the value of the size variable for that vertex. The response rate is the ratio Response/Size and a hotspot is a collection of vertices for which the overall response rate is unusually large.

2.1.3 ULS scan statistic

We have a new version of the spatial scan statistic designed for detection of hotspots of arbitrary shapes and for data defined either on a tessellation or a network. Our version looks for hotspots from among all connected components of upper level sets of the response rate and is therefore called the upper level set (ULS) scan statistic. The method is adaptive with respect to hotspot shape since candidate hotspots have their shapes determined by the data rather than by some *a priori* prescription like circles or ellipses. This data dependence is taken into account in the Monte Carlo simulations used to determine null distributions for hypothesis testing. We also compare performance of the ULS scanning tool with that of the traditional spatial scan statistic. The key element here is enumeration of a searchable list of candidate zones *Z*. A zone is, first of all, a collection of vertices from the abstract graph. Secondly, those vertices should be connected (Figure 19-2) because a geographically scattered collection of vertices would not be a reasonable candidate for a "hotspot." Even with this connectedness limitation, the number of candidate zones is too large for a maximum likelihood search in all but the smallest of graphs. We reduce the list of zones to searchable size in the following way. The response rate at vertex *a* is $G_a = Y_a / A_a$. These rates determine a function $a \to G_a$ defined over the vertices in the graph. This function has only finitely many values (called levels) and each level *g* determines an upper level set U_g defined by $U_g = \{a : G_a \geq g\}$. Upper level sets do not have to be connected but each upper level set can be decomposed into the disjoint union of connected components. The list of candidate zones *Z* for the ULS scan statistic consists of all connected components of all upper level sets. This list of candidate zones is denoted by Ω_{ULS}. The zones in Ω_{ULS} are certainly plausible as potential hotspots since they are portions of upper level sets. Their number is small enough for practical maximum likelihood search—in fact, the size of Ω_{ULS} does not exceed the number of vertices in the abstract graph (e.g., the number of cells in the tessellation). Finally, Ω_{ULS} becomes a tree under set inclusion, thus facilitating computer representation. This tree is called the ULS-tree (Figure 19-3); its nodes are the zones $Z \in \Omega_{\text{ULS}}$ and are therefore collections of vertices from the abstract graph. Leaf nodes are (typically) singleton vertices at which the response rate is a local maximum; the root node consists of all vertices in the abstract graph.

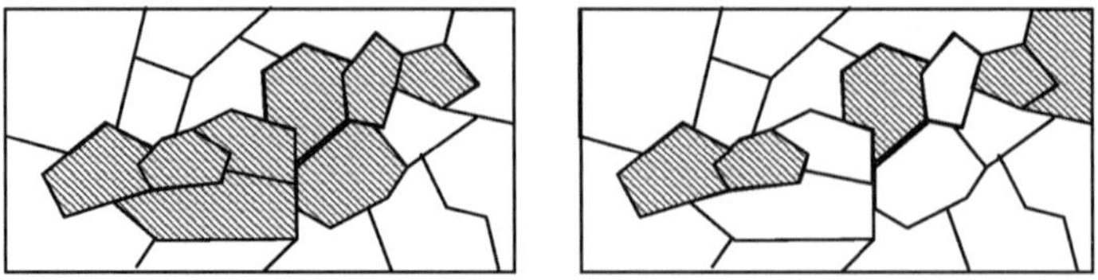

Figure 19-2. Connectivity for tessellated regions. The collection of shaded cells on the left is connected and, therefore, constitutes a zone. The collection on the right is not connected.

Finding the connected components for an upper level set is essentially the issue of determining the transitive closure of the adjacency relation defined by the edges of the graph. Several generic algorithms are available in the computer science.

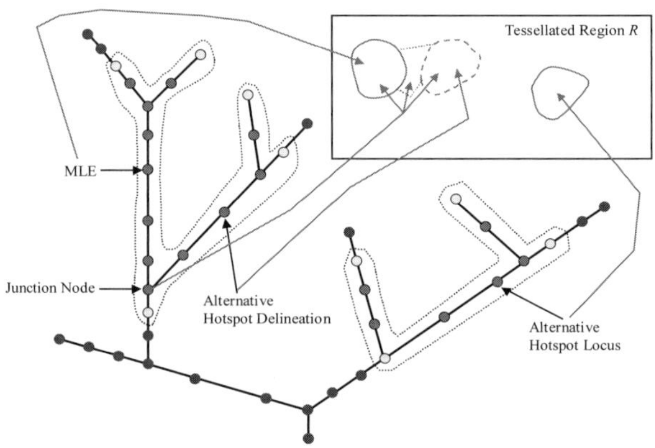

Figure 19-3. A confidence set of hotspots on the ULS tree. The different connected components correspond to different hotspot loci while the nodes within a connected component correspond to different delineations of that hotspot.

2.1.4 Hotspot confidence sets

The hotspot MLE is just that—an estimate. Removing some cells from the MLE and replacing them with certain other cells can generate an estimate that is almost as plausible in the likelihood sense. We will express this uncertainty in hotspot delineation by a confidence set of hotspot zones—a subset of the ULS tree (Figure 19-3). We will determine the confidence set by employing the standard duality between confidence sets and hypothesis testing in conjunction with the likelihood ratio test. The confidence set also lets us assign a numerical hotspot-membership rating to each cell (e.g., county, zip code, census tract).

The rating is the percentage of zones (in the confidence set) that include the cell under consideration (Figure 19-4). A map of these ratings, with superimposed MLE, provides a visual display of uncertainty in hotspot delineation.

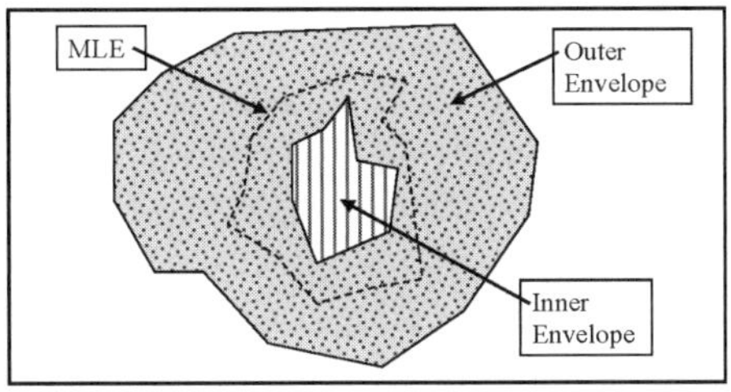

Figure 19-4. Hotspot-membership rating. Cells in the inner envelope belong to all plausible estimates (at specified confidence level); cells in the outer envelope belong to at least one plausible estimate. The MLE is nested between the two envelopes.

2.1.5 Typology of space-time hotspots

Scan statistic methods extend readily to the detection of hotspots in space-time. The space-time version of the circle-based scan employs cylindrical extensions of spatial circles and cannot detect the temporal evolution of a hotspot (Figure 19-1). The space-time generalization of the ULS scan detects arbitrarily shaped hotspots in space-time. This lets us classify space-time hotspots into various evolutionary types—a few of which appear on the left hand side of Figure 19-5. The merging hotspot is particularly interesting because, while it comprises a connected zone in space-time, several of its time slices are spatially disconnected.

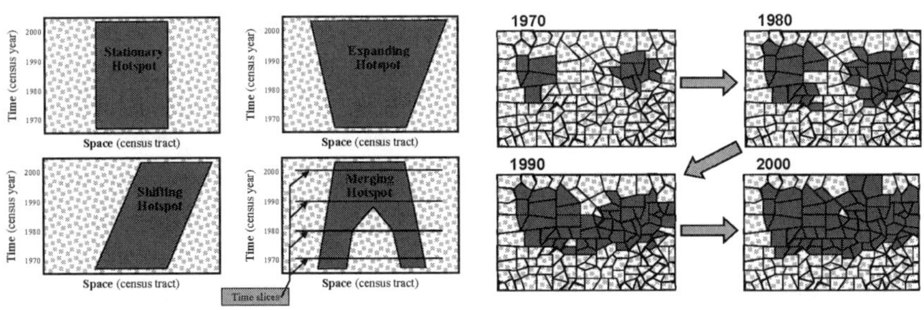

Figure 19-5. The four diagrams on the left depict different types of space-time hotspots. The spatial dimension is shown schematically on the horizontal and time is on the vertical. The diagrams on the right show the trajectory (sequence of time slices) of a merging hotspot.

2.2 Prioritization Methodology

We address the question of ranking a collection of objects, such as initial hotspots, when a suite of indicator values is available for each member of the collection. The objects can be represented as a cloud of points in indicator space, but the different indicators typically convey different comparative messages and there is no unique way to rank the objects. A conventional solution assigns a composite numerical score to each object by combining the indicator information in some fashion. Every such composite involves judgments (often arbitrary or controversial) about tradeoffs among indicators. We take the view that the relative positions in indicator space determine only a partial ordering (Neggers and Kim 1998) and that a given pair of objects may not be inherently comparable. Working with Hasse diagrams (Neggers and Kim 1998) of the partial order, we study the collection of all rankings that are compatible with the partial order.

2.2.1 Multiple indicators and partially ordered sets (Posets)

The scan statistic ranks hotspots based on their statistical significance (likelihood values). But, other factors need to be considered in prioritizing hotspots, such as mean response, peak response, geographical extent, population size, economic value, etc. We therefore envision a suite of indicator values attached to each hotspot with large indicator values signifying greater hotspot importance. Different indicators reflect different criteria and may rank the hotspots differently. In mathematical terms, the suite of indicators determines a partial order on the set of hotspots. Thus, if *a* and *b* are hotspots, we say that *b* is inherently more important than *a* and we write $a \prec b$ if $I(a) \le I(b)$ for *all* of the indicators *I*. If distinct hotspots are distinct in indicator space, the $\prec$ relation has the three defining properties of a partial order: (i) transitive: $a \prec b$ and $b \prec c$ implies $a \prec c$; (ii) anti-symmetric: $a \prec b$ and $b \prec a$ implies $a = b$; and (iii) reflexive: $a \prec a$. Certain pairs *a*, *b* of hotspots may not be comparable under this importance ordering since, for example, there may be indicators such that $I_1(a) < I_1(b)$ but $I_2(a) > I_2(b)$. In this case, hotspot *b* would be located in the fourth quadrant of Figure 19-6. Because of these inherent incomparabilities, there are many different ways of ranking the hotspots while remaining consistent with the importance ordering. A given hotspot *a* can therefore be assigned different ranks depending upon who does the ranking. It turns out that these different ranks comprise an interval (of integers) called the rank interval of *a*. Rank intervals can be calculated directly from the partial order.

First, define *B*(*a*) to be the number of hotspots *b* for which $a \prec b$, i.e., the count of the first quadrant in Figure 19-6. Next, define *W*(*a*) as *B*(*a*) plus the number of hotspots that are not comparable with *a*; this is the total count for quadrants 1, 2, and 4 in Figure 19-6. The rank interval of *a* then consists of all integers *r* such that $B(a) \le r \le W(a)$. The length, $W(a) - B(a)$, of this interval is called the rank-ambiguity of hotspot *a*.

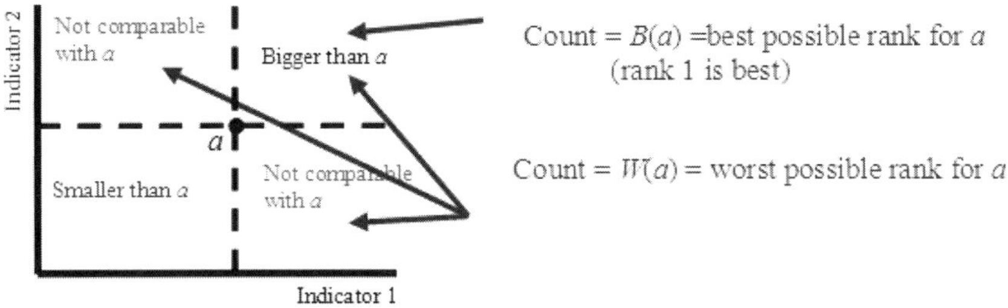

Figure 19-6. Regions of comparability and incomparability for the inherent importance ordering of hotspots. Hotspots form a scatterplot in indicator space and each hotspot partitions indicator space into four quadrants.

2.2.2 Hasse diagrams and linear extensions

Posets can be displayed as Hasse diagrams (Figure 19-7).

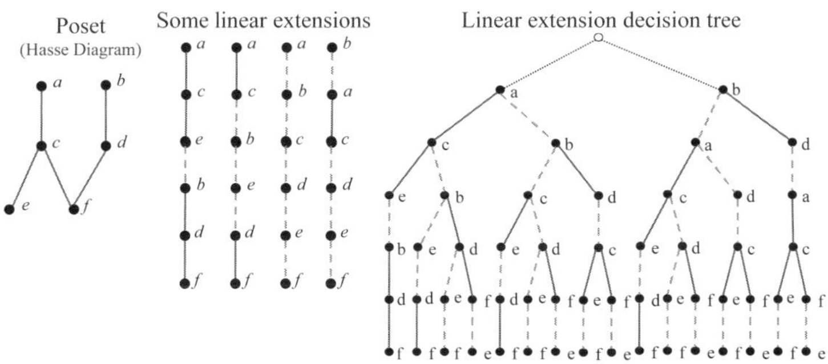

Figure 19-7. Hasse diagram of a hypothetical poset (left), some linear extensions (middle), and a decision tree giving all 16 possible linear extensions (right). Links shown in dashed/red (called jumps) are not implied by the partial order. The six members of the poset can be arranged in 6!=720 different ways, but only 16 of these are valid linear extensions.

A Hasse diagram is a graph whose vertices are the hotspots and whose edges join vertices that cover one another in the partial order. Hotspot *b* is said to *cover a* in the partial order if three things happen: (i) $a \prec b$; (ii) $a \neq b$; and (iii) if $a \prec x \prec b$ then either $x = a$ or $x = b$. In words, *b* is strictly above *a* and no hotspots are strictly between *a* and *b*. Each of the many possible ways of ranking the elements of a poset is referred to as a linear extension. The Hasse diagram of each linear extension appears as a vertical graph (Figure 19-7). Enumeration of all possible linear extensions can be accomplished algorithmically as follows. The top element of a linear extension can be any one of the maximal elements of the Hasse diagram. Select any one of these maximal elements and remove it from the Hasse diagram. The second ranked element in the linear extension can be any maximal element from the reduced Hasse diagram. Select any of these and proceed iteratively. The procedure can be arranged as a decision tree (Figure 19-7) and each path through the tree from root node to leaf node determines one linear extension.

2.2.3 Linearizing a poset

The suite of indicators determines only a partial order on the hotspots, but it is human nature to ask for a linear ordering. We ask: Is there some objective way of mapping the partial order into a linear one? Our solution treats each linear extension in Figure 19-7 as a voter and we apply the principle of majority rule. Focus attention on some member *a* of the poset and ask how many of the voters give *a* a rank of 1? 2? Etc. The results are displayed in Figure 19-8, where each row of the table is called a rank-frequency distribution. The cumulative forms of these rank-frequency distributions form a new poset with stochastic ordering of distributions as the order relation. For this example, the new poset is already a linear ordering (see Figure 19-8).

	Rank						
Element	1	2	3	4	5	6	Totals
a	9	5	2	0	0	0	16
b	7	5	3	1	0	0	16
c	0	4	6	6	0	0	16
d	0	2	4	6	4	0	16
e	0	0	1	3	6	6	16
f	0	0	0	0	6	10	16
Totals	16	16	16	16	16	16	

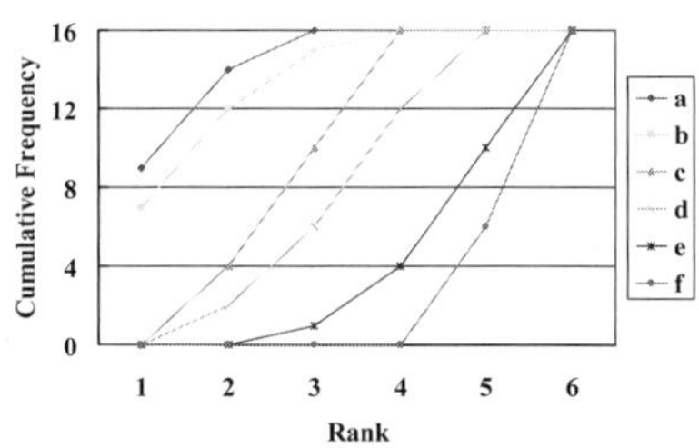

Figure 19-8. (Left) Rank-frequency table for the poset of Figure 19-7. Each row gives the number of linear extensions that assign a given rank r to the corresponding member of the poset. Each row is referred to as a rank-frequency distribution. (Right) Cumulative rank-frequency distributions for the poset of Figure 19-7. The curves are stacked one above the other giving a linear ordering of the elements.

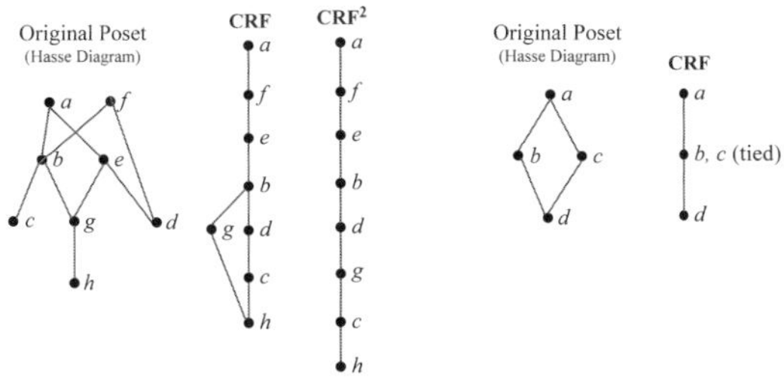

Figure 19-9. (Left) Two iterations of the CRF operator are required to transform this partial order into a linear order. (Right) A poset for which the CRF operator produces ties.

We refer to the above procedure as the cumulative rank-frequency (CRF) operator. In general, it does not transform a partial order into a linear order in a single step; instead, multiple iterations may be required (Figure 19-9). The CRF operator can also produce ties in the final linear ordering.

3. ILLUSTRATIVE APPLICATIONS AND CASE STUDIES

3.1 Network Analysis of Biological Integrity in Freshwater Streams

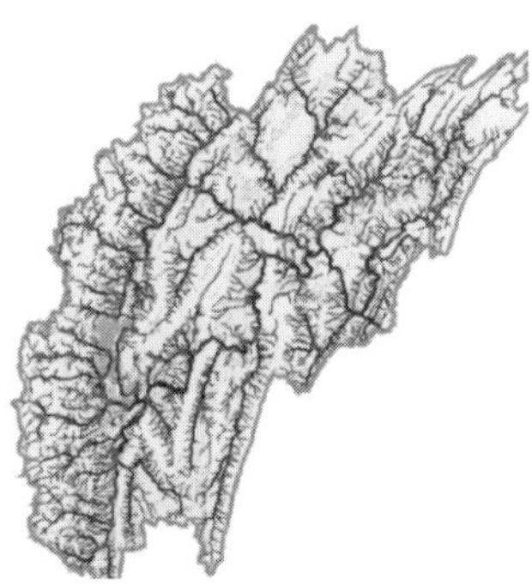

This study will employ the network version of the upper level set scan statistic to characterize biological impairment along the rivers and streams of Pennsylvania and to identify subnetworks that are badly impaired. The state Department of Environmental Protection is determining indices of biological integrity (IBI) at about 15,000 sampling locations across the Commonwealth. Impairment will be measured by a complemented form of these IBI values. We will also use remotely sensed landscape variables and physical characteristics of the streams as explanatory variables in order to account for impairment hotspots. Critical stream subnetworks that remain unaccounted for after this filtering exercise become candidates for more detailed modeling and site investigation. See Wardrop et al. (2005).

3.2 Watershed Prioritization for Impairment and Vulnerability

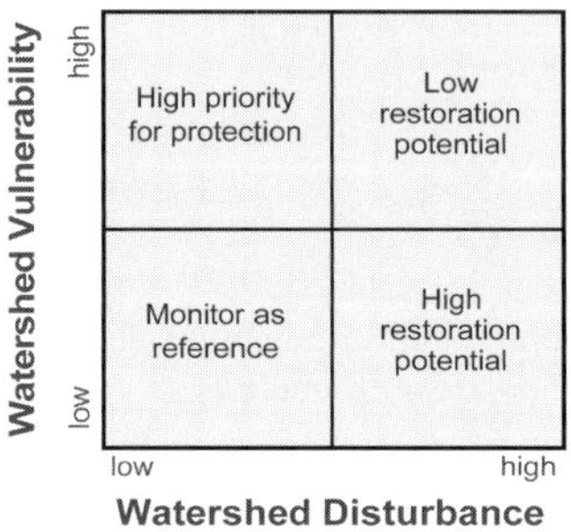

This study will develop a prioritization model for watersheds (12-digit HUCs) of the Mid-Atlantic Highlands. A suite of indicators will be identified to assess each watershed's susceptibility to impairment (vulnerability). A second suite of indicators will measure actual stress or disturbance for each watershed. The watersheds will then beranked according to each of the two separate sets of indicators. The proposed prioritization methodology will be used for ranking purposes. Each watershed is thus assigned a pair of ranks indicating its vulnerability status and its disturbance status. The pairs of ranks yield a scatter plot in the disturbance × vulnerability plane. The four quadrants in this plot have distinctly different management implications, as depicted in the accompanying diagram. Disturbance will be measured by stressor variables such as: excess sediment, riparian degradation, mine drainage, excess nutrients, exotic species, agriculture (esp. on slopes), road crossings, forest fragmentation, and indices biological impairment. Vulnerability primarily reflects physical characteristics and natural features of the watershed and can be measured by: hydrogeomorphology (HGM), climate, aspect, slope, stream sinuosity, soil type, bedrock, and water source. Products include: a procedure for classifying watersheds by their features and condition, a taxonomy of Mid-Atlantic watersheds, and a set of monitoring and restoration options for each watershed class that can assist managers in developing TMDL (total maximum daily load) plans, Patil et al. (2000).

3.3 Tasking of a Self-organizing Oceanic Surveillance Mobile Sensor Network

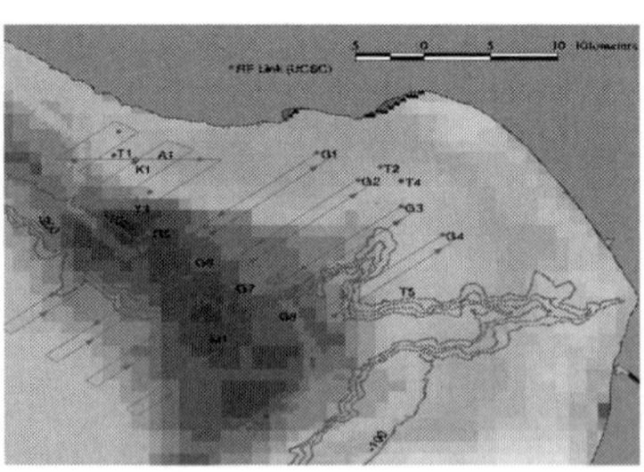

The Autonomous Ocean Sampling Network Simulator (AOSN) is used to study coordination and control strategies for high-resolution, spatio-temporally coordinated surveys of oceanographic fields such as bathymetry, temperature and currents using autonomous unmanned undersea vehicles. Currently, the network of mobile sensor platforms is autonomous and self-organizing once given high-level tasking from an external tactical coordinator. This case study proposes to use upper level set scan statistic theory to identify hotspots in data gathered by the sensor network and use this information to dynamically task mobile sensor platforms so that more data can be gathered in the areas of interest. By detecting hotspots and tasking accordingly, network resources are not wasted on mapping areas of little change. The ability of the sensor network to dynamically task its own components expands the network's mission and increases the reactivity to changing conditions in a highly dynamic environment. See Phoha et al. (2001).

3.4 Persistent Poverty Patch Dynamics and Poverty Eradication Policy

As Glasmeier (2004) puts it, "the United States is a nation pulling apart to a degree unknown in the last twenty-five years. Despite more than a decade of strong national economic growth, many of America's communities are falling far behind median national measures of economic health."

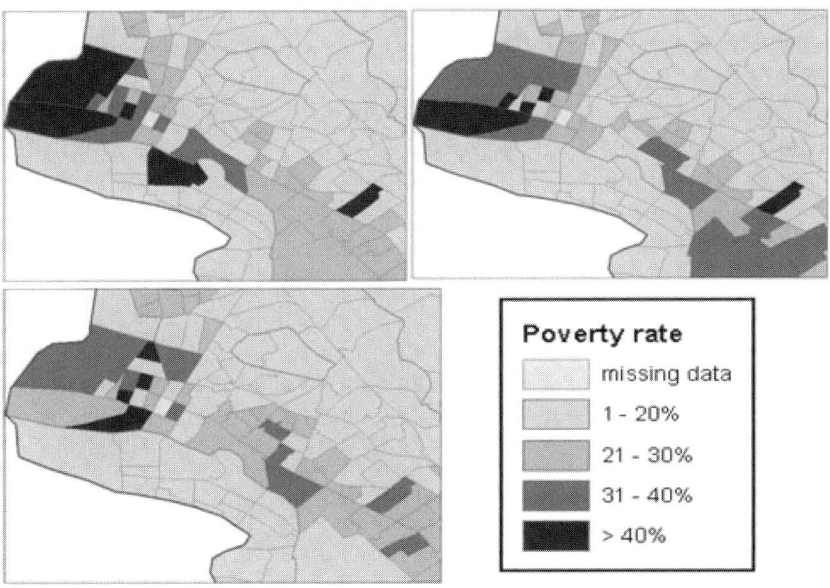

Figure 19-10. Shifting poverty, Oakland, CA, 1970-1980-1990.

The federal anti-poverty programs have had little success in eradicating pockets of persistent poverty. In order to help formulate promising policies, it has become important to analyze spatial and temporal compositions of persistent poverty at multiple scales and examine the persistent poverty patch trajectories over the years in various urban and rural regions. Glasmeier (2004) speaks of several dimensions of tract poverty in metropolitan areas during 1970-90, such as, persistent, concentrated, growing, and shifting (Figure 19-10).

The case study under consideration is motivated to answer the following question: can spatial-temporal patterns of poverty hotspots provide clues to the causes of poverty and lead to improved location-specific anti-poverty policy? Our approach will be used to detect shifting poverty hotspots, coalescence of neighboring hotspots, or their growth for this case study.

3.5 Cyber Security and Computer Network Diagnostics

Securing the nation's computer networks from cyber attacks is an important aspect of national Homeland Security. Network diagnostic tools aim at detecting security attacks on computer networks. Besides cyber security, these tools can also be used to diagnose other anomalies such as infrastructure failures, and operational aberrations. Hotspot detection forms an important and integral part of these diagnostic tools for discovering correlated anomalies. The project research can be used to develop a network diagnostic tool at a functional level. The goal of network state models is to obtain the temporal characteristics of network elements such as routers, typically in terms of their physical connectivity, resource availability, occupancy distribution, blocking probability, etc. We have done prior work in developing network state models for connectivity, and resource availability. We have also developed models for studying the equilibrium behavior of multi-dimensional loss systems (Acharya, 2003). The probabilistic finite state automaton (PFSA) describing a net element can be obtained from the output of these state models. A time-dependent crisis-index is determined for each network element, which measures their normal behavior pattern compared to crisis behavior. The crisis-index is the numerical distance between the stochastic languages generated by the normal and crisis behavior. The crisis-index is the numerical distance between the stochastic languages generated by the normal and crisis automata. We plan to use the variation distance between probability measures, although other distances will also be considered. The crisis behavior can be obtained from past experience. The crisis indices over a collection of network elements are then used for hot-spot detection using scan statistic methodology. These hot spots help to detect coordinated security attacks geographically spread over a network.. See Figure 19-11.

Additional application of PFSA include the tasking of the self-organizing surveillance mobile sensor networks, geotelemetry with wireless sensor networks, video-mining networks, and syndromic surveillance in public health with hospital networks.

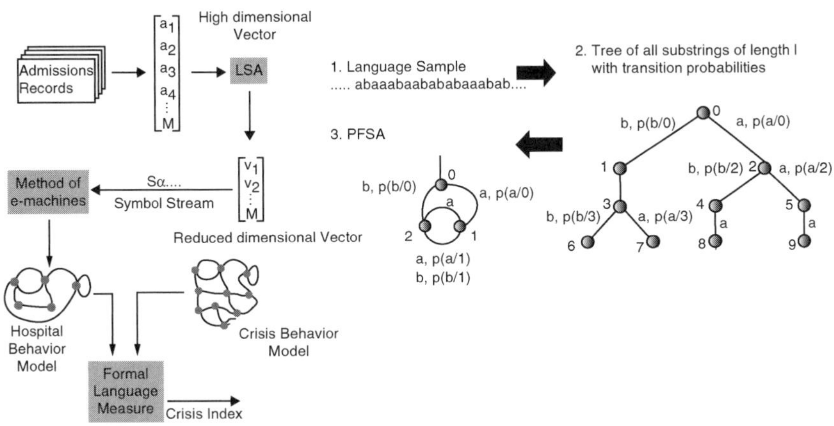

Figure 19-11. (left) The overall procedure, leading from admissions records to the crisis index for a hospital. The hotspot detection algorithm is then applied to the crisis index values defined over the hospital network. (right) The-machine procedure for converting an event stream into a parse tree and finally into a probabilistic finite state automaton (PFSA).

3.6 Network Applications and New York City Subway System Syndromic Surveillance Data

For certain problems, there is an underlying network structure on which we will want to perform the cluster detection and evaluation. For example, the New York City Health Department is monitoring the New York subway system and water distribution networks for bioterrorism attacks. In such a scenario, a circular scan statistic is not useful as two individuals close to each other in Euclidian distance may be very far from each other along the network. However, the ULS methods will be employed for the detection and evaluation of clusters on a predefined network. The essentially linear structure of these networks, compared with tessellation-derived networks, is expected to have a major impact on the form of the null distributions and their parametric approximations.

The New York City Department of Health (DOH) and Metropolitan Transportation Authority (MTA) began monitoring subway worker absenteeism in October 2001 as one of several surveillance systems for the early detection of disease outbreaks. Each day the MTA transmits an electronic line list of workers absent the previous day, including work location and reason for absence. DOH epidemiologists currently monitor temporal trends in absences in key syndrome categories (e.g., fever-flu or gastrointestinal illness). Analytic techniques are needed for detecting clustering within the subway network.

4. CONCLUSION

We now live in the age of geospatial technologies. The age old geographic issues of societal importance are now thinkable and analyzable. The geography of disease is now just as doable as genetics of disease, for example. And it is possible to pursue it in an intelligent manner with the rapidly advancing information technology around.

Government agencies continue to require meaningful summaries of georeferenced data to support policies and decisions involving geographic assessments and resource allocations. So also the public with initiatives of digital governance in the country and around the world. Surveillance geoinformatics of spatial and spatiotemporal hotspot detection and prioritization is a critical need for the 21st century.

This chapter briefly describes a prototype geoinformatic hotspot surveillance system for hotspot delineation and prioritization and provides a variety of case studies and illustrative applications of societal importance. The prototype system consists of modules for hotspot detection and delineation, and for hotspot prioritization.

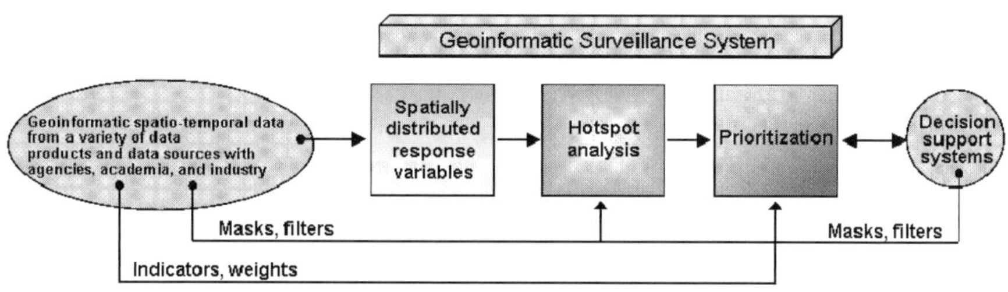

Figure 19-12. Framework for the Geoinformatic Hotspot Surveillance (GHS) system.

5. ACKNOWLEDGEMENTS

This material is based upon work supported by (i) the National Science Foundation Grant No. 0307010, (ii) the United States Environmental Protection Agency under Grant No. R-828684 and Grant No. RD-83244001 and (iii) the Pennsylvania Department of Health using Tobacco Settlement Funds under Grant No. ME 01324. Any opinions, findings, and conclusions or recommendations expressed in this material are those of the author(s) and do not necessarily reflect the views of the agencies.

REFERENCES

Glasmeier A (2004) An atlas of poverty in America: One nation, pulling apart, 1960-2003, Routledge, Oxford, UK.

Kulldorff M (1997) A spatial scan statistic. Communications in Statistics: Theory andMethods, 26:1481–1496.

Kulldorff M, Nagarwalla N (1995) Spatial disease clusters: Detection and inference. Statistics in Medicine, 14:799–810

Neggers J, Kim HS (1988) Basic Posets. World Scientific, Singapore.

Patil GP, Johnson GD, Myers WL, Taillie C (2000) Multiscale statistical approach to critical-area analysis and modeling of watersheds and landscapes. Pages 293-310 in *Statistics for the* 21st Century: Methodologies for Applications of the Future, C. R. Rao and G. J. Szekely, eds. Marcel Dekker, New York.

Patil GP, Taillie C (2004a) Upper level set scan statistic for detecting arbitrarily shaped hotspots. Environmental and Ecological Statistics, 11:183-197.

Patil GP, Taillie C (2004b) Multiple indicators, partially ordered sets, and linear extensions: Multi-criterion ranking and prioritization. Environmental and Ecological Statistics, 11:199-228.

Patil GP, Duczmal L, Haran M, Patankar P (2006a) On PULSE: The progressive upper level set scan statistic system for geospatial and spatiotemporal hotspot detection. In: The 7th Annual International Conference on Digital Government Research, San Diego, CA, May 21-24, 2006.

Patil GP, Bhat KS, Kase M (2006b) Multicriterion prioritization and differential weights, stepwise aggregation, Hasse diagrams, and Poset cumulative rank frequency operators. In: The 7th Annual International Conference on Digital Government Research, San Diego, CA, May 21-24, 2006.

Phoha S, Peluso E, Culver RL (2001). A high fidelity ocean sampling mobile network (SAMON) simulator tested for evaluating intelligent control of unmanned underwater vehicles. Revised version submitted to IEEE Journal for Ocean Engineering, Special Edition, June 2001.

Wardrop DH, Bishop JA, Easterling M, Hychka K, Myers WL, Patil GP, Taillie C (2005) Use of landscape and land use parameters for classification and characterization of watersheds in the Mid-Atlantic across five physiographic provinces. Environmental and Ecological Statistics, 12:209-223.

SUGGESTED READINGS

- Patil GP, Taillie C (2004a) Upper level set scan statistic for detecting arbitrarily shaped hotspots. Environmental and Ecological Statistics,

11:183-197. (A basic proof of concept paper for upper level set scan system.) At: http://www.stat.psu.edu/~gpp/pdfs/TR2002-0601.pdf

- Patil GP, Taillie C (2004b) Multiple indicators, partially ordered sets, and linear extensions: Multi-criterion ranking and prioritization. Environmental and Ecological Statistics, 11:199-228. (A basic proof of concept paper for poset prioritization and ranking system.) At: http://www.stat.psu.edu/~gpp/pdfs/TR2001-1204.pdf
- Kulldorff M, Nagarwalla N (1995) Spatial disease clusters: Detection and inference. Statistics in Medicine, 14:799–810. (A basic paper for circular spatial scan.)

ONLINE RESOURCES

- http://www.stat.psu.edu/hotspots
  A project website providing project activities, products, publications, and events.
- http://www.dgrc.org/dgo2006/papers/workshops.jsp#hotspot
  Article on the workshop program on hotspot geoinformatics.)
- http://www.satscan.org
  (Freeware for circular spatial scan program and information.
- http://www.getsynapsed.de/
  Freeware for academia for Hasse program for Windows.
- http://www.stat.psu.edu/~gpp
  Website of the Penn State Center for Statistical Ecology and Environmental Statistics—Home base of the digital government research project for hotspot geoinformatics.

QUESTIONS FOR DISCUSSION

1. How to improve the quality and quantity of the ULS nodal tree and thus introduce PULSE – Progressive ULS Scan.
2. How to formulate and conduct a comparative study of performance evaluation of suitably different hotspot detection procedures.
3. How to improve the poset prioritization MCMC program by giving it a clever start, rather than the random start of a linear extension.
4. Is poset-prioritization-based ranking represented by an appropriate index-based ranking?

Chapter 20

GEOINFORMATION TECHNOLOGIES TO SUPPORT COLLABORATIVE EMERGENCY MANAGEMENT

Sven Fuhrmann[1], Alan MacEachren[2], and Guoray Cai[3]

[1]Texas State University, Department of Geography, San Marcos, Texas, U.S.A. (fuhrmann@txstate.edu); [2]The Pennsylvania State University, GeoVISTA Center, University Park, Pennsylvania, U.S.A. (maceachren@psu.edu); [3]The Pennsylvania State University, College of Information Sciences and Technology, University Park, Pennsylvania, U.S.A (cai@ist.psu.edu)

CHAPTER OVERVIEW

In today's emergency management environments geoinformation technologies play a vital role, but their potential has not been fully exploited. Key decision makers usually do not have direct access to Geographic Information Systems and if they receive access, complex user interfaces often hinder performance for high pressure tasks. In order to provide decision makers with direct and easy access to geoinformation in emergency situations and support group collaboration, we developed three collaborative geoinformation platforms: the Multimodal Interface Platform for Geographic Information Systems (GeoMIP), the GeoCollaborative Crisis Management platform for mobile collaboration and a web-portal for humanitarian relief logistics. The technologies developed are intelligent, multimodal (speech and gesture-based) user interfaces that allow synchronous and asynchronous collaboration between decision makers; support GIS use by mobile emergency management teams; and provide open standards-based web portal technologies.

1. INTRODUCTION

The use of geoinformation technologies is broadly established in academia, business and governmental agencies. Within emergency management, Geographic Information Systems (GIS) have been used for over 20 years (Cova and Church 1997). Examples for GIS utilization in natural and man-made disasters are to support flood mapping, hurricane prediction, and environmental clean-ups after industrial accidents. GIS use in emergency management cuts across multiple domains and user groups and many definitions are available to describe the concepts, techniques and impacts of GIS. For the emergency management domain, Geographic Information Systems can be best described as software for integrating and analyzing geospatial data relevant to individuals and teams who carry out a range of key emergency management tasks (e.g., situation assessment, evacuation planning and execution, logistics planning and supply delivery, damage assessment, etc).

Today, emergency management applies geoinformation technologies in all five phases of the emergency management process, i.e. planning, mitigation, preparedness, response, and recovery (Johnson 2000). In 2001 GIS was prominently used in the rescue, relief and recovery process after the World Trade Center attack. Although New York City's Emergency Operation Center and GIS infrastructure was destroyed, city officials were able to set up a backup facility and use GIS to produce maps for emergency response purposes by the evening of 9/11 (Kevany 2003).

Despite the recent popularity in using Geographic Information Systems for emergency management, their potential has not been fully explored because most systems do not support direct multi-user access and require highly trained operators that produce analysis and mapping results for the decision makers. In most emergency situations, GIS operators receive their orders via runners (staff members) who are asked by the decision makers to inquire about maps (Brewer 2005). The GIS specialists usually react to mapping and spatial analysis requests from decision makers, e.g. after the World Trade Center attack GIS specialists, supported by company consultants, were operating Geographic Information Systems and producing maps on demand (Greene 2002) and, after Hurricane Katrina, GIS experts from Louisiana State University provided support to evacuation and relief efforts (Curtis et al. 2006). In larger communities, state and federal agencies GIS operations have become an integral part of Emergency Operation Centers (EOCs), but in some instances, e.g. smaller and/or rural communities, special GIS operators might not be available or are not part of the Emergency Operation Center staff. Even in New Orleans, a major metropolitan area, GIS use was hindered during Hurricane Katrina because the mapping requests overwhelmed the EOC capabilities and outdated computers caused frustration (Curtis et al. 2006).

Geographic Information Systems have been demonstrated to provide major benefits to emergency management, but the technology has also shortcomings and constraints. Kevany (2003) identifies eight different shortcoming categories each with at least five individual challenges. The most prominent constrains identified by Cutter (2003), ESRI (2000, and Kevany (2003) are that (1) users need extensive training to operate a GIS, (2) group work functions have not been implemented, (3) real-time data are often not accessible, (4) data formats are sometimes incompatible, and (5) the data quality frequently does not match the requirements. In the light of 9/11 many researchers and developers are working on the removal of these shortcomings, e.g. the integration of real time data (Kwan and Lee 2005; Baldus and Kim 2005), interoperable GIS (Rocha, Cestnik, and Oliveira 2005) and improvements in spatial data infrastructure (Mansourian et al. 2006; Maguire and Longley 2005).

This chapter will focus on developing relevant and usable geoinformation technologies. We begin with an overview of the field that addresses three themes: the current status of GIS for emergency management, efforts to extend GIS to support collaboration across teams and organizations, and efforts to make GIS easier to use so that non-specialists can access the information they need to carry out emergency management work. We follow this overview with a set of case studies from our own Digital Government research. These case studies highlight our research on: intelligent, multimodal user interfaces that allow more natural access to GIS-based information by individuals without special training and that enable synchronous and asynchronous collaboration between decision makers; support for GIS use by mobile emergency management teams; and open standards-based web portal technologies to support multi-organization humanitarian relief activities.

2. OVERVIEW OF THE FIELD

2.1 GIS in Emergency Management

Disasters strike unexpectedly. In the context of emergency management, disasters are any event that results in large scale and high impact emergency situations. These events, natural or human-generated, are ones that have high death tolls and/or substantial damage to property and infrastructure. The 2004 Indian Ocean earthquake and the resulting tsunamis resulted in over 185,000 deaths (United Nations 2006), Hurricane Katrina killed over 1800 people in 2005 (Wikipedia 2006), the 2006 earthquake in Indonesia caused over 6000 deaths (International Federation of Red Cross And Red Crescent Societies 2006) and in the 2001 World Trade Center attack over 2700 lives were lost (CNN.com 2005). These and other disasters resulted in calls to develop and use new technologies for better emergency management (U.S. Department of Homeland Security 2004).

The initial response to disasters happens on a local level. It is usually the city or county that needs to cope with emergency situations (Gunes and Kovel 2000). Emergency management is concerned with reducing potential human and material losses from crisis events, assuring immediate rescue and relief efforts, and supporting effective recovery (FEMA 2005). The emergency response cycle by Cutter (2003) schematically represents the different stages in emergency management (Figure 20-1).

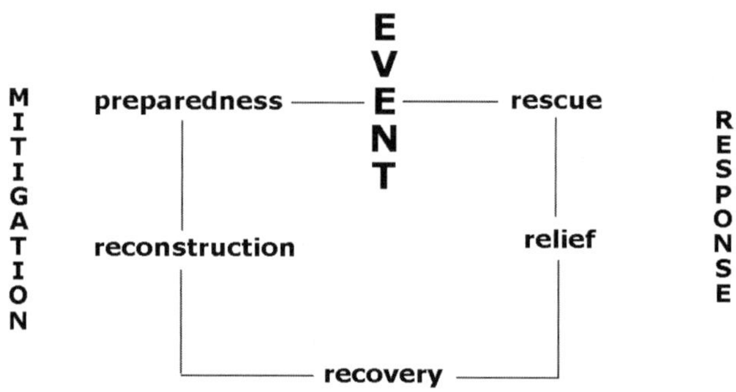

Figure 20-1. The emergency response cycle (Cutter 2003)

The emergency response cycle (Figure 20-1) illustrates the process by which federal, state and local agencies, private businesses and citizens react to disasters, recover, and prepare for a possible new disaster. In recent years, emergency management was mostly concerned with reacting to emergency situations. Lessons learned, particularly from recent major disasters, indicate that it is important to be proactive and mitigate the potential for disasters before they strike. After the World Trade Center attack President Bush established the Disaster Management E-Government Initiative (White House 2006) intended to do just this. The Disaster Management Initiative investigates and develops State of the Art technology and standards to support disaster information and services. Its focus is on the development of Internet-based services and protocols that will help the emergency management domain to manage incidents, share information and gain common situational awareness by providing Disaster Management Interoperability Services or DMIS. DMIS is an open and interoperable platform that currently can provide basic maps that can be edited and shared through access protocols, tactical information exchange, and weather information (see https://interop.cmiservices.org/).

The Disaster Management E-Government Initiative (White House 2006) and the National Incident Management System (U.S. Department of Homeland Security 2004) encourage the use of geoinformation technology in emergency management. GIS provides functions, e.g. disaster forecasts, impact modeling, vulnerability analysis, damage assessment, resource management, etc. that support essential emergency management tasks (Gunes and Kovel 2000; Cova et al. 2005; Zerger and Smith 2003).

The most prominent GIS technology development in emergency management in recent years is HAZUS (Hazards U.S.), a multi-hazard risk assessment and loss estimation software program. The Federal Emergency Management Agency (FEMA) started to develop HAZUS in 1997 focusing on estimating losses from earthquake related events (Quinn 2000). Over the next years HAZUS was further developed and in 2003 HAZUS-MH (Multi-Hazard) was released. HAZUS-MH not only models earthquake losses but also helps to make forecasts and risk assessment decisions for flooding and hurricane events. HAZUS-MH can prioritize potential losses so that rescue activities can focus on areas with the greatest needs. HAZUS-MH was successfully applied during Hurricane Isabel in 2003 and Hurricane Katrina in 2005 (Levitan and Hill 2005; Oliver 2004; Srinivasan 2003).

HAZUS-MH and DIMS can be considered success stories about application of GIS in emergency management. But geoinformation technology still has two major shortcomings in the fast paced emergency management domain: (a) emergency management is fundamentally an activity carried out by teams (and teams of teams) but current GIS does not support collaboration and (b) current GIS is hard to use, requiring a substantial amount of specialized training, thus it does not allow direct access to geospatial data, analysis and mapping abilities by the decision makers (few of whom have specialized GIS knowledge). Most likely HAZUS-MH and DIMS will be operated by a trained specialist who reacts to the requests of the decision makers. In a typical workflow, the GIS specialist will acknowledge the request for spatial analysis and mapping products, walk to his/her workstation and return with mapping products for the decision makers about 10-25 minutes later (Brewer 2005). Such workflows limit the potential access to geospatial information and take extra time, two limitations that are critical in emergency management.

2.2 Supporting Collaboration in Emergency Management

Difficulties in multi-jurisdictional emergency agencies working together during and after 9/11, led to the creation of the National Incident Management System (NIMS). Historically many emergency responders and their departments/agencies have dealt with emergencies by themselves, mostly in a non-standardized fashion. Major disasters such as 9/11 and Hurricane Katrina made clear that large (and smaller) disasters that cross single-jurisdictions require an overarching incident management structure. In 2003, President Bush issued the Homeland Security Presidential Directive 5 that states: "NIMS will include a core set of concepts, principles, terminology, and technologies covering the incident command system; multi-agency coordination systems; unified command; training; identification and management of resources; qualifications and certification; and the collection, tracking, and reporting of incident information and incident resources" (U.S. Department of Homeland Security 2004). NIMS outlines a framework for interoperability and compatibility that allows flexibility and standardization within the organizational structure of emergency management. It encourages the use of geoinformation technology (U.S. Department of Homeland Security 2004), but does not provide detail about the GIS design requirements. Since 2003, NIMS has been adopted in many jurisdictions to improve emergency planning and response. All federal departments, agencies, state, local, and tribal governments are required to comply with NIMS implementation requirements by October 1, 2006, i.e. use the NIMS-based Incident Command System (ICS) organizational structures and operational procedures to manage emergency incidents. (NIMS Integration Center 2005b, 2005a).

The most obvious role for geoinformation technology in emergency management is to enable collaborative geoinformation access and decision making within the organizational structure. GIScience research has begun to address the challenges and opportunities associated with extending geoinformation technology to use by groups (Armstrong 1993; Al-Kodmany 2000; Jankowski and Nyerges 2001a; MacEachren 2000, 2001; MacEachren and Brewer 2004; Schafer et al. 2005). However, researchers still have limited knowledge about the dynamics of collaborative group work with geospatial information technologies, particularly in emergency management where these technologies may have a central role in time-critical decision making. Here, we will focus on shared visual interfaces to geospatial information.

Although Armstrong and Densham (1995), and Armstrong (1997) predicted that GIS would be used in group settings for decision making and developed a prototype visual aide for facility location, follow-up research was somewhat slow to materialize. Jankowski and Nyerges (2001a, 2001b) have been among the most active researchers in this domain, focusing particular attention on development and testing of a theory-based approach to understanding the process of group decision making in the context of urban and regional planning. In relation to the role of maps and visual display, their empirical research reached a conclusion that maps were more often used if decision making involved a conflict. In subsequent work, Jankowski collaborated with other colleagues to develop highly interactive visual tools to support decision making (Andrienko, Andrienko, and Jankowski 2003).

Drawing upon perspectives from computer supported cooperative work, collaborative visualization, group work with GIS, and other domains, MacEachren (2005) proposes that visual artifacts have three fundamental roles in facilitating group work with geospatial information. Specifically, visual artifacts can function: (a) as objects of collaboration (e.g., maps depicting entities to discuss, create or manipulate), (b) to support dialogue (e.g. between decision makers who might draw a diagram to illustrate a relationship they are trying to explain), and (c) to support coordinated activities (e.g. dynamic maps that help an EOC team monitor and adjust executing plans). Research findings in these areas would enable multi-user geocollaboration: the synchronous or asynchronous collaboration of numerous users with geospatial information through geospatial technologies (MacEachren and Brewer 2004).

2.3 Making GIS Easier to Use Through New Interaction Techniques

GIS user interfaces continue to evolve, from early command line mode interaction to graphical (point and click) user interfaces – but still these interfaces do not bridge the gap between expert users and novice/once-in-a-while GIS users. Especially in time critical situations, i.e. emergencies, GIS should provide direct access to geospatial data and support the situation awareness of decision makers who are typically not expert GIS users. Overall, strategies that have potential to address this issue include giving more attention to understanding how innovations diffuse and what the impediment to up-take are as well as taking a user-centered approach to design of GIS as a whole and of the user interface that new and occasional users must master (MacEachren et al. 2005).

Numerous factors contribute to GIS acceptance and usability barriers and many strategies for solving this problem have been suggested. One category of possible solutions might consist of multimodal interfaces. In our daily tasks and conversations, verbal descriptions and gestures have become essential communication vehicles. In emergency management we use gestures and verbal commands to direct people, request information, make decisions and give explanations. Our human senses, i.e. hearing, sight, smell, touch, taste, and equilibrium allow us to perceive and communicate information about our environment. Nowadays computers have the ability to simulate this information for the human senses and also perceive information via different modalities (Dix et al. 1998; Shneiderman 1998). Oviatt (2003) describes multimodal systems as systems that process two or more combined user input modes, such as speech, touch, gesture, gaze or body movements. Systems that allow only one input modality are considered to be unimodal (Schoemaker et al. 1995). Multimodal interfaces might provide a solution to better GIS interfaces by supporting more natural interaction with maps and the information behind them.

Research about multimodal interfaces (Lamel et al. 1998; Rasmussen, Pejtersen, and Goodstein 1994) emphasizes the use of natural and conversational human-computer interfaces, e.g. speech and free-hand/pen-based gestures but little research has focused on multimodal GIS interaction (Schlaisich and Egenhofer 2001; Jeong and Gluck 2003). Cohen et al. (1997) developed a pen and speech-based multimodal interface to interact with maps. They adopted a multimodal approach because previous research showed that speech-only interfaces were not effective for specifying spatial relations. In usability assessments, Cohen and colleagues found that, with a multimodal interface, participants were able to express spatial relations more efficiently than with speech-only interfaces (Cohen et al. 1997). In subsequent research Cohen, McGee, and Clow (2000) found that users of interactive multimodal maps even solved tasks faster and had shorter error correction times than users of common GUI-based maps. In complementary research, Jeong and Gluck (2003) studied the feasibility of adding haptic and auditory displays to GIS. They discovered that (a) haptic displays produced faster and more accurate results than auditory and auditory/haptic displays and (b) users liked the combined auditory/haptic displays much better although there performance was less good. Sharma et al. (1999) and Kettebekov and Sharma (2001) solved a variety of speech-gesture capture problems, analyzing weather broadcasts in which individuals talk and gesture at large screen maps. Their research has been leveraged in the GeoMIP and GCCM development.

3. CASE STUDIES

Our Digital Government research is focused on advance GIS to better support emergency management activities. The research addresses two overarching issues: (1) developing a more comprehensive understanding of geospatial information technology-enabled individual and group work in emergency situations and (2) the development of advances in geospatial information technology that support coordinated same-place and distributed crisis management activities. Here, we provide a brief overview of three prototypes developed within the overall research effort and that (a) enable GIS in emergency management, (b) support synchronous and asynchronous collaboration and decision making between decision makers, (c) provide map-mediated decision support between groups that work in the same place (room) and different places (mobile components) and support multilingual logistic tasks in multi-national emergency events. The prototype applications that will be introduced are (a) the Dialog-Assisted Visual Environment for Geoinformation (DAVE_G), (b) the Mobile Environments for Geo-Collaborative Crisis Management, and (c) the Humanitarian Relief Logistics Web Portal.

3.1 The Multimodal Interface Platform for Geographic Information Systems

Imagine an emergency operation center (EOC) of a government organization at 2:00 AM in which a group of emergency managers try to reach a decision about how to respond to a flash flood that occurred after an intense rainstorm and at the same time cope with a weakening dam that is threatening a city with its residents and infrastructures. Unfortunately the existing paper maps generated by GIS do not support the creation of a common operational picture and the group needs to request help from the off-duty GIS analyst to find out about potential hazards and solutions. The contact information for the GIS analyst is not on the EOC contact list, since the GIS branch is part of the urban planning division. About one hour later the GIS analyst receives the call for duty and arrives at the EOC after a long commute. At 5:00 AM the first situation maps are printed and transferred to the EOC.

Such a scenario could happen at almost any time in any place. It indicates many important points in emergency management that relate to geoinformation technology development. Emergency management requires decision makers in an EOC to (a) gain fast access to critical geospatial data, (b) rely on team work and derive information from geospatial data collaboratively, and (c) coordinate and execute decisions quickly. Successful geoinformation technology needs to meet these requirements; otherwise the technology might not be used in response and rescue missions.

To meet the needs of the EOC context requires tools that allow personnel to gain fast access to geospatial data and to collaborate in decision making.

We believe that natural interfaces to GIS, that make use of integrated (freehand) gesture and natural dialog, have the potential to enable efficient access to and work with geoinformation technology for non-GIS specialists, i.e. decision makers. We approached the system development from a human-centered system perspective that focused on users, their knowledge, and their tasks as fundamental input to the tool design process. Analysis of the emergency management tasks and interactions was essential to develop an intelligent system that recognizes the natural dialog of emergency managers and understands their tasks and requirements in different situations (Sharma et al. 2003; MacEachren et al. 2005). Domain knowledge (including spoken domain-specific phrases) and tasks of emergency managers were captured using a cognitive systems engineering (CSE) approach (Rasmussen et al. 1994). Some of the knowledge elicited was represented in concept maps that detailed connections among information, technology, people, and decision-making tasks (Brewer 2002). These concept maps provided a basis for scenario development. Several scenarios were designed to frame development, e.g. a hurricane threat in Florida and a chemical incident in the New York metro area. Besides task identification, the designed scenarios were essential for identifying generic and domain-specific GIS requests that the system must support.

To overcome single user constrains of GIS and support group work, a single-user system developed in earlier research, the Dialog-Assisted Visual Environment for Geoinformation (DAVE_G1) was extended to support group work and more flexible dialogue. DAVE_G1, developed through an NSF small ITR grant, implemented core, proof-of-concept ideas to achieve a working prototype multimodal interface to GIS using integration of speech and free-hand gesture (Sharma et al. 2003). DAVE_G2, developed as part of our current NSF Digital Government project implemented a range of advanced strategies for supporting natural interaction with GIS (MacEachren et al. 2005) (see Figure 20-2, next page). These advances included improved speech processing (using grammar-based parsing to extract content-carrying phrases), better semantic interpretation for understanding user intentions to match them with GIS commands, and the addition of dialogue control that supports user-system interaction to determine user intention (rather than the simpler strategy of one-pass system interpretation of user requests used in DAVE_G1). Building on this progress, industry partner Advanced Interfaces, Inc. (now VideoMining) then developed a more robust commercial version of the system, the Geospatial Multimodal Interface Platform (GeoMIP).

DAVE_G (both 1 and 2) was designed to accept simple voice and freehand gesture-based commands. Both modalities allow the users to query data sets, navigate through the environment (zoom and pan), and draw points, lines and circles on a large screen display (Figure 20-2).

Figure 20-2. The Dialog-Assisted Visual Environment for Geoinformation (DAVE_G2)

Two different types of requests can be distinguished; one that relies on spatial references that need to be specified by gesturing (e.g. pointing and outlining), and a second that allows requests to be expressed solely by speech. The current DAVE_G2 version features the following requests

- Data query (show/hide features, select/highlight features)
- Buffering (create/show buffers),
- Map navigation (pan left/right/up/down, center at, zoom in/out/area/full extend) and Drawing (points, circle, line, free hand) (MacEachren et al. 2005).

For fulfilling a successful task, e.g. visualizing a theme, the user does not need to provide all required information at once. DAVE_G2 incrementally collects information about the intended task by supporting a human-computer-based dialog. As an example, the user might want to display population data, DAVE_G2 might have different kinds of population information available (e.g., for census tracts, counties), thus DAVE_G2 would ask which of the available population data sets the user wants to have displayed (Cai, Wang, and MacEachren 2003).

The DAVE_G2 architecture is based upon three modules: Human Interaction Handling, Human Collaboration and Dialog Management, and Information Handling (Figure 20-3, next page).

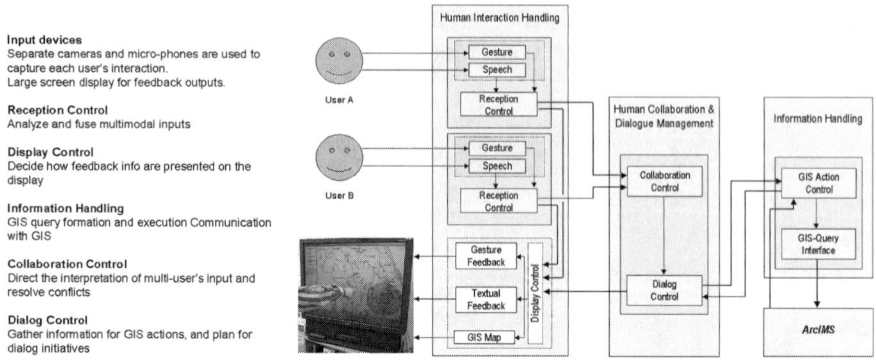

Figure 20-3. The DAVE_G2 architecture (after MacEachren et al., 2005)

The Human Interaction Handling Module consists out of two components: (1) the human reception control that captures speech and gesture input through cameras and microphones and generates descriptions of recognized words, phrases, sentences, and gestures, (2) the display control that receives the processed system responses, e.g. maps and textual messages. It coordinates the direct feedback in response to users' actions, e.g. cursor movements.

The Human Collaboration and Dialog Management Module receives the gesture descriptions and verbal utterances from the reception control components. It coordinates the execution of these commands through the collaboration manager and the dialog manager. The collaboration manager is involved in the conflict management if two or more persons are interacting with DAVE_G2. The dialog manager checks the received information for consistency and ambiguity and establishes a dialog with the users to resolve interpretation problems. When sufficient information is collected the Information Handling Module initiates a GIS query and sends the query, through the GIS query interface, to ArcIMS, which is located on a remote server (ESRI 2003). The GIS action control takes care of all GIS related queries and maintains information regarding the current status of the GIS. Successful GIS queries return a map and relevant metadata to the Information Handling Module that passes the returned information (including error messages) to the display control.

In 2005 the commercial adaptation of some of the ideas developed in DAVE_G1 and 2, GeoMIP, was successfully deployed as demo system at the Port Authority of New York and New Jersey and will be further developed and distributed by VideoMining, Inc. Working with the Port Authority of New York and New Jersey has helped identify long-term tasks to make adoption of the GeoMIP system easier for emergency management. Examples include: (a) integrating the GeoMIP system with existing EOC software tools, (b) dynamically synchronizing GeoMIP system GIS data with master GIS datasets, and (c) providing role-specific, expertise collaboration to enable seamless group decision-making.

3.2 Synchronous GeoCollaborative Crisis Management with Mobile Teams

The DAVE_G implementations and their transition to the Multimodal Interface Platform for Geographic Information Systems (GeoMIP) was a first step towards making geoinformation technology accessible and available in emergency management settings typically found in Emergency Operations Centers (EOC). However, most emergency management activities involve cooperation among EOCs and teams of emergency responders in the field. Such settings are exemplified by the scenario depicted in Figure 20-4 in which a package of chemical substance generates suspicion of a terrorist attack.

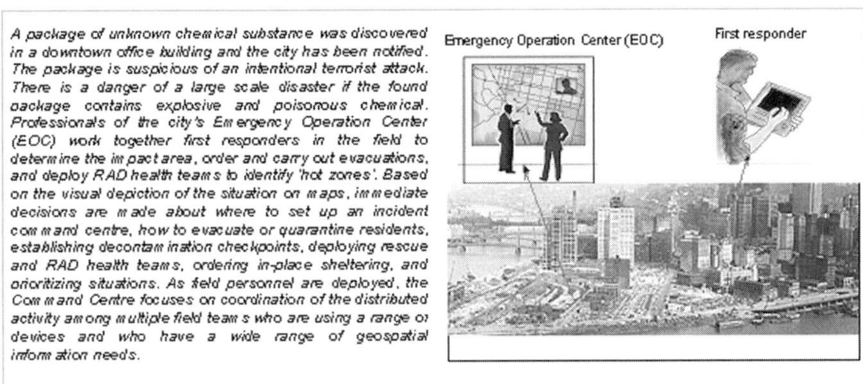

Figure 20-4. A scenario of GeoCollaborative Crisis Management (GCCM) (after Cai and MacEachren, 2005)

Geographical intelligence gathered in the field and decisions and actions made in the EOC must be shared across the team, creating team awareness on an emergency situation. Yuan and Detlor (2005) pointed out the potentials for networked mobile devices to enhance the crisis response team in their ability to monitor crisis dynamics, assess damage, constructing team knowledge, and coordinating collaborative actions, but effective technology for crisis response support does not exist yet. Hence, our next step in the GeoCollaborative Crisis Management project (GCCM) was concerned with supporting multimodal and map-mediated collaboration among EOCs and mobile teams. The GCCM research team developed a multi-agent system that is designed to mediate collaborative activities among emergency managers in EOCs and first responders in the field.

The challenges of supporting synchronous collaboration among distributed emergency response teams are many-folds. Emergency management teams are often formed dynamically in an ad-hoc manner according to the situation. Some members may be constantly on the move, while others stay in relatively stable environments. Members may be equipped with a diverse range of devices that need to communicate with each other reliably. Irrespective of the team configuration, technology support should facilitate information flows among team members. Map-mediated geocollaboration goes beyond simple sharing of geographical information, and should include workspace awareness and activity awareness to enable coordination and cooperation.

We have developed a map-enabled groupware environment called GCCM (Figure 20-5, next page). GCCM is designed to mediate collaborative activities among emergency managers in Emergency Operation Centers (EOCs) and first responders in the field. It assumes that the EOCs are equipped with a large-screen display together with microphones and cameras to capture human speech and free-hand gestures. The EOC coordinates with field teams through multimodal dialogues mediated by GCCM. Field teams have access to hand-held devices that run a GCCM client. Using GCCM mobile client, a crisis manager in the field can access geographical intelligence gathered over the network as well as communicating and collaborating with other team members, using natural multimodal dialogues (natural speech and pen-based gestures). All communications are through XML-based web service protocols. Mobile devices use wireless connections, while the EOC system(s) use high-speed network connections.

During an interactive session, GCCM mediates all the message flows among team members and reasons about the role of maps in the ongoing tasks in order to determine map contents, presentation format, and sharing requirements. Currently, GCCM support crisis response teams by allowing each member to work with geospatial information individually or collaboratively with others. To support first responders, GCCM can also interpret stylus input from tablet PC as deictic or iconic gestures. Examples include the ability to: select cities that are on one side of a position (spatial component indicated with a linear gesture), highlight a critical facility (spatial component indicated by a pointing gesture), exclude locations outside of a region from consideration (spatial component indicated with an area gesture). More generally, users can indicate any specific location or extent through gesture (e.g. "zoom to include *this* area" – with a pointing or area gesture indicating the referent for *this* and the interpretation of the request based on which kind of gesture is sensed).

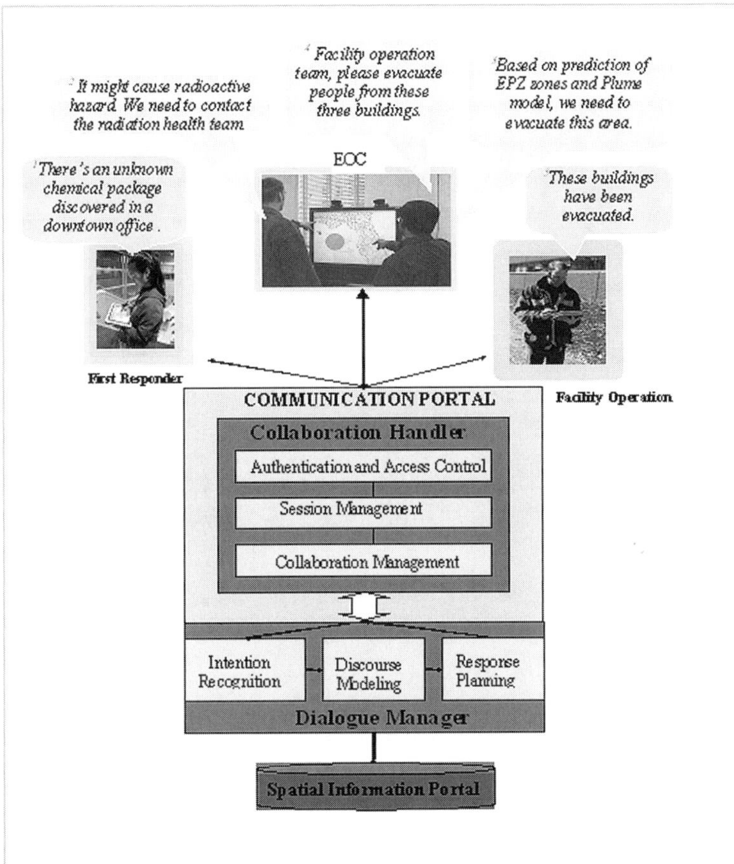

Figure 20-5. GCCM environment (after Cai and MacEachren, 2005)

As a reconfigurable prototype, GCCM employs a web service based distributed architecture. The architecture of a system refers to the description of components, connectors, and their configurations. From the perspective of geocollaboration support, the architecture of GCCM has to cope with a GIS service specification model, a groupware specification model, and their dynamic integration based on task knowledge. The result of this work has been detailed in a paper by Cai (2005) and illustrated in the Figure 20-6. It extends distributed GIS with groupware and intelligent communication agents. In addition to the architectural choice, special attention is given to the computational approach for enabling collaborative geographical information dialogues in spatial decision-making contexts. Collaboration requires representation and reasoning on a team mental model, which must be constructed from dialogue contexts and shared knowledge.

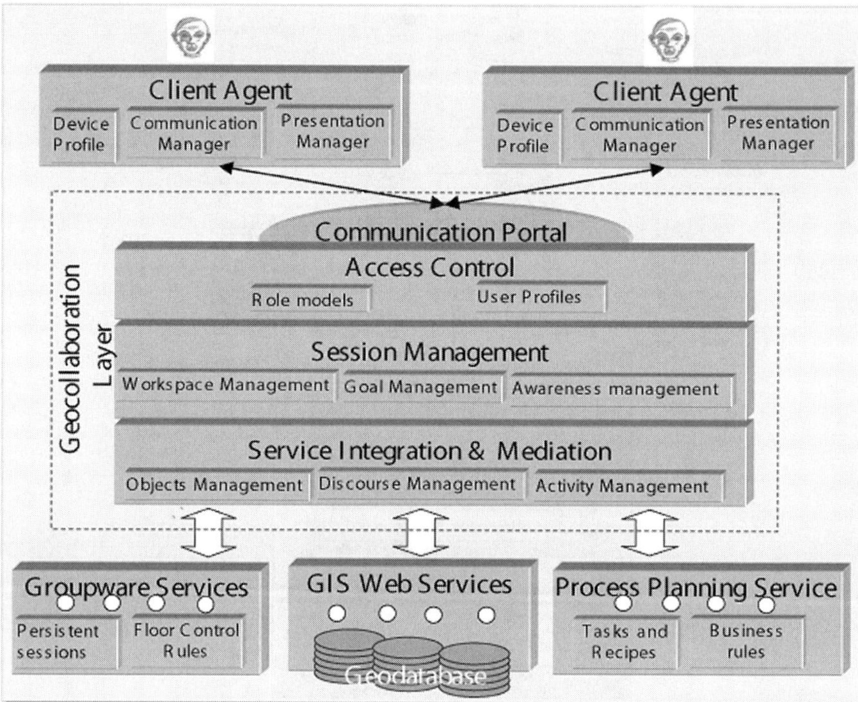

Figure 20-6. A distributed architecture of GCCM environment (after Cai 2005)

3.3 The Humanitarian Relief Logistics Web Portal

A massive tsunami strikes the coast of Thailand. Teams need to remove rubble; rescue efforts are being complicated by electric power outages in the area and a shortage of heavy equipment and generators. "We are in dire need of assistance and relief," particularly antibiotics and medical staff, the Foreign Ministry says. UNICEF deploys staff to Thailand and says it has prepared emergency supplies that include: 9,000 tarpaulins, 850 hygiene kits, 1,165 small tents, 753 large tents, 4,000 lanterns, 160 collapsible water tanks, 1,707 school kits, 50 school tents, 152 recreation kits, and 90 school-in-a-box school supplies. "A planeload of relief supplies also is on the way with more than 5,000 pounds of medical supplies and two portable water treatment facilities," the Foreign Ministry spokesperson says.

This scenario gives just a brief introduction into the essential logistics that go along with large-scale disasters. The Indian Ocean Tsunami that rippled across the globe on December 26, 2004, the 2005 hurricane season and other recent natural disasters have indicated the need for geospatial infrastructures that effectively support humanitarian logistics and response and facilitate planning and mitigation efforts on a national and international level. In order to meet these requirements we developed the Geo-collaborative Web Portal (GWP) as a prototype testbed for studying the potential of map-based, different place collaboration and coordination strategies and technologies. The goal of the GWP is to provide a common and intuitive interface through which asynchronous, geocollaborative activities can be conducted in support of humanitarian relief logistics operations (Figure 20-7).

The GWP is an active research effort for which an early prototype has been implemented. GWP development extends our GCCM efforts for useful

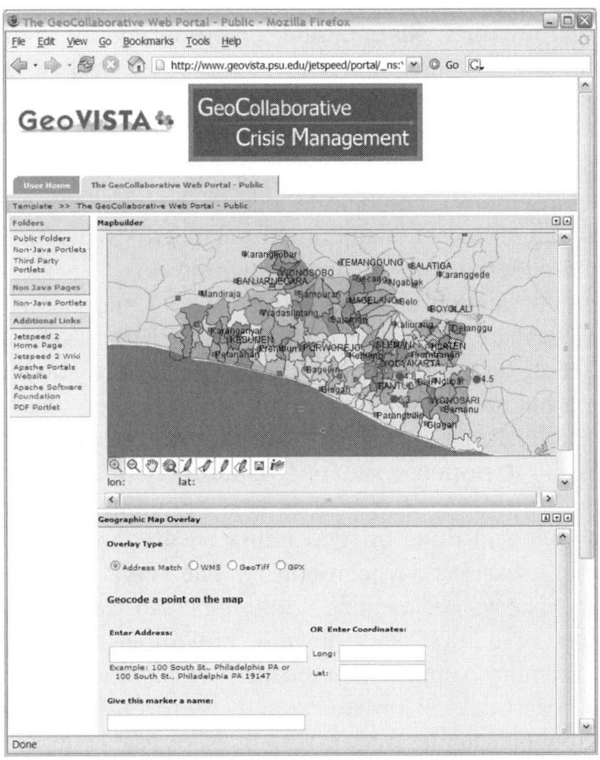

Figure 20-7. The Geocollaborative Web Portal (GWP)

and usable geoinformation technologies in emergency management to the context of international, multiorganization coordination, with a focus on support of relief and recovery efforts. The near-term goals for the GWP are to support situation assessment, positioning teams and distribution sites, and routing supplies. Special emphasis is being placed on supporting international group interaction through collaborative map annotation procedures, support for group activity awareness and transactive memory (through action histories), multi-lingual map feature labeling, organization-specific symbol sets to overcome communication barriers, and upload of photos and GPS feeds from the field. The GWP will facilitate asynchronous group knowledge development through: (a) integrating external resources (Web Map Services and Web Feature Services), (b) providing interactive concept maps with operation and command structures, (c) retrieving and storing of internal and external data and (d) displaying web syndications (news and blogs) through RSS (Really Simple Syndication 2.0) and GeoRSS (RSS feeds described by location).

The intention is that the web portal can be used as a central online location for information sharing and reporting by all parties (national and international) that are involved in response activities. Additional functionality that has been identified thus far as desirable includes: tracking of situational urgency at various locations (lack of food, medical supplies, etc.), support for efficient and relevant resource allocation, tools to enable relocating response crews, and help in identifying hierarchy issues that arise from coordinating different institutional perspectives (government agency policies vs. non-governmental organization policies).

The current application provides three different map-based collaboration components. They are discussed in detail elsewhere (Tomaszewski et al. 2006; Turton et al. submitted) with a brief summary provided here. The first component is a mapping session in which multiple users interact via a web map. Map administrators can add or remove collaborators, tools and functionalities as the response situation requires. Both single user and group interaction is controlled. Responders can be online at the same time interacting in near real time, or (depending on the time zone or workload) conduct mapping sessions asynchronously. The GWP functionality records the interaction history, i.e. panning, zooming, map extent, and annotation. This capability is a first step toward providing more comprehensive transactional memory support that enables collaborators (who may have never met) to keep track of (or execute a query to find out) who is likely to know details about particular places, resources, or past actions.

Another suite of tools in the GeoCollaborative Web Portal allows users to input a diverse range of geospatial data into the portal and subsequently share it with other collaborators using a variety of methods. Functions include real-time address geocoding, GPS data exchange (waypoints, routes, and tracks) through GPX (the GPS Exchange Format), geospatial image overlays, and dynamic Web Map Service and Web Feature Service data integration. These capabilities are based on Open Geospatial Consortium standards (for details see: Turton et al. (submitted).

Besides geographic maps, the GWP also enables concept map-based group work (for additional details, see: MacEachren et al. (working paper). The goal of the concept maps is to help collaborators to structure and share knowledge about relief logistics operations by understanding responsibilities and procedures, displaying different organizational policies in relief efforts and identifying logistics solutions. Dynamic links between the concept maps and the geographic map allow users to employ the concept map as an interface to information that may have a geographic component and to use the concept map to refocus the geographic map on the appropriate context.

The long term goal for the GWP development effort is to demonstrate (and empirically study) how geocollaborative technologies coupled with effective, intuitive information sharing can bridge potential language and cultural constraints between team members and lead to coordinated perspectives through the construction of team knowledge that can overcome issues inherent in disaster response collaboration.

4. DISCUSSION

Geoinformation technologies provide essential functions and methods for effective emergency management but these rather complex functionalities are usually available only to one GIS specialist at a time. Emergency management is a collaborative effort: it involves the police forces, fire departments, EMS, transportation planners, politicians and depending on the scale of the emergency many other individuals and agencies. Currently geoinformation technology restricts the range of potential users and narrows the chances for effective problem recognition and solving. This shortcoming needs to be overcome to meet the challenges of NIMS and in broader perspective support homeland preparedness and security requirements for future natural and human-generated disasters.

We outlined three geoinformation technology developments that support asynchronous and synchronous collaboration with geospatial data and enable communication, analysis, discussion, and decision-making within the emergency management group. The technologies we introduced are intelligent, multimodal user interfaces that allow synchronous and asynchronous collaboration between decision makers; support GIS use by mobile emergency management teams; and provide open standards-based web portal technologies to support multi-organization humanitarian relief activities. The developed applications replace traditional views on human-computer interaction. Mouse and keyboard interaction are replaced by natural language and gesture recognition, the advantages of multimodal interfaces have been extended to support mobile use of GIS, and we are beginning to work on support for international interfaces to map-based information.

Introducing useful and usable geoinformation technologies into emergency management represents a great challenge that can not be fulfilled without guidance and feedback from first responders and emergency managers. The applied human-centered design approach taken in the research summarized above, proved to support application design and implementation in an effective fashion. The quality of the applications was improved using an iterative design process that made extensive use of close interaction with domain specialists that enabled requirements and tasks analysis and collection of quantitative and qualitative feedback in usability testing sessions.

Rapid advances in geoinformation technologies are creating new opportunities and challenges and many research questions have not been answered, yet. Our evolving research on novel geoinformation and geovisualization technologies is being continued through the North-East Visualization & Analytics Center (NEVAC). The NEVAC is one of the five Regional Visualization Analytics Centers, funded by the Pacific Northwest National Laboratory through their Department of Homeland Security's National Visualization and Analytics Center (NVAC). The fundamental scientific objectives underlying the NEVAC are to: (a) understand how individuals and teams carry out analytical reasoning and decision making tasks with complex geoinformation technology and (b) using this understanding to develop and assess geoinformation technologies that enable these processes. The research results will influence and foster national and international geoinformation technology development for better emergency management and homeland security.

ACKNOWLEDGEMENTS

This material is based upon work supported by the National Science Foundation under Grants No. BCS-0113030, EIA-0306845; PI: Alan M. MacEachren, CoPIs: Rajeev Sharma, Guoray Cai, Michael McNeese, Sven Fuhrmann. Grateful appreciation goes to the following individuals for their assistance and support: Rajeev Sharma, Michael McNeese, Levent Bolelli, Isaac Brewer, Adrian Cox, Timothy Frazier, Marc Friedenberg, Xiaoyan

Liu, Bita Mortazavi, Joaquin Obieta, Scott Pezanowski, Ingmar Rauschert, Michael Stryker, Brian Tomaszewski, Ian Turton, Hongmei Wang, and Yinkun Xue. Any opinions, findings and conclusions or recommendations expressed in this material are those of the author(s) and do not necessarily reflect the views of the funding agency.

ACRONYM TABLE

Acronym	Short Description
DAVE_G	Dialog-Assisted Visual Environment for Geoinformation, developed at Penn State's GeoVISTA Center to enable speech and gesture-based GIS collaboration during emergencies.
EOC	Emergency Operation Center, central facility to manage a range of emergency situations.
GCCM	GeoCollaborative Crisis Management, a project at Penn State's GeoVISTA Center to support multimodal and map-mediated collaboration among EOCs and mobile teams.
DIMS	Disaster Management Interoperability Services, open platform that provides maps, tactical information exchange and weather information.
GeoMIP	Multimodal Interface Platform for Geographic Information Systems, commercial adoption of DAVE_G components.
GIS	Geographic Information Systems, software for integrating, analyzing and visualizing geospatial data.
GWP	GeoCollaborative Web Portal, developed at Penn State's GeoVISTA Center, prototype testbed for studying map-based, different place collaboration and coordination.
HAZUS-MH	Hazards U.S. Multi-Hazard, pre-event risk assessment and loss estimation software, developed by FEMA.
NIMS	National Incident Management System, core set of concepts, principles, terminologies, and technologies covering the incident commend system, multi-agency coordination, management of resources and additional topics in unified emergency management.

REFERENCES

Al-Kodmany, K. 2000. Extending Geographic Information Systems to Meet Neighborhood Planning Needs: The Case of Three Chicago Communities. *URISA Journal* 12 (3):19-37.

Andrienko, G., N. Andrienko, and P. Jankowski. 2003. Building Spatial Decision Support Tools for Individuals and Groups. *Journal of Decision Systems* 12 (2):193-208.

Armstrong, M. P. 1993. Perspectives on the development of group decision support systems for locational problem-solving. *Geographical Systems* 1 (1):69-81.

———. 1997. Emerging technologies and the changing nature of work in GIS. Paper read at American Congress on Surveying and Mapping, at Bethesda, MD.

Armstrong, M. P., and P. J. Densham. 1995. Collaborative spatial decision-making: A look at the dark side. Paper read at Proceedings of GIS/LIS '95, at Bethesda, MD.

Baldus, G., and J. Kim. 2005. Integrating GIS and real-time vehicle tracking for county emergency response. Paper read at 2005 ESRI International User Conference Proceedings, at San Diego.

Brewer, I. 2005. Understanding work with geospatial information in emergency management: A Cognitive Systems Engineering approach in GIscience, Department of Geography, The Pennsylvania State University, University Park, PA.

Cai, G. 2005. Extending distributed GIS to support geo-collaborative crisis management. *Geographic Information Science* 11 (1):4-14.

Cai, G., and A. M. MacEachren. 2005. Supporting effective human interactions with geographic information during crisis response. *GeoMatica* 59 (4):415-425.

Cai, G., H. Wang, and A. M. MacEachren. 2003. Communicating Vague Spatial Concepts in Human-GIS Interactions: A Collaborative Dialogue Approach. Paper read at COSIT 2003: Conference on Spatial Information Theory, 24-28 September, at Ittingen, Switzerland.

CNN.com. 2006. *Identification of 9/11 remains comes to an end* 2005 [cited 05/12/2006 2006]. Available from http://www.cnn.com/2005/US/02/22/wtc.identifications/.

Cohen, P., M. Johnston, D. McGee, S. Oviatt, J. Pittman, I. Smith, L. Chen, and J. Clow. 1997. QuickSet: Multimodal interaction for distributed applications. Paper read at Proceedings of the Fifth International Multimedia Conference (Multimedia '97), at Seattle.

Cohen, P., D. R. McGee, and J. Clow. 2000. The efficiency of multimodal interaction for a map-based task. Paper read at Proceedings of the Applied Natural Language Processing Conference, April 29 - May 4, at Seattle, WA.

Cova, T. J., and R. L. Church. 1997. Modelling community evacuation vulnerability using GIS. *International Journal of Geographical Information Science* 11 (8):763-784.

Cova, T. J., P. E. Dennison, T. H. Kim, and M. A. Moritz. 2005. Setting wildfire evacuation trigger points using fire spread modeling and GIS. *Transactions in GIS* 9 (4):603-617.

Curtis, A., J. W. Mills, J. K. Blackburn, and J. C. Pine. 2006. Hurricane Katrina: GIS response for a major metropolitan area, 7. Baton Rouge: Louisiana State University.

Cutter, S. L. 2003. GI Science, Disasters, and Emergency Management. *Transactions in GIS* 7 (4):439-445.

Dix, A. J., J. E. Finlay, G. D. Abowd, and R. Beale. 1998. *Human-Computer Interaction*. 2 ed. Englewood Cliffs: Prentice Hall.

ESRI. 2000. Challenges for GIS in emergency preparedness and response, 34. Redlands: ESRI.

FEMA. 2006. *IS-1 Emergency Manager: An Orientation to the Position*. Federal Emergency Management Agency 2005 [cited 05/12/2006 2006]. Available from http://training.fema.gov/EMIWeb/IS/is1lst.asp.

Greene, R. W. 2002. *Confronting Catastrophe: A GIS Handbook*. Redlands: ESRI Press.

Gunes, A. E., and J. P. Kovel. 2000. Using GIS in Emergency Management Operations. *Journal of Urban Planning and Development* 126 (3):136-149.

International Federation of Red Cross And Red Crescent Societies. 2006. *Indonesia: Yogyakarta Earthquake - Operation Update no.2*. ReliefWeb 2006 [cited 06/02/2006 2006]. Available from http://www.reliefweb.int/rw/RWB.NSF/db900SID/ABES-6QDPLM?OpenDocument.

Jankowski, P., and T. L. Nyerges. 2001a. *Geographic Information Systems for Group Decision Making: Towards a participatory, geographic information science*. New York: Taylor & Francis.
———. 2001b. GIS-supported collaborative decision making: Results of an experiment. *Annals of the Association of American Geographers* 91 (1):48-70.
Jeong, W., and M. Gluck. 2003. Multimodal Geographic Information Systems: Adding haptic and auditory display. *Journal of the American Society for Information Science and Technology* 54 (3):229-242.
Johnson, R. 2000. GIS technology for disasters and emergency management, 12. Redlands: ESRI.
Kettebekov, S., and R. Sharma. 2001. Toward natural gesture/speech control of a large display. Paper read at Engineering for Human-Computer Interaction, May 11 - 14, at Toronto.
Kevany, M. J. 2003. GIS in the World Trade Center attack - Trial by fire. *Computers, Environment and Urban Systems* 27:571-583.
Kwan, M.-P., and J. Lee. 2005. Emergency response after 0/11: the potential of real-time 3D GIS for quick emergency response in micro-spatial environments. *Computers, Environment and Urban Systems* 29:93-113.
Lamel, L., S. Bennacef, J. L. Gauvain, H. Dartiguest, and J. N. Temem. 1998. User Evaluation of the MASK Kiosk. Paper read at ICSLP 1998, at Sydney.
Levitan, M. L., and C. Hill. 2005. Residential wind damage in Hurricane Katrina - Preliminary estimates and potential loss reduction through improved building codes and construction practices, 9. Baton Rouge: LSU Hurricane Center, Louisiana State University.
MacEachren, A. M. 2000. Cartography and GIS: facilitating collaboration. *Progress in Human Geography* 24 (3):445-456.
———. 2001. Cartography and GIS: Extending collaborative tools to support virtual teams. *Progress in Human Geography* 25 (3):431-444.
———. 2005. Moving geovisualization toward support for group work. In *Exploring geovisualization*, eds. J. Dykes, A. M. MacEachren and M.-J. Kraak, 445-461. Amsterdam: Elsevier.
MacEachren, A. M., and I. Brewer. 2004. Developing a conceptual framework for visually-enabled geocollaboration. *International Journal of Geographical Information Science* 18 (1):1-34.
MacEachren, A. M., G. Cai, R. Sharma, I. Rauschert, I. Brewer, L. Bolelli, B. Shaparenko, S. Fuhrmann, and H. Wang. 2005. Enabling collaborative geoinformation access and decision-making through a natural, multimodal interface. *International Journal of Geographical Information Science* 19 (3):293-317.
MacEachren, A. M., X. Liu, S. Pezanowski, and B. M. Tomaszewski. working paper. Bridging forms of knowledge for crisis management: Concept maps to geographic maps.
Maguire, D. J., and P. A. Longley. 2005. The emergence of geoportals and their role in spatial data infrastructures. *Computers, Environment and Urban Systems* 29 (1):3-14.
Mansourian, A., A. Rajabifard, M. J. Valadan Zoej, and I. Williamson. 2006. Using SDI and web-based system to facilitate disaster management. *Computers & Geosciences* 32:303-315.
NIMS Integration Center. 2005a. State and territorial compliance activities: Federal fiscal year 2006, 13: DHS/FEMA.
———. 2005b. Tribal government and local jurisdiction compliance activities: Federal fiscal year 2006, 13: DHS/FEMA.

Oliver, C. 2004. FEMA employs new state-of-the-art technology to predict losses from hurricane Isabel, 11: FEMA.

Oviatt, S. 2003. Multimodal interfaces. In *The Human-Computer Interaction Handbook: Fundamentals, Evolving Technologies and Emerging Applications*, eds. J. A. Jacko and A. Sears, 286-304. Mahwah: Lawrence Erlbaum.

Quinn, B. B. 2000. HAZUS - Getting back to business. *Geospatial Solutions* October 2000.

Rasmussen, J., A. M. Pejtersen, and L. P. Goodstein. 1994. *Cognitive engineering: Concepts and applications*. New York: J. Wiley & Sons.

Rocha, A., B. Cestnik, and M. A. Oliveira. 2005. Interoperable Geographic Information Services to Support Crisis Management. In *Lecture Notes in Computer Science - Web and Wireless Geographical Information Systems: 5th International Workshop, W2GIS 2005, Lausanne, Switzerland, December 15-16, 2005. Proceedings* eds. K.-J. Li and C. Vangenot, 246-255. Berlin: Springer.

Schafer, W. A., C. H. Ganoe, L. Xiao, G. Coch, and J. M. Carroll. 2005. Designing the next generation of distributed, geocollaborative tools. *Cartography and Geographic Information Science* 32 (2):81-100.

Schlaisich, I., and M. J. Egenhofer. 2001. Multimodal spatial querying: What people sketch and talk about. Paper read at 1st International Conference on Universal Access in Human-Computer Interaction, at New Orleans.

Schoemaker, L., J. Nijtmans, A. Camurri, F. Lavagetto, P. Morasso, C. Benoit, T. Guiard-Marigny, B. Le Goff, J. Robert-Ribes, A. Adjoudani, I. Defee, S. Munch, K. Hartung, and J. Blauert. 1995. A taxonomy of multimodal interaction in the human information processing system. Miami: Esprit Basic Research Action 8579.

Sharma, R., I. Poddar, E. Ozyildiz, S. Kettebekov, H. Kim, and T. S. Huang. 1999. Toward interpretation of natural speech/gesture: Spatial planning on a virtual map. Paper read at Proceedings of ARL Advanced Displays Annual Symposium, at Adelphi, MD.

Sharma, R., M. Yeasin, N. Krahnstoever, I. Rauschert, G. Cai, I. Brewer, A. M. MacEachren, and K. Sengupta. 2003. Speech-gesture driven multimodal interfaces for crisis management. *Proceedings of the IEEE* 91 (9):1327-1354.

Shneiderman, B. 1998. *Designing the user interface - Strategies for effective human-computer interaction*. 3 ed. Reading: Addison-Wesley Publishing Company.

Srinivasan, D. 2003. Battling hazards with a brand new tool. *Planning* February 2003:10-13.

Tomaszewski, B. M., A. M. MacEachren, S. Pezanowski, X. Liu, and I. Turton. 2006. Supporting Humanitarian Relief Logistics Operations through Online Geocollaborative Knowledge Management. Paper read at Proceedings of The National Conference on Digital Government Research, May 21-24, 2006, at San Diego, CA.

Turton, I., B. M. Tomaszewski, S. Pezanowski, and A. M. MacEachren. Submitted. An OGC standards approach to web-based geocollaboration.

U.S. Department of Homeland Security. 2004. National Incident Management System, 139. Washington D.C.: U.S. Department of Homeland Security.

United Nations. 2006. *The human toll*. Office of the Secretary-General's Special Envoy for Tsunami Recovery 2006 [cited 05/12/2006 2006]. Available from http://www. tsunamispecialenvoy.org/ country/humantoll.asp.

White House. 2006. *The Presidential Disaster Management Initiative*. White House 2006 [cited 05/12/2006 2006]. Available from http://www.whitehouse.gov/omb/e-gov/c-2-2-disaster.html.

Wikipedia. 2006. *Hurricane Katrina*. Wikipedia 2006 [cited 06/02/2006 2006]. Available from http://en.wikipedia.org/wiki/Hurricane_Katrina.

Yuan, Y., and B. Detlor. 2005. Intelligent Mobile Crisis Response Systems. *Communications of the ACM* 48 (2):95-98.
Zerger, A., and D. I. Smith. 2003. Impediments to using GIS for real-time disaster decision support. *Computers, Environment and Urban Systems* 27:123-141.

SUGGESTED READINGS

- Longley, P. A., M. F. Goodchild, et al. (2005). Geographic Information Systems and Science. Chichester, John Wiley & Sons. *Gives an essential* introduction into the field of GIScience and the geoinformation technology.
- Dykes, J., A. M. MacEachren, et al., Eds. (2005). Exploring Geovisualization. Amsterdam, Elsevier. Provides an exclusive overview about cutting-edge geovisualization research.
- Greene, R. W. (2002). Confronting Catastrophe: A GIS Handbook. Redlands, ESRI Press. Introduces the use of GIS in emergency management and lists development challenges.
- Oviatt, S. (2003). Multimodal interfaces. The Human-Computer Interaction Handbook: Fundamentals, Evolving Technologies and Emerging Applications. J. A. Jacko and A. Sears. Mahwah, Lawrence Erlbaum: 286-304. Narrates over the design and integration of multimodal interfaces in IT products.
- Thomas, J. J. and K. A. Cook, Eds. (2005). Illuminating the path - The research and development agenda for visual analytics. Los Alamitos, IEEE Computer Society. The latest research agenda in the important field of visual analytics.

ONLINE RESOURCES

- Department of Homeland Security:http://www.dhs.gov
- Official Web Portal of 26 U.S. government agencies that are concerned with emergency management and homeland security: http://www.disasterhelp.gov
- GeoVISTA Center, The Pennsylvania State University: http://www.geovista.psu.edu
- HAZUS - FEMA's Software Program for Estimating Potential Losses from Disasters: http://www.fema.gov/plan/prevent/hazus/index.shtm

- The National Incident Management System (NIMS) Integration Center: http://www.fema.gov/emergency/nims/nims.shtm
- United Nations website providing information to humanitarian relief organizations: http://www.reliefweb.int

QUESTIONS FOR DISCUSSION

1. Which emergency management tasks would benefit the most from provision of more current, relevant information available where and when it is needed?
2. For what aspects of emergency management is collaboration most critical and what kinds of collaboration need to be supported?
3. How does the role of geospatial information (and GIS) vary across the emergency management stages and among different kinds of emergencies? Give examples.
4. Why are Geographic Information Systems essential for emergency management?
5. What are the major shortcomings of Geographic Information Systems in emergency management?
6. What are the benefits of multimodal user interfaces for Geographic Information Systems?

Chapter 21

SUSTAINABLE CROSS-BOUNDARY INFORMATION SHARING

Theresa A. Pardo, J. Ramon Gil-Garcia, and G. Brian Burke

Center for Technology in Government, University at Albany, State University of New York, Albany, New York, U.S.A. ([tpardo, jgil-garcia,bburke]@ctg.albany.edu)

CHAPTER OVERVIEW

Information is one of the most valuable resources in government. Government managers are finding however, that information needed to plan, make decisions, and act is often held outside their own organizations, maintained in disparate formats, and used for widely different purposes. Efforts to bring this data together across boundaries have provided new understanding into just how difficult cross-boundary information sharing is. Finding ways to bring together information and integrate it for use in solving pressing public problems is fast becoming a focus of attention for digital government practitioners and researchers alike. This chapter reports on one such study[1] of cross-boundary information integration that revealed three important lessons for creating and sustaining cross-boundary information sharing: 1) interoperability is key, 2) a shift in agency culture is necessary, and 3) the role of policy-makers is central to this type of project. Four recommendations for action derived from the case studies are presented as well. Government executives and policy-makers need to ensure the creation of enterprise-wide mechanisms and capabilities such as (1) governance structures, (2) resource allocation models, (3) scalable strategies, and (4) non-crisis capacity.

[1] The project is funded in part through a grant from the National Science Foundation, grant number ITR-0205152.

1. INTRODUCTION

Information is one of the most valuable resources in government. Anderson and Dawes characterize information as the primary input to, and product of, government activity. They identify collecting it, housing it, protecting and using it as fundamental responsibilities of the public sector (Anderson and Dawes, 1991). Information sharing is key to government's ability to work effectively across organizational boundaries. Agency heads and program managers are finding that information needed to plan, make decisions and act is often held outside their own organizations, maintained in disparate formats and used for widely different purposes. Finding ways to bring together information and integrate it for use in solving pressing public problems is fast becoming a focus of attention for digital government practitioners and researchers alike. Efforts to create resources for practitioners are underway at federal, state and local levels (See the list of related readings and online references). And information integration as a topic of study has receiving increasing attention from funding organizations in the US, such as the National Science Foundation, the Office of Homeland Security, the Department of Health and Human Services, and the Department of Justice.

Overcoming the challenges to information integration requires managers and policy-makers from multiple organizations and levels of government to come together to create new capabilities to share information across boundaries. This chapter reports on a study[2] of cross-boundary information integration that revealed three important lessons for creating and sustaining cross-boundary information sharing: 1) interoperability is key, 2) a shift in agency culture is necessary, and 3) the role of policy-makers is central to this type of project (Pardo and Burke, 2005). Four recommendations for action derived from the case studies are presented as well. Government executives and policy-makers need to ensure the creation of enterprise-wide mechanisms and capabilities such as (1) governance structures, (2) resource allocation models, (3) scalable strategies, and (4) non-crisis capacity.

2. INTERORGANIZATIONAL INFORMATION INTEGRATION

Information integration (1) is a critical component in the design and implementation of several advanced information technologies, such as data

[2] The project is funded in part through a grant from the National Science Foundation, grant number ITR-0205152.

mining and visualization, (2) involves phenomena and theoretical frameworks in several disciplines, and (3) is a lynch pin in a substantial range of IT use in critical public policy areas such as public safety, environmental protection, crisis response and management, and health care. In a simple conceptualization, information integration allows managers to work at the same time, with the same information drawn from multiple disparate sources. In a more complex form, it has the potential to support the transformation of organizational structures and communication channels between and among multiple agencies working in different locations. It requires radical technical and organizational process and behavior changes for the individuals and organizations involved (Pardo, et al., 2006). Organizations must establish and maintain collaborative relationships in which knowledge sharing is critical to resolving numerous issues relating to data definitions and structures, diverse database designs, highly variable data quality, and incompatible network infrastructure. These integration processes often involve new work processes and significant organizational change. They are also embedded in larger political and institutional environments which shape their goals and circumscribe their choices (Center for Technology in Government, 2002).

While many acknowledge the importance of information integration for health care and other policy domains, the 2004 bipartisan *9/11 Commission Report* presented a sobering picture of the public sector's current ability to leverage information. It emphasized that a weak system for processing and using information impedes the U.S. government's ability to best use the vast amount of information to which it has access. It seems clear that governments could be more efficient and effective if they had the capability to integrate and use the information they already collect and store (Caffrey, 1998 and Dawes and Pardo, 2002).

Despite its numerous challenges, support for information integration transcends partisan politics and crosses multiple policy areas or enterprises. In an August 2004 op-ed in *The Washington Post*, Senators Hillary Clinton and Bill Frist called on the United States to realize the information revolution's full potential to improve the nation's health-care system. Both senators wrote that using technology to integrate information would improve care, lower costs, improve quality and empower consumers.

Integrating and sharing information across traditional government boundaries involves complex interactions among technical and organizational processes. From a technical perspective, system designers and developers must regularly overcome problems related to the existence of multiple platforms, diverse database designs and data structures, highly variable data quality, and incompatible network infrastructure (Ambite and Knoblock, 1997 and Krishnan, et al., 2001). From an organizational perspective, these technical processes often involve new work processes, mobilization of limited resources, and evolving interorganizational relationships (Davenport, 1993 and Fountain, 2001). These necessary changes are influenced by specific types of social interaction, which take the form of group decision-making, learning, understanding, trust building, and conflict resolution, among others (Chua, 2002, Powell, et al., 1996, and Wastell, 1999).

Government executives are leading agency efforts to integrate information resources across agency boundaries, across levels of government and across governmental jurisdictions. However, while armed with the most advanced IT in the world, they are finding the task exceedingly difficult, leading to serious problems, quick disintegration, or outright failures (Fountain, 2001 and Dawes and Pardo, 2002). Moreover, the difficulty that government agencies face increases proportionally with the increases in the number of boundaries to be crossed, the number and type of information resources to be shared, and the number of technical and organizational processes to be changed or integrated.

Information integration, as well as information sharing, offers organizations a greater capacity to share information across organizational boundaries, to discover patterns and interactions, and to make better informed decisions based on more complete data (Dawes, 1996). Increased productivity, improved decision-making, reduced costs, increased revenues, and integrated services have been identified as positive results as well (Gil-Garcia and Pardo, 2005).

Understanding the type of information sharing being pursued and the challenges associated with achieving the stated objectives is important to understanding the benefits that organizations can expect to realize. The benefits realized from information integration differ from organization to organization and according to characteristics of specific projects. However, there are certain types of benefits that can be expected in almost any information integration or information sharing initiative. Dawes classifies these benefits into three categories: technical, organizational, and political (Dawes, 1996).

2.1 Technical Benefits

Technical benefits are those related to data processing and information management. For instance, information integration reduces duplicate data collection, processing, and storage, and therefore reduces data processing costs that attend every public program (Caffrey, 1998). An information integration initiative can also promote better standards and shared technical resources.

2.1.1 Organizational benefits

Organizational benefits are related to the solution of agency-wide problems or the enhancement of organizational capabilities. Improving the decision making process, broadening professional networks, improving coordination, increasing the quality of services, and reducing costs are some examples of organizational benefits (Anderson and Dawes, 1991 and Gil-Garcia and Pardo, 2005).

2.1.2 Political benefits

Political benefits might include better appreciation for government-wide policy goals, more public accountability, more comprehensive public information, integrated planning, and service delivery (Anderson and Dawes, 1991). Political benefits can also be considered as individual benefits for public officials as a result of the use of specific technology characteristics or applications.

2.2 Understanding the Complexity of Integration Initiatives

Information integration, like many other IT-related initiatives, presents organizations with tremendous challenges. These challenges result from the reality that integrating information ultimately involves large parts, if not the whole, of an enterprise or policy domain. This situation is made even more challenging by the fact that these enterprises differ greatly among states and localities. Those involved in integration initiatives must be aware of the differences and the implications of those differences as they look to their colleagues for guidance and best practices.

For instance, some initiatives focus on a specific problem while others focus on building systemic capacity. Table 21-1 shows one way to classify integration initiatives in terms of their focus and the associated level of organizational involvement. Without oversimplifying the important factors contributing to the success of an information integration initiative, there seems to be a logical progression of complexity. Specific characteristics of each initiative, such as the number of participants or the institutional framework, will influence the final result.

In general terms these dimensions help to characterize the challenges being faced by government practitioners seeking to share information across boundaries. For example, an inter-governmental initiative with a focus on building systemic capacity can be generally understood as more complex than an intra-organizational initiative focusing on a specific need or problem. The cases presented in this chapter can be classified as D, E, or F type integration initiatives. Therefore, they are high complexity initiatives.

Table 21-1. Types of integration initiatives*

Organizational Level	Focus on meeting a specific need or problem	Focus on building a systemic capacity
Inter-Governmental	E	F
Inter-Organizational	C	D
Intra-Organizational	A	B

**Adapted from Gil-Garcia, et al., 2005*

3. STUDY METHODOLOGY

This study examines cross-boundary information sharing through a case study methodology encompassing documentation analysis and semi-structured interviews. This research project concentrates on information integration activities in criminal justice and public health, since they include a full range of functions across all three levels of government. These are also areas in which significant integration initiatives are underway and available for study.

Semi-structured interviews were conducted with public managers and other actors involved in criminal justice and public health information integration initiatives at the state and local level. The public health cases focused on the immediate response to and subsequent preparation for the West Nile Virus outbreaks in Colorado, Oregon, Connecticut, and New York. The criminal justice cases included cross-boundary information integration initiatives in the states of New York, North Carolina, Colorado, and New York City. The interviews addressed three basic questions:

1. What are the critical factors and processes involved in integrating information across levels and agencies in government? In particular we are interested in analyzing how IT and social factors interact to influence the effectiveness of interorganizational information integration.
2. How do the factors and processes vary for different types and degrees of integration?
3. Can the processes be modeled in ways that improve our understanding of information system development and of interorganizational collaboration? Do these models contribute to new theoretical insights for developing and implementing advanced applications of IT?

The research team developed a coding scheme following an inductive logic and using grounded theory techniques (Glaser, 1992, Glaser and

Strauss, 1997, and Strauss and Corbin, 1998). Atlas.ti, a qualitative analysis software tool, was used to support coding and analysis activities. First, based on a sample of interview transcripts, an initial coding scheme was developed by the research team. Second, using this coding scheme, researchers carefully read and coded the rest of the transcripts, always having coordination meetings to make additions and refinements to the initial list of codes. Third, the research team looked for concepts and categories that were well represented in the data as well as the relationships among them. Fourth, a preliminary theoretical model was developed and refined through several iterations to ensure that each variable and relationship was grounded in the interview data. Finally, a high-level conceptual model was developed and the research team derived lessons and recommendations for practice.

4. INFORMATION INTEGRATION IN CRIMINAL JUSTICE AND PUBLIC HEALTH

The arguments for creating capability for sustainable information sharing programs in public health and safety are compelling. As a result, agencies in these domains tend to be early adopters of integrated information resources. In fact, public health and criminal justice are examples of domains that have recognized the value of sharing data across organizational boundaries and already boast of many successful information integration initiatives.

In the public health enterprise, for example, the Centers for Disease Control and Prevention (CDC) spent the last five years promoting information integration to provide timely, high-quality data and information at all levels of government. Information integration presents great benefits not only for daily operation activities, but also for public health emergency response. Gathering, handling and sharing information in response to a public health crisis, such as the emergence of the West Nile Virus (WNV), requires not only great interorganizational coordination and communication, but also adequate technical capacity for sharing information across organizational boundaries and among multiple levels of government.

The U.S. Department of Justice (DOJ), also an early adopter, has encouraged and supported enterprise-wide criminal justice information integration between and among federal, state and local justice agencies. Information sharing, according to Domingo Herraiz, director of the Bureau of Justice Assistance in the DOJ's Office of Justice Programs, is the "cross-cutting prevention piece" that will allow communities to reduce crime and fight terrorism. The DOJ is investing in information sharing in the justice enterprise by developing technical tools such as XML standards for justice information sharing. Information integration can provide important benefits to this type of initiative, which have the objective of creating systemic capacity for the medium and long term. Public health and safety, as stated above, illustrate compelling benefits of information integration. The complexity of these environments, however, makes the challenges quite compelling as well. To better understand these complexities, we examined

Table 21-2. Basic Characteristics of the Cases

Case Site	Focus of Effort	Involved Parties
Justice Cases		
New York State	Create a portal for delivery of integrated justice services.	New York State Division of Criminal Justice Services, the Director of Criminal Justice, New York State Police, New York State Department of Corrections, and various other state agencies.
New York City District Attor-ney's Office	Integrate 70+ disparate databases into a single usable information repository.	Several units of the New York City District Attorney's Office
North Carolina	Develop an integrated justice information repository.	North Carolina Justice Agencies, various county and municipal agencies.
Colorado	Expand a nationally recognized information sharing model to other areas of the criminal justice enterprise.	State of Colorado Justice Agencies, Colorado Legislature
Public Health Cases		
New York State	Develop and implement a strategy for responding to the reemergence of WNV.	New York State Department of Health, the New York City Health Department, The Center for Disease Control, State Wildlife pathologist, various county and municipal govern-ments as well as other state agencies.
Colorado	Develop and implement a strategy for responding to the reemergence of WNV.	Colorado Department of Health, The Center for Disease control, various county and municipal governments as well as other state and federal agencies.
Oregon	Develop and implement a strategy for responding to the reemergence of WNV.	Oregon Department of Health, State Veterinarian, various state, county, and municipal govern-ments as well as other federal agencies.
Connecticut	Develop and implement a strategy for responding to the reemergence of WNV.	Central Connecticut Health District, Connecticut Department of Public Health, Department of Environmental Protection

eight public health and integrated justice projects. The project sites (see Table 21-2) were selected based on three criteria: complexity, integration status, and the availability of a governance body. An effort was also made to include various geographic regions of the US.

One interesting and important variation among the cases was the focus of effort. The public health cases all had the same focus – to develop and implement a strategy for responding to the reemergence of WNV. The capability of each state, however, to develop a fully integrated, sustainable information resource varied considerably. In the justice cases, both focus and capability varied considerably. The one characteristic the justice cases had in common was that none of the states were in crisis response. The public health cases were in crisis-response mode; they were all responding to an imminent threat. The similarities and differences among the cases provide a robust set of conclusions about lessons learned and recommendations for action that apply across variations in information integration project focus, the complexity of the project, the stage of integration and the form and format of current governance structures. The recommendations appear to be relevant to both crisis and non-crisis-based responses.

5. MAIN LESSONS

Government leaders and IT executives increasingly recognize cross-boundary information sharing as a critical and complex process. These executives and the agencies they lead are finding their involvement in these efforts goes much deeper than adopting new suites of IT software and hardware. They realize that successful information sharing requires a cross-agency evaluation of how individual agencies acquire and mobilize a wide range of resources, including IT. The difficulty of this task boils down to the ability of a cross-agency group to resolve conflict among organizations and make decisions and mobilize organizational resources across intergovernmental and interorganizational boundaries. Three lessons in particular stand out from the others in terms of value to practitioners as they pursue governmental reform objectives through cross-boundary information integration. These lessons are presented below, followed by specific recommendations for action.

5.1 The Key Is Interoperability

Technological advances made data integration possible, but research and practical experience tell us that technology alone cannot solve information integration problems. The solution also requires management and policy interoperability. Creating processes that span organizations — in a sense, achieving management interoperability — requires a wide range of skills and tenacity. Paul Hutcheon, health director for the Central Connecticut Health District, drew on these skills in his efforts to develop a health district among several towns in central Connecticut. Health districts in Connecticut are designed to maximize public health services by integrating scarce public health resources and attracting additional state funding. They provide an organizing framework, and in some cases, are precursors to full health information integration. Hutcheon faced significant resistance in trying to get local legislative leaders on board. "Each town council member was concerned about losing local control. It's always the biggest initial issue, but it never turns out to be a real issue," he said. "It's really a fear of the unknown."

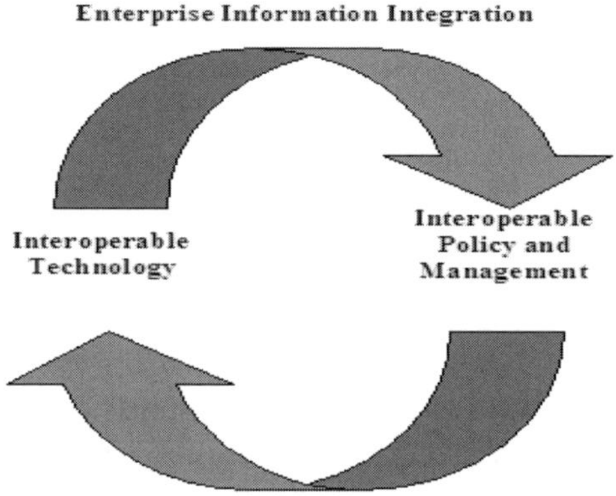

Figure 21-1. Interoperability and Information Integration

Making the argument about the return on investment for resource integration within one agency is difficult enough, but making it across many localities is daunting. Local officials had to decide whether to spend money on local efforts versus investing in an integrated approach with an unclear direct benefit. Responsible officials must ask questions, such as: Do we have to spend more money to be a part of the district? How much will it cost? What are we going to get from it? Are we going to get more than we have now?

Hutcheon mentioned that communicating directly with local officials, over a period of four years, was the only way to succeed. "Not that everybody gets sold on it," he said, "but you get enough votes to say, OK." For each potential integration partner, Hutcheon worked to allay local concerns. Hutcheon's challenge was showing how investment in a health district, which required the integration of town public health resources, including information, would serve local constituencies' needs.

5.2 Shifting Agency Culture

Changing old work models, according to Martin Cirincione, executive deputy commissioner at the New York State Division of Criminal Justice Services, is a critical step in integration processes. Agency culture presented an initial barrier to New York's enterprise-wide justice information integration initiative, eJusticeNY. "The culture within criminal justice agencies is inherently conservative. If you look at all the different functions performed by government, probably the oldest and most basic is public safety and the maintenance of order in society. Justice agencies have been around for a long time with this same mission."

It is not always easy to keep the right balance between a strong mission-driven culture and innovative uses of information technologies. "Our challenge is adopting new tools along the way that enable us to continue to achieve this mission. Realizing the full potential of information as a tool requires new ways of working and new technologies. We want one point of access that enables us to remain focused on our mission — while taking advantage of new ways to support that mission." Breaking through the conservative nature of most agencies, justice or otherwise, is what makes things work.

5.3 The Central Role of Policy-Makers

Managers can successfully face many of these challenges, but there are others that require the intervention of policy-makers. One of the most powerful lessons learned is that only legislators and government policy-makers have the power to alleviate key constraints on enterprise-wide, sustainable information integration strategies. These constraints are of particular concern as integration teams expand their efforts beyond agency-based, single problem-focused initiatives to enterprise-wide information integration. For information integration's value to be realized at the enterprise level, CIOs must work with elected officials and policy-makers to bridge the gap between what can be accomplished through project-level innovation and what is necessary for enterprise-wide change.

Past legislation and executive policies, often enacted in response to a specific set of conditions, can inadvertently create institutional constraints that make already difficult management tasks even more problematic. Since 1998, according to Theresa Brandorff, former director and CIO for the Colorado Integrated Criminal Justice Information System (CICJIS), criminal justice agencies in Colorado have worked within a legislated initiative enacted to improve the matching of criminal dispositions across local and state law enforcement, and legal organizations in Colorado. The legislation, however, tied funding and decision-making to this single issue, and did not allow for future needs, said Brandorff. "It hampers agency efforts to expand Colorado's nationally recognized information sharing model to other areas of the criminal justice enterprise and to other enterprises, such as homeland security." As CIO, Brandorff played a critical role in translating the needs of public managers into action recommendations for legislators and government policy-makers. This translation resulted in a new bill that was passed by the Colorado General Assembly and signed by Governor Bill Owens.

6. TAKING ACTION

Policy-makers, with the help of CIOs, can begin to back up their calls for sustainable integrated information resources through the development of policies that eliminate environmental constraints. Four recommendations present a starting point for the policy-making.

6.1 Create Effective Cross-Boundary Governance Processes

Information integration projects often blur lines of authority and conflict with existing agency decision-making mechanisms. Cross-boundary governance structures need their own clear lines of authority and realistic membership rosters that recognize the political realities of public-sector decision-making. These should not arbitrarily replace existing lines of authority with cross-boundary governance structures that disregard how decision-making flows through agencies and branches of government. Rather, they must complement traditional mechanisms with transparent, realistic and flexible cross-boundary governance structures that, over time, can handle more and more challenging needs.

CIOs play a critical role in initiating legislative and executive policy changes — changes that will enable governance structures to adapt to changing information integration needs. Brandorff noted that CIOs played a crucial role in Colorado's efforts to expand its successful information sharing model. "After acknowledging that the current statutes limited the CICJIS governance body in its efforts to expand operations with others as opportunities arise," she said, "the CIOs of our justice agencies were able to work with their executive directors to craft new statutory language that would enable the executive directors to expand the CICJIS model."

6.2 Create Enterprise-Oriented Resource Allocation Models

Many government managers are hesitant to participate in information integration projects due to demands the projects make on funds already committed to agency-based programs. Past experience tells decision-makers that new cross-boundary integration projects drain people and money from already overstretched budgets, and most existing resource allocation models do not allow for the movement of money or people across agency lines. The National Governors Association pointed out in a 2002 report that stovepiped funding mechanisms often hinder integration projects. Consequently, even when agencies recognize the value of integration efforts and are willing to commit resources, they can do so only in fits and bursts. But as projects become more complex and long term, they are stymied by the inevitable limitations of the old models. Even in situations where integration initiatives are sanctioned by key leaders, participation and commitment are severely limited by these conditions.

Many recognize that legislation must lay the foundation for resource allocation models that recognize and account for this new way of working. In the Central Connecticut Health District, Hutcheon regularly saw his efforts challenged by traditional rules. "Another challenge we've been facing throughout the state of Connecticut is to get the state Legislature to address the existing insufficient capacity of local health departments to provide day-to-day basic public health functions, much less during a public health emergency," he said. Current legislation under committee review in the Connecticut General Assembly proposes a resource allocation model that would perpetuate public health "stovepipes" at the local government level by funding numerous part-time public health directors throughout Connecticut to provide specific emergency response functions.

Unfortunately emergency response is only one of 10 public health service areas mandated by the U.S. Centers for Disease Control and Prevention. Alternative legislation, also under committee review and supported by the Connecticut Association of Directors of Health, includes a different resource allocation model that would facilitate the integration of public health resources across localities so towns could draw on full-time health departments that provide the full range of public health services rather than just emergency response.

6.3 Invest in Scalable Strategies

Many information integration projects unintentionally create new information silos in the form of horizontal "islands of information." An island of information is a collection of information related to a single problem or issue that only a select group of agencies may access. Past legislation and executive policies have often failed to recognize that enterprises are not static or forever tied to a single issue. Enterprises and their member agencies change and will continue to change based on the needs of the government and its citizens. While policies related to information integration often stem from the need to solve a specific problem, they also present leaders with the opportunity to make policies scalable to new issues and sustainable over time.

Dr. Amy Sullivan, Epidemiologist with Oregon's Multnomah County Health Department's Disease Prevention and Control Division, described her challenges collaborating with external agencies on problem-specific and temporary or seasonal programs, such as West Nile Virus (WNV), compared to broader systemic programs, such as bio-terrorism. "In planning for a WNV outbreak, I know the specific people in the specific agencies I need to work with to get the information my health department needs to most effectively support our county leadership and public. In support of my agency's bio-terrorism mission, I'm often dealing with agencies on a much more institutional level," she said. "And honestly, the interactions with individual people in problem-specific situations are just fine, whereas the institutional interactions on larger programs, such as bio-terrorism, can be more complicated."

6.4 Reduce Barriers to Noncrisis Capacity Building

Government agencies react well to crises, in part because they loosen the institutional and organizational constraints on multiorganizational efforts, such as information integration. Crisis response is myopic, however, because resources are targeted to respond to a specific situation. Committing resources to build government's overall response readiness becomes a priority on the public agenda following a crisis, but then tends to recede as quickly as it emerged. Government leaders have the exclusive ability to sustain investments in overall response readiness by creating an environment that enables enterprise-wide integrated information to be cultivated and improved over time so they are available to help avoid and respond to future crises. Investment in readiness requires tangible resources, such as personnel, equipment and infrastructure, but less tangible resources, such as capacities for collaboration among various government agencies, can be even more critical.

Multnomah County's Dr. Sullivan has also found that for agencies to achieve information integration on a more systemic and institutional level, they must understand each other's missions and needs. To achieve this level of understanding, she said, agencies go through several stages of collaboration. The first stage is "shake hands." Meet and get to know the people from agencies you will be working with. The second stage is to coordinate planning and training with agencies through exercises and routine responses. Only after going through these first two stages can agencies reach the stage of true information integration. Building this collaboration capacity takes time and resources, and only through legislative and executive support can individual agencies begin to work through the first two stages and be prepared for information integration when and wherever it's needed.

7. CONCLUSION

While government managers play their own essential roles in government information integration, legislators and government executives alone have the power to change environmental constraints that impede the ultimate success of information sharing initiatives. Public-sector executives, in particular chief information officers, can be the bridge between agency efforts to put information to work and policy-makers' efforts to create the environment necessary for this work to succeed. Policy-makers must be made aware that the very legislation they put forward in pursuit of better government may, in fact, constrain efforts to deliver exactly the results they seek.

REFERENCES

Aldine de Gruyter; Strauss, A., & Corbin, J. (1997). Grounded theory in practice. Thousand Oaks, CA: Sage Publications.

Ambite, J. L., and Knoblock, C. A. "Agents for Information Gathering," *IEEE Expert Intelligence Systems & Their Applications* (12:5), 1997, pp. 2-5; Krishnan, R., Li, X., Steier, D., and Zhao, L. "On Heterogeneous Database Retrieval: A Cognitively Guided Approach." *Information Systems Research* (12:3), 2001, pp. 286-301.

Andersen, D. F., and Dawes, S. S. *Government information management. A primer and casebook*. Prentice Hall, Englewood Cliffs, NJ, 1991; Gil-García, J. R., and Pardo, T. A. "E-government success factors: Mapping practical tools to theoretical foundations," Government Information Quarterly (22:2), 2005.

Bardach, E. *Getting agencies to work together: The practice and theory of managerial craftsmanship*. Brookings Institution Press, Washington, DC, 1998.

Caffrey, L. *Information sharing between & within governments*. Commonwealth Secretariat, London, 1998.

Chua, A. "The influence of social interaction on knowledge creation," *Journal of Intellectual Capital* (3:4), 2002, pp. 375-392.

CTG (2002). Modeling interorganizational information integration: Project description. Albany, NY. http://www.ctg.albany.edu/projects/miii?proj=miii&sub=summary.

Davenport, T. A. *Process Innovation: Reengineering Work Through Information Technology*. Harvard Business School Press, Boston, MA, 1993.

Dawes, S. S. "Interagency information sharing: Expected benefits, manageable risks," *Journal of Policy Analysis and Management* (15:3), 1996, pp. 377-394.

Dawes, S. S., & Pardo, T. A. (2002). Building collaborative digital government systems. Systematic constraints and effective practices. In W. J. McIver & A. K. Elmagarmid (Eds.), *Advances in digital government. Technology, human factors, and policy* (pp. 259-273). Norwell, MA: Kluwer Academic Publishers.

Dawes, S. S., Pardo, T. A., Simon, S., Cresswell, A. M., LaVigne, M., Andersen, D., and Bloniarz, P. A. *Making smart it choices: Understanding value and risk in government it investments*. Center for Technology in Government, Albany, NY, 2004.

Fountain, J. E. *Building the virtual state. Information technology and institutional change*. Brookings Institution Press, Washington, D.C., 2001.

Gil-García, J. R., and Pardo, T. A. "E-government success factors: Mapping practical tools to theoretical foundations," *Government Information Quarterly* (22:2), 2005, pp. 187–216.

Gil-García, J. R., Schneider, C., Pardo, T. A., and Cresswell, A. M. *Interorganizational information integration in the criminal justice enterprise: Preliminary lessons from state and county initiatives*. Paper presented at the 38th Hawaii International Conference on System Sciences (HICSS), Mãnoa, Hawaii, 2005, January 3-6.

Glaser, B. G. (1992). Basics of grounded theory analysis: Emergence vs. Forcing. Mill Valley, CA: Sociology Press.

Glaser, B. G., & Strauss, A. L. (1967). Discovery of grounded theory: Strategies for qualitative research. Chicago, IL.

Strauss, A., & Corbin, J. (1998). Basics of qualitative research. Techniques and procedures for developing grounded theory. Thousand Oaks, CA: Sage Publications.

Pardo, T.A. and Burke, G.B., "Solving the Integration Puzzle" *Pubic CIO Magazine*, Summer 2005 (www.public-cio.com/story.php?id=2005.04.28-93830).

Pardo, T. A., Cresswell, A. M., Thompson, F., & Zhang, J. (forthcoming). Knowledge sharing in cross-boundary information sharing innovations. *Journal of Information Technology and Management*, special issue on Information Sharing across Multiple Organizations.

Powell, W. K., Koput, K. W., and Smith-Doerr, L. "Interorganizational collaboration and the locus of innovation: Networks of learning in biotechnology," *Administrative Science Quarterly* (41), 1996, pp. 116-145.

Wastell, D. G. "Learning Dysfunctions in Information Systems Development: Overcoming the Social Defenses With Transitional Objects," *MIS Quarterly* (23:4), 1999, pp. 581-600.

SUGGESTED READINGS

- Cresswell, A.M., Pardo, T.A., & Hassan, S. (2007). Assessing Capability for Justice Information Sharing. Paper presented at the 8th Annual International Digital Government Research Conference, Philadelphia.
- Cresswell, A.M., Pardo, T.A., & Canestraro, D.S. (2006). Digital Capability Assessment for e-Government: A Multi-Dimensional Approach. Paper presented at the 5th International E-GOV Conference, Krakow, Poland.
- Gil-García, J.R. & Pardo, T. A. (2005). e-Government Success Factors: Mapping Practical Tools to Theoretical Foundations. *Government Information Quarterly*, 22(1), 187-216.

- Harrison, T., Gil-García, J.R., Pardo, T.A., & Thompson, F. (2006). Learning about Interoperability for Emergency Response: Geographic Information Technologies and the World Trade Center Crisis. Paper presented at the 39th Hawaiian International Conference on System Sciences (HICSS), Hawaii.
- Pardo, T. A., Cresswell, A. M., Thompson, F., & Zhang, J. (2006). Knowledge Sharing in Cross-Boundary Information Systems Development. *Journal of Information Technology and Management*, 7(4) (Special Issue on Information Sharing Across Multiple Organizations).
- Pardo, T.A., Gil-Garcia, J.R. & Burke, G.B. (2006). Building Response Capacity Through Cross-Boundary Information Sharing: The Critical Role of Trust. Paper presented at the EChallenges Conference, Barcelona, Spain.

ONLINE RESOURCES

- Making Smart IT Choices: Understanding Value and Risk in Government IT Investments, April 2004: http://www.ctg.albany.edu/publications/guides/smartit2
- Sharing Justice Information: A Capability Assessment Toolkit, November 2005: http://www.ctg.albany.edu/publications/guides/sharing_justice_info
- Center for Technology in Government: http://www.ctg.albany.edu
- National Association of State Chief Information Officers: http://www.nascio.org/publications/index.cfm
- US Department of Justice Office of Justice Programs Information Technology Initiatives: http://www.it.ojp.gov/index.jsp
- US General Services Administration Intergovernmental Solutions: http://www.gsa.gov/Portal/gsa/ep/channelView.do?pageTypeId=8203& channel Id=-13227
- The E-government Executive Education (3E) project at Harvard's John F. Kennedy School of Government: http://www.ksg.harvard.edu/exec_ed/3e/
- The National Center for Digital Government: http://www.umass.edu/digitalcenter/
- The European Union's the e-Government Economics Project (eGEP): http://217.59.60.50/eGEP/Static/E_Description.asp
- SEARCH The National Consortium for Justice Information and Statistics Information Sharing: State and Local Profiles: http://www.search.org/programs/info/resources.asp

- US Department of Health and Human Services, October 2005: http://www.dhhs.gov/news/press/2005pres/20051006a.html
- Public Health Information Network (PHIN), US Department of Health and Human Services, Centers for Disease Control and Prevention: http://www.cdc.gov/phin/
- The Sawyer Principles: Digital Government Service Delivery and the Lost Art of Whitewashing a Fence, Center for Digital Government, 2005: www.centerdigitalgov.com/publications.php?pub_id=27
- NIEM, the National Information Exchange Model, U.S. Department of Justice and the Department of Homeland Security, June 2006: http://niem.gov/
- National Criminal Intelligence Sharing Plan, United States Department of Justice, March 2002: http://www.it.ojp.gov/topic.jsp?topic_id=93

QUESTIONS FOR DISCUSSION

1. Why is cross-boundary information sharing important to the work of government agencies?
2. How do new requirements for information use change our current understanding of government operations?
3. What are the critical factors and processes involved in cross-boundary information sharing?
4. How can policy makers eliminate environmental constraints on sustainable cross-boundary information sharing?
5. What role can public managers play in reducing organizational constraints on sustainable cross-boundary information sharing?
6. How can chief information officers facilitate a dialogue about cross-boundary information sharing between policy makers and public managers?
7. How do information technology and social factors interact to influence the effectiveness of cross-boundary information sharing?

Chapter 22

URBANSIM

Using Simulation to Inform Public Deliberation and Decision-Making

Alan Borning[1], Paul Waddell[2], and Ruth Förster[3]

[1]Dept. of Computer Science & Engineering, University of Washington, Seattle, Washington U.S.A. (borning@cs.washington.edu); [2]Evans School of Public Affairs, University of Washington, Seattle, Washington U.S.A.(pwaddell@u.washington.edu); [3]Institut für Raum- und Landschaftsentwicklung, ETH (Swiss Federal Institute of Technology), Zürich, Switzerland, (ruth.foerster@irl.baug.ethz.ch)

CHAPTER OVERVIEW

Decisions regarding urban transportation investments such as building a new light rail system or freeway extension, or changes in land use policies such as zoning to encourage compact development and curb low-density urban sprawl, have significant and long-term economic, social, and environmental consequences. Further, land use and transportation decisions interact. Integrated simulation models can help government agencies and citizens make more informed decisions about such issues. We briefly describe the history of urban models, and present a taxonomy of needed refinements to them. We then present a case study of the UrbanSim model system and a significant application of it to the Puget Sound Area in Washington State. We also situate this effort in the digital government research arena, in which is presents a significant research opportunity: hard technical problems, unmet demand from government users, and important issues around supporting a more democratic planning process.

1. INTRODUCTION

Decisions regarding major urban transportation investments, as well as regarding policies to improve air quality and to manage urban development to reduce the adverse effects of low-density urban sprawl, are critical, interdependent choices that shape the long-term quality of life in urban areas. These choices and the problems they attempt to address have important social, economic and environmental impacts that spill over jurisdictional boundaries and that are impacted by decisions made by a wide range of institutions. In the United States, they fall into the scope of metropolitan governance, where the institutional frameworks for forming and implementing policy are less robust than at higher or lower levels of government. These metropolitan governance structures hover between the vise-grip of local governments' control of land use decisions, and the state and federal control of resources for transportation and environmental regulations. In the gap, Metropolitan Planning Organizations (MPOs) have been created by states under federal requirements to better coordinate the allocation of federal investments in transportation, and air quality planning. These MPOs generally do not have any taxing or direct implementation or operational responsibility, but are charged with creating regional transportation plans and coordinating these with land use and air quality planning. It is a tall order.

Putting institutional difficulties aside for the moment, the task of developing regional transportation plans is complex enough at a technical level. How can an almost infinite list of alternative transportation investments proposed by local governments, states, and other entities be examined systematically and an investment plan adopted that reflects a democratic process based on a robust assessment of the alternatives? Over the past several decades, MPOs and their predecessor institutions have used simulation models to predict the volumes of traffic on the transportation network, given assumptions about the land use patterns that would generate patterns of travel demand on this network. The traditional models are called 'four-step models' because they break this task into (1) predictions of the number of trips generated and attracted in each zone of the metropolitan area, (2) the trip distribution patterns from zone to zone, (3) the mode choice of trips (automobile, transit, etc.) between any two zones, and ultimately, (4) how these trips are assigned to the capacity-constrained network, leading to patterns of travel time and congestion. These four-step models were originally developed within the discipline of civil engineering in the late 1950s and early 1960s to address a very specific problem: how to estimate the amount and location of additional road capacity needed to satisfy a given demand for transportation. They became ingrained into the planning process for transportation, reinforced by federal investment and regulation.

In the 1960's and 1970's, the four-step travel models were brought into mainstream use and became the mainstay analysis tool used to support decisions on alternative road investments.

Since the 1980's, however, the models and the decision-making process have come under increasing scrutiny and criticism, leading to substantial pressure to revise both [3]. One of the central criticisms is that the models, and the way they have been generally used, assume that changes in land use result in different demands on the transport system, but that changes in the transportation system do not cause land use changes to occur. Aside from the mountain of theoretical and empirical evidence to the contrary, this assumption violates common sense. Building a major highway through farmlands cannot be expected to have absolutely no impact on the probability that sites along the new highway, or accessible to it, will develop. And if there is an impact on development, the logical extension is that it will in turn impact travel demand. This idea is what has been referred to as induced demand, and one of the reasons scholars have become increasingly skeptical that it is possible to "build your way out of congestion" (see [10] for example). Since the U.S. Clean Air Act Amendments of 1990 and the Intermodal Surface Transportation Efficiency Act of 1991, federal policy has recognized the need to link transportation and land use, in order to account for this relationship. Since that time, refinement of transportation planning practice has been slow, partly due to the technical difficulties of accounting for the interactions, and partly due to political constraints and the increasing role of public involvement in decision-making processes such as these.

Early use of technology such as transportation models to support transportation investments dates to a conception of planners as technocrats who provide answers that are to be taken at face value and used as an objective basis for public decisions. Public participation in these decisions, and in the technical analyses behind them, was decidedly not on the agenda. Much has changed since then, especially at the local government level. An increasingly sophisticated and skeptical set of stakeholders demands public participation, as well as transparency and access to information about the decision-making process and the assumptions and analyses behind it. Conflicting interests are played out in public meeting after public meeting and in committee after committee that is deliberating land use policies or transportation investments. Environmental advocates have increasingly come to use the courts to prod planning agencies to refine their analyses to address shortcomings such as the omission of land use feedback effects [16].

1.1 Urban Modeling as a Digital Government Research Area

The domain of land use and transportation modeling thus provides a significant opportunity for digital government research: it is of great interest to government agencies, and it includes a set of hard, open problems, both technical and procedural. This chapter is intended for digital government researchers and students who are generally computer- and policy-literate, but who are not necessarily expert in either the domain of urban modeling or of land use and transportation policy. In this chapter, we first present a taxonomy of needed refinements to urban models themselves, and to the process of applying them. We then present a case study of UrbanSim, an urban modeling system that our group has been developing at the University of Washington, including a short history, more recent research initiatives, and some significant applications to planning activities. Our focus in this chapter is primarily on the U.S. context. However, controversies regarding land use and transportation occur world-wide, and analogous issues arise around using models to inform decision-making in other countries.

1.2 A Taxonomy of Model and Process Refinements

Our research is intended to contribute both to improving the technical modeling capacity to address issues such as the land use consequences of transportation investments, as well as to improving the process of using models in a democratic decision-making context.

Table 22-1. Model and process refinements

Refinement of Models
- Validity
• Accuracy
• Handling of uncertainty
• Policy sensitivity
- Comprehensiveness
• Real estate development and prices
• Employment location
• Household location
• Transportation system
• Environmental impacts
Refinement of Process
- Refinement of the model construction and application process
• Feasibility of data preparation
• Performance
• Usability
• Support for software evolution
- Support for a more effective democratic process
• Responding to stakeholder interests and concerns
• Transparency
• Fairness
• Facilitating stakeholder access to models and their output

To help structure this case study, as well as providing a framework for evaluating urban models, we offer the above taxonomy of model and process refinements (Table 22-1).

We hope that this taxonomy will be of value beyond this particular case study as well, for other studies of modeling and simulation in the policy arena. In developing this framework, we draw on and extend earlier work that has criticized earlier urban models (for example [18]). We then describe how our project and several research initiatives within it have emerged to address these challenges.

1.2.1 Refinement of models

At the top level, we distinguish between *refinement of models* and *refinement of process*. Refinement of models focuses on the models themselves. In turn, we can classify the work on refinement of models as work on *validity* and on *comprehensiveness*.

Validity includes improving the accuracy of the models, and also their sensitivity to policies of interest. Accuracy means that the predicted values (for example, of population density in different neighborhoods) are close to the observed values.

This raises the obvious problem of how to evaluate the accuracy of predictions of events in the future. One technique is *historical validation*, in which the model is run on historical data, and the results compared with what actually transpired (see [27] for example). This has the clear merit of comparing with real outcomes. There are difficulties as well, however. First, in many cases the needed historical data is not available. Also, for the relatively small number of regions for which data is available, there may not have been major land use and transportation changes over the period being tested, so that the model in effect isn't being used to simulate major decisions. An alternative technique that is often used is to run the model system with fairly extreme scenarios (e.g. doubling the capacity of selected roadways, or removing zoning restrictions on height limits in a neighborhood). The results are then evaluated by an expert review panel.

Predicting the future is a risky business. There are numerous, complex, and interacting sources of uncertainty in urban simulations of the sort we are developing, including uncertainty regarding exogenous data, the model structure and specification, the parameters of the model, and from the stochastic nature of the simulation. Nevertheless, citizens and governments do have to make decisions, using the best available information. Ideally we should represent the uncertainty in our conclusions as well as possible, both for truthfulness and as important data to assist in selecting among alternatives. However, to date there has been only a small amount of work done on handling uncertainty in urban modeling in a principled fashion [24].

We often also want to improve the sensitivity of the model to policies of interest. For example, if a region is interested in policies that foster walkable neighborhoods, then the model should be able to model walking for transportation as well as for health and recreation. Which policies are of interest is of course a political and societal question; but given such policies, whether the model responds suitably to them becomes a question of validity.

Yet another sort of refinement of the models is increasing their comprehensiveness to include other actors and processes in the urban environment. For example, for households, we might model additional demographic processes, such as household formation and dissolution. Or for environmental impacts, we might model consumption of additional kinds of resources, or the impacts of decisions on biodiversity as well as on particular species of interest (for example, due to Endangered Species Act considerations).

There are important pitfalls and tensions associated with the goal of increasing the comprehensiveness of models: namely what Lee [18] called the problem of hyper-comprehensiveness. One aspect of this is pressure to model more and more aspects of the urban environment because these aspects are important to someone — even though they might have little relation to land use and transportation. For example, there might be demands to model voter turnout rates. These pressures are relatively straightforward to deal with, by reminding stakeholders of the purpose of the modeling work and the need to remain focused. A more difficult issue is that a seemingly endless number of factors influence urban land use and transportation.

For example, crime is clearly an important factor in residential location choice, in transportation choice, and others. But we need not just data on current crime rates — and perhaps more importantly, on people's perceptions of crime — but also a predictive model of crime in the future under different possible scenarios. This is both difficult and controversial. For example, what are the major determinants of the crime rate? Economic conditions? Family stability and moral instruction? The nature of the criminal justice system? How far should the modeler go down this path? Or as another example (relevant to the region around Seattle), suppose we want to model the return rate of wild salmon in rivers and streams that flow through urban regions. There are many factors affecting this: the amount of impervious surface, pollutants from agricultural runoff, the number of fish caught by both commercial and sport fishers, oceanic conditions (including temperature, since the salmon grow to maturity in the ocean before returning to fresh water streams to spawn), and many others. Among the pitfalls of overly ambitious modeling are increasing model complexity, additional data requirements, and in some cases the credibility of the overall modeling effort.

1.2.2 Refinement of process

Returning to the top level of the taxonomy, refinement of process includes first, improving the process of developing, extending, and applying models; and second, supporting their more effective use in a democratic society. The first of these is concerned with instrumental values such as usability and feasibility: data preparation issues, adequate performance, usability of the software, and accommodating changes in requirements, data, and the like. It must be feasible to prepare the data needed to run the model. Typically, this implies that the data must already be in hand — collecting new data is enormously expensive. But the data in hand may be of varying quality, or in the wrong format, and so forth. Performance should be adequate, and the software must be usable by the technical staff at the planning organization. Also, the model system architecture should allow for the system to evolve as requirements and the questions asked change over time.

Another set of process issues revolve around the desire to use modeling as part of a more participatory, open, and democratic process, rather than in a technical, back-room exercise. One aspect of this is improving the relevance of the modeling and output to the diverse range of stakeholder concerns (in other words, increasing its comprehensiveness in response to stakeholder values). Transparency of the model itself, of the input data preparation process, and of the overall context in which it is used also play an important role as well. Another aspect of this is improving the fairness of the model (for example, in not omitting an important transportation mode, or short-changing the interests of renters as compared with home owners). Again, this can result in additional demands for refinement of the model (either its validity, comprehensiveness, or both). The results of running the model, and ideally even the ability to experiment with alternatives, should be opened up to a wider range of stakeholders, rather than being restricted to the technical modelers. System performance is relevant here also: for example, if the model takes weeks to run, clearly this would make it difficult to use to support deliberation, in which model results are discussed, and in response new questions are asked of the model or new scenarios are proposed for testing.

There are some obvious tensions among these objectives for refinement of models and process. Pressures to increase policy sensitivity in order to avoid bias from omission of certain policies from consideration, for example pedestrian and bicycling modes, increase the need for a very high level of behavioral and spatial detail. This will certainly come at a cost in performance, and quite possibly also at a cost of some reduction in the accuracy of the results. How can model sensitivity, data requirements, transparency, computing performance, and accuracy be compared against each other? How are the interests of different stakeholders served by alternative compromises among these? How do these choices affect the legitimacy of the model system and the process for using it in the decision-making process? These are difficult problems, and ones that have not received sufficient attention to date. We seek to address these concerns in our project in addition to the more purely technical issues of model refinement.

2. THE URBANSIM PROJECT: A CASE STUDY

UrbanSim is an open-source land use modeling system, which integrates with an external travel model to provide a capability for integrated modeling of urban land use, transportation, and environmental impacts. It is reusable, in the sense that it can be applied to a new region by supplying the appropriate data, as opposed to being for a single region only. Its development has been motivated by the desire to refine both the models and processes, as described in Section 1.2.

Our research agenda draws broadly from the academic fields of urban planning and design, public policy, economics, geography, sociology, civil engineering, and computer science, and balances academic research interests with pragmatic relevance in addressing important social problems and public policy choices. Engagement with local and metropolitan governments and planning processes has been essential to this agenda. This engagement informs the research in numerous ways, and motivates it. We therefore devote attention in this chapter to the process of adoption of UrbanSim by public agencies for operational use, and examine two case studies of applying UrbanSim in the metropolitan regions around Salt Lake City and Seattle. In this section we first review the initial development of the UrbanSim project, and then describe some of the significant research initiatives that we have launched in response to lessons learned along the way.

2.1 Related Work

UrbanSim has been developed over the past decade, and has both benefited from prior work and, we think, substantially extended prior modeling approaches. While space prevents a complete treatment of how UrbanSim compares to other modeling approaches, we offer here a concise treatment, along with pointers to more in-depth reviews of urban models, including UrbanSim itself [9, 20, 25, 31]. We begin by contrasting UrbanSim with two alternative modeling approaches that were available by the mid-1990s, when the design and development of UrbanSim began. The approach that has been most widely used to do land use modeling is based on the Lowry gravity model [19], which adapted the law of gravity from physics and applied it to predict the flow of travel between locations as a function of the sizes of origin and destination and the ease of travel between them. This approach, also widely referred to as a spatial-interaction approach, was used widely in transportation modeling to predict trip distribution patterns, was later refined and adapted to predict land use patterns in the DRAM/EMPAL model system developed around 1970 [22]. This approach has been criticized as over-emphasizing the role of transportation in location choices, and lacking behavioral content such as a representation of real estate markets (housing supply, demand, and prices are not considered, only household and job locations in zones). An alternative approach is the spatial input-output approach that was also initially developed around 1970, adapting the input-output models developed to describe monetary flows in the U.S. economy to predict monetary flows between economic sectors and between zones [8, 11]. This is roughly analogous to an international trade model in which the countries are replaced by some geographic subdivisions of the study area. These spatial input-output models translate from monetary flows into tons of freight, and by dividing the monetary flow from labor to a sector by the average wage rate in the sector, derive the number of workers and the implied commuting flows. While this approach is intriguing for large-scale areas where there is interest in predicting inter-metropolitan freight movement, it seems less suited to developing a behaviorally-transparent model of how households choose where to live or business choose to locate, or of the behavior of real estate developers. Unlike the spatial-interaction approach, the spatial input-output approach does recognize the role of markets, and treats demand, supply, and prices. Both of these modeling approaches share the approach used by virtually all previous urban models: they formulate an equilibrium set of conditions and solve for an equilibrium that is not path-dependent, rather than attempting to predict dynamic changes over time.

UrbanSim differs significantly from these and other earlier modeling approaches in several respects. First, it emphasizes behavioral theory and transparency. This leads to a more explicit treatment of individual agents such as households, jobs, and locations, and to a microsimulation of the choices that these agents make over time. UrbanSim was the first operational modeling system to use very small geographic units such as parcels or small grid cells, and to microsimulate individual agents and their choices in a framework that includes an explicit representation of real estate demand, supply, and prices and their evolution over time. One other approach that has emerged recently warrants comment. The use of rule-based models that are embedded in highly graphical environments such as Geographic Information Systems has increased in the past several years. These are not behavioral models in the sense that they do not attempt to reflect the pattern of agent behavior observed in the real world. Instead, these tools allow a user to impose on the system a set of assumptions, such as the distribution of population twenty years in the future, and then to visually examine the result of applying those assumptions. While the intent is quite different than the ones we have outlined above, there is some risk that users may misinterpret the output of such tools as containing more behavioral information than it in fact does. (In the above example, simply asserting that a given neighborhood will have a given population density is very different from simulating the results of policies, such as transportation and zoning changes, designed to achieve that result. After all, the policies might or might not achieve the desired result.) There may in fact be some useful complementarity between these kinds of visually-engaging tools and more behaviorally-focused models: the visual tools could provide a useful interface to obtain information from stakeholders about their preferences, and the behavioral models could provide stakeholders feedback about how effective alternative policy actions might be in achieving those objectives, and to help examine what the trade-offs are among the objectives.

2.2 Early Development of UrbanSim

Paul Waddell originally became interested in the problem of land use and transportation modeling in the 1980's, when he worked for a metropolitan planning organization and encountered first-hand the unsatisfactory state of modeling practice. At that time (and it is still widely the case today), the models available for use in metropolitan planning lacked behavioral realism, had insufficient theoretical underpinnings, were largely insensitive to important public policies, and as a cumulative result of these considerations, lacked credibility with both technical planners and with policy-makers. These models were, in short, ineffective.

In the mid-1990's Waddell began designing and developing UrbanSim to address some of the clear shortcomings of existing models to support metropolitan planning. The design choices in this early work focused on improving behavioral realism, validity, and policy relevance. UrbanSim was designed based on a micro-simulation approach to modeling household choices of residential location, business location choices, and real estate development and prices, and the use of a dynamic, annual simulation of the evolution of cities over time. It attempted to make explicit the role of policy inputs, such as comprehensive land use plans and transportation infrastructure, in order to support the evaluation of alternative policy scenarios and their effects. Waddell supervised the development of a prototype version in Java for testing in Eugene, Oregon [26], supported by a contract with the Oregon Department of Transportation.

In 1998, Alan Borning began collaborating with him on this work, based on common interests in using information technology to improve the process of metropolitan planning. In 1999 we obtained the first of a series of grants from the National Science Foundation to support the project, this one from the Urban Research Initiative. This more flexible funding allowed us to put together a team consisting of graduate and undergraduate computer science students, along with students from urban planning, civil engineering, and economics, who rewrote the model and its interface (still in Java).

2.3 Subsequent Research Initiatives

After the initial development work on the UrbanSim prototype and a first effort to improve the software engineering and design of the system, three priorities emerged. First, we wanted to further refine the models, to improve their validity and comprehensiveness (see the taxonomy in Section 1.2). Second, we wanted to explore more systematically the issues around opening the process of using the model to more participation, as well as carefully considering issues of transparency, fairness, and the range of stakeholders affected by the decisions that were to be informed by information coming from the model system. These priorities in turn gave rise to the third priority, namely, addressing the significant computational and software engineering challenges that then arose due to the level of detail the system was attempting to represent, the complexity of the models, and the need to support system evolution and change.

Guided by these priorities, we submitted two additional NSF proposals. In 2001 we were fortunate enough to be awarded a 5-year NSF grant under the Information Technology Research Initiative, administered through the NSF Digital Government program, along with a companion grant from the Digital Government program itself. This increased level of funding and longer funding period enabled us to take on a substantially larger and more risky research agenda, while still pursuing our overall strategy of integrating the research with close collaboration with local and metropolitan governments and planning processes. In the remainder of this section we summarize these initiatives. Relating back to the taxonomy, these initiatives all apply to various items in the taxonomy of refinements, but often an initiative will pertain to several — there is usually not a one-to-one mapping between initiatives and items in the taxonomy.

2.3.1 Improving model validity

A significant amount of the work in the past several years has concerned improving the validity of the models. Much of this work has been quite technical, and for purposes of this case study, we mention two of these activities, along with providing references to papers that provide additional detail.

The location choice models (for Household Location Choice and Employment Location Choice), for example, have undergone a series of improvements. Despite this, throughout the UrbanSim 3 efforts these two models suffered from a problem of dispersion. For example, highly desirable residential areas — e.g. with a lake or ocean view — typically have higher real estate values and wealthier residents. Absent some significant external cause we would expect this to continue; yet in the simulation results we were seeing a dispersion of wealthy households from these neighborhoods, as well as poorer households moving into these desirable areas. (While for policy reasons we might desire more mixed neighborhoods, achieving this would require policy changes — the effect we were seeing was due to some combination of model specification and software implementation.) This shortcoming was an issue in an assessment of the application of UrbanSim in Salt Lake City (see Section 2.4, and a full description in reference [30]). It was only in our most recent version of the system, UrbanSim 4 (Section 2.3), that we were able to address this. This problem was one of several that precipitated a complete redesign of the software implementation, since diagnosing and addressing it proved to be too challenging in the UrbanSim 3 implementation.

The Developer Model, which simulates the actions of real estate developers, is one of the most complex of UrbanSim's component models. We have had more versions of this model component than any other. In part this reflects the relatively smaller amount of academic research on real estate supply than on demand. Two approaches are discussed in the real estate literature: the site looking for a use and the use looking for a site. The former approaches the problem from the land owner's perspective: whether to develop a parcel, and if so, into what use. The latter approaches the problem from the perspective of a specialized developer, say, of office space, who needs to choose a profitable location for the project. Through UrbanSim 3 we adopted the site looking for a use perspective, which was consistent with the literature in land cover change. We learned through several model applications, however, that this approach was problematic from the perspective of policy sensitivity. If we significantly changed the land area available for development, for example, modeling the introduction of an Urban Growth Boundary to constrain low-density development, then the amount of development was significantly reduced, which does not conform to expectations. Instead, we would expect development to continue, but at higher prices, and focused in the areas available for development. So in the development of UrbanSim 4, we re-designed the developer model from the use looking for a site perspective, which has a natural and behaviorally-correct response to a significant change in the area of land available for development: it scales the probabilities among the remaining available sites.

2.3.2 Increasing model comprehensiveness — modeling environmental impacts

Another aspect of model refinement is increasing the comprehensiveness of UrbanSim's component models to encompass additional phenomena. In some cases this is of primary interest as a means of improving model validity. For example, one such effort has concerned improving the Demographic Transition Model, which simulates the creation and removal of households (to simulate the real world processes of births, deaths, children leaving home, and movement into and out of the study area). The primary purpose of this activity is to improve the validity of the location choice models.

Another reason to model additional phenomena is to capture important impacts of land use and transportation decisions, even if these impacts don't feed back directly into the operation of the other component models. Environmental impacts are the most significant class of such phenomena. In our current implementation, we produce indicators of greenhouse gas emissions from transportation, and have a component model that simulates land cover change. (Land cover is important in its own right, and is also useful as a factor in producing other environmental indicators — for example, impervious surface affects water runoff characteristics.) We plan to add additional indicators in the near future, beginning with air quality and resource consumption indicators.

As noted above, these indicators do not currently feed back into the operation of the other component models — although adding such feedback (e.g. to the residential location choice model) is a research topic for the future. In any case, these indicators of environmental impact become important considerations in the deliberative process in which the model is used.

2.3.3 Value sensitive design

The domain of urban planning is both value laden and rife with long-standing disagreements. In addition, as described in the introduction, there is increasing desire to move the modeling and planning process from a technically-focused "back room" operation to a more open and participatory one, which immediately leads to questions of who are the stakeholders and who should participate, along with other issues of transparency, accountability, and openness. In terms of our taxonomy, these issues initially fall into the category of "Support for a more effective democratic process," but fairly quickly lead to issues regarding the process of constructing and applying the models, as well as to pressures for refinements to the model.

To approach these value issues in a principled fashion, we rely on the Value Sensitive Design theory and methodology [14]. Value Sensitive Design is an approach to the design of information systems that seeks to account for human values in a principled and comprehensive way throughout the design process. Key features are its interactional perspective, tripartite methodology (consisting of conceptual, empirical, and technical investigations), and emphasis on indirect as well as direct stakeholders.

For UrbanSim in its current form, the direct stakeholders are the urban modelers and technical planners who use UrbanSim and manipulate its results. The indirect stakeholders are those who do not use the system directly, but who are affected by it. They include for example elected officials, members of advocacy and business groups, and more generally all the residents of the region being modeled, as well as residents of nearby regions. One way of framing our goal of opening up the planning process and use of models to wider participation is to move more people from the indirect to the direct stakeholder category: to provide meaningful direct access to the results from the models, and ultimately to the tools for simulating other possible plans and futures.

Early in our conceptual investigations, we made a sharp distinction between explicitly supported values (i.e., ones that we explicitly want to support in the model system) and stakeholder values (i.e., ones that are important to some but not necessarily all of the stakeholders). Next, we committed to several key moral values to support explicitly: fairness and more specifically freedom from bias [15], representativeness, accountability, and support for a democratic society. In turn, as part of supporting a democratic society, we decided that the system should not a priori favor or rule out any given set of stakeholder values, but instead should allow different stakeholders to articulate the values that are most important to them, and evaluate the alternatives in light of these values. We identified comprehensibility, and subsequently legitimation and transparency, as key instrumental values to be supported explicitly as well.

In terms of specific Value Sensitive design research activities, one project involved carefully documenting and presenting the indicators that portray key results from the simulations [4] using a web-based Indicator Browser. We also developed the Indicator Perspective framework, which allows a set of organizations with a diverse set of positions and interests to put forth different perspectives on what is most important in the results from UrbanSim, and how it should be interpreted. Our design for the Indicator Browser and Indicator Perspectives addresses a number of challenges, including responding to the values and interests of diverse stakeholders, and providing relatively neutral technical information and at the same time supporting value advocacy and opinion. A third activity has been the development of "Personal Indicators" that allow individuals and households to ask how different alternatives will affect them personally, for example, in terms of housing costs or individual commute times [6, 7]. Together, these projects represent a significant set of steps toward making the modeling components of the planning process more open and participatory, supported by a solid theoretical foundation.

2.3.4 Software engineering

The significant performance demands of the system that arise due to the level of detail being represented, the complexity of the models, the close scrutiny of the simulation results, and the need to support system evolution and change, all give rise to pressures for good software engineering and software development practices. The ITR grant, with its funding level and five-year term, enabled us to hire two software engineering professionals with substantial industry experience, who were then able to provide much stronger guidance on our software development process, as well as being able to work closely with the students involved with the software side of the project over the years, including a large number of computer science and computer engineering undergraduates.

We put into place an agile software development process [1], which relies on small, incremental development steps, automated testing, and responsiveness to change. *Unit tests* — small, self-contained tests that exercise a particular part of the code — play an essential role in the process [17, 21]. Following a modified extreme Programming approach [2], we carry this further and use a test-first development strategy, in which the software developer first writes the unit tests, and then writes the code to be tested. We also rely on an automatic build system that runs all the tests whenever new code is checked into the code repository. A novel feature of our development environment is a set of traffic lights (real ones), placed in the hallway of our lab and in developers' offices. When the light is green, the checked-in code has passed all tests; when it is yellow, the tests are currently being run on newly-submitted code; and when it is red, one or more tests have failed. A green light serves as a reassuring status indicator of the state of the software, while a red light is a powerful social incentive to fix the software problem, as a top priority. The traffic light and other novel features of our development methodology are described in a paper in the 2003 Agile Development Conference [13], while another novel feature of our process, the use of 'today' messages as a coordination tool for software developers, is discussed in more detail in reference [5]. Finally, a recent paper [23] describes a novel extension to the unit testing framework to handle testing stochastic models (such as many of the UrbanSim models).

2.3.5 Opus and UrbanSim 4

In 2002 we rewrote UrbanSim again (still in Java), resulting in UrbanSim 3, which was our production system for several years. The use of Java as an implementation language for UrbanSim was a good choice in many respects, but there were some problems as well, in particular, inaccessibility of the code to domain experts, and performance issues. Regarding accessibility, our hope was that, by using suitable abstractions and a very clear coding style, that modelers (domain experts), as well as software engineers, could experiment with the models. Alas, due to the inherent complexities of the Java implementation of UrbanSim 3 and the Java development environment, this did not happen. There were also some intractable modeling problems (regarding dispersion of housing and employment) that we were having great difficulty with in the Java version — but which we were able to quickly resolve in some experimental code in the Python programming language. We also found that, unlike Java, the domain experts (the modelers) *were* willing to read and modify Python code. Python itself has poorer performance than Java. However, in recent years, a number of packages have been developed, including Numeric and numarray, that can be called from Python and that allow one to manipulate large arrays and matrices very efficiently. UrbanSim simulations usually process a huge amount of data, which in the Java version was done using iterations written in Java, and is now handled using calls to these efficient packages.

Another problem was the existence of a set of independent research projects at different institutions, all working in the domain of land use and transportation modeling, but that had incompatible platforms and implementations, making it hard to share and build on each other's work. A growing consensus emerged among researchers in the urban modeling community that a common, open-source platform would greatly facilitate sharing and collaboration. In response, an international group of researchers, including groups at the University of Toronto, the Technical University of Berlin, and ETH (the Swiss Federal Institute of Technology in Zurich), began collaborating with the UrbanSim team to develop a new software architecture and framework — Opus, the Open Platform for Urban Simulation [29].

At the same time that we were designing and implementing Opus, we began implementing UrbanSim 4 using the new platform (using UrbanSim as one of the test cases for the design and implementation of Opus). We continued using our agile, test-driven development methodology with Opus/UrbanSim. We now have a well-functioning system, written in Python, that makes heavy use of efficient matrix and array manipulation libraries. Opus and UrbanSim 4 contain far less code than the previous implementation, yet implement a much more modular and user-extensible system that also runs faster. UrbanSim 4 also incorporates key functional extensions such as integrated model estimation and visualization. In terms of our taxonomy (Section 1.2), these extensions are process refinements that address technical and engineering issues. Model estimation, for example, was formerly an error-prone process involving using external econometric packages, which required several months of skilled staff time. With the integrated estimation capabilities, models can now be estimated in less than a day. The integrated visualization facilities don't provide quite such a dramatic gain in efficiency, but nevertheless make it much easier to produce simple visualizations of indicator results for diagnosis and policy application.

Another component of the Opus work — our data storage representation — illustrates the ongoing tension between ease of use and transparent access on the one hand, and efficiency on the other. In UrbanSim 2, input data for the simulation was held in a single large binary file that used a format specific to UrbanSim (and similarly for output data). This was efficient but not particularly transparent. In addition, we regularly changed the format to meet new requirements, introducing versioning problems. For UrbanSim 3, we moved to an SQL database, using MySQL, an efficient, widely-used open source database. The database schema was carefully documented in our web-based documentation. Indicators were defined using SQL queries, which were part of "live" technical documentation [4]. This greatly enhanced transparency, but at a cost to efficiency. In particular, computing a set of indicators could take longer than the run time for the simulation itself. In Opus and UrbanSim 4, we support a variety of data storage formats, including a SQL database, binary files (using the format defined by the numarray package), tab-delimited files, and others. Indicators can now be defined using Opus variable definitions in addition to SQL queries. This is currently a considerably less transparent format, but indicator values can now be computed in minutes rather than hours. We expect to be able to design ways to increase the transparency of this more efficient approach by developing appropriate user interfaces for browsing and computing indicators.

We released Opus and UrbanSim 4 in June 2006. UrbanSim is currently in use in projects in the U.S. for the metropolitan regions around Detroit, El Paso, Honolulu, Houston, and Seattle, and internationally in Amsterdam, Paris, Tel Aviv, and Zurich. Additional projects have been launched in Burlington, Durham, Phoenix, and San Francisco, and internationally in Melbourne, Australia. Many of the current projects, as well as all of the new ones, are now using UrbanSim 4. In July 2006 we hosted the second UrbanSim Users Group meeting, which included 35 participants from across the U.S., as well as Netherlands and Israel. The primary purpose of this meeting was to assist current users in transitioning to UrbanSim 4.

2.3.6 Uncertainty

We recently started a project to provide a principled statistical analysis of uncertainty in UrbanSim, and to portray these results in a clear and useful way to the users of the system. In this work, we are leveraging a promising technique, Bayesian melding, which combines evidence and uncertainty about the inputs and outputs of a computer model to yield distributions of quantities of policy interest. From this can be derived both best estimates and statements of uncertainty about these quantities. This past year we have had some initial success in employing this technique, applying it to calibrate the model using various sources of uncertainty with an application in Eugene-Springfield, Oregon. These results are reported in a recent journal article [24]. Once the analysis infrastructure is in place, we will extend the Indicator Browser and other interaction and visualization tools to include appropriate depictions of uncertainty. We also intend to extend the uncertainty analysis to address simultaneously the problems of developing data for use in modeling (which is currently a very tedious and error-prone process) and analyzing the role of uncertainty in input data on model estimation and on simulation results.

2.4 Applying UrbanSim

An important part of our research agenda has been close collaborations with a number of regional government agencies in applying UrbanSim to their regions. In this subsection we call out the Salt Lake City and Puget Sound applications in particular. These two cases present substantially different aspects, both in terms of characteristics of the region, and of the legal and political context. The Salt Lake City application is described in detail in reference [30], and more briefly in reference [28]. The PSRC application is being studied, particularly with respect to the PSRC/UW collaboration, the decision-making regarding adoption, and their implications for use of the model in practice, as a component of Ruth Förster's forthcoming Ph.D. dissertation [12].

During 2002–20003, we worked intensively with the Wasatch Front Regional Council in applying UrbanSim to Salt Lake City and the surrounding areas, building on earlier work with the agency. The Greater Wasatch Area, containing 80% of Utah's population and centered on Salt Lake City, is a rapidly growing metropolitan area, with population predicted to increase by 60% in the year 2020. In order to deal with projected increases in population and travel, Utah officials developed a series of transportation improvement plans, one component being the Legacy Parkway, a controversial four-lane highway extending 14 miles north from Salt Lake City. The highway project precipitated a lawsuit, which ultimately resulted in a settlement that included terms requiring the Wasatch Front Regional Council to test the integration of UrbanSim with their regional travel model system, and if successful, to bring this into their operational use in transportation planning.

The assessment of the integration of UrbanSim with the regional travel model system was launched in 2003 with the formation of a Peer Review Panel, consisting of technical experts in land use and transportation modeling, along with a Management and Policy Committee and a Scenarios Committee. A very tight schedule was specified in the out-of-court settlement, requiring that the entire review be completed by the end of 2003. The Peer Review Panel decided on a validation of the combined UrbanSim – Travel Model System using a series of tests. One test was to model the effects of the existing long-range plan (LRP) in 2030. There were also five other "sensitivity tests," each of which involved making a simulated major change to the adopted plan and assessing the results, for example, removing a major highway link included in the LRP, removing a major transit link, or adding a significant land use policy such as an urban growth boundary. The overall evaluation focused on issues of model validity and usability.

The Peer Review Panel concluded that UrbanSim produced credible results for tests involving large changes (e.g. the urban growth boundary test), but not for relatively smaller changes (e.g. removing a major highway link). It was during this process that we discovered the dispersion problem mentioned earlier. Their summary assessment supported the implementation and application of UrbanSim by the WFRC, with the understanding that important refinements and improvements were needed. Subsequently, during 2004, staff of the WFRC made additional efforts to improve the data and the model specification, and the agency decided to move the model into operational use.

Another important collaboration has been with the Puget Sound Regional Council (PSRC), to apply UrbanSim to that region (which includes Seattle and other surrounding cities). In this project, a collaborative agreement was developed between the PSRC and the Center for Urban Simulation and Policy Analysis (CUSPA), to develop the database and apply UrbanSim to the Central Puget Sound region containing Seattle. A Technical Advisory Committee, consisting of planners and analysts from cities and counties in the region, was engaged with the process to review the development of the data and model, and to provide refinements to the data and feedback on the model development. The process was managed closely by two staff members of the PSRC, and during the project two PSRC staff members were hired by CUSPA for the intensive database development effort, and then re-hired by PSRC afterwards. The project was funded by the PSRC and structured in annual contracts with clear work scope for each period. The first two years were essentially spent on database development and refinement, and the third on model estimation and testing.

During this period, as we learned from both the Salt Lake City project and the Puget Sound project about several problems in the model specification and software implementation in UrbanSim 3, we confronted a difficult choice of whether to attempt to resolve these problems in the production system (UrbanSim 3 in Java), or invest all of our effort on completing more quickly the conversion to the more modular Python implementation in OPUS and UrbanSim 4. We had already learned that we could more readily solve modeling problems using the incomplete Python version that we had been unable to address in the UrbanSim 3 code base (mainly due to the complexity of debugging the code). At the same time, there were considerable risks to attempting to rapidly complete and test the conversion to Python without putting the PSRC project well behind schedule. Ultimately, after extensive consultation with the PSRC, we made the decision to freeze further investment in the UrbanSim 3 code, other than minor maintenance, and to put all our effort into the new platform. Since that decision, we have fully implemented the PSRC model application using the new UrbanSim 4 code in OPUS, and have done extensive testing with the system. It may have added as much as a year to the project schedule over what had been expected, but it is not clear that the schedule would have been any earlier if we had continued working on the UrbanSim 3 platform to attempt to resolve the problems we faced.

PSRC staff worked with CUSPA to develop criteria for evaluating the model results and to determine when it would be ready to put into production use. Unfortunately, longitudinal data were not available to undertake a historical validation as was done in Eugene-Springfield [27], so the focus of the evaluation was shifted to sensitivity analysis and comparison with previous results. The PSRC has used the DRAM/EMPAL model to prepare land use allocations for use in its transportation planning process for many years, and though they have numerous concerns about it, they have managed to find workable solutions by overriding the model results based on local review procedures using their Technical Advisory Committee and a Regional Technical Forum. The assessment of UrbanSim involved comparing the predictions from 2000 (the base year) to 2030 using UrbanSim with the heavily reviewed and adjusted predictions of DRAM/EMPAL. Since the two models use different levels of geography (DRAM/EMPAL uses approximately 200 Forecast Analysis Zones and UrbanSim uses approximately 800,000 grid cells), UrbanSim data were aggregated to levels that could be compared to the previous results. The initial focus was on population and employment predictions, since these are the data used in the travel model system. A set of indicators was selected for use in diagnosing the performance of the model and to identify issues and problems, in a process of negotiation among the participants.

Based on this, the UW/PSRC team classified the issues into critical, significant, and cosmetic. (Critical issues were ones that had to be resolved before the PSRC would be comfortable placing the model system into operational use. Significant issues were ones that PSRC regarded as important, but would not block putting the system into operational use.)

In addition to comparing the predictions of UrbanSim with previously adopted forecasts, a series of sensitivity tests were conducted to determine if the results from the model were sensitive in the direction and magnitude experts would expect when an input was changed significantly. For these tests, we compared results for the baseline scenario, which was based on currently adopted land use policies and the adopted Regional Transportation Plan, with results for scenarios that included doubling highway capacity in Snohomish County on the north end of the study area, relaxing the Urban Growth Boundary, and constraining development capacity in King County (the central county in the study area). These tests were selected to probe both the scientific robustness of the model and its sensitivity to policies of interest in the region. This can thus be seen as addressing both the accuracy and policy sensitivity aspects of model validity, as discussed in the taxonomy presented in Section 1.2.

The land use policies showed the expected effects, but the highway scenario showed less sensitivity than was expected, in the sense that it did not produce much redistribution of population and employment into Snohomish County. This was consistent with a pattern in the comparison of the UrbanSim baseline scenario against previously adopted forecasts, which showed considerably lower growth rates in Snohomish County than the earlier results did. These remain on the agenda for further examination to determine whether these results are plausible or are an artifact of the model specification or input data. In spite of these remaining issues, the PSRC is moving ahead with the process of bringing UrbanSim into operational use, and is preparing for a final phase of work to do so during 2006-07.

In addition to the Salt Lake City and Puget Sound applications, we have worked with other agencies in applying UrbanSim in the urban areas around Detroit, Eugene, Honolulu, and Houston. There have also been research and pilot applications in Amsterdam, Paris, Phoenix, Tel Aviv, and Zurich. We have also been working actively to form a user community. The first UrbanSim Users Group Meeting was in San Antonio, Texas, in January 2005. This meeting attracted some 30 participants from Metropolitan Planning Organizations around the country, a number of academic researchers, and one participant from Europe. The second UrbanSim Users Group meeting will be held in July

2006, with one important goal being to help existing UrbanSim 3 users to migrate to UrbanSim 4. We hope to increasingly engage model users and other research groups in the collaborative development of Opus and of UrbanSim itself, by extensions and refinements to the current model system, and the addition of new tools and models.

3. CONCLUSION AND FUTURE WORK

In this chapter we have presented an introduction to the domain of urban modeling and to some of the uses and controversies around employing these models to inform public decision-making, including a taxonomy of refinements to urban models and to the process of applying them. We then presented a case study of the UrbanSim model system, including principal areas of research and some applications to planning activities in different regions. This domain represents a significant opportunity for digital government research: hard technical problems, unmet demand from government users, and important issues around supporting a more democratic planning process.

There is work that remains to be done. Most importantly, our goal of producing a system that is in routine and widespread use in informing the planning process is not yet achieved. UrbanSim is being transitioned to operational use in a number of regions, and there are a fair number of additional research applications of the system. However, it is not yet in routine policy use. Beyond that, the development of the Opus platform should enable a rich set of collaborations among researchers world-wide, including the development of open-source travel models and environmental models closely integrated with the land use models in UrbanSim. Finally, we have touched on two other major open areas of ongoing research: first, increasing access to the results of modeling for a wide range of stakeholders, and ultimately to simulating additional alternatives; and second, providing a principled modeling of uncertainty in land use and transportation simulations.

ACKNOWLEDGMENTS

We would like to thank all of the UrbanSim research team members and collaborators. This research has been funded in part by grants from the National Science Foundation (EIA-0121326 and IIS-0534094), in part by a grant from the Environmental Protection Agency (R831837), in part by a partnership with the Puget Sound Regional Council, and in part by gifts from IBM and Google.

REFERENCES

1. K. Beck. *Extreme Programming Explained: Embrace Change*. Addison-Wesley, Reading, Mass., 2000.
2. K. Beck. *Test-Driven Development – By Example*. Addison-Wesley, Reading, Mass., 2003.
3. E. Beimborn, R. Kennedy, and W. Schaefer. Inside the blackbox: Making transportation models work for livable communities. Citizens for a Better Environment and Environmental Defense Fund, 1996. Available from Environmental Defense Fund, Washington D.C., http://www.edf.org
4. A. Borning, B. Friedman, J. Davis, and P. Lin. Informing public deliberation: Value sensitive design of indicators for a large-scale urban simulation. In *Proc. 9th European Conference on Computer-Supported Cooperative Work*, Paris, Sept. 2005.
5. A. B. Brush and A. Borning. 'Today' messages: Lightweight support for small group awareness via email. In *Hawaii International Conference on System Sciences* (HICSS 38), Jan. 2005.
6. J. Davis. Household indicators: Design to inform and engage citizens. In *CHI 2006 Work-in-Progress Papers*. ACM Press, Apr. 2006.
7. J. Davis. *Value Sensitive Design of Interactions with UrbanSim Indicators*. PhD thesis, Dept. of Computer Science & Engineering, University of Washington, 2006.
8. T. de la Barra. *Integrated Land Use and Transportation Modeling: Decision Chains and Hierarchies*. Cambridge University Press, 1995.
9. R. Dowling, R. Ireson, A. Skabardonis, D. Gillen, and P. Stopher. Predicting air quality effects of traffic-flow improvements: Final report and user's guide. Technical Report 535, National Cooperative Highway Research Program, Transportation Research Board, National Research Council, 2005.
10. A. Downs. *Still Stuck in Traffic: Coping with Peak-hour Congestion*. The Brookings Institution, Washington, D.C., 2004.
11. M. Echenique, A. Flowerdew, J. Hunt, T. Mayo, I. Skidmore, and D. Simmonds. The MEPLAN models of Bilbao, Leeds and Dortmund. *Transport Reviews*, 10(4):309–322, 1990.
12. R. Förster. *Bridging the gap between scientifically-based information and its application in planning for sustainable regional development: The role of computer models*. PhD thesis, Department of Environmental Engineering, ETH Zurich, 2007. In preparation.
13. B. Freeman-Benson and A. Borning. YP and urban simulation: Applying an agile programming methodology in a politically tempestuous domain. In *Proceedings of the 2003 Agile Development Conference*, Salt Lake City, Utah, June 2003. Available at http://www.urbansim.org/papers.
14. B. Friedman, P. H. Kahn Jr., and A. Borning. Value Sensitive Design and information systems: Three case studies. In *Human-Computer Interaction and Management Information Systems: Foundations*. M.E. Sharpe, Armonk, NY, 2006.
15. B. Friedman and H. Nissenbaum. Bias in computer systems. *ACM Transactions on Information Systems*, 14(3):330–347, 1996.
16. M. Garret and M. Wachs, editors. *Transportation Planning on Trial: The Clean Air Act and Travel Forecasting*. Sage Publications, Thousand Oaks, CA, 1996.
17. A. Hunt and D. Thomas. *Pragmatic Unit Testing*. The Pragmatic Programmers, LLC, 2003.
18. D. B. Lee. Requiem for large-scale models. *Journal of the American Institute of Planners*, 39:163–178, 1973.
19. I. Lowry. A model of metropolis. Technical Report RM-4035-RC, Rand Corporation, Santa Monica, CA, 1964.
20. E. Miller, D. Kriger, and J. Hunt. Integrated urban models for simulation of transit and land use policies. Final Report, Project H-12. TCRP Web Document 9, Transit

Cooperative Highway Research Project, National Academy of Sciences: Washington, DC. http://books.nap.edu/books/tcr009/html, 1999.
21. R. E. Noonan and R. H. Prosl. Unit testing frameworks. In *SIGCSE '02: Proceedings of the 33rd SIGCSE Technical Symposium on Computer Science Education*, pages 232–236, New York, 2002. ACM Press.
22. S. Putman. *Integrated Urban Models: Policy Analysis of Transportation and Land Use.* Pion, London, 1983.
23. H. Ševčíková, A. Borning, D. Socha, and W.-G. Bleek. Automated testing of stochastic systems: A statistically grounded approach. In *Proceedings of the ACM International Symposium on Software Testing and Analysis*, 2006. In press.
24. H. Ševčíková, A. Raftery, and P. Waddell. Assessing uncertainty in urban simulations using Bayesian melding. *Transportation Research B*, 2006. Accepted subject to modest revision - draft available from www.urbansim.org/papers/_BMinUrbansim.pdf
25. F. Southworth. A technical review of urban land use-transportation models as tools for evaluating vehicle reduction strategies. U.S. Department of Energy, 1995.
26. P. Waddell. A behavioral simulation model for metropolitan policy analysis and planning: Residential location and housing market components of UrbanSim. *Environment and Planning B: Planning and Design 2000*, 27(2):247–263, 2000.
27. P. Waddell. UrbanSim: Modeling urban development for land use, transportation, and environmental planning. *Journal of the American Planning Association*, 68(3):297–314, Summer 2002.
28. P. Waddell and A. Borning. A case study in digital government: Developing and applying UrbanSim, a system for simulating urban land use, transportation, and environmental impacts. *Social Science Computer Review*, 22(1):37–51, 2004.
29. P. Waddell, H. Ševčíková, D. Socha, E. Miller, and K. Nagel. Opus: An open platform for urban simulation. Presented at the Computers in Urban Planning and Urban Management Conference, London, June 2005. Available from www. urbansim.org/papers.
30. P. Waddell, G. Ulfarsson, J. Franklin, and J. Loeb. Incorporating land use in metropolitan transportation planning. Submitted for publication – draft available from www.urbansim.org/papers, Feb. 2006.
31. P. Waddell and G. F. Ulfarsson. Introduction to urban simulation: Design and development of operational models. In P. Stopher, K. Button, K. Haynes, and D. Hensher, editors, *Handbook of Transport, Volume 5: Transport Geography and Spatial Systems*. Pergamon Press, 2004.

SUGGESTED READINGS

- Paul Waddell and Gudmundur F. Ulfarsson, "Introduction to Urban Simulation: Design and Development of Operational Models," *Handbook of Transport, Volume 5: Transport Geography and Spatial Systems*, P. Stopher et al., eds., Pergamon Press, 2004. Available from www.urbansim.org/papers. An introduction to urban simulation (interpreted broadly to mean operational models that attempt to represent dynamic processes and interactions of urban development and transportation).

- Paul Waddell, "UrbanSim: Modeling Urban Development for Land Use, Transportation, and Environmental Planning," *Journal of the American Planning Association*, Vol. 68 No. 3, Summer 2002, pages 297–314. An early but accessible overview of the UrbanSim system.

- Paul Waddell and Alan Borning, "A Case Study in Digital Government: Developing and Applying UrbanSim, a System for Simulating Urban Land Use, Transportation, and Environmental Impacts," *Social Science Computer Review*, Vol. 22, No. 1, February 2004, pages 37–51. As the title suggests, presents UrbanSim as a case study in digital government research. Emphasizes the various tensions between conducting university research and applying it to a regional government application in Salt Lake City in a highly visible, contested domain.
- Batya Friedman, Peter H. Kahn Jr., and Alan Borning, "Value Sensitive Design and Information Systems: Three Case Studies," in *Human-Computer Interaction and Management Information Systems: Foundations*, Ping Zhang and Dennis Galletta, eds., M.E. Sharpe, Armonk, NY, 2006. A description of the Value Sensitive Design theory and methodology, including an UrbanSim case study.

ONLINE RESOURCES

- The UrbanSim website, including papers, downloads, and other information: http://www.urbansim.org
- The home page for the Value Sensitive Design project: http://www.ischool.washington.edu/vsd

QUESTIONS FOR DISCUSSION

Here are a number of questions that would be suitable for classroom discussion (as well as future research).

1. Consider D. B. Lee's 1973 critique "Requiem for Large-Scale Models" [18]. Which of the problems raised by Lee have been addressed by current models, and which are still open problems? Of the open problems, which will it be feasible to address in the next decade?
2. What issues arise in applying UrbanSim to urban regions in countries other than the United States, including both developed and developing countries? Consider issues of alternate land use laws and ownership, transportation patterns, data availability, and others.
3. There are huge uncertainties about some of the exogenous assumptions used by UrbanSim, including the future price of oil, the macroeconomy,

possible technological shifts in transportation or telecommuting, and others. How should these uncertainties best be communicated to users of UrbanSim? What are appropriate controls for allowing them to change these assumptions?

4. Suppose UrbanSim were being designed for use by authoritarian governments rather than in a democratic context. Are there things that the designers should do differently? If so, what?

UNIT 3

Case Studies

Chapter 23

TAKING BEST PRACTICE FORWARD

Helene Gieber[1], Christine Leitner[2], Gerti Orthofer[1], and Roland Traunmüller[1]

[1]Institute of Informatics in Business and Government, Johannes Kepler University Linz (surname@iwv.jku.at); [2]Center for European Public Administration (CEPA), Danube University Krems, previously Head of eEurope Awards Programme

CHAPTER OVERVIEW

Grading Best Practice model cases paves the way for wide-reaching improvements in e-Government applications. This contribution provides a short overview of the eEurope Awards for e-Government 2005, including details on their objectives, the process and the awarded projects. Then some lessons learned from the e-Government Awards 2005 in relation to Best Practice transfer are summarised. In this context, key issues pertinent to using Best Practice model cases in practice and knowledge transfer are explored. The salient point is how to put model cases into practice. Four points have to be considered: finding suitable model cases, evaluating the feasibility of a project, entering a learning process and using various knowledge transfer mechanisms.

1. THE eEUROPE AWARDS: PROMOTING BEST PRACTICE

Knowledge transfer to build better e-Government solutions is in demand. This interest is due to different stages of maturity in eTransformation. Many institutions are still in initial stages of e-Government development (as a whole or in a particular field of application), and thus they seek advice and information from experienced partners. In that way Best Practice (or Good Practice - a less pretentious notion which has become a widely used term) paves the way for development. One has to see the evaluation of e-Government projects as a crucial part of the public governance cycle which starts with democratic deliberation, involves planning and policy making and is concluded by the assessment of governmental work. In some way, ideas that date back to the political cybernetics from the Sixties have matured by now.

Award programmes are an effective way to identify high quality cases. For this reason, in 2001 the European Commission launched a good practice awards programme within the framework of the eEurope initiative. The objective of the eEurope Awards for Innovation in e-Government[1] was to stimulate and facilitate the exchange of good practice and experience in the public sector across Europe by identifying and promoting excellence and creativity with a view to supporting the mutual recognition and adoption of good practices. Such has been the success of this initiative that the e-Government Awards 2005 have been designated an i2010 event. In June 2006, the Council of Ministers of Telecommunication welcomed the i2010 e-Government Action Plan adopted by the European Commission in April 2006 which emphasises the importance of good practice exchange and knowledge transfer in e-Government across Europe. Furthermore, in its conclusions the Council confirmed the strategic role of the Awards within the framework of the Action Plan.

2. THE eEUROPE AWARDS PROCESS

The Awards aim to highlight and inform about the efforts made by a wide variety of European national, regional and local actors in the public sector. Through the use of information and communication technologies (ICT) they have increased efficiency and performance and improved the quality and accessibility of public services. For the four sets of Awards (two

[1] The eEurope Awards Programme was funded by the IST programme for the years 2003-2005.

for e-Government and two for eHealth), a total of 880 projects were submitted from almost 30 countries. In each competition, the shortlisted candidates (finalists) were invited to exhibitions at high-level conferences where the winners were presented to the public.

The Awards themselves promote the use of innovative technology by electronically managing the application and evaluation process. The winning entries are evaluated and ranked by experts from a variety of European countries with multidisciplinary backgrounds. The eEurope Awards are an IST[2] accompanying measure (Framework Programme 5) and are managed by the eEurope Awards Secretariat (hereafter called "Secretariat") based at the European Institute of Public Administration (EIPA) in the Netherlands. The Secretariat ensures transparency, fairness and the smooth running of the process. It has produced good practice catalogues which include a brief analysis of the shortlisted cases for each award (finalists) and state of affairs reports related to each award. In addition, it publishes a summary and conclusions of each conference and compiles the evaluation reports for all awards.[3] The Institute of Informatics in Business and Government of Linz University was invited to provide support for both e-Government Awards (in 2003 and 2005).

3. THE eEUROPE AWARDS FOR e-GOVERNMENT 2005

The e-Government Awards 2005 formed part of the third Ministerial e-Government Conference, "Transforming Public Service," in Manchester on 24-25 November 2005. The conference, which was jointly organised by the European Commission and the UK Presidency of the European Union, was dedicated to analysing the future trends of e-Government in Europe. It brought together ministers and politicians responsible for e-Government in Europe as well as top managers and practitioners from public administrations and industry. Thus, as was the case at the 2003 Ministerial Conference in Como, Italy, the second e-Government Awards received attention at the highest level of European administration.

The main goal of the third Ministerial e-Government Conference in Manchester in November 2005 was to demonstrate the benefits that European, national and regional e-Government initiatives had delivered to their stakeholders so far. This implied a shift in focus compared to the 2003 event, where clearly the maturity of online provision of government services

---

[2] Information Society Technologies

[3] Details on winners, honourable mentions, finalists, reports, conclusions: www. e-europeawards.org

was at the centre of discussions, with limited attention to (economic and social) impact. The deliberate choice of themes and selection criteria for the e-Government Awards 2005 summarised below reflect these developments, and in that sense the projects identified through the awards process provide evidence of efforts made at the grassroots level.

One of the prior goals of the Awards was to identify and disseminate good practice in transforming public services. They were organised in close cooperation with the European Commission and the UK Presidency of the European Union. Preparations had already started at the end of 2004. The submissions (hereafter called "cases") were received and evaluated electronically via the eEurope Awards web application (www. e-europeawards.org).[4] In order to ensure the timely and effective dissemination of the call across Europe and all levels of administration, thus achieving a critical mass of applications, extensive online marketing was conducted and administrations were invited to pre-register their interest in the period from mid February until mid March. The eEurope Awards Helpdesk registered 106 entries from 25 countries. Moreover, the Secretariat made use of its extensive network and was invited to present the Awards at various conferences as well as in the European Public Administration Network (EPAN) and the e-Government subgroup of the eEurope Advisory Board. Two hundred and thirty four cases from 28 countries (out of the 33 eligible ones) were submitted in response to the 2005 call.

4. THE SELECTION PROCESS

Based on the experience and methodology of the previous Awards, the cases were evaluated in a three-step process. Furthermore, to ensure continuity, the same eligibility criteria as in 2003 were applied: The case had to be from a member State of the European Union, a candidate country or a member of EFTA; the case had to be operational; and the first applicant had to be a public sector actor. Comprehensive and complete documentation had to accompany the submission. A new criterion was introduced for cases already submitted for previous Awards, whereby they had to demonstrate significant progress compared to the last submission.

In the first phase the cases were evaluated on a remote and anonymous basis by a panel of independent experts. In a second phase, consensus meetings and a plenary session of the expert panel were held in Maastricht in July 2005. Fifty two cases were shortlisted as finalists and thus invited to exhibit at the Manchester Ministerial e-Government Conference in November 2005. All decisions taken by the expert panel were consensual. In addition, the 52 finalists plus an additional 24 cases received the

[4] Annotation: the Manchester 2005 Competition used the notion Good Practice.

e-Government Good Practice Label awarded by the European Commission via the e-Government Good Practice Framework.[5] The next step was the final Judging which took place the day before the conference in Manchester. From the shortlist identified in phase 2 fifteen nominees were selected by the panel of experts, and out of those the experts voted four winners (one per theme).

Evaluation is a complex task that requires thorough consideration, especially when it comes to defining criteria. In the case of the e-Government Awards 2005 the following three main evaluation criteria were applied during the selection process: (1) innovation and effective management, (2) real practical results and impact, and (3) relevance and transferability (Leitner 2005).

Criteria relevance: For a case to be relevant an innovative approach to tackling a problem was required. Furthermore, high scores were given to exemplary project development, accurate documentation and sound engineering. Generally, the compliance with e-Government strategy goals will distinguish a project, e.g.:

- citizen-centred services achieving high take-up and customer satisfaction
- high integration and collaboration of different systems and entities
- effective collaboration between public administration and citizens
- mobile Government and the extension of broadband usage
- establishment of Public-Private-Partnerships

Criteria transferability: The applicants had to provide a valuable and sufficiently detailed list of advice for potential recipients. The case should show that the underlying principles can be examined and adapted by others or used as inspiration and/or guidelines. Transferability of best practice has to consider both the supply side and the demand side (i.e. what can be learned and who can learn from the experience). Thus, achieving transferability of a given solution is not easy. Various aspects have to be taken into account. Government structures may vary, e.g. depending on the degree of centralisation/decentralisation, the roles of agencies and the specificities of administrative cultures.

5. THEMES AND WINNERS OF THE e-GOVERNMENT AWARDS 2005

The e-Government Awards 2005 aimed at identifying and disseminating good practice in transforming public services within four themes: "Enabling

[5] www.egov-goodpractice.org

e-Government – The Right Environment," "Transformation – Government Readiness," "Businesses and Citizens Service Use" and "Impact." The four themes corresponded to the themes of the Ministerial e-Government Conference held in Manchester in November 2005, where the Awards were presented. The following section summarises the focus of each theme and briefly describes the winners.

Theme 1: Creating the right environment to enable government, businesses and citizens to benefit from transformation.

The questions addressed by this theme concern how information technology can enable better government, and how it can create the right environment to transform public administrations for the benefit of government, businesses and citizens. The 71 cases (30% of all applications for the e-Government Awards) submitted in this theme demonstrated good practice in establishing infrastructure, frameworks for modernisation, standards and methodologies, government services, government-to-business solutions, organisation of services and community development.

The winner in this theme came from Poland, i.e. KSI ZUS – Complex Computer Systems for the Social Insurance Institution, which according to the Jury "[...] is an extremely impressive initiative involving large-scale institutional change. Despite the short time period in which the project has been active, it already has a high impact on agencies, employers and insured persons. There is significant potential for transfer to other sectors and countries." KSI ZUS is the first public institution in Poland that has made it possible to submit documents by secure email. Small enterprises may still use traditional hard copy, with advanced technology document scanners being used to digitise and store paper-based information. More than 75% of payees file eDocuments via "Payer" software, which is a part of the KSI ZUS system. This accounts for 90% of all information submitted to ZUS. The electronic data transmission channel communicates with Open-End Pension Funds (OFEs), financial intermediaries and the National Healthcare Fund (NFZ). Thus an infrastructure is provided that enables workers in Poland to better plan saving for their pensions before they retire.

Theme 2: Transformation of the organisation and innovation in the back office.

This theme concerns the transformation and innovation of the back office with e-Government acting as a catalyst for the transformation in public administrations and embraces a number of different topics. The 44 cases (19% of the total) submitted under this theme demonstrated a wide range of examples of good practice in information and knowledge management, such as secure data processing and transmission between administrations and departments, change management or multiple citizen service and training tools. Cases demonstrated that the effective use of ICT in a public administration redesigned by business process re-engineering can result in significant improvements in public sector effectiveness, both in customer services and internal matters.

The winner in this thematic group came from Denmark, i.e. EID – Electronic Invoicing Denmark, an example of a national government showing readiness for e-Government and demonstrating how organisational transformation and back-office innovation takes place across the public sector. According to the Jury, "The project is a good example for all European governments. It focuses on electronic invoicing that was mandated by law and put into practice with an XML-based standard. Business processes both in government and business have been improved significantly since it was introduced in early 2005 achieving 95% take-up rate. An important value-added is that provision was made for SMEs to comply with the eInvoicing through service providers." The system has resulted in savings of an estimated € 120-150 million per year. Electronic Invoicing is compulsory in Denmark. It is supported by a recent legislative framework. EID was the result of a public-private partnership that made use of successfully established technology. Fifteen million transactions that were previously handled on paper are now managed electronically.

Theme 3: Businesses and Citizens Service Use – Transformation and innovation in external facing services, putting citizens and businesses at the centre, driving use and participation

Theme 3 is concerned with the transformation and innovation in external facing services. By putting citizens and businesses at the centre, real benefits for users should be delivered. More specifically, this thematic group explores citizen and business-centred service innovations that achieve efficiency savings. The 102 cases (44%) submitted under this theme encompassed a variety of services such as e-Government portals for citizens, e-Government portals for business, local city interfaces, multi service delivery mechanisms, fiscal management, national and local e-democracy initiatives, as well as community service.

The winner in this theme came from the Netherlands. Kadaster On-line compiles data about registered properties and makes it available to business clients and citizens through public registers and cadastral maps. It supports the objective of the Dutch government to have 65% of public services online by 2007. The Jury described this project as "[...] an excellent project that provides significant benefits to administration and users through the integration of cadastral information and services. The integration and collaboration of different systems and entities is impressive, and there is high potential for replication in different regions and European countries."

The service is used by 6,000 registered clients and enables 45,000 users to access up-to-date land registry information. Over 60,000 products are provided. The most important extensions are online products for citizens, the use of automated data traffic, which enables clients to incorporate land registry information into their own applications automatically, and EULIS, a project that involves several countries cooperating to make land registry information accessible on a pan-European level.

Theme 4: Impact – Measuring the impact on and benefits to government, businesses and citizens

The delivery of clear and measured benefits to government, businesses and citizens is the core of this theme. Although each of the first three themes required demonstrable outcomes, this fourth theme focused explicitly on the analysis and measurement of impact. The 17 submitted cases (7% of the total of submissions) encompassed a variety of topics like efficiency, value added, cost and time savings, government services to citizens and business, government assessment, measuring and evaluation systems, and benefits realisation aspects. The cases selected as finalists illustrate how, by setting indicative objectives/indicators/targets and defining quantitative and qualitative approaches, the analysis of major benefits either to users or the public administration can be assessed by common measurement frameworks. Social and economic impact can also be measured by user feedback.

The winner of this theme was the Irish Revenue On-line Service (ROS). The Jury concluded that "The project has impressive and well-documented results in terms of service take-up and process re-engineering. There is an excellent business case that is convincing for both administrations and users. With the high level of interest in eTaxation in many EU and candidate countries, the well-documented processes and lessons learned from this project provide an excellent guideline for both technical development and change management." In 2004, over 1.1 million returns were filed with ROS representing € 8.3 billion in payments. In addition, 53% (157,218) of timely filed income tax returns and 79% of all new vehicle registrations were filed with ROS during the year. There were 2.1 million enquiries to the ROS customer information service in the same period. As ROS is a fully automated back-end integrated service, staff resources have been moved from routine processing work to more rewarding and productive compliance and investigative work. Providing online access to customer information substantially reduces customer contacts for the Inland Revenue, and automated payment systems mean earlier bank payments for the Inland Revenue and speedier repayments for customers.

In terms of numbers of submissions, Theme 3, "Businesses and Citizens Service Use" appeared to be most appealing with 44% of all submissions (i.e. 102 cases), followed by Theme 1 "Enabling e-Government – The Right

Environment" with 30% (i.e. 71 cases) and Theme 2 "Transformation – Government Readiness" with 19% (i.e. 44 cases). Only 17 cases (i.e. 7%) were submitted under Theme 4 – "Impact." The reason for the rather low response to this thematic group may be that these developments are still in their early stages. Not only were applicants asked to describe the tools they had used to measure impacts but they also had to present the actual evidence collected in applying these tools. Projects that had been submitted for previous Awards were encouraged to participate in this thematic group. In those cases applicants were asked to demonstrate significant progress since the previous Awards in addition to the requirements described before. The above mentioned theme distribution was reflected in the group of the 52 finalists: 20 cases (38%) under Theme 3, 18 (35%) under Theme 1, 8 (15%) under Theme 2, and 6 (11.5%) under Theme 4 were invited to take part as exhibitors at the Manchester conference.

To better understand the context of a given case, a new category – "policy issues addressed by the case" – was introduced in the case description template. It is interesting to note that apart from general purpose initiatives (16.9%), i.e. core administrative services, the policy issues addressed point towards increased interest in projects related to state and society issues, such as e-democracy and/or e-Participation (15.8%), followed by social affairs (13.1%), economy and labour (12.8%), and tax and customs (10.7%). This trend is also reflected among the group of 52 finalists: 17.9% refer to general purpose, 14.5% to state and society, 13.8% to economy and labour, and 12.4% to social affairs.

6. LESSONS LEARNED FROM THE e-GOVERNMENT AWARDS 2005

The lessons learned from the 2005 Awards have been analysed and consolidated in the report on "Transforming Public Services: The case for the e-Government Awards" which is part of the project deliverables (Leitner 2005). A summary of the findings is presented here.[6]

The cases submitted for the 2005 Awards demonstrate that:

- the momentum for transformation of public services is still increasing;
- re-organisation is at least as important as new technologies;

[6] For other literature and the state of the art we refer to some current collective volumes and the proceedings of the Annual EGOV Conference series: Grönlund 2002, Traunmüller and Lenk 2002, Traunmüller 2003, Traunmüller 2004, Wimmer et al. 2005, Wimmer et al. 2006.

- it is important to make sure that citizens and businesses are benefiting; and
- quantification of benefits is possible.

e-Government is an essential tool for modernising Europe's public administrations. Awards, rankings and good practice case collections are ingredients of government modernisation policies. The fundamental question in this context is what European public administrations will look like in the future. Will there be convergence, or will each country follow a path of its own? Experience with New Public Management has shown that, while concepts and blueprints tend to be similar worldwide, their implementation and final outcome point to a high degree of diversity, which reflects the basic institutional characteristics of the respective national politico-administrative systems.

Creativity is an essential component for modernisation which can be stimulated by good practice, even though the best practice examples have to be carefully chosen and properly assessed. While the concepts underlying good practice solutions can be copied, their implementation takes place in environments which are shaped by the prevailing forces and institutional traditions of a given administrative culture. In this context, the e-Government Awards are not really about competition, but about learning, recognising creativity and identifying innovation that others can use.

Overall there appears to be a common understanding that the e-Government Awards 2005 have played a successful role in stimulating the sharing of experience in Europe.[7] This is inherent in the stated goal of the programme which aims to identify good practice in e-Government and to provide a European-wide platform for the recognition of achievement in transforming government through the use of ICT. More specifically, one can conclude from the 2005 experience: The Awards facilitate the exchange of good practices and shared learning with European partners, providing an opportunity for the recognition of successful case histories. Nonetheless some suggestions for improvement can be made:

Lessons learned from failures need to be included:

- A more structured approach is required which takes into account the context, the needs of recipients and face-to-face interaction.

---

[7] Direct feedback from stakeholders is essential to understand the issues at stake. Therefore – in addition to the data received through the applications – an attempt was made to use the Awards process to develop a deeper understanding of stakeholder needs by actively involving the 52 shortlisted candidates. Feedback was collected in the workshop for finalists; from the finalists' questionnaires distributed during the exhibition at the Ministerial eGovernment Conference 2005; and in the parallel session "Taking good practice forward" on 25 November 2005 at the Ministerial eGovernment Conference 2005.

- The problems of common standards for comparison and the constant need to update databases have to be addressed.

On a more global scale, the Awards provide a mechanism for a positive experience of shared learning referring to e-Government issues for conference attendees, the finalists themselves and – via various media – a wider audience of professional specialists. In this context, it is important to demonstrate that lessons have been learned from problems and failure. There is a balance to be struck between claiming legitimate credit for past achievements and being honest in admission of any shortcomings.

- Exercises such as the Awards exhibition and the direct involvement of the stakeholders are important for networking, awareness, knowledge enhancement, motivation and acknowledgement. Moreover, they are essential components of frameworks for good practice exchange.
- Databases are a good help, still, they are just one possible (however useful) tool for dialogue and learning. Looking at the feedback received during the 2005 Awards, one clearly sees that there is a need for an environment in which stakeholders can share their views and visions not only on a virtual platform but also face to face. The exchange of new solutions and the importance of personal contacts were ranked the top two benefits of the Awards exhibition.
- The challenge to create an environment for mutual learning, along with the need for common standards for comparison, was emphasised, as was the plea for a common understanding that each problem is individual and requires an individual solution in its context.
- Finally, one should consider providing actual examples of the successful transfer of good practices and making the transfer process in itself a subject for case studies of good practice.

The research report EIPA presented at the Ministerial Conference in Como in 2003 identified "the way to learn from each other" as one of the key challenges for e-Government in Europe and thus suggested "to [establish] a framework for the exchange of good practices and experience at the European and international level [...] in order to foster strong commitment and continuity in the practical implementation of e-Government." Furthermore it emphasised that "[since] continuity is a key factor in the process of exchanging good practices, it is indispensable to establish such a framework to avoid a mere one-off "copying" of an awarded application which might not be suitable in a given socio-cultural context" (Leitner 2003). Much work has been done in this respect; however, as indicated in this paper, a number of issues still need to be addressed in order to take good practice exchange forward to support government modernisation policies across and beyond Europe.

7. THE CHALLENGE OF USING GOOD PRACTICE

For public authorities transferring knowledge means a continuous and effective exchange of experience. Best Practice is the pivot around which all activities spin; yet knowledge transfer goes far beyond reading a database of Best Practice cases and copying smooth running applications. To put it boldly: Best Practices from other organisations cannot simply be "replicated." This would mean that one underestimates the role of the concrete environment as well as the diversity of cultural, social and political backgrounds.

We are turning to the salient point now, the use of Best Practice cases. Landmark projects as model cases are the starting point; however, knowledge transfer means entrepreneurship. Three questions will be addressed in more detail:

1. How to find suitable model cases
2. How to evaluate the feasibility of a project
3. How to embark on learning processes and transfer mechanisms

Further reference is made to other publications, e.g. on the procedure (Gieber et al. 2006) and on a framework for feasibility (Traunmüller and Orthofer 2005).

8. FINDING SUITABLE MODEL CASES

Due to the diversity of cases, analysis and comparison may sometimes be quite difficult. Ideally a model case´s substantial parts are relevant for the analyzer's own project; furthermore, a model case will give insights into the project history that may be used as guidance and inspiration.

Seeking model cases: Consideration starts with the gathering of information on suitable model cases with relevance for the planned project. Examples could be the before-mentioned eEurope Awards Competitions, but also other best practice compilations for e-Government established by the EU.[8] Several model cases may be found as there are a lot of different projects with similar goals and conditions.

[8] http://europa.eu.int/information_society/activities/egovernment_research/gpf/cases/index_en.htm.

Deficiencies in documentation: Commonly, the main obstacle for analysis is insufficient documentation of model cases. Project descriptions are often very short and not sufficiently detailed, which makes it difficult to relate the content to the situation at hand. Furthermore, specific guidelines for use are required. For example, a good description would give hints on how a project could be split in smaller parts. Another obstacle is that the development stages of a project are insufficiently documented. Most documentation does not allow finding out reasons for certain design and implementation decisions within a model case.

Glossy descriptions are red herrings: Official documentation may mislead when it lacks substance. An important point is the fact that in reality we learn from both good cases and bad cases. There are many forces that avoid disclosure. People are afraid to talk about their failures, and even if street-level-bureaucrats would dare to admit mistakes, the higher ranks would "smooth" the text: Officially all projects are always successful. As the analysis of the eEurope Awards has shown, lessons learned from failures provide highly valuable information.

9. A FRAMEWORK FOR EVALUATING FEASIBILITY

For assessing a planned project, a framework may help to evaluate the feasibility. It puts a proposed system in the context of experiences gained from good practice. Here a framework is given sketching some important factors.

Goals of a project: Technology should not be considered as dominant System thinking will help to balance technology, organisational and societal goals. The aims in focus may be different: promoting the economy, offering services to citizens, involving citizens in participation, etc.

Strategies: There is a compelling need for developing visions and strategies. Imagination beyond short-term is necessary, often only innovative solutions may work. Here we suggest some aspects for planning: seeking public-private partnerships (PPPs) may further the project; bringing in NGOs is an essential help; mentoring might be beneficial. Overall, it is important to develop a proper strategy together with a well-defined and realistic set of goals and criteria. This is a pre-requisite to ensure that the right objectives are reached in response to actual social and economic demands. Having the right vision will ensure innovative concepts of ICT usage.

Existing structures and resources: A main step is building on the structures and resources at hand. There is a wide diversity of actions: using infrastructure and premises, coming together with interested groups, assembling active persons, etc. A general advice should be given: In system design continuity is as important a point as sustainability and affordability. For this careful deliberation is required.

Funding: Economic risks call for cost-benefit assessment which may not always be viable. It has to be stated that an economic viability assessment is not all; quite often it has to be balanced with other considerations. One reason for starting a project is an emerging and urgent need; other causes may be strategic significance or political considerations.

Assessing benefits: Costs and benefits imply a lot of different aspects that should be considered. However, in this context we only mention a few criteria: number of access channels and services, greater accountability, openness, transparency, etc.

Public-private partnerships: Generally, funding is a difficult task for which innovative solutions have to be found. This often leads to partnerships. PPPs offer many opportunities for funding as well as for the collaborative development of projects. There is always a need to balance the interests of the private partner, who expects a return on investment, and the public interest. This is not an easy task as potential benefits, such as access to and quality of services, are by nature rather intangible.

Actors: A prime question is: Who are the key actors - institutions and individuals - and how can we engage them? Commonly many persons, groups and institutions are involved in a concrete empowerment activity, e g. politicians, officials, NGOs and citizens. One has to be aware that actors are embedded in different situations and structures and may have different policies, visions and attitudes. So a divergence in viewpoints will occur even if not apparent at first glance.

Cooperation situations: Constellations of actors are important. There are a lot of negotiations going on in different project phases. Typical situations are making decisions on design or implementation. There is a need to create win-win approaches; actors should perceive that the benefits are balanced. For cooperation, common goals and a shared understanding of tasks should be established; openness builds the ground for innovation and success.

Technology: There is a clear motto: The use of technologies should be vision-driven rather than simply follow installation instructions for ready-made technical systems. For this problem, comprehension of the existing situation has to be combined with a good understanding of the opportunities opened up by technology. It is misleading to perceive problems and solutions only in the light of available and viable technical systems. Summing up, a balanced view is needed.

Design: Design has to take into account the characteristics of the public sector as features that are inherent and will not change (dominance of legal norms, transparency and safeguarding legal validity, etc.). Furthermore, a sound engineering approach is indispensable. This implies building suitable and user-friendly systems, looking for standards, safeguarding unimpeded communication, etc.

Legal and regulatory framework: Often legal rules and internal regulations need to be adapted to enable administrative procedures to be carried out electronically. Also, with regard to governmental needs on planning and emergency situations, the regulations have to strike a balance between privacy and openness.

Transforming administrative culture: Institutional settings influence the nature of innovation, administrative culture being an important aspect of these settings. So design has to focus on both staff qualification and cultural issues. Change management has to ensure a smooth transition of the organisation.

10. COLLECTIVE LEARNING PROCESSES AND TRANSFER MECHANISMS

According to Viviane Reding, "We are starting to see benefits from Europe's investments in 'e-Government' over the last few years, but we need to be more active in learning lessons from each other and getting the benefits of scale from adopting common approaches across borders." However, collective learning processes and transfer mechanisms are not fully established.

Proceeding to organisational learning: Best Practice examples should not mean replication in the sense of a mere transposition of experience, for this is likely to fail. Best practice should spur and somehow guide an evolutionary process within the institution. Therefore, organisational learning becomes the real agenda. In this respect, each institution has to develop its own roadmap to progress.

There are quite a lot of definitions of organisational learning, such as describing it as a process of detecting and correcting errors. As Ray Stata states, "...Organizational learning occurs through shared insights, knowledge, and mental models … and builds on past knowledge and experience – that is, on memory..." (Stata 1989). Thus a learning organisation is an organisation skilled in creating, acquiring, and transferring knowledge, as well as modifying its behaviour to reflect new knowledge and insights. This means learning from one's own practice and past as well as learning from experiences of others.

Fostering communication: Generally, communication with others is crucial for the use of Best Practice. In deliberating model cases several questions may arise. Conversation may also help to clarify emerging queries on the feasibility of transfer. The diversity of persons involved ensures different perspectives. The aim is to create knowledge through communication.

Learning to share[9]: The individuals start to discover what they know and share it; this will stimulate a learning process. It is a turning point when knowledge sharing becomes the rule. Surely selfishness will not die, but if we begin to see the advantages of sharing, it becomes distributed in a creative way.

Creating a learning situation: Organisational learning is hard work as it affects the whole organisation. Some points that make institutional learning a success are:

- Transferring knowledge quickly and efficiently throughout the organisation is crucial. Knowledge has to flow as a continuous act. Last but not least, the persons involved have to be taken into consideration.
- Several modes of learning have to be blended, comprising individual learning, learning by communication and the use of knowledge repositories.
- Learning has to be planned. One needs a defined project and an adequate allocation of persons, time and budget. A policy defining learning only in vague terms is risky, since it would result in weak commitment.
- Inter-institutional transfer shows certain hindrances. In any organisation several barriers emerge when it comes to incorporating knowledge created elsewhere. This has to be recognised as a problem which makes commitment from the top essential.
- Participation is crucial. The actual situation must be analysed and this means involving various stakeholders. Often stakeholders have difficulties defining a vision, yet they are quite good at spotting weak points of existing applications.

Championing innovation: You have to want innovation. As Patrick Corsi states: “innovation does not come by decree: you need to champion it” (Corsi 2001). Having a champion who blazes the trail is essential in any transfer project.

Invention seeds change, yet it is transfer that makes change happen, and there are several transfer mechanisms, documenting Best Practice examples

---

[9] At the World Economic Forum 2005 it was declared that “Learning to share” is the ultimate challenge for knowledge. (Newsweek Special Edition on the World Economic Forum 2005.)

being the most important of them. Still, Best Practice should not be used exclusively. It is advisable to have several methods of transfer which supplement each other.

Knowledge transfer conferences: Here institutions with highly different levels of experience come together; transfer from institutions with mature experience to those with less experience is intended. Transfer conferences have a particular agenda including cases studies and practice collections as well as policies and strategies for improvement.[10]

Learning journeys and virtual transfer spaces: These are two solutions greatly differing in cost and effort. The first one offers the participants the opportunity to explore first-hand innovative governmental programmes and their implementation – often in the form of organised on-site visits. Virtual transfer forums are less effective but provide easily accessible information.

Involving facilitators and mentors: Human experience is a key factor. A very strong and formally defined way of mentorship is found in twinning projects. These constitute a particular mechanism involving a special commitment between two institutions, thus creating an intensive learning situation, with the more advanced partner acting as mentor. The Institute of Informatics in Business and Government at Linz University has gained experience in two twinning activities.[11]

11. THE FUTURE: PROCEEDING TO HIGHER ORDER MODEL SOLUTIONS

There are many processes and capabilities that are common across public authorities. Having shared accepted model solutions would revolutionise the public sector. This would mean proceeding to higher order model solutions, thus defining standard paradigms for the public realm. These would include the following items:

- Generalised interfaces of high usability
- Common process modules for services (initiation, case handling, provision, payment, etc.)
- A sophisticated systems integration with an architectural tier that connects the diverse agencies within the public area

[10] As an example the Institute of Informatics in Business and Government at the Linz University has organised the Eastern European e|Gov Days in cooperation with the Austrian Computer Society and Eastern European Partners.

[11] Involvement comprises working as systems analyst for a Migration Information System for Lithuania, and experiences on the cooperation between Stuttgart and Sankt Petersburg.

- Systems safeguarding security and identity management
- Systems managing human resources, public procurement, etc.
- Training and qualification capabilities for staff.

At present we focus on individual model cases that can be followed as examples, thus providing inspiration for projects to be implemented. Compared to the situation some years ago this is already considerable progress; however, for the future it will not suffice to dispose of a portfolio of model prototypes. We have to head towards standardisation.

REFERENCES

COM (2006) 173 final, i2010 e-Government Action Plan: Accelerating e-Government in Europe for the Benefit of All, Brussels, 25 April 2006

Corsi P, Dulieu M (2001) The Innovation Drive. The Marketing of Advanced Technologies. Knowledge 2 Know-how Ltd, London

Dovifat A, Kubisch D, Brüggemeier M, Lenk K, Reichard Ch (2004) Explaining Successes and Failures of E-Government Implementation with Micropolitics. In: Traunmüller R (ed) Electronic Government. Third International Conference E-GOV 2004, Proceedings, Springer, Berlin Heidelberg, pp 308-312

European Commission, 5th Framework Program, User-friendly Information Society (IST) (2001) Key Action I - Systems and Services for the Citizen. Retrieved August 8, 2006 http://www.cordis.lu/ist/ka1/home.html

Gieber H, Orthofer G, Traunmüller R (2006) Best Practice in e-Government: Some Reflections on Usage In: Wimmer MA, Traunmüller R, Orthofer G (eds) Knowledge transfer across Europe: 4th Eastern Europe e|Gov Days and 5th e|Gov Days, OCG, Wien

Grönlund A (ed) (2002) Electronic Government - Design, Applications and Management. Idea Group Publishing, Hershey

Lei-da C et al (2004) Consumer acceptance of virtual stores: a theoretical model and critical success factors for virtual stores. ACM SIGMIS Database, vol 35, pp 8 - 31

Leitner C (ed) et al (2003) e-Government in Europe: The State of Affairs, presented at the e-Government Conference in Como, EIPA, Maastricht

Leitner C (ed) et al (forthcoming 2007) Transforming Public Services: The Case for the e-Government Awards, EIPA, Maastricht. (http://www.eipa.eu/eEurope_Awards/ index.htm)

Lenk K, Traunmüller R, Wimmer MA (2002) The Significance of Law and Knowledge for Electronic Government. In: Grönlund A (ed) Electronic Government - Design, Applications and Management. Idea Group Publishing, Hershey, pp 61-77

Newsweek Special Edition (2005) The Knowledge Revolution, Special Edition to the World Economic Forum 2005, Newsweek

Press release 10042/06, 2735th Council Meeting. Transport, Telecommunications and Energy. Luxembourg, 8th and 9th June 2006. e-Government for all Europeans. Council Conclusions. p 20. www.consilium.europa.eu/ueDocs/cms_Data/docs/pressData/en/trans/ 89954.pdf

Stata R (1989) Organisational learning – The Key to Management Innovation. Sloan Management Review

Traunmüller R (ed) (2003) Electronic Government. Second International Conference E-GOV 2003, Proceedings, Springer, Heidelberg

Traunmüller R (ed) (2004) Electronic Government. Third International Conference E-GOV 2004, Proceedings, Springer, Berlin Heidelberg

Traunmüller R, Lenk K (eds) (2002) Electronic Government. First International Conference E-GOV 2002, Proceedings, Springer, Heidelberg

Traunmüller R, Orthofer G (2005) Knowledge Transfer in e-Government - Mechanisms and Experiences from Eastern European Cases. In: e-Government: European Strategies Compared, COM-PA Conference Proceeding, Bologna

Wimmer MA (ed) (2005) E-Government 2005: Knowledge Transfer and Status. OCG Schriftenreihe, Wien

Wimmer MA, Traunmüller R, Grönlund A, Andersen KV (eds) (2005) Electronic Government. 4th International Conference E-GOV 2005, Springer, Berlin Heidelberg

Wimmer MA, Traunmüller R, Grönlund A, Andersen KV (eds) (2006) Electronic Government. 5th International Conference E-GOV 2006, Springer, Berlin Heidelberg.

SUGGESTED READINGS AND ONLINE RESOURCES

- Traunmüller Roland (ed.): Knowledge Transfer for e-Government. Seeking Better e-Government Solutions. Trauner Verlag, Linz. 2006.
- Leitner Christine (ed) et al (2003) e-Government in Europe: The State of Affairs, presented at the e-Government Conference in Como, EIPA, Maastricht (http://www.eipa.eu/eEurope_Awards/eEurope_Website_Documentation%20Section/e-gov_Research%20Report_2003.pdf)
- Leitner Christine (ed) et al, (2007, forthcoming) Transforming Public Services: The Case for the e-Government Awards, EIPA, Maastricht. (http://www.eipa.eu/eEurope_Awards/index.htm)
- Corsi P, Dulieu M The Innovation Drive. The Marketing of Advanced Technologies. Knowledge 2 Know-how Ltd, London. 2001
- Wimmer Maria (ed) Knowledge Management in Electronic Government
- Springer Verlag. Heidelberg. 2645. LNAI. 2003
- Newsweek: The Knowledge Revolution, Special Edition, December 2005

QUESTIONS FOR DISCUSSION

1. Which criteria are valuable for Knowledge Transfer?
2. Which factors are key to running a successful project?
3. Why will a mere replication of projects fail?

4. What methodologies/instruments exist that better analyse the demand side of knowledge transfer?
5. What are some ways to better match the demand side (i.e. recipients) with the supply side of knowledge transfer?
6. How can awards schemes contribute to enhanced knowledge transfer?

Chapter 24

EPETITIONING IN THE SCOTTISH PARLIAMENT

Ann Macintosh[1], Nick Adams[1], Angus Whyte[1], and Jim Johnston[2]

[1]International Tele-democracy Research Centre, Napier University, Edinburgh, UK; [2]The Scottish Parliament, Edinburgh, UK.

CHAPTER OVERVIEW

This case study focuses on the use of an online petitioning system for the Scottish Parliament. The system, called ePetitioner, was developed through a partnership between Napier University in Edinburgh and BT Scotland. The objective of ePetitioner is to provide a service for citizens to raise concerns and have them addressed through the formal processes of parliament. Traditional petitioning merely allows citizens to add their name and address to a petition if they support it, typically without the opportunity to consider and reflect on the issue and also with no mechanism to register opinion against the petition. Adding technology to support such a push-button process is recognized by many as running counter to supporting democracy and therefore not enhancing participation. Therefore ePetitioner was designed from the outset to allow background information on the petition and links to third party websites to be added to better inform potential visitors to the petition web pages. Additionally, a discussion forum is integrated into each petition to facilitate discussion on the petition and allow arguments for and against to be voiced. We argue that these additional features added to the traditional petition process can be viewed as technology design aiming to enable more participative democracy.

1. INTRODUCTION

This chapter focuses on the introduction and use of information and communication technology (ICT) in the form of an online petitioning system in the Scottish Parliament to give citizens an opportunity to participate in the democratic decision making of Scotland. The system is called ePetitioner.

One of the main issues to emerge from the European Conference of Members of National Parliaments in Information and Communication Technologies was the need to strengthen parliamentary democracy with better involvement of citizens in political and democratic processes. The Scottish Parliament's ePetitions system which was formally launched in February 2004 is an exemplary use of ICTs to achieve these aims.

In the UK in 1997 the concept of devolution had begun to reshape government, providing opportunities to form new national governments in Scotland, Wales and Northern Ireland. A 'Yes vote' in the Scottish devolution referendum in 1997 predicated the arrival of a Scottish Parliament in May 1999. The Scottish Parliament gave devolved power for specific areas of government from the Westminster Parliament in London to a new Scottish Parliament based in Edinburgh. The development of ePetitioning should be viewed within the Parliament's founding principles which were drawn up by the Consultative Steering Group (CSG). This group of distinguished parliamentarians and civic leaders was set up in November 1997 to develop ways of working for the new Parliament. The CSG identified four key principles in its final report (HMSO 1999): sharing the power; accountability; access and participation; and equal opportunities. In particular, it stated that the Parliament: 'should be accessible, open, responsive, and develop procedures which make possible a participative approach to the development, consideration and scrutiny of policy and legislation.' The CSG also established an expert panel on ICTs who reported that: 'Encouraging and fostering democratic participation is a very important part of the Parliament's objectives of promoting openness and accessibility, and of working in partnership with the people of Scotland.'

The CSG report called for a development of a culture of genuine consultation and participation, to include citizens not currently engaged in the political process. Integral to this was the establishment of a Pubic Petitions Committee (PPC) whose remit consists solely of the consideration of petitions. The Committee provides an avenue for individuals, community and pressure groups and other organizations to participate fully in the democratic process in Scotland by raising issues of public concern with the Parliament. There are no restrictions on who can submit a petition or the number of signatures required for a petition to be considered by the Committee. Petitions can also be lodged in any language. ePetitioning is seen as a means of enhancing accessibility to participation in the political process which in turn will strengthen the accountability of Members of the Scottish Parliament (MSPs) to the people of Scotland.

2. LITERATURE REVIEW

The practice of interest groups and individuals lobbying elected representatives is often viewed as running counter to principles of open government, particularly where influence goes unseen and unaccounted for. Nevertheless, if lobbying can be seen as the boundary between formal structures of governance and the informal influence of organized civil society (Nixon and Johanssen 2000) then it possible that ICT may help to make this process more transparent.

Petitioning is well recognised as a form of political action across European democracies. Within a UK context the right of the subject to petition the Monarch for redress of grievances has probably been exercised since Saxon times. It was recognised in Magna Carta and more explicitly in an Act of 1406. In 1571 a Committee for Motions of Griefs and Petitions was first appointed. The Bill of Rights of 1688 reaffirmed "the right of the subjects to petition the King" and stated that "all commitments and prosecutions for such petitioning are illegal". ePetitioner in the Scottish Parliament is therefore concerned with applying technology to a rich historical tradition of political engagement with which citizens can easily identify.

Petitioning is a simple and straightforward means of democratic participation and citizens have long used this mechanism as a means of raising issues of concern with their elected representatives. Indeed, within the UK, recent research by the Electoral Commission found that apart from voting in elections, signing petitions is the most frequently undertaken political activity. The survey which involved interviews with a representative sample of 2,605 adults aged 18+ across the UK and reported that: 'The past 12 months have seen a statistically significant increase in the number who say they have signed a petition over the past two or three years (from 39% in December 2003 to 44% in December 2004).' (The Electoral Commission 2005: p19) It is, therefore, significant that despite increasing concern regarding voter apathy the number of citizens signing petitions is actually increasing.

However, traditional petitioning merely allowed citizens to add their name and address to a petition if they supported it, typically without the means to become better informed on the subject matter and usually without the opportunity to consider and reflect on the issue. Also, there was also no mechanism to register opinion against the petition. Adding technology to support such a push-button process is recognized by many authors as running counter to supporting democracy. Barber (1984) clearly highlights the dangers of merely re-enforcing a questionable process with technology. Similarly, Fishkin (1992) argues the need to turn away from instant reaction politics and provide spaces for citizens to deliberate on issues. Budge (1996) argues that democratic political participation must involve both the means to be informed and the mechanisms to take part in democratic decision making. In the following section we demonstrate how the Scottish Parliament is using ePetitioner to address citizen participation through these joint perspectives of informing and participating. ePetitioner was designed from the outset to allow the principal petitioner to add background information on the petition and links to third party websites. Here the notion was to try to better inform potential visitors to the petition web pages. Additionally, a discussion forum is integrated into each petition in an attempt to facilitate discussion on the petition and allow arguments for and against to be voiced. These additional features added to the traditional petition process can be viewed as technology design aiming to enable more participative democracy however.

It is now widely recognized that ICTs have the potential to enhance democratic participation. The OECD (2001) states in its handbook on public participation in policy-making that: 'ICTs can provide powerful tools for strengthening government-citizen relations.' However, other authors (e.g. Sclove 1995; Mansell & Silverstone 1998) have drawn attention to the importance of correct technology design and its potential to also constrain democratic action. The Scottish Parliament's approach, addressed by ePetitioner in particular, is in keeping with the OECD report Citizens as Partners (2001), which described an urgent need for transparency, accountability and participation in political decision-making. The OECD Report proposed three strategies for enhancing citizen participation including 'partnership':

"Citizens can make an active and original contribution to policy-making, when their relationship with government is founded on the principle of partnership. Active participation represents a new frontier in government-citizen relations for all OECD Member countries." (p. 41)

A later study on behalf of the OECD (Macintosh, 2003) specifically looked at how ICT could be applied to enhance citizen participation in the policy process. The report provided an initial analytical framework for e-Participation and gave examples of best practice in a number of OECD member states. When considering ground-up participation it found few countries were addressing this aspect of citizen engagement. However, it cites the Scottish Parliament as addressing e-Participation through ePetitioning.

Lastly, ePetitioner also supports the European Commission's view of the *Role of e-Government for Europe's Future* in working towards: 'governments that are understandable and accountable to the citizens, open to democratic involvement and scrutiny' (COM (2003) 567).

3. EPETITIONING IN SCOTLAND

3.1 Specific Objectives

The objectives of ePetitioner, and the processes in place for its effective management, are to provide a service for citizens to raise concerns and have them addressed through the formal processes of parliament. Specifically, ePetitioner aims to enhance citizens' *access* to the petitioning process which can be realized in terms of these specific requirements:

- Any citizen should be able to raise an ePetition provided it adheres to admissibility criteria, e.g. that it is on an issue that the Scottish Parliament has powers to deal with. This contrasts with the approach of the Legislative Assembly of Queensland, for example, where ePetitions may only be presented through a representative.
- Citizens should be enabled to *discuss an ePetition*, regardless of whether they add their name in support of it. There is a need to *moderate* this discussion. Petitions should be regarded as topics of public debate by a geographically dispersed population, rather than simply as online documents to be delivered to representatives. EPetitioner aims to add to the participative element of the traditional petitioning process by allowing the possibility to sit down and think about the petitions key points in depth before making an informed choice as to whether or not to support and sign the petition and whether to add any comment.

To develop the petitioning *process*, the Public Petitions Committee (PPC) of the Scottish Parliament had to formulate information about the procedures in easily understandable and usable *guidelines* for the submission of petitions, both generally and for ePetitions specifically. A requirement for ePetitioner was therefore to provide online access to these guidelines. They describe the kind of issues that can be raised, what citizens should do before starting a petition, the form and content of the petition, how the PPC would consider the petition and who to contact for further information. Citizens also need to know about online security and privacy, about how to start an ePetition, the additional information they may provide to inform other citizens, about the issues they want to raise, and what may happen subsequently.

Academic research has suggested that one of the main reasons why those who have participated in the work of public bodies have come away dissatisfied is lack of information regarding the outcomes of participation exercises. ePetitioner provides citizens with the opportunity to track Parliament's response to the matters raised through a link to a progress page on each petition on the Parliament's website.

3.2 Design and Use

ePetitioner was developed through a partnership between BT Scotland, Napier University and the Scottish Parliament. Their shared interest in online public participation struck a chord with the NGO *WWF Scotland*, who saw an opportunity for more effective lobbying, and raised the first ePetition to enhance the public profile of a campaign on marine national parks in December 1999. ePetitioner was initially available as a pilot on the University's server (Macintosh et al. 2002). Following the success of the pilot, the system was re-engineered to fully integrate it with the Scottish Parliament's own website, and specifically the Public Petition Committee's pages and database of received petitions (Adams et al. 2005).

Ordinarily a person (or organization) wishing to raise a petition would contact the PPC clerking team and agree with them the text for the petition. This is necessary to ensure the petition is admissible within the Guidance on the Submission of Public Petitions[1]. Once the text of the ePetition has been agreed with the individual or organization raising it (the 'principal petitioner'), it is then entered into ePetitioner through a form in the online administration section. The petition is then live and runs for the prescribed period (usually 4–6 weeks), during which the signature list is regularly checked for spurious signatures, and the discussion forum moderated by the PPC clerking team on a daily basis. In particular, comments are checked to ensure that they are relevant to the aims of the petition and not potentially defamatory or inflammatory. Signatures are simply the name and location given by a citizen who wishes to support a petition. While it would be technically possible to require citizens to provide digital signatures, that would be inconsistent with the objective of maximizing accessibility since it would add to the technical competences required of citizens. Furthermore, duplicate names and addresses can occur, either through accidentally submitting the 'sign petition' form more than once, or a person may sign a petition on multiple occasions. These are monitored and automatically

[1] htttp://www.scottish.parliament.uk/business/petitions/guidance/index.htm

marked as duplicates by the software. Bogus signature or address detection is less easy to do automatically, so facilities to manually moderate signatures are included, which are assisted by metrics that are built in to the administration section. These help identify where individuals have, for example, repeatedly signed from the same IP address. It is relevant to note that there is no minimum number of signatures, thus there is little incentive for lobbying groups to fake ePetition signatures.

The ePetitioner System comprises 2 sections: the Front-End is the publicly accessible web pages where the citizens interact with the system. It has ten basic ePetition functions which are shown in Figure 24-1; the Back-End is the private Administrative Section which comprises password protected web pages for all administrative functions. It provides five high-level commands through which non-technical staff can support and maintain the ePetitioning processes. These are shown in Figure 24-2 (next page).

The system is integrated with the Parliament's own database of petitions (which includes petitions received on paper), to enable the progress of ePetitions to be automatically included under "Progress in Parliament".

Since the system was formally launched in February 2004 the Public Petitions Committee has agreed a rolling program of events aimed at promoting the public petitions system including ePetitioning especially to citizens who have been traditionally marginalized from the political process. This involves the Committee traveling to different towns and cities across Scotland in order to provide practical advice on how to petition the Parliament.

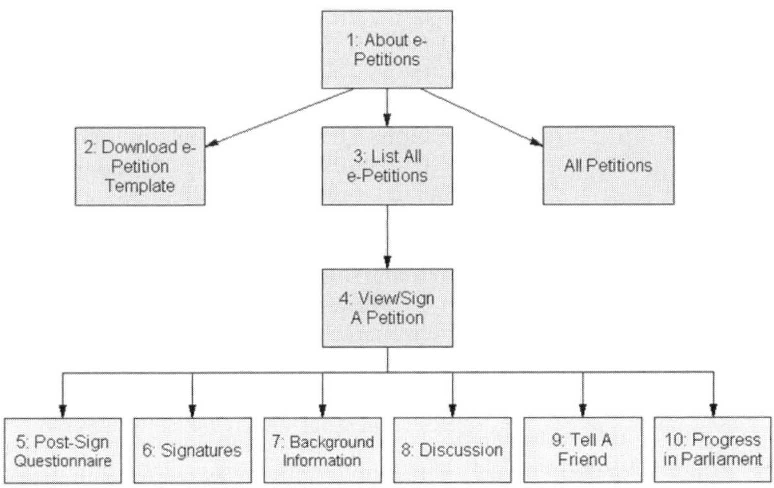

Figure 24-1. ePetitioner front-end

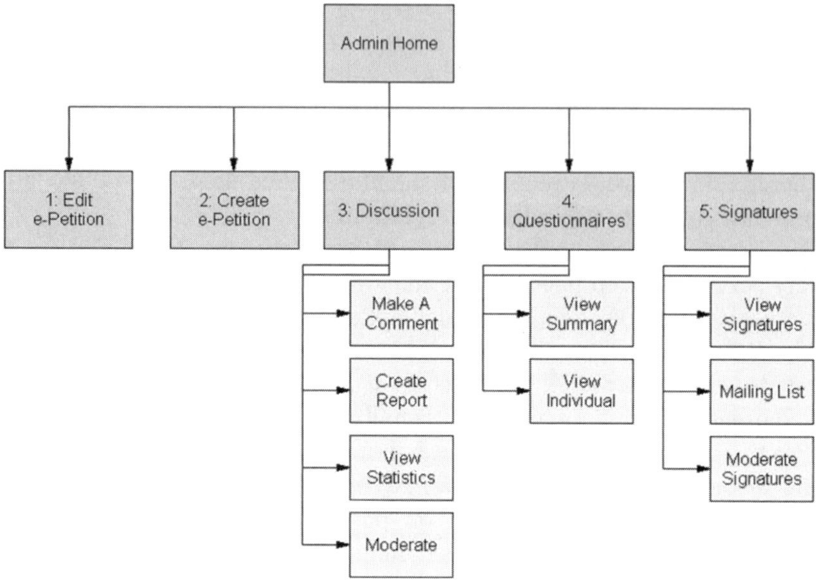

Figure 24-2. ePetitioner back-end

The Committee has also sought to maximize local media coverage for these events with the aim of publicizing the system widely. The success of these events can be seen in the feedback which the Committee has received from participants as summarized in the reports of each event which can be found on the Parliament website at:
http://www.scottish.parliament.uk/business/committees/petitions/index.htm
In order to make more explicit how e-Participation systems fit into different democratic contexts, a framework to characterize e-Participation initiatives has been developed based on previous OECD work (Macintosh 2004). This framework, developed around ten key dimensions for government-led initiatives and in particular for citizen participation in policy-making, enables tools and projects to be described in different democratic contexts. ePetitioner is described using these key dimensions in Table 24-1.

Table 24-1. Key dimension characterising ePetitioner

Level of engagement:	Addresses the ground-up perspective of citizen participation, empowering citizens to influence decision-making.
Stage in decision-making:	Provides a genuine opportunity for individual citizens to directly access the political process and have an impact on policy making and legislative change.
Actors:	Various civil society organizations and individuals have made use of the system to petition the Parliament. The Public Petitions Committee in the Parliament 'own' the process.

(Continued)

Table 24-1. (Continued)

Level of engagement:	Addresses the ground-up perspective of citizen participation, empowering citizens to influence decision-making.
Technologies used:	Implemented in Microsoft Active Server Pages (ASP) and uses a SQL Server database to hold the petitions data. It uses the open standard XHTML 1.0 for web page markup, and ODBC (Open DataBase Connectivity standard) to connect to the database.
Rules of engagement:	As the system is collecting names and addresses, there is a very clear privacy statement which is in line with the practices of the Parliament. Terms and conditions of use are also clearly displayed.
Duration and sustainability:	First used in December 1999 by special agreement of the Public Petitions Committee. After an extended pilot period it was re-engineered in Spring 2003 to provide a seamless integration between it and the Scottish Parliament website.
Accessibility:	The e-petitioner system is accessed from the top-level pages of the Public Petitions Committee of the Parliament website and is consistent with the Web Access Initiative's (WAI) Level 2 compliance specifications.
Resources and promotion:	The 'Admin' functions allow non-technical staff to support the system It is directly promoted from the Scottish Parliament web pages and the Public Petitions Committee run a series of outreach programs across Scotland
Evaluation and outcomes:	Initial evaluation undertaken during 2000 and 2001. In the current session of the Scottish Parliament 98 e-petitions have been raised.
Critical success factors:	The Convener of the Public Petitions Committee, and the Clerk to the Committee are very supportive and enthusiastic about e-petitions. Management procedures are in place to incorporate the submission of e-petitions into the normal workflow of the Committee.

3.3 Results

In the 2005-2006 session of the Scottish Parliament 98 ePetitions have been raised on a number of issues ranging from 'Broadband for all of Scotland by 2005', 'Coastal and River erosion' and 'Culture and Tourism Policies regarding Robert Burns.' One of the strengths of the system is the range of issues which are raised by citizens many of which may otherwise not be considered by the Parliament. Over 50,000 signatures have been added in support of petitions during this period and over 1200 comments have been posted on the discussion forums.

The most successful ePetition to date is a petition calling on Parliament to urge the Scottish Executive to review its proposals for the controversial Aberdeen Western peripheral Route in light of the growing public concern with this project. This ePetition which is on-line until 31 August 2006 has at the time of writing collected 3811 signatures and 150 comments have been posted on the discussion forum.

There has also been a steady increase in the number of signatories adding their support to ePetitions and in addition posting comments on the discussion forum. When ePetitioner was first launched, few citizens appreciated how the discussion forum could be used to support their cause. These early ePetitions typically received one or two comments. That situation has gradually changed and now users see the discussion forum as a means to tell their own story of how they have been affected by policy (or lack of it).

For example, a petition raised in July 2004 requesting "that the Scottish Parliament urge the Scottish Executive to ensure the provision of acute 24hr a day all-year-round consultant-led services across Scotland, including rural communities" received 89 comments from 1906 signatories. Comments such as the following were received:

> "Our Grandmother lives in Fort William and we visit Fort William a lot and we have heard everyone talking about how important it is to have consultancy services in the Belford. We also know what is happening in PRI in Perth and think it is awful."

And:

> "My wife underwent major surgery at the Belford recently and we have only praise for the care, skill and dedication of the staff. The Belford is a major asset of the West Highlands and it is important that the expertise it offers remains accessible to the locality."

ePetitioner also provides the opportunity to for petitioners to gather support for their petition globally. For example, an ePetition calling on the Scottish Parliament to review the policy and commitment of the Scottish Executive to place Robert Burns and his legacy at the heart of its culture and tourism policies ran over a 6 week period and collected 1810 signatures. Although the majority, 1000, were from Scotland, 260 were from the United States; 144 from Canada, 142 from England the remainder from a further 35 countries ranging from Poland to Brazil. This information is provided in a briefing for the Committee and is useful in demonstrating the breadth of support for a specific issue.

The success of ePetitioner as an innovative tool in driving use and participation in the political process is best illustrated by the extent to which it allows citizens to have an influence on the policy-making agenda. For example, the ePetition referred to above in relation to Health provision in rural areas was considered by the Public Petitions Committee and the petitioners invited to the Committee to give oral evidence. The petitioners were allowed to make a brief presentation and were then questioned by Members of the Committee on the issues raises by the petition. Having heard from the petitioners the Committee agreed to formally refer the petition to the Health Committee for further consideration and to pass copies of the petition to the Minister for Health and Community Care and the National Advisory Group on Service Change for information.

The Health Committee subsequently agreed to take forward the issues raised by the petition within its consideration of its report on workforce planning in the NHS. The Committee noted the work of the Belford Action Group and the West Highland Health Services Solutions Group and agreed to invite the groups to submit written evidence to its inquiry. The Committee further agreed to direct the petitioner to the work being undertaken by the Kerr Group on the National Framework for the NHS. Finally, the Committee agreed to invite representatives of the Belford Action Group and the West Highland Health Services Solutions Group to attend any event or events the Committee may hold to debate the conclusions of its workforce planning inquiry.

The ePetitioner who initially lodged the petition was subsequently invited to participate in a public debate organised by the Health Committee in the Parliamentary Chamber on the issue of ‘Reshaping the NHS in Scotland?’ During this debate the ePetitioner stated: ‘I am in a position today—standing among delegates—in which I did not expect to find myself. I am one of the ordinary people who, through the Public Petitions Committee process and the Belford action group, can participate today. I ask Mr Norris how we move away from the proposition that groups such as the Belford action group centre on only a few people. My group came to the Parliament on the back of a meeting that was attended by a vast number of people on a cold November night. I was privileged to be involved with MSPs who put us on the path to the Public Petitions Committee and the Health Committee, and we are here today. The people of Scotland should be well proud of this institution..’.www.scottish.parliament.uk/business/committees/health/reports-05/her05-nhs-01.htm). This ePetition demonstrates how citizens through ePetitioner can find themselves at the heart of the policy-making process.

3.4 Monitoring

Visitors to the ePetitioner site who choose to add their name to a petition are presented with an ‘exit questionnaire’. This facilitates a degree of monitoring what users think of the system, and is a way to assess user reaction. As the exit questionnaire is voluntary it has been completed by only

11,671 of the 52,679 ePetition signers – just over 22%. Table 24-2 gives an overview of some of the responses to a few of the questions

Table 24-2. Summary of exit questionnaire results

Question	Highest response	Percent	Second highest	Percent
Where have you been using this website today?	From home	47.9%	From work	36.7%
Did you require help with this website?	No	89.5%	Yes	2.6%
Did you find that signing the petition was ...	Easy enough	91.3%	Not sure	0.8%
Did you find that reading the information provided was ...	Easy enough	88.4%	Didn't look at it	2.0%
Could you see yourself using this website again for other petitions?	Yes	72.5%	Not sure	16.9%

The final question asked is "Is there anything you think we should change about ePetitioner?". Here there were a large number of open responses, the majority of which indicated there were no serious problems.

The results will not include any site users who visited but found ePetitioner either uninteresting or too difficult to use, since they will not have signed an ePetition, so cannot be solely used as a basis for comprehensive evaluation, but the results make a valuable contribution.

4. CONCLUSION AND DISCUSSION

Integral to the success of ePetitioner is the existence of a robust parliamentary procedure which is easily accessible to citizens and in which citizens can have confidence that the issues which they raise will be fully considered by the administration. In particular, it is essential that adequate and transparent feedback mechanisms are developed to ensure a steady communication flow between the PPC and the petitioner. As such, sufficient resources are required to manage the process and to ensure that petitioners are advised of the progress of petitions and in particular are advised of the reasons as to the outcome of petitions. Some key learning points have been:

- The need for a shared willingness to innovate in methods of public involvement;
- Clearly worded and easy to follow guidelines need to be published in the interests of transparency and process management;
- To enhance accessibility of the process, the petitioning 'front end' must also be accessible and usable;

- Building online discussion capabilities into the ePetitions addresses the need for the online process to open up the possibilities for public discussion, including discussion with elected representatives where appropriate, around topics that concern citizens.
- The confidence of citizens in the ability of the system to have a real impact on the political process is a key element for long term sustainability of ePetitioning as a public engagement mechanism. This means that a key element of the ePetitioning system is the ability to track progress of an ePetition through the decision-making process, and that the management process must also meet the need to update the progress information so that citizens and others can monitor the political process.

The System has attracted growing interest from the Public to the point that to date in the 2006 Session there were a total of 52,679 signatures and 1296 discussion comments made on 98 petitions through the System.

During 2004 and 2005, the ePetition system was successfully transferred to two English Local Authorities and over the course of the year evaluations were undertaken (Whyte et al. 2005). These early evaluation results indicate that ePetitioner is a useful tool in enabling citizens to better engage with political processes at a local government level also. In 2005 ePetitioner was transferred to the German Bundestag. Here again early successes have been seen with 171 petitions lodged since October 2005 with a total of 284,384 signatures and attracting 12,343 discussion comments. Although in-depth evaluations and comparative studies have still to be undertaken, it appears that online petitioning with an integrated discussion forum has the potential flexibility to support citizens at all levels of government, whether a large national parliament, (the German Bundestag represents a population of 80 million people); a devolved parliament, (the Scottish Parliament represents a population of 5 million people); or at local government level where the authorities represent less than 0.5 million people.

REFERENCES

Adams, N. J., Macintosh, A., and Johnston, J. (2005); 'e-Petitioning: Enabling Ground-up Participation'; Challenges of Expanding Internet: E-Commerce, E-Business and E-Government; Matohisa Funabashi and Adam Grzech (eds); 5th IFIP Conference on e-Commerce, E-Business and E-Government (I3E'2005); October 26-28 2005, Poznan, Poland, pp265-279 Barber, B. (1984). *Strong democracy: Participatory politics for a new age.* Berkeley: University of California Press.

Budge, I. (1996). *The new challenge of direct democracy.* Cambridge: Polity Press

Fishkin, J. S. (1995), The Voice of the People. Public Opinion and Democracy, Yale University Press.

HMSO (1999), Shaping Scotland's Parliament. Report of the Consultative Steering Group.

Macintosh, A. (2003); "Using information and communication technologies to enhance citizen engagement in the policy process"; in *Promises and Problems of E-Democracy: Challenges of online citizen engagement*. Paris: OECD. Available at: http://www1.oecd.org/publications/e-book/4204011E.PDF

Macintosh, A. (2004) 'Characterizing E-Participation in Policy-Making'. System Sciences, 2004. Proceedings of the 37th Annual Hawaii International Conference (HICSS-37), on 5-8 Jan. 2004 Page(s):117 – 126. ISBN: 0-7695-2056-1

Macintosh, A.; Malina, A.; and Farrell, S. (2002); Digital Democracy through Electronic Petitioning; In McIver, W. and Elmagarmid, A.K. (2002) (eds). Advances in Digital Government: Technology, Human Factors, and Policy; Boston/Dordrecht/London: Kluwer Academic Publishers. pp. 137-148.

Mansell, R. & Silverstone, R. (1998). (eds). *Communication by Design*, UK: London: University Press.

Nixon, O. and Johansson, H. (1999) 'Transparency through technology: the internet and political parties' In Hague, B and Loader, B. (eds.) Digital Democracy: Discourse and Decision Making in the Information Age London: Routledge.

OECD (2001), Citizens as Partners: Information, consultation and public participation in policy-making: OECD, Paris.

Sclove, R. E. (1995). *Democracy & technology*, New York: Guildford Press.

The Electoral Commission (2005), An audit of political engagement 2, Research Report March 2005. ISBN: 1-904363-60-1; available at http://www.electoralcommission.org.uk/templates/search/document.cfm/11652.

Whyte, A., Renton, A. and Macintosh, A. (2005) e-democracy from the Top Down: An Evaluation of e-democracy Activities Initiated by Councils and Government Bristol City Council. Published by Bristol City Council for The Local e-democracy National Project. Available at: http://www.e-democracy.gov.uk/products

SUGGESTED READING

The OECD 2001 report provides useful background to citizen participation in policy-making providing a number of guiding principles for off-line engagement. The follow-on OECD report (Macintosh 2003) provides the technology enabled approach to citizen participation. The "Digital Democracy through Electronic Petitioning" by Macintosh et al., provides an overview of the original system, while the paper "e-Petitioning: Enabling Ground-up Participation" by Adams et al. provides an up to date description of the current system and its use ion the Scottish Parliament.

ONLINE RESOURCES

The Scottish Parliament website for ePetitioner is at: http://epetitions.scottish.parliament.uk/ (accessed 6 July 2006). ePetitioner for the German Bundestag can be found at: http://itc.napier.ac.uk/

e-Petition/bundestag/ (accessed 6 July 2006). Finally the two English local authority ePetitioner sites are:

http://www.bristol-city.gov.uk/item/epetition.html, and
http://e-petitions.kingston.gov.uk/ (accessed 6 July 2006).

QUESTIONS FOR DISCUSSION

1. Can ePetitioner address the democratic deficit and re-engage the public in activities such as voting?
2. To what extent can ground-up e-Participation systems, such as ePetitioner, be integrated into democratic processes at national, federal and local levels of government?
3. What additional features, such as access by mobile devices, could be added to ePetitioner to better facilitate public engagement?

Chapter 25

CITIZEN ACCESS TO GOVERNMENT STATISTICAL INFORMATION

Alan F. Karr

National Institute of Statistical Sciences Research, Triangle Park, North Carolina, U.S.A.

CHAPTER OVERVIEW

Modern electronic technologies have dramatically increased the volume of information collected and assembled by government agencies at all levels. This chapter describes digital government research aimed at keeping government data warehouses from turning into data cemeteries. The products of the research exploit modern electronic technologies in order to allow "ordinary citizens" and researchers access to government-assembled information. The goal is to help ensure that more data also means better and more useful data. Underlying the chapter are three tensions. The first is between comprehensiveness and understandability of information available to non-technically oriented "private citizens." The second is between ensuring usefulness of detailed statistical information and protecting confidentiality of data subjects. The third tension is between the need to analyze "global" data sets and the reality that government data are distributed among both levels of government and agencies (typically, by the "domain" of data, such as education, health, or transportation).

1. INTRODUCTION

Modern electronic technologies have dramatically increased the volume of information collected and assembled by government agencies at all levels. Computer-directed data collection is ubiquitous, by means of telephone surveys, web forms and passive but sometimes invasive technologies such as radio-frequency identifiers (RFID), credit cards, cellular telephones, video surveillance of streets and buildings, and global positioning system (GPS) transmitters.

That government agencies have *more* (in most cases, vastly more) data is beyond dispute. Whether these agencies have *better*, or *more useful*, data is much less clear. Data quality is, ultimately, determined by uses and users of the data, and is a complicated, multi-faceted issue (Karr, Sanil and Banks 2006; OMB 2002). Electronic collection and assembly of data have increased some facets of data quality, for example, timeliness. Other facets, such as accuracy, relevance and accessibility, are more problematic. Privacy of data subjects such as individuals and establishments, and confidentiality of the data itself are also concerns.

Indeed, no positive aspect of "more data" seems to lack a corresponding negative side. Electronic data, whether reviewed by humans or not, may be rife with errors, and the more data there is, the less likely it is to be reviewed. Despite pervasive use of search engines such as Google, the more data there is, the harder it is to find what one wants, or to determine whether what has been found is what is wanted. If survey respondents feel that their privacy is threatened, they may decline to participate or may provide incorrect information. Re-purposing of data—using it for purposes other than the original, designed one—has become commonplace, often with unintended, and sometimes disastrous, consequences.

There is real danger, therefore, that vast and growing government data warehouses will instead become data cemeteries, rather than being used properly to yield great individual and social benefit.

This chapter focuses digital government research aimed at preventing data warehouses from turning into data cemeteries. It addresses three central tensions. The first is between comprehensiveness and understandability of information available to non-technically oriented "private citizens" for non-research purposes, which is discussed in Section 2. The second tension is between ensuring usefulness of detailed statistical information and protecting confidentiality of data subjects, as discussed in Section 3. The clientele for such information is the research and public policy communities. The third tension is between the need to analyze "global" data sets and the fact that government data are distributed among levels of government (federal, state, local and others) and within levels among agencies (typically, by the "domain" of data, such as education, health, or transportation). Systems to cope with this are described briefly in Section 4.

To illustrate, consider the following three questions, each of which requires access to government statistical information:

1. A family is considering moving to Chapel Hill, NC. How can it obtain reliable, up-to-date, understandable information about public schools, the housing market, environment and safety in a way that does not consume enormous amounts of time sifting through irrelevant information? Can it trust the information it locates?
2. A researcher would like to understand the effect of class size and teacher training on the performance of students at the K-12 level. Doing so requires detailed data that allow the researcher to separate effects of class size and teacher training from confounding factors such as family structure, parental engagement and community economic characteristics. Even if explicit identifying information such as names and addresses is removed, data at this level may be "re-identified" by linking them to databases containing identifiers. How can the government agencies holding the data make it available to this researcher?
3. County health agencies in North Carolina need to protect against a bird flu pandemic that is "visible" only at the state level. For example, a slightly elevated number of cases in each county may not be significant in is own right, but that all counties have elevated numbers may be highly significant. Yet, counties may be unwilling or unable to pool their data in order to conduct the analysis. Can the analysis be performed in some virtual manner instead?

Underlying all three tensions and all three questions is how to exploit modern electronic technologies in order to allow "ordinary citizens" or researchers, access to information. There is also one underlying assumption that is so obvious that it is rarely stated—that "the government," possibly unlike other organizations that disseminate information, is seeking to tell the truth insofar as possible. In this chapter, digital government means digital, truth-telling government.

There are many related issues not discussed here. For example, there are populations, such as the vision- or hearing-impaired, for whom conventional means of presenting information—which today and in the context of this chapter means standard web browsers operating on high-speed Internet connections—are not appropriate. Federal websites must comply with Section 508 of the US Rehabilitation Act, but this act specifies minimal standards, not always effective functionality. Technical and non-technical considerations may conflict. For instance, medians are well-known to be superior to means as indicators of central tendencies in data, in the sense of being less influenced by means by extreme values, but are not well understood among the general public. Hardware is a limiting factor: a 1280 × 1024 computer display contains only 1,310,720 pixels, and cannot display remotely that many "pieces of information."

Most of the data we consider are "official statistics" data pertaining to individuals, households or establishments such as schools and businesses. Large-scale scientific databases (for example, satellite images) present quite different issues. We also do not consider classified data such as counter-terrorist or intelligence information, the "physical security" against hacking of computer systems or inside threats. These are challenging issues that ought to be taken up by digital government researchers.

Finally, because there is not space to do them justice, we do not consider geographically referenced data and the use of maps and other visualizations to display them. These have been important threads of digital government research. Alan McEachern of Pennsylvania State University and Hanan Samet of the University of Maryland have been leaders of this research.

2. BROAD ACCESS

Section 3 focuses on dissemination of detailed information to communities of researchers, in order to support possibly very sophisticated statistical analyses of the data. However, most citizens are not researchers, and their needs—as well as ways of meeting them—differ from those of researchers. In particular, confidentiality is rarely a driving issue, because of the nature or granularity of the information sought. Instead, the problems are highly user-centric: finding, accessing, manipulating and understanding information.

Because of the digital government focus of this book, we restrict attention to information held or provided by government agencies. More so than in Section 3, however, multiple agencies may be involved. The principal means of dissemination is agency-operated web sites.

We illustrate with two rather different kinds of information searches. The first, from Section 1, is to obtain information about a community to which a family is considering moving, or, more generally, to compare such information about several communities. We term these searches for *information specifics*, and they are discussed in Section 2.1.

The second type of search, which overlaps to some extent the uses of information discussed in Section 3, is for *information summaries*. For example, a citizen might be interested in health status of individuals (as measured, say, by annual per capita days of hospitalization) as a function of their county of residence, age and race. Conceptually, this information is a three-way table, but the user's needs are quite different from those of a statistical researcher. Information summaries are discussed in Section 2.2.

The very complex question of how to facilitate locating information is discussed briefly in Section 2.3.

2.1 Information Specifics

As noted previously, these searches are for particular kinds of information about particular entities. Much of this information resides in state- or lower-level, as opposed to federal, databases. We continue to use the "information about a community" example.

The person seeking information specifics wants them to be:

- Easy to find. This does not mean a Google search on the name of the community, which will return too many (or "the wrong") hits to be useful, but rather being able to find the state- or county- or municipality-level web site containing the information.
- Accurate. This issue is as subtle as it seems innocuous. Citizen users may presume that there is a "gold" standard whereby accuracy can be judged, but this is almost never true (Karr, Sanil and Banks 2006). Judging accuracy of one imperfect database by comparing to another that may be equally flawed is a hazardous strategy at best, but often nothing else is possible. Other information consists of statistical estimates and is therefore uncertain (as the result of sampling rather than enumeration, for example). Statistical uncertainty is not, however, a concept that is well understood among the general public.
- Timely. This can be a major problem. A state-level web site containing information about all communities in the state might reasonably be up-to-date. A federal-level counterpart might be less timely, because it takes longer to assemble information across states. But timeliness might not be uniform across information types: school information might be from last year, but housing information from three years ago. Timeliness may vary across states. Simply making clear the "age" of information without also obscuring it is not trivial.
- Interpretable. A researcher working with data might be presumed to be knowledgeable about how variables are defined and how the data were collected. To non-researchers, though, the very meaning, for instance, of concepts such "housing value" may not be clear. Is it assessed value? Estimated market value? Or something else entirely? Do per-pupil expenditures in the public school system include capital expenditures? Qualifications about the data (for instance, that

standardized test scores exclude students with certain learning disabilities) may be obscure or absent.

- Consistent. As implied already, consistency is a profound issue, which overlaps many of the other issues. Different databases need not be uniformly accurate, uniformly timely or uniformly interpretable. Some problems are "legacy" ones: databases of fatal automobile and trains accidents assembled by the US federal government do not use the same criterion for how long following the accident a death must occur in order to be considered accident-related. Others are "units" problems, many of which arise from the US not using metric units of measurement. Still others are simply inexplicable.

Many of these are the same data quality issues raised again in Section 3, but in a wholly different context and with different consequences. While some statistical analyses can tolerate modest data quality problems (Karr, Sanil and Banks 2006), the seeker of information specifics who receives a low quality response to his or her one query is doomed, without even knowing it. There is also the overarching issue of how to convey data quality information, as opposed to data content, without overwhelming users.

Treatment of the issues is in only the early stages. The National Infrastructure for Community Statistics (NICS) (see http://www.nicsweb.org/) is one very promising initiative, which seeks to use various digital government technologies to promote dissemination of community-level information. Digital government researchers have provided significant input to the creators of NICS.

2.2 Information Summaries

Recall from the beginning of this section the example of health status of individuals (measured, for concreteness, by annual per capita days of hospitalization) as a function of their county of residence, a categorical age variable, and race. As noted previously, this information summary is simply a three-dimensional table. At one level, this is precisely the problem: that table is not two-dimensional, and thereby not readily displayed in a web browser (or on a page of paper). It is large, indexed by the approximately 3,100 counties in the US, 20 five-year age ranges and (in the 2000 decennial census), as many as 64 race categories. It does not fit on either a computer screen or a normal-sized piece of paper. The table is also hierarchical: counties are grouped into states, and state-level summaries are also of interest. The table is inefficient for answering some queries. For example, without some capability to re-order the table cells, finding the county with the largest hospitalization rate for each (age, race) combination is tedious at best. Finally, the table is but one summary of a larger database. Another user might be interested in a different response tabulated differently.

In addition, all of the data quality issues raised in Section 3.1 are pertinent.

So one can ask, what kinds of software tools can serve the need for information summaries? Most official statistics agencies maintain web sites providing tabular information summaries. Figure 25-1 shows the US Census Bureau's American Fact Finder web site (http://factfinder.census.gov/home/saff/main.html?_lang=en). The query whose response is shown there is for county-level populations in the US at seven points in time—a two-dimensional table. The scale issue is handled by converting one national query to 51 state queries; Figure 25-1 shows the results for North Carolina. Even so, scrolling is still required.

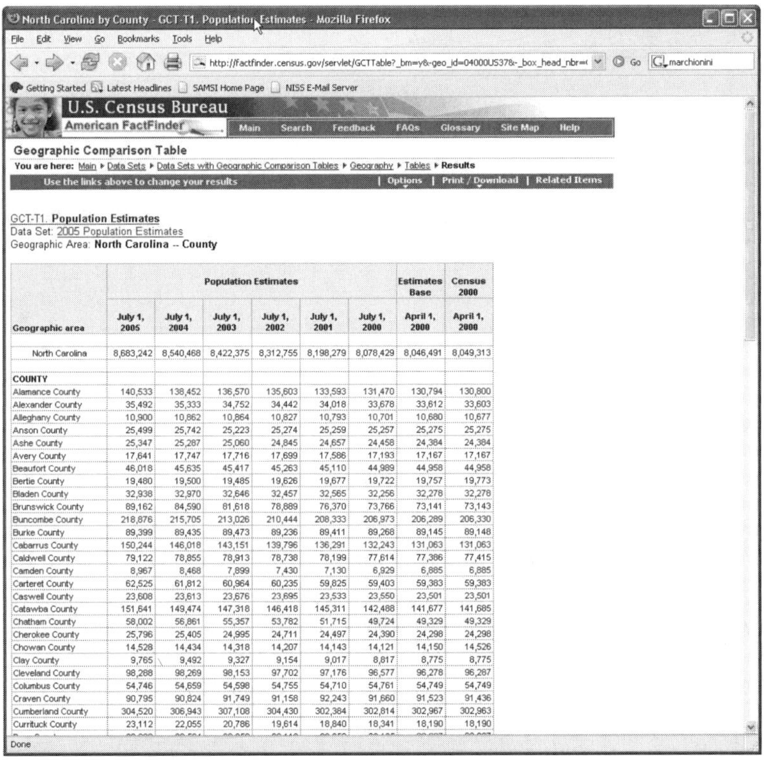

Geographic area	Population Estimates July 1, 2005	July 1, 2004	July 1, 2003	July 1, 2002	July 1, 2001	July 1, 2000	Estimates Base April 1, 2000	Census 2000 April 1, 2000
North Carolina	8,683,242	8,540,468	8,422,375	8,312,755	8,198,279	8,078,429	8,046,491	8,049,313
COUNTY								
Alamance County	140,533	138,452	136,570	135,603	133,593	131,470	130,794	130,800
Alexander County	35,492	35,333	34,752	34,442	34,018	33,678	33,612	33,603
Alleghany County	10,900	10,862	10,864	10,827	10,793	10,701	10,680	10,677
Anson County	25,499	25,742	25,223	25,274	25,259	25,257	25,275	25,275
Ashe County	25,347	25,287	25,060	24,845	24,657	24,458	24,384	24,384
Avery County	17,641	17,747	17,716	17,699	17,586	17,193	17,167	17,167
Beaufort County	46,018	45,635	45,417	45,263	45,110	44,989	44,958	44,958
Bertie County	19,480	19,500	19,485	19,626	19,677	19,722	19,757	19,773
Bladen County	32,938	32,970	32,646	32,457	32,565	32,256	32,278	32,278
Brunswick County	89,162	84,590	81,618	78,889	76,370	73,766	73,141	73,143
Buncombe County	218,876	215,705	213,026	210,444	208,333	206,973	206,289	206,330
Burke County	89,399	89,435	89,473	89,236	89,411	89,268	89,145	89,148
Cabarrus County	150,244	146,018	143,151	139,796	136,291	132,243	131,063	131,063
Caldwell County	79,122	78,855	78,913	78,738	78,199	77,614	77,386	77,415
Camden County	8,967	8,468	7,899	7,430	7,130	6,929	6,885	6,885
Carteret County	62,525	61,812	60,964	60,235	59,825	59,403	59,383	59,383
Caswell County	23,608	23,613	23,676	23,695	23,533	23,550	23,501	23,501
Catawba County	151,641	149,474	147,318	146,418	145,311	142,488	141,677	141,685
Chatham County	58,002	56,861	55,357	53,782	51,715	49,724	49,329	49,329
Cherokee County	25,796	25,405	24,995	24,711	24,497	24,390	24,298	24,298
Chowan County	14,528	14,434	14,318	14,207	14,143	14,121	14,150	14,526
Clay County	9,765	9,492	9,327	9,154	9,017	8,817	8,775	8,775
Cleveland County	98,288	98,269	98,153	97,702	97,176	96,577	96,278	96,287
Columbus County	54,746	54,659	54,598	54,755	54,710	54,761	54,749	54,749
Craven County	90,795	90,824	91,749	91,158	92,243	91,660	91,523	91,436
Cumberland County	304,520	306,943	307,108	304,430	302,384	302,814	302,967	302,963
Currituck County	23,112	22,055	20,786	19,614	18,840	18,341	18,190	18,190

Figure 25-1. The US Census Bureau's American Fact Finder. The tabular information is population in North Carolina as a function of county and time.

Determining that Mecklenburg County has the largest population requires perusing the entire table. Finding the fifth-largest county takes more work, but would be simple if rows of the table could be sorted interactively on the basis of one column. Finding the most populous county in the US requires examining 51 tables. Although some values in the table are statistical estimates, there is no detail about uncertainties. For most users this seems acceptable, but for others it is not.

The Toxic Release Inventory (TRI) Explorer web site of the US Environmental Protection Agency (http://www.epa.gov/triexplorer/), shown in Figure 25-2, provides more interactivity than the American Fact Finder.

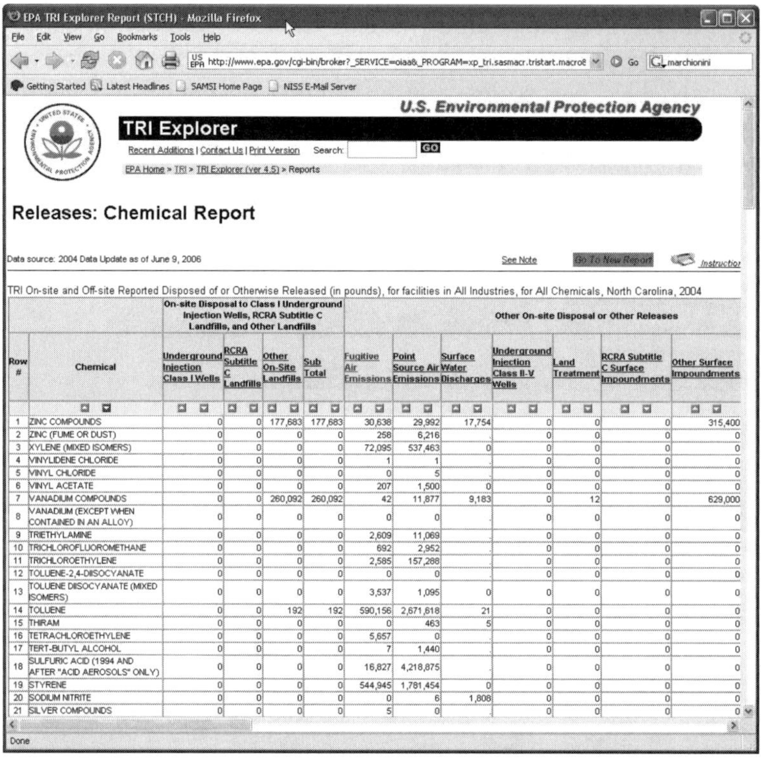

Row #	Chemical	On-site Disposal to Class I Underground Injection Wells, RCRA Subtitle C Landfills, and Other Landfills				Other On-site Disposal or Other Releases						
		Underground Injection Class I Wells	RCRA Subtitle C Landfills	Other On-Site Landfills	Sub Total	Fugitive Air Emissions	Point Source Air Emissions	Surface Water Discharges	Underground Injection Class II-V Wells	Land Treatment	RCRA Subtitle C Surface Impoundments	Other Surface Impoundments
1	ZINC COMPOUNDS	0	0	177,683	177,683	30,638	29,992	17,754	0	0	0	315,400
2	ZINC (FUME OR DUST)	0	0	0	0	258	6,216	.	0	0	0	0
3	XYLENE (MIXED ISOMERS)	0	0	0	0	72,095	537,463	0	0	0	0	0
4	VINYLIDENE CHLORIDE	0	0	0	0	1	1	.	0	0	0	0
5	VINYL CHLORIDE	0	0	0	0	0	5	.	0	0	0	0
6	VINYL ACETATE	0	0	0	0	207	1,500	0	0	0	0	0
7	VANADIUM COMPOUNDS	0	0	260,092	260,092	42	11,877	9,183	0	12	0	629,000
8	VANADIUM (EXCEPT WHEN CONTAINED IN AN ALLOY)	0	0	0	0	0	0	.	0	0	0	0
9	TRIETHYLAMINE	0	0	0	0	2,609	11,069	.	0	0	0	0
10	TRICHLOROFLUOROMETHANE	0	0	0	0	692	2,952	.	0	0	0	0
11	TRICHLOROETHYLENE	0	0	0	0	2,585	157,288	.	0	0	0	0
12	TOLUENE-2,4-DIISOCYANATE	0	0	0	0	0	0	.	0	0	0	0
13	TOLUENE DIISOCYANATE (MIXED ISOMERS)	0	0	0	0	3,537	1,095	0	0	0	0	0
14	TOLUENE	0	0	192	192	590,156	2,671,618	21	0	0	0	0
15	THIRAM	0	0	0	0	0	463	5	0	0	0	0
16	TETRACHLOROETHYLENE	0	0	0	0	5,657	0	.	0	0	0	0
17	TERT-BUTYL ALCOHOL	0	0	0	0	7	1,440	.	0	0	0	0
18	SULFURIC ACID (1994 AND AFTER "ACID AEROSOLS" ONLY)	0	0	0	0	16,827	4,218,875	.	0	0	0	0
19	STYRENE	0	0	0	0	544,945	1,781,454	0	0	0	0	0
20	SODIUM NITRITE	0	0	0	0	0	6	1,808	0	0	0	0
21	SILVER COMPOUNDS	0	0	0	0	5	0	.	0	0	0	0

Figure 25-2. US EPA's TRI Explorer. The table is indexed by chemical and characteristics of release. Clicking on either of the arrow symbols at the head of each column sorts the rows on the table in ascending or descending order based on that column.

The underlying data, aggregated to the state level (North Carolina), are releases of toxic chemicals at industrial sites, indexed by chemical and the location of the release (to water, air, …). The rows in the table in Figure 25-2 can be sorted in ascending or descending order, on the basis of the values in any column, by clicking on up- and down-arrows icons at the head of the column. The need for scrolling remains, and the columns containing totals, at the right edge of the table, are invisible without scrolling.

We note in passing that the TRI, some of whose data quality problems are discussed in Karr, Sanil and Banks (2006), is an example not of re-purposed data, but of purposeless data. That no uses of the data are specified (year-to-year comparisons, for example, are a natural one) has significant impact on data quality.

Figure 25-3 shows one final example, from the Health Data for All Ages (HDAA) system of the US National Center for Health Statistics (NCHS), available at http://www.cdc.gov/nchs/health_data_for_all_ages.htm.

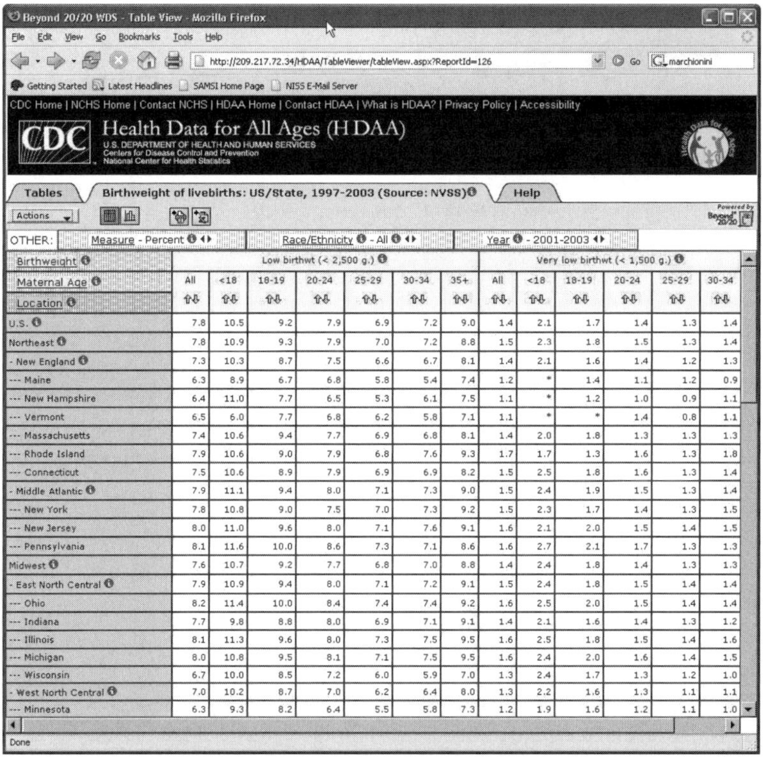

Birthweight	Low birthwt (< 2,500 g.)							Very low birthwt (< 1,500 g.)					
Maternal Age / Location	All	<18	18-19	20-24	25-29	30-34	35+	All	<18	18-19	20-24	25-29	30-34
U.S.	7.8	10.5	9.2	7.9	6.9	7.2	9.0	1.4	2.1	1.7	1.4	1.3	1.4
Northeast	7.8	10.9	9.3	7.9	7.0	7.2	8.8	1.5	2.3	1.8	1.5	1.3	1.4
- New England	7.3	10.3	8.7	7.5	6.6	6.7	8.1	1.4	2.1	1.6	1.4	1.2	1.3
--- Maine	6.3	8.9	6.7	6.8	5.8	5.4	7.4	1.2	*	1.4	1.1	1.2	0.9
--- New Hampshire	6.4	11.0	7.7	6.5	5.3	6.1	7.5	1.1	*	1.2	1.0	0.9	1.1
--- Vermont	6.5	6.0	7.7	6.8	6.2	5.8	7.1	1.1	*	*	1.4	0.8	1.1
--- Massachusetts	7.4	10.6	9.4	7.7	6.9	6.8	8.1	1.4	2.0	1.8	1.3	1.3	1.3
--- Rhode Island	7.9	10.6	9.0	7.9	6.8	7.6	9.3	1.7	1.7	1.3	1.6	1.3	1.8
--- Connecticut	7.5	10.6	8.9	7.9	6.9	6.9	8.2	1.5	2.5	1.8	1.6	1.3	1.4
- Middle Atlantic	7.9	11.1	9.4	8.0	7.1	7.3	9.0	1.5	2.4	1.9	1.5	1.3	1.4
--- New York	7.8	10.8	9.0	7.5	7.0	7.3	9.2	1.5	2.3	1.7	1.4	1.3	1.5
--- New Jersey	8.0	11.0	9.6	8.0	7.1	7.6	9.1	1.6	2.1	2.0	1.5	1.4	1.5
--- Pennsylvania	8.1	11.6	10.0	8.6	7.3	7.1	8.6	1.6	2.7	2.1	1.7	1.3	1.3
Midwest	7.6	10.7	9.2	7.7	6.8	7.0	8.8	1.4	2.4	1.8	1.4	1.3	1.3
- East North Central	7.9	10.9	9.4	8.0	7.1	7.2	9.1	1.5	2.4	1.8	1.5	1.4	1.4
--- Ohio	8.2	11.4	10.0	8.4	7.4	7.4	9.2	1.6	2.5	2.0	1.5	1.4	1.4
--- Indiana	7.7	9.8	8.8	8.0	6.9	7.1	9.1	1.4	2.1	1.6	1.4	1.3	1.2
--- Illinois	8.1	11.3	9.6	8.0	7.3	7.5	9.5	1.6	2.5	1.8	1.5	1.4	1.6
--- Michigan	8.0	10.8	9.5	8.1	7.1	7.5	9.5	1.6	2.4	2.0	1.6	1.4	1.5
--- Wisconsin	6.7	10.0	8.5	7.2	6.0	5.9	7.0	1.3	2.4	1.7	1.3	1.2	1.0
- West North Central	7.0	10.2	8.7	7.0	6.2	6.4	8.0	1.3	2.2	1.6	1.3	1.1	1.1
--- Minnesota	6.3	9.3	8.2	6.4	5.5	5.8	7.3	1.2	1.9	1.6	1.2	1.1	1.0

Figure 25-3. NCHS' Health Data for All Ages (HDAA) System. The underlying data structure is a five-dimensional table. The multiple forms of interactivity are discussed in the text.

The table presents percentages (among all live births) of low birth weights as a function of five categorical variables: birth weight, maternal age, hierarchically structured location, race and time. The data source is the National Vital Statistics System (LVSS). This is a five-dimensional table. The degree of interactivity is high. Three dimensions—birth weight, maternal age and geography—are displayable simultaneously because one (birth weight) is comprised of only two categories. The geographical hierarchy is made clear graphically. Race and time are handled by multiple tables, which can be changed by means of mouse clicks. Rows can be sorted in ascending or descending order by any column. (The arrow symbols are arguably clearer here than in Figure 25-2.) Information about any term can be obtained by clicking on the icon next to it. Figure 25-4 shows this "metadata" (data about data) for the term "Maternal Age."

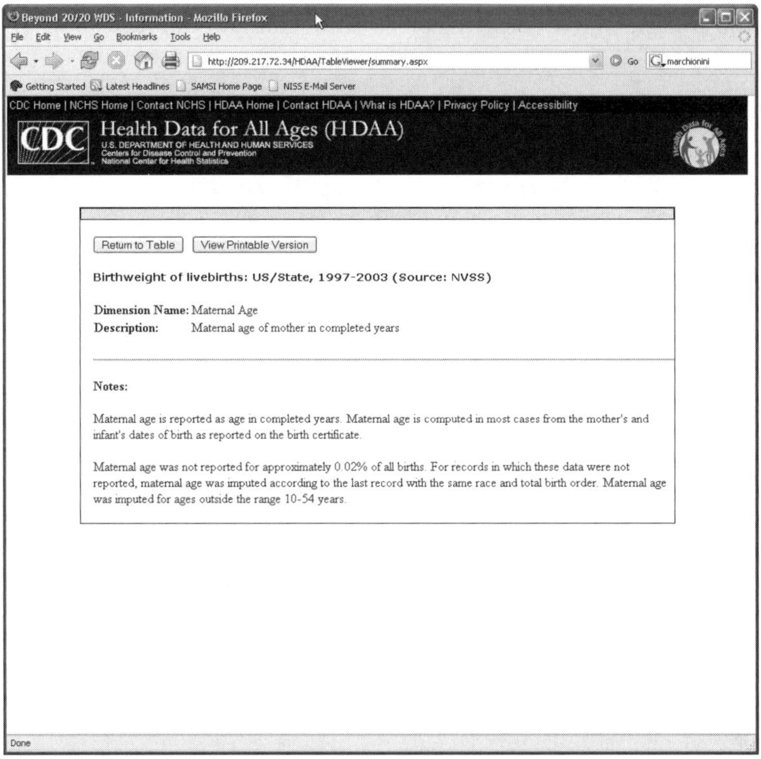

Figure 25-4. HDAA metadata (data about data) for the variable "Maternal Age." This view is accessed by clicking in the corresponding icon in the view in Figure 25-3.

There is overlap between systems for information summaries and for information specifics. The National Center for Education Statistics' Common Core of Data (CCD) web site (http://nces.ed.gov/ccd/schoolsearch/), shown in Figure 25-5, provides access to both information about specific public schools and summary information. One, possibly non-obvious, question raised by Figure 25-5 is how someone interested in either information about a specific school or summary information (at the district, county or state level, for example) is supposed to know to go to the CCD web site to find it. We discuss this question of locating statistical information next.

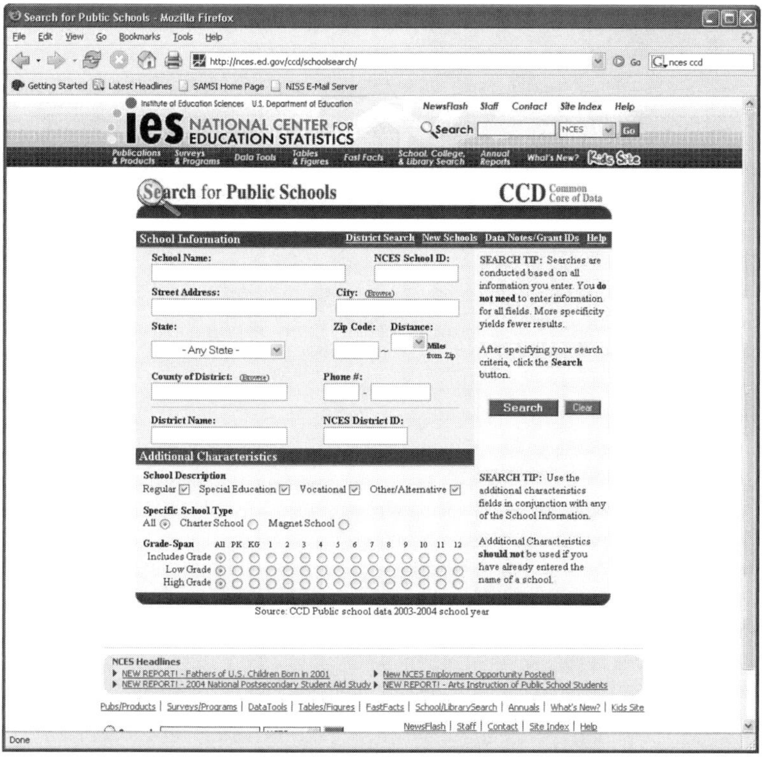

Figure 25-5. NCES' Common Core of Data (CCD) web site, which provides both information specifics and information summaries.

2.3 Locating Statistical Information

While it may be clear to expert users in the setting of Section 3 where to find particular data sets, the same is surely not true in the setting of this section. Many citizens are not even aware that the US federal statistical system is compartmentalized on the basis of domain (agricultural, demographic, economic, education, energy, health, …) of data. (In countries there is a single national statistics agency, such as Statistics Canada.) Broad-based tools such as Google are not (yet, in any event) truly effective at locating statistical information, although the CCD web site is fifth entry returned by a Google search for "School Information."

The "FedStats" web portal (http://www.fedstats.gov/), whose home page is shown in Figure 25-6, is one means of accessing information from more than 100 (!) US federal statistical agencies. In part, this web site was developed with input from the digital government program.

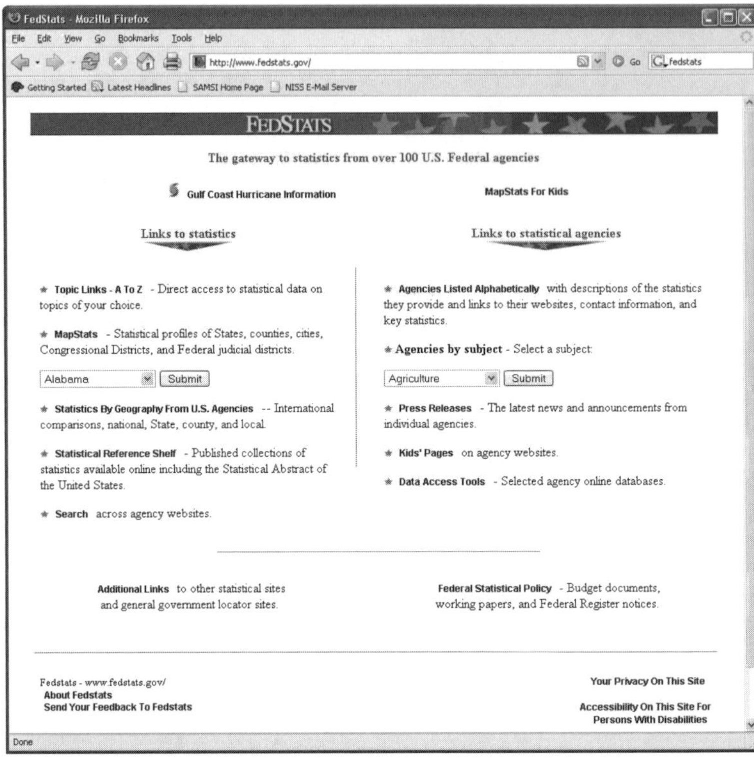

Figure 25-6. The FedStats home page, which provides links to statistical agency data by selecting from drop-down lists.

A more ambitious, interactive and powerful software tool developed by Gary Marchionini of the University of North Carolina at Chapel Hill and numerous colleagues (see Ceaparu 2003, Haas 2003, Marchionini and Brunk 2003 and Marchionini et al. 2000) is shown in Figure 25-7. (A demonstration is available at: http://idl53.ils.unc.edu/~junliang/rb_nchs.html.) Underlying the Java applet in Figure 25-7 is information about more than 4,000 web pages from the NCHS web site. The user may interactively filter the search by topic and/or geographical coverage.

An especially challenging problem is for statistical agencies to learn whether users have located the information they sought. This is a generic problem for many web sites, which is complicated for government sites for both technical and other reasons. Federal websites cannot use "cookies" to track repeat visits by users, which are sort of evidence that useful information has been found. Nor do they ask explicitly for user feedback, which may be a mistake.

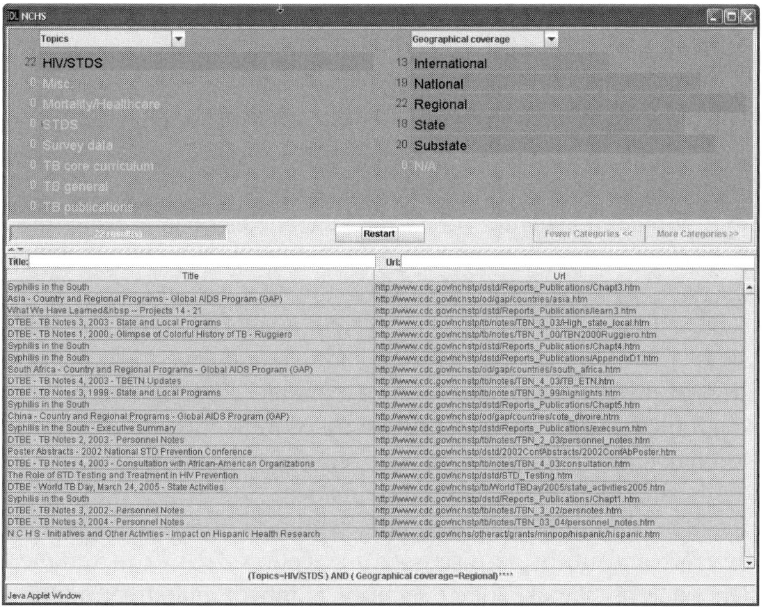

Figure 25-7. Relational data browser developed by Marchionini and colleagues, populated with information about more than 4,000 NCHS web pages.

3. RESEARCHER ACCESS

As compared with Section 2, the problems discussed here are more technical, but there is more history to build on. The fundamental tension addressed is between researcher demand for detail and accuracy in released information and the need to preserve privacy of data subjects and confidentiality of the data. Except in Section 3.4, we focus on releases of "microdata," that is, (possibly altered) individual data records. One reason why researchers seek microdata is that this enables them to conduct analyses of their own choosing.

3.1 Statistical Disclosure Limitation

Government data collections, the most familiar of which is the decennial census, are conducted under express or implied promises of confidentiality, some of which carry the force of law. A Census Bureau employee or contractor who reveals an identified record is guilty of a felony. Protecting confidentiality is also judged essential to the quality of the data: although the evidence is more anecdotal that scientific, almost everyone believes that respondents will lie if they feel that confidentiality is threatened.

Official statistics agencies have a long history of attention to statistical disclosure limitation (SDL), which is sometimes known as statistical disclosure avoidance or statistical disclosure control (Doyle, et al. 2001, Willenborg and de Waal, 2001). At the highest level, strategies for SDL on microdata fall into two classes: those based on *restricting access* to the data and those based on *restricting the data* themselves.

Many US federal statistics ("Fedstats") agencies operate restricted access data centers, to which researchers can come and conduct analyses on unaltered data. Typically, the researcher, the analysis and the results of the analysis are all vetted manually. The system is expensive, inequitable (some researchers live near centers, others don't) and overlooks entirely the interaction of different analyses with one another. An alternative, emerging approach, remote access servers, are discussed in Section 3.4.

Restricted data, in general, means removing portions of the data, and perhaps altering others, in way that reduces the risk of disclosure but decreases the utility of the released information as little as possible. (What is meant by risk and utility is discussed in Section 3.2.) For example, direct identifiers such as names, social security numbers and street addresses are easily and almost always removed from data. More subtle identifiers such as "Occupation = Mayor" in a database of residents of New York City must also be considered.

Even more problematic is that in many cases, the (non-identifier) data values themselves determine records uniquely. For example, more than 90% of people in the US are uniquely identified by their date of birth, gender and 5-digit ZIP code.[1] Extreme values of variables such as age or income can also create problems. Bill Gates can be identified in a database of Washington residents on the basis of income alone.

To cope with these and other issues, statistical agencies have traditionally altered data in various ways. Methods that actually change data values are illustrated in Section 3.3. Others are so ubiquitous that some data users are not even aware that they are disclosure limitation devices. For example, *top-coding* could replace the actual values all incomes exceeding (say) $1,000,000 by "$1,000,000 or more." In the same way, age in years can be replaced by age in five-year-long intervals (0-5, 6-10, ...). Counties can be replaced by states. These SDL strategies tell the truth, but not the whole truth.

---

[1] Readers who are interested may wish to try the following experiment. Assuming that you know nothing about yourself other than your name and state of residence, see how long it takes to locate these three pieces of information on the web (and whether they are right!). Hint: start with a voter registration or property ownership database.

3.2 Risk-Utility Formulations

A fundamental issue is how a statistical agency should think about the information it releases. Researchers at the National Institute of Statistical Sciences (NISS), as well those at many other organizations, advocate a risk-utility approach employing concepts from microeconomics. Just as a consumer cannot simultaneously optimize consumption of both automobiles and houses (Because of budget constraints, more of one implies less of the other!), an agency cannot simultaneously minimize disclosure risk and maximize data utility. Instead the agency must trade one for the other; the point is to do so in a principled manner.

A risk-utility formulation requires, for each candidate release, both a quantified measure of disclosure risk and quantified measure of data utility (Gomatam et al. 2005; Karr, Kohnen, et al. 2006). Then, given a set of candidate releases, a statistical agency may select one in at least two possible ways. First, given an upper bound on disclosure risk, the agency may choose the release that maximizes data utility subject to that bound.

A more general approach is to define the *risk-utility frontier* of candidate releases that are undominated with respect to the partial order defined by saying that R_2 is "better than" R_1 if it has *both* higher data utility *and* lower disclosure risk. The key point is that all releases for which there is some other release with both lower risk and higher utility can be dropped from further consideration. The remaining releases constitute the risk-utility frontier, which is analogous to production possibility frontiers in micro-economics. The great value of the risk-utility frontier is that it reduces, in some cases dramatically, the number of candidate releases requiring further consideration. Moreover, for almost any tradeoff function between risk and utility, the optimal solution will lie on the frontier.

3.3 Examples of SDL Methods

Here we give a brief summary of some common methods for SDL. The descriptions are largely heuristic, and some are principally pictorial. Many methods are omitted altogether.

3.3.1 Categorical data

Categorical data, as the name suggests, take such values as "Sex = Male" or "State of Residence = NC." They can arise directly (Think of many survey forms!) or from numerical data. For instance, "Age = 15-20" may come directly from a survey form, or may be derived from an "Age in

Years" or "Date of Birth" variable. Nearly always (see also Section 3), categorical data are presented, explicitly or implicitly, in tabular form.

Techniques for SDL for categorical data include category aggregation (Example: "Age in Years" is replaced by "Age = 0-5, 6-10, …"), deletion of attributes, replacing high-dimensional tables by lower-dimensional "marginals" (Dobra, et al. 2002, 2003); suppressing sensitive cell values; and data swapping, where fixed or randomly selected variables are exchanged between randomly selected pairs of data records.

A NISS-developed system (Karr, et al. 2002) for geographical aggregation of risky county-level data on chemical (e.g., pesticide) usage on farms is illustrated in Figure 25-8.

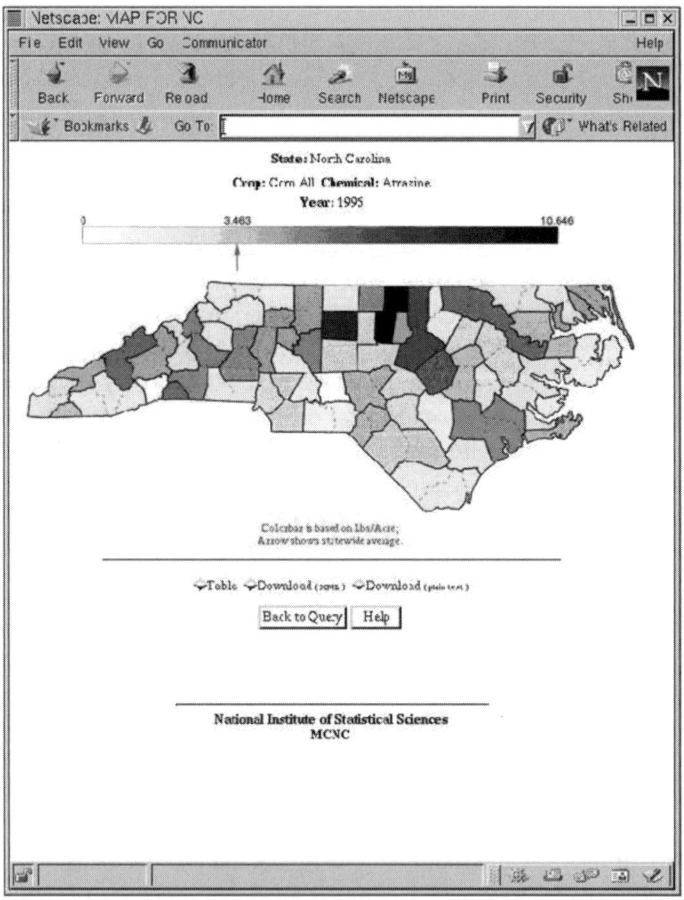

Figure 25-8. NISS-developed system for geographical aggregation of data that is too risky to release at the county level. County boundaries within "supercounties" are shown by dashed lines.

The client was the National Agricultural Statistics Service (NASS). County-level data are unreleasable if too few surveyed farms contribute to them or if they are dominated by one farm (so that a country total is effectively the value for that farm). The computational engine behind Figure 25-8 uses heuristic optimization algorithms to aggregate unreleasable counties into releasable "supercounties." Unfortunately but unavoidably, in the process some counties whose data could have been released separately are incorporated into larger supercounties.

Cell suppression has a lengthy and somewhat controversial history. In its simplest form, risky (almost always, low count) cell values are simply suppressed from a table prior to release. But things are not this simple: if marginal totals (in a two-dimensional table, row and column sums) are also be released, or have been released elsewhere, then to protect one suppressed, risky cell, additional, secondary suppressions are necessary. The required number of such secondary suppressions increases with the dimension of the table, and even recognizing that enough secondary suppressions have been made entails significant computational effort. A further disadvantage is that cell suppression hinders or prevents statistical analysis of tabular data.

Figure 25-9 illustrates data swapping for an 8-variable data set derived from the US Current Population Survey (CPS). The categories there are actually coarsened versions of the original categories, showing that it is possible to use more than one method of SDL prior to releasing data.

Record	Age	EmplType	Educ	MarStat	Race	Sex	AveHours	Salary
1	<25	Gov	HS	Marr	W	M	40	<$50K
2	25–55	SE	Bach	Marr	NW	M	>40	<$50K
3	25–55	Gov	Bach+	Unmarr	NW	F	>40	>$50K
4	>55	Priv	Bach	Unmarr	W	F	>40	<$50K
5	<25	Other	SomeColl	Marr	W	M	40	>$50K
6	>55	Priv	Bach+	Marr	NW	F	40	>$50K

Record	Age	EmplType	Educ	MarStat	Race	Sex	AveHours	Salary
1	>55	Gov	HS	Marr	W	M	40	<$50K
2	25–55	SE	Bach	Marr	NW	M	>40	<$50K
3	<25	Gov	Bach+	Unmarr	NW	F	>40	>$50K
4	>55	Priv	Bach	Unmarr	W	F	>40	<$50K
5	25-55	Other	SomeColl	Marr	W	M	40	>$50K
6	<25	Priv	Bach+	Marr	NW	F	40	>$50K

Figure 25-9. Example of data swapping. The swapped variable is "Age," which is swapped between records 1 and 6 and records 2 and 5.

To exemplify the risk-utility formulations of Section 3.2, an agency that has decided to employ data swapping must select: (1) Which variable(s) (the *swap variables*) are to be swapped, (2) The percentage of records (the *swap rate*) for which these variables will be swapped, and (3) Possible constraints (for example, that records may not be swapped "across state lines"). Rationales for swapping more than one variable include preserving important relationships in the data and preventing detectably swapped records, such as men undergoing hysterectomies. Gomatam, Karr and Sanil (2006) contains several examples of data swapping viewed as a decision problem, in which disclosure risk relates to unswapped records in small-count cells and data utility is the inverse of distortion.

The NISS Data Swapping Toolkit (Gomatam, Karr and Sanil, 2006), is publicly available software (downloadable from the NISS web site, at http://www.niss.org/software/dstk.html) for performing data swapping and visualizing risk-utility frontiers, as shown in Figure 25-10. The data set consists of the 8 CPS variables shown in Figure 25-9 for 48,842 records. The experiment underlying that figure considers two swap rates—1% and 2% of the data, and, for each of these, 36 choices of swap attributes—8 single attributes and 28 pairs of attributes. Only 8 of the 72 cases considered lie on the risk-utility (in this case, risk-distortion) frontier.

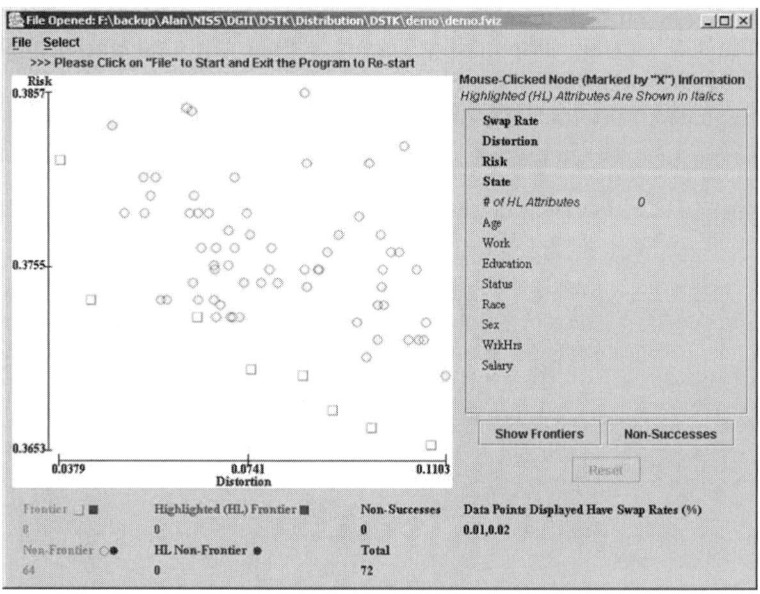

Figure 25-10. Visualization of a risk-utility frontier for data swapping, produced by the NISS Data Swapping Toolkit. Two swap rates and for each, 36 choices of one or two swap attributes, are shown. Combinations on the risk-utility frontier are symbolized by squares.

3.3.2 Numerical data

Methods for SDL for numerical data include addition of random noise, data swapping (possibly with restrictions on how far apart the values of swapped variables may be, to avoid, for example, swapping an income of $40,000 for one of $700,000,000), and microggregation, in which data records are grouped into clusters containing small numbers of relatively homogeneous records, and then all records in each cluster are replaced by their centroid. Figure 25-11 illustrates adding noise to a two-variable—age and income—data set. Initially (and unrealistically), the age-income relationship was perfectly linear. Following addition of noise to income, the linear relationship is still discernible, but less precise and therefore less risky.

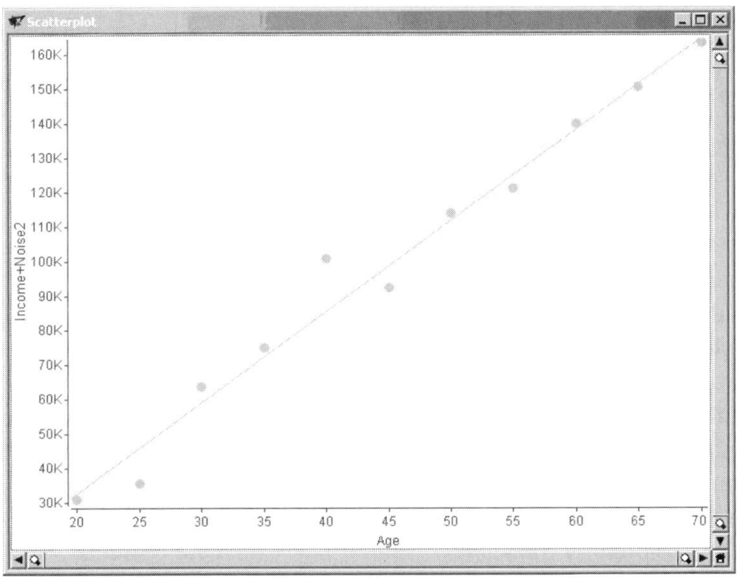

Figure 25-11. Addition of random noise to a numerical variable. Original values of the income variable lay on a straight line. Noise-perturbed values preserve the nature but not the specific details of the original relationship.

Figure 25-12 illustrates microaggregation with a cluster size of three. Karr, Kohnen et al. (2006) contains several utility measures for this setting, ranging from measures tied to one specific regression analysis on the data to very general measures of data distortion.

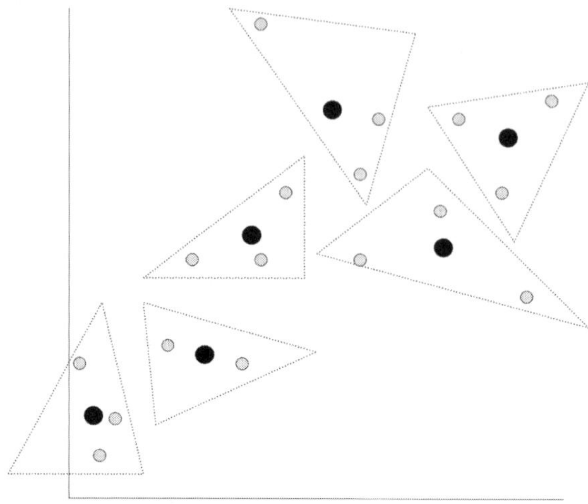

Figure 25-12. Microaggregation for two-dimensional data with clusters of size three. The triangles show the clusters, and in each cluster, the original, light gray data records are replaced by the black centroid. One cluster contains only two records.

3.4 Remote Access Servers

An emerging technology for dealing with confidential data is not to release data at all, even using any of the altered forms discussed in Section 3.3. Instead, a web-based, remote access server responds (Although not necessarily as the user wishes, because the server may decline to answer the query.) to electronically submitted queries for statistical analyses of the data. Such analyses may be as sophisticated as linear regressions (Gomatam et al. 2005) or as simple as tabular summaries (Dobra et al. 2002, 2003). The attraction is that analyses are *performed on the original data*, on a secure computer operated by the agency, so that the results are correct.

Figure 25-13 shows a NISS-developed table server. The underlying data set is the same 8-variable, 48,842-element CPS-derived data set underlying Figures 25-10 and 25-11. The associated 8-dimensional contingency table contains 2,880 cells, of which 1,695 contain non-zero counts. This table is neither realistically large nor realistically sparse: the table associated with the 52-question US Census long form contains on the order of 10^{47} cells, of which only approximately 10^9 are non-zero, and cannot even be thought of, let alone manipulated computationally, as an array. Queries are for "marginal" sub-tables of the 8-way table, such as the 3-way table of "Age cross Education cross Marital Status." There are $2^8 = 256$ sub-tables. Of course, answering one query also answers others. (Releasing the Age cross

Education cross Marital Status table also releases its three two-dimensional "children"—the Age cross Education, Age cross Marital Status and Education cross Martial Status tables, as well as the one-dimensional tables for Age, Education and Marital Status individually.)

Research on remote access servers has revealed a number of subtle (and not-so-subtle) issues. It is no surprise that, as noted in Section 3.1, query interaction is a major problem: several queries are collectively risky in ways that none of them is individually. While a remote access server can simply ignore query interaction, this is at least irresponsible and (one hopes!) unnecessary. For the table server in Figure 25-13, knowledge of all 28 six-way sub-tables provides very tight bounds on the entries in the full table, even though none of the individual six-way tables is nearly as risky. (For a simple illustration, write down a two-by-two table containing positive or zero integer entries, calculate the row and column sums, and then erase the table. The row and column sums are together much more revealing about the table than either alone.)

Figure 25-13 visualizes the hypothetical effect of releasing the 4-way table of Age cross Education cross Marital Status cross Work Hours in light of having previously released several other 3-way tables, which appear as black squares in the lower left-hand portion of the display.

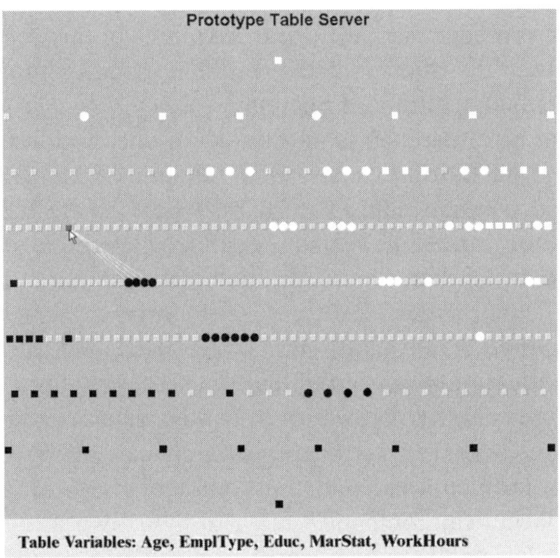

Figure 25-13. NISS-developed table server, showing the effect of responding to a query for the four-way table pointed to by the cursor. Previously released tables are black squares in the lower left-hand corner. What would be additional releases are the black circles radiating southeast from the table in question. Previously unreleasable tables are the white squares in the upper right-hand corner. Tables that would become unreleasable are the white circles.

What is perhaps more striking, and less anticipated, is that whenever a query is answered, other queries become *permanently unanswerable.* An agency operating a remote access server must, therefore, devise release rules that account not only for the risk of answering a query in light of previously answered queries but also for the dis-utility that answering one query precludes ever answering many others.

Release rules for remote access servers should also ensure user equity. Because each answered query creates unanswerable queries, some mechanism is necessary to prevent a group of users, or a single user, from bombarding the server with queries it finds interesting, which may rule out the queries of interest to many other users. Mediating mechanisms include some form of "voting" to determine the queries of greatest interest, which raises many problems of its own, and money, which is currently not seen as acceptable by statistical agencies.

4. DISTRIBUTED DATA

Underlying nearly all of Sections 2 and 3 is that inescapable reality that government data are distributed, in the US across both agencies and levels of government. As discussed in Section 2, simply locating the "right" information is a problem that still needs research. In this section we discuss briefly how the "distributed data" problem maps into the statistical analysis/confidentiality setting of Section 3.

Suppose that a researcher is interested in the performance of school children, say on standardized tests, as a function of family characteristics such as size and parental education. It may be that the best relevant data reside in 51 or more state-level databases. Indeed, even the states themselves may be interested in performing a detailed statistical analysis to determine which family characteristics affect pupil performance, which would clearly be most informative if all states' data were used. But at the same time, because of confidentiality concerns, they may be unwilling or forbidden to share data with one another, or to turn over their data to a trusted third party. To illustrate how digital government research can go beyond its "home" context, similar problems exist in the commercial world. For example, a group of pharmaceutical companies may, to their own and societal benefit, wish to conduct an analysis of adverse drug effects on the union of their individual chemical databases.

NISS has developed, and continues to develop, Internet-based technologies for secure, privacy-protecting, valid statistical analysis of distributed databases. Full description of these methods and the software system that implements them is beyond the scope of this chapter. Briefly (see, for example, Karr, et al. 2004 and Karr, Fulp, et al. 2006), the techniques employ concepts of secure multi-party computation (SMPC) from computer science to perform analyses of "horizontally partitioned data." By this we mean that the data records are distributed, as opposed to the variables. The "vertically partitioned" case (Karr, et al. 2005, Sanil et al. 2004) is considerably more challenging, and it is relevant to US statistical agencies! The analyses that can be performed easily are those requiring only summaries (in technical language, sufficient statistics) that are *additive across the agencies*. Many common techniques, such as construction of contingency tables and linear regression, fit this paradigm.

For such analyses, the relevant concept from SMPC is secure summation Imagine a group of people who wish to determine their average income without revealing their individual incomes to each other. (A popular-media version of this is a puzzle to determine their total weight.) To calculate the total income, which divided by the number of people gives the average, the people use a round-robin procedure. The first person adds his or her income to a large random number, and passes that sum to the second person, who adds his or her income, passes the new running sum on, and so forth. When the sum arrives back at the first person, it consists of the random number plus the sum of everyone's incomes, so the person subtracts the random number and shares the result.

Of course, in reality, the process is fraught with shortcomings. It is vulnerable to collusion, lying and, without proper implementation, corruption by outsiders. Further research is needed and is being done.

5. CONCLUSION: THOUGHTS ABOUT THE FUTURE

The threads of research described in Sections 2, 3 and 4 seem to hold rather different prognoses for the future.

The broad access needs discussed in Section 2 seem likely to grow for the foreseeable future. Although impressive, initial research has raised more questions than it has resolved, and research needs will continue to increase for years. While the "audience" for manipulating large, high-dimensional tables may be limited, the demand for accessing and manipulating multiple smaller marginals is virtually unlimited. Systems such as HDAA (Figures 25-3 and 25-4) are held back by current hardware, communication and software. (HTML contains no abstraction of a table of more than two dimensions, for example.) It seems short-sighted to presume that hardware and software systems alone will solve the problem. Data quality may be the major issue.

For reasons discussed below, government agencies may at some point no longer be the providers of choice for statistical data in the context of Section 3. It seems more likely that they will remain the providers of choice in the setting of Section 2, if only because this is a service that no organization other than the government will supply.

It is not entirely obvious that federal statistical agencies will continue to disseminate data for purposes of statistical analysis in the manner described in Section 3, except possibly using remote access servers (Section 3.4) to disseminate the results of analyses instead. Among the reasons for this are that tools and external databases for record linkage may become so powerful and readily available that no releasable have any utility. A second reason is that the information may be available elsewhere (ChoicePoint, for example) without any SDL applied to it. Agencies may hold a cost advantage for a while and a quality advantage for longer, but not necessarily forever. SDL technologies may become solutions to problems that no longer exist. The Section 3 problems are also driven by difficult-to-predict public attitudes about privacy and confidentiality. For instance, many people in the US have been willing to sacrifice some (personal) privacy in the name of (collective) homeland security, although there are already signs of decreased tolerance. Currently, medical records may be the "hot button" issue. Potentially more profound changes, for example, a shift from concern about releasing information to resultant harm, are possible.

There is almost no way not to see the distributed data setting of Section 4 as a wave of the future. The need for systems such as those described briefly there is not driven solely by confidentiality. Such systems are a viable means of conducting statistical analyses integrating large, dynamic databases that are impossible or even just inconvenient to transmit to a central location. Although communication speeds will continue to increase, FedEx can move a petabyte of data from point A to point B overnight, but today's networks cannot.

ACKNOWLEDGMENTS

This research was supported by NSF grants EIA-0131884 and SES-0345441 to the National Institute of Statistical Sciences (NISS). Any opinions, findings, and conclusions or recommendations expressed in this publication are those of the author and do not necessarily reflect the views of the National Science Foundation. Fedstats agencies that are partners in the research described here include the Bureau of Labor Statistics, Bureau of Transportation Statistics, Census Bureau, National Agricultural Statistics

Service, National Center for Education Statistics and National Center for Health Statistics.

REFERENCES

Ceaparu I (2003) Finding governmental statistical data on the Web: A case study of FedStats. IT and Society 1(3):1-17

Dobra A, Fienberg SE, Karr AF, Sanil AP (2002) Software systems for tabular data releases. International J. Uncertainty, Fuzziness and Knowledge Based Systems 10(5):529-544

Dobra A, Karr AF, Sanil AP (2003) Preserving confidentiality of high-dimensional tabulated data: Statistical and computational issues. Statistics and Computing 13:363-370

Doyle P, Lane, JI, Theeuwes JJM, Zayatz LV (2001) Confidentiality, disclosure and data access: Theory and practical application for statistical agencies. Elsevier, Amsterdam

Gomatam S, Karr AF, Sanil AP (2006) Data swapping as a decision problem. J. Official Statistics (to appear).

Gomatam S, Karr, AF, Reiter JP, Sanil AP (2005) Data dissemination and disclosure limitation in a world without microdata: A risk-utility framework for remote access analysis servers. Statistical Science 20(2):163-177.

Haas SW (2003). Improving the search ernvironment: Informed decision making in the search for statistical information. J. American Society for Information Science and Technology 54(8): 782-797.

Karr, AF, Lee, J, Sanil AP, Hernandez J, Karimi S, Litwin K (2002) Web-based systems that disseminate information from data but preserve confidentiality. In: Elmagarmid E, McIver WM (eds) Advances in digital government: Technology, human factors, and policy, Kluwer, Boston, pp. 181-196

Karr AF, Lin X, Reiter JP, Sanil AP (2004) Secure regression on distributed databases. J. Computational and Graphical Statistics 14(2):263-279

Karr AF, Lin X, Reiter JP, Sanil AP (2005) Privacy preserving analysis of vertically partitioned data using secure matrix products. J Official Statistics (submitted)

Karr AF, Fulp WJ, Lin X, Reiter JP, Vera F, Young SS (2006) Secure, privacy-preserving analysis of distributed databases. Technometrics (to appear)

Karr AF, Kohnen CN, Oganian A, Reiter JP, Sanil AP (2006) A framework for evaluating the utility of data altered to protect confidentiality. The American Statistician 60(3):224-232

Karr, AF, Sanil AP, Banks DL (2006) Data quality: A statistical perspective. Statistical Methodology 3(2):137-173

Marchionini G, Brunk B, (2003) Toward a general relation browser: A GUI for information architects. J. Digital Information 4(1)

Marchionini G, Hert CA, Shneiderman B, Liddy ED (2000) Extending understanding of federal statistics in tables. In: Scholtz J, Thomas J (eds) Conference on universal usability 2000 proceedings. ACM, New York, pp. 132-138

Sanil AP, Karr AF, Lin X, Reiter JP (2004) Privacy preserving regression modelling via distributed computation. In: Proceedings of the Tenth ACM SIGKDD International Conference on Knowledge Discovery and Data Mining, pp. 677-682

US Office of Management and Budget (2002) Guidelines for ensuring and maximizing the quality, objectivity, utility, and integrity of information disseminated by federal agencies. Available on-line at http://www.whitehouse.gov/omb/fedreg/reproducible.html.

Willenborg LCRJ, de Waal T (2001) Elements of statistical disclosure control. Springer-Verlag, New York

SUGGESTED READINGS

- Doyle P, Lane, JI, Theeuwes JJM, Zayatz LV (2001) Confidentiality, disclosure and data access: Theory and practical application for statistical agencies. Elsevier, Amsterdam: statistical disclosure limitation from a statistical agency perspective.
- Duncan GT, Jabine TB, de Wolf, VA (1993) Private lives and public policies: Confidentiality and accessibility of government statistics. National Academy Press, Washington: report of a National Research Council panel on confidentiality and data access, with a strong policy orientation.
- Fienberg SE, Willenborg LCRJ (1998) (eds) Special issue of the Journal of Official Statistics on disclosure limitation methods for protecting the confidentiality of statistical data: a set of papers addressing many aspects of statistical disclosure limitation.
- Willenborg LCRJ, de Waal T (2001) Elements of statistical disclosure control. Springer-Verlag, New York: an accessible introduction to techniques for statistical disclosure limitation.

ONLINE RESOURCES

- *Web sites for digital government projects.* Those most directly associated with the material presented here are located at the National Institute of Statistical Sciences (http://www.niss.org/dgii/index.html) and the University of North Carolina at Chapel Hill (http://www.ils.unc.edu/govstat/).
- *Web sites of the Federal Statistical agencies.* These can be reached from the FedStats portal at http://www.fedstats.gov/.

QUESTIONS FOR DISCUSSION

1. Does one form of access—web browsing, and one technology—HTML, so dominate our concepts of access to government information that possibly more effective alternatives are being overlooked? If so, what are they?
2. Section 4 focuses on how the "researcher access" setting of Section 3 relates to distributed databases. How does the "citizen access" context of Section 2 relate? Think especially of data quality issues.

3. In the Section 2 context of users who are not statistical experts, how might it be possible to convey uncertainties associated with values, such as those derived from surveys, that are statistical estimates? Color has been proposed in the visualization community: red for highly uncertain values, moving to blue as the uncertainty is decreases. Would this work? What else is possible?
4. Does information privacy exist today in any meaningful sense? Instead of controlling access to information, is it more feasible to record who accesses what information, and to notify people, as well as give them the opportunity to view and correct information about themselves?
5. In what ways are the risk-utility formulations of Section 3.2 relevant in the context of Section 2?
6. Given the constraints mentioned in Section 5, how can government agencies attempt to determine if the information needs of users of their web sites are being fulfilled?
7. How do any of the issues in Sections 2-4 translate to new forms of data such as images, audio and video?

Chapter 26

INFECTIOUS DISEASE INFORMATICS AND SYNDROMIC SURVEILLANCE

Daniel Zeng[1], Hsinchun Chen[1], and Ping Yan[1]

[1]Management Information Systems Department, University of Arizona, Tucson, Arizona, U.S.A.

CHAPTER OVERVIEW

Infectious disease informatics (IDI) is an emerging field that studies data collection, sharing, modeling, and management issues in the domain of infectious diseases. This chapter discusses various technical components of IDI research from an information technology perspective. Syndromic surveillance is used to illustrate these components of IDI research, as it is a widely-adopted approach to detecting and responding to public health and bioterrorism events. Two case studies involving real-world applications and research prototypes are presented to illustrate the application context and relevant system design and data modeling issues.

1. INTRODUCTION

In highly-mobile modern societies, infectious diseases, either naturally occurring or caused by bioterrorism attacks, can spread at a rapid rate, resulting in potentially significant loss of life and economic assets (Pinner, Rebmann et al. 2003; Zeng, Chen et al. 2004; Zeng, Chen et al. 2005).

Information systems are increasingly playing a significant role in developing an effective approach to prevent, detect, respond to, and manage infectious disease outbreaks of plants, animals, and humans (Buehler, Hopkins et al. 2004; Zeng, Chen et al. 2005). A large amount of data related to infectious disease detection and response is being collected by various laboratories, health care providers, and government agencies at local, state, national, and international levels (Pinner, Rebmann et al. 2003). A number of information access, analysis, and reporting systems have also been developed and adopted in various public health and homeland security application contexts. For example, in its role as the key agency responsible for human reportable diseases in the U.S., the U.S. Centers for Disease Control and Prevention (CDC) has developed computerized reporting systems for local and state health departments and is also playing a central role in coordinating standardization efforts with an aim for interoperable messaging and data/system integration. Similarly, the U.S. Department of Agriculture (USDA) is enhancing data systems for certain animal diseases (e.g., mad cow disease and foot-and-mouth disease), and the U.S. Geological Survey (USGS), through its National Wildlife Health Center (NWHC) and numerous partners, manages databases for wildlife diseases.

A significant portion of recent work, from the perspectives of both academic research and real-world system implementation, on public health and bioterrorism event detection and response, has been focused on syndromic surveillance (Lawson and Kleinman 2005; Wagner, Moore et al. 2006). Syndromic surveillance is defined as an ongoing, systematic collection, analysis, and interpretation of "syndrome"-specific data for early detection of public health aberrations. The rationale behind syndromic surveillance lies in the fact that specific diseases of interest can be monitored by syndromic presentations that can be shown in a timely manner such as nurse calls, medication purchases, and school or work absenteeism. In addition to early detection and reporting of monitored diseases, syndromic surveillance also provides a rich data repository and highly active communication system for situation awareness and event characterization.

This chapter introduces infectious disease informatics (IDI), an emerging subfield of biomedical informatics that systematically studies information management and analysis issues in the domain of infectious diseases (Zeng, Chen et al. 2005; Hu, Zeng et al. 2007). The objective of IDI research can be summarized as the development of the science and technologies needed for collecting, sharing, reporting, analyzing, and visualizing infectious disease data and for providing data and decision-making support for infectious disease prevention, detection, and management. IDI research directly benefits public health agencies in their infectious disease surveillance activities at all levels of government and in the international context. It also has important applications in national security concerning potential bioterrorism attacks (Siegrist 1999).

This chapter emphasizes various technical components of IDI research with detailed discussions on the design and various system components of an infectious disease information infrastructure. Considering the importance of syndromic surveillance as a widely-adopted approach to detect and respond to public health and bioterrorism events, we use syndromic surveillance systems as the representative IDI application to frame the discussion.

The rest of the chapter is organized as follows. Section 2 provides a brief overview of IDI, discussing its overall objectives and the key motivating technical and policy-related challenges. In Section 2, we also present the basic technical components of an IDI system and related design considerations from an information systems perspective. Section 3 presents an introduction to syndromic surveillance systems, covering issues ranging from applicable data sources, related data analysis and modeling work, to data visualization. In Section 4 we use two real-world IDI projects to provide the readers with a concrete sense of what IDI systems look like and how they are used in specific application contexts. A major purpose of this section is to illustrate in an integrated manner how the technical issues discussed in Sections 2 and 3 are treated in applications. We conclude in Section 5 by summarizing the chapter and pointing out several ongoing trends in IDI research and application.

2. INFECTIOUS DISEASE INFORMATICS AND ITS MAJOR TECHNICAL COMPONENTS

2.1 Objectives and Challenges

IDI is an emerging field of study that systematically examines information management and analysis issues related to infectious diseases (Zeng, Chen et al. 2004; Hu, Zeng et al. 2007). The specific technical objectives of IDI research can be summarized as the development and evaluation of frameworks, techniques, and systems needed for collecting, sharing, reporting, analyzing, and visualizing infectious disease data and for providing data and decision-making support for human, animal, and plant infectious disease prevention, detection, and management. IDI research is also concerned with studying technology adoption issues to promote real-world application of these IDI frameworks, techniques, and systems.

IDI research is inherently interdisciplinary, drawing expertise from a number of fields including but not limited to various branches of information technologies such as information integration, knowledge representation, data sharing, Geographic Information Systems (GIS), data mining, text mining, and visualization; and other fields such as biostatistics, bioinformatics, dynamical systems, operations research, and management information systems. It also has a critical policy component dealing with issues such as data ownership and access control, intra- and inter-agency collaboration, and data privacy and data confidentiality. Because of its broad coverage, IDI research and practice rely on broad participation and partnership between various academic disciplines, public health and other disease surveillance, management, diagnostic, or research agencies at all levels, law enforcement and national security agencies, and related international organizations and government branches.

The basic functions required of any IDI system are data entry, storage, and query, typically implemented as computerized record management systems deployed by local public health agencies or at local hospitals and laboratory facilities. To enable information sharing and reporting across record management systems maintained at different sites, system designers and operators need to agree on a common technical approach. This technical approach should include data sharing protocols based on interoperable standards and a Web-enabled distributed data store infrastructure to allow easy access. It also needs to provide a scalable and effective reporting and alerting mechanism across organizational boundaries and provide important geocoding and GIS-based visualizations to facilitate infectious disease data analysis.

To maximize the potential payoff of an IDI system, advanced information management and data analysis capabilities need to be made available to the users. Such information management capabilities include visualization support to facilitate understanding and summarization of large amounts of data. An important aspect of data analysis is concerned with outbreak detection and prediction in the form of spatio-temporal data analysis and surveillance. New "privacy-conscious" data mining techniques also need to be developed to better protect privacy and patient confidentiality (Kargupta, Liu et al. 2003; Wylie and Mineau 2003; Ohno-Machado, PS et al. 2004).

From a policy perspective, there are mainly four sets of issues that need to be studied and related guidelines developed (Zeng, Chen et al. 2004). The first set is concerned with legal issues. There exist many laws, regulations, and agreements governing data collection, data confidentiality and reporting, which directly impact the design and operations of IDI systems. The second set is mainly related to data ownership and access control issues. The key questions are: Who are the owner(s) of a particular dataset and derivative data? Who is allowed to input, access, aggregate, or distribute data? The third set concerns data dissemination and alerting: What alerts should be sent to whom under what circumstances? The policy governing data dissemination and alerting needs to be made jointly by organizations across jurisdictions and has to carefully balance the needs for information and possibility of information overflow. The fourth set is concerned with data sharing and possible incentive mechanisms. To facilitate fruitful sharing of infectious disease data on an ongoing basis, all contributing parties need to have proper incentives and benefit from the collaboration.

To summarize, from an application standpoint, the ideal IDI system would include a field deployable electronic collection instrument that could be synchronized with server based information systems in public health departments (Zeng, Chen et al. 2005). Biological specimen processing would be handled in laboratory information systems that were integrated completely with epidemiological and demographic information collected from the field and with the electronically submitted data from non-public health clinical laboratory information systems. The integrated laboratory, demographic, and epidemiological information would be available for statistical and GIS analyses in real time as the data are collected. The data collected would be available to authorized users of a system that would protect identifying information of any individuals using role based user access and permissions. Data could be shared across public health jurisdictions and between public health and nonpublic health agencies where such sharing was appropriate and where only appropriate data was provided. The ideal data system would use standards for metadata, terminologies, messaging formats, and security to maintain true semantic interoperability. Data analysis, altering, and decision support would be integrated into the data stream for data validation, message routing, and data de-duplication.

2.2 Basic Technical Components and Design Considerations

This section summarizes basic technical components of an IDI system needed to provide essential data support. More advanced functionalities of IDI systems tend to be application-specific; some of these functionalities and related technological support will be discussed in Section 3.

The following technical considerations are critical to the design of a basic IDI system: data standards, system architecture and messaging standards, and data ingest and access control. In this section, we briefly discuss them in turn at the conceptual level. In Section 3, these issues will be revisited in the specific context of syndromic surveillance.

Data Standards. Data standards enable interoperability between information systems involved in disease reporting and surveillance. Data standards are also critical to provide unambiguous meaning to data and form the foundation that enables data aggregation as well as data mining. Many data standards have been developed in health care and public health informatics, causing considerable confusion and implementation difficulties. Fortunately, the swarm of data standards applicable to IDI is beginning to narrow to a manageable group by the combined efforts of the National Center for Vital Health Statistics (NCVHS) and the Consolidated Health Informatics (CHI) E-Gov initiative (Goldsmith, Blumenthal et al. 2003). See Table 26-1 for some of the key standards.

Table 26-1. CHI Standards Applicable to IDI (Zeng, Chen et al. 2005)

CHI Adopted Standard	*Domain*
Health Level 7 (HL-7) messaging	messaging
Laboratory Logical Observation Identifier Name Codes (LOINC)	laboratory test orders
SNOMED CT	laboratory result contents; non-laboratory interventions and procedures, anatomy, diagnosis and problems
RxNORM	describing clinical drugs
HL-7 clinical vaccine formulation (CVX) and manufacturer codes (MVX)	immunization registry, terminology

While these standards are currently required only for federal government information systems, in all likelihood, data standards adopted by the federal government will be assimilated and adopted by private industry over a relatively short period of time due to the combination of payor (Medicare, Medicaid, and the Civilian Health and Medical Program of the Uniformed Services (CHAMPUS)) pressures, the sheer size of the federal government health care sector, and the need for private industry to communicate with these government systems. The Health Resources and Services Administration (HRSA) has also provided funds for encoding hospital laboratory information systems with the intention of helping migrate the systems from local code sets or CPT4 and ICD-9 code systems to LOINC and SNOMED codes that will allow interoperability with local, state, and federal health information systems adhering to CHI standards.

In the public health sector, the CDC has led the way in the push for data standardization through the National Electronic Disease Surveillance System (NEDSS) and the Public Health Information Network (PHIN) initiatives. These initiatives define a set of vocabularies, messaging standards, message and data formats as well as the architectural components required for public health jurisdictions utilizing the federal Bioterrorism grants for funding information systems development. The National Library of Medicine brokered contract with the American College of Pathologists for the United States licensure of the SNOMED vocabulary, the naming of the first National Health Information Technology Coordinator, and the ongoing work on the National Health Information Infrastructure (NHII) provides the means for accelerating the pace for data standardization.

System Architecture and Messaging. There are fewer messaging standards relevant to IDI. Among them, Health Level 7 (HL7) is the dominant messaging standard for transfer of clinical information. Almost all hospital information systems exchange HL7 messages and the majority of large private clinical labs have adopted the HL7 standard as well. The current ANSI approved version of HL7 is 2.5; however, several new Version 3 messages for public health reporting have been developed and are being reviewed for implementation as a normative standard. The HL7 Version 3 specification represents a paradigm shift from the flat file structure of the 2.x HL7 versions to an object oriented Reference Information Model (RIM) foundation. This change provides the necessary structure to disambiguate the detailed information in the message and maintain the contextual relationships between data elements that are critical in infectious disease and bioterrorism system to system communication. The CDC has set a goal of using Version 3 messages for morbidity reporting from states to the CDC. Additionally, the HL7 Clinical Document Architecture (CDA) standard is being considered in a variety of reporting and data collection scenarios including the CDC Outbreak Management System.

Data Ingest and Access Control. Data ingest control is responsible for checking the integrity and authenticity of data feeds from the underlying information sources. Access control is responsible for granting and restricting user access to potentially sensitive data. Data ingest and access control is particularly important in IDI applications because of obvious data confidentiality concerns and data sharing requirements imposed by data contributors. Although ingest and access control issues are common in many application domains, IDI poses some unique considerations and requirements. In most other applications, a user is either granted or denied access to a particular information item. In IDI applications, however, user access privilege is often not binary. For instance, a local public health official has full access to data collected from his or her jurisdiction but typically does not have the same access to data from neighboring jurisdictions. However, it does not necessarily mean that this official has no access at all to such data from neighboring jurisdictions. Often he or she can be granted access to such data in some aggregated form (e.g., monthly or county-level statistics). Such granularity-based data access requirements warrant special treatment when designing an IDI system.

3. SYNDROMIC SURVEILLANCE SYSTEMS

In the previous section, we briefly introduced the field of IDI and discussed the basic components of IDI systems. We noted that the discussion of many advanced functionalities of IDI systems needs to be framed in an application-specific manner. This section provides such an application context, i.e., syndromic surveillance, which allows us to have an extended discussion of these basic IDI system components along with advanced IDI data analysis and visualization techniques. Syndromic surveillance by itself represents a major trend in both research and real-world implementation and is arguably the most active and important IDI application in the current practice.

3.1 Background

Public health surveillance has been practiced for decades and continues to be an indispensable approach for detecting emerging disease outbreaks and epidemics. Early knowledge of a disease outbreak plays an important role in improving response effectiveness. While traditional disease surveillance often relies on time-consuming laboratory diagnosis and the reporting of notifiable diseases is often slow and incomplete, a new breed of public health surveillance systems has the potential to significantly speed up detection of disease outbreaks. These new, computer-based surveillance systems offer valuable and timely information to hospitals as well as to state, local, and federal health officials (Pavlin 2003; Bravata, McDonald et al. 2004; Dembek, Carley et al. 2005; Yan, Zeng et al. 2006). These systems are capable of real-time or near real-time detection of serious illnesses and potential bioterrorism agent exposures, allowing for a rapid public health response (Mandl, Overhage et al. 2004). This public health surveillance approach is generally called syndromic surveillance, an ongoing, systematic collection, analysis, and interpretation of "syndrome"-specific data for early detection of public health aberrations.

In the literature, the discussion of syndromic surveillance systems usually falls under the following functional areas: 1) data sources and acquisition, 2) syndrome classification, 3) anomaly detection, and 4) data visualization and data access. The surveillance data are first collected from the data providers to a centralized data repository where the raw data are categorized into syndrome categories to indicate certain disease threats. Anomaly detection employing time and space data analysis algorithms characterizes the syndromic data to detect the anomalies (for example, the surge of counts of clinic visits aggregated by days, or anomalous spatial clusters of medical records aggregated by ZIP codes). The data visualization and data access module is used to facilitate case investigations and support data exploration and summarization in a visual environment. The rest of this section is dedicated to these four functional areas, respectively.

3.2 Data Sources and Acquisition

Syndromic surveillance is a data-driven public health surveillance approach which collects and processes a wide array of data sources. These data sources include chief complaints, emergency department (ED) visits, ambulatory visits, hospital admissions, triage nurse calls, 911 calls, work or school absenteeism data, veterinary health records, laboratory test orders, and health department requests for influenza testing, among others (Lombardo, Burkom et al. 2004; Ma, Rolka et al. 2005). For instance, one of the most established syndromic surveillance projects, the Real-time Outbreak Detection system (RODS), uses laboratory orders, dictated radiology reports, dictated hospital reports, poison control center calls, chief complaint data, and daily sales data for over-the-counter (OTC) medications for syndromic surveillance (Tsui, Espino et al. 2003).

Preliminary investigations have evaluated the effectiveness of different data sources in syndromic surveillance and studied the difference among them in terms of information timeliness and characterization ability for outbreak detection, as they represent various aspects of patient health-care-seeking behavior (Lazarus, Kleinman et al. 2001; Ma, Rolka et al. 2005). For example, school absenteeism comes to notice relatively earlier as individuals take leave before seeking health care in hospitals or clinics, but specific disease evidence provided by the absenteeism type of data is limited. Table 26-2 provides a rough-cut classification of different data sources used for syndromic surveillance organized by their timeliness and the capability to characterize epidemic events.

Data acquisition is a critical early step when developing a syndromic surveillance system. The particular data collection strategy is obviously dependent on the data providers' information system infrastructure. Such strategies range from direct manual entry on paper or using hand-held devices (Zelicoff, Brillman et al. 2001) to automated data transmission, archiving, query and messaging (Lombardo, Burkom et al. 2003; Espino, Wagner et al. 2004).

Table 26-2. Data sources organized by data timeliness and epidemic characterization (Yan, Zeng et al. 2006)

Timeliness	Characterization	
	High	Low
High	• Chief complaints from ED visits and ambulatory visits • Hospital admission • Test orders • Triage nurse calls, 911 calls • Prescription medication data	• OTC medication sales • School or work absenteeism • Veterinary health records
Low	• ICD-9 code • Laboratory test results • Clinical reports	• Public sources (local or regional events)

Many practical challenges exist that still hinder data collection efforts, including the following: (a) different coding conventions among the health facilities need to be reconciled when integrating the different data sources; (b) providing and transmission of data either requires staff intervention or dedicated network infrastructure with relatively high security level, which are often viewed as extra cost to data providers; (c) data sharing and transmission must comply with HIPAA and others, to be secure and assure privacy; and (d) there is a time lag getting data from data providers to syndromic surveillance systems. Data quality challenges (e.g., incompleteness and duplications) often pose additional challenges.

3.3 Syndrome Classification

The onset of a number of syndromes can indicate certain diseases that are viewed as threats to the public health. For example, influenza-like syndrome could be due to an anthrax attack, which is of particular interest in the detection of bioterrorism events.

A syndrome category is defined as a set of symptoms, which is an indicator of some specific diseases. For example, a short-phrase chief complaint "coughing with high fever" can be classified as the "upper respiratory" syndrome. Table 26-3 summarizes some of the most commonly-monitored syndrome categories. Note that different syndromic surveillance systems may monitor different categories. For example, in the RODS system there are 7 syndrome groups of interest for bio-surveillance purposes;

whereas EARS defines a more detailed list of 43 syndromes (http://www.bt.cdc.gov/surveillance/ears/). Some syndromes are of common interest across different systems, such as respiratory or gastrointestinal syndromes.

Table 26-3. Syndrome categories commonly monitored

Influenza-like	Respiratory	Dermatological
Fever	Neurologic	Cold
Gastrointestinal	Rash	Diarrhea
Hemorrhagic illness	Severe illness and death	Asthma
Localized cutaneous lesion	Specific infection	Vomit
Lymphadenitis	Sepsis	Other/none of the above
Constitutional		
Bioterrorism agent-related diseases		
Anthrax	Botulism-like/botulism	Plague
Tularemia	Smallpox	SARS (Severe Acute Respiratory Syndrome)

Currently the syndrome classification process is implemented into syndromic surveillance systems either manually or through an automated system. Note, however, automated, computerized syndrome classification is essential to real-time syndromic surveillance. Syndrome classification is thus one of the first and most important steps in syndromic data processing. The software application that evaluates the patient's chief complaint or ICD-9 codes and then assigns it to a syndrome category is often known as a syndrome classifier (Lu, Zeng et al. 2006).

A substantial amount of research effort has been expended to classifying free-text chief complaints into syndromes. This classification task is difficult because different expressions, acronyms, abbreviations, and truncations are often found in free-text chief complaints (Sniegoski 2004). For example, "chst pn," "CP," "c/p," "chest pai," "chert pain," "chest/abd pain," and "chest discomfort" can all mean "chest pain." As we observed in the previous section, a majority of syndromic surveillance systems use chief complaints as a major source of data; as a result, syndrome classification has wide applications. Another syndromic data type often used for syndromic surveillance purposes, i.e. ICD-9 or ICD-9-CM codes, also needs to be grouped into syndrome categories. Processing such information is somewhat easier as the data records are structured.

Classification methods that have been studied and employed can largely be categorized into four groups: 1) Natural language processing; 2) Bayesian classifiers; 3) Text string searching; and 4) Vocabulary abstraction. We summarize existing classification methods in Table 26-4.

Table 26-4. Syndrome classification approaches (Yan, Zeng et al. 2006)

Approach	Description	Example Systems
Manual grouping	Medical experts in syndromic surveillance, infectious diseases, and medical informatics perform the mapping of laboratory test orders into syndrome categories (Ma et al., 2005).	The BioSense system (Bradley et al., 2005; Sokolow et al., 2005) and Syndromal Surveillance Tally Sheet program used in EDs of Santa Clara County, California.
Natural language processing (NLP)	NLP-based approaches classify free-text CCs with simplified grammar containing rules for nouns, adjectives, prepositional phrases, and conjunctions. Critiques of NLP-based methods include lack of semantic markings in chief complaints and the amount of training needed.	As part of RODS, Chapman et al. adapted the MPLUS, a Bayesian network-based NLP system, to classify the free-text chief complaints (Chapman et al., 2005) (Chapman et al., 2005; Wagner, Espino et al., 2004).
Bayesian classifiers	Bayesian classifiers, including naïve Bayesian classifiers, bigram Bayes, and their variations, can classify CCs learned from the training data consisting of labeled CCs.	The CoCo Bayesian classifier from the RODS project (Chapman et al., 2003).
Text string searching	A rule-based method that first uses keyword matching and synonym lists to standardize CCs. Predefined rules are then used to classify CCs or ICD-9 codes into syndrome categories.	EARS (Hutwagner et al., 2003), ESSENCE (CDC, 2003), and the National Bioterrorism Syndromic Surveillance Demonstration Program (Yih et al., 2005).
Vocabulary abstraction	This approach creates a series of intermediate abstractions up to a syndrome category from the individual data (e.g., signs, lab tests) for syndromes indicative of illness due to an agent of bioterrorism.	The BioStorm system (Crubézy et al., 2005) (Buckeridge et al., 2002; Monica Crubézy, Martin O'Connor, Zachary Pincus, & Musen, 2005; Shahar & Musen, 1996).

*ESSENSE: Electronic Surveillance System for the Early Notification of Community-Based Epidemics; #EARS: Early Aberration Reporting System

Evaluations have been conducted to compare various classifiers' performance for certain selected syndrome types. For instance, experiments conducted on two Bayesian classifiers for acute gastrointestinal syndrome demonstrate a 68 percent mapping success against expert classification of ED reports (Ivanov, Wagner et al. 2002). Several technical challenges to syndromic classification remain. There are no standardized syndrome definitions employed universally by different syndromic surveillance systems. Different computerized classifiers, or human chief complaint coders, are trained to prioritize and code symptoms differently following different coding conventions. Studies demonstrate that the comparisons between two syndrome coding systems show low agreement in most of the syndrome classifications (Mikosz, Silva et al. 2004).

3.4 Data Analysis and Outbreak Detection

Automated data analysis for aberration detection is essential to real-time syndromic surveillance. These algorithms, spanning from classic statistical methods to artificial intelligence approaches, are used to quantify the possibility of an outbreak observed from the surveillance data. For instance, such models have been employed to predict outbreaks of West Nile virus (Eidson, Miller et al. 2001; Wonham, de-Camino-Beck et al. 2004) and of influenza (Hyman and LaForce 2004).

Usually, a detection system employs more than one algorithm, as no single algorithm can cover the wide spectrum of possible situations. Below we sample representative algorithms organized as temporal, spatial, and spatial-temporal methods (Buckeridge, Burkom et al. 2005).

Another category, which is not shown in Table 26-5, includes "data-fusion" approaches where multiple data sources (e.g., ED visits and OTC sales data) are combined to perform outbreak detection. The idea of such "data-fusion" approaches is that multiple data streams are analyzed with the extensions of analytical techniques, such as MCUSUM or MEWMA, to increase detection sensitivity while limiting the number of false alarms.

Table 26-5. Outbreak Detection Algorithms

Algorithm	Short Description	Availability and Applications	Features and Problems
Temporal Analysis			
Serfling method	A static cyclic regression model with predefined parameters optimized through the training data	Available from RODS (Tsui, Wagner et al. 2001); used by CDC for flu detection; Costagliola *et al.* applied Serfling's method to the French influenza-like illness surveillance (Costagliola, Flahault et al. 1981)	The model fits data poorly during epidemic periods. To use this method the epidemic period has to be pre-defined.
Autoregressive Integrated Moving Average (ARIMA)	A linear function learns parameters from historical data. Seasonal effect can be adjusted.	Available from RODS	Suitable for stationary environments.

(Continued)

Table 26-5. (Continued)

Algorithm	Short Description	Availability and Applications	Features and Problems
Exponentially Weighted Moving Average (EWMA)	Predictions based on exponential smoothing of previous several weeks of data with recent days having the highest weight (Neubauer 1997)	Available from ESSENCE	Allowing the adjustment of shift sensitivity by applying different weighting factors.
Cumulative Sums (CUSUM)	A control chart-based method to monitor for the departure of the mean of the observations from the estimated mean (Das, Weiss et al. 2003; Grigoryan, Wagner et al. 2005). It allows for limited baseline data.	Widely used in current surveillance systems including BioSense, EARS (Hutwagner, Thompson et al. 2003) (Hutwagner, Thompson et al. 2003) and ESSENCE, among others	This method performs well for quick detection of subtle changes in the mean (Roger-son 2005); it is criticized for its lack of adjustability for seasonal or day-of-week effects.
Hidden Markov Models (HMM)	HMM-based methods use a hidden state to capture the presence or absence of an epidemic of a particular disease and learn probabilistic models of observations conditioned on the epidemic status.	Discussed in (Rath, Carreras et al. 2003)	A flexible model that can adapt automatically to trends, seasonality covariates (e.g., gender and age), and different distributions (normal, Poisson, etc.).
Wavelet algorithms	Local frequency-based data analysis methods; they can automatically adjust to weekly, monthly, and seasonal data fluctuations.	Used in NRDM to indicate zip-code areas in which OTC medication sales are substantially increased (Espino and Wagner 2001; Zhang, Tsui et al. 2003)	Account for both long-term (e.g., seasonal effects) and short-term trends (e.g., day-of-week effects) (Wagner, Tsui et al. 2004).
Spatial Analysis			
Generalized Linear Mixed Modeling (GLMM)	Evaluating whether observed counts in relatively small areas are larger than expected on the basis of the history of naturally occurring diseases (Kleinman, Lazarus et al. 2004; Kleinman, Abrams et al. 2005)	Used in Minnesota (Yih, Abrams et al. 2005)	Sensitive to a small number of spatially focused cases; poor in detecting elevated counts over contiguous areas as compared to scan statistic and spatial CUSUM approaches (Kleinman, et al. 2004).

(Continued)

Table 26-5. (Continued)

Algorithm	Short Description	Availability and Applications	Features and Problems
Spatial scan statistics and variations	The basic model relies on using simply-shaped areas to scan the entire region of interest based on well-defined likelihood ratios. Its variation takes into account factors such as people mobility	Widely adopted by many syndromic surveillance systems; a variation proposed in (Duczmal and Buckeridge 2005); visualization available from BioPortal (Zeng, Chang et al. 2004).	Well-tested for various outbreak scenarios with positive results; the geometric shape of the hotspots identified is limited.
Bayesian spatial scan statistics	Combining Bayesian modeling techniques with the spatial scan statistics method; outputting the posterior probability that an outbreak has occurred, and the distribution of this probability over possible outbreak regions	Available from RODS (Neill, Moore et al. 2005)	Computationally efficient; can easily incorporate prior knowledge such as the size and shape of outbreak or the impact on the disease infection rate.
Spatial-temporal Analysis			
Space-time scan statistic	An extension of the space scan statistic that searches all the sub-regions for likely clusters in space and time with multiple likelihood ratio testing (Kulldorff 2001).	Widely used in many community surveillance systems including the National Bioterrorism Syndromic Surveillance Demonstration Program (Yih, Caldwell et al. 2004)	Regions identified may be too large in coverage.
What is Strange About Recent Event (WSARE)	Searching for groups with specific characteristics (e.g., a recent pattern of place, age, and diagnosis associated with illness that is anomalous when compared with historic patterns) (Kaufman, Cohen et al. 2005)	Available from RODS; Implemented in ESSENCE	In contrast to traditional approaches, this method allows for use of representative features for monitoring (Wong, Moore et al. 2002; Wong, Moore et al. 2003). To use it, however, the base-line distribution has to be known.

(Continued)

Table 26-5. (Continued)

Algorithm	Short Description	Availability and Applications	Features and Problems
Prospective Support Vector Clustering (PSVC)	This method uses the Support Vector Clustering method with risk adjustment as a hotspot clustering engine and a CUSUM-type design to keep track of incremental changes in spatial distribution patterns over time	Developed in BioPortal (Zeng, Chang et al. 2004; Chang, Zeng et al. 2005)	This method can identify hotspots with irregular shapes in an online context

Another challenging issue for real time outbreak detection is that the surveillance algorithms rely on historic datasets that span a considerable length of time against which to measure the anomaly of observed data. Few methods demonstrate reliable detection capability with short-term baseline data. Measurements on timeliness, specificity, and sensitivity of the detection algorithms have been reported; however, existing evaluation studies are quite limited, as they are either reliable only for one specific disease (Kleinman and Abrams 2006) or are biased by simulation settings as very few bioterrorism attacks for real testing are available.

3.5 Data Access and Visualization

To facilitate interactive data exploration, maps, graphs, and tables are common forms of helpful visualization tools. Below we briefly review some sample implementations in IDI contexts. Section 4 contains several more detailed case studies with screenshots.

The RODS system employs the GIS module to depict data spatially. In BioSense and ESSENSE, a geographical map consisting of individual zip codes is marked with different colors to represent the threat level. Stratification can be applied for different syndrome categories, and individual case details can be accessed by "drill down" functions. The BioPortal project makes available an advanced visualization module, called the Spatial Temporal Visualizer (STV) to facilitate exploration of infectious disease case data and to summarize query results (Hu, Zeng et al. 2005). STV is a generic visualization environment that can be used to visualize a number of spatial temporal datasets simultaneously. It allows the user to load and save spatial temporal data in a dynamic manner for exploration and dissemination.

4. IDI AND SYNDROMIC SURVEILLANCE SYSTEM CASE STUDIES

To better illustrate the earlier discussion on the data sources used and technical components of IDI systems, and related implementation issues, we present two case studies in this section.

4.1 RODS

The first case study examines the Realtime Outbreak and Disease Surveillance (RODS) system, which has been deployed across the nation. The RODS project is a collaborative effort between the University of Pittsburgh and Carnegie Mellon University. It provides a computing platform for the implementation and evaluation of different analytic approaches for outbreak detection, among other data collection and reporting functions.

The RODS project was initiated by the RODS Laboratory in 1999. The system is now an open source project under the GNU license. The RODS development effort has been organized into seven functional areas: overall design, data collection, syndrome classification, database and data warehousing, outbreak detection algorithms, data access, and user interfaces. Each functional area has a coordinator for the related open source project effort and there is an overall coordinator responsible for the architecture, overall integration of components, and overall quality of the source code. Figure 26-1 illustrates the RODS' system architecture.

The RODS system as a syndromic surveillance application was originally deployed in Pennsylvania, Utah, and Ohio. It is currently deployed in New Jersey, Michigan, and several other states. By June 2006, about 20 regions with more than 200 health care facilities connected to RODS in real-time. It was also deployed during the 2002 Winter Olympics (Espino, Wagner et al. 2004).

The RODS data are collected in real-time through HL7 messages from other computer systems such as registration systems and laboratory information systems, over a Secure Shell–protected Internet connection in an automated mode. The National Retail Data Monitor (NRDM) is a component of the RODS system, collecting and analyzing daily sales data for OTC medication sales. It also collects and analyzes chief complaint data from various hospitals. The RODS system currently monitors 8 syndrome categories: Gastrointestinal, Hemorrhagic illness, Constitutional, Neurologic, Rash, Respiratory, Botulism-like/botulism, Others.

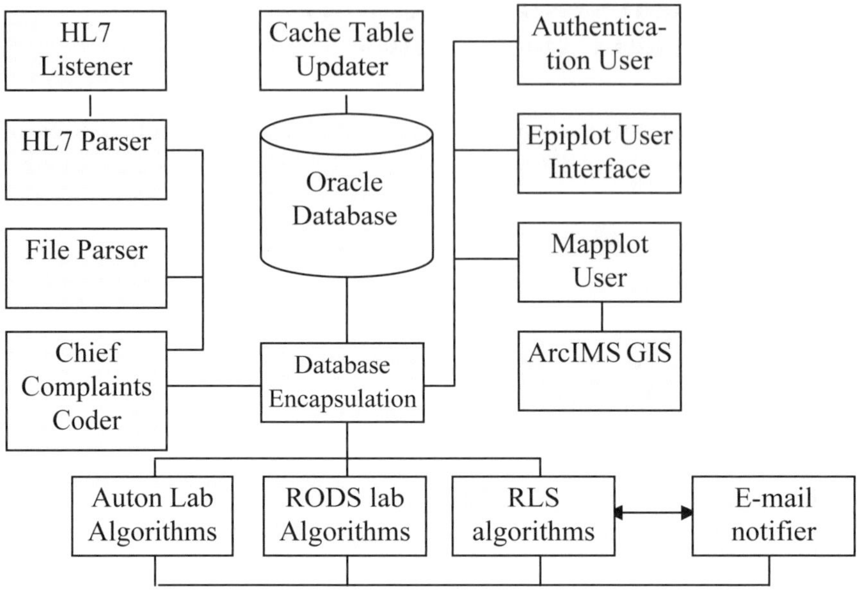

Figure 26-1. RODS system architecture (Espina, Wagner et al. 2004)

One of the major strengths of RODS is in data analysis. A number of syndrome classification approaches have been tested and implemented in the RODS system. It applies a keyword classifier and an ICD-9 classifier to chief complaint data. The CoCo module, a syndrome mapping component, has been tested in multiple settings (Olszewski 2003). For the respiratory syndrome, based on manually-classified results, CoCo's sensitivity level achieves 77% and specificity level 90%. A Bayesian network-based semantic model has been shown to classify free-text chief complaints effectively at the expense of added system complexity and computational overhead (Chapman, Christensen et al. 2005). The performance of the classifier represented by the ROC curve for each syndrome category varies between 0.95 and 0.99.

The current open source release of the RODS system includes implementations of several outbreak detection algorithms: wavelet-detection algorithms, CUSUM, SMART, scan statistics, RLS, and WSARE.

RODS provides multiple graphing techniques with both time-series and geographical displays available via an encrypted, password-protected Web interface. Three different data views — Main, Epiplot, and Mapplot — are supported. The main RODS screen shows time-series plots updated on a daily basis for each syndrome. The user can also view these graphs by county or for the whole state. The Epiplot screen is highly interactive; the user can specify the syndrome, region, start dates, and end dates, to generate customized time-series plots. A "get cases" button allows users to view case-level detail for encounters making up the specific time-series. The Mapplot screen provides an interface to the ArcIMS package, to display disease cases' spatial distribution using patients' zip code information.

4.2 BioPortal

The second case study is about the BioPortal system. The BioPortal project was initiated in 2003 by the University of Arizona and its collaborators in the New York State Department of Health and the California Department of Health Services under the guidance of a federal inter-agency working group named the Infectious Disease Informatics Working Committee. Since then, its partner base has expanded to include the USGS, University of California, Davis, University of Utah, the Arizona Department of Health Services, Kansas State University, and the National Taiwan University. BioPortal provides distributed, cross-jurisdictional access to datasets concerning several major infectious diseases, including Botulism, West Nile virus, foot-and-mouth disease, livestock syndromes, and chief complaints (both in English and Chinese). It features advanced spatial-temporal data analysis methods and visualization capabilities.

Figure 26-2 shows its system architecture. BioPortal supports syndromic surveillance of epidemiological data and free-text chief complaints. It also supports analysis and visualization of lab-generated gene sequence information.

Figure 26-3 illustrates how epidemiological and genetic data analyses are integrated from a systems perspective.

As to data collection, emergency room chief complaint data in the free-text format are provided by the Arizona Department of Health Services and several hospitals in batch mode for syndrome classification. Various disease-specific case reports for both human and animal diseases are another source of data for BioPortal. It also makes use of surveillance datasets such as dead bird sightings and mosquito control information. The system's communication backbones, initially for data acquisition from New York or California disease datasets, consist of several messaging adaptors that can be customized to interoperate with various messaging systems. Participating syndromic data providers can link to the BioPortal data repository via the PHINMS and an XML/HL7 compatible network.

BioPortal provides automatic syndrome classification capabilities based on free-text chief complaints. One method recently developed uses a concept ontology derived from the UMLS (Lu, Zeng et al. 2006). For each chief complaint (CC), the method first standardizes the CC into one or more medical concepts in the UMLS. These concepts are then mapped into existing symptom groups using a set of rules constructed from a symptom grouping table. For symptoms not in the table, a Weighted Semantic Similarity Score algorithm, which measures the semantic similarity between the target symptoms and existing symptom groups, is used to determine the best symptom group for the target symptom. The ontology-enhanced CC classification method has also been extended to handle CCs in Chinese.

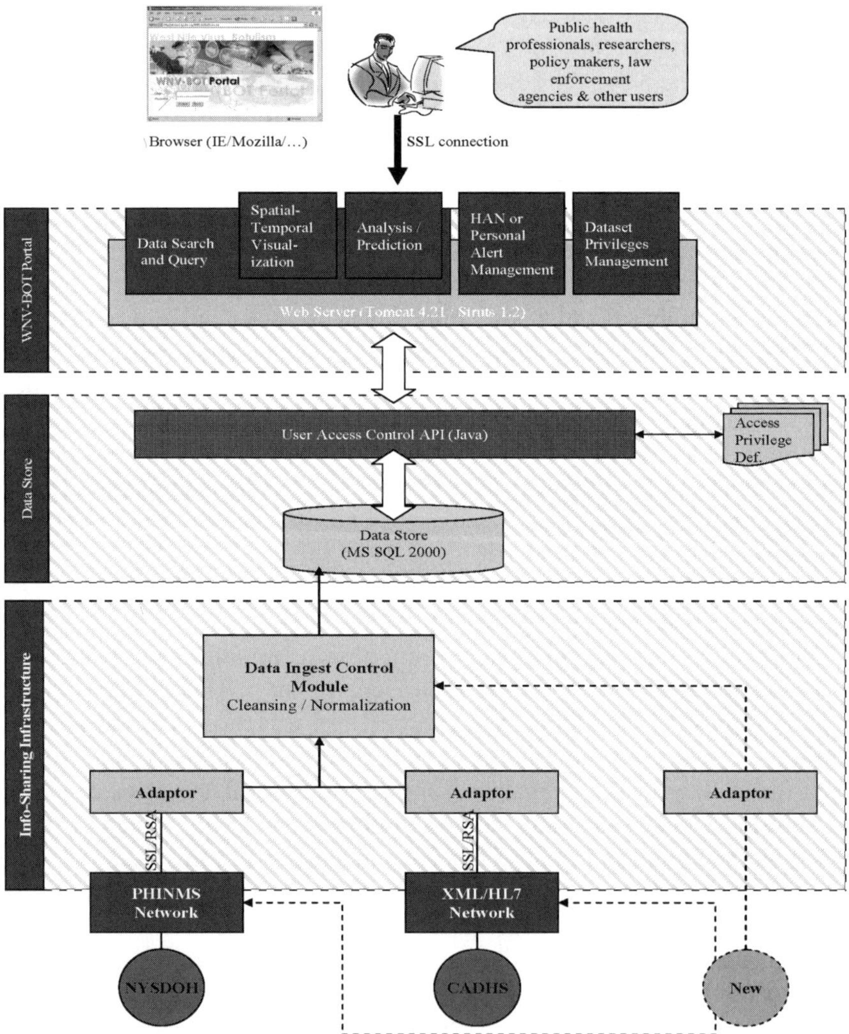

Figure 26-2. BioPortal information sharing and data access infrastructure

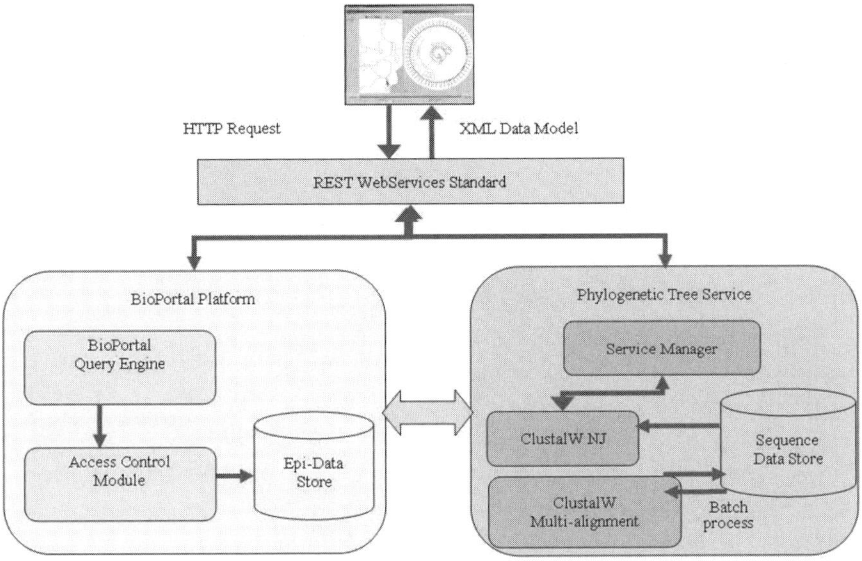

Figure 26-3. Integrating epidemiological data and gene sequence data analysis in BioPortal

BioPortal supports outbreak detection based on spatial-temporal clustering analysis, also known as hotspot analysis, to identify unusual spatial and temporal clusters of disease events. BioPortal supports various scan statistic-based methods through the SaTScan binary, which has been widely used in public health; the Nearest Neighbor Hierarchical Clustering method initially developed for crime analysis; and two new artificial intelligence clustering-based methods (Risk-Adjusted Support Vector Clustering, and Prospective Support Vector Clustering) developed in-house, which can support detection of areas with irregular shapes (Zeng, Chang et al. 2004; Chang, Zeng et al. 2005).

BioPortal makes available a visualization environment called the Spatial-Temporal Visualizer (STV), which allows users to interactively explore spatial and temporal patterns, based on an integrated tool set consisting of a GIS view, a timeline tool, and a periodic pattern tool.

Figure 26-4 illustrates how these three views can be used to explore an infectious disease dataset. The GIS view displays cases and sightings on a map. The user can select multiple datasets to be shown on the map in different layers using the checkboxes (e.g., disease cases, natural land features, and land-use elements). Through the periodic view the user can identify periodic temporal patterns (e.g., which months or weeks have an unusually high number of cases). The unit of time for aggregation can also be set as days or hours. The timeline view provides a timeline along with a hierarchical display of the data elements, organized as a tree. A new gene sequence-based phylogenetic tree visualizer (not shown in Figure 26-4) has been recently added to the STV interface for diseases with quick mutation rates such as the foot-and-mouth disease. This allows BioPortal users to explore epidemiological and sequence data concurrently.

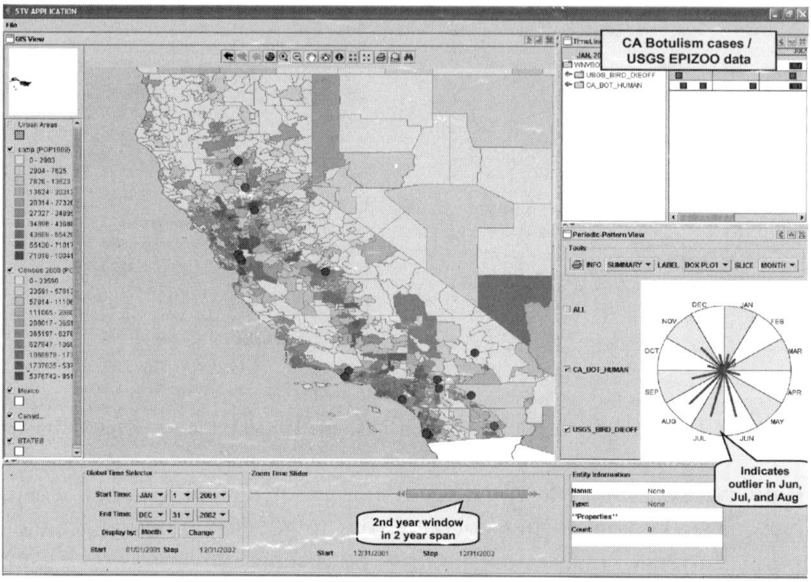

Figure 26-4. Spatial-temporal visualizer

Data confidentiality, security, and access control are among the key research and development issues for the BioPortal project. A role-based access control mechanism is implemented based on data confidentiality and user access privileges. The project has also developed a consortium type of data sharing Memoranda of Understanding (MOU) to reduce the barrier of sharing information among data contributors including local and state public health agencies.

5. CONCLUDING REMARKS

This chapter provides a brief review of infectious disease informatics (IDI) with a particular focus on its application in syndromic surveillance. Traditional disease surveillance systems are based on confirmed diagnoses, whereas syndromic surveillance makes use of pre-diagnosis information for timely data collection and analysis. The main IT-related topics and challenges in IDI and syndromic surveillance are presented in this chapter.

With regards to ongoing trends in IDI and syndromic surveillance, we see significant interest in informatics studies on topics ranging from data visualization, further development and comprehensive evaluation of outbreak detection algorithms, data interoperability, and further development of response and event management decision models based on data and predictions provided by syndromic surveillance systems.

From an application domain perspective, the following areas can potentially lead to new and interesting innovations and research. First, public health surveillance can be a truly global effort for pandemic diseases such as avian influenza. Issues concerning global data sharing (including multilingual information processing) and the development of models that work over a wide geographical area need to be addressed. Syndromic surveillance concepts, techniques, and systems are equally applicable to animal health besides public health. We expect to see significant new work to be done to model animal health-specific issues and deal with zoonotic diseases.

ACKNOWLEDGEMENTS

This work is supported in part by the U.S. National Science Foundation through Digital Government Grant #EIA-9983304, Information Technology Research Grant #IIS-0428241, by the U.S. Department of Agriculture through Grant #2006-39546-17579, and by the Arizona Department of Health Services. We would like to thank the members of the BioPortal project for insightful discussions. The first author is an affiliated professor at the Institute of Automation, the Chinese Academy of Sciences, and wishes to acknowledge support from a research grant (60573078) from the National Natural Science Foundation of China, an international collaboration grant (2F05N01) from the Chinese Academy of Sciences, and a National Basic Research Program of China (973) grant (2006CB705500) from the Ministry of Science and Technology.

REFERENCES

Bradley, C. A., H. Rolka, et al. (2005). "BioSense: Implementation of a National Early Event Detection and Situational Awareness System." MMWR (CDC) 54(Suppl): 11-20.

Bravata, D., K. McDonald, et al. (2004). "Systematic review: Surveillance Systems for Early Detection of Bioterrorism-Related Diseases." Annals of Internal Medicine 140: 910-922.

Buckeridge, D., H. Burkom, et al. (2005). "Algorithms for Rapid Outbreak Detection: a Research Synthesis." Journal of Biomedical Informatics 38: 99-113.

Buckeridge, D., J. Graham, et al. (2002). Knowledge-Based Bioterrorism Surveillance. American Medical Informatics Association Symposium, San Antonio, TX.

Buehler, J., R. Hopkins, et al. (2004). "Framework for evaluating public health surveillance systems for early detection of outbreaks: Recommendations from the CDC working group." MMWR (CDC) 53(RR-5): 1-13.

Chang, W., D. Zeng, et al. (2005). A Novel Spatio-Temporal Data Analysis Approach based on Prospective Support Vector Clustering. Proceedings of the Fifteenth Annual Workshop on Information Technologies and Systems (WITS'05), Las Vegas, NV.

Chang, W., D. Zeng, et al. (2005) "Prospective Spatio-Temporal Data Analysis for Security Informatics." Proceedings of the 8th IEEE International Conference on Intelligent Transportation Systems Vienna, Austria.

Chapman, W. W., L. Christensen, et al. (2005). "Classifying Free-text Triage Chief Complaints into Syndromic Categories with Natural Language Processing." Artificial Intelligence in Medicine 33(1): 31-40.

Christensen, L., P. Haug, et al. (2002). MPLUS: a Probabilistic Medical Language Understanding System. Workshop on Natural Language Processing in the Biomedical Domain.

Cooper, G. F., D. H. Dash, et al. (2004). Bayesian Biosurveillance of Disease Outbreaks. Twentieth Conference on Uncertainty in Artificial Intelligence, Banff, Alberta, Canada.

Costagliola, D., A. Flahault, et al. (1981). "A routine tool for detection and assessment of epidemics of influenza-like syndromes in France" American Journal of Public Health 81(1): 97-99.

Crubézy, M., M. O'Connor, et al. (2005). "Ontology-Centered Syndromic Surveillance for Bioterrorism." IEEE INTELLIGENT SYSTEMS 20(5): 26-35.

Das, D., D. Weiss, et al. (2003). "Enhanced Drop-in Syndromic Surveillance in New York City Following September 11, 2001." J Urban Health 80(1(suppl)): 176-188.

Dembek, Z., K. Carley, et al. (2005). "Guidelines for Constructing a Statewide Hospital Syndromic Surveillance Network." MMWR (CDC) 54(Suppl): 21-26.

Duczmal, L. and D. Buckeridge (2005). "Using Modified Spatial Scan Statistic to Improve Detection of Disease Outbreak When Exposure Occurs in Workplace — Virginia, 2004." MMWR (CDC) 54(Suppl): 187.

Eidson, M., J. Miller, et al. (2001). "Dead Crow Densities and Human Cases of West Nile Virus, New York State, 2000." Emerging Infectious Diseases 7: 662-664.

Espino, J. U. and M. M. Wagner (2001). "The Accuracy of ICD-9 Coded Chief Complaints for Detection of Acute Respiratory Illness." Proc AMIA Symp: 164-168.

Espino, J. U., M. M. Wagner, et al. (2004). "Removing a Barrier to Computer-Based Outbreak and Disease Surveillance — The RODS Open Source Project." MMWR (CDC) 53(Suppl): 34-41.

Goldsmith, J., D. Blumenthal, et al. (2003). "Federal Health Insurance Policy: A Case of Arrested Development." Health Affairs 22(4): 44-55.

Grigoryan, V. V., M. M. Wagner, et al. (2005) "The Effect of Spatial Granularity of Data on Reference Dates for Influenza Outbreaks." RODS Laboratory Technical Report, 2005

Hu, P.-J. H., D. Zeng, et al. (2007). "A System for Infectious Disease Information Sharing and Analysis: Design, Implementation and Evaluation." IEEE Transactions on Information Technology in Biomedicine in press.

Hu, P. J.-H., D. Zeng, et al. (2005). Evaluating an Infectious Disease Information Sharing and Analysis System. Intelligence and Security Informatics (ISI), Atlanta, Georgia, USA.

Hutwagner, L., W. Thompson, et al. (2003). "The Bioterrorism Preparedness and Response Early Aberration Reporting System (EARS)." J Urban Health 80(2 suppl 1): 89-96.

Hyman, J. and T. LaForce (2004). Modeling the spread of influenza among cities. Bioterrorism: Mathematical Modeling Applications in Homeland Security. H. Banks and C. Castillo-Chàvez, Society for Industrial and Applied Mathematics: 211-236.

Ivanov, O., M. M. Wagner, et al. (2002). Accuracy of Three Classifiers of Acute Gastrointestinal Syndrome for Syndromic Surveillance. AMIA Symp.

Kargupta, H., K. Liu, et al. (2003). Privacy Sensitive Distributed Data Mining from Multi-Party Data. Proc. of the first NSF/NIJ Symposium on Intelligence and Security Informatics, Springer LNCS 2665.

Kaufman, Z., E. Cohen, et al. (2005). "Using Data on an Influenza B Outbreak To Evaluate a Syndromic Surveillance System — Israel, June 2004 [abstract]." MMWR (CDC) 54(Suppl): 191.

Kleinman, K. and A. Abrams (2006). "Assessing surveillance using sensitivity, specificity and timeliness." Statistical Methods in Medical Research, Vol. 15, No. 5, 445-464 (15(5): 445-464.

Kleinman, K., A. Abrams, et al. (2005). "A Model-adjusted Spacetime Scan Statistic with an Application to Syndromic Surveillance." Epidemiol Infect 2005(119): 409-19.

Kleinman, K., R. Lazarus, et al. (2004). "A Generalized Linear Mixed Models Approach for Detecting Incident Cluster/signals of Disease in Small Areas, with an Application to Biological Terrorism (with Invited Commentary)." Am J Epidemiol 2004 159: 217-24.

Kulldorff, M. (2001). "Prospective Time Periodic Geographical Disease Surveillance Using a Scan Statistic." Journal of the Royal Statistical Society, Series A(164): 61-72.

Lawson, A. B. and K. Kleinman, Eds. (2005). Spatial and Syndromic Surveillance for Public Health, John Wiley & Sons.

Lazarus, R., K. Kleinman, et al. (2001). "Using Automated Medical Records for Rapid Identification of Illness Syndromes (Syndromic Surveillance): the Example of Lower Respiratory Infection." BMC Public Health 1(9).

Lombardo, J., H. Burkom, et al. (2003). "A systems overview of the Electronic Surveillance System for the Early Notification of Community-based Epidemics (ESSENCE II)." Journal of Urban Health: Bulletin of the New York Academy of Medicine 80(2): 32-42.

Lombardo, J., H. Burkom, et al. (2004). "Electronic Surveillance System for the Early Notification of Community-Based Epidemics (ESSENCE II), Framework for Evaluating Syndromic Surveillance Systems." Syndromic surveillance: report from a national conference, 2003. MMWR 2004 53(Suppl): 159-165.

Lu, H.-M., D. Zeng, et al. (2006). Ontology-based Automatic Chief Complaints Classification for Syndromic Surveillance. Proceedings of the IEEE Systems, Man, and Cybernetics, Taipei, IEEE Press.

Ma, H., H. Rolka, et al. (2005). "Implementation of Laboratory Order Data in BioSense Early Event Detection and Situation Awareness System." MMWR (CDC) 54(Suppl): 27-30.

Mandl, K. D., J. M. Overhage, et al. (2004). "Implementing Syndromic Surveillance: a Practical Guide Informed by the Early Experience." J Am Med Inform Assoc. 11(2): 141-50.

Mikosz, C. A., J. Silva, et al. (2004). "Comparison of Two Major Emergency Department-Based Free-Text Chief-Complaint Coding Systems." MMWR (CDC) 53(Suppl).

Moore, A. W., G. Cooper, et al. (2002) "Summary of Biosurveillance-relevant Statistical and Data Mining Techniques." RODS Laboratory Technical Report Volume, DOI:

Neill, D., A. Moore, et al. (2005). "A Bayesian Spatial Scan Statistic." Accepted to Neural Information Processing Systems 18.

Neubauer, A. (1997). "The EWMA Control Chart: Properties and Comparison with Other Quality-control Procedures by Computer Simulation." Clinical Chemistry 43(4): 594-601.

Ohno-Machado, L., P. S. S. PS, et al. (2004). "Protecting Patient Privacy by Quantifiable Control of Disclosures in Disseminated Databases." International Journal of Medical Informatics 73(7-8): 599-606.

Olszewski, R. T. (2003). Bayesian Classification of Triage Diagnoses for the Early Detection of Epidemics. 16th Int FLAIRS Conference.

Pavlin, J. A. (2003). "Investigation of Disease Outbreaks Detected by "Syndromic" Surveillance Systems." Journal of Urban Health: Bulletin of the New York Academy of Medicine 80(2): 107-114.

Pinner, R., C. Rebmann, et al. (2003). "Disease Surveillance and the Academic, Clinical, and Public Health Communities." Emerging Infectious Diseases 9(7): 781-787.

Rath, T. M., M. Carreras, et al. (2003). Automated Detection of Influenza Epidemics with Hidden Markov Models. Lecture Notes in Computer Science Springer Berlin/ Heidelberg 521 - 532

Rogerson, P. A. (2005). Spatial Surveillance and Cumulative Sum Methods. Spatial & Syndromic Surveillance for Public Health. K. K. Andrew B Lawson, John Wiley & Sons, Ltd: 95-113.

Siegrist, D. (1999). "The Threat of Biological Attack: Why Concern Now?" Emerging Infectious Diseases 5(4): 505-508.

Sniegoski, C. A. (2004). "Automated Syndromic Classifi cation of Chief Complaint Records." JOHNS HOPKINS APL TECHNICAL DIGEST 25(1): 68-75.

Sokolow, L. Z., N. Grady, et al. (2005). "Deciphering Data Anomalies in BioSense." MMWR (CDC) 54(Suppl): 133-140.

Tsui, F.-C., J. U. Espino, et al. (2003). "Technical Description of RODS: a Real-time Public Health Surveillance System." J Am Med Inform Assoc 2003 10: 399-408.

Tsui, F.-C., M. M. Wagner, et al. (2001). "Value of ICD-9–Coded Chief Complaints for Detection of Epidemics." Symposium of Journal of American Medical Informatics Association.

Wagner, M. M., A. W. Moore, et al. (2006). Handbook of Biosurveillanec, Elsevier.

Wagner, M. M., F.-C. Tsui, et al. (2004). "National Retail Data Monitor for Public Health Surveillance." MMWR (CDC) 53(Suppl): 40-42.

Wong, W. K., A. Moore, et al. (2003). "WSARE: What's Strange about Recent Events?" Journal of Urban Health 80((2 Suppl. 1)): 66-75.

Wong, W. K., A. Moore, et al. (2002). Rule-based Anomaly Pattern Detection for Detecting Disease Outbreaks. AAAI-02, Edmonton, Alberta

Wonham, M., T. de-Camino-Beck, et al. (2004). "An epidemiological model for West Nile virus: invasion analysis and control applications." Proceedings of Royal Society: Biological Sciences 271(1538): 501-507.

Wylie, J. E. and G. P. Mineau (2003). "Biomedical Databases: Protecting Privacy and Promoting Research." Trends in Biotechnology 21(3): 113-116.

Yan, P., D. Zeng, et al. (2006). A Review of Public Health Syndromic Surveillance Systems. ISI 2006, San Diego, CA, USA, Springer.

Yih, W., B. Caldwell, et al. (2004). "The National Bioterrorism Syndromic Surveillance Demonstration Program." MMWR (CDC) 53(Suppl): 43-6.

Yih, W. K., A. Abrams, et al. (2005). "Ambulatory-Care Diagnoses as Potential Indicators of Outbreaks of Gastrointestinal Illness — Minnesota." MMWR (CDC) 54(Suppl): 157-162.

Zelicoff, A., J. Brillman, et al. (2001). The rapid syndrome validation project (RSVP). AMIA Symp.

Zeng, D., W. Chang, et al. (2004). Clustering-based Spatio-Temporal Hotspot Analysis Techniques in Security Informatics. IEEE Transactions on Intelligent Transportation Systems.

Zeng, D., W. Chang, et al. (2004). A Comparative Study of Spatio-Temporal Data Analysis Techniques in Security Informatics. Proceedings of the 7th IEEE International Conference on Intelligent Transportation Systems, Washington, DC.

Zeng, D., H. Chen, et al. (2005). Disease Informatics and Outbreak Detection. Advances in Medical Informatics: Knowledge Management and Data Mining in Biomedicine. H. Chen, S. Fuller and A. McCray, Springer.

Zeng, D., H. Chen, et al. (2004). Towards A National Infectious Disease Information Infrastructure: A Case Study in West Nile Virus and Botulism. Proceedings of National Conference on Digital Government.

Zeng, D., H. Chen, et al. (2004). West Nile virus and botulism portal: A case study in infectious disease informatics. Intelligence and Security Informatics, ISI-2004, Lecture Notes in Computer Science.

Zhang, J., F. Tsui, et al. (2003). "Detection of Outbreaks from Time Series Data Using Wavelet Transform." AMIA Symp 748-52.

SUGGESTED READINGS

- "Handbook of Biosurveillance," M. M. Wagner, A. W. Moore, R. M. Aryel (eds.), 2006. Academic Press. This edited volume provides a comprehensive review of the theory and practice of real-time human disease outbreak detection. Its discussion on statistical outbreak detection methods is particularly informative.
- "Monitoring the Health of Populations: Statistical Principles and Methods for Public Health Surveillance," R. Brookmeye and D. F. Stroup (eds.), 2004. Oxford University Press. This text is primarily concerned with statistical models as applied to health surveillance data and related analysis and interpretations challenges.
- "Public Health Informatics and Information Systems." P. O'Carroll, W. Yasnoff, E. Ward, L. Ripp, and E. Martin (eds.), 2002. Springer. This

edited book covers all aspects of public health informatics and presents a strategic approach to information systems development and management.

- “Bioterrorism: Mathematical Modeling Applications in Homeland Security,” H.T. Banks and C. Castillo-Chàvez (eds.), 2003. The Society for Industrial and Applied Mathematics. This edited volume covers recent research on bio-surveillance, agroterrorism, bioterrorism response logistics, and assessment of the impact of bioterrorism attacks. The specific emphasis of this book is on mathematical modeling and computational studies relevant to bioterrorism research.

ONLINE RESOURCES

- CDC’s NEDSS homepage at http://www.cdc.gov/nedss/index.htm
- CDC’s PHIN homepage at http://www.cdc.gov/phin/, including the BioSense project homepage at http://www.cdc.gov/PHIN/component-initiatives/biosense/index.html
- Health Level Seven standards and software implementation at http://www.hl7.org
- Scan statistics-related outbreak detection software, datasets, and selected publications http://www.satscan.org
- The RODS project’s homepage at http://rods.health.pitt.edu/
- The ESSENCE project’s homepage at: http://www.geis.fhp.osd.mil/aboutGEIS.asp.
- The BioPortal project’s homepage at http://www.bioportal.org
- http://statpages.org/ and http://www.autonlab.org/tutorials/, for related statistical and data mining tutorials.

QUESTIONS FOR DISCUSSION

1. What patient confidentiality, and data ownership and access control issues need to be considered in the IDI context?
2. What is the current status of IDI data and messaging standard development? What role should government play in the standardization effort?

3. Scan statistics and hotspot analysis techniques can identify unusual clustering of events or cases in space and time. How can one interpret the findings based on these techniques in the IDI context?
4. What role can visualization play in IDI data analysis? What are the types of visualizations commonly used by public health officials (not necessarily computerized) in disease surveillance?
5. What are the potential policy and organizational barriers to the deployment of syndromic surveillance systems? How can we overcome these barriers?
6. What are the technical obstacles associated with developing a syndromic surveillance system with international coverage? What are the non-technical obstacles?

Chapter 27

SUPPORTING DOMAIN-SPECIFIC DIGITAL LIBRARIES IN GOVERNMENT

Two Case Studies

Mathew Weaver[1], Lois M. L. Delcambre[2], Marianne Lykke Nielsen[3], Susan Price[2], David Maier[2], and Timothy Tolle[4]

[1] EarthSoft, Inc, Uikiah, Utah; [2]Portland State University, Portland, Oregon; [3]Royal School of Library and Information Science, Denmark; [4]Formerly with the USDA Forest Service.

CHAPTER OVERVIEW

Government agencies often provide web-accessible collections of documents for use by government employees as well as the general public. In our work, we focus on domain-specific digital libraries where the subject matter of the documents is restricted to the topics of concern in the government work; our goal is to assist government users who are knowledgeable in the domain(s) represented in the collection. We report here on two digital government projects: a project with the United States Department of Agriculture (USDA) Forest Service with a focus on providing comprehensive access to documents produced by the agency for Forest Service managers, and a second project with the national health portal in Denmark, sundhed.dk, with a focus on meeting the information needs of family practice physicians as they treat patients. In this chapter, we describe how the use of a digital library application, Metadata++, can improve document and information retrieval, and we explore other aspects that contribute to project success, such as involvement of government partners, agency commitment, technology transfer, and evaluation.

1. INTRODUCTION

Government agencies often provide web-accessible collections of documents for use by government employees as well as the general public. In our work, we focus on domain-specific digital libraries where the subject matter of the documents is restricted to the topics of concern in the government work.[1] We are developing mechanisms to assist government users as they search for information in domain-specific digital libraries as part of their professional work. Our goal is to assist government users who are knowledgeable in the domain(s) represented in the collection. Our mechanisms may also be useful to other users, particularly as they become familiar with the documents and terminology used in the domain-specific digital library. We report here on two digital government projects.

In the first project, we partnered with Region 6 of the United States Department of Agriculture (USDA) Forest Service with a focus on providing comprehensive access to documents produced by the agency for natural resource managers in the Forest Service and other natural resource management agencies. This multi-year project, completed in 2005, is the primary focus of this chapter.

In the second project, our current project, we are partnered with the national health portal in Denmark, sundhed.dk, with a focus on meeting the information needs of family practice physicians as they treat patients. The goal for this second project is providing quick access to documents with highly relevant information.

In our first project, we targeted the needs of natural resource managers in the Pacific Northwest in the US, with input from federal, state, and local agencies involved in natural resource management including the United States Department of Interior (USDI) Bureau of Land Management, the USDI Fish and Wildlife Service, the USDI National Park Service, and the Adaptive Management Areas of the Pacific Northwest, in addition to the USDA Forest Service. Documents generated by natural resources managers are very often of use to these and other natural resource managers grappling with similar issues or situations. These documents are heterogeneous in nature and of varying lengths 14 (sometimes hundreds of pages) including reports mandated by the US National Environmental Policy Act (e.g., *Decision Notices*, *Environmental Assessments*, and *Environmental Impact Statements*). Note that almost every project involves a range of scientific disciplines and other subject areas such as soil, forestry, vegetation, climatology, hydrology, wildlife and fish biology, fire, recreation, and range land.

---

[1] Thus, we are not working in an open environment such as the World Wide Web where arbitrary subject matter can be addressed in arbitrary documents.

We observed that many classification systems and controlled vocabularies were already in wide use in natural resource management. These vocabularies represent the perspectives of the disciplines in play and include the terminology or professional jargon in use in natural resource management. Note that multiple vocabularies, each in common use by at least a subset of the users, exist to describe the same phenomena and that some terms appear in multiple vocabularies. Our approach was to develop a digital library system that could accommodate and exploit the variety and richness of these existing vocabularies. The challenge was to define a model that could accommodate the same term appearing in multiple vocabularies and thus avoid the high cost 10 typically required to build a new, perhaps comprehensive, concept-based thesaurus or ontology. It is unlikely that a single, new ontology would be widely adopted in this environment because the use of many of the existing vocabularies is widespread and may even be mandated or legislated.

We defined a thesaurus model and an associated software system called Metadata++ to represent the various vocabularies of interest. This model is able to accommodate existing terminologies and vocabularies "as provided," without requiring any change in the terms or the structure of the vocabulary. Thus we are able to represent existing terminology and allow the same term to appear in different contexts.

A term that appears two or more times is called a *multiple occurrence*. Figure 27-1 shows multiple occurrences for the term "Riparian," each with a distinct path, where the paths preserve the structure in the original vocabulary.

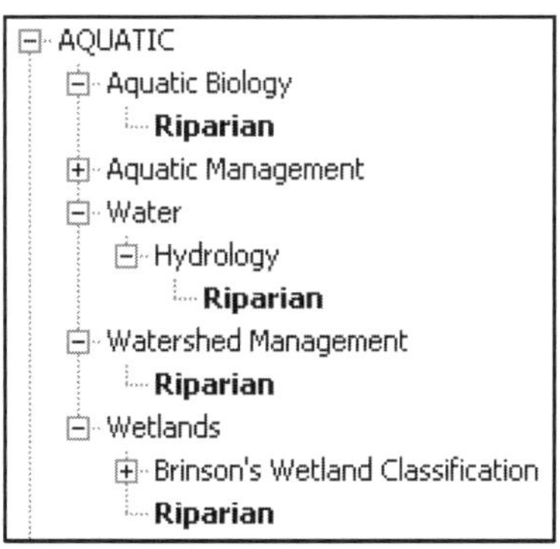

Figure 27-1. Multiple occurrences of the term "Riparian," with their respective paths

Note that "Aquatic/Aquatic Biology/Riparian" as well as "Aquatic/ Watershed Management/Riparian" are considered distinct terms. Since each term is always represented with its associated path, we refer to the model as a path-based thesaurus model. The top-level (i.e., first) term in each path represents the top-level subject area of the vocabulary. The top-level subject areas included in Metadata++ for this project are shown in Figure 27-2.

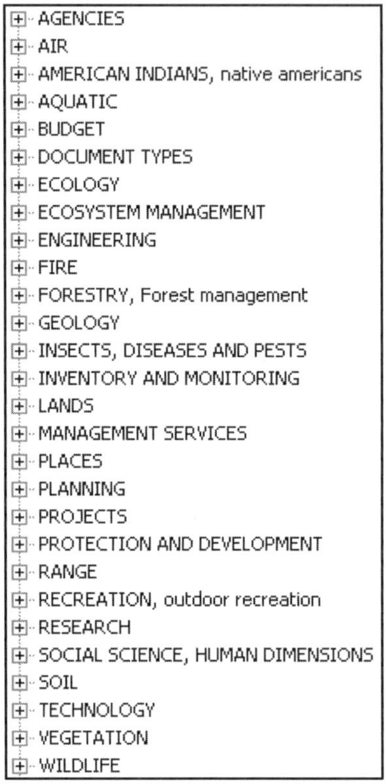

Figure 27-2. Top-level subject areas

Each occurrence of the term "riparian" shown in Figure 27-1 is in the "Aquatic" top-level subject area.

The Metadata++ digital library application allows users to:

- browse and search the various terminologies and vocabularies,
- find terms of interest and understand the context of those terms,
- index documents using path-based terms as keywords,
- browse documents associated with path-based terms,
- search for documents using path-based search terms, and
- view search results within the context of the terminologies.

In the next section, we briefly present work related to our research in the first project. In the third section, we describe the Metadata++ model and its associated software system, along with our evaluation of four successive implementations of the system. We also briefly summarize our current project with sundhed.dk, the health portal in Denmark. In the final section, we summarize our research contributions and discuss our experience in the conduct of these projects.

2. LITERATURE OVERVIEW

A long-standing debate in the field of information retrieval pits human indexing (believed to be high-quality and expensive) against machine indexing 4 (believed to be lower-quality and inexpensive). But research suggests that the two indexing methods are complementary and should be used in combination 3. Metadata++ supports human indexing using path-based terms and as well as full-text indexing (using Microsoft® Indexserver). There are two reasons why full-text indexing, on its own, might not be sufficient for natural resource documents. First, since some natural resource documents are mandated by law, they may contain "boilerplate" with nearly identical text that may lessen the effectiveness of automatic searching algorithms based on full-text indexing and term occurrence 4. Second, since these documents typically lack the kind of hyperlink structure used in a Google-style page ranking algorithm 7, the most relevant documents might not be highly ranked in a search result.

One important advantage of human indexing is that the indexer can analyse and judge the importance of the content and relate it to the perspective and needs of the domain context. Mai suggests what he calls a *domain-centered* approach to indexing where the indexer considers how the document relates to the collective domain knowledge instead of the common approach (what he calls a *document-centered* approach) where indexers consider (only) the content of the document itself 13. When a term in Metadata++ has multiple occurrences, the human indexer can select one or more of the multiple occurrences for a term as an index term thus allowing the same document to be indexed from multiple perspectives. Thus Metadata++ is supporting domain-centered indexing, in an interdisciplinary context. Note that the automatic, full-text indexing in Metadata++ is based only on the term; there is no consideration of the path.

A controlled vocabulary (consisting of terms typically selected by a group of expert users for use in a particular domain) is useful in information retrieval 12 and can improve consistency in indexing. The Metadata++ model is similar to a typical model for a thesaurus 1 in that it represents hierarchical (*broader term/narrower term*), *synonym*, and *related term* relationships between terms.

The distinct path associated with each occurrence of a multiple occurrence in Metadata++ provides a mapping to the original vocabularies contributed to Metadata++. Thus the multiple occurrences support a mapping between vocabularies, much like approaches to mapping between vocabularies that produce a temporary union list based on word matching as described by Zeng and Chan 28. Also, since Metadata++ represents multiple vocabularies, the *synonym* links from one path-based term to another can be used to represent a mapping from one vocabulary to another.

3. THE METADATA++ DIGITAL LIBRARY

The basic framework of the Metadata++ digital library is the hierarchy[2] of terms, which faithfully represent multiple controlled vocabularies from a variety of top-level subject areas within the natural resource management domain. Metadata++ is able to store and present each vocabulary "as is," i.e., as provided by the domain experts.[3]

3.1 Using Path-based Terms

In Metadata++, a term is always presented with its corresponding path in the hierarchy. Path-based terms give more context than a simple list of keywords. Our hypothesis, which was confirmed in our usability tests with Forest Service personnel, was that users would be able to easily infer the meaning or connotation intended for each term based on the associated path (without requiring a dictionary or glossary definition). Metadata++ allows a user to search for a particular term using the Find window, as shown in Figure 27-3. Here we see the terms that contain the text "old growth" with their corresponding paths.

Metadata++ also allows multiple terms to be grouped together in what we call a *polyterm.* In Figure 27-3, "Late successional forest," "old growth forest," and "late seral stage forest" are separated by commas and grouped together with a common path. In a traditional thesaurus 2, when multiple terms are used to represent the same concept, one of the terms is chosen as the so-called "preferred" term and the remaining terms are called "non-preferred," "lead-in", or "entry" terms. When indexing using such a

---

[2] To be more precise, Metadata++ represents a forest (no pun intended) of terms because there are multiple trees, i.e., multiple top-level nodes. See Figure 27-2.

[3] Note, in the prototype system for the USDA Forest Service, some vocabularies (such as the taxonomic description of plants and animals) were provided in their original form and others (such as simple lists of commonly used terms) were merged and adjusted by our collaborators from the USDA Forest Service.

thesaurus, typically only preferred terms are associated with documents. When such a thesaurus is used during searching, if a user enters a non-preferred term it can automatically be replaced by the preferred term (in a system where documents are indexed using only preferred terms) or the search expression can be expanded to include the preferred and all of the non-preferred terms (in a system where documents are indexed using a full-text index). In Metadata++, terms are not designated as preferred or non-preferred terms. Each term or polyterm with its associated path can be used to index a document and can be used in a search. The Metadata++ model serves as a searching thesaurus, as described by Bates 6, because it helps the user explore topics and terminology, make their own mental associations, discover topics related to their interests and discover the various terms under which material might be found.

In Metadata++, terms with paths are always displayed hierarchically, by merging the prefix of their paths. Thus terms, e.g., in the Find window, are displayed in the same order and position as they appear in the full Metadata++ hierarchy.

3.2 Exploring Terms

Metadata++ supports browsing controlled vocabularies beginning with the top-level subject areas shown in Figure 27-3 in what we call the Browse window.

And Metadata++ supports searching for text within terms using the Find window as shown in Figure 27-3. For any term in the Browse or Find window, the user can right-click on the term to see a popup context menu as shown in Figure 27-3. The context menu allows the user to display other terms for the same subject (i.e., synonyms), related topics (i.e., related terms), document titles that have been indexed with a specific term (i.e., *explicit documents* for the term) and documents titles for documents where the term appears in the text (i.e., *implicit documents* for the term).

The first option on the context menu shown in Figure 27-4, "Multiple Occurrences, Synonyms, and Related Terms", shows other related terms with their associated paths. The second and third options show the explicitly referenced documents and implicitly referenced documents, respectively. Clicking on a document in either list will open a separate window that contains document metadata, including path-based keywords and summary information as shown in Figure 27-5.

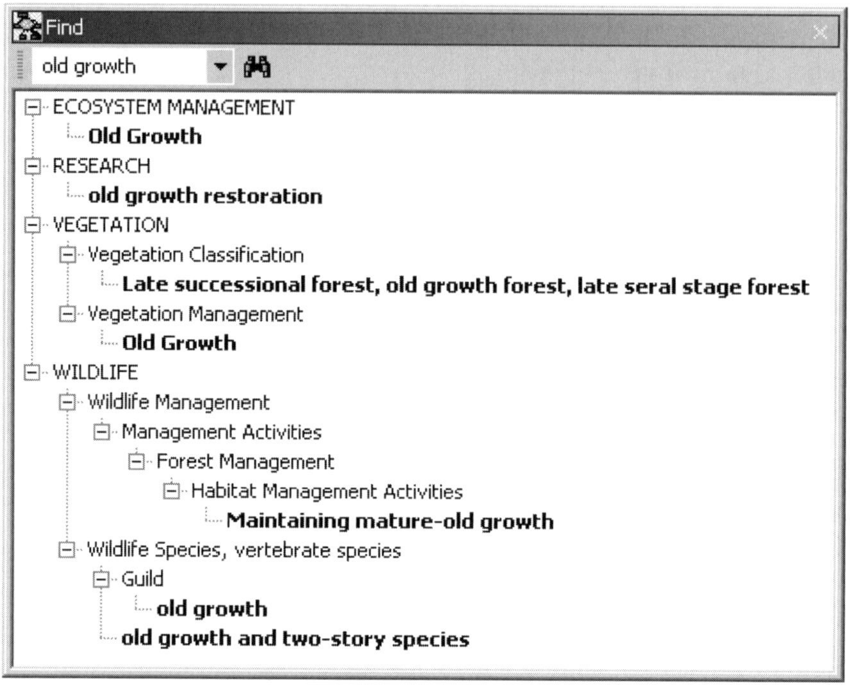

Figure 27-3. Screenshot of Find window (showing terms containing "old growth")

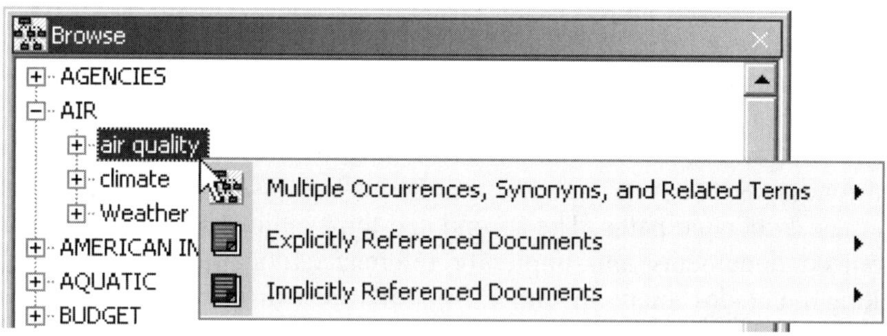

Figure 27-4. Screenshot of right-click context menu for terms

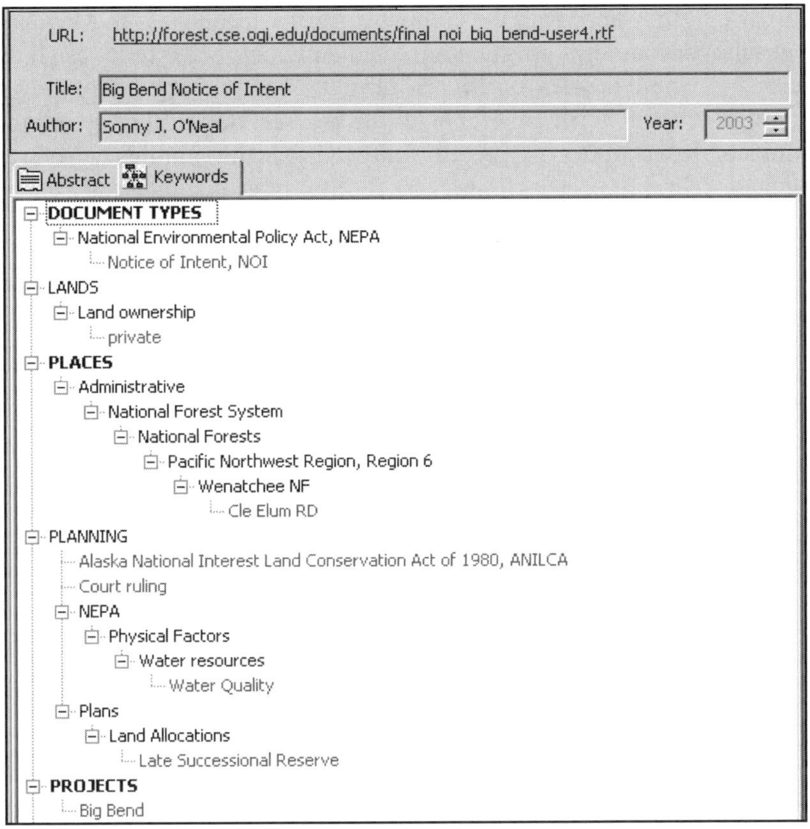

Figure 27-5. Cropped screenshot of document metadata

Any term in the hierarchy may be used as a document keyword, regardless of where it appears and whether or not it has narrower terms. The indexer may drag terms from either the Browse window or the Find window to the Keywords tab shown in Figure 27-5.[4]

3.3 Searching for Documents

The user may type any search string into the Find window to find possible path-based terms that may then be added to a search. Searchers add search terms by dragging a term from the Browse or Find window and dropping it (anywhere) on the Search window. As mentioned above, the terms dropped onto a Search window are displayed with their full path, in

[4] The DOCUMENT TYPES, PLACES, and PROJECTS top-level subjects are shown in **boldface** font (whenever they appear) as a subtle reminder to the user that they should select terms from these subjects when indexing the document.

the order that they appear in the complete set of vocabularies in Metadata++. The results for that term are shown immediately below the term, as shown in Figure 27-6 where the *AIR/air quality* term has been dropped onto the search window. For each term in Figure 27-6, we see the explicitly referenced documents listed first (in green) followed by the implicitly referenced documents (in blue). (In Figure 27-6, the first document is explicitly referenced (green) and the remaining are implicitly referenced (blue).)

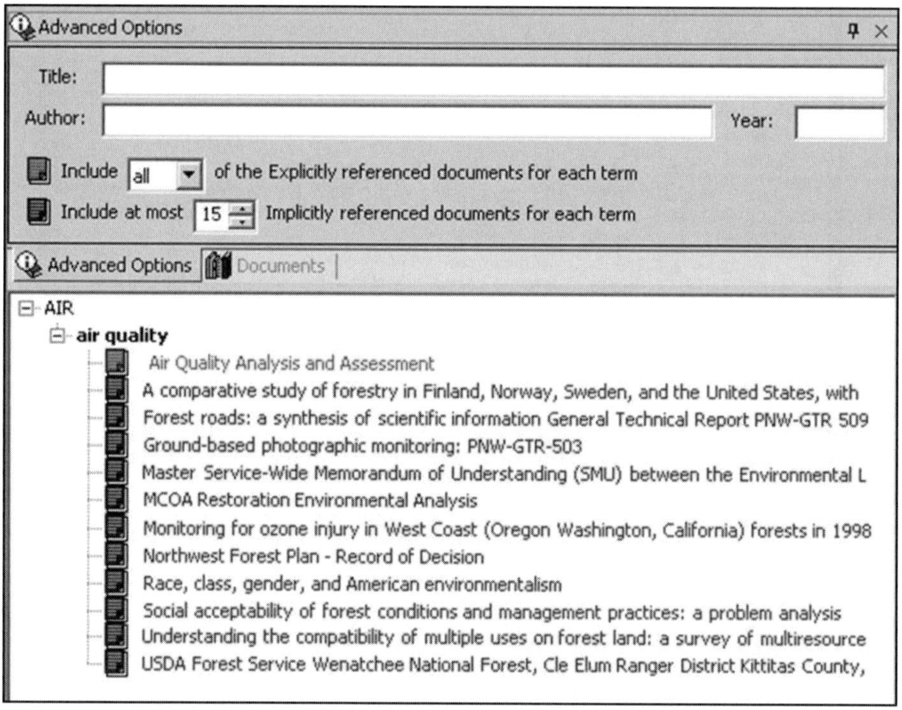

Figure 27-6. Cropped screenshot of Search menu

Research shows that query expansion is useful and that users prefer interactive query expansion 21. Metadata++ allows the user to interactively expand the search. Right-clicking on any search term in the Search window allows the user to add any of the related terms for the selected term using the first menu item shown in Figure 27-7. The second item in this context menu allows the user to add all multiple occurrences of a term to the search and the third menu item expands the search to include all narrower terms of the current search term. The user may remove an unwanted search term by simply deleting it from the Search window (by clicking on the term in the hierarchy and pressing the <DELETE> key).

Figure 27-7. Cropped screenshot showing the context menu for Search term

Results from this project include a description of the Metadata++ model 24 an investigation and evaluation of several storage management options for the vocabularies 26, an architecture and implementation for using a geographic information system (GIS) with Metadata++ to find synonymous terms for locations based on overlapping spatial footprints 25, and a companion project[5] that considered the facilitators and inhibitors to information sharing across government agencies 9. Weaver provides an extensive description of the work 23 and recent work describes the results from our usability tests 17.

4. THE SOFTWARE ARCHITECTURE FOR METADATA++

One important aspect of a software application intended for use by government partners is the software architecture. In an effort to support the varied requirements of this application, as shown in Table 27-1, we implemented the Metadata++ system four times over a period of about five years. Here we examine and evaluate the software architecture of these implementations with regard to the how they meet these requirements. The Availability and Library Size requirements are routine and thus did not significantly impact our architectural evaluation. Note that our implementation of these four software architectures respectively used four successive implementations for storing the hierarchy of terms 26.

[5] This work was supported in part by the National Science Foundation, Grant Number, 0204796.

Table 27-1. Software Quality Requirements for Metadata++, as articulated by the USDA Forest Services

Accessibility	System must be accessible from locations with broadband or dialup Internet connection. System must run on a typical desktop computer running Microsoft Windows®.
Availability	Availability during "normal business hours" is important, but not mission critical. Periodic system failure or offline maintenance is acceptable.
Performance	System performance, comparable to a typical web-based system, is required. There are no hard real time performance requirements.
Multi-user scalability	System must support hundreds of concurrent users, including the distribution and maintenance of the application to these users.
Library size	System is expected to manage hundreds or even thousands of documents.
Usability	System must be usable by people with ordinary computer skills.

Deployment of a web application is simple and efficient; the updated files are copied to the web server, and subsequent client sessions automatically use the updated version of the application. Using a web application is also simple with a web browser-based interface – often referred to as a thin client. But, web browser-based applications can be quite limited in the user interface functionality they provide. An alternative to a web application is a thick-client application, typically supporting a rich user interface. But deployment is difficult because the executable file and supporting libraries must be downloaded and installed on each client machine.

The accessibility requirement in Table 27-1 suggests a web application because the application would be available from any machine with a web browser and an Internet connection. But the usability requirement suggests a thick-client application with a rich user interface. We consider here our implementations of the Metadata++ application and their levels of success in satisfying the architectural objectives.

Our **first** implementation was a thin client based on Microsoft® Active Server Pages (ASP). These server-side scripts, hosted within Microsoft® Internet Information Server (IIS), contain logic for obtaining data from Microsoft® SQL Server 2000 and constructing a hierarchical display of terms represented in HTML. Client-side Javascript enables the user to select a search term by clicking on the text of the term within the hierarchy. Search results are displayed in a separate browser window using an HTML table. In this implementation, the server is completely stateless. That is, no session or user information is retained on the server between requests.

Because it uses a thin-client architecture, this application satisfies the accessibility, availability, and multi-user scalability objectives. But the performance is noticeably poor due to the numerous round-trips to the server particularly while exploring the hierarchy. Also, user actions are rather awkward. For example, exploring the hierarchy requires double-clicking the node of interest rather than using the traditional expand (+) and collapse (-) icons.

To improve usability, we developed a **second** implementation with a thick-client architecture using Microsoft® Visual Basic.NET® and Windows Forms. The application makes a direct TCP/IP connection (on port 1433) to Microsoft® SQL Server 2000 (running on a server) to retrieve the hierarchy and search for documents and stores all session information on the workstation (the server is stateless). The user interface provides familiar methods of interaction – including expanding and collapsing nodes (while exploring the hierarchy) and dragging and dropping terms (when expressing searches).

Since this is implemented as a thick client, each user machine needs to be upgraded with new software updates, limiting the scalability. Another drawback is that the application will not run if a firewall is blocking communication on port 1433, the typical TCP/IP database connection port. VPN access is unreasonable due to common use of limited bandwidth connections, such as dialup. Yet another problem is that when the database resides within the agency firewall, public access is limited.

To address the lack of accessibility caused by the firewall restriction, our **third** implementation uses a thin-client approach based on Microsoft® ASP.NET. The server is not completely stateless – minimal session information (including user authentication) is retained on the server between requests. This application sufficiently satisfies the accessibility, availability, and multi-user scalability objectives and the performance is also much better – mainly due to an improved back-end storage mechanism 26. However, each user interaction with the application, e.g., expanding a node in the hierarchy, requires a round-trip to the server. When the user is browsing several levels deep within the hierarchy, where expanding a single node may only add a few nodes to the visible hierarchical display, the entire display must nevertheless be created, transmitted, parsed, and displayed with each interaction.

The usability of this application is better than that of the first thin-client application in that the user can explore the hierarchy by expanding and collapsing nodes using the "plus" and "minus" symbols. But the application does not support other desired interactions, such as drag-and-drop for selecting terms and right-clicking for additional contextual information about a specific term. Another issue is that each term has an extra "information" node (as shown by the 'i' icon in Figure 27-8) to allow the user to view explicitly referenced documents, implicitly referenced documents, and all related terms. This extra node is cumbersome and non-intuitive, especially for beginners.

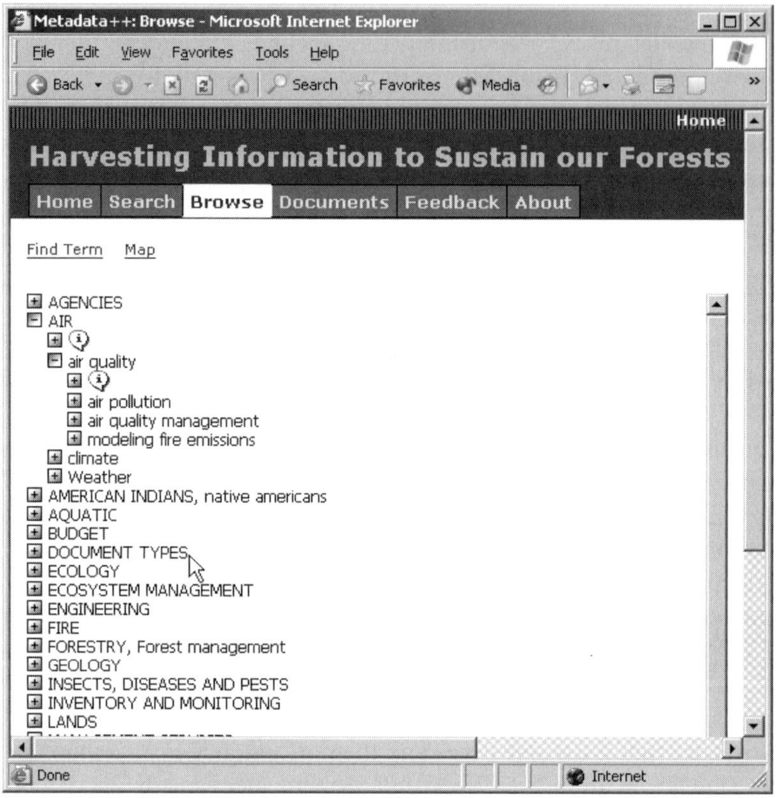

Figure 27-8. Screenshot of ASP.NET Thin Client

Table 27-2. Summary of Architectures with Regard to Objectives

	Accessibility	Availability	Performance	Multi-user Scalability	Usability
HTML/ASP Thin-Client	Good	Good	Poor	Good	Poor
VB.NET Thick-Client	Poor	Good	Good	Poor	Good
ASP.NET Thin-Client	Good	Good	Moderate	Good	Moderate
VB.NET Smart-Client	Good	Good	Good	Good	Good

Our **fourth** and final implementation of the Metadata++ application, illustrated in Figure 27-9, combines both thin-client and thick-client advantages using the smart client 22 technology (in the Microsoft® .NET Framework) with the deployment and accessibility advantages of a web application using techniques described by Glenwright 11 and Sells 19. The application uses .NET Web Services 27 to communicate with the Microsoft Windows NT® file system back-end storage system on the server.

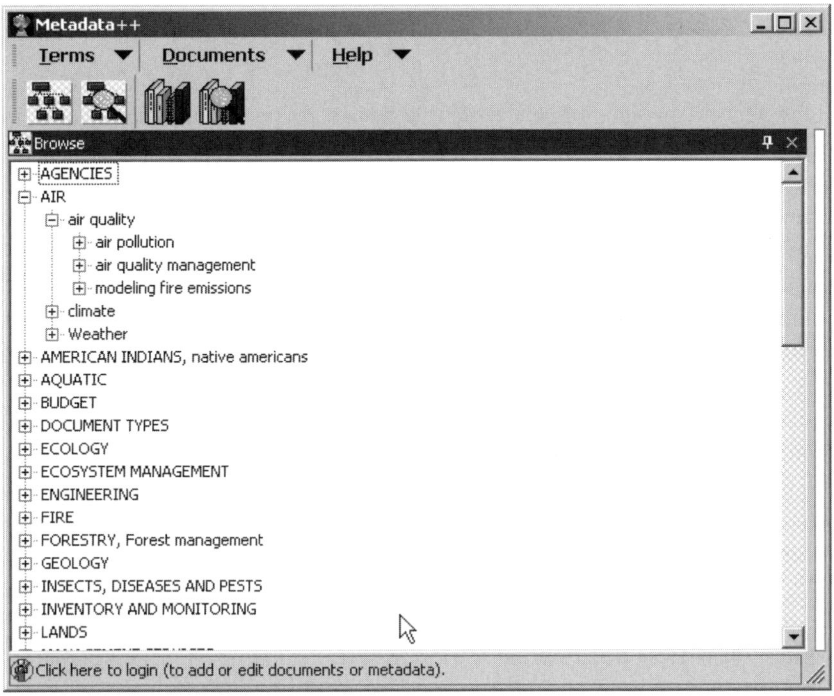

Figure 27-9. Screenshot of VB.NET Smart Client

The thick-client features of this application (including drag-and-drop, right-click, etc.) make it easy to use. Unlike a traditional thick-client application, this application also satisfies the accessibility, availability, and multi-user scalability objectives because the application is easily deployed (by visiting a URL with automatic updates). The auto-update process and the web services communicate over the standard HTTP port (port 80), which eliminates the problems caused by firewalls blocking the database connection.

This application also resolves the performance issues related to thin-client implementations. Because the application is running as a standalone application on the client machine, it maintains its own process state (and the server is stateless). For example, when a user expands a node, the server only needs to send the children of that node because the rest of the hierarchy is already on the client. The client receives the new nodes (from the web service) and adds them to the hierarchical display. Table 27-2 summarizes our evaluation of the four software architectures considered for Metadata++; our fourth implementation best meets the goals for this application and is the one currently operational.

5. OUR CURRENT PROJECT

Our second project began with the desire to test Metadata++ in a new domain. Our government partner, the national Danish healthcare portal, sundhed.dk, serves three main constituencies: citizens, family practitioners, and hospital-based healthcare practitioners. Many documents in the portal are manually indexed using three controlled vocabularies intended to represent the perspectives of these three constituencies, respectively. Sundhed.dk asked us to focus primarily on supporting the needs of family practitioners, typically with very targeted information needs, that arise during daily patient care. We decided not to use Metadata++ in this project because we learned that, unlike the natural resource managers, many users are unfamiliar with the vocabularies. Also, the vocabularies do not cover important topics that commonly appear in users' information needs. Further, since physicians need to find relevant information in 30 seconds or less, we felt that asking them to navigate a search thesaurus was inappropriate.

We are developing a new model that describes the documents that appear in a domain-specific digital library. Our model, called Semantic Components, classifies documents into *document classes*, i.e., categories of documents that contain similar types of information. Examples of document classes in sundhed.dk are *Clinical Problem* (documents about clinical diseases or conditions) and *Clinical Method* (documents about diagnostic or therapeutic procedures or tests). Documents within a class contain information about one or more of a small set of aspects of the main topic called *semantic components*. For example, two of the semantic components in *Clinical Problem* documents are *treatment* and *diagnosis,* while semantic components in *Clinical Method* documents include *risks* (possible complications or side effects) and *aftercare* (follow-up care, restrictions on diet or activity). A semantic component instance is one or more segments of text, that are not necessarily contiguous, that contain information about a semantic component in a particular document. A semantic component instance may or may not be associated with a structural element of the document, such as a subheading, to indicate its presence.

We anticipate that a list of the semantic component instances present in a document, along with the size of each instance, can serve as a document profile to help a searcher choose from among a set of documents returned from a search. Also, we believe that it will be useful to allow a user to search for a term that occurs within a particular semantic component. For example, a search for the term “penicillin” within the *treatment* semantic component of documents about endocarditis might return different documents than a search for “penicillin” within the *prevention* semantic component. We hypothesize that indexing semantic components (indicating the presence and location of semantic component instances within documents) will be less expensive than keyword indexing, especially in the absence of existing suitable vocabularies, yet will result in improved search results compared to automated full-text indexing alone. Experiments planned for the near future will investigate the usefulness of this approach. Vibeke Luk, information specialist and librarian for sundhed.dk, is our primary government partner for the second project. She interfaces with the rest of the sundhed.dk staff, the outside vendors, and the regional governments in Denmark.

6. DISCUSSION

Our research in our first project focused on the domain-specific terminology that is characteristic of the natural resource management domain, with many different classification schemes (e.g., the taxonomic description of plants and animals, various vegetation classification schemes, soil classification series, and various location schemes including watersheds using the Hydrologic Unit Codes, Ranger Districts/National Forests in the Forest Service, and Resource Areas/Districts/States in the Bureau of Land Management). The main research goal of this project was the representation and disambiguation of terms that can appear in multiple controlled vocabularies, with slightly or significantly different meanings. The unique features of the Metadata++ thesaurus model, in addition to the decision to always display a path with every term, are *multiple occurrences* and *polyterms*.

We have observed that natural resource managers sometimes seek documents that discuss issues from their own, disciplinary perspective, e.g., when a soil scientist is looking for similar issues regarding soil in other projects. And they sometimes seek information from multiple perspectives, e.g., when a natural resource manager charged with updating an existing Watershed Analysis wants to see current information about the watershed from a variety of perspectives: forestry, recreation, wildlife, transportation, etc. By combining a variety of domain-specific vocabularies and using path-based terms, we facilitate domain-centered indexing 13, as well as searching within and across knowledge domains.

Multiple occurrences in Metadata++ provide an automatic mapping among the original vocabularies; the presence of a term in multiple locations, with distinct paths, implies a mapping. This connection is particularly useful when multiple occurrences refer to the same basic concept from slightly different perspectives (as shown in Figure 27-3, above, for the term "Old Growth") as opposed to distinct concepts (such as "dolphin," the term that represents a mammal, a fish, and a partially submerged, man-made structure). The vast majority of our multiple occurrence terms are in the former case, likely because we are working in a domain-specific setting.

The Metadata+ model handles synonyms in two ways: interchangeable synonyms are handled by the use of polyterms, whereas synonym relationships among terms with distinct paths (including a mapping between two terms in distinct vocabularies) can be represented with the explicit synonym relationship in Metadata++. For instance, scientific and common names for the same species are treated as individual terms, presented in independent hierarchies, related appropriately by synonym links. Searchers can thus see the same topic, the species, from the perspective of a layman or a scientist. A similar solution has been used in a corporate, domain-specific thesaurus within the domain of pharmaceuticals, where related terms used to describe a drug (i.e., the chemical structure, the generic drug name, the trade name, and acronym variants) were all represented as preferred terms, connected through synonym links 16. In this case, the searcher was able to specify his or her search from a research, clinical, or marketing perspective.

One of the strengths of our project was the detailed, in-depth involvement of our government partners. Tolle, our primary partner in the project, coordinated the participation of many different groups of domain specialists to articulate the requirements for the system. These groups represented many different subject areas including climate, fire, wildlife biology, fish biology, soil, vegetation, and recreation specialists. Tolle worked very closely with the research team to communicate the requirements and to develop and provide important artifacts such as vocabularies and documents. Another strength of the project was the robustness of the prototype software system. Each prototype described above was fully operational and available for users to try out, over an extended period of time.

The Metadata++ software is not yet in use by the Forest Service or related agency; possible reasons for this include the following.

- The National Forests experienced approximately a 40% cut in funding at about the time we were trying to deploy our digital library.

- The Forest Service was not yet widely using digital libraries or a content management system to mange their project-related documents. It may be easier to deploy a new capability resulting from a research project when it can be added to an existing operational system rather than when one must first introduce a complete system (e.g., for managing documents, in this case).
- The best possible research prototype, once deployed for use by real users, needs both software maintenance (e.g., to adapt to operating system and other changes) and user support (e.g., to answer questions as they arise). We were not able to identify a recipient organization to receive and deploy our software, perhaps because it is more usual for a natural resource agency to purchase software products rather than develop and maintain their own proprietary solutions. Metadata++, as written, is a custom application that would require software development and maintenance expertise.

One important issue in a digital government research project is the level of government partner personnel that participate in the project. Partners at a relatively high-level can offer broad endorsement and authorize financial and other support, but are less likely to be engaged in the details of the project. Conversely, personnel who are closer to the operational level of the agency can provide invaluable assistance to the project but may not have the signature or decision-making authority to commit resources for the project. Perhaps a useful strategy would be to have multiple project liaisons within the same government partner agency with one or more at a somewhat higher level (to offer financial and in-kind support) and one or more at a somewhat lower level (to participate directly in the research project).

Another important issue concerns technology transfer. There are a number of mechanisms that one might use including: (a) launching or collaborating with a start-up company to develop and market a commercial product, (b) releasing the software under an open source licensing agreement, (c) releasing the software directly to the government agency where it could be (perhaps completely) re-implemented within the context of existing software systems, (d) transferring the software to an existing vendor of products used by the agency, and (e) hiring a team of software consultants to develop the production version of the system, tailored to the needs of the government agency. One suggestion that might facilitate deployment is to identify the recipient IT or other group for the deployed software at the beginning of the deployment effort.

Finally, particularly for research prototypes that are intended to be used as part of a new process or a new way of doing business, there is a need to evaluate the associated costs, benefits, and risks. Such analysis is typically outside the expertise of a computer science research team.

7. ACKNOWLEDGEMENT OF SPONSORS AND PARTNERS

We acknowledge the broad range of participants from the natural resource agencies associated with this project; their insight and experience was invaluable. We acknowledge members of our technical advisory board, who provided invaluable advice early in the project.

We also acknowledge the Forest Service personnel that served as test subjects in our usability tests, with the endorsement of their respective supervisors. We acknowledge the additional faculty, Drs. David Hansen, Marianne Koch, Fred Phillips, Leonard Shapiro, Nicole Steckler, and Patricia Toccalino; additional consultants, Eric Landis and Craig Palmer; additional graduate students, Lacey Baldwin, Balbinder Banga, Shawn Bowers, Ashley Burt, Bill Howe, Sudarshan Murthy, Julia Norman, Rupini Tumala, and Kirsten Zillman; undergraduate students, Dan Behlings, Jason Brewster, and Afrem Gutema; and high school students, Emily Langston, Jordan Wirfs-Brock, Kinley Campbell, and Qing Dong, who were part of this project.

We acknowledge the broad range of participants in our current project including Vibeke Luk, Peter Vedsted, Jens M. Rubak, and Frans Lacour in Denmark. And we acknowledge funding from the Århus Region in Denmark to pay for the family practice physicians that will participate in our upcoming usability test.

We gratefully acknowledge the support the National Science Foundation[6] and the insight and support from the program directors of the Digital Government Research Program, Lawrence Brandt and Valerie Gregg (formerly with NSF). Any opinions, findings, conclusions, or recommendations expressed here are those of the author(s) and do not necessarily reflect the views of the National Science Foundation

REFERENCES

1. Jean Aitchison, Alan Gilchrist, David Bawden. Thesaurus construction and use: a practical manual. London : Aslib. (2000).
2. American National Standards Institute – ANSI/NISO Z39.19 "Guidelines for the Construction, Format, and Management of Monolingual Thesauri" *NISO Press* (2003).
3. James D. Anderson, José Pérez-Carballo. "The nature of indexing: how humans and machines analyze messages and texts for retrieval. Part I: Research, and the nature of human indexing." *Information Processing & Management* Volume 37, Issue 2, Pages 231-254, March 2001.

---

[6] NSF Grant Numbers 9983518 (Project with the Forest Service in the US) and 0514238 (Project with sundhed.dk in Denmark)

4. Ricardo Baeza-Yates, Berthier Ribeiro-Neto. *Modern Information Retrieval.* Addison-Wesley (1999).
5. Balbinder Banga, Eric Landis, Timothy Tolle, Lois Delcambre, Fred Phillips. "User needs assessment for the adaptive management portal." *National Conference on Digital Government Research.* Los Angeles, California, Pages 329-334, May 2002.
6. Marcia J. Bates. "Subject Access in Online Catalogs: A Design Model." *Journal of the American Society for Information Science.* Volume 37, Issue 6, Pages 357-376, 1986.
7. Sergey Brin, Lawrence Page. "The Anatomy of a Large Scale Hypertextual Web Search Engine." *Computer Networks and ISDN Systems.* Volume 30, Issues 1-7, Pages 107-117, April 1998.
8. Lois Delcambre, Timothy Tolle, et al. "Harvesting Information to Sustain Forests." *Communications of the ACM.* Volume 46, Issue 1, Pages 38-39, January 2003.
9. David B. Drake, Marianne J. Koch, Nicole A. Steckler. "Scientist, Politician, and Bureaucrat Subcultures as Barriers to Information-Sharing in Government Agencies." *National Conference for Digital Government Research* DG.O 2003.
10. Raya Fidel. "Searchers' Selection of Search Keys: II. Controlled Vocabulary or Free-Text Searching." *Journal of the American Society for Information Science.* Volume 42, Number 7, Pages 501-514, 1991.
11. Anthony Glenwright. "Automatically Upgrade Your .NET Applications On-The-Fly" http://www.devx.com/dotnet/Article/10045/0/page/1 Date Viewed: May 2004.
12. Lancaster, F W. "*Indexing and abstracting in theory and practice.*" London: Library Association, 2003.
13. Jens-Erik Mai. "Analysis in indexing: document and domain centered approaches." *Information Processing & Management.* Volume 41, Pages 599-611, 2005.
14. Robert E. McGrath, Joe Futrelle, Ray Plante, Damien Guillaume. "Digital Library Technology for Locating and Accessing Scientific Data." *ACM Conference on Digital Libraries.* Berkeley, California, Pages 188-194, August 1999.
15. Marianne Lykke Nielsen. "A framework for work task based thesaurus design." *Journal of Documentation.* Volume 57, Issue 6, Pages 774 – 797, 2001.
16. Marianne Lykke Nielsen. "Task-based evaluation of associative thesaurus in real-life environment." *American Society for Information Science and Technology.* Providence, Rhode Island, November 2004.
17. Marianne Lykke Nielsen, Lois Delcambre, Timothy Tolle, Mathew Weaver. "Indexing and retrieval challenges in digital government systems – summary of an empirical research project." *2nd Scandinavian Workshop on e-gov. Copenhagen: CBS,* 2005.
18. Gordon H. Reeves, David B. Hohler, David P. Larsen, David E. Busch, Kim Kratz, Keith Reynolds, Karl F. Stein, Thomas Atzet, Polly Hays, Michael Tehan. "Aquatic and Riparian Effectiveness Monitoring Plan for the Northwest Forest Plan." *Regional Ecosystem Office*, Portland, Oregon, USA (2002).
19. Chris Sells. ".NET Zero Deployment: Security and Versioning Models in the Windows Forms Engine Help You Create and Deploy Smart Clients." *MSDN Magazine,* http://msdn.microsoft.com/msdnmag/issues/02/07/NetSmartClients/default.aspx Date Viewed: August 2002.
20. Leonard Shapiro, Lois Delcambre, Timothy Tolle, Mathew Weaver, David Maier, Dale Guenther, Jason Brewster, Afrem Gutema. "G-Metadata++: Rich Keyword Search Enhanced with a GIS." *International Conference on Geographic Information Science.* Boulder, Colorado, September 2002.
21. Shiri, C. Revie. "Query expansion behaviour within a thesaurus-enhanced search environment: a user-centered evaluation." *Journal of the American Society for Information Science*. Volume 57, Issue 4, Pages 462–478, 2006.
22. Smart Client Developer Center. http://msdn.microsoft.com/smartclient/Date Viewed: October 2004.

23. Mathew Weaver. "Enhancing a Domain-Specific Digital Library with Metadata Based on Hierarchical Controlled Vocabularies." Doctoral Dissertation, OGI School of Science & Technology, Oregon Health and Science University, September 2005.
24. Mathew Weaver, Lois Delcambre, David Maier. "A Superimposed Architecture for Enhanced Metadata." *DELOS Workshop on Interoperability in Digital Libraries European Conference on Digital Libraries*. Darmstadt, Germany, September 2001.
25. Mathew Weaver, Lois Delcambre, Leonard Shapiro, Jason Brewster, Afrem Gutema, Timothy Tolle. "A Digital GeoLibrary: Integrating Keywords and Place Names." *European Conference on Digital Libraries*. Trondheim, Norway, Pages 422-433, August 2003.
26. Mathew Weaver, Lois Delcambre, Timothy Tolle. "Metadata++: A Scalable Hierarchical Framework for Digital Libraries." *International Symposium on Digital Libraries and Knowledge Communities in Networked Information Society*. Tsukuba, Japan, March 2004.
27. Web Services Developer Center. Microsoft Developer Network (MSDN). http://msdn.microsoft.com/webservices/ Date Viewed: May 2005.
28. Marica Lei Zeng and Lois Mai Chan. "Trends and Issues in Establishing Interoperability Among Knowledge Organization Systems." *Journal of the American Society for Information Science and Technology*, 55(5):377-395, 2004.

SUGGESTED READINGS

- Aitchison, J, Gilchrist, A & Bawden, D (2000). Thesaurus construction and use: a practical manual. London: Aslib.
- ANSI/NISO. "Guidelines for the Construction, Format, and Management of Monolingual Controlled Vocabularies," ANSI/NISO Z39.19-2005 ISBN: 1-880124-65-3. The standard for constructing controlled vocabularies (Z39.19). http://www.niso.org/standards/resources/Z39-19-2005.pdf
- Caplan, P. (2003). Metadata fundamentals for all librarians. Chicago: American Library Association.
- Communications of the ACM, Volume 38, Issue 4 (April 1995). SN:0001-0782, Special Issue on digital libraries. The introduction to it is here: htp://portal.acm.org/citation.cfm?id=205325
- Haynes, D. (2004). Metadata for information management and retrieval. London: Facet Publishing.
- International Conference on Digital Libraries, Proceedings of the fifth ACM conference on Digital libraries, San Antonio, Texas, United States, Pages: 113 – 121, 2000. "Greenstone: a comprehensive open-source digital library software system"http://portal.acm.org/citation.cfm?id=336650
- Lancaster, F. W. (2003). Indexing and abstracting in theory and practice. London: Library Association.

ONLINE RESOURCES

- The International Journal on Digital Libraries, http://www.dljournal.org/
- The Journal of Digital Information, http://journals.tdl.org/jodi
- Medical Subject Headings (MeSH®), http://www.nlm.nih.gov/mesh/
- The National Science Digital Library, United States federated digital library to support K-12 science education. http://nsdl.org/
- The Getty Art and Architecture Thesaurus Online, http://www.getty.edu/research/conducting_research/vocabularies/aat/
- WordNet, A Lexical Database for the English Language. http://wordnet.princeton.edu/

QUESTIONS FOR DISCUSSION

1. In this project we focused on the use of domain-specific terminology because it was very well-known and widely used by the natural resource managers. As is typical in a technical field, there are a number of terms consisting of ordinary English words that have specialized meaning, such as the term "adaptive management" or "old growth." We believe that support for specialized terminology or controlled vocabularies can be highly useful in a domain-specific digital library as opposed to an open, diverse collection such as the Web, for example. Consider a range of document collections and discuss whether they use domain-specific terminology and whether the collections are narrow enough to permit the exploitation of such terminology.
2. We implemented four distinct Metadata++ systems, as well as multiple storage options for the vocabularies and multiple interconnections with a geographic information system. Yet, our innovative software features are not (yet) deployed in an operational system. Discuss possible mechanisms for deployment as well as the factors or issues that might contribute to or prevent the uptake of research contributions in a digital government project.
3. One of the strengths of both of our projects discussed in this chapter is the in-depth engagement of multiple participants from our partner government agencies. Discuss the positive and negative aspects of such in-depth involvement, both to the quality of the research work and to the resulting software solutions.

Chapter 28

BUSINESS-TECHNOLOGY ALIGNMENTS IN E-GOVERNMENT

A Large-Scale Taiwan Government Electronic Record Management Systems Study

Fang-Ming Hsu[1], Paul Jen-Hwa Hu[2], and Hsinchun Chen[3]

[1]*Associate Professor and Chairman, Department of Information Management, National Dong Hwa University, Taiwan, R.O.C. (fmhsu@mail.ndhu.edu.tw);* [2]*Associate Professor and David Eccles Faculty Fellow, Accounting and Information Systems, David Eccles School of Business, University of Utah, U.S.A. (actph@business.utah.edu);* [3]*McClelland Professor, Department of Management Information Systems, University of Arizona, U.S.A. (hchen@eller.arizona.edu)*

CHAPTER OVERVIEW

Advances in information technology are bringing about fundamental changes in the way governments work, share information, and deliver services. For e-government to succeed, government agencies must manage records and archives, but the sheer volume and diversity of such documents/archives necessitate the use of electronic record management systems (ERMS). Using an established business–technology alignment model, we analyze an agency's strategic alignment choice and examine the agency performance outcomes associated with that alignment. The specific research questions addressed in the study are as follows: (1) Do strategic alignment choices vary among agencies that differ in purpose, geographic location, or position within the overall government hierarchy? (2) Do agencies' alignment choices lead to different outcomes? and (3) Does performance in implementing, operating, and using ERMS vary among agencies that follow different alignment choices? We conducted a large-scale survey study of 3,319 government agencies in Taiwan. Our data support the propositions tested. Based on our findings, we discuss their implications for digital government research and practice.

1. INTRODUCTION

The advent of information technology (IT), which has reshaped the modern business landscape, is now bringing about drastic changes in the fundamental processes that define how governments work, share information, and deliver services. As Grover and Kettinger (2000) point out, efforts to initiate process changes are difficult to attain without technology enablers. Increasingly, governments around the world thus are embracing exciting technological opportunities for digitizing their processes and operations to provide innovative e-government services that are conveniently accessible to citizens, constituencies, and various government agencies (Dawes and Prefontaine 2003). E-government practices have matured at a steady pace, gradually advancing from novel e-option concepts to well-conceived e-channels capable of meeting the mounting demands for improved service accessibility, agility, flexibility, and quality.

E-government thus is becoming a crucial but challenging area for information systems (IS) researchers and practitioners (Chen et al. 2006). Information technology has been shown to be important for government administration, including collaboration and coordination among different agencies or functional areas (Kelly 1998). However, technology availability represents a necessary but often insufficient condition for ensuring the success of an e-government initiative. Effective management also is critical and indispensable.

The IT expenditures by the United States government, for example, have increased significantly in recent years, but the benefits accrued from these investments have been ambiguous and often questioned (Ault and Gleason 2003). Similar criticisms prevail in various e-government initiatives, whose results are mixed at best. Government agencies often organize their services and operations into programs that may be changed in response to a host of factors, including budgetary constraints, political priorities, and new technology implementations (Walker 2001). As Fountain (2001) and Mullen (2003) cautiously note, government agencies must have a clear "big picture" and focus on interagency collaborations and fully leveraging their IT capabilities.

The alignment between business and technology strategy represents a fundamental challenge facing agencies in e-government contexts. As Crittenden et al. (2004) conclude, government agencies will continue to struggle to generate appropriate actions and desired outcomes until they can align business/management decisions and technology opportunities. The business–technology alignment indeed represents a critical challenge to managers in both public and private organizations (Pollalis 2003). In light of their resource constraints and performance expectations, many nonprofit organizations (including government agencies) have become increasingly concerned with actual program effectiveness for organizational performance (Fine et al. 2000; Kaplan 2001).

Hence a critical question remains: What leads to agency-effective e-government? Within a governmental system, agencies are endowed with defined autonomy and appropriated resources that make them largely comparable to private organizations, whose performance is greatly affected by the alignment of their business and technology strategies (Henderson and Venkatraman 1993). The important but distinct components of an agency's management system and the way it functions and interacts with citizens and other agencies therefore must align with its strategic intent, as far as possible (Scott 2003). A review of extant literature suggests few empirical studies of the relationship between an agency's strategic alignment and its performance, with the exceptions of Crittenden et al. (2004) and Stone and Crittenden (1994). However, strategic alignment requires a systematic, coherent analysis across major decision-making areas of the agency (Scott 2003), which demands an examination of the key factors that affect strategic alignment in an agency and an assessment of the outcomes and agency performance associated with that alignment.

In this chapter, we investigate agencies' business–technology alignments in the implementation of electronic record management systems (ERMS). We analyze each agency's strategic alignment choice, then examine its outcome and effects on agency performance, using a large-scale survey study of 3,319 Taiwanese agencies at both central and local governmental levels. To develop our propositions, we synthesize relevant prior research and important contextual characteristics pertinent to ERMS, target agencies, and the overall government structure. We then test our propositions using the participating agencies' responses and assessments. Operationally, we evaluate business–technology alignment outcomes in terms of key problem areas and satisfaction scores and measure agency performance by examining contests for prestigious awards that signify national best practices for implementing, operating, and using ERMS. Overall, our study addresses the following questions.

1. Do strategic alignment choices vary among government agencies that differ in purpose, geographic region, and position within the overall government hierarchy?
2. Do agencies' alignment choices lead to different outcomes associated with the use of ERMS?
3. Does performance in the implementation, operations, and actual use of ERMS vary among agencies that follow different alignment choices?

The organization of the rest of this chapter is as follows: Section 2 describes the e-government developments in Taiwan and provides an overview of the pertinent policies, regulations, and technology opportunities accessible to agencies. Section 3 reviews relevant previous research and highlights our motivation. Section 4 describes the overall research framework and the specific propositions, which we test in an empirical study whose design and data collection details appear in Section 5. We highlight the key analysis results in Section 6 and discuss their implications to research and practice. Section 7 concludes with a summary and discussion of our study's contributions and limitations.

2. BACKGROUND OVERVIEW

The Taiwanese central government revealed its grand vision of e-government in 1997, laying out a master plan for establishing a national infrastructure for e-government and identifying important administrative reforms necessary for transforming government agencies in the emerging information/knowledge economy. The National Information Infrastructure initiative was launched in November 1997 to create a national platform for rapidly expanding e-government programs that deliver innovative government-to-government, government-to-citizen, and government-to-business services. Most, if not all, e-government services involve and are supported by various documents, records, or archives and thus require the use of ERMS. Typically, an ERMS contains voluminous official records, documents, and archives that are digitalized and can be easily searched and accessed with 24/7 availability that overcomes any geographic boundaries.

When preparing or delivering a service, a government agency often references pertinent records or documents and, in most cases, creates new records to reflect and document the service rendered. The management of these government documents, records, and archives is critical but tedious, often challenging government agencies that essentially are in information businesses. A system approach is desirable, particularly considering the diversity of government documents, the sheer volume of the records and archives, and the frequency with which they are created, accessed, or updated. Several trends are emerging to address this issue, including a fundamental shift from paper-based storage to computer-based systems, from paper to electronic documents, from managing information to supporting its access and retrieval, and from a cost-reduction focus to continued process improvement (Stephens 1998). These trends all point to government agencies' need for ERMS.

In December 1999, the Taiwanese government passed the Archives Act, which established the legal foundation and technology standards for managing government records and archives electronically. The National

Archives Administration (NAA) was established in November 2001 as the supreme governing entity charged with educating, promoting, and advancing the use of ERMS among government agencies at all levels. To improve administrative efficiency and service quality, the NAA revealed a "Ten-Year Strategic Plan" in 2002, outlining its goals for digitalizing government documents and records, together with a master plan for developing, implementing, and disseminating ERMS to all agencies before 2011. Prior to the creation of the NAA, government records and archives were predominantly paper-based and often scattered among different agencies, which meant both citizens and government agencies had great difficulty locating and accessing particular records, documents, or archives efficiently or effectively. As a result of the National Electronic Archives Retrieval system, which is supported by a centralized catalog database, government documents/records are now easily and conveniently accessible by the general public, business communities, and agencies.

3. LITERATURE REVIEW AND MOTIVATION

E-government implements cost effective models for citizens, industry, federal employees, and other stakeholders to conduct business transactions online and therefore requires the effective integration of strategy, process, organization, and technology (Whitson and Davis 2001) to link government information infrastructures to the necessary digital domains (Tapscott 1995). In this section, we review relevant previous research, describe the business–technology alignment in government, detail the development of electronic record/archive management in Taiwan, and highlight our motivation.

3.1 Previous Electronic Records Management Research

Electronic record/archive management is critical to government services and has been examined by both public administration and research communities. On the public administration front, the Freedom of Information Act was fully implemented by the British government in January 2005, thereby legitimating the right of access to government information and demanding that public authorities publish and disseminate information in accordance with "publication schemes." This Act encourages all public authorities (agencies) to organize and store their records and archives in compliance with the provisions of a Code of Practice, which focus on desirable practices for gathering, managing, and destroying records. The National Archives is responsible to assist public authorities by evaluating their conformance with the Records Management Code (Blake 2005).

Similar developments have taken place elsewhere. For example, the Australian government, in complying with the Public Records Act effective since 1973, created the Public Record Office Victoria (PROV) as the principal architect and implementer of public records in Australian. This office establishes standards for public records to support their management, including creation, access, and update, and provides assistance and recommendations to various agencies through a record management program for their compliance with the standards established under the Public Records Act. An initial version of the Victorian Electronic Records Strategy was revealed in April 2000 to assist agencies managing their electronic records; an updated version appeared in July 2003. Together, these programs and strategies provide blueprints for developing ERMS in the Australian government system by noting essential system requirements, system specifications, metadata schema, standardized record formats, and record exporting formats.

Meanwhile, the technology that enables e-government is evolving rapidly, which introduces challenges into the design and implementation of compatible system infrastructures that can support electronic record/archive management (Sprague 1995). As Young (2005) has commented, an electronic record management program must include an understanding of how an agency's business operates and establishes rapport. Documents must be integrated into a management process that provides desirable transparency to users and creates auditable trails for internal and external control purposes (Thurston 1997). A good case in point is a network-based image system for archival storage, commonly used to replace aging microfilm systems, that eliminates physical storage and shipments (Sprague 1995).

Similar developments have been observed in the United States, where the National Archives and Records Administration (NARA) is charged with addressing these problems and challenges, including lost data in computer-based systems and divergent record/document formats, many of which are outdated (Weinstein 2005). Technology standards are still evolving and cannot meet the storage and retrieval needs of government agencies satisfactorily (Sprague 1995). In response, NARA has proposed a Records Management Profile in the Federal Enterprise Architecture and supports requirements analyses for Records Management Service Components, both of which are critical to electronic record management by agencies.

Despite the attention and efforts, current practices are far from perfect and need to respond to a host of challenges that pertain to both technology and management (Weinstein 2005). Among them, the implementation and actual use of ERMS are essential but have not received adequate attention in previous research. The International Records Management Trust has developed an objective system, the Records Management Capacity

Assessment System, to assess the strengths and weaknesses of different ERMS (Griffin 2004). According to this system, the most primitive capacity level lacks any management policies and processes, formal or ad hoc, whereas at the highest capacity level, the ERMS creates a knowledge management environment that effectively supports the agency's objectives and functions. Advancements between these capacity levels require mature, delicate, sophisticated integrations of records/archive management and business processes, enabled by technological solutions (Griffin 2004).

3.2 Business–Technology Strategy Alignment in Government

Pollalis (2003) shows the importance of aligning business and technology strategies and their integrations in the overall organization system. As described by Venkatraman et al. (1993), management practices act as "alignment mechanisms" that can meet the challenge of translating strategic choices into administrative practices and operational decision making. Growing academic research and practice guidelines suggest that investments in technology alone cannot warrant success in e-government. That is, agencies must invest in processes and human capital (and training) to ensure effective technology implementation and use (Chircu and Kauffman 2001). New technology implementations also can initiate and facilitate important business transformations. Soh and Markus (1995) suggest that performance enhancements enabled by technology assets must be accompanied by appropriate technology use, which often requires process changes. Such strategic alignment can be conceptualized with an internal or external focus (Henderson and Venkatraman 1993). From an enterprise perspective, government agencies are similar to functional departments in an organization, and legislation and policymaking can facilitate cooperative efforts among them (Ault and Gleason 2003). In turn, an appropriate alignment between the agency and the policymaking institution may induce desirable performance.

Several factors affect technology investment decisions by governments, including the value to agencies; the value to taxpayers, lawmakers, or other stakeholders; and the technology risks (Chircu and Lee 2003). Public organizations take into account the value a technology creates within the investing agency as well as for external partners or users. Whereas technology investment decision making in the private sector usually is shaped by strategic goals, that in the public sector often is influenced by political considerations and motives, which define resource allocations directly and indirectly in response to the needs of agencies and their stakeholders (Chircu and Lee 2003).

According to Bacon (1991), an organization needs an IS/IT strategy to (1) achieve business objectives, (2) improve current use of technology, and (3) comply with regulations and other external requirements. An agency's business strategy for implementing and operating an ERMS can be analyzed according to the perspective of internal versus external resources. In terms of internal resources, an agency can employ its financial and personnel resources to acquire a customized ERMS through outsourcing or in-house development efforts. Alternatively, agencies can rely on external resources to acquire ERMS, such as free systems developed and made available by other government organizations.

3.3 Development of Electronic Record/Archive Management Systems in Taiwan

Motivated by improved document and record management, the increasing accessibility of records and archives, and an enhanced realization of the benefits of knowledge embedded in documents and archives, the NAA initiated the National Archives Information System (NAIS) project for 2003–2006. Specifically, the NAA attempted to address several core implementation challenges, such as creating baseline rules for computerized record management and developing an electronic record cataloging system to support a national electronic archives retrieval system that would meet security and authentication requirements. The central government's commitment to electronic record/archive management is strong; it allocated a total budget of US $17 million between 2003 and 2006.

According to the NAA, the official documents or records created by a government agency must be made accessible to other agencies. When issuing or receiving an official document, an agency must create the necessary electronic records and, in some cases, send important records to archives. Each agency must catalog its records and archives and send them electronically to the NAA, which maintains a centralized database to support queries and retrievals by the general public or other agencies. At the time of our study, the computerization of government documents, records, and archives was in progress, and a vast majority of agencies had implemented or gained access to various ERMS. In this study, we define strategic alignment specifically as the extent to which the NAA's technology strategy supports and is supported by an agency's business strategy to meet regulations and mandated requirements. We posit that an appropriate fit between the technology and business strategies will lead to desired outcomes and improved agency performance.

3.4 Motivation

According to Heeks (2000), approximately 20–25% of e-government projects in developed countries are either never implemented or abandoned immediately after implementation, and a further 33% fail because they fall short of their major goals or result in significant undesirable outcomes. Government records and archives are critical to both citizens and agencies and encapsulate organizational knowledge and memory that is indispensable to government services and operations. Current practices involve an obvious emphasis on technology considerations (e.g., technology investment, deployment), whereas issues that pertain to business or management receive little attention. For example, continued federal spending on computerization in the United States has failed to generate convincing results and suffers abundant criticism (Ault and Gleason 2003). Understandably, effective electronic record management requires formal control of the records/archives, efficient record sharing among various agencies, and adequate planning by the agencies at both service-delivery and policymaking levels. Because records and archives are valuable resources and assets of agencies, the agencies must design, construct, and employ integrated systems in accordance with established standards, policies, and procedures (PROV 2003).

Some previous e-government research has examined technology deployment for the relationships between government and citizens (e.g., Chircu and Lee 2003). Considering government as a whole, we attempt to investigate business–technology strategy alignment between an agency and the policymaking organization. Common e-government contexts are typified by considerable resource constraints, which make the business–technology alignment increasingly essential in the implementation and satisfactory use of ERMS by agencies. Henderson and Venkatraman (1993) and Tallon and Kraemer (1999) propose a strategic alignment model for producing desirable outcomes and improved organizational performance. In our context, this model suggests an agency must align its business strategy and the NAA's technology strategy to succeed in its implementation and use of an ERMS. Thus, it is important to examine an agency's business strategy, analyze its ERMS implementation choices, and evaluate the outcomes associated with the alignment choice, as well as the resultant agency performance.

4. RESEARCH FRAMEWORK AND PROPOSITIONS

In this section, we describe our research framework and discuss the propositions to be tested.

4.1 Research Framework

Our research framework (see Fig. 28-1) adapts the strategic alignment model by Tallon and Kraemer (1999), which suggests that an organization can derive favorable outcomes and improved performance by aligning its business and technology strategies. In this model, management practices represent alignment mechanisms for translating strategic choices into administrative decision making and operational details (Venkatraman et al. 1993). We analyze the business–technology alignment in an agency from a "shortfall" perspective. A shortfall occurs when an agency's business strategy cannot be supported adequately by the NAA's technology capability or fails to take full advantage of the NAA's technology capability. If an agency's business strategy fits well with the NAA's strategy for implementing ERMS, the alignment may affect the agency's performance in electronic record/archive management directly and significantly. That is, an adequate alignment can greatly facilitate an agency's favorable outcomes or improved performance in e-government services. In this study, we specifically define strategic alignment as the extent to which an agency's business strategy is congruent with the NAA's technology strategy and thereby meets the regulatory requirements and fully leverages the governmental system resources.

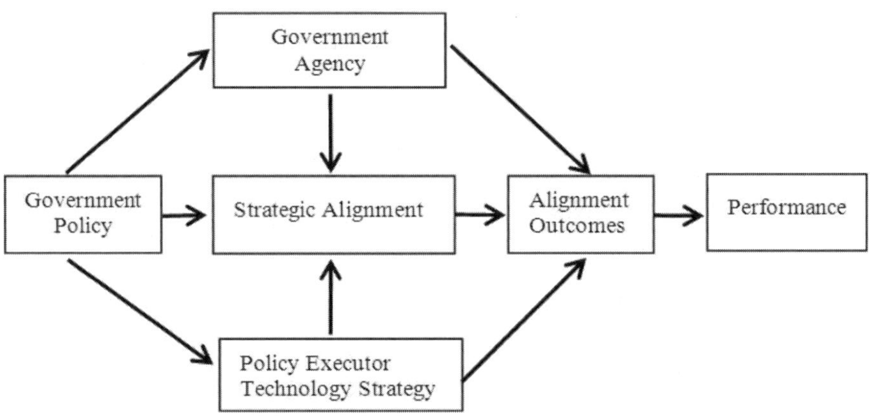

Figure 28-1. Research Framework

On the basis of Tallon and Kraemer's (1999) model, we analyze individual agencies' business strategies for computerizing records and archives, assess their alignment with the technology strategy of the NAA, and examine the associated outcome and resulting agency performance. As part of their business strategy, some agencies develop ERMS in-house, whereas others acquire proprietary ERMS from outsourcing vendors or adopt the free ERMS, whether in simple or complex form, provided by the NAA. Regardless of their strategic choices, agencies must comply with the related policies and regulations and the NAA's general guidelines. The strategic alignment anchor enables us to examine the outcomes associated with each alignment choice, such as common problems encountered by agencies or their satisfaction with the assistance and services provided by the NAA.

According to the Archive Act, each government agency is responsible for collecting and managing its official records and archives electronically, with the necessary accessibility and security. A host of core operations is critical, including record/archive capturing/gathering, declaration, classification, cataloging, preservation, retrieval/access support, disposal, exporting/transfer, updating or destruction, and security control. Classification and cataloging of records and archives are particularly crucial for agencies that must comply with the classification scheme and guidelines. All agencies must provide a catalog of their records and archives periodically to the NAA, which then includes and aggregates these catalogs into the national electronic archives system, conveniently accessible by the general public and all government agencies through the "National Electronic Archives Retrieval (NEAR)" system available on the NAA website. To foster the use of official records and archives managed by individual agencies, the NAA has enacted a rule for computerized record management that establishes a necessary regulatory baseline for the adoption of ERMS by agencies.

4.2 Analysis of Strategic Alignments

Before the promulgation of the Archives Act, record management was not an essential process for government agencies. Most record management practices were manual and could not provide effective access support. An important modern requirement of systems is cataloging; all agencies must use a catalog file compliant with a prespecified XML data format that can deliver the catalog of their records/archives to the NAA, via its website, e-mail, or post services.

The NAA assumes multiple roles in fostering electronic record/archive management practices among agencies: policymaker, architect, regulator, and auditor. In terms of the NAA's technology strategy, an agency can choose from a range (I–IV) of strategic alignments. If it selected alignment type I, an agency would develop an ERMS in-house using its own IT staff, funding, and existing system resources. In this case, the NAA assumes a supportive role and helps the agency use the "Electronic Records Cataloging System (ERCS)" and online submission function with "Electronic Records Catalog Checking System (ERCCS)" (developed and maintained by the NAA) to meet the mandated format requirements for delivering the catalog file. Government agencies that subscribe to alignment type I maintain their ERMS themselves.

In alignment type II, an agency acquires an ERMS through outsourcing arrangements that may include system design, implementation, and testing by the chosen vendor. In this case, the NAA provides a mandatory baseline for functional specifications that must be noted in the agency's request for quotes or bid assessments. During the outsourcing process, the NAA assists agencies in identifying preferred vendors and assessing their capability and systems. At the time of our study, the NAA was about to certify preferred vendors considered competent and reliable for developing and implementing ERMS in government agencies.

With alignment type III, an agency adopts ERCS, a simplified ERMS developed and made available by the NAA. Agencies can download and install this system, which already possesses the functionality required by the NAA, including cataloging.

Finally, an agency that follows alignment type IV adopts RecordsOnline, a comprehensive ERMS developed by the NAA. This system has a full range of functionality to support record/archive management and operates in an Internet-based environment supported by a backend, centralized database system maintained by the NAA. After implementing RecordsOnline, ERCS, or ERCCS, agencies receive system administration and end-user training support from the NAA. Figure 28-2 (next page) summarizes the strategic alignments between an agency and the NAA.

For cost effectiveness and external controls, records managers often use existing software packages (Young 2005). However, an agency also should select an appropriate business strategy with respect to its competence and services/operations scope. Such strategies straddle internal and external domains (Henderson and Venkatraman 1993) and, in the case of acquiring ERMS, can be assessed according to internal versus external controls. An agency can gain increasing internal control by developing an ERMS specific to its needs and operations. In contrast, an agency can allow external control by adopting the ERMS developed and maintained by the NAA. Alternatively, agencies can balance the internal and external controls through outsourcing arrangements.

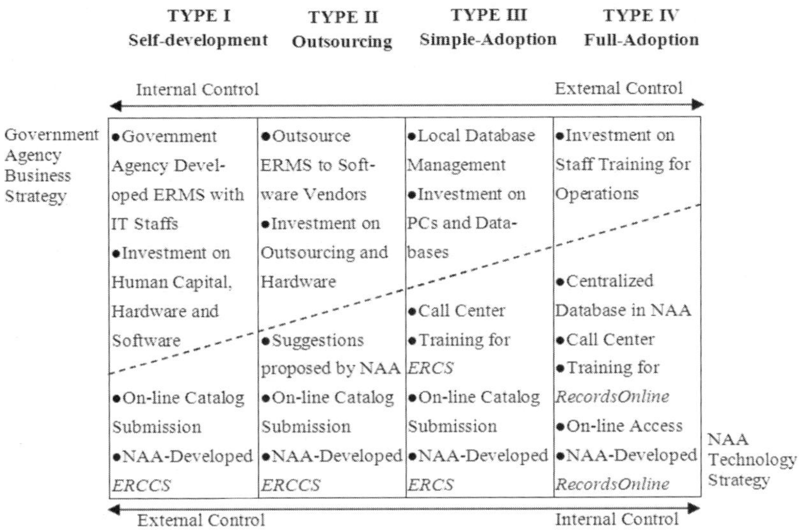

Figure 28-2. Summary of Strategic Alignments by Government Agencies

4.3 Propositions

The success of electronic record/archive management demands substantial efforts from an agency to ensure desired system usage and service enhancement (Griffin 2004). Government agencies vary considerably in their resources, such as funding, specialized skills, and manpower. As a result, they must choose adequate strategies to meet their regulatory and operational requirements.

Agencies also differ in their operational purposes, geographic locations, and relative positions in the government hierarchy. E-government can overcome agency and jurisdictional barriers and thereby enable integrated, whole-government services across central and local agencies (Chen et al. 2006). On the basis of its primary purpose or function, an agency can be categorized as administration, business, or public school. For example, business agencies generally have a profit orientation and access to more resources than do public schools. Furthermore, agencies that pertain to the central government are relatively more resourceful than are their local counterparts. Finally, the exact position or level of an agency within the overall government structure can affect its technology deployment (Caudle et al. 1991). Agencies at higher administrative levels often influence agencies at lower administrative levels, partially because of the chain of command and budgetary controls. For example, the National Police Agency has direct administrative influence over the Municipal Police Agency and may exert pressure regarding its adoption of a particular ERMS. Interorganizational network centrality also is germane to any increases in resource contributions (Crittenden et al. 2004). Von Hippel (1994), in a study of information stickiness, shows that problem solving and system support often proceed from the locus. Accordingly, agencies with similar purposes, geographic locations, or positions within the government hierarchy are likely to follow the same alignment choices in acquiring ERMS. Thus, we test the following proposition:

> Proposition 1: Government agencies that vary in purpose, geographic location, or position within the government hierarchy are likely to follow different strategic alignments in their implementation of ERMS.

Previous research surrounding nonprofit organizations has highlighted the importance of key stakeholders in defining and assessing organizational performance (Fine et al. 2000; Kaplan 2001; Crittenden et al. 2004). The long-term success of records management requires agencies to allocate resources and actually use the system, in addition to maintaining the records and archives to support their functions or services (Griffin 2004). Hence, an organization should avoid internal managerial informality and respond to external interdependence using a planning process (Crittenden et al. 2004). An agency also must attend to relevant policies and regulations when assessing and selecting its appropriate strategic alignments with respect to its operations and resource constraints. Such strategic assessments and choices likely relate to particular outcomes (Henderson and Venkatraman 1993). In our case, agencies can choose from a range of alignment types—RecordsOnline, ERCS, ERCCS, and an online submission system by the NAA. These alignment choices may lead to different outcomes, which we measure in terms of the problems commonly encountered by an agency and its satisfaction with the assistance and services by the NAA. Satisfaction offers a critical outcome measure for assessing strategic alignments (Arino 2003). In addition, external interdependence, which reflects how the concerns of clients and external agencies influence an agency's decision making, may be important for satisfaction and resource changes (Crittenden et al. 2004). Similarly, unsatisfactory technology use and common problems in system support, operations, and integration represent important measures of strategic alignment outcomes (Bacon 1991). Thus, we test the following proposition:

> Proposition 2: Government agencies that vary in their strategic alignments for ERMS are likely to experience different outcomes in terms of common problems and satisfaction with the assistance and services by the NAA.

Pollalis (2003) notes the importance of aligning business and technology strategies for improved organizational performance. Similarly, Reich and Benbasat (2000) argue that technology implementation and its connection to the business strategy defines the strategic alignment, which in turn affects management performance and actual technology usage. Garg et al. (2005) suggest that technology investments alone cannot guarantee performance; rather, the business–technology alignment influences organizational performance. Organizations can realize and capitalize on greater payoffs from their technology investments by aligning their business and technology strategies (Tallon et al. 2000). In our context, agencies that implement ERMS to manage their records/archives are monitored and evaluated by the NAA on a regular basis. According to the NAA's evaluation scheme, recognizing business and technology objectives is critical for assessing agencies' strategic alignments (Reich and Benbasat 2000). To ensure all agencies' compliance with the Archive Act, the NAA examines their archive/record management practices and operations and grants prestigious Golden Archives Awards to officially recognize those that clearly demonstrate outstanding practices and services. Thus, we test the following proposition:

> Proposition 3: Agencies that vary in their strategic alignments are likely to differ in their performance, as manifested by their standing in the assessment rankings for Golden Archives Awards.

5. STUDY DESIGN AND DATA COLLECTION

We conducted a large-scale survey study to test our propositions. In this section, we detail our study design and data collection methods.

5.1 Measurements

On the basis of our research framework, we identified the specific constructs to be examined, then operationalized them using relevant measures from prior research. Specifically, we evaluate strategic alignment choices using three items adapted from the internal and external concept by Henderson and Venkatraman (1993). The outcome of strategic alignment is measured with 20 items adapted from relevant previous research (Markus and Keil 1994; Bhattacherjee 2001; Feinberg et al. 2002). These question items pertain to common problems regarding ERMS and satisfaction with the assistance and services from the NAA. We use technology leadership to approximate agency performance and measure individual agencies' performance according to their standing in the Golden Archives Awards contest. In Table 28-1, we summarize the items used to measure the alignment outcome, together with their respective Cronbach's alpha values, eigenvalues, and factor loadings.

Table 28-1. Summary of Question Items Used to Measure Alignment Outcome, Alpha Values, Eigenvalues, and Factor Loadings

Factor	Cronbach's Alpha	Eigenvalue	Loading
Problems in Resources	0.82	1.18	
• Deficiency on Financial Budget			0.71
• Deficiency on Human Resources			0.63
Problems in Literacy	0.94	1.68	
• Deficiency on Information Literacy			0.83
• Deficiency on Archives Knowledge			0.83
Problems in Systems Integration	0.68	1.30	
• Deficiency on Software Functions			0.68
• Deficiency on Hardware Capability			0.59
• Deficiency on Systems Integration			0.47
Problems in Digital Archives	0.83	1.85	
• Deficiency on Digital Archives Management			0.78
• Deficiency on Information Security			0.71
• Deficiency on Digital Archives			0.63
Satisfaction with ERMS by NAA	0.91	3.92	
• Satisfaction with Online-Submission			0.82
• Satisfaction with RecordsOnline			0.80
• Satisfaction with NEAR			0.72
• Satisfaction with ERCS			0.71
• Satisfaction with ERCCS			0.70
• Satisfaction with NAA Information Services			0.68
• Satisfaction with NAA Training			0.51
Satisfaction with Call Centers of NAA	0.93	3.08	
• Satisfaction with Expertise of Call Centers			0.89
• Satisfaction with Services by Call Centers			0.88
• Overall Satisfaction with Call Centers			0.75

5.2 Instrument Validation

Several domain experts reviewed a preliminary questionnaire and provided their evaluative feedback. These experts include IS managers and NAIS project managers who are highly knowledgeable about electronic record management practices in government agencies. On the basis of their assessments and suggestions, we made several wording changes, fine-tuned the language to better reach the targeted agencies and their respondents, and revised the layout design to make it visually appealing. We then conducted a pilot study to assess our survey instrument with key personnel from 10 agencies. Results from the pilot study suggest adequate validity of our instrument, which we therefore use in our formal study.

5.3 Participating Agencies and Data Collection

The e-government policy in Taiwan requires all government agencies to implement ERMS. For this study, a government agency refers to an entity within the governing body that has an annual budget from the Ministry of Audit and is autonomous in its resource allocation decision making. We contacted a total of 8,029 government agencies and sent the questionnaire packets via postal mail. The survey packet consisted of a cover letter describing our objectives and data management plan, a support letter from the NAA, and the questionnaire. Through the official reporting channel, we collected completed questionnaires and signatures from the chief officer of the participating agency. A total of 3,319 agencies completed the survey, for an effective response rate of 41.5%. We took a key informant approach by targeting records management staff, who understand the implementation and current practice of ERMS within the agency. This study also includes agencies designated as administration, business, and public school, at both central and local locations in the overall governing structure in Taiwan.

We used 20 items to assess the outcomes associated with each strategic alignment choice. We first assessed the reliability of our measurements by examining the Cronbach's alpha of each construct. As summarized in Table 28-1, all investigated outcome dimensions exhibit an alpha value greater than or close to the common threshold of 0.7, evidence of adequate reliability. We then performed a principal component factor analysis to evaluate the construct validity of the alignment outcome dimensions. As shown in Table 28-1, six factors—representing problems in capital, problems in literacy, problems in systems integration, problems in digital archives, satisfaction with ERMS, and satisfaction with call centers of the NAA—are extracted. These factors correspond to the outcome dimensions and show satisfactory convergent and discriminant validity, in that the loadings of the items measuring the same construct are considerably higher than those for any different construct, with eigenvalues greater than 1.0, a common threshold.

6. ANALYSIS RESULTS AND DISCUSSION

Our sample includes 1,450 administration agencies, 190 business agencies, and 1,679 public schools. The agencies' purposes are summarized in Table 28-2. According to our analysis, 564 participating agencies are at the central level, and the remaining (2,755) agencies pertain to local government. Representative types of the participating agencies are depicted in Table 28-3. As it shows, 1,555 of 3,319 agencies have separate record management departments, and 620 have a part-time records management staff. A total of 1,758 agencies have separate computer departments, and 988 have support staff for records management operations. We also summarize the characteristics of the respondents from the participating agencies in Table 28-4. A total of 212 agencies developed their own ERMS, 359 agencies outsourced ERMS development, 2,746 adopted the ERCS made available by the NAA, and the remaining 2 agencies used the NAA's RecordsOnline system. We also analyzed the agencies (43 central and 37 local) that received Golden Archives Awards between 2003 and 2005. Only two participating agencies followed the full-adoption alignment strategy (alignment type IV); because of this small number, we do not include this alignment type in our analysis and discussion.

Table 28-2. Summary of Participating Agencies by Purpose

Administration (n=1450)	Count	Business (n=190)	Count	Public Schools (n=1679)	Count
General Administration	775	Petroleum, Power, Tobacco	27	University	26
Police and Army	84	Liquor, Water	8	College	4
Finance and Tax	67	Transportation	116	Military School	7
Culture and Education	61	Bank	14	Police School	2
Justice	47	Hospital	25	General High School	70
Economic Affairs	80			Vocational High School	33
Traffics	59			Special Education School	6
Health	211			Junior High School	322
Social Welfare	66			Elementary	119
				School	8
				Kindergarten	11

Table 28-3. Participating Agencies: Central vs. Local Government and Levels

Central Government (n=564)	Count	Local Government (n=2755)	Count
Level 1		Level 1	
Executive Yuan	1	Taiwan Provincial Government	6
Legislative Yuan	1	Taipei City Government	73
Examination Yuan	1	Kaohsiung City Government	141
Academia Sinica	1		
Level 2 and its subsidiary		Level 2 and its subsidiary	
Ministry of Audit	25	Taipei County Government	142
Ministry of Interior	31	Yilan County Government	101
Ministry of National Defense	24	Taoyuan County Government	168
Ministry of Finance	68	Hsinchu County Government	69

(Continued)

Table 28-3. (Continued)

Central Government (n=564)	Count	Local Government (n=2755)	Count
Ministry of Education	51	Miaoli County Government	18
Ministry of Justice	42	Taichung County Government	180
Ministry of Economic Affairs	28	Changhua County Government	186
Ministry of Transportation & Communications	155	Nantou County Government	19
Department of Health	16	Yunlin County Government	119
Veterans Affair Commission	32	Chiayi County Government	154
Council of Agriculture	41	Tainan County Government	221
Central Election Commission	8	Kaohsiung County Government	175
Council of Labor Affairs	8	Pingtung County Government	183
Others	31	Taitung County Government	70
		Hualien County Government	103
		Penghu County Government	66
		Kinmen County Government	44
		Leanjan County Government	13
		Keelung City Government	56
		HsinChu City Government	47
		Taichung City Government	67
		Chiayi City Government	29
		Tainan City Government	57
		Others	248

Table 28-4. Summary of Respondents by Job Category

ERM Staffs	Count
Contracted Full-time ERM Staff	128
Dedicated Full-time ERM Staff	1889
Professional Personnel Part-time in ERM	708
Teacher Part-time in ERM	579
Computer Engineer Part-time in ERM	15

By design, central government agencies deal with issues, activities, or affairs pertinent to the national level. In Taiwan, the central government consists of agencies at four levels, whereas local government agencies are classified by three different levels. Within the central government, level 1 agencies have the ultimate administrative power and include the Executive Yuan, under which fall the Ministry of National Defense, the Ministry of Finance, and the Ministry of the Interior, the level 2 central government agencies. The National Fire Agency falls under the Ministry of the Interior and is an example of a level 3 central government agency, whereas the Keelung Harbor Fire Brigade under the National Fire Agency represents a level 4 central government agency. For local governments, the Taipei City Government is a level 1 agency, whereas the Zhongshan District Office, under the Taipei City Government, is a level 2 agency, and the Da-An Elementary School in the Da-An District is a level 3 local agency. Typically, central government agencies have larger staffs and more resources than local government agencies.

6.1 Strategic Alignments of Government Agencies in Implementing ERMS

As shown in Table 28-5, central and local government agencies obviously differ in their strategic alignment choices. Results of the Chi-square tests indicate a significant difference between central and local agencies ($p < 0.001$), as well as between agencies at different levels ($p < 0.001$). Most local agencies choose alignment type III, whereas many central agencies adopt alignment type II, which offers them more direct control. According to our findings, local agencies tend to use the ERMS provided by the NAA instead of using their own resources to build ERMS or outsource the system development. In addition, agencies at lower levels, both central and local, appear to favor alignment type III. For instance, a total of 2,500 level 3 local agencies adopted the ERCS available from the NAA at no cost.

Table 28-5. Analysis of Agencies' Alignment Choices by Administrative Hierarchy

		Alignment Type I	Alignment Type II	Alignment Type III
Central Government Agencies	Level 1	1	2	0
	Level 2	8	19	5
	Level 3	45	105	85
	Level 4	90	93	110
	Total	144	219	200
Local Government Agencies	Level 1	0	2	2
	Level 2	3	13	44
	Level 3	65	125	2,500
	Total	68	140	2,546

As summarized in Table 28-6, agencies that have a business purpose or function are more likely to adopt alignment types I or II than are agencies responsible for administration or education, as suggested by the p-value less than 0.001 in the Chi-square test.

Table 28-6. Analysis of Alignment Choices by Agencies by Agency Purpose

	Alignment Type I	Alignment Type II	Alignment Type III	Total
Administration	79 (5.5%)	201 (13.9%)	1168 (80.6%)	1448 (100%)
Business	67 (35.2%)	49 (25.8%)	74 (39.0%)	190 (100%)
Public Schools	66 (3.9%)	109 (6.5%)	1504 (89.6%)	1679 (100%)

Business-oriented agencies, such as the Bank of Taiwan, have the necessary resources and autonomy to develop and implement their own

ERMS and therefore are more likely to develop or outsource ERMS (i.e., alignment types I or II).

Table 28-7 summarizes the different alignment choices with respect to geographic regions. Results of the Chi-square tests show significant differences among the alignment choices adopted by agencies located in various geographic regions ($p < 0.001$). Agencies located in the northern region are more likely to adopt alignment types I or II than are agencies elsewhere. This finding may be partially explained by their convenient access to the technical support and system development capabilities offered by the extensive information industry that is geographically based in this region.

Table 28-7. Analysis of Alignment Choices by Agencies by Geographic Regions

	Alignment Type I	Alignment Type II	Alignment Type III	Total
Northern Region	100 (10.5%)	168 (17.8%)	680 (71.7%)	948 (100%)
Central Region	48 (6.1%)	87 (11.1%)	648 (82.8%)	783 (100%)
Southern Region	48 (3.8%)	84 (6.6%)	1,140 (89.6%)	1,272 (100%)
Eastern Region	15 (6.2%)	18 (7.4%)	210 (86.4%)	243 (100%)
Offshore Islands	1 (1.4%)	2 (2.8%)	68 (95.8%)	71 (100%)

In analyzing the specific ERMS adopted or vendors outsourced, we observe similarities, or clusters, among agencies based on their purposes or geographic locations. For example, local agencies located in the same city or county often adopt the same ERMS. Similarly, public schools located in the same city or county tend to adopt the same ERMS system. Central government agencies that serve the same purpose (e.g., administration or business) also are likely to adopt the same ERMS, perhaps because they have highly comparable functional needs and often exchange information. The satisfactory experience of one agency seems to propagate to related agencies at lower levels, such that, for example, most of the agencies under the Ministry of Interior implement the ERMS system used by the Ministry of Interior. Similar phenomena are observed among the agencies under the Ministry of Finance, the Ministry of National Defense, and the Council of Agriculture.

Our overall results, as summarized in Tables 28-5 through 28-7, support our first proposition: Government agencies that vary in purpose, geographic location, or position are likely to follow different strategic alignments in their implementation of ERMS.

6.2 Outcomes of ERMS in Government Agencies

We use ANOVA and Scheffe's posterior analysis to evaluate the difference among the alignment outcomes associated with the various choices. Table 28-8 summarizes the mean and standard deviation of each factor, together with the *p*-value and Scheffe test. As shown, agencies that choose alignment type III experience more problems in capital, literacy, and integration than in other areas. Agencies that adopt alignment type II (i.e., outsourcing) seem more satisfied with ERMS and the NAA's call centers and report fewer problems than agencies following other alignment types. The use of outsourcing services to achieve desired system integration therefore is understandably common (Pollalis 2003). As suggested by a *p*-value less than 0.001 in the Chi-square test, the data support our second proposition: Government agencies that vary in their strategic alignments for ERMS are likely to have different alignment outcomes in terms of their common problems and satisfaction with the assistance and services provided by the NAA.

Table 28-8. Analysis of Alignment Choices and Outcomes

	Alignment Type I	Alignment Type II	Alignment Type III	p-value
Problems in Capitals	5.63 (1.28)	5.49 (1.24)	6.05 (1.11)	<0.001 III > I = II
Problems in Literacy	5.75 (1.11)	5.88 (1.06)	5.96 (1.03)	0.010 III > I
Problems in Systems Integration	4.76 (1.25)	4.52 (1.36)	5.20 (1.11)	<0.001 III > I > II
Problems in Digital Archives	5.02 (1.08)	5.25 (1.12)	5.11 (1.13)	0.023 II = III = I
Satisfaction with NAA ERMS and Assistance	4.86 (0.99)	5.02 (1.03)	4.76 (1.04)	0.001 II > III
Satisfaction with NAA Call Centers	5.10 (1.11)	5.33 (1.14)	4.99 (1.16)	<0.001 II > I = III

Notes: I, II, and III in Scheffe test denote alignment types I, II, and III, respectively.

Of the 80 agencies that received Golden Archives Awards, 42 of them participated in our study. Table 28-9 shows the alignment choices by the award-winning agencies and other agencies. According to the Chi-square test, agencies that choose alignment type II are more likely to win Golden Archives Awards than are other agencies ($p < 0.001$). The winning ratio is significantly higher among agencies that outsource ERMS developments than among those that develop the system in-house or adopt the ERMS from the NAA. These agencies provide financial support for outsourcing efforts and must comply with the NAA's system requirements, functional specifications, and vendor selection criteria. According to our analysis, coordination between an agency following alignment type II and the NAA is critical. Apparently in recognition of this criticality, the NAA is expected to initiate an accreditation program in July 2006 to certify vendors qualified to develop ERMS for various agencies. Although record/archive management is not a primary activity in Porter's (1985) value chain, it is critical to government agencies, for which the development or acquisition of adequate ERMS demands significant monetary investments, specialized personnel, management involvement, and strong administrative support.

Table 28-9. Analysis of Alignment Choice and Agency Performance Measured by Winning NAA Golden Archives Awards (GAA)

	Alignment Type I	Alignment Type II	Alignment Type III
Agencies with GAA	4 (1.89%)	26 (7.24%)	12 (0.44%)
Agencies without GAA	208 (98.11%)	333 (92.76%)	2,734 (99.56%)
Total	212 (100%)	359 (100%)	2,746 (100%)

For our measurement of an agency's performance according to whether it won a Golden Archives Award, we performed stepwise discriminate analysis, in which winning the award is the target class and important alignment outcome factors are predictor variables. Among the alignment outcome dimensions studied, we find that problems in systems integration, problems in digital archives, and satisfaction with the NAA call centers are significant for distinguishing individual agencies' performance. Table 28-10 summarizes the mean and standard deviation of each alignment outcome dimension among agencies, regardless of whether they received Golden Archives Awards.

Table 28-10. Analysis of Alignment Outcomes and Agency Performance

	Agencies without GAA	Agencies with GAA
Problems in Capitals	5.976 (1.158)	6.085 (1.071)
Problems in Literacy	5.945 (1.034)	6.011 (1.192)
Problems in Systems Integration	5.104 (1.168)	4.722 (1.634)
Problems in Digital Archives	5.120 (1.132)	5.569 (1.123)
Satisfaction with NAA ERMS and Assistance	4.793 (1.035)	4.708 (1.109)
Satisfaction with NAA Call Centers	5.024 (1.160)	5.608 (1.023)

According to our analysis, agencies that received awards have fewer problems in systems integration than other agencies. Data in a record management system are exported from backend document systems, and the strategic alignment between business and technology can create favorable outcomes and improved agency performance when the agency's ERMS is integrated into the overall system (Pollalis 2003). By improving the integration between an ERMS and the related backend (document) systems, an agency can reduce human involvement, a common source of errors. Digital archives represent a logical extension in agencies' management of their official records and archives. Analysis of qualitative comments from 26 participating agencies suggests that the award-winning agencies, as a group, have greater concerns about and a better appreciation of future trends in record/archive management. From a coadaptation aspect, people adapt to a system that also evolves to meet their needs (Ackerman 2000). The call centers allow the NAA to maintain positive working relationships with agencies by providing relevant information, answering inquiries, or solving problems in a timely manner. In this vein, higher satisfaction with the call centers leads to more positive working relationships between an agency and the NAA. According to our analysis, the alignment outcome factors can explain differential performance among agencies—namely, winning versus not winning Golden Archives Awards. Hence, our data support our third proposition: Agencies that vary in their strategic alignments likely differ in their performance, as manifested by their standing in the assessment rankings for Golden Archives Awards.

7. SUMMARY

The alignment between business and technology strategies is important and can affect outcomes and organizational performance. Such alignments represent a process of continuous adaptation and change (Henderson and Venkatraman 1993) and therefore should not be considered discrete, one-time events. In e-government contexts, agencies that differ in purpose or resources should analyze and select appropriate alignment strategies for favorable (alignment) outcomes and improved agency performance. Our study shows that the alignment between the agency's business strategy and the NAA's technology strategy is essential and that different alignment choices lead to various outcomes and agency performance.

The agency's purpose, geographic region, and position within the overall government structure affect its alignment choice in implementing ERMS. Because agencies in charge of similar tasks or affairs need to exchange information routinely and frequently, their alignment choices must support commonality and interorganizational working relationships through the ERMS electronic channel and related systems (Blake 2005). It is therefore not surprising that most choose the same alignment strategy and ERMS.

Virtual agencies retain their core activities and outsource others. Their use of outsourcing arrangements may improve organizational efficiency and knowledge sharing/transfer and possibly provide better alignment between the agency's mission and national policy with greater implementation flexibility (Castro et al. 2003). Agencies also vary considerably in the resources they can expend to acquire and implement ERMS. Agencies with a business orientation often have more resources, and many adopt an outsourcing strategy. Agencies with convenient access to abundant technology support also are likely to follow the outsourcing path. In general, agencies that select the outsourcing alignment type have fewer problems and are more satisfied with the assistance and services of the NAA than are other agencies that follow self-development or adoption alignment choices. Meanwhile, local agencies that have relatively stringent resource constraints tend to adopt the ERMS made available by the NAA.

The NAA grants Golden Archives Awards to agencies that are outstanding in the operations, services, and use of ERMS. These recognized agencies are required to share their best practices with other agencies for benchmark purposes and host onsite visits. The NAA mandates all agencies visit at least one award-winning agency to be considered for Golden Archives Awards. All award-winning agencies must share their experiences and practices with agencies at the levels below them with which they interact or cooperate routinely.

Seamless integration among related systems is crucial to the ultimate success of ERMS. Typically, input to ERMS comes from backend document management systems and database systems. Such systems are autonomous and have limited compatibility, which necessitates an analysis of the different specifications needed to transfer data into an ERMS. The interface between an ERMS and a backend image system also is important and must comply with both the ERMS and existing systems. Although they may recognize the criticality of a seamless integration among document systems, database systems, image systems, and ERMS, most (if not all) government agencies in Taiwan are far from achieving ultimate integration. Some award-winning agencies proactively promote the concept of record flow, advocating a common platform for simplifying the record flow process among agencies through record capturing and confirmation. Therefore, continued efforts must advance current ERMS practice toward seamless integration.

ACKNOWLEDGMENTS

This research is partially funded by the National Archives Administration, Taiwan, the Republic of China.

REFERENCES

Ackerman MS (2000) The Intellectual Challenge of CSCW: The Gap Between Social Requirements and Technical Feasibility. Human-Computer Interaction 15: 179-203.

Arino A (2003) Measures of Strategic Alliance Performance: An Analysis of Construct Validity. Journal of International Business Studies 34: 66-79.

Ault JT, Gleason JM (2003) U.S. Government Decision Makers' Expectations and Patterns of Use of Emerging and Existing Information Technologies. Government Information Quarterly 20: 63-76.

Bacon N (1991) Information Systems Strategies in Government: Recent Survey Evidence. Journal of Information Technology 6: 94-107.

Bhattacherjee A (2001) Understanding Information Systems Continuance: An Expectation–Confirmation Model. MIS Quarterly 25: 351-370.

Blake R (2005) Complying with the Records Management Code: Evaluation Workbook and Methodology–Consultation Draft. The National Archives, UK.

Castro M, Foster RS, Gunn K, Roberts EB (2003) Managing R&D Alliances Within Government: The 'Virtual Agency' Concept. IEEE Transactions on Engineering Management 50: 297-306.

Caudle SL, Gorr WL, Newcomew KE (1991) Key Information Systems Management Issues for the Public Sector. MIS Quarterly 15: 171-188.

Chen YN, Chen HM, Huang W, Ching RKH (2006) E-Government Strategies in Developed and Developing Countries: An Implementation Framework and Case Study. Journal of Global Information Management 14: 23-46.

Chircu AM, Kauffman RJ (2001) Limits to Value in Electronic Commerce-Related Information Technology Investments. Journal of Management Information Systems 17: 61-82.

Chircu AM, Lee HD (2003) Understanding IT Investments in the Public Sector: The Case of E-Government. In: Proceedings of the Ninth Americas Conference on Information Systems (AMCIS), FL.

Crittenden WF, Crittenden VL, Stone MM, Robertson CJ (2004) An Uneasy Alliance: Planning and Performance in Nonprofit Organizations. International Journal of Organization Theory and Behavior 7: 81-106.

Dawes SS, Prefontaine L (2003) Understanding new models of collaboration for delivering government services. Communications of The ACM 46: 40-42.

Feinberg RA, Hokama L, Kadam R, Kim I (2002) Operational Determinants of Caller Satisfaction in Banking/Financial Service Call Center. The International Journal of Bank Marketing 20: 174-180.

Fine AH, Thayer CE, Coghlan AT (2000) Program Evaluation Practice in the Nonprofit Sector. Nonprofit Management and Leadership 10: 331-339.

Fountain JE (2001) Building the Virtual State: Information Technology and Institutional Change. Washington, DC: Brookings Institute.

Garg AK, Joubert RJO, Pellissier R (2005) Information Systems Environmental Alignment and Business Performance: A Case Study. South African Journal of Business Management 36: 33-53.

Griffin A (2004) Records Management Capacity Assessment System. Archival Science 4: 71-97.

Grover V, Kettinger WJ (2000) Business Process Change: A Reflective View of Theory, Practice, and Implications. In: Zmud R (ed.) Framing the Domains of IT Management: Projecting the Future Through the Past. Cincinnati, OH: Pinnaflex Educational Resources.

Heeks R (2000) Reinventing Government in the Information Age. London: Routledge Press.

Henderson JC, Venkatraman H (1993) Strategic Alignment: Leveraging Information Technology for Transforming Organizations. IBM Systems Journal 32: 4-16.
Kaplan RS (2001) Strategic Performance Measurement in Nonprofit Organizations. Nonprofit Management and Leadership 11: 353-370.
Kelly KL (1998) A System Approach to Identifying Decisive: Information for Sustainable Development. European Journal of Operational Research 109: 452-464.
Markus ML, Keil M (1994) If We Build It, They Will Come: Designing Information Systems that People Want to Use. Sloan Management Review 35: 11-25.
Mullen PR (2003) The Need for Government-wide Information Capacity. Social Science Computer Review 21: 456.
Pollalis YA (2003) Patterns of Co-Alignment in Information-Intensive Organizations: Business Performance through Integration Strategies. International Journal of Information Management 23: 469-492.
Porter M (1985) Competitive Advantage. New York: The Free Press.
Public Record Office Victoria (PROV) (2003) PROS 99/007 (Version 2) Management of Electronic Records. Public Record Office Victoria, Australia.
Reich BH, Benbasat I (2000) Factors that Influence the Social Dimension of Alignment between Business and Information Technology Objectives. MIS Quarterly 24: 181-113.
Scott G (2003) The Learning Government. OECD Journal on Budgeting 3: 55-69.
Soh C, Markus ML (1995) How IT Creates Business Value: A Process Theory Synthesis. In: Proceedings of the Sixteenth International Conference on Information Systems, 29-41.
Sprague RH Jr. (1995) Electronic Document Management: Challenges and Opportunities. MIS Quarterly 19: 29-49.
Stephens DO (1997) Demark: Toward Global Leadership in Electronic Archives and Records Management. ARMA Records Management Quarterly 31: 62-71.
Stephens DO (1998) Megatrends in Records Management. ARMA Records Management Quarterly 32: 3-9.
Stone MM, Crittenden WF (1994) A Guide to Strategic Management in Nonprofit Organizations. Nonprofit Management and Leadership 4:193-213.
Tallon P, Kraemer KL (1999) Process-oriented Assessment of the Alignment of Information Systems and Business Strategy: Implications for IT Business Value. University of California, Irvine, Center for Research on Information Technology and Organizations. I.T. in Business. Paper 142.
Tallon P, Kraemer KL, Gurbaxani V (2000) Executives' Perceptions of the Business Value of Information Technology: A Process-Oriented Approach. Journal of Management Information Systems 16: 145-173.
Tapscott D (1995) Digital Economy: Promise and Peril in the Age of Networked Intelligence. New York: McGraw-Hill.
Thurston A (1997) Records Management as a Public Sector Accountability Function. International Journal of Government Auditing 24: 7-9.
Venkatraman N, Henderson JC, Oldach S (1993) Continuous Strategic Alignment: Exploiting Information Technology Capabilities for Competitive Success. European Management Journal 11: 139-149.
Von Hippel E (1994) 'Sticky Information' and the Locus of Problem Solving: Implications for Innovation. Management Science 40: 429-439.
Walker RG (2001) Reporting on Service Efforts and Accomplishments on a 'Whole of Government' Basis. Australian Accounting Review 11: 4-16.
Weinstein A (2005) NARA Enters New 'ERA' of Electronic Records Management. Information Management Journal 39: 22-24.

Whitson TL, Davis L (2001) Best Practices in Electronic Government: Comprehensive Electronic Information Dissemination for Science and Technology. Government Information Quarterly 18: 79-91.

Young J (2005) Electronic Records Management on a Shoestring: Three Case Studies. Information Management Journal 39: 58-60.

SUGGESTED READINGS

- Blake R (2005) Complying with the Records Management Code: Evaluation Workbook and Methodology–Consultation Draft. The National Archives, UK.
- Chen YN, Chen HM, Huang W, Ching RKH (2006) E-Government Strategies in Developed and Developing Countries: An Implementation Framework and Case Study. Journal of Global Information Management 14: 23-46.
- Crittenden WF, Crittenden VL, Stone MM, Robertson CJ (2004) An Uneasy Alliance: Planning and Performance in Nonprofit Organizations. International Journal of Organization Theory and Behavior 7: 81-106.
- Pollalis YA (2003) Patterns of Co-Alignment in Information-Intensive Organizations: Business Performance through Integration Strategies. International Journal of Information Management 23: 469-492.
- Public Record Office Victoria (PROV) (2003) PROS 99/007 (Version 2) Management of Electronic Records. Public Record Office Victoria, Australia.

ONLINE RESOURCES

- Electronic Records Management, The National Archives, UK, http://www.nationalarchives.gov.uk/electronicrecords
- Victorian Electronic Records Strategy (VERS), Public Record Office Victoria (PROV), Australia, http://www.prov.vic.gov.au/vers/vers/default.htm
- The Electronic Records Archives Program Management Office (ERA-PMO), National Archives and Records Administration (NARA), USA, http://www.archives.gov/era/program-mgmt.html
- National Archives of Australia, http://www.aa.gov.au
- National Archives Administration (NAA), Taiwan, http://www.archives.gov.tw
- Association of Records Managers and Administrators (ARMA), http://www.arma.org/

- Center for Technology in Government, State University of New York-Albany, http://www.ctg.albany.edu/
- Dawes S S, Burke B, Dadayan L, Embar S, and Kwon H, "Building State Government Digital Preservation Partnerships: A Capability Assessment and Planning Toolkit, Version 1.0," http://www.ctg.albany.edu/publications/guides/digital_preservation_partnerships
- Pardo T A, Burke G B, and Kwon H, "Preserving State Government Digital Information: A Baseline Report," http://www.ctg.albany.edu/publications/reports/digital_preservation_baseline
- National Electronic Commerce Coordinating Council, "Regulatory Impacts on E-Records Management Decision," http://www.ec3.org/Downloads/2005/e-records_management.pdf
- National Electronic Commerce Coordinating Council, "Creating and Maintaining Proper Systems for Electronic Record Keeping," http://www.ctg.albany.edu/publications/reports/proper_systems
- Pardo T A, Dawes S S, and Cresswell A M, "Opening Gateways: A Practical Guides for Designing Electronic Records Access Programs," http://www.ctg.albany.edu/publications/guides/gateways
- The National Digital Information Infrastructure and Preservation Program at the US Library of Congress, http://www.digitalpreservation.gov

QUESTIONS FOR DISCUSSION

1. How can a policy regulator evaluate the requirement of individual agencies to develop a global information infrastructure?
2. How can a government agency maintain a balance when allocating resources between core and supportive activities, e.g., documentation?
3. The biggest challenge in implementing an electronic records management system is the culture shift for electronic records management. How can administrators and managers in government agencies encourage their employees' involvement in the development, implementation, and actual use of ERMS?
4. This study represents a point of departure for examining agencies' business–technology alignments in e-government. What additional investigations are needed to analyze such alignments and empirically assess their effects on agency performance and service quality?

Chapter 29

RESEARCH AND DEVELOPMENT OF KEY TECHNOLOGIES FOR E-GOVERNMENT[1]

Case Studies in China

Chunxiao Xing, Jijiang Yang, Wei He, Yong Zhang, and Chen Chen

Research Institute of Information Technology,Tsinghua University, Beijing, China, 100084 (xingcx@mail.tsinghua.edu.cn)

CHAPTER OVERVIEW

Government informatization has become an important component of the national information infrastructure and a major factor affecting international competitive power. E-government construction is regarded as one of the most important tasks for the national economy and society informatization in China today. TH-DGRC has been researching and developing e-government projects since 2003. In this chapter, we first introduce China's e-government history, progress, challenges, and plans. Next we propose a methodology for an e-government plan and design – GIA (Government Informatization Architecture) – and discuss its key reference models. Third, we present the government information resource catalog and exchange systems. Finally, we describe two case studies in Beijing's municipal government.

[1] Supported by the National Natural Science Foundation of China under Grant (No. 60473078); and the Beijing Science and Technology Program under Grant (No. Z0004029040811).

1. INTRODUCTION

Since the 1980's, the rapid development and wide application of information technology have brought new innovation to global industry. Informatization [6] is a process of change that features (a) the use of informatization and IT [information technologies] to such an extent that they become the dominant forces in commanding economic, political, social, and cultural development; and (b) unprecedented growth in the speed, quantity, and popularity of information production and distribution. Informatization is a major trend in international economics and social development. It is also an important flag for measuring a country's or region's modernization. The Chinese government is pushing for the informatization of government, economics, and society. Informatization has become the inevitable choice for accelerating China's industrialization and modernization. It is also the key to promoting China's productivity, enhancing its national comprehensive strength and international competitive power, and protecting national security.

1.1 E-Government History in China

The development of China's e-government has experienced four phases as follows [1,2]:

- The pilot phase (1973-1983). The informatization of Chinese government can be traced back to 1975, when the central government first applied electronic computers to economic planning and data statistics.
- The startup phase (1984-1990). During the sixth five-year plan (1981-1985), computers were mainly used for data processing and management information systems. During the seventh five-year plan (1986-1990), 12 application systems were proposed, including the Police Information System and the National Economic Information System, and the design/construction process began. During the later period, office automation (OA) grew into fashion.
- The development phase (1991-2000). In 1992, the government sectors in China were required to construct OA systems. In 1993, the Chinese central government and the former Ministry of Electronics Industry (now part of the Ministry of Information Industry) launched the "Golden Projects" as a series of separate administrative capabilities. Initially, there were three projects known as Golden Bridge, Golden Card, and Golden Customs. Many other projects were subsequently announced, but the first three were the most remarkable and the most important in China. In January 1999, the Government Online Project

was formally launched by China Telecom and the State Economic and Trade Commission's Economic Information Center along with the information offices of more than 40 central government ministries and commissions. It interconnects the government offices of every province, autonomous region, and municipality.

- The full-scale promoting phase (2000-now). In December 2001, the first meeting of the National Informatization Leading Group (NILG) was held and government's informatization was proposed. In fact, e-government was regarded as the chief task of the NILG. From then on, e-government construction entered a new period of overall advancement and rapid development. The NILG met again in 2002 and 2003. They issued a framework of e-government and promulgated several official documents to guide China's e-government practice.

1.2 E-Government Progress in China

Nowadays, the main contents and tasks of China's e-government are:

- To construct an integrated network platform for central and local governments;
- To construct portals for local governments, which are led by the central portal;
- To build four public fundamental databases: population fundamental database, corporation fundamental database, macro/social economics developing fundamental database, spatial and natural resources fundamental database;
- To construct and enhance twelve business systems (i.e. "Twelve Golden Projects");
- To enhance standardization of e-government;
- To enhance construction of e-government network and information security, including publishing "Governmental Information Public Regulation" and "Electronic Signature Law of PRC";
- To encourage development and utilization of government information resources;
- To enhance training of civil servants.
- By 2005, the main areas of progress in China's e-government were:
- Strategy: the National Informatization Leading Group (NILG) passed "National Informatization Strategy 2006-2020" at their fifth meeting, on November 3, 2005, which highlighted several targets:
- Regulation: "Electronic Signature Law of PRC" on April 1, 2005;

- Evaluation: according to the UN Global E-government Readiness Report 2005 [7], China's e-government preparation index was 0.5078, moving up 10 positions to 57th position.
- Portal construction: The central portal, http://www.gov.cn, opened on January 1, 2006. "Government Web Sites' Performance Evaluation in 2005" states that in 2005 96.1% of the Ministries and Commissions had web sites, up by 2.7 percentage points over 2004; 81.3% of local governments had web sites, up by 8.4 percentage points over 2004.
- Standards: On December 26, 2005, the National E-government Standardization General Working Group published the records of the published e-government standards.
- Demonstration projects: In June 2006, the e-government demonstration project was accepted. This is a key science and technology project of the 10th five-year plan which includes 23 sub-projects, 16 demonstration sites, and 7 local governments.

E-government in China is developing steadily and has become an effective approach to transform government functions and improve administrative efficiency. Government sectors use information technology to extend publicity, strengthen information resource sharing and collaboration, and improve public services. The framework of China's e-government has been promulgated, construction of the web sites and applications have made clear progress, the central government portal is formally underway, the web site functions are becoming richer, and portals are becoming an important window for the government to provide management and services. The effects of informatization in customs, taxes, audit, finance, public security, and social labor protection are obvious and have played important roles in enhancing the government's supervision and management capabilities and increasing the capabilities of law enforcement and public service.

1.3 E-Government Challenge Issues in China

Although China has made great progress in e-government construction, there are still many challenges.

- The strategic plan and top design, legislation, and standardization of e-government lag behind the e-government construction. Some officers blindly regard the e-government construction as prestige projects, which leads to many repetitions and "stove-pipe" projects.
- The vertical systems (such as "Golden Projects") are strong and horizontal systems (such as cross-agency projects) are weak, which creates isolated systems—"Information Islands."

- The information resources of the government have not been fully developed and utilized yet.
- The security of e-government information, network, systems of e-government is still a difficult problem. The performance evaluation of e-government projects has not been taken seriously.
- There is an imbalance in e-government development between the east and the west of China, and between city and rural area as well.
- Many e-government developers focus on information systems implementation and pay little attention to government affairs.

Solving the above-mentioned problems will remain a major research focus in the next few years.

1.4 E-Government Plan in China

The Chinese government has recognized the challenges and made concrete plans. In the "11th five-year plan" (2006-2010), the main e-government goal is: the e-government network will cover most of the country and the information resource publicity and sharing schemas will come into being. Government portals will become an important channel of government information publicity, and more than 50% of administration admission projects will be processed online. To achieve such goals, five transformations must be promoted:

- For e-government, to change the emphasis from one-sided infrastructure construction to deep applications;
- For information networks, to change from separate construction to integrated utilization of resources;
- For information systems, to change from isolated running to interconnecting and resource sharing;
- For information management, to change from emphasizing self-service to emphasizing public service;
- For information sites, to change from self-construction and self-management to depending on social powers.
- Seven tasks have to be accomplished to enhance construction of e-government:
- Deepen the application of e-government, further expand the scope and content of government affair publicity, and publish government information in a timely and correct manner.
- Promote interconnection and exchange between application systems and fully explore the efficiency of e-government.

- Promote information sharing and business collaboration and improve the application level of e-government.
- Set up a national unified e-government network, make master plans by taking all factors into consideration, and integrate the resources.
- Protect information security and execute the "Active and Integrated Preventing" policy
- Promote legislation and emphasize training.
- Set up a proper operational mechanism for construction, scientific management, efficient operation, and maintenance of e-government.

Top leaders of the central government have recognized the importance of e-government and related projects. At China's e-government working meeting on June 12, 2006, Wen Jiabao, the Premier, emphasized the importance of accelerating e-government construction and pushing innovation in administrative systems. He also highlighted the role of e-government in improving government efficiency and public service, as well as in creating conditions for better public participation in economic and social activities. Huang Ju said that enhancing e-government construction promotes the self-innovation and construction of government agencies, enhances the capability of government administration, raises operational efficiency, and improves the quality of public service. To date, this work has achieved great success and gained important preliminary results. All central and local governments are required to implement e-government carefully, to enhance collaboration and protect security. The goal is to enhance national economics and social projects with systematic development of e-government. Zeng Peiyan, another vice Premier, stated that for the purpose of sustainable development, government sectors should adapt the institution of e-government according to relevant policies and try to find a development approach for e-government that fits in with China's specific environment.

1.5 Digital Government Research Center at Tsinghua University

The Digital Government Research Center (TH-DGRC) of Tsinghua University is a virtual research center based at the Research Institute of Information Technology (RIIT), School of Public Management, School of Economic Management, which researches way and means to apply information technology in government, to reconstruct government management, and to develop advanced systems to meet government requirements. The center carries out research on e-government theory and practice for efficient s e-government projects from multiple perspectives, including:

- Providing technology consultation and master planning and deployment schema for central and local governments.
- Participating in key government informatization projects.
- Setting up the communication network for e-government and assisting with the journal "E-Government."
- Training high-level professionals and government information officers (CIO).
- Developing software component library for e-government.
- Applying and researching national and enterprise's projects on E-government.

The groups in the center include: optimized management of the governmental workflow, performance evaluation, government resource management, government information security, architecture design, government network, and software components. In addition there is a training unit, mainly aimed at the government information officers, which teaches an introduction to the basic thoughts on international and domestic e-government, e-government architecture design and planning, data model in e-government, the component model of the basic software, case studies, and so on.

The chapter is organized as follows. In Section 1 we briefly introduced China's e-government history, progress, challenges, and plans. Then in Section 2 we propose a methodology for an e-government plan and design, including a discussion of GIA (Government Informatization Architecture) and its key reference models. Thirdly, we present government information resource catalog and exchange systems in Section 3. Finally, we describe two case studies in Beijing's municipal government in Sections 4 and 5.

2. GIA: GOVERNMENT INFORMATIZATION ARCHITECTURE

2.1 Introduction

As described above, more and more problems are emerging as information technologies are applied to government. The strategic plan and top design for e-government construction is becoming a major priority for China. In order to guide government informatization processes in China, in March 2006 the State Council Informatization Work Office proposed and promulgated a comprehensive state e-government framework, including five parts (Figure 29-1): Service and Application systems, Information Resource, Infrastructure, Legislation and Standardization, and Management mechanism.

The framework gives a blueprint of the whole e-government and guidelines for its construction on a very macro level. It also provides the foundation for IT investment analysis. Although it provides policy direction and a strategic plan, it does not give a concrete solution for building e-government and integrating the different parts.

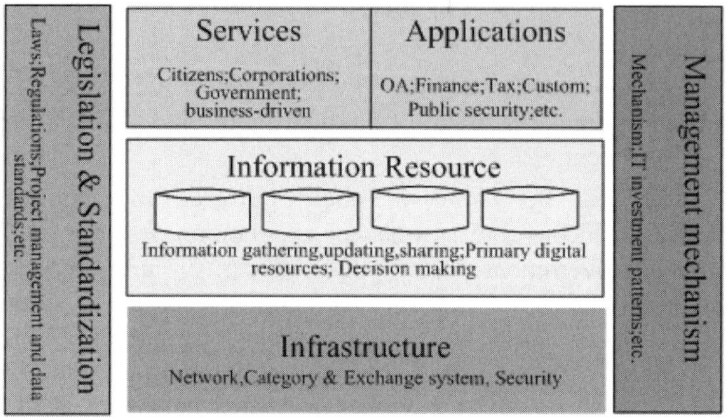

Figure 29-1. State E-Government Framework

2.2 GIA (Government Informatization Architecture) Project

The GIA project, supported by Beijing's government, tries to propose a comprehensive solution to direct e-government implementations at the operational level. Its main objectives are:

- To propose a systematic and unified theory and methodologies to guide e-government implementations, including supporting technologies and related standards.
- To build a business-driven architecture to describe e-government and enhance collaboration among government agencies.

GIA is a three-dimension structure:

- Reference models dimension: To describe six reference models, including Performance Reference model, Business Reference model, Service component Reference model, Technology Reference model, Data Reference model, and Security Reference model.
- Lifecycle dimension: This dimension describes the lifecycle of system integration when carrying out an IT project. When the system is implemented, the government informatization goes up to a new

stage. Maturity models can be used to evaluate the level of e-government.

- Implementation dimension: This dimension describes the main methodologies of enterprise modeling. In different phases of carrying out a project, different methods can be used to depict the model and system structure.

2.3 Reference Models

E-government reference models provide a common communication platform among different domain experts when a government is implementing informatization. They are the benchmarks for building actual models and realizing target models. The GIA project follows the Zachman framework [3] and uses FEA (Federal Enterprise Architecture) and e-GIF (e-Government Inter-operationality Framework) for reference [4] [5]. A framework of six reference models is proposed for China's e-government.

The following paragraphs give a brief description of each reference model. Each model is referred to by FEA structure and description, but its real contents are based on China's realities.

2.3.1 Business Reference Model (BRM)

The BRM provides a framework facilitating a functional (rather than organizational) view of the government's lines of business (LoBs), including its internal operations and its services for citizens, independent of the agencies performing them.

The BRM is structured into a tiered hierarchy representing the business functions of the government.

2.3.2 Service component Reference Model (ScRM)

The ScRM is a business-driven, functional framework classifying Service Components according to how they support business and performance objectives. It serves to identify and classify horizontal and vertical Service Components supporting government agencies and their IT investments and assets. The model aids in recommending service capabilities to support the reuse of business components and services across the government.

The ScRM is organized across horizontal service areas, independent of the business functions, providing a leverage-able foundation for reuse of applications, application capabilities, components, and business services.

2.3.3 Technology Reference Model (TRM)

The TRM is a component-driven, technical framework categorizing the standards and technologies to support and enable the delivery of Service Components and capabilities. It also unifies existing agency TRMs and e-government guidance by providing a foundation to advance the reuse and standardization of technology and Service Components from a government-wide perspective.

Aligning agency capital investments to the TRM leverages a common, standardized vocabulary, allowing interagency discovery, collaboration, and interoperability. Agencies and the government will benefit from economies of scale by identifying and reusing the best solutions and technologies to support their business functions, mission, and target architecture.

2.3.4 Data Reference Model (DRM)

The DRM is a flexible, standards-based framework to enable information sharing and reuse across the federal government via the standard description and discovery of common data and the promotion of uniform data management practices.

2.3.5 Performance Reference Model (PRM)

The PRM framework is designed to clearly articulate the cause-and-effect relationship between inputs, outputs, and outcomes. The framework builds from the value chain and program logic models. This "line of sight" is critical for IT project managers, program managers, and key decision-makers to understand how, and to what extent, key inputs are enabling progress toward outputs and outcomes. The PRM captures this "line of sight" to reflect how value is created as inputs (such as Technology) and used to create outputs (through Processes and Activities) which, in turn, impact outcomes (such as, Mission, Business, and Customer Results).

2.3.6 Security Reference Model (SRM)

SRM is also a component-driven framework. It is used for technologies that support and enable the delivery of service components and capabilities, and also for service components that support and enable business processes. It categorizes the standards, security components, and infrastructures. It gives a guideline for building secure systems when implementing e-government, from hardware to software.

2.4 Comprehensive Architecture for Government Informatization

A comprehensive architecture for government informatization is illustrated in Figure 29-2. This architecture has been described by Dr. Li and Dr. Chen in their book "The Overall Design for Enterprise Informatization," but there are some new elements added. The architecture is based on a series of reference models, with a maturity model to judge the e-government level at a more macro level.

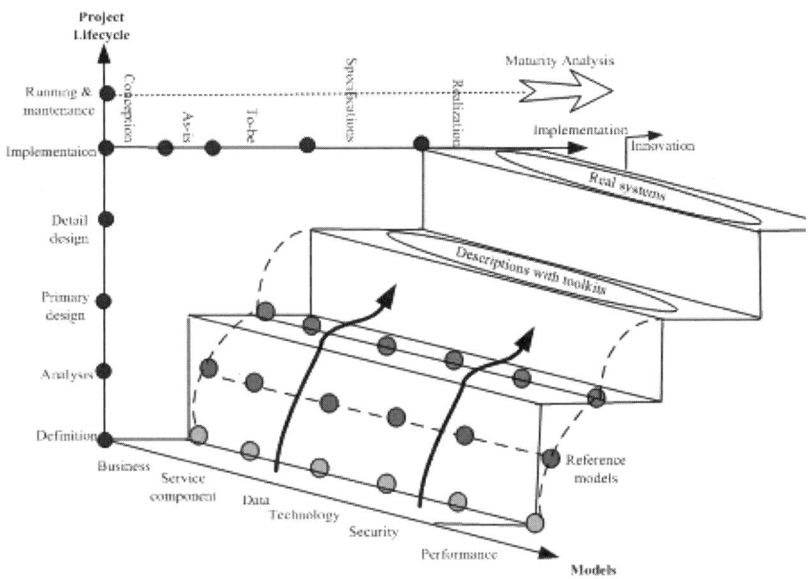

Figure 29-2. Comprehensive Government Informatization Architecture

First is the model dimension which describes the different models of government or its sections. In different phases, the models are exhibited as different patterns.

The second dimension is the lifecycle dimension. There are six phases, including project definition, analysis, primary design, detailed design, implementation, and running and maintenance. When the system has been implemented, a maturity model is used to evaluate the level of e-government.

Third is the implementation dimension. It describes the different methodologies used in different phases. After analyzing the conceptual model, "as-is" models are built based on six models. Under the mission and strategy direction, "to-be" models are designed based on the "as-is" model and reference models. With the help of variant modeling tools, the different models are mapped to systems' specifications. The new systems are built according to these specifications.

The whole architecture is a stair structure meant to reflect the processes and levels of the government system. It must be emphasized that the 'stairs' are repetitious, that is to say, all of the processes are continuously iterative. A maturity model is used to evaluate the result of each iteration.

3. GOVERNMENT INFORMATION CATALOG AND EXCHANGE SYSTEM

3.1 Introduction

GIA mainly focuses on high-level strategic plans and architecture designs for e-government. This section describes the technology, standards, and solutions for information sharing and exchange. An important task in China's e-government construction is to develop and utilize government information resources. In order to collaborate and share information resources across agencies, China has launched a project to establish a standard Catalog system and an Exchange system. Under the direction of the Chinese State Council Informatization Work Office and the State Standardization Management Board, universities and research institutes have collaborated with enterprises to do pre-research on each system. Two drafts have been worked out: "The Catalog System of Government Information Resources" and "The Exchange System of the Government Information Resources." TH-DGRC is one of the main members of the working group.

Government Information Resources refers to the information generated, collected, invested, or managed through government administration processes. To construct an infrastructure of government information resources and exchange resources between agencies, it is necessary to solve the following basic questions (3WH):

- What resources need to be exchanged across agencies?
- Where is the content of government information resources?
- Who provides or uses the resources? How could the services for these resources be publicized? How will people find and use them?

3.2 Catalog System

The Catalog system for government information resources can organize, store and manage their metadata. The sharing of government information resources can be implemented through publishing, searching, locating, and managing the metadata.

3.2.1 System Architecture

The Catalog system architecture is shown in Figure 29-3. A catalog system primarily consists of a catalog service system of government information resources. Its supporting environment includes software, hardware, and networks, standards and specifications, and a security system.

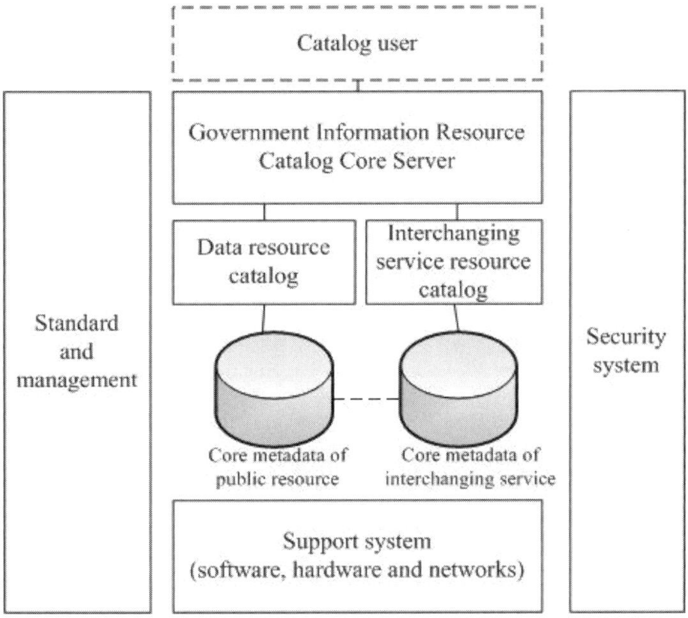

Figure 29-3. Architecture of Catalog System

3.2.2 Business model of catalog system

The business model of the Catalog system is shown in Figure 29-4. Every government agency depends on its business systems to build the public resource database and exchange resource database, from which the provider will extract the characteristics of the public resources and exchange services to generate the public resource catalog and exchange service catalog. The user will query the catalog through the one-stop government information resource catalog system.

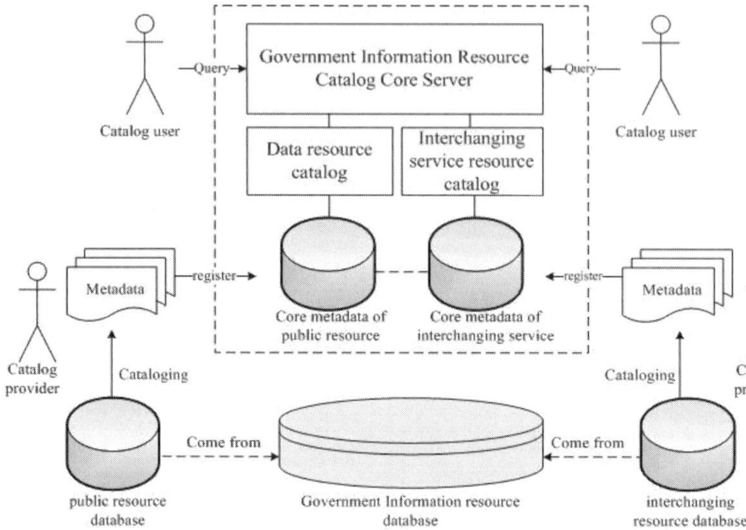

Figure 29-4. Catalog System Business Model

3.2.3 Functions of catalog system

The basic functions of the Catalog system include catalog, registration, publication, search, and maintenance. Catalog provides function to edit the core metadata of the public resources and exchange service resources. Registration means that the catalog provider must register with the resource manager including resource metadata and service metadata. Publication allows publication of the metadata content through the catalog server. Search invokes the standard interface to applications and supports querying the metadata.

3.2.4 Workflow of catalog system

The Catalog system's workflow is shown in Figure 29-5. The central and local governments catalog core metadata of public resources and exchange service resources, registering with the manager through the metadata registration system. The manager publishes the registered catalog contents. The user sends catalog queries to the manager through the government resource catalog's one-stop service and results are receives results in turn.

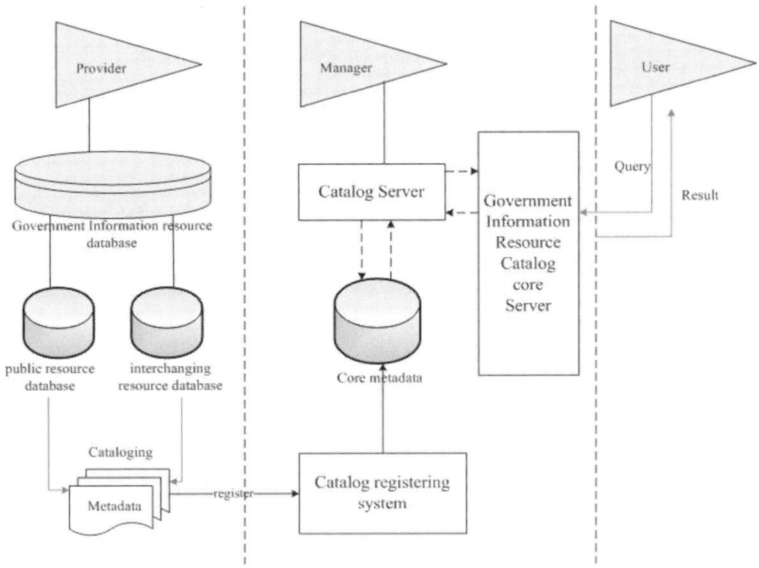

Figure 29-5. Workflow of the Catalog System

3.3 Exchange System

Based on the national e-government network and the security infrastructure, the Exchange system for government information resources provides an infrastructure for the exchange and sharing of government information resources across agencies and projects.

3.3.1 System Architecture

There are three roles in the Exchange system: provider of resources, user of resources, and catalog center of resources. The provider is responsible for making resources available by publishing them in the catalog. Users can search and query the resource catalog. The catalog center manages the catalog organization (by category) and user services. Users can also exchange information with providers directly without querying the catalog.

The Exchange system architecture consists of service models, exchange platforms, information resources, and technical standards and administration mechanisms, as shown in Figure 29-6. The business applications of different service models access and operate resources by invoking the exchange service provided by the exchange platform. Technical standards and administration mechanisms guarantee exchange and share resources.

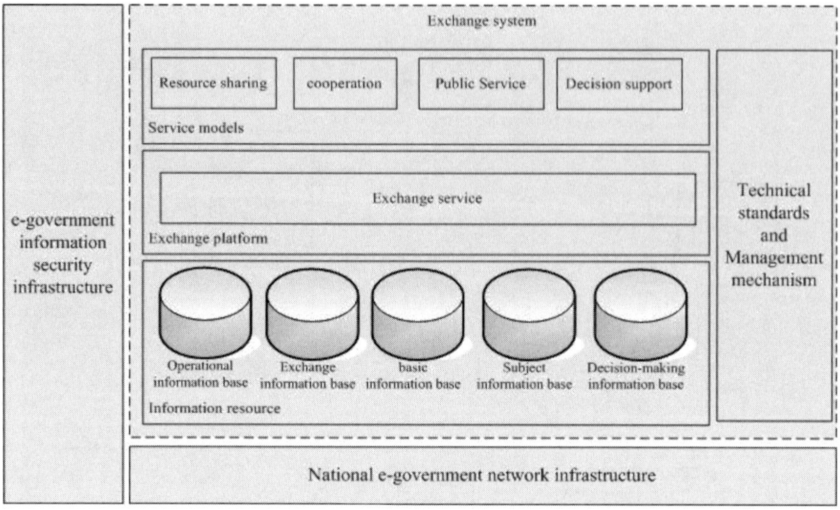

Figure 29-6. Architecture of Exchange System

Service models are the representation of the main government information resources provided by the exchange system for governmental applications, which include resource sharing, business collaboration, public service, and decision-making support.

The information resources refer to the shared information that is involved in exchange, and includes:

- Business information database – an information database for the business information systems of every government agency.
- Exchanging information database – a temporary information database built for information exchange between government agencies.
- Fundamental information database – including Population database, Corporation database, Natural Resources and GeoSpatial Information database, Macro-economy database.
- Shared theme database – a shared information database designed for every kind of business application theme.
- Decision-making support database – the shared information database provides information to aid decision-making and analysis.
- There are three types of technical standards:
- Standards related to information resources, such as the sharing of indicators and information coding.
- Standards related to interconnection and interoperation of technical platforms.
- Standards related to technical management.

The management mechanism refers to the management regulations and rules for construction, operation, and management of the Exchange system.

3.3.2 Concept model of exchange system

The concept model (shown in Figure 29-7) consists of a central exchange node and terminal exchange nodes. The central node manages the information exchange service between terminal nodes and can generate a shared information database if required.

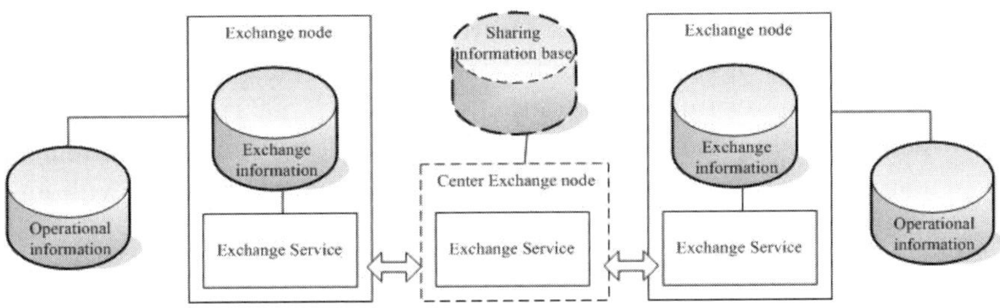

Figure 29-7. Concept Model of Exchange System

- Business information is the government information resource that is produced and managed by central and local governments;
- Exchange information is the government information resources stored by terminal nodes to be exchanged.
- The shared information database provides consistent government information resource storage for many terminal nodes. Each terminal node can access the database according to certain rules. In the Exchange system the shared database is optional.
- A terminal exchange node is the starting point or destination for exchange of government information resources. It can execute transformation between business information and exchange information, and realizes the transportation and process of government information resources through the exchange service.
- The central node provides a point-to-point or point-to-multipoint information routing, reliable information transportation, and other functions. There can be zero or several central exchange nodes between two terminal nodes.
- The exchange service is a collection of operations that includes the transportation between the exchange nodes and the processing of

government information resources. Different combinations of exchange services support different service models.

3.3.3 Exchange models

There are three main exchange models for information resources across agencies.

- Central exchange model: Information resources are stored in a shared database; the information provider or the user can exchange information resources by accessing the shared database.
- Distributed exchange model: Information resources are stored in all of the business information databases; the provider and the user of information resources can directly transport the resources between them by using the exchange service provider through the exchange nodes. This exchange mode includes exchange with or without a center.
- Mixed model: Combines the central exchange mode and distributed exchange mode. Information exchange can be accomplished not only by shared information database but also through direct access or through the central exchange node.

3.4 Applications of Catalog System and Exchange System

The Catalog system and Exchange system have been investigated and tested in Shanghai, Tianjin, Beijing, and Foshan in the Guangdong province in China. The initial results have been implemented through the practice of local informatization processes, based on business requirements and directed by actual government applications. The prototypes have proven the standards of the Catalog and Exchange systems and provided important guidelines for further promotion and implementation.

4. MEDW: MACRO-ECONOMY DATA WAREHOUSE

The "11th five-year plan" (2006-2010) described earlier in section 1.4 also calls for building four large-scale basic databases, which will include information on population, juridical persons, resource environment geographic information, and the macro-economy. Beijing MEDW is one of the key node databases in the state macro-economy basic database. In this section, we will discuss the design, development, and implementation of MEDW.

4.1 Introduction

The MEDW project, supported by the Beijing Statistics Bureau, is a comprehensive information management system. By using data warehouse technology, metadata specifications, and classification technology, MEDW can provide all kinds of information on various aspects of Beijing's macro-economy and social development. The functions include ETL (extract, transform, and load), search, query, OLAP/OLTP, forecast, decision-making, document content management, and personalized information display based on a web-based report tool.

MEDW includes the following information:

- Relating to the the national statistics and survey system: national gross economy, agriculture, industry, construction, transportation and postal industries, wholesale and retail trade, catering industry, population, employment, labor wages, investment, science and technology, price, urban and rural living standards, urban socio-economic development, prosperity, and international statistics results.
- Relating to government agencies' statistic and survey systems: finance, banking, insurance, taxation, balance of payments, foreign trade, customs statistics, labor protection, tourism, education, culture, sports, health, civil, jurisdiction, land resources, water resources, environment, meteorology, and etc.
- Other non-conventional investigations.

4.2 System Architecture

MEDW has been designed with four layers: collection layer, data layer, logical layer, and representation layer (shown in Table 29-1 and Figure 29-8).

Table 29-1. The Description of MEDW Architecture

Layer	Function
Presentation layer	• Provide multiple classified navigations • Support queries on the raw data or information integrated indicators • Provide ad hoc queries • Provide visualization and interactive analysis • Offer customized user interface
Logic layer (platform layer)	• A uniform service interface based on Web Service • Uniform log-on and privileges management • Uniform modules management

(Continued)

Table 29-1 (Continued)

Layer	Function
Data layer	• Neutral data model • Immigration tool based on XML • Data modeling tool
Collection layer (Data Source)	• Harvest system based on the data exchange system • Customized interface for data harvesting • Manual data reporting system

4.3 System Functions

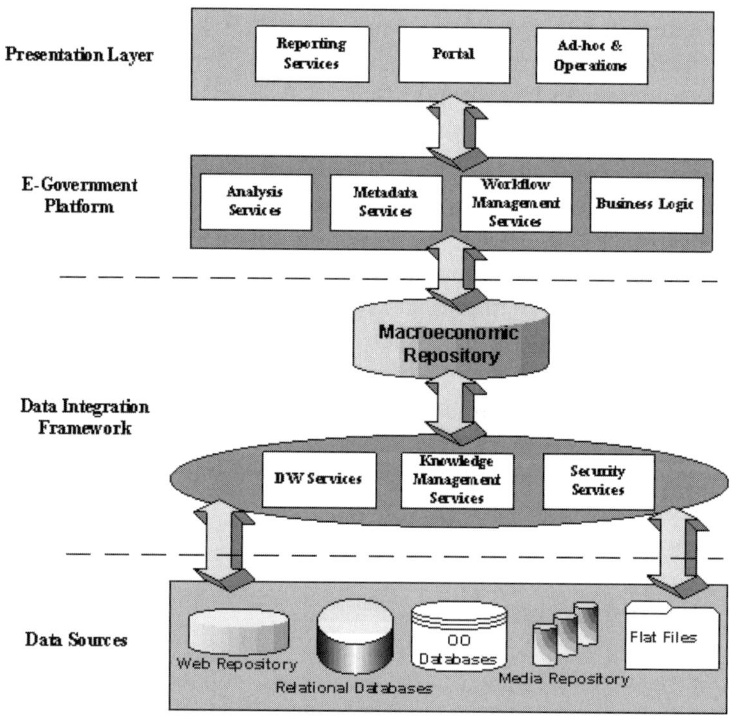

Figure 29-8. System Architecture

1. Statistical processing
   This function has the following capabilities:
   - Provide statistical methods that are used to generate macro-economic indicators from lower level data, calculate formulas, and coverage.
   - Build the corresponding data processing and calculation capabilities, including server/mainframe system, massive data central storage system, relational database management system, logical component

set of statistical data processing algorithms, and application server that is a middleware system to deploy computing logic components.

2. Knowledge base

This function can analyze the trend of the various macro-economic indicators, and give the statistics results on a year-to-year basis or month-to-month basis.

By using data warehouse technologies and a multi-dimensional database, it can do further mining of macro-economic indicator data; focus on the logic relationships of constraints, influence, and interaction; and perform all kinds of relativity analysis.

3. Monitoring and alerting

Macro-economy forecasting provides perspective on overall national development, investigating and predicting the size, growth rate, scale, and development level of the national economy.

Macro-economy decision-making refers to the processes that decide how to manipulate the macro-economy variables and realize them based on current national economic development. The intent is to efficiently adjust the relationship between total demand and total supply, and to keep the development of the national economy healthy and sustainable way.

The system can set a threshold for each macro-economic indicator and separate different operating areas with different colors. If an indicator exceeds the threshold, it will give warning automatically (such as flashing on the screen).

Options include the ability to select, combine, and sort alerting indicators, adjust thresholds, and define and modify the operating area.

4. Public information publishing and service

- Information portal
- Publishes the major macro-economic indicators dynamically
- Provides detailed query service on the relevant macro-economic indicator data
- Defines and auto generates reports
- Provides online analysis of the macro-economic indicators (OLAP)
- Defines and assists with generating the report template showing the macro-economy situation.

The macro-economy data integration platform and the MEDW homepage are shown in Figures 29-9 and 29-10 respectively.

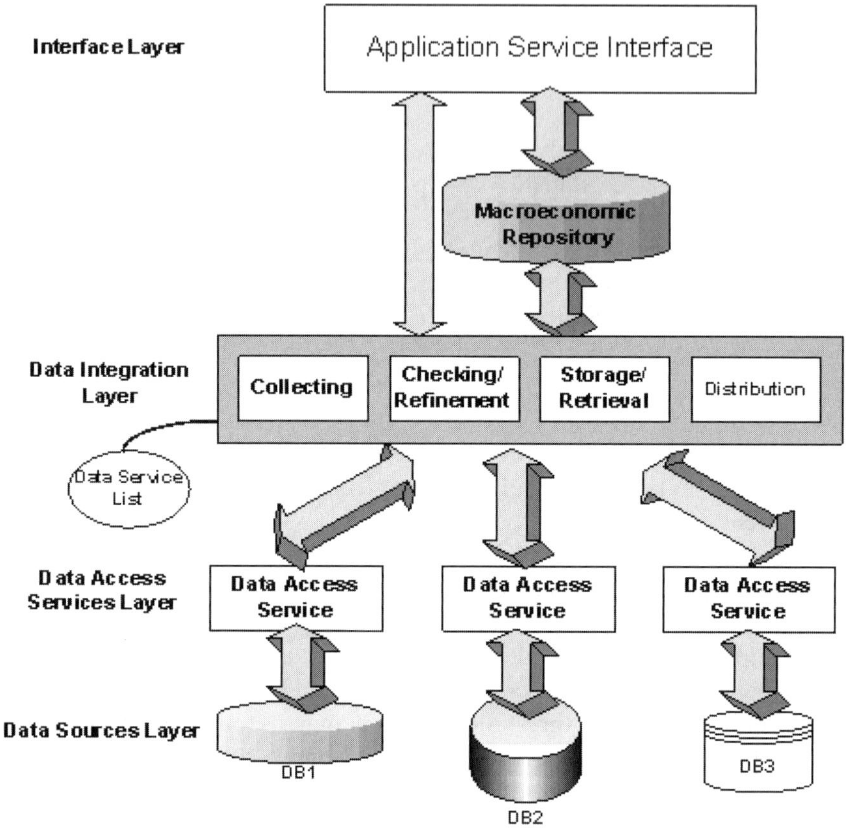

Figure 29-9. Data Integration Platform

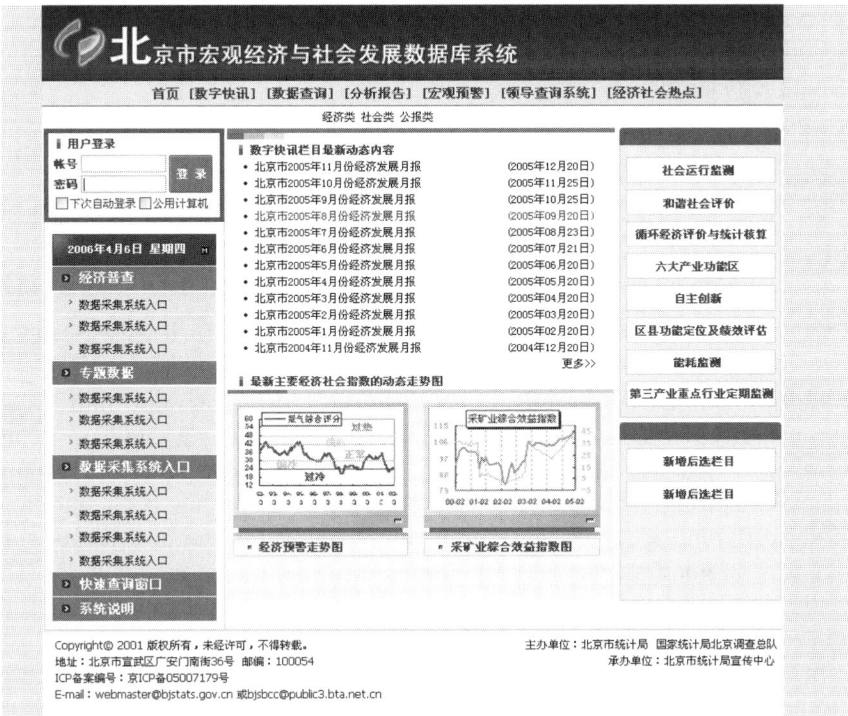

Figure 29-10. Homepage of MEDW

5. MEANS: MODEL OF EXAMINATION AND APPROVAL ON NETWORK

In this section, we will discuss another case study – MEANS – for e-government construction in Beijing's municipal government.

5.1 Introduction

Administrative license is a very important function at different levels in China's government. It means that administration agencies license citizens, enterprises, and other organizations to do specific activities based on related laws. For example, if one wants to set up a company, he/she applies to the Industry and Commercial Management (ICM) agency. After being verified and registered by ICM, a person gets licensed and can start their business. With the recent development of market economies, China's government has eased up on licensing regulations. But in order to enhance market supervision and management and increase the capability of public resources allocation, the government still retains licensing authority for some matters through legislation.

The key characteristics of administrative license are:

- it is based on requisitions;
- it is a government checkup behavior based on related laws;
- it is a kind of activity to manage society;
- it should be approved by formal document, format, date, stamp, etc;
- different projects need to be approved by different levels of government.

Before China's "Administrative License Law" was put into effect, Administrative License was called "Administrative Examination and Approval." Usually, the processes to license a project involved multiple agencies. Getting a project licensed thus involved going back and forth among different agencies and filling out various information forms since there was no good mechanism for sharing information among agencies. This greatly decreased the government's efficiency and the customers' (citizens and corporations) satisfaction level.

In Beijing, there are more than one thousand matters that require licenses. Different matters stand for different business processes in or across government agencies.

5.2 Administrative License Platform

In order to improve quality of service and increase government efficiency, Beijing built the "Administrative License Platform (ALP)" which can optimize the business licensing processes. It uses standard and unified models (including data and processes, etc) to integrate different agencies that are involved in licensing activities. The architecture of ALP is illustrated in Figure 29-11.

The architecture consists of three main parts:

- Online service platform (OSP): its main functions are to provide a unified portal for requisitions. Customers (including citizens and corporations) can submit their required documents, inquire on progress and results, and receive the government notification.
- Collaborative work platform (CWP): its main functions are to share information and other data assets among different agencies. When the system receives a requisition, it harmonizes the work processes according to process models. The documents and related information are transferred to the distributed working systems (including different agencies and low level governments). The working system can

exchange data with other related agencies through CWP. The processes' states and results are returned back to OSP for customer inquiry and tracking.

- Online management platform (OMP): used to manage the above two systems.

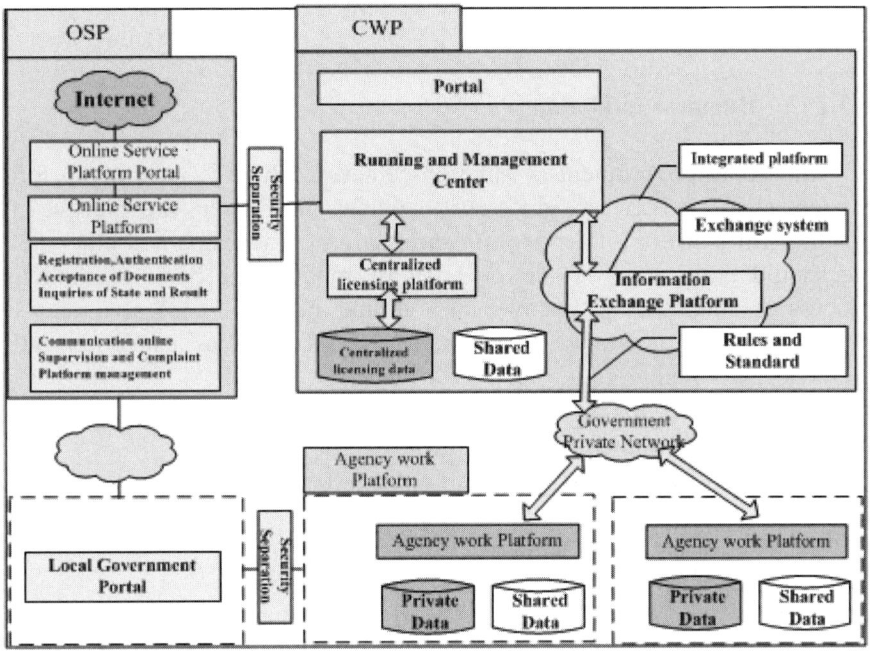

Figure 29-11. Architecture of ALP

5.3 Business Modeling for Administrative License

5.3.1 Objects

The administration licensing processes are very complex, especially those that involve several agencies. The goals of the MEANS project, which was supported by the Beijing Economical Information Center (BEIC), included:

1. Public service-oriented business modeling. Currently, the business modeling is still agency-centered. Customers still need to know which agencies provide what kind of services. It is especially difficult for business analyzers and system designers to find a main threshold from

among thousands of complicated business processes (corresponding to different matters).

2. Developing a business model for Administrative License in Beijing. A standard and exact business model can help government make sense of what they are really doing and what customers really want and then optimize or reengineer the work processes. It can also aid system designers to design the system from the government point of view.

5.3.2 Business modeling

Traditional government is function-centered. There is little or no information sharing between different agencies. In order to improve the government's quality of service in Administrative Licensing and other areas, we should build a service-driven business model. The business modeling process is intended to uncover and define business processes that are provided to customers by government and its agencies using normative methodologies and tools.

The following list of AL business questions can help to model the service-oriented business.

1. What business service can government deliver to customers?
2. How can customers quickly find the service that they need?
3. Which business process links with the service?
4. What kind of documents should customers prepare?
5. Are there sub-functions that involve different agencies?

1. Data collection

Before developing the service-oriented Administrative License business model, BEIC, who is responsible for the ALP project, collected matters that required licensing. The collections are agency-based. For each matter, the main information included:

- The name of the matter and its identification (defined by law and local regulations);
- Who is responsible for the matter?
- What processes are required from the customer point of view?
- What documents and forms are submitted?

It should be indicated that so-called matters collected from agencies are different from the matters mentioned by customers. The matters mentioned by customers might be the composite of a few governmental matters (accomplished by different agencies). Usually, 'To do a matter' means a customer wants to apply for an Administrative License from the government. From the government viewpoint, it might be business processes across different agencies. Each governmental matter is just one of many processes to accomplish a customer's matter.

2. Analysis

There are more than one thousand matters that are involved in customer service from the government point of view. Governmental matters should be mapped to customers' matters. Each governmental matter can be analyzed by the following questions.

- Whom does the governmental matter serve?
- What matter does the governmental matter help the customer "to do"?
- Who should accomplish the matter (i.e., this process is executed by whom, agencies level)

In order to cover all the government business (in the license area) from the customer viewpoint, analyzing business itself is not enough. The service targets should also be considered.

This can be expressed by Figure 29-12. In the figure, the horizontal axis represents the services offered by government; the vertical axis represents the service targets. Each cross-point in the figure represents one matter the customer needs to do. For example, Point A represents a non-local resident who does matters related to tax. There is little or no relativity between the different cross-points.

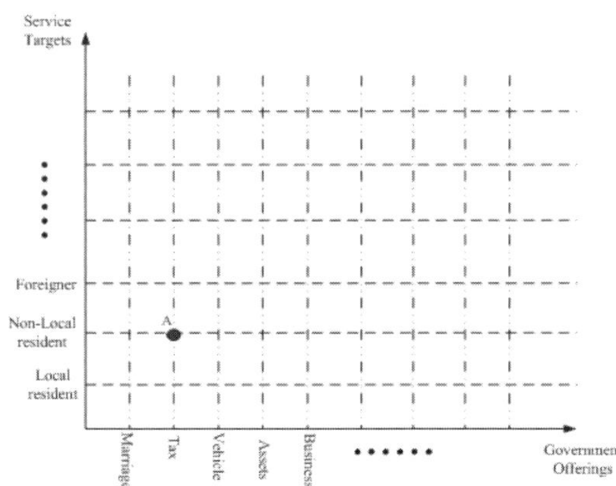

Figure 29-12. Two-dimension Administrative License Business Model

3. Grouping and mapping

According to the above analysis, service targets and government offerings are categorized respectively.

- Service targets are classified as two types: Individual and Corporation. Each category is described as a three or four-tiered hierarchical structure. For example, individual citizens consist of local resident, non-local resident, foreigner, etc. For corporations, we have two steps. Firstly, we decompose it in terms of types. Then we decompose each type in terms of industries. For example, corporations consist of inner-capital, outer-capital, private, state-owned, foreign-capital, etc. Each type of corporation can decompose as different industries, such as Medicine, Restaurant, Mine, etc.
- Government offerings are described as the line of business (LoB) and sub-functions. LoBs are grouped according to lifecycle methods. That is to say, from the beginning (birth for individuals or set up for corporations) to the end (death for individuals or closing for corporations), what kinds of matters that individuals or corporations involve government matters? Sub-functions are the more detailed classifications.

Combining the above two aspects can make up a complete service-oriented and function-driven business model. The governmental matters (defined by laws and regulations) can be mapped to sub-functions. Each sub-function represents a specific business process for a specific type of service object (citizens or corporations).

5.3.3 Unified business process models

Business process models reflect the operations of sub-functions. The unified business process model combines different information in one model, including data, performance, and roles. In Front-office, the model can tell customers how to do a matter, what they should submit, and when they get results. In Back-office, the model can be the foundation of system analysis. Each sub-function can be constructed as a service component in ALP.

5.4 Practice on ALP

Currently, on ALP (Administrative License Platform), the government matters (offerings) are still agency-centric, not customer-centric. Although they also categorized the government business, it is still not easy for customers to find what they want. According to the model described above, the customers can easily find what they want. They don't need to know who is responsible for the matter. Even if they have to interact with the government directly, they can easily know exactly where they should go and what they should prepare. Organizational borders have become much less relevant.

6. CONCLUSIONS

In this chapter, we introduced China's e-government history, progress, challenge issues, and plans. GIA is proposed based on the State E-Government Framework and other developed countries' experiences. Two of the key technologies in e-government implementation were introduced, i.e., government information resource Catalog system and Exchange system, Two case studies were given: the Macro-economy Data Warehouse and a business model for Administrative License in Beijing's municipal government.

In the future, we will further investigate the theory, methods, and technologies for e-government construction in China. Based on China's needs and realities, we will develop components for e-government implementations. We will consider business reconstruction, performance evaluation, and combining ICT with government businesses.

ACKNOWLEDGEMENTS

This work was supported by the National Natural Science Foundation of China, the Beijing Science and Technology Program, Beijing Municipal Commission of Development and Reform project, and Beijing Municipal Statistics Bureau project. We would like to thank Hu Qingcheng, Chen Zaiben, Chen Cheng, Zhang Xiaohu, Lin Demiao, and Cao Jiawei for their helpful research and development work on the case studies. We would also like to thank Li Yong and Gao Jing for drawing and translating some of the figures in the chapter.

REFERENCES

1. Changsheng Wang, E-government Blue Book China E-Government Development Report, Social Science Literature Press, 2004
2. Zhiguang Shan, Xinyou Li, Zhongming Wang, Jiajun Ning. Policies and practice of e-government construction in China. IEEE International Conference on E-Commerce Technology for Dynamic E-Business, 2004. pp:366 - 369
3. Zachman, Enterprise Architecture, http://www.zifa.com/framework.html, Accessed in 2006.2 .

4. http://www.e-gov.gov
5. http://www.govtalk.gov.uk
6. Wang, Georgette. Treading different paths: informatization in Asian nations. Norwood, NJ: Ablex. 1994
7. http://www.unpan.org/e-govkb/global_reports/05report.htm

SUGGESTED READINGS

- Li Qing, Chen Yuliu, "Overall Design for Enterprise Informatization (Chinese)", Tsinghua University Press, 2004.
- Changsheng Wang, "Blue Book of Electronic Government: China e-Government Development Report No.1," Social Sciences Documentation Publishing House, 2003
- Raghu Ramakrishnan, Johannes Gehrke. Database Management Systems. The McGraw-Hill Companies, Inc. 2003
- Pan-ning Tan, Michael Steinbach, and Vipin Kumar, "Introduction to Data Mining", Pearson Education, Inc. 2006
- Carol O'Rourke, Neal Fishman and Warren Selkow, "Enterprise Architecture Using the Zachman Framework", published by Course Technology, a division of Thomson Learning, Inc. Boston, MA (2003). ISBN: 0-619-06446-3. Publication date: April 2003.
- Jiawei Han, Micheline Kamber., "Data mining". Morgan Kaufmann Publishers, 2001
- Finn V. Jensen, "Bayesian Networks and Decision Diagrams", Springer. 2001.
- Spirtes, P.,Glymour,C., and Scheimes, R. Causation, "Prediction and Search", New York. 1993
- Roger S. Pressman, "Software Engineering – A Practitioner's Approach", Six Edition. McGraw-HILL, 2005
- Subhash Bhatnagar, "E-Government: From Vision to Implementation: A Practical Guide with Case Studies", Sage Publications, 2005
- Irwin Miller, Marylees Miller. "John E.Freund's Mathematical Statistics with Applications". Prentice Hall,2003
- Roger S. Pressman, "Software Engineering – A Practitioner's Approach", Six Edition. McGraw-HILL, 2005
- Subhash Bhatnagar, "E-Government: From Vision to Implementation: A Practical Guide with Case Studies", Sage Publications, 2005

ONLINE RESOURCES

- Beijing Administrative License Platform, http://eservice.beijing.gov.cn/helpservlet?command=ABOUT (Chinese)
- BIRT (Business Intelligent Report Tool) project, http://www.eclipse.org/birt/
- China e-Government Standards. http://www.egs.org.cn/
- Beijing municipal government portal, http://www.beijing.gov.cn/
- Beijing Statistical Information Net Portal, http://www.bjstats.gov.cn/
- Federal Enterprise Architecture (FEA), http://www.whitehouse.gov/omb/e-gov/a-1-fea.html
- E-Government Interoperability Framework Version 6.1 e-Government Interoperability Framework Version 6.1. http://www.govtalk.gov.uk/interoperability/egif.asp
- SOA and Web services, http://www-128.ibm.com/developerworks/webservices
- Digital Resources Management System, http://drms.riit.tsinghua.edu.cn
- SOA and Web services. http://www-128.ibm.com/developerworks/webservices
- Digital Resources Management System. http://drms.riit.tsinghua.edu.cn

QUESTIONS FOR DISCUSSION

1. What is GIA? How can GIA be used for e-Government practice?
2. Describe how to best design a strategic plan and design for e-Government projects. What are some of the practical and effective methods and steps?
3. What is FEA architecture? What differences are there among EA, FEA, E-GIF, and GIA?
4. What's the relationship between data elements and a metadata registry?
5. What is a Catalog system and an Exchange system? How are they used?
6. Describe an approach for designing a massive Macro-economy database or data warehouse. How are data models of statistic databases built?

Chapter 30

NEW ZEALAND'S 2006 CENSUS ONLINE

A Case Study

Rowena Cullen

School of Information Management, Victoria University of Wellington, Wellington, New Zealand (rowena.cullen@vuw.ac.nz)

CHAPTER OVERVIEW

For the first time, in 2006, the five yearly New Zealand Census was made available for completion and return online. This chapter discusses the grounding of the Online Census project within Statistics New Zealand's overall strategy for the 2006 census, as well as New Zealand's e-government goals, its multi-channel strategy, and its Bicultural and Disability strategies. The chapter then outlines how the project was set up, how the teams were established, and their relationship with other aspects of the overall Census project. The chapter describes the details of the Online Census option itself, the distribution of user ids, the construction of the web site and interface design, user support, and how the data was collected. Critical decisions related to estimates of uptake, load demand, and the choice of technology partners are discussed as well as the technology itself. Key factors in the success of the project, such as the identification of potential risks, especially risks associated with key stakeholder groups, and the communications strategy employed are also covered. In conclusion, the final uptake of the Online Census option, post-census evaluation undertaken, and some comparisons with other countries are presented.

1. INTRODUCTION

Statistics New Zealand conducts a census of population and dwellings every 5 years, in accordance with the New Zealand Statistics Act (1975). Until the current year, data collection for the census has been a manual process in which a form for each individual, and a dwelling form for each discrete dwelling, is delivered to each private household and other types of accommodation and residential institutions in the country (such as motels, hospitals and prisons). Completion of the forms is mandatory for each individual and household, although the individual form may be completed on behalf of children or incapacitated adults. The forms are collected shortly after Census night, and the data entered into a database for analysis. The data collection stage of the census, Statistics New Zealand's largest field-based activity, is an obvious candidate for enhancement by the use of information and communication technologies.

The 2001 census coincided with the formation of the E-government Unit within the State Services Commission and the launch of the first New Zealand e-Government strategy, which included in its mission statement: "*By 2004 the Internet will be the dominant means of enabling ready access to government information, services and processes*" (State Services Commission 2003*)* Immediate deliverables included as many government forms online as possible. (State Services Commission 2001) In 2003, the Mission was extended to include goals for 2007 and 2010:

- By June 2007, networks and Internet technologies will be integral to the delivery of government information, services and processes.
- By June 2010, the operation of government will have been transformed through its use of the Internet.

At the same time, it was realised that not all citizens would want, or were able to engage with government online, and a Channel Strategy was developed that would endorse the principle that: "People will have a choice of channels to government information and services that are convenient, easy to use and deliver what is wanted. (State Services Commission 2004)." Throughout its entire development period the Online Census 2006 was required to be grounded in the developing e-government strategy, and meet these various e-government goals.

The significance of the Online Census project derives from its place within the New Zealand e-government strategy, but also from the fact that the Census is one of the few compulsory activities that the entire New Zealand public is required to carry out (while voter registration is mandatory for all citizens 18 years and over, not all citizens are required to complete a tax return, and the census also includes overseas visitors in the country on Census night.) In addition, New Zealand was one of the first countries in the world to attempt to offer a multimodal census form, both online and in print, in both the national languages, (English and Maori, the language of the indigenous people of New Zealand), and in a form accessible by screen readers for those with visual disabilities.[1] The final, and perhaps most significant factor in the project is the fact that census data is collected on one nominated day in a five year period, and that everyone in New Zealand at the time, citizens and visitors, are required to complete their form on that date or as close to it as possible. As a project, it presents a microcosm of planning, implementation and evaluation, focused on a few key objectives, that must either deliver within a tightly defined time frame, or be deemed to fail. Government, in such circumstances, cannot afford to fail.

This chapter discusses the lengthy planning process that led to the offering of the New Zealand Census Online in 2006, the way in which the project was managed, the selection and application of technology, the development of the teams working on it, organisational development factors, and aspects of knowledge management and knowledge sharing that emerged during its implementation. The chapter then reports on its reception by the citizens of New Zealand, and concludes with some reflections on factors identified as critical to its success by Statistics New Zealand staff, and a brief discussion on its contribution to the New Zealand e-government strategy.

2. LITERATURE REVIEW

Given the uniqueness of a project such as the Online Census, there is little literature available on this specific activity of government in a digital environment. Only a few other jurisdictions have attempted a trial let alone a full scale implementation of an online census. This is partly because of the developmental state of e-government globally, and the periodic timetabling of census activity. Spain, Norway, Australia and Canada and the United States were known to have conducted trials, and Switzerland to have completed a full option. (Reuters 2006). Singapore successfully offered its citizens the option in their 2000 census. Advantages in the Singapore online exercise were identified as follows:

> The advantages of Internet Enumeration outweigh the potential risk factors. Respondents enjoy greater privacy, as their information will be transmitted directly to the Department's database. Furthermore, the form-filling experience over the Internet will be a positive and interactive one.

---

[1] In the two previous censuses, 1996 and 2001, the forms had been available in both English and a bilingual Maori and English version.

> User-friendly help features and explanatory notes will be provided instantaneously when required. The system will also perform simple on-line checks, and prompt the respondent to re-enter data that are clearly wrong or inconsistent. For further convenience, partially completed questionnaires could be saved and retrieved at a later time for completion.
>
> From an operational perspective, Internet enumeration has many advantages. Most of the data collected from the Internet would already be electronically coded, thus reducing data entry and coding at the back end. Furthermore, there are substantial manpower savings since interviewers are not required to "canvass" information from the population. (Geok and Leong 1999)

In their 2006 census, to be conducted shortly after the New Zealand census, Australia and Canada were planning to offer the online option country-wide.

Such developments represent something between the second and third stages of e-government development in Darrell West's taxonomy: "2) the partial service delivery stage; (3) the portal stage, with fully executable and integrated service delivery" although the characteristics of an online census exercise perhaps represent more the second stage where [citizens] can request and use online services and manipulate informational databases to a limited extent. Still, the offering of online services is sporadic and their number is limited. Furthermore, there is infrequent posting of privacy and security statements on homepages, and accessibility of Web sites to people with either disabilities or poor English-language skills is limited. (West 2004)

West's four stages, from simple electronic bill-board to interactive democracy with public outreach and accountability enhancing features, outline some aspects of the transformation of government that the development of interactive e-government services is predicted to lead to. But this anticipated transformation is difficult to define.

As West notes, digital delivery systems, which are 'non-hierarchical', nonlinear, interactive, and available twenty four hours a day have led some commentators to predict the Internet will transform government within what he describes as "the classic model of large-scale transformation" producing "revolutions in individual behavior and organizational activities." (West 2005, 5) However, as he also notes, "not all technological innovation leads to large-scale transformation. An alternative model stresses incrementalism." (West 2005, 5) While a project such as this, in which an interactive online experience is offered alongside traditional channels, may raise the expectations of citizens for further and more regular online interaction with government, the question of the extent to which this occurred in this case, and the extent to which a project narrowly focused on one specific interaction with citizens, rather than agency to agency interaction, or within agency interaction, must be considered carefully. As West further notes, government agencies' use of technology is affected by many other factors, including "institutional arrangements, budget scarcity, group conflict, cultural norms, and prevailing patterns of social and political behavior. These may favor more gradual change, which is not in itself to be ignored".

The successful implementation of an online census requires an understanding of many issues, some of which relate to the use of online forms, and, in particular, internet security and privacy. While a number of jurisdictions at both state and national level have successfully implemented online tax filing and payment systems, albeit with relatively low uptake in some cases (West 2005a, Wang 2003), reports on the success or otherwise of online options for other mandatory citizen requirements, such as compulsory voter registration, are relatively rare. (de Vuyst and Fairchild 2005) But implementation of online systems on this scale usually entail consideration of additional factors that are now being discussed in the emerging e-government literature, socio-economic and cultural factors affecting citizens' ability and willingness to interact electronically with government, barriers and motivators to doing so, and the digital divide. (Cullen 2006) High rates of usage are necessary to achieve predicted cost savings and efficiencies for both state and citizens, government must meet rising expectations of citizens for electronic services equal to those available in the private sector, and public acceptance depends on clearer communication of both the benefits, and developing confidence in the systems themselves. (West 2005, 100)

Finally, the successful implementation of a one chance project such as the online census is grounded more in good project management, than in emerging concepts of e-government, and the transformation of government. Any transformational value of the exercise may lie as much in the introduction of good business practice to government than in anything related to the changing relationship between citizens and government. And yet, if that relationship is to change, the practices that lead to trust and an ongoing business relationship in the commercial world may turn out to be a valuable lesson for government agencies. The basic tenets of project management and IT vendor relationships are as critical to e-government projects as they are to any enterprise information system or e-commerce project, including the establishment of wide-ranging project teams, inclusive of key stakeholders. (Krysiak et al. 2004)

As academic management consultant Kathy Schwalbe notes, good project management depends on attention to four domains:

- project human resource management, is concerned with making effective use of the people involved with the project;

- project communications management involves generating, collecting, disseminating, and storing project information;
- project risk management includes identifying, analyzing and responding to risks related to the project;
- project procurement management involves acquiring or procuring goods and services for a project from outside the performing organisation. (Schwalbe 2004, 10)

Each of these requires the application of well established project planning tools, and techniques, in order to cope with the stringent demands arising from the nature of projects - defined as unique temporary undertakings, involving considerable uncertainty, within constraints of scope, time and cost. (Schwalbe 2004, 4-5) This particular project, constrained by the nature of a 5 yearly census, which is especially unique in that it required participation in some form from every human being in the country on one specific night, across all socio-economic and ethnic groups, and developed within an ambitious e-government programme, would require close attention to all four domains.

3. SETTING UP THE PROJECT

Statistics New Zealand began planning for an online option in the 2006 Census almost immediately after the completion of the 2001 Census. Clear objectives were set for the project within the wider objectives of the Census itself. The specific objectives of the online census option were:

- improving participation in the census process;
- improving aspects of census data quality;
- building capability for the 2011 census and beyond;
- reducing costs and freeing resources to maximise value for money.

In addition, wider societal and cross-government objectives were also defined:

- [meeting] the expectation of citizens for an electronic method of interacting with government; and
- [complying with] Government strategic direction, including E-government strategy, Maori Language Strategy, and Disability Strategy.

Social benefits of the project identified in relation to these key drivers focused on providing choice and convenience to respondents, reducing a trend towards lower participation in the census, and providing access [online] in both the Maori language and to the visually impaired. Economic benefits anticipated included "spreading the cost and risk of a future technology 'big hit' by undertaking development and learning in the 2006 Census," achieving fiscal savings, and gaining experience in statistical data collection for Statistics New Zealand's other projects, as well as other large scale e-government interactions with citizens. The fiscal savings anticipated included reducing collection and data entry costs, form production and warehousing costs associated with the collection and storage of the printed forms. This would enable Statistics New Zealand to shift resources to activities focused on enhancing the participation of social groups more difficult to reach. Internally, objectives constantly kept in mind by the teams working on the project, and articulated by the General Manager, Census, are simply stated as:

- choice (for respondents);
- learning (for Statistics New Zealand);
- knowledge sharing (with other agencies and other jurisdictions); and
- data integration (across the paper-based and online data collection processes).

Throughout 2002 an organisational structure was developed to respond to these objectives, and teams with appropriate skills put in place under the leadership of the General Manager, Census 2006. Staff were recruited with appropriate skills where necessary, and members of other groups within Statistics New Zealand were co-opted for the development period. One critical and very deliberate appointment was that of a Project Manager for the Online Census (within the Methods and Operations Business Unit), who brought extensive IT and project management skills to the core team. Members of the other teams related to the project had responsibility for all aspects of the Census within their field of control, as well as for the Online Census. Thus, the Project Manager of the Field Management Operation, within the Data Collection Unit, had responsibility for liaising with, and setting in place procedures for Area Managers and District Supervisors, in relation to both the delivery and collection of the physical forms, and the online option. Similarly, the Census Communications Manager, had responsibility for communicating with the general public and news media information concerning the whole of the census project, including the online option.

3.1 The Online Census

The system being developed emerged as follows: the printed census forms, one of which was to be completed for each dwelling in the country (the dwelling form), and the individual form, to be completed by or on behalf of every individual in the country, were to be delivered to each dwelling in the country, beginning on the 20 February, in preparation for Census night, March 7 2006. Census collectors were required to visit every private household/property and other types of residential accommodation or institutions, enquire how many people lived there, code and hand over the appropriate number of forms (including additional dwelling forms if there was more than one dwelling on the property), note the name of the person to whom they were given, and enquire if anyone would want to complete the forms online. A five-point script was given to each collector, and was to be followed exactly. Those who indicated they wanted to complete the form(s) online were given a sealed envelope containing an Internet PIN number, which in conjunction with the Internet ID provided on the census form, would provide a unique logon for each individual. Forms were still assigned and left for those who stated they would like to use the online form, in case anything prevented them from doing so. The envelope carried details of minimum system requirements on the outside and instructions on the inside, in both English and Maori, the URL of the census form, and the Internet PIN.

The web site itself (http://www.stats.census2006.govt.nz), maintained separately from the general census information web site (http://www.stats.census.govt.nz) for security reasons, was made available from three days before the census form delivery operation commenced on February 20th 2006, until the end of March 2006. In order to fulfil the objective of choice, and inclusiveness, the form was able to be accessed and completed by anyone with a Windows, Mac or Linux operating system who had an internet browser that was either Internet Explorer v4.0 and above (excluding Macintosh platforms), Netscape Navigator v6.0 and above, Mozilla v1.0 (including Firefox), Safari v1.2, or Opera v7.10 and above, and whose computer was SSL 128bit enabled.[2] A toll-free helpline prominently displayed on both the unfolded envelope and every single web page of the online form, was available to assist anyone who encountered problems logging on or completing the form. An email accessible helpdesk was also available on the web site.

The site was available for a period of six weeks, although users were required to enter data relevant to their location, means of travel to work etc., in relation to the Census night itself. After logging on to the form, users were able to spend up to an hour completing the form before the session terminated, primarily for security reasons. The form was designed by the Statistics New Zealand's Questionnaire Design Consultancy as a single scrolling page, with minimal graphics, to encourage completion, provide a

---

[2] That is, with Secure Socket Layer encryption

sense of control to the user, reduce download times, and support dial-up access. It was a dynamic form; in response to completion of some data elements, responses might be queried if they conflicted with other responses, (through a pop-up dialogue box) or questions which were no longer relevant (e.g. marital status if the respondent was under 16 years of age) would become less visible. The form was also designed so that responses could be corrected before submission, and selected options that a user wanted to change could be reversed. A final submission section gathered and offered key data for confirmation, and if these key fields had not been completed, requested this information again. These items matched the key items on the printed form, that collectors were required to check for when they collected completed forms. A final pop-up screen specifically requested formal confirmation of the validity of data submitted.

Respondents wishing to complete their form using New Zealand's other official language, Maori, could access on the home page the alternative Maori version of either the dwelling form or the individual form. All menu options, help buttons, etc. appeared in Maori, although English translations were available by clicking on an English language button (Reo Ingarihi) on each section, or through mouse rollover. Responses for which free text was permitted (18 questions out of 47) could be entered in English or Maori. The screen reader version of the English online form was available from a hidden selection on the initial screen.

The form itself was designed to replicate as closely as possible the printed form, so as to eliminate any possible impact on the quality of the data based on the medium being used, while still maintaining a user friendly, and platform-neutral user interface. Additional concerns in the design of the form centred around maintaining data quality (it is easier to mistype a response than to do so in long hand), while at the same time not introducing bias by constraining or directing user response in the online environment. The objective of effective integration of data across the two data collection systems was paramount.

Once an online form had been submitted to the central data collection system, notification was entered into the Field Response Database, and that information sent to the collector so that the household need not be revisited. Collectors were able to establish whether all forms from each household had been completed online, or whether there was a need to return for additional printed forms. Only the address, the household ID and the number and type of forms completed (dwelling or individual) was sent to the collector, who thus had no access to the data on the actual submitted online forms themselves. Training was given to Area Managers and District Supervisors in the use of the Field Response Database, and field staff had access to the practice online census form well before the official online census form was publicly available, in order to familiarise themselves with it before interacting with the general public as they delivered the forms.

Upon submission of the online census form, data was immediately encrypted (at 128 bits) and sent to the servers, in Wellington and Auckland, of the company engaged to operate the electronic data collection, Datacom, decrypted, and instantaneously re-encrypted at 256 bit. It was stored on Datacom's server for a maximum of 24 hours, while being transferred to the Statistics New Zealand server in Christchurch, backed up, then wiped from Datacom's server upon confirmation of secure arrival, decryption and backup at Statistics New Zealand. The data was then ready to be integrated with data being entered from the paper-based form, with normal procedures for back-up and security (which is at a very high level, as it is for all the data held by Statistics New Zealand). At the same time, the Field Response Database, recording all field staff, areas, mesh blocks (the geographical units used by Statistics New Zealand to manage their geographical information systems) was updated, and receipt of the form was notified to the census collector for that block, by means of a text messaging system.

3.2 The Planning Process

Throughout 2002, in the early stages of the planning process, the focus was on defining objectives, and identifying key skills needed to meet these. An initial feasibility study was completed in March 2003, to prepare a budget request for a full feasibility study and business case to be presented to government. A prototype system was built for these feasibility studies using Lotus Notes, and tested in field tests in March and November 2003. This enabled a full business case to be put to Cabinet in time for resources to be allocated in the 2004 budget for the July 2004-05 year and beyond.

An early problem in establishing the teams and getting the project underway, was the fact that those involved in the online census, apart from the small team under the Online Census Project Manager were members of other teams with responsibilities to the full census project, of which the online census was only part. Breaking down silos between units coming together for this project, but with other competing demands on their time, required a conscious effort to bring people on board, consult and involve as widely as possible, and start an internal training process in the techniques of project management. At the same time, key personnel were carrying out what research they could about other jurisdictions that had trialled an online Census, as well as any reports on potential user response (such as research commissioned by the State Services Commission, or E-government Unit (Curtis et al. 2004, Cullen and Hernon 2004, GO2003). As a result of much of the early testing, two key points about uptake emerged. While receptiveness to the concept of an online census form had been shown to be high, it was not expected that in reality uptake would be at the same level. From field tests, it was projected that around 15-20 percent of people might take up the option, although in the dress rehearsal conducted in March 2005, uptake of the online option was only 6%. (Pink and Smith 2005) Given this uncertainty, it was decided that the system should be able to cater for 35% of households opting for online completion over the entire period, and peak loads (on Census night itself, between 8 and 10pm) able to cope with 10-12% of that uptake, that is, 35,000 concurrent users.

3.3 Selection of Technology Solution and Partner

Given the green light for implementation of an online census option in the 2006 Census a full tender process was embarked on using the New Zealand government e-procurement system, GETS (Government Electronic Tendering System), for an IT partner who could deliver this capability, with all the attendant requirements for security and confidentiality. Statistics New Zealand did not perceive that it had the computing capacity or internal skills to develop a solution capable of handling this peak load, and did not want to develop these skills as a core competency. A three stage tender process was used, starting with a Registration of Interest (ROI), followed by an RFI (Request for Information), and finally an RFP (Request for Proposal). Four companies went through to the RFP stage, and the selected company, Datacom, was required to prepare a solution ready for the dress rehearsal in March 2005. Presentations to interested vendor partners stressed the need for 100% success, 100% availability 24/7, 100% security, and 100% reliability. The selection was based on the company that could offer a robust solution, and with a reputation for reliability, rather than the proposed technology itself.

While no new technology was used, it was applied in an innovative and challenging way. The system was developed using ASP.NET and JavaScript. Three versions of the online form were prepared, one with JavaScript, one using plain HTML for respondents not JavaScript enabled, and one screen reader version for the visually impaired. The system was required to be accessible across a range of operating systems (including Windows, Apple Mac and Linux), browser interfaces (see above), and bandwidth. Authentication was required to be robust without losing respondents because of draconian requirements, and to be able to overcome user error and low level technical skills. A validation application was thus developed for the project to cope with user error in entering allocated IDs and PINs.

The authentication process itself, based on the household Internet ID supplied on the census form and the Internet PIN, checked the data elements against the database for non-duplication, and then locked the two numbers together for use by any future session, (e.g. by additional household members).

Where an error was made in entering the household ID, a process was set up to re-allocate the erroneous ID to the household. This created a problem for the household originally allocated that ID, a situation that was resolved through contact with the helpdesk. The helpdesk would then check the household ID and the allocated PIN against the household ID-PIN validation system, using only the first character and the last four characters of the alphanumeric PIN. This was sufficient to identify that another PIN had already been locked against the household ID without the helpdesk operator being able to access the full PIN or any personal data already stored in the database. The user was then advised to enter their household ID, with the final digit changed to an X, which would alert the system to the correction that had been made, but allow the householder to continue with the online form. The application, developed in-house by Statistics New Zealand's IT group, thus maintained the privacy and security of the data entry system, the integrity of the household ID and PIN validation system, with a high level of scalability (the five digits available for the checking process account for up to 25 million variations). Thus, the risk of incorrect ID or PIN entry by respondents was catered for without breaching the integrity of the data entry system, a key performance measure for the project.

A second key measure related to points in the transmission and storage of the data entered by respondents that could cause unacceptable response times for users. An anticipated point of weakness was in the time taken to replicate data across the three regional data centres. If delays in the replication process (replication latency) reached 20 seconds for five minutes, further users would be asked to logon later. These critical system performance measures were built into the business requirements the partner vendor company was required to meet, and thoroughly negotiated with them. The relationship between Statistics New Zealand staff and the primary system vendor Datacom was described as excellent, and from many examples given of solutions to problems identified and resolved by Datacom in a timely way, appears to have been a close and cooperative relationship.

4. MANAGING THE PROJECT

From the start, Statistics New Zealand identified the Online Census Project as a project in which "failure was not an option."[3] Management of the online census project was consciously based on the key tenets of project

---

[3] Ian Smith. Personal communication with author, 27 April, 2006.

management: in particular it focused on the recruitment and training of personnel, communication between groups involved in the project, careful procurement of the needed technology solutions, and a thorough approach to risk management.

While the responsibility for securing appropriate skills in project management, and establishing the core teams lay in the hands of the General Manager of the Census, training was also put in place for all permanent staff contributing to the project in project management systems and techniques. On the understanding that the effective integration of the online option into the very carefully managed 5-yearly Census process would require a higher level of cross team cooperation, a serious attempt was made to break what were perceived to be barriers between the roles of the vertical teams, described by several participants as a ''silo mentality,' and pull together horizontal teams, where the impact that decisions made in one area would have on other processes and decisions was more fully understood. Extensive training was also developed for the Area Managers, District Supervisors, and the field staff who would deliver and collect the census forms (the census collectors). A system of cascade training was set up within tight guidelines to ensure that census collectors used a predetermined script when communicating with householders about the census requirements overall, as well as the online option.

A very thorough approach was taken to identifying and anticipating risks to the success of the project. Risks which were sufficiently likely as to be almost inevitable (e.g. user error in inputting data), were dealt with as issues. Risks were closely aligned with the identification of key stakeholders in the projects, and the relationship with each stakeholder group. Some key stakeholders and associated risks included:

- the government and its monitoring agencies - notably the State Services Commission, and Treasury- regarding the overall success of the project, its ability to deliver on the benefits promised to government, meet its objectives on time and within budget, and provide appropriate learning for other Statistics New Zealand projects and projects in other agencies;
- respondents - changes in the New Zealand demographic, social attitudes less positive towards compliance, perceptions of risks to security and privacy in the online environment, wide range of technology platforms used by respondents, and varying degrees of IT competence. A major issue here was the use of a private company for the initial collection of data, the risk of a negative public perception of the vulnerability of personal data in the hands of a private company, and the consequent requirement that the data remained on

company servers for the minimum amount of time, and only in encrypted form;

- system risk, in terms of robustness, availability 24/7 throughout the period of availability, and its ability to manage load and maintain acceptable response times if uptake was high;
- support for users via the helpdesk, and the online help system to ensure that problems were quickly resolved. Performance of the helpdesk staff was also an issue here;
- performance of field staff - the accuracy of what householders were told about the census requirements, and the online option, and the impact of their performance on the credibility of Statistics New Zealand, e.g. if print forms were demanded of those who had submitted an online form;
- the media, the advertising campaign and its impact, the general news media, and also the computer/Internet media community, watching the project with considerable interest, and keen to pick up any negative feedback from the public;
- telecommunications companies, and ISPs, who needed to be warned early of the potential load on their systems on census day;
- communicating with and managing the expectations of the disability community;
- communicating with and managing the expectations of Maori, and the involvement of the Maori Language Commission in translating the existing bilingual form to online an online format.

While risk management was primarily the responsibility of the General Manager, Census, each team was required to compile its own risk register, address each risk in terms of likelihood and impact, and report on their risk management strategies and actions. Within the various teams, analysis of lower level risks, e.g., back-up systems in the event of a technology failure, and people related issues such as the motivators and barriers affecting uptake by respondents or the performance of field staff, and strategies for reducing them, were set in place. With all external partners, including the primary external partner, Datacom, a risk management register was developed and reviewed monthly, covering network, application, infrastructure, security, and external risks such as natural disasters, and an extensive programme of usability testing, acceptability testing, and load testing was carried out on the system, in addition to the field tests noted earlier. Risk management was therefore a component of the business requirements for each tendering process, part of ongoing service delivery between Statistics NZ and the vendor partners, and built into field staff performance measures (affecting remuneration).

4.1 Communications

Communications with key stakeholders, especially the media, and the management of public and media awareness of the Census generally, and the online census option, was in the hands of the Census Communications Manager. In planning the communications campaign for the 2006 Census consideration was given first and foremost to motivating New Zealanders to participate in the Census, and only then to positioning the online form as one of the ways of participating. The online form introduced an element of the unknown into the campaign for 2006 given the lack of certainty concerning the level of uptake, and the impact of this on the system's ability to respond. The main television advertising campaign was focused on 'brand awareness' and motivating participation in the census itself. The campaign relating to the online option was conceived as a public information campaign, rather than an overtly promotional campaign. Primary concerns were the need to manage uptake and avoid overloading the system if use exceeded predictions, and to place some boundaries around the expertise of those attempting to use the online form.

Within the overall framework of getting the critical messages about the requirements of the census out to the public, and the processes that would follow, the media were the preferred medium; news releases were used rather than advertising where possible. A statement about the online census was included in all media releases, but based on the consideration that most people wanting to complete the form online would be regular users of the Internet, promotion of the online option was primarily in the online arena. One commercial web site (TradeMe), two news media web sites (Stuff and the *New Zealand Herald*), and the home page of Xtra, the largest ISP in the country, were selected for this campaign, in addition to technology focused publications such as *InfotechWeekly* and *Computerworld*. The Statistics New Zealand census web site, the page about the online census, and the media pack available from the Census web site outlined how the online option would work, and stressed the high level security surrounding submission of the form. Key benefits gained from completing online that formed the basis of the public information campaign included the convenience, and ease of completion of the online form, the fact that no-one saw your submitted data, and that there was no need to wait for the census collector to return for your form. Communications concerning the online Maori option, and the screen reader version of the form, were mainly carried out through the relevant community organisations. The online census option was also included in information and activities in the Statistics New Zealand Schools Corner (see http://www.stats.govt.nz/schools-corner/).

4.2 Knowledge Management and Knowledge Sharing

As the online census project developed, knowledge was shared vertically and horizontally both within the group, and internationally. At the level of the General Manager, international contact was primarily with those jurisdictions which had a similar option, e.g. Canada, Australia, and Singapore. This is within the context of regular communication between statistical agencies, and Census managers around the English speaking world. This relationship was also useful at the level of several of the Project Managers, who had regular communication with their counterparts in Australia and Canada, the United States and England. Some of this knowledge sharing included other bureaus seeking advice, or information, about New Zealand experience, as well as Statistics New Zealand seeking solutions to problems others might have already encountered or resolved. Informal, workshop style conferences were also held among these groups.

Within the New Zealand government system, knowledge gained in the project was shared with a number of other agencies including, the Privacy Commission, the State Services-ICT forum, and the Ministry of Education. Knowledge within Statistics New Zealand and other agencies about the administration (and to a lesser extent the design) of online forms was also sought, but much of the knowledge that went into early scoping studies was based on the published research reports cited earlier. Advice was received from the State Services Commission, and presentations made throughout the process to a variety of groups, e.g. the monthly meetings of government CIOs (GOVIS), and the Conference of European Statisticians. (Pink and Smith 2005)

Within Statistics New Zealand, considerable effort was made to document the progress, and the learning emerging in the developing project, through the project management process, and short policy documents. Extensive documentation of the planning process captured much of the informal knowledge sharing that went on in meetings as the various teams gained expertise in project management, and in the technical problems, and solutions that were emerging. Minutes of all meetings were entered into a Lotus notes database. The project was also managed using the standard project management methodology, which was used across the programme. As the projects got closer to implementation, this documentation was enhanced with programme-wide risks and issues management techniques. Statistics New Zealand has also more recently adopted a more comprehensive Project Management Framework (PMF) – however, this was introduced when most census projects were well underway, and the costs of transition to the framework were judged to be too high. However, the key elements of the PMF have been used in the project documentation.

4.3 Meeting the Objectives

Following the actual Census night, when the majority of citizens and visitors to the country completed their census forms, and either submitted them online or set them aside to await the visit of the field collector, the staff of Statistics New Zealand began their evaluation of the process with debrief sessions, and a formal evaluation process. A stratified random survey of citizen respondents was also undertaken to ascertain their awareness of the census, the online option, and their attitudes to several dimensions of the census (awareness of advertising, preferred mode of completion, use of the bilingual form etc.). It is estimated that 7% of the population took up the online option, submitting almost 400,000 forms online (of which nearly 500 were in Maori). Preliminary counts, issued on May 29, indicated that the number of people in New Zealand on Census night was 4,116,900 persons, and that there were 1,469,700 occupied dwellings

Among the senior Statistics New Zealand staff involved in the project, and amongst the project managers involved, there is a sense of a project well completed. Census night came and went with no failure, and very little adverse comment. Most media comment has been favourable, commenting on the ease, and lack of delay in completing the Census online. The project was perceived to have delivered on time, on budget, and to meet requirements. The internal objectives of the project, to offer choice to citizens, to ensure that the system did not fail technically, to successfully integrate data from the two systems, and to share knowledge in developing the project, and learn from it, were all considered to have been met. The question of how well the higher level objectives were met (improving participation, data quality etc.) will have to wait until the census data has been analysed; they are not answerable at this point. Internal predictions based on field trials and the dress rehearsal of a potential uptake of 15-20% of respondents were not met, given the actual uptake of around 7%. However, it is possible that the 6% uptake of the online option in the dress rehearsal conducted in March 2005 was a more realistic figure than believed at the time, and there is some reflection going on about social and other factors that might have impacted on this outcome, some of which related to the specific nature of the census, e.g., it is a standalone task where the printed form is as convenient as online for many people, families might find it a useful social/educational activity to undertake together, and hotels, hostels and boarding houses would have no incentive to offer residents an online option.

Lower level objectives

Overall the New Zealand 2006 Census successfully collected data from nearly everyone in New Zealand on Census night in spite of what is clearly a more challenging social environment for the collection of census data than in the past. There were some internal system issues, some back office systems related to the overall Census itself that didn't work as well as intended, but the contingency plans put in place, and the census operation itself worked well. The effort that had gone into the planning process, and the risk management process were considered to have been well justified Each Business Unit involved in the online census project was able to point to successes, and key objectives that had been met, e.g. getting information out fast to field collectors via the text messaging system. Underlying these achievements is the organisational learning, the knowledge sharing, and the improvement in internal processes, seen by staff as a result of pulling the right teams together (from both internal and external appointments), the adoption of very thorough planning procedures, and enhanced HR management in relation to the six and a half thousand contract field workers (e.g. getting key performance indicators in place for field staff to enhance compliance). The ability of the helpdesk to sort out problems that occurred when collectors or respondents supplied or used incorrect IDs was another success noted.

5. THE PUBLIC RESPONSE

A telephone survey of a stratified, randomly selected sample of 1501 respondents was conducted for Statistics New Zealand by Research New Zealand between 6 and 9 April, 2006, 4-6 weeks after the Census night.[4] The interim findings from the survey show that while 95% of respondents had seen or heard information about the census before Census night, (the majority primarily through television advertising), only 74% indicated that they were aware that they could complete the form online, and only 66% recalled being offered a PIN to compete the form online. Of those who reportedly did not know that they could have completed online, only 43% stated that they would, in fact, have done so. Of those who were aware of the online option, only 19% reported that someone in their household had taken a PIN, and only 79% of that group reported that someone in their household had actually used it. (This is approximately 12% of the total number of

[4] Interim topline data has been made available for this case study. The full report was not due until June 19 2006.

people surveyed, which is slightly higher than the 7% uptake reported by Statistics New Zealand at this stage.)

Findings from the interim survey data supplied indicate that amongst those who did complete the census online there are some interesting demographics. Actual use of the online form, as a percentage of those households which requested the PIN, was higher, at 80%, among the majority ethnic group, New Zealand Europeans, than among Maori (70%), Pacific people (54%), and Asians (75%), but also surprisingly high among 65+ year olds (at 91%). Household income emerged as an apparent factor in both whether the household accepted PIN, and in whether a member of the household completed the online form. Of those who did complete the form online, 97% rated it as easy or very easy (a very high 77% responded 'very easy'), with 45-64 year olds, and 65+ year olds, finding it easier than younger age groups. Of the total group surveyed, 51% of respondents indicated they were likely in future to complete the forms online, the main reasons given being convenience (42%), ease of use (40%), no need to wait for the form to be collected (21%), and less time consuming (20%). Reasons selected by those who thought it was unlikely they would complete the form online in future focused on confidentiality/security (30%), they were used to or prefer paper forms (24%), don't know how to use computers (17%), have no computer access (13%), have no Internet access (12%), are not Internet savvy (10%). The majority of 65+ year olds surveyed (70%) indicated they were unlikely or very unlikely to complete online in future; Asians were the ethnic group that indicated they were most likely to complete online in future.

6. LESSONS LEARNED, CHANGES ADVOCATED

6.1 Evaluation of Planning and Implementation

There has been a high degree of self-reflection evident in both the planning and implementation of the project, and the evaluation currently taking place. While many questions focus on addressing perceived points of weakness in the project, and identifying how these arose and how they could be better handled next time, some, inevitably are about higher level policy issues such as the positioning of the online census option in the 2011 census, and whether to make it the first option for respondents at that time.

The online census form and the data capture and transmission system are perceived to have worked well, with no significant technology problems beyond some minor user input problems which were addressed by the helpdesk.[5] In relation to this, the recruitment of experienced IT project managers, bringing high level project management skills, that were taken on board by other teams, is seen as a major factor in the success of the project, and a lasting benefit to Statistics New Zealand. Equally, the high level of commitment from all involved, including the chief vendor partner, Datacom, is seen by most involved as a critical factor in achieving the main goals of the online Census project. In its implementation of this project Statistics New Zealand have paid attention to all four domains of project management, human resources, risk management, procurement management, and communications, but it is the last that is perceived to be an area needing attention.

It is noted by the various project managers and teams, a view endorsed by the General Manager, Census, that there is room for even more and better communication, further breaking down of silos, and that further effort in this direction, on top of the efforts made so far, would have eliminated some of the problems perceived. Secondly, and this is a view held perhaps more tentatively, that the approach to the question of uptake, and the conservative promotion of the online option may have been one of the factors that contributed to the low level of uptake compared with predictions. At the same time, it is acknowledged that there are many social and demographic factors that may impact on the citizen's willingness to interact online with government, and that these need to be further explored and understood.

There will be considerable interest in reviewing the New Zealand experience in the light of the experiences of the other countries conducting censuses in 2006 - especially Canada (which ran its Census in May 2006 and extensively promoted the on-line option) and Australia, which conducted its Census in August, and which included a PIN number for the online option with every census form. To date, uptake of the Australian online census option is estimated at about 774,000 online forms, or 9% of all census forms received. Statistics Canada report that 23% of Canadian Households had responded to the 2006 Census using the Internet, at the time field non-response follow-up efforts commenced in mid-May. By the end of the Census collection period in August, 2.26 Million households had responded on the internet, which amounts to approximately 18.2% of the total number of occupied dwellings. The actual response exceeded Statistics Canada's planning assumptions. (McBeth, 2006) Significant differences in the way that the online option was promoted in each case, different levels of broadband access, and the use of mail-out/mail-in delivery in the Canadian census, rather than house to house delivery, may have impacted on this result.

---

[5] These were relatively minor - problems experienced with the Safari browser, and a separate problem experienced by some respondents who had a pop-up blocker turned on in their system took some time to resolve.

There is a sense within the organisation that the leadership and vision of the Government Statistician, (a former CIO of the Australian Statistics Bureau), and from the General Manager, Census, were critical to the entire planning and implementation of the project. This leadership enabled all teams to keep the larger organisational objective in mind while focusing on the detail of project and risk management. There is also a sense of confidence going into the 2011 Census that many of the necessary lessons have been learned.

6.2 Lessons for e-government

The major contribution to the e-government strategy in New Zealand that has emerged from this project is the successful roll-out of the system, and the perception of success. As Russell Brown (a well-regarded IT commentator in the country) noted

> Those involved with the online Census form, filled in by about 345,000 New Zealanders this month, deserve a pat on the back.
>
> That a substantial minority of New Zealanders would be likely to take the option of providing the information online was obvious enough – look how many of us now bank online. Actually getting such an important job right was another matter. But the online form, devised and designed at Statistics New Zealand, was not only easy, it was also easier than the paper form.
>
> The hardest job in internet engineering is to create a system to be used by a great number of people in a short time. . . but the system (engineered and tested by local company Datacom) never seemed under load. And the PIN number scheme worked: I watched the Census collector walk past our house because a text message had already told him that we had responded online.
>
> Statistics New Zealand studied the experiences of several countries that have already offered a trial or an internet option for their censuses, and is sharing information with its counterparts in Canada and Australia, where similar projects are pending this year. New Zealand's effort has provided a useful lead in the way that the state can communicate with the people it serves. (Brown 2006)

Every success of this kind builds confidence in citizens that they can interact with government in the same way as they can with the corporate sector, and builds confidence in the public sector that, with planning, it can deliver a successful project, and is making progress towards the June 2007, goal that "networks and Internet technologies will be integral to the delivery of government information, services and processes." The 2010 goal of transforming government is perhaps more difficult. The breaking down of 'silos', both within and between agencies is clearly a part of this, as is the enhanced interaction with government through the Internet, but perhaps the bigger change is the adoption of good project management practice, something that we have not seen as much in the public sector to date. Finally, this project, another positive achievement for e-government in New Zealand, may well be part of an incremental change in the adoption of online interactions between citizens and government, a change that will be driven more by citizens' choices, than a government agenda.

ACKNOWLEDGEMENTS

This chapter was prepared with the invaluable assistance of Statistics New Zealand staff, namely: Nancy McBeth, General Manager, Census 2006; Ian Smith, Online Census Project Manager; Philippa Kidd, Manager, Field Collections; Sarah Minson, Manager, Methods and Operations; Penny Collinson, Communications Manager, Census 2006; and was approved for publication by Brian Pink, Government Statistician.

REFERENCES

Brown R (2006) Right first time. New Zealand Listener 203 March 25-31 2006.

Cullen, and Hernon, P (2004) Wired for well-being: citizens' response to e-government. State Services Commission, Wellington, available at: http://www.e.govt.nz/resources/research/channel-surfing-200409/research/vuw-report-200406/, accessed May 19 2006.

Cullen, R (2006) E-government and the digital divide, In: Hernon P, Cullen R, Relyea H (eds) Comparative perspectives on e-government: serving today and building for tomorrow. Scarecrow Press, Lanham, MD, pp289-313.

Curtis C, Vowles J, and Curtis B. Channel surfing: how New Zealanders access government, State Services Commission Wellington, available at: http://www.e.govt.nz/resources/research/research/channel-surfing-200409, accessed May 19 2006.

de Vuyst B, Fairchild, AM (2005) Experimenting with voting registration: the case of Belgium. Electronic journal of e-government 3:87-89.

Geok LB, Leong BCW (1999) Singapore's approach to Population Census 2000. United Nations ESCAP. Working Group of Statistical Experts, 11th session, 1999. Bangkok.

GO2003 (2003) Government Online, a national perspective 2003 - New Zealand. Taylor Nelson Sofres, available at: http://www.e.govt.nz/resources/research/go-survey-2003, accessed May 19 2006.

Krysiak M, Tucker C, Spitzer D, and Holland, K. E-procurement: state government learns from the private sector. In: Pavlichev A, and Garson GD (eds) Digital government: principles and best practices, Idea Publishing, Hershey, pp 149-168.

McBeth, N (2006) Personal email communication with the author, based on email correspondence with the Australian Bureau of Statistics and Statistics Canada.
Pink B, and Smith I (2005) Using both Internet and field collection methods for the 2006 Census of population and dwellings - the New Zealand experience so far. United Nations. Economic and Social Council. Conference of European Statisticians. CES/2005/13, Geneva.
Reuters (2006) Canadian census counts on online responses. May 2, 2006. http://news.zdnet.com/2100-9588_22-6067362.html, accessed 16 May 2006.
Schwalbe K (2004) Information technology project management. 3rd edn. Thomson, Boston.
State Services Commission. E-government Unit (2001) Government@your.service: E-government strategy. State Services Commission, Wellington. Available at http://www.e-government.govt.nz/docs/e-gov-strategy-apr-01/index.html, accessed April 8, 2005.
State Services Commission (2003) E-government vision, mission, goals and outcome. State Services Commission, Wellington. Available at http://www.e-government.govt.nz/docs/e-gov-strategyjune-2003, accessed April 10, 2005.
State Services Commission (2004) Participation - channel strategy. Scoping study, Ch 8. State Services Commission, Wellington. Available at: http://www.e.govt.nz/policy/participation/channel/, accessed 19 May, 2006.
Wang, Y-s (2003) The adoption of electronic tax filing systems: an empirical study. Government Information Quarterly 20:333-352.
West, D (2004) E-government and the transformation of service delivery and citizen attitudes. Public administration review 64:15-27.
West, D (2005) Digital government: technology and public sector performance, Princeton University Press, Princeton.
West, D (2005a) The Case of online tax filing. In: Digital government: technology and public sector performance. Princeton University Press, Princeton.

SUGGESTED READING

- Schwalbe, K. (2004) *Information technology project management.* 3rd edn. Thomson, Boston.
- Heeks, Richard. e-Government risk: assessment and mitigation. pp.216-239, in *Implementing and managing e-government.* Sage, London.

ONLINE RESOURCES

- Australian eCensus: http://www.abs.gov.au/websitedbs/d3310114.nsf/home/2006%20Census:%20eCensus
- Canada. 2006 census online: http://www22.statcan.ca/ccr_r000_e.htm
- Heeks, Richard. Achieving Success/Avoiding failure: http://www.e-devexchange.org/e-gov/topic1.htm; http://www.e-devexchange.org/e-gov/riskassess.htm

- New Zealand. 2006 census at: http://www.stats.govt.nz/census/2006-census/default.htm
- Singapore. Department of Statistics. Census of Population 200, Administrative report: http://www.singstat.gov.sg/pdtsvc/pubn/softcopy/cop2000admin.pdf

QUESTIONS FOR DISCUSSION

1. What are the critical success factors in this project, and how important was each?
2. Which aspects of project management were managed well in this project, and which should Statistics New Zealand be looking to improve in the next census?
3. To what extent should possible media response drive decision-making in a project such as the online census?
4. What are some of the specific risks that would have been identified as the project developed, and how could they have been minimised or eliminated?
5. Where do you see this project taking New Zealand in terms of e-government? Does it represent the second or third phase of Darrell West's taxonomy?
6. To what extent does this project contribute to the advancement of e-government goals of the New Zealand government?

Chapter 31

MULTIDISCIPLINARY E-GOVERNMENT RESEARCH AND EDUCATION AS A CATALYST FOR EFFECTIVE INFORMATION TECHNOLOGY TRANSFER

Bienvenido Vélez-Rivera, Manuel Rodríguez-Martínez, Walter Díaz, Mario Núñez-Molina, and Pedro I. Rivera-Vega

University of Puerto Rico, Mayagüez

CHAPTER OVERVIEW

The Digital Government Project at the University of Puerto Rico Mayagüez is an attempt to leverage research in information technologies and computer science to identify and help overcome some of the most pervasive barriers to the adoption of IT by small and regional governments. We present a survey study that measures the level of penetration of IT in general and internet technology in particular by the citizens of the city of Mayagüez, Puerto Rico. We then proceed to present our experience in helping this small city adopt IT to enhance its systems and processes with the end goal of improving the internal work environment as well as the quality of services to the citizens. We hope that this experience will both help and stimulate similar ongoing and future efforts by universities to improve the quality of government and thus life in their surrounding communities.

1. INTRODUCTION

Electronic government systems have an unprecedented potential to improve the responsiveness of governments to the needs of the people that they are designed to serve. To this day, this potential is barely beginning to be exploited, more so in smaller towns of limited economic resources. Significant barriers hinder the effective integration of information technologies into government practices and their adoption by the public. Government agencies often find themselves in a disadvantaged position to compete with the private sector for information technology workers, a workforce whose shortage at a national level is well recognized. The need to abide by rigid procurement practices makes it virtually impossible for agencies to keep their technology infrastructure up to date with the fast pace of technological advances. For instance, Moore's Law, a well known technological trend, predicts that processing speed doubles approximately every two years. Today, this trend shows no sign of slowing down in the near future. Local and regional governments are particularly affected by this state of affairs.

A multidisciplinary group including researchers from the University of Puerto Rico Mayagüez (UPRM) and personnel from the municipal government from the city of Mayagüez has worked for the last three years to combine their talents in Public Administration, Computer Science, Engineering, and Social Sciences, in order to identify significant barriers to the effective transfer of information technology into government practices and their adoption by the public, engineer novel solutions to help overcome these barriers, and test their solutions in a real municipal governmental environment. The team from the city of Mayagüez included experts on Information Systems, Engineering, and Public Administration. The technical side of the UPRM group encompassed faculty members with expertise in Distributed Database Systems, Information Retrieval, and High Performance Computing. From the Social Sciences the UPRM group includes faculty members with expertise in Political Sciences and Psychology.

The UPRM Digital government project has three main components: a research component, a technology transfer component, and a dissemination component. The research component focused in the areas of semantically-rich document management, heterogeneous database integration, and social barriers to adoption of IT. The technology transfer component involved senior students in the analysis and design of IT solutions to help ameliorate the most pressing information needs as jointly determined by the UPRM and Mayagüez teams. The dissemination component consisted of a yearly workshop in which students and faculty presented the results of the previous year.

Located on the west coast of the island of Puerto Rico, the Municipality of Mayagüez has a population of one hundred thousand citizens and a budget of approximately fifty million dollars. The city hosts the University of Puerto Rico Mayagüez campus, the main Engineering School on the island with over ten thousand students, and is considered the leading governmental city within the western region. Of all the people old enough to go to college only 20% have obtained a degree. Moreover the median household income for the municipality is only $12,042. In addition 24% of all homes lack phone service.

We begin the chapter with a presentation (Section 2) of the results of a survey study conducted at the beginning of the project and designed to assess the degree of IT and e-government technology penetration within the community of Mayagüez. This study sets the stage for a discussion of the various technology transfer projects developed during the collaborative effort and their impact on the municipality. Due to space limitations we present a brief discussion of one of the research projects as an illustration of the type of effort that can result in a win-win situation benefiting academia, industry, government, and the population at large. We conclude with a discussion of the most important lessons learned during the Digital Government project and suggestions for future projects.

2. SOME SOCIOECONOMIC BARRIERS TO THE DEPLOYMENT AND UTILIZATION OF E-GOVERNMENT INITIATIVES IN MAYAGÜEZ, PUERTO RICO

According to Pavlichev and Garson 12 e-government can be described as the use of Information Technology by governmental institutions to improve services and information flows to citizens, improve both the efficiency and effectiveness of the public sector, and substantially increase the government's transparency to the public while providing greater opportunities and venues for citizen participation in democratic governance. On the other hand, political participation has been defined in many ways, but a particularly useful definition was proposed by Nagel 11: "Participation refers to actions through which ordinary members of a political system influence or attempt to influence outcomes." Joining these views, it is clear that e-government initiatives in fact create new forms of political participation.

The development of e-government initiatives can be seen as a three stage process. The first stage is comprised by efforts to make as much governmental information as possible available to citizens. This may include everything from contact information for public officials, statistical data, calls for bids, contracts, and so on. The second stage consists of developing systems allowing citizens to perform governmental transactions online. The third and final stage involves the implementation of procedures to maximize citizen interaction with governmental decision makers and decision making 2.

All three stages are potentially beneficial in that they increase transparency in government, efficiency, and citizen opportunities to obtain services. However, it is the third stage that is most critical if e-government initiatives are to fulfill their promise of increased democracy. This is to be achieved by democratizing both the dissemination and accessing of information 3. The central thesis of this view is that until the late 20th century, the relatively high costs of information and communication favored the development of hierarchical bureaucratic organizations wherein access to and control of information was the key to power. This certainly extends to government wherein it has been amply shown that policy outcomes sharply favor actors, such as interest groups and political parties, who are better organized, informed, and capable of participating in such ways that permit them to reward or punish incumbents based on said policy outcomes 10 13. However, it is now argued that the ascendancy of the internet has resulted in a changed information market wherein the marginal costs of information have been greatly reduced. If this is correct, it would in turn mean that larger well organized hierarchical groups and organizations have relatively less inherent informational advantages over smaller organizations or even unorganized majorities 3.

Although reduced marginal costs of information induced by information technology and e-government initiatives have a potential to significantly enhance democracy 83, it has been shown that, in relation to other forms of political participation, even large reductions in the marginal costs of participating often do not necessarily lead to the expected increased participation 1310. Therefore it may very well be the case that policy outcomes will still favor the already better informed and politically active. It follows then that for e-government efforts and the information technologies that make it possible to become truly democratizing factors, it is first necessary that present day biases in political interest, knowledge, and participation be reduced.

Following the literature on political participation we therefore argue that democratization will occur only to the extent that the following conditions are met:

1. There must be a reasonable degree of equality of access to the technology necessary to make use of the IT revolution and e-government initiatives.
2. The different subpopulations and demographic groups in society must have knowledge of these opportunities and know how to exploit them.
3. There should not be major biases in the extent to which different groups make use of these opportunities.

These conditions do not constitute an exhaustive list of the criteria necessary for democratization to occur; rather they are intended as a set of necessary, but not sufficient, criteria 13 7 10 15.

Research into political participation shows that the social and economically privileged participate more extensively, and effectively, in politics than do the less well off 13 10 15. If we consider the use of e-government options to be a form of political participation, it follows that, although decreasing in extent, due to the continued existence of the digital divide in the United States, wherein the more economically privileged and educated have greater access to both computers and the internet, these individuals will also accrue a greater proportion of the benefits of e-government initiatives and will further increase their advantageous position with respect to public policy outcomes 4 3 10.

We examine these issues within the context of ongoing e-government initiatives by the city of Mayagüez, Puerto Rico in order to identify the nature of some of the socioeconomic and behavioral barriers to the utilization of e-government initiatives. This research addresses the following questions:

1. Which subpopulations stand to benefit more from these efforts and what does this mean for the promise of greater democracy through e-government initiatives? How is this related to the socioeconomic and demographic characteristics of the population?
2. What is the significance of these biases for democratic governance?

3. METHODOLOGY

Our data were obtained through a mixed mode survey of Mayagüez residents aged 18 and over. The core survey consisted of 401 telephone interviews with respondents selected through the use of random digit dialing techniques. Given that according to the US Census of Population and Housing a substantial 24% of households in Mayagüez do not have telephone service, we also implemented a face to face survey with residents of housing units in which there was no phone service. This was achieved by sampling census block groups with probability of selection proportional to the amount of housing units without phones within them. Once the block groups were selected, blocks, housing units (without phone service), and respondents were randomly selected from each one. This procedure resulted in an additional 146 interviews, for a total sample size of 547 interviews of which 73.3% were phone interviews and 26.7% were face to face.

The data were analyzed using both bivariate and multivariate methodologies as described in the following section.

4. RESULTS

We examine three different but obviously related indicators of the potential for e-government efforts to achieve the goal of facilitating citizen access to services and information and to increase citizen participation in decision making: computer ownership, internet access, and actual use of e-government services and information.

Though having a computer or internet access in the house is not indispensable for citizens to make the most of the opportunities provided to them by e-government initiatives, it is highly convenient for doing so. Citizens who do not have access to a computer or other medium to connect to the internet from home have to depend on the availability of the necessary technology at their place of work, school, or some other public or private facility. Our data show that 47% of our respondents indicated that they had a computer at home whereas 34% say that they have internet access at home. The corresponding figures for the United States are 68% and 61%, respectively 4. Given that the median annual family income for the US in 2003 was approximately $45,000 4 while it was only $15,000 for Mayagüez 15 these differences are not at all surprising. Furthermore, 36% of our respondents indicated that they have access to a computer at their place of work or school while 28% indicate that they have internet access at work or school. Overall, 56% of our respondents have access to a computer at home or work or school whereas 48% say they have internet access from home, work, or school[1].

The data also indicate heavy socioeconomic biases in both computer ownership and internet access. Tables 31-1 and 31-2 summarize the relationship between these variables and income and education. The digital gap is clearly observed. Wealthier and more educated individuals are much

---

[1] The 146 respondents who lacked phone service were asked whether they had ever used a publicly available computing facility. Only 2.4% of them indicated they had ever used a municipal or state operated facility while less than 1% (n=1) indicated he or she had used a privately operated one (e.g. internet café).

more likely to own computers, have internet access, and make use of e-government resources than are the less privileged.

Table 31-1. Computer and internet access at home, school, or work by income in Mayagüez, Puerto Rico * **

	$0-$14,999	$15,000-$34,999	$35,000-
Has computer access	40.6%	79.0%	97.3%
	n=114	94	71
Has internet access	37.1%	68.1%	90.4%
	89	81	66

*p<.05 for both computer and internet access; ** Source: Authors' survey

Table 31-2. Computer and internet access at home, school, or work by education in Mayagüez, Puerto Rico* **

	Less than high school degree	High school degree	Associate degree or more
Has computer	15.8%	52.8%	79.1%
access	n=18	102	186
Has internet	8.8%	45.1%	68.9%
access	10	87	162

* p<.05 for both sets of relationships; ** Source: Authors' survey

Though not exactly comparable because it summarizes only computer and internet access at home, Table 31-3 shows that the same pattern holds for the relationship between education and access to computers and to the internet in the United States.

Table 31-3. Computer and internet access at home by education in the United States* ** ***

	Less than high school degree	High school degree	Associate degree or more
Has computer at home	46.6%	63.7%	83.6%
Has internet access at home	38.2%	55.6%	78.4%

* p<.05 for both sets of relationships; ** Sample weighted to US population size;

*** Source: US Bureau of the Census, Current Population Survey, October 2003

We now examine the relationship between the use of e-government services and SES. As an indicator for e-government service or information use, we created a variable which indicates whether the respondent has ever accessed information or services from either the Federal or Puerto Rican government or had ever sent an email message to any official of either government. Tables 31-4 and 31-5 summarize the relationship between this variable and respondents' income and education, respectively.

Table 31-4. Use of e-government services or information by income in Mayagüez, Puerto Rico* **

	\$0-14,999	\$15,000-\$34,999	\$35,000-
Has used e-government services	9.6%	19.3%	30.1%
	n=27	23	22

* p<.05; ** Source: Authors' survey

Table 31-5. Use of e-government services or information by education in Mayagüez, Puerto Rico* **

	Less than high school degree	High school degree	Associate Degree or more
Has used e-government services	1.8%	9.8%	23.8%
	n=2	19	56

* p<.05; ** Source: Authors' survey

We observe that both income and education are strongly related to the use of e-government resources. However, we expect that, as is often the case with other forms of participation, the effect of income is, to a degree, an artifact of its correlation with education.

We further explore these results using a multivariate approach. Following Bimber 3 we utilize logistic regressions to model computer ownership, internet access, and the use of e-government services or information as a function of respondents' age, work status, education, income, gender, and whether they are university students or not. These variables encompass indicators for the ability to meet the costs associated with acquiring and using information technology, the knowledge and interest necessary to do so, and exposure to the technology.

We expected age to be negatively associated with computer ownership and internet access, but not necessarily with use of e-government services or information. In other words we expect the young will have greater access to technology, but will not necessarily be more likely to use it with political ends. This is so because, we expect that, all else being equal, younger respondents will have had greater exposure to information technology than older ones. However, the literature on political participation shows that the young are often less likely to participate in politics than older individuals 13 5. For the same reasons, we expected working outside the house to be positively correlated with all three dependent variables.

We expected education to also be positively associated with all three dependent variables as it contributes in various ways to increase their likelihood. First, the more educated will have an easier time meeting some of the information costs associated with both purchasing and using IT and also of e-government services. For example, if all else is equal, one would expect the more educated to be better able to decide which technologies to purchase as a means to achieve IT related goals. Furthermore, they will also be more likely to understand the importance, possibilities, and limitations related to different forms of political participation, including the use of e-government resources, and should also be more likely to know about the availability of e-government options to interact with the governmental apparatus 14 13 10 3.

Income is also a powerful predictor of some forms of political participation, particularly those that require a monetary investment. For example, income is an important predictor of making contributions to political campaigns and membership in groups which require the payment of dues. However, once education is accounted for, it is only weakly associated with voting 13 5. Following this line of thought, we expect income to be strongly and positively associated with computer ownership, less strongly with having internet access, and weakly, if at all, with use of e-government resources.

Finally, we include a dummy variable identifying university students because Mayagüez has various university campuses with a total of approximately 18,000 students among them. Given that we did not exclude university students from our samples even if they were not permanent residents of Mayagüez (because even then they are consumers of municipal services), and that we expected them to be more likely to own computers and to access the internet than would otherwise be predicted, we included a variable identifying them in the analysis. We also include a dummy variable to account for access to computers and the internet at home, work, or school in the models for internet access and e-government service usage.

Table 31-6 clearly shows that the more educated and financially better off have clear advantages over the less privileged in relation to computer ownership. This is not surprising given that, as expected, the more educated and wealthier individuals should be better able to deal with the costs associated with purchasing and owning computers.

Furthermore, the younger respondents are more likely to report having computers at home than older ones, even when controlling for factors such as education, income, and currently being a university student. Working outside the home has a positive effect on access to computers whereas gender had no bearing on it.

When we consider internet access (Table 31-7) we once again find evidence for the primacy of income and education. Those with higher incomes or greater education are more likely to be able to pay for internet access or to have access to it at either school or work.

On the other hand, we once again find that gender is not a significant variable; males are no more or less likely than females to report having internet access. This is noteworthy in that males are almost twice as likely to report having internet access than are females (62% and 36%, respectively). Furthermore, we also observe that working outside the home has no independent effect on internet access.

Table 31-6. Computer access at home, work, or school*

	B	Standard Error	P
Age in years	-.039	.009	.000
Work outside home or not	.966	.282	.001
Ln(Education)	2.395	.544	.000
Ln(Income)	1.342	.242	.000
Gender	-.064	.279	.817
University student	2.320	.584	.000
Constant	-3.381	.998	.001

N=470, chi-sq.=265; p=0.000, Nagel. r2 = .582

*Note: Logit coefficients. Work variable is coded 1 for those who work outside the house, 0 otherwise; gender is coded 1 for males, 0 females. Income refers to household income and is coded as follows: 1 $0 to $4,999, 2 $5,000 to $9,999, 3 $10,000 to $14,999, 4 $15,000 to $24,999, 5 $25,000 to $34,999, 6 $35,000 to $44,999, 7 $45,000 to $59,999, and 8 $60,000 and greater. University student is coded 1 for respondents who are university students, 0 otherwise. A logarithmic transformation is used for both the education and income variables in all multivariate analysis.

Table 31-7. Internet access at home, work, or school

	B	Standard Error	P
Age in years	-.014	.014	.311
Work outside home or not	.029	.402	.943
Ln(Education)	1.362	.680	.045
Ln(Income)	.749	.318	.018
Gender	-.466	.370	.207
University student	3.248	.912	.000
Access to a computer at home, work, or school	5.660	.843	.000
Constant	-6.091	1.480	.000

N=470, chi-sq.=434;p=0.000, Nagel. r^2 = .804

Table 31-8 summarizes our findings for having used e-government resources to obtain either services or information from the federal or Puerto Rican governments. The first important point is that the model, though significant, explains only a relatively small amount of the variance in the dependent variable. Furthermore, it is noteworthy that the only independent variables with statistically significant coefficients were education and having internet access, whereas the income variable ceased to be significant.

Table 31-8. Respondent made use of e-government resources to access government services or information

	B	Standard Error	P
Age in years	-.015	.011	.194
Work outside home or not	.127	.332	.703
Ln(Education)	2.705	.883	.001
Ln(Income)	.154	.172	.572
Gender	-.219	.302	.462
University student	.295	.375	.432
Internet access	1.246	.438	.004
Constant	-6.668	1.324	.000

N=470, chi-sq.=71; p=0.000, Nagel. r^2 = .245

5. DISCUSSION

The multivariate analysis provides some key insights into our understanding of barriers to the use of e-government services by the general public. The first is that as we move on from the determinants of access to computers towards internet access and ultimately to the use of e-government resources, we find that the importance of income decreases. This is consistent with the reduction in costs thesis. Once one has obtained access to a computer, the cost of internet access becomes relatively trivial and, in turn, once one has obtained internet access, the, additional monetary cost of using it to obtain governmental services and information becomes practically negligible. This finding is consistent with Bimber's 3 argument on the declining marginal costs of information.

The second key point is the role played by education. Compared to its role in determining access to computers, the magnitude of the education coefficient decreases markedly when one considers its role in relation to internet access. However, the importance of education greatly increases as a determinant of e-government usage. This suggests that even though advances in IT and e-government may have greatly decreased many of the costs of at least some forms of political participation and of information seeking, it also appears that the use of e-government resources remains costly in terms of either, or both, the informational burdens that must be met to make use of them or the opportunity costs associated with doing so. This means that, at least at present, the promise of enhanced democracy and citizen participation in public affairs through the application of IT is not being fulfilled as the privileged, particularly the more educated and presumably better informed, will continue to have greater access to the State. In fact, e-government initiatives, at least in Mayagüez, Puerto Rico, are likely to increase preexistent biases in political participation which are already favorable to the better off. In other words, at least at present, e-government efforts may actually serve to increase political inequality and therefore hinder democratization.

However, we also found that the usual SES variables associated with the so-called digital divide explain very little about e-government usage. Our thesis for future work is that e-government usage is a form of political participation and as such, cannot be adequately explained by predominantly SES-based models. Rather, we must also look at issues such as citizen engagement, issue salience, feelings of personal efficacy, trust in government, contextual factors such a mobilization efforts by activists, governmental efforts at promoting its use, and very importantly, understanding the opportunity costs involved in these forms of participation 5 13 10.

On the other hand, the positive and significant effect of having internet access, even when controlling for education and income, suggests that present day efforts by the Puerto Rican state government and the Municipality of Mayagüez to promote the use of e-government resources by placing digital libraries in the midst of less privileged communities may have at least some effect on increasing e-government usage by less privileged populations. Future research needs to explore this in much greater detail as our present understanding of this topic is rather limited. As stated previously, this exploration must be undertaken from the perspective of modeling political participation.

Following this line of thought, our findings also suggest that to substantially increase the use of e-government options would require strategies analogous to those used to increase other forms of political participation. This is important not only for extending the use of e-government resources throughout different social groupings, but also for e-government to make the critical transition from its 2nd stage of development and its emphasis on governmental transactions to its 3rd stage in which the emphasis is on communication and interaction between citizens, decision makers, and decision making processes which must be achieved for e-government efforts to reach their democratizing potential.

6. DEPLOYMENT OF E-GOVERNMENT INFORMATION SYSTEMS TO THE CITY OF MAYAGÜEZ

One of the goals of the UPRM Digital Government Project was to transfer modern information technology to the Municipality of Mayagüez by designing and developing computer-based information systems to process government transactions and support automated services to citizens. We looked for cost-effective solutions that were based on modern open source systems and tools requiring little or no licensing fees. The systems were to be Web-based, providing new avenues for citizens to interact with government agencies.

Once these systems are in place and in regular use, important benefits would be derived by all the parties involved. From the government side, these solutions improve efficiency in bringing services to constituents, in broadening the type of services available, and in reaching reliable means of facilitating the collection of statistical data that can be used in the assessment of the quality of services and the formulation of proposals to obtain external funds to support their programs. The citizens, on the other hand, receive more efficient services with improved capabilities for following up their requests and better accountability. Academia benefits from an opportunity for students and faculty to get involved in a practical engineering project with a potential to improve the quality of life in their surrounding communities.

Local city governments usually have only a relatively small budget to support the development of this kind of IT solution, making it more difficult to consider modern computer systems and tools to facilitate interaction with the general public. Furthermore, there is the general idea that open source systems and tools are not reliable or that the services provided will be unavailable if the systems happen to fail; hence, the common vision is that, in order to be able to implement and deploy these systems, proprietary solutions that often come with elevated costs are required. This common belief usually stops regional governments, and low budget enterprises, from taking advantage of the availability of systems and tools that are public domain to implement systems to automate day-to-day operations. It is therefore another important contribution of this project to promote a change of this mentality. All the computer applications that we have implemented are constructed upon open standards and open source tools and systems.

In this section, we discuss the approach that we followed to develop information systems for three agencies in the city of Mayagüez.

6.1 Identifying the Opportunity to Exploit IT

The selection of the agencies that would be impacted by the technology transfer project was mainly conducted by the administration of the city. The decision to give the city the greatest weight in this decision was critical as it would improve the chances that the administration will provide adequate support to the projects if they gave them high priority. The agencies initially selected were the Housing Office, the Citizen's Services Office, and the Public Works Office. The specifics of each application are described in a subsequent section. Together, these three agencies handle thousands of citizens' requests per month. The objective was to eventually provide citizens a direct mechanism to apply for services and follow up on pending requests online. Although at the time of this writing this objective has not been achieved, critical steps in this direction have already been accomplished.

6.2 Computing and Networking Infrastructure

The Digital Government project has served as an important catalyst in the deployment of the basic infrastructure required to support modern information systems. The project has provided the municipality with guidance and knowledge in the selection of adequate technologies resulting in the most efficient investments. It is common practice for small governments to rely on sales personnel to gather information on available IT. These vendors often try to push a complete line of technology with less regard for efficiency and cost savings. Vendors are often represented by sales people with rather superficial knowledge of the technologies that they represent. The project has empowered the administration with additional vendor-independent expertise. One of the biggest challenges has been the provision of an adequate networking infrastructure to connect all the geographically dispersed municipal agencies. The UPRM team is currently helping the city in the design and deployment of a city intranet interconnecting offices using widely available ISP technology such as DSL yet providing compliance with the current regulations on IT usage.

6.3 Requirements Elicitation – Project Scope Delimitation

Each software development project started with a customer centric requirements elicitation process. One UPRM team consisting of one faculty member and two to three undergraduate students was assigned to each agency. Each agency team met several times with personnel from the corresponding agency to understand the scope of the process that the agency thought should be automated in order to yield the highest payoff in efficiency and quality of service. The UPRM team was critical in helping delimit the scope of the project according to their knowledge of the software development process while the city personnel contributed their knowledge of the processes, which in many cases were based more on common practices than in well documented standard operating procedures. More importantly, the requirements elicitation process served to begin the cultivation of a long term personal relationship and a solid foundation of trust among UPRM and Mayagüez personnel that we believe was critical to the success achieved by the project. When we approached the city for the first time it was not uncommon for us to perceive an atmosphere of pessimism towards IT, possibly founded on past failed promises and attempts to adopt similar technology.

6.4 Adopting a Standard Open Architecture

The architecture selected for all the information systems follows the three tier model as shown in Figure 31-13. This model, referred to as *Model-View-Controller (MVC) 69,* is considered the modern standard for the development of dynamic Web-based applications or GUI-oriented applications in general.

The *View* component consists of the graphical interface of the system, which in the Web-based application are created using HTML tools and Java Server Pages (JSP). The *Model* component encapsulates all the access and management logic of data records in the system. The *Controller* manages the required access controls so that user commands at the *View* level are executed by the appropriate component at the *Model* layer.

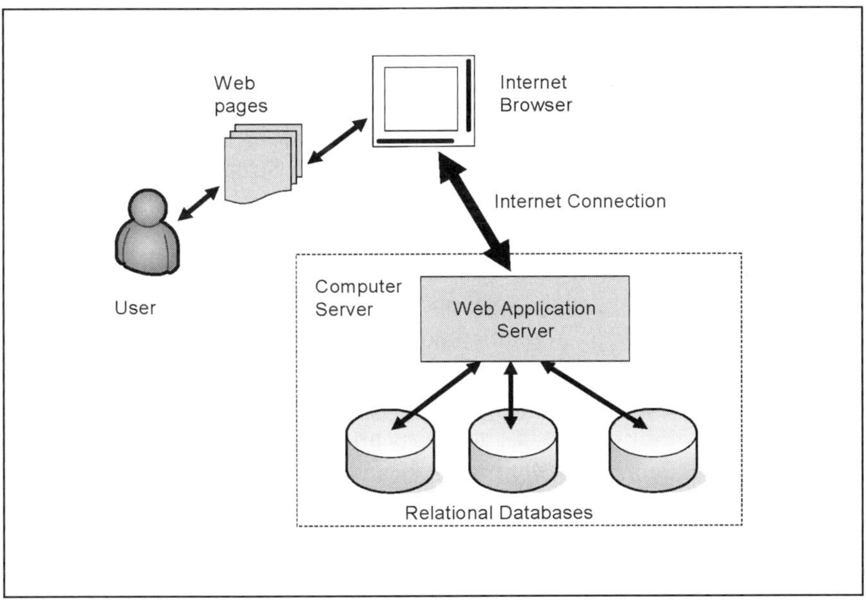

Figure 31-13. Three Tier Model-View-Controller Architecture

This architecture offers several important benefits:

- It is a well known architecture, and as such its adoption offers the opportunity of an open and competitive market of service providers that could offer long term support.

- Facilitates maintenance of the application by separating the maintenance of each layer of software.
- Enables the adoption of the best technology available for each layer at each point in time and as the system grows and matures.

For the database management system we have selected MySQL. This DBMS is open source and is free. It has also proved to be robust and efficient, with capacity to manage a moderate number of concurrent transactions. A large number of well-ranked companies and government agencies actually use this DBMS, including: Continental Airlines, NASA, Yahoo, Ticketmaster, The Weather Channel, etc. In the event that a more robust or efficient RDBMS is eventually required, the application can be easily ported as all communication between the model layer and the RDBMS is carried on via the standard JDBC API. An important component of all e-government systems is the reporting subsystem. We experimented with a variety of reporting technologies and finally selected the JasperReports open source platform. This platform offers a wide variety of reporting formats and supports multiple means for exporting information into helper applications such as spreadsheets, word processing, and presentation software. A strong yet flexible reporting subsystem offers opportunities for significant cost savings in human hours dedicated to manual data entry, processing, and analysis. In some cases, we dramatically reduced the time required to generate a report from days to seconds.

The view layer uses Java custom tags technology supported by Java Server Pages (JSP), enhanced with the use of Java Struts. The JSP pages are compiled by Apache Tomcat Server 1 (http://tomcat.apache.org), which runs on the Apache Web Server. In this way Apache Tomcat and Apache Web Server can be integrated under the same computing Server, hence providing the whole environment needed to support all the Web applications.

The controller layer is implemented by *Java Beans*, which are connected under the specifications of *Struts*. These *Beans* are used to control access to system resources, guaranteeing the security policies that have been defined by the corresponding agency. They also allow the proper management of errors of the system. The controller beans are executed by the Apache Tomcat server.

6.5 Adopting an Agile Software Development Approach

Once the initial requirements elicitation process was completed, each UPRM development team proceeded to design and develop a first prototype of the system. We used an agile development process and did not generate detailed specification documents. Instead we interleaved our development time with several interactions with real end users. At each interaction we demonstrate a more complete version of the system and collect feedback which will be incorporated into the next version. Our experience confirmed the effectiveness of the agile process in developing a sense of ownership and involvement in the development of the systems from its early stages of the process that we believe is critical in the eventual acceptance and support of the new system by the employees. Early involvement also helps in reducing the anxiety caused by the sudden adoption of an unfamiliar system and gives the agency an early start on conducting any process and policy changes necessary to maximize the benefit obtained from the new system. These changes may require time consuming administrative or even legislative actions. An agile process conveniently blurs the separation between the development and deployment phases.

The UPRM team was also instrumental in the identification of and emphasis on adopting requirements that would yield significant direct benefits to their users. Surprising as it may sound, our experience was that a first set of requirements will often focus on using the computer system to imitate the existing processes. The UPRM team was instrumental in helping city officials think about ways to streamline processes to save time and resources and expedite customer service. City employees constantly provide feedback on what changes would be too radical to be accepted at the moment. The process helped to continue nurturing the strong human relationship of trust begun at the requirements elicitation phase.

6.6 Deployment, Training, and Support

The agile development process in most cases made the process of final deployment rather seamless. Once available at their desktops, key employees immediately began to experiment with the systems. By this time they were, for the most part, anxious to begin using their new tool. They pretty much knew what to expect. The agile process served to feed their expectations. The project was able to radically turn an initial sense of pessimism into realistic hope for significant improvements to their working conditions as well as to the quality of service provided to their customers. The big lesson is that improving the quality of governmental services provided to citizens should begin with improving the quality of working conditions and level of active involvement from employees providing these services. Developing a sense of ownership appears to be a necessary condition for the success of deploying new digital government services.

An agile software development process also dramatically facilitated training of personnel to use the new systems. Many of them had already been involved in the design of the system and knew what to expect. Some of the key employees required little or no training. The UPRM team developed a two-tier training approach consisting of training sessions on fundamentals of computer usage and training sessions specific to the application developed for each agency. Basic computer training was offered during our annual Digital Government Congress free of charge to all employees of the city. Application specific training was offered in a small sequence (3-4) of training sessions offered exclusively to employees of each agency. Most employees required less than 10 hours of training to become fully proficient on their corresponding systems. We are aware of other digital government efforts that have had considerable trouble getting enough employees to accept training to use new systems that they haven't had a say in designing.

The UPRM team has provided continuous technical support during the duration of the NSF grant. However, the team has made the city administration aware that this support will not be sustainable once NSF funds stop. We have begun conversations on alternative sustainable approaches to provide long term support to the effort and discuss this issue further in Section 7.4. We are happy to report that the robustness of the system has surpassed all our initial expectations. At the time of this writing the systems continue to operate with less than one failure per month.

7. DESCRIPTION OF SPECIFIC E-GOVERNMENT SYSTEMS

At the beginning of the UPRM Digital Government project the Municipality of Mayagüez did not have any web-enabled information systems available. At the time of this writing the city is currently operating web-enabled systems at two of its agencies providing the most direct services to its citizens: Public Works and Citizen's Services. The system at the Housing Office has suffered delays, mostly due to the availability of the computing infrastructure, but it is planned to go into production use early in 2007. The networking infrastructure required to provide online access is expected to be deployed in early 2008 as well.

In this section we provide an overview of the systems developed for the three Mayagüez government agencies: Citizen's Services Office, Public Works Office, and Public Housing Office. Each of these systems is based upon the framework discussed in the previous section. Our discussion concentrates on the needs of each of these agencies that our systems addressed, on their implementation, and on their adoption by city personnel.

Although each of the systems have particular needs and require different implementation approaches in several instances, they all addressed common needs in many aspects. The most noticeable is that they all are targeted to manage the process that is required for citizens to submit requests, or applications, to receive some type of government service. This process goes from the moment that an application or request is initiated up to the moment when it is rejected, or, in the case when it is granted, the service is completely offered. Hence, each of these three systems has the objective of facilitating the process to collect data that is required from an applicant, to facilitate the process of evaluating an application, and, for those cases in which the service is granted, to facilitate the process to guarantee an efficient service. The systems further collect data for auditing purposes and to produce reports.

In terms of more detailed operations, the particular system in each of the three agencies includes the following:

1. *Capture requests initiated by an employee or by any particular citizen* – this is accomplished by providing specialized forms that the citizens, or agency officials, fill in with the details of the individuals participating in the application and the services being requested. All the data that is collected as part of this process is internally stored in the system's database and linked to the particular service application for future processing.
2. *Validate that the request has satisfied all the requirements* – the system includes the appropriate knowledge to be used in the process of determining if an application form has been successfully completed.
3. *Route the request to the proper government official for evaluation* – after an application or request is submitted, the system routes it to the appropriate official or agency program for evaluation. The official or program that receives the application is chosen based on the services requested. How to properly do this match is part of the knowledge that is stored in the internal database of the system.
4. *Facilitate the evaluation process* – the evaluation process is simplified by the system in several aspects. First, applications are electronically transferred to its evaluator person. The system contains data that establishes the steps that need be followed when evaluating each type of service. It also contains all the knowledge about the particular requirements that must be satisfied during the evaluation process of the particular services requested.
5. *Register the final decision about each particular request* – when the evaluation is completed, the final decision about each particular request is stored in the corresponding database.

6. *Register any action concerning those requests that are approved* – when services requested are approved, the system facilitates the day to day operations that are needed in order for the particular service to be successfully implemented. It is important that data is collected about this process since it is required for auditing purposes and also to identify deficiencies in the process.
7. *Allow the verification of the status of a request that has been submitted* – at any moment the status of an application can be verified, either by the main applicant or by officials from the agency.
8. *Produce statistical reports* – statistical reports are important for the government in order to identify future needs and improvements that may be required in the process of evaluation or offering services. These reports include statistics about mean time to complete crucial steps of the whole process, services offered per regions, services offered per time period, services offered to particular individuals, etc. Each system collects the appropriate data in order for this type of report to be produced.
9. *Management of user accounts* – user accounts are required for each type of government official that is assigned to work with the system. The users fall into one of several possible categories, among them: administrators, common citizens, evaluators, and other personnel in charge of managing services approved. The final privileges that a particular user has depend on the category he/she belongs to and the position occupied in the agency. For example, the agency may include several programs, each offering in charge of supporting different types of services. An evaluator working for a particular program has the right to evaluate only services that are managed for that particular program that he/she works for.
10. *Manage waiting lists* – the management of waiting lists is important in order for the services to be offered in a fair manner and according to legal rules established. In some cases the agency is required to follow strict rules when determining the order of evaluation of applications and offering of the services. These may not only depend on chronological ordering, but on several attributes of the participant in the application.

In each one of the systems, our solutions include the creation of an internal database to be managed by the system. These databases are designed to include data that captures the internal business rules of the agencies: personnel, services that are offered, programs that support those services, and requirements that need to be satisfied. In addition, they are designed to store all the data that is collected from applications submitted, the evaluation conducted, and the administration of the services approved. All the data collected is stored in the system's database in order to be able to use it during the evaluation of future requests from the same person and for auditing purposes. Furthermore, the data collected is never erased, and any action registered in the system is always linked to the particular user that initiated it.

Each system allows the efficient management of the budget that has been allocated to each possible service. When a particular citizen submits an application for a particular service, such application is evaluated to determine if such person qualifies to receive such service, and if funds are available to support it. If the service is finally approved, the system facilitates the tracking of all the activities that need to be executed in order for the service to be offered. An important element of this validation is the avoidance of assigning to an individual more resource than he is entitled to by regulation or law. These policies are extremely hard, if not impossible, to implement on paper systems.

What follows is a more specific description of the services offered by each of the three government agencies included in this project.

7.1 Citizen's Services Office

The Citizen's Services Office at the Mayagüez city government manages financial support services that are offered to low income citizens. These services have the specific purpose of dealing with certain urgent needs requiring disbursement that the person cannot afford. Among others, the following needs may be supported by these services: payment for utilities, cover funeral costs, provide prepaid coupons for food, support the acquisition of health-related equipment, cover funeral costs, pay for eye glasses, pay for medicines, pay for medical appointments, pay for professional counseling, etc. The system developed aims to facilitate the process of submitting applications from citizens, to evaluate the applications, and to eventually administer the services offered in those cases that are approved.

7.2 Public Works Office

The Mayagüez City Public Works Department, identified as OPM (from its name in Spanish), has the duty to offer several different services to citizens in the region of Mayagüez with the ultimate goal of improving quality of life in the area. Among those services we can distinguish the following: debris clean-up, side-walks construction, road or street asphalting, public illumination construction, etc. The system developed has the following general capabilities: citizens are able to submit service requests online, system routes each request to the different working groups in the office which are qualified to handle the particular type of request it belongs to, the citizens themselves and the officials from the agency are able to use the system to give follow up to the process of solving the situation corresponding to a particular complaint, citizens are kept informed about the progress or the work, and the system is available to be used over the Web. The system is also capable of assigning priorities to services that need to be provided depending on the urgency of the situation, allows officials to assign resources, and must collect the appropriate data for auditing purposes.

7.3 Public Housing Office

The main goal of the Public Housing Department is to provide housing-related services to low income residents of Mayagüez. The services that are provided include house reconstructions, rent payments, emergency support, etc. They are sponsored by different federal programs, such as HOME, Section 8, CDGB, etc. The system developed has the main task of processing applications that constituents submit requesting services offered by the agency. If the particular service is finally awarded, then the system supports the management of the service being granted. The system maintains relevant data of the applicants and applications submitted, even if the services requested are not granted.

The application process requires collecting data from all the members of the family unit the applicant is part of. Once an application is completed, the system routes it to the proper program for its evaluation. The program finally evaluating an application is determined by the type of services being requested in the application.

7.4 Long Term Sustainability Plan

Although continued funding from NSF has facilitated the initial design and development effort, an alternative must be devised to provide continuous long term support to the effort initiated by this project. This alternative must guarantee the timely provision of technical support and training to the city at minimal cost. We proposed to the city the creation of a private company founded by UPRM students and faculty that would provide a comprehensive service package including technical support and software maintenance based on an application hosting model. The company will provide and maintain the computing platform that will host all the web applications. The company will sign a confidentiality agreement guaranteeing that all governmental information will be kept confidential.

The company will be able to provide the service package at an affordable price for several reasons. First, most of the supporting software used will be open source running off-the shelf standard hardware. Second, the company will aggressively seek to provide a similar package to other municipalities in the region in order to amortize common recurrent costs such as space, electricity, equipment, and bandwidth. Third, the company will amortize the cost of human resources by offering a comprehensive package including a myriad of services that would cost significantly more if offered by separate providers. These services include web site design and maintenance, backup maintenance, and equipment maintenance contracts among others.

8. SUMMARY

Although the UPRM Digital Government project has achieved significant advances in the transfer of information technology into one small city in Puerto Rico, it remains to be shown that these advances translate into a long term sustainable effort that extends beyond the city of Mayagüez. The UPRM will continue to collaborate with the city towards deploying an adequate networking infrastructure capable of supporting the provision of online services directly to citizens. The city has promised to continue investing towards this goal and consequently to improve the responsiveness and transparency of its government that would translate into improved quality and quantity of services and, as a result, an improved quality of life. The UPRM team has already spun off a private company to continue supporting the project through a social entrepreneurship endeavor. The central guiding principle throughout the development of the project has been the genuine interest from all participants in understanding and leveraging the particular interests and reward systems of the other parties to formulate opportunities generating significant value for all its participants. We strongly encourage other University/Government collaborations to seek similar opportunities and make the best of them.

REFERENCES

1. Apache Tomcat. The Apache Jakarta Project. http://*jakarta.apache.org/tomcat/*
2. Ballard, R. E-Government: An overview of what it is, benefits and issues. Land Information, New Zealand, 2001.
3. Bimber, B. Information and American Democracy. Cambridge UP, Cambridge, UK, 2003.

4. Bureau of Labor Statistics and United States Census Bureau. October 2003 Current Population Survey: Computer Use Supplement. http://www.bls.census.gov/cps/computer/computer.htm.
5. Cámara-Fuertes, L. The Phenomenon of Puerto Rican Voting. University Press of Florida, Gainesville, FL, 2004.
6. Chopra, V. et. al. Beginning JavaServer Pages. Wiley Publishing Inc. 2005.
7. Dahl R. A Preface to Democratic Theory. University of Chicago Press, Chicago, IL, 1956.
8. Dahl R. Democracy and its Critics. Yale University Press, New Haven, CT, 1989.
9. Freeman, E. *Head First Design Patterns.* O'Reilly. 2004.
10. Lijphart, A. Unequal Participation: Democracy's Unresolved Dilemma. The American Political Science Review. 91:1-14.
11. Nagel, J. Participation. Prentice Hall, Engelwood Cliffs, NJ, 1986.
12. Pavlichev, A and Garson, G. (eds.). Digital Government: Principles and Best Practices. Idea Group Publishing, Hershey, PA, 2003.
13. Rosenstone, S. and Hansen, M. Mobilization, Participation and Democracy in America. Mcmillan, New York, NY, 1993.
14. Rosenstone, S. and Wolfinger, R. The Effect of Voter Registration Laws on Voter Turnout. The American Political Science Review. 72:22-45.
15. US Bureau of the Census. Census of Population 2000, Detailed Characteristics: Puerto Rico. U.S. Government Printing Office, Washington, D.C. 2000.
16. Verba, S., Schlozman, K. and Brady, H. Voice and Equality: Civic Voluntarism in American Politics. Harvard UP, Cambridge, MA, 1995.

ACKNOWLEDGMENTS

This work has been supported by NSF Digital Government Grant EIA-0306791 and by the Puerto Rico Industrial Development Company (PRIDCO) under grant 2003-15. We would also like to thank the Municipality of Mayagüez, Puerto Rico, its mayor, Hon. Jose Guillermo Rodriguez, their liaison officer Eng. Jose Quiñones, and all their employees for their kind and energetic support to our project.

SUGGESTED READINGS

- Bhatnagar, Subhash. E-Government: From Vision to Implementation–A Practical Guide with Case Studies. Sage Publications Pvt. Ltd, 2004.
- Curtin, Gregory G., Michael H. Sommer, and Veronika Vis-Sommer. The World of E-Government. Haworth Press, 2004.
- Fountain, Jane E. Building the Virtual State: Information Technology and Institutional Change. Brookings Institution Press, 2001.

- Pavlichev, Alexei, and G. David Garson. Digital Government: Principles and Best Practices. Idea Group Publishing, 2003.
- West, Darrell M. Digital Government: Technology and Public Sector Performance. Princeton University Press, 2005.

ONLINE RESOURCES

- Cook, M. Making a case for local E-government. Center for Technology in Government, 2002: http://www.ctg.albany.edu/publications/guides/making_a_case/making_a_case.pdf
- Dada, D. (Editor) The failure of e-Government in developing countries, The Electronic Journal of Information Systems 2006, 26,7:1-10 http://www.ejisdc.org/ojs2/index.php/ejisdc/article/viewFile/277/176
- Bannister, F. Electronic Journal of e-Government: http://www.ejeg.com/index.htm

QUESTIONS FOR DISCUSSION

1. What particular advantages can e-government provide to smaller regional and municipal governments?
2. What are the implications of equality of access to government information and services?
3. In what ways can e-government enhance digital democracy?
4. How does the digital divide affect the successful implementation of e-government?
5. How can e-government help bridge the digital divide?
6. Can you think of novel ways to make collaborative digital government projects more self-sustainable?

Chapter 32

A HYBRID E-GOVERNMENT MODEL

Case Studies in Shanghai

Pengzhu Zhang[1], Xiaoning Mao[1], Xieping Tang[1], and Daniel Zeng[2]

[1]*Aetna School of Economics and Management, Shanghai Jiaotong University, Shanghai, China(email: pzzhang@sjtu.edu.cn, philipmao@online.sh.cn, and xieping@yahoo.com.cn);* [2]*Management Information Systems Department, University of Arizona, Tucson, Arizona, U.S.A., and Chinese Academy of Sciences, Beijing, China*

CHAPTER OVERVIEW

A wide range of e-government services is being made available in both online (through Web-based portals) and offline (through physical administrative service centers with backend computer support) settings. This chapter examines issues related to developing hybrid e-government projects leveraging both online and offline channels to maximize their impact. Three case studies based on ongoing projects initiated by various government branches in the Shanghai area are presented. The first case study focuses on Shanghai's online portal "China Shanghai." The second case study discusses a successful offline e-government project undertaken by the Qingpu District Government of Shanghai. The third case study is focused on a "Letters-and-Visits" (government customer relation and complaint processing) information system developed by the Xuhui District Government of Shanghai. The main findings of our studies indicate that hybrid e-government provides a convenient, timely, and implementable mechanism to bridge the digital divide. Its wide application is expected in developing countries.

1. INTRODUCTION

Most current e-government research emphasizes the use of the Internet and Web as the vehicle of e-government information and service delivery. In developed countries, this certainly reflects the practice as broadband connections and computer use are wide-spread (Al-Tawil and Sait 2002; Fang 2002; Graafland-Essers, Ettedgui et al. 2003; Reddick 2004). In a 2001 study, Layne and Lee summarize different phases of e-government project development, mostly on website development, and propose a four-stage model based on e-government project experience in the United States (Layne and Lee 2001). In their model, the first stage of e-government system development is mainly concerned with catalogue, which is characterized by online presence, a description and catalog of different types of services provided, and the availability of various forms that can be directly downloaded from the government website. The second stage is focused on transaction, providing various government services online with backend database support. The third stage is about vertical integration, linking local systems with complementary capabilities to develop an integrated system in a functional area. The last and fourth stage concerns horizontal integration, in which systems are integrated across functional areas to offer a one-stop environment to serve the users. Progressing in this sequence of stages entails an increased level of system integration and more complex coordination within and across organizations.

In a 2002 study, Ronaghan defines the goal of e-government projects as utilizing the Internet and Web for delivery of government information and services to citizens (Ronaghan 2002). In his study, a five-stage model, as summarized in Table 32-1, is proposed.

Table 32-1. A Five-Stage Model of E-Government Project (Ronaghan 2002)

	Stage	Description
1	Emerging	An official online presence is established
2	Enhanced	Website content are enhanced; information becomes increasingly dynamic
3	Interactive	Users can download forms, send e-mails to officials, and interact with service providers through the Web
4	Transactional	Users can pay for services and conduct other transactions online
5	Seamless	E-services are integrated across organizational boundaries

E-government system development in developing and developed countries shares many similarities. At the same time, due to differences in infrastructure (e.g., telecommunication infrastructure and Internet accessibility), user base (e.g., educational level), and political and governance system (e.g., the maturity level of various types of governmental service offerings), issues unique to developing countries need to be systematically studied. Research in this area is still sporadic but is attracting increasing attention (Backus 2001; Ndou 2004). Based on a survey of Chinese government Web portals, Zhao proposes a six-phase Chinese e-government model with a focus on e-government website (Zhao 2003). These six phases are as follows: online presence and informing the citizens of the portal effort; information dissemination; information search; online transactions for various government agencies; government project management; and information classification and service catalogues. Another broader six-stage model is proposed in (Wang 2004), trying to capture e-government projects and inter-agency collaboration beyond Web portals. These six stages are preparation, internal coordination, acceptance and transaction, mutual transaction, vertical integration, and horizontal integration.

This chapter is aimed at summarizing lessons learned from three real-world e-government projects in Shanghai. Although not an attempt to mount a comprehensive investigation of e-government development issues in developing countries, this chapter tries to provide insights as to the factors that are crucial to successful implementation of e-government projects in environments different from those studied in the current digital government literature on developed countries. A recurring theme when discussing these case studies is how to deal with the digital divide from the perspective of e-government in a rapidly-growing economy such as China.

The rest of the chapter is organized as follows. In Section 2, we provide some background information on Shanghai and its e-government initiatives. Section 3 discusses the first case study focusing on Shanghai's online portal "China Shanghai." The second case study, presented in Section 4, discusses an offline e-government project undertaken by the Qingpu District Government of Shanghai. Section 5 reports the third case study on a "Letters-and-Visits" – government customer relation and complaint processing – information system developed by the Xuhui District Government of Shanghai. The application context surrounding the development of this system is somehow unique to the Chinese governance model and raises interesting research questions about Government-to-Citizen (G2C) relation management (Carter and Belanger 2004; Lau and Chu 2004; Wang 2004). We conclude in Section 6, summarizing lessons learned and raising some future research questions.

2. SHANGHAI AND ITS E-GOVERNMENT INITIATIVES

Shanghai is located along the East Coast of China. It is a major economic, financial, trading, and tourism center of China, and an important international port city in Pacific Asia. The city covers about 6,340 square kilometers, of which 610 square kilometers are the suburban area. The city comprises 18 administrative districts and 1 county. Among them, 11 districts are in the urban area while the remaining 7 districts and 1 country are mainly in the suburban area.

According to recent official statistics, in 2004, the average GDP per capita in Shanghai was about USD 6,700, a level similar to that in a middle-tier developed country. The Lujiazui area in the Pudong District is one of the most active and affluent areas in Shanghai. In this area, 67% of the residents use computers and 40% of the residents have broadband Internet connections (Chen and Zhang 2004).

The Qingpu District is located in Shanghai's western suburban area. This district covers about 670 square kilometers, about one tenth of the city area. In 2004, the GDP in the Qingpu District reached USD 3.22 billion and the average GDP per capita was about USD 4,500. Measured by the average GDP per capita (only two thirds of the city average), Qingpu's economic condition is below average when compared to other districts (especially those in the downtown area).

Qingpu has a population of about 710,000, among which 456,000 are permanent residents and the remaining are immigrant workers from less-developed parts of the city and neighboring provinces. Among the permanent residents, 345,000 people are engaged in the agricultural sector. A large percentage of the immigrant and agricultural workers are illiterate, making computer or Internet accessibility irrelevant. The contrast between Qingpu and the Lujiazui area clearly demonstrates the enormous digital divide challenge Shanghai and China (among other developing countries) are facing.

In the 1990s, Shanghai started its e-government projects. Since then, Shanghai has developed a fairly comprehensive networking infrastructure to link governments at various levels including the municipal level, the district level, and the community/neighborhood level. The three Shanghai projects discussed in this chapter are representatives of a wide array of e-government initiatives that are being actively developed.

The first e-government project is the "China Shanghai" website (www.shanghai.gov.cn), which became operational in 2002. This e-government portal provides an online platform for Government-to-Citizen (G2C), Government-to-Business (G2B), Government-to-Employee, and

Government-to-Government (G2G) interactions (Fang 2002). In a recent competition organized by the United Nations on government websites, the "China Shanghai" website was ranked fifth.

The second e-government project studied in this chapter is an offline project by the Qingpu District. The purpose of this project is to integrate various government service functions in one physical location such that citizens can have a one-stop, convenient service "shopping" experience.

The third project is a G2C project initiated by the Xuhui District of Shanghai. As one of its most affluent urban districts, Xuhui has the highest concentration of cultural and scientific institutions in Shanghai and is home to many international corporations. This G2C project is being undertaken by a government branch in the Xuhui District Government, which is in charge of handling citizen complaints.

3. CASE STUDY I: "CHINA SHANGHAI"

"China Shanghai" is the Web portal for the Shanghai Municipal Government. It has been attracting a lot of Web traffic, with more than 400,000 average daily visits. This Web portal, developed and continuously refined over the course of the past five years, provides a communication channel for various departments and agencies within the Shanghai Municipal Government to disseminate information to the general public. It integrates many specialized government information sources and provides many transactional functions for people to conduct business and receive services from the government. In addition, as an exemplary e-government project, this portal serves many educational and public relation purposes.

"China Shanghai" is offered in three versions. The simplified Chinese version aims at people from mainland China; the traditional Chinese version is intended to be used by visitors from other regions of China and overseas Chinese; the English version targets at foreigners. The main components of this portal, as illustrated in Figure 32-1, include: the Shanghai news, Mayor's corner, information and announcements from government branches, key statistics, business transactions online, consultation and information online, investing in Shanghai, tourist information, citizen services, FAQ, and citizens' comments and feedback.

In order to provide better online service experience, the portal allows a user to assume one of the five different roles including ordinary resident, enterprise, investor, tourist, and special-need group (including senior citizens and children, among others). Depending on the role, different interfaces and service items will be presented. A user can also create a personalized page after registering with the portal and specifying a number of preferences regarding screen layouts, information contents, etc. The portal also offers advanced search functions to perform in-site searches.

"China Shanghai" has links to almost all of the 240+ government departments and agencies in Shanghai. Based on the classification scheme proposed by Ronaghan (Ronaghan 2002), e-government efforts in Shanghai at the municipal level have achieved Stage 4 (transactional). Tables 32-2 and 32-3 list the types of transactions that can be conducted through the portal and the number of related service items for citizens and businesses, respectively.

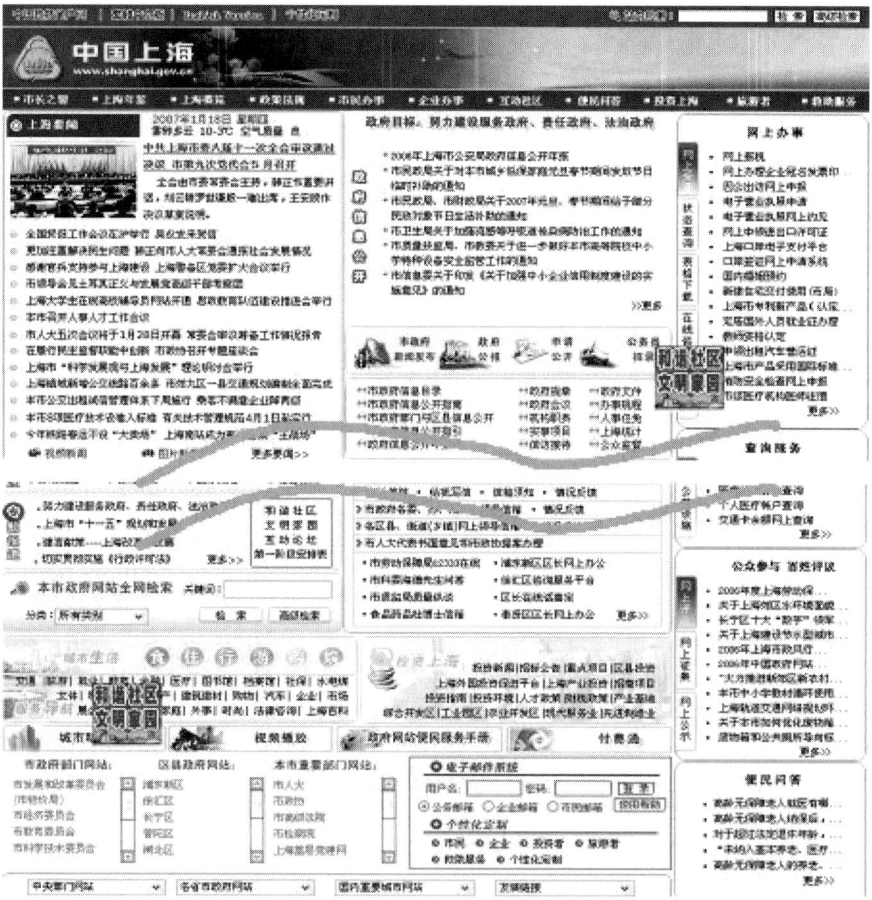

Figure 32-1. China Shanghai – www.shanghai.gov.cn

Table 32-2. Online transaction offerings for citizens

Service Types	# of Service Items
Family Planning	30
Real Estate	6
Transportation	52
Tourism	6
Documents and Certificates	23
Social Security and Services	17
Health	11
Personal Finance	11
Public Utilities	5
Legal Services and Consultation	13
Education	14
Public Safety and Police	40
Entry and Exit	13
Consumer Rights	4
Marriage	4
Jobs and Employment	38
Death	2
Total	**329**

Table 32-3. Online transaction offering for businesses

Service Types	# of Service Items
Registration of New Companies	25
Changes of Business	20
Business Certificates	63
Annual Verifications and Checkings	10
Taxation	24
Business Administration	22
Quality Control	63
Imports and Exports	56
Environmental Protection	86
Intellectual Property	15
Human Resources and Training	55
Labor Protection	8
Public Safety and Police	49
Legal Supervision	3
Natural Disaster Preparation and Response	24
City Development	79
Water Resources	27
Transportation	135
Project Approval	51
News Media and Publications	45
Broadcasting, Movies, and TV	63
Bankruptcy and dissolution	15
Others	104
Total	**1043**

As a citizen-oriented Web portal, "China Shanghai" offers a range of convenient services. For illustration purposes, we provide one example below. Two citizens wanting to get a marriage license can log on to "China Shanghai" and choose the "Online Marriage" function, managed by the Civil Affairs Bureau of the Shanghai Municipal Government. After providing necessary information such as the groom and the bride's names, national ID numbers, dates of birth, ages, addresses, contact information, etc., as shown in Figure 32-2, the users can proceed to make an appointment with a local marriage license office close to their home addresses. Before reservations are made, the backend system will verify the marital status of both parties and check other applicable rules. If everything is in order and the requested date is confirmed, the "Online Marriage" system will present the appointment page, as shown in Figure 32-3, providing detailed information about the appointment and the local marriage license office including its address and contact phone number. It even automatically calculates the bus route.

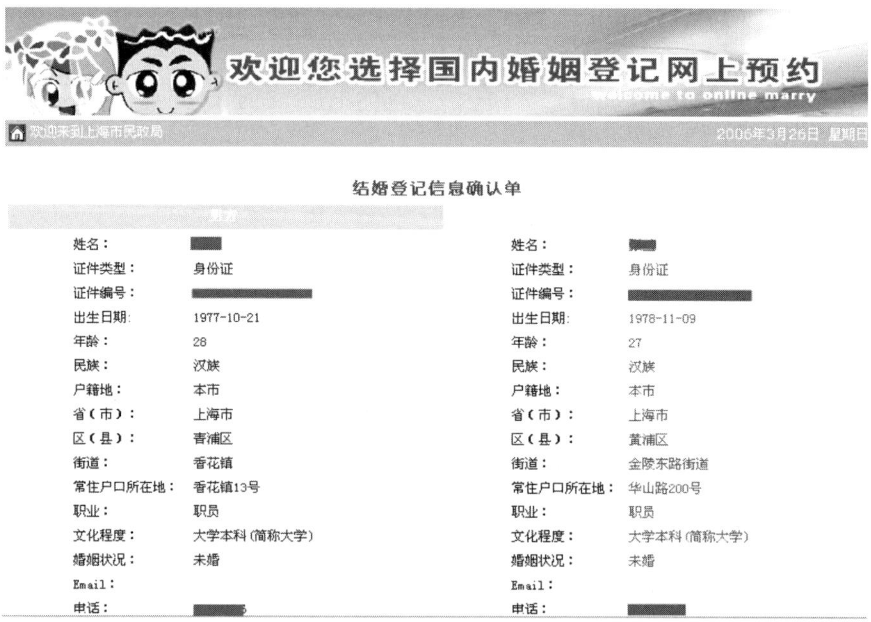

Figure 32-2. "Online Marriage" Service: Information Collection

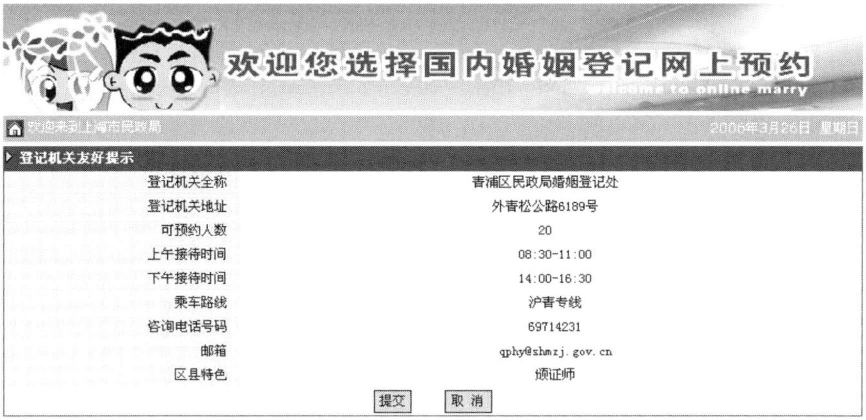

Figure 32-3. "Online Marriage" Service: Reservations Made

In addition to serving individual citizens, "China Shanghai" also serves local businesses by offering a variety of online transactions. We use the "Taxation Online" subsystem, accessible through "China Shanghai," to illustrate this type of G2B service. Shanghai has developed this "Taxation Online" system under a national-wide e-government initiative called the "Golden Tax" project. Figure 32-4 shows the primary information flow involved in this system.

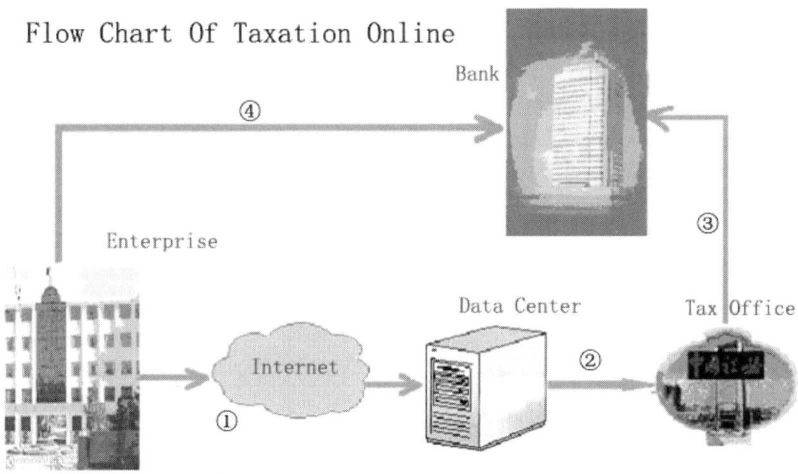

Figure 32-4. Taxation Online

From a procedural standpoint, online tax filing proceeds as follows. A local business first submits information online on "Taxation Online." At the backend, the portal forwards the collected information to an internal data center, which in turns pushes the business' request and related information to an appropriate taxation office based on the type of the tax filed. Officials in the taxation office process the request and if all the conditions are met, a participating bank will deduct tax money from the designated account. After the bank transaction is completed, the taxation officials will issue the receipt to the business.

Note that to complete the online transactions as described above, close coordination across organizational boundaries are necessary. The taxation office is responsible for processing the data entered by the business and applying applicable tax regulations and rules. The participating bank needs to manage the tax-related accounts and balance transfers. The "China Shanghai" portal manages the front-end part of user interaction, ensures the security of the portal system and data transfers, and logs all user activities. The Shanghai Electronic Certificate Authority Center Co., Ltd. is responsible for issuing the CA digital certificates for online taxation and providing third-party authentication services, to prevent data losses or sniffing.

District governments in Shanghai all participate in the "China Shanghai" project by developing their own local portals. In the next section, we will focus on an offline effort by the Qingpu District. In the remainder of this section, we briefly introduce Qingpu's online effort. As shown in Figure 32-5, as part of "China Shanghai," Qingpu has its own customized local one-stop Web portal to meet the specific needs of the citizens in the Qingpu District. This portal is offered in Simplified Chinese and English. It covers all the departments and agencies within the District Government. It also offers a range of services including District Commissioner's Corner, Letters-and-Visits (see Section 5), local news and announcements, local government contracts, local government regulations, tourist information, in-site Web search, among others.

4. CASE STUDY II: QINGPU'S ADMINISTRATIVE SERVICE CENTER

The Qingpu District's offline e-government project was partially motivated by the fact that many citizens do not yet have access to the Internet, or do not have sufficient education or training to use computers and the Web. It is particularly true for the population the Qingpu District Government serves, as discussed in Section 2.

Figure 32-5. Shanghai Qinpu District's Portal─www.shqp.gov.cn

As such, this e-government initiative is designed to partially address the significant challenge of the growing digital divide between the developed urban areas and less developed suburban areas in the Shanghai area. In effect, this challenge is applicable to many other parts of China as well as developing economies in other parts of the world.

Qingpu's offline project is centered around a one-stop Administration Service Center (ASC). This physical service center offers a range of services on governmental approvals, licenses, and certificates for both citizens and businesses. Before the ASC became operational, to conduct business or receive services, citizens and businesses often needed to visit multiple branches of the government located at different sites. When the ASC started to operate, however, these multiple visits can be consolidated into one visit, saving time and effort. For some complicated service items, for instance, registering for a new company which involves approvals from and coordination among several government branches, such savings can be really significant. To further streamline various administration service processes, the ASC has also implemented a consolidated one-stop payment system. The concept behind the ASC represents an innovation on government operations and its positive impact has been well-received.

The Qingpu ASC started its operation in 2002. It now has grown to cover 31 departments and 6 social service units of the District Government. Operated by more than 200 staff members, the ASC can handle 516 types of approvals, licenses, and other service items. In 2005, the center processed more than 90,000 service requests, representing a 20% jump from 2004, and approved 88,600 licenses, a 21.5% jump from 2004. The total number of citizens it served in 2005 reached more than 102,000.

Tables 32-4 and 32-5 list the departments and agencies offering services through the ASC to citizens and local businesses, respectively.

Table 32-4. Departments and Agencies Servicing Citizens through ASC

water resources bureau	municipal engineering bureau
marriage administration center	civil affairs bureau
union administration office	social welfare office
population and family planning office	tobacco monopoly office
coal and gas administration office	public health office
farming machine office	agricultural technology center
sports bureau	fishery office
police station	exit and entry administration office
price monitoring office	information committee
finance bureau	medical and health office
culture and media bureau	

Table 32-5. Departments and Agencies Servicing Businesses through ASC

development and reform committee	foreign trading committee
construction committee	planning bureau
housing and land planning bureau	firefighting office
economic committee	environment protection bureau
science and technology commission	statistical bureau
water resources bureau	industrial and commercial bureau
taxation bureau	civil air defense office
power bureau	work security and supervision bureau
telecommunication bureau	weather bureau
public health office	technical service bureau

In addition to various government departments and agencies, the Qingpu ASC also houses a number of business and social service entities to further reduce the citizens and local businesses' time and effort when doing business with the government. A partial list of these entities is given in Table 32-6.

Table 32-6. Sample Business and Social Service Entities Housed in ASC

several banks	Jieqiang construction company
foreign investment service center	Changxin accounting firm
Qingzhen engineering service center	Ronghao special equipment company
business center	Taikang life assurance company
representatives from the industrial park	

For quality assurance purposes, the ASC trains its staff members, whose primary employment is with different district government departments and agencies, on public service and professionalism [13]. It also implements an electronic evaluation system to collect feedback on the quality of service provided by each staff member who has direct contact with the customers. For instance, every transaction/service window has an electronic evaluation machine. After a transaction is completed, the citizen who just received the service can provide immediate feedback about his or her experience with the agent who provided the service. These machines have evaluation buttons labeled as "fully satisfied," "somewhat satisfied", and "dissatisfied." If the citizen deems the service as not fully satisfied, he or she can provide further feedback about why it is the case. Some sample reasons for the citizen to choose from are: "the service agent has a bad attitude," "the process takes too long", and "the service agent is not familiar with the task." All these evaluations are transmitted to a central server managed by the ASC. At the end of every month, the ASC will publicize the evaluation results on each participating government department or agency.

As many of these participating government departments have already had their own vertical information or transactional systems, the ASC has necessitated a district-level horizontal integration, at least in the backend computing sense. The ASC information system by itself represents a major e-government application. This system cuts across departmental boundaries and can monitor the status of each transaction along its entire life cycle. Its basic system architecture is shown in Figure 32-6.

We now use one example application concerning registering a new company to show the operations of the ASC. In China, registering a new company is complicated and time-consuming. The ASC has been proven to accelerate this process significantly through enabling parallel processing across government departments. Figure 32-7 shows the process of applying for the business license for a restaurant. This diagram was actually produced by the ASC management system, showing the entire workflow and expected time needed for each of the approvals (by different governing bodies).

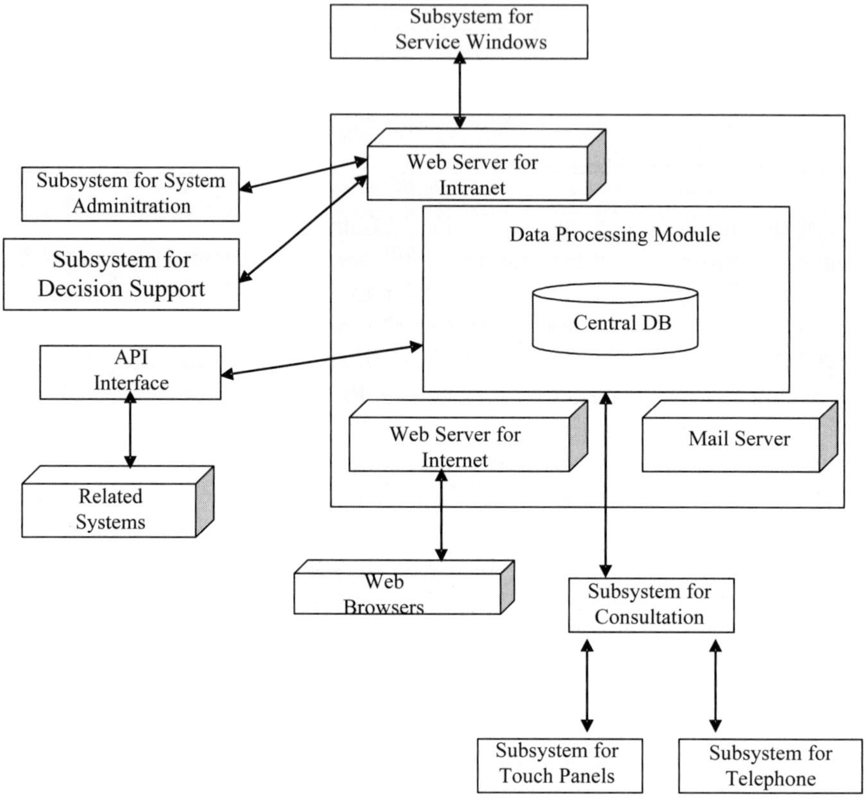

Figure 32-6. Qingpu ASC Management System

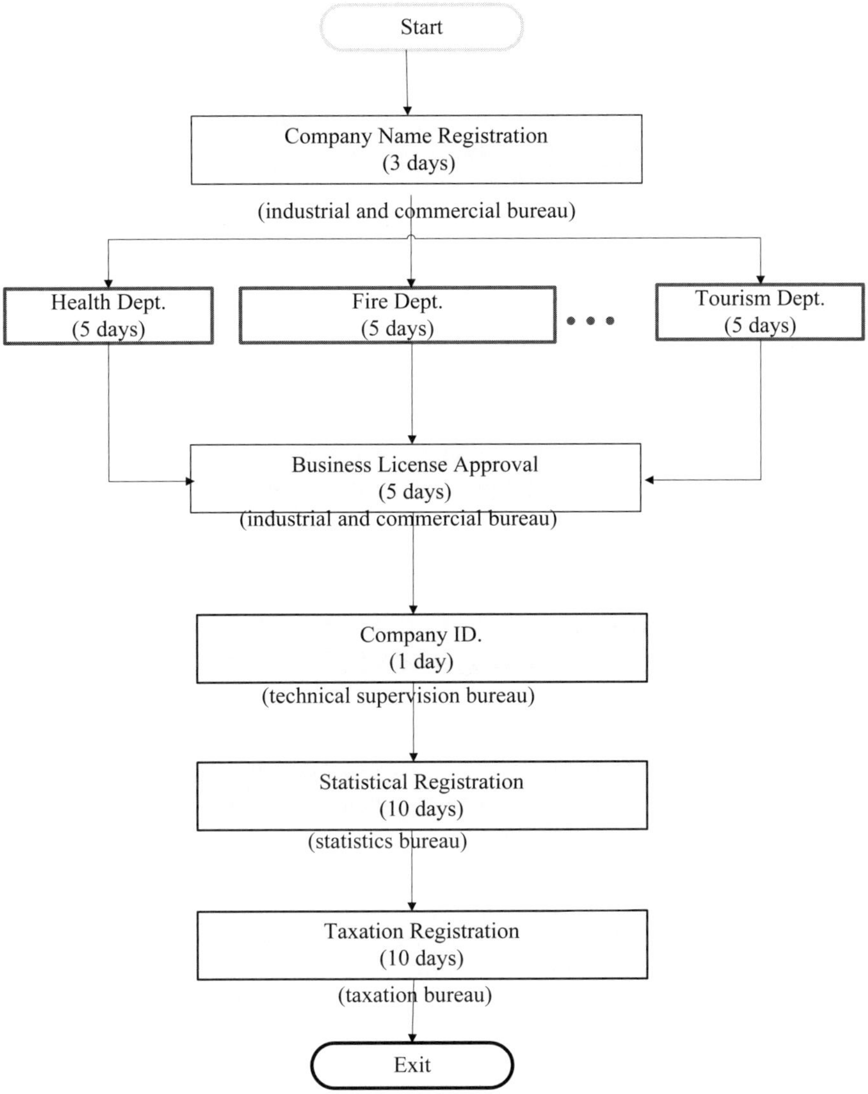

Figure 32-7. Process of Registering for a New Company

The Qingpu ASC has been operational for more than 4 years now. The advantages of such offline e-government projects have been evident. First, in developing countries, labor costs are low, while relatively speaking, massive investment in online e-government projects (including computing hardware, network infrastructure, and software) can be a big burden for local governments. Offline e-government projects in many cases are easier to get off the ground from an investment perspective. Second, in China, the governance model is rapidly moving towards citizen/business-centered, transparent, and service-oriented. The ASC provides a potentially low-cost environment to test drive e-government model changes and new ideas, which in a later stage may find their way to a fully-automated online implementation. Third, e-government projects are partially driven by the geographical distribution of the population being served. In many parts of China including Shanghai, population density is high, making the centralized ASC model cost-effective and appealing to the citizens and local businesses (Wei and Zhao 2005).

5. CASE STUDY III: A G2C "LETTERS-AND-VISITS" INFORMATION SYSTEM

The Central Government of China has been promoting service-oriented government operations for years. G2C relation management plays a critical role in this effort and e-government technology provides an enabling platform to improve the effectiveness and efficiency of G2C relation management (Lee, Tan et al. 2005; Jiang, Wu et al. 2006; Streib and Navarro 2006).

An important aspect of G2C relation management is concerned with how to handle citizens' complaints. In almost all levels of governments in China, there is a dedicated office called "Letters-and-Visits" that is in charge of handling citizens' complaints. These offices accept complaints either through mails (and more recently emails) or face-to-face meetings. In recent years, because of the fast-paced economic development and resulting social and economic structural changes, the number of the complaints submitted to various Letters-and-Visits offices has increased sharply. Some of the leading causes for these complaints are unemployment, land use, city development projects, apartment building demolition and re-development, and environmental concerns. How to improve the effectiveness and efficiency of the operations of Letters-and-Visits offices, given the limited availability of funding and man power, becomes a pressing issue nation-wide.

We summarize below the main problems with the current, largely manually-driven Letters-and-Visits process. (a) As almost every level of government has a Letters-and-Visits office, the duties of these offices often overlap and in many cases are ill-defined. This has created a lot of confusion to the citizens. (b) The current process of handling complaints is not efficient and an effective tracking and logging system is lacking. As a result, many citizens bypass the local Letters-and-Visits offices and visit the Letters-and-Visits Bureau in the Central Government. When the central office receives these complaints, they send them back to the local branches for investigation. This costly and time-consuming process is known to result in major dissatisfaction from the citizens. (c) More often than not, a complaining citizen will send the same complaint letter to multiple Letters-and-Visits offices at once. Processing these duplicated letters leads to a great deal of lost productivity. Furthermore, the citizen can be very frustrated when different offices, without knowing they are handling the same case, provide different answers and responses.

As a national response, the Chinese Central Government issued the New Letters and Visits Act in 2005, calling for the development of interoperable Letters-and-Visits information systems and both vertical and horizontal system integration.

The case in point is the Letters-and-Visits information system developed by the Xuhui District in Shanghai. This system is aimed at (a) integrating complaint reporting and processing functions, (b) providing full data analysis capabilities, (c) improving the portion of the complaint cases being successfully resolved in the first round of processing, (d) making the entire handling process transparent to the citizens, (e) providing additional channels for complaint submission (e.g., by email and Web), and (f) providing quantifiable measures and statistics to assess the performance of the Letters-and-Visits office.

Figure 32-8 shows a typical business process before the Letters-and-Visits system was adopted. The problems discussed above concerning the general problems of the current Letters-and-Visits handing approach manifest themselves in this local context: overlapping duties, dispersed data, duplicated processing, potentially conflicting responses, etc.

Figure 32-9 illustrates a typical business process after the Letters-and-Visits information system was implemented. This represents a much-improved, cleaner, and more efficient work flow. A complaining citizen just needs to access one government Web portal, a component of "China Shanghai," which is linked to the Letters-and-Visits system, to report and track the progress of his or her case. In an offline situation, visiting any of the Letters-and-Visits offices will allow this citizen to learn about the current status of his or her case. Government officials can receive real-time updates about cases and related statistics. Communications between different functional departments can be done and logged through the system as well.

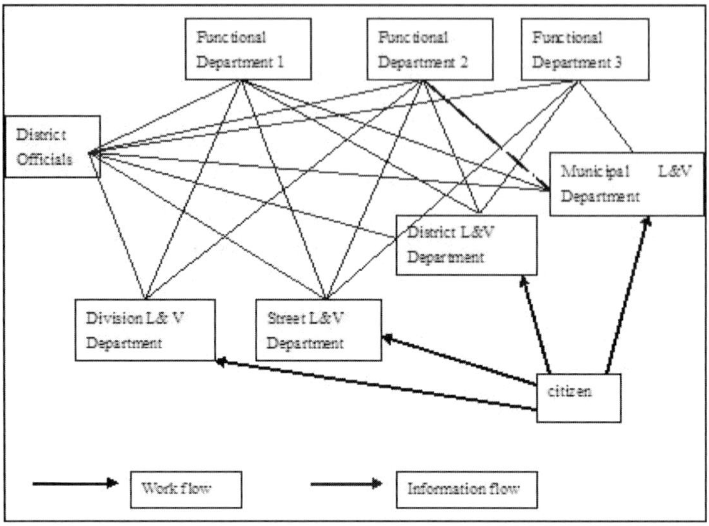

Figure 32-8. Business Process before the Implementation

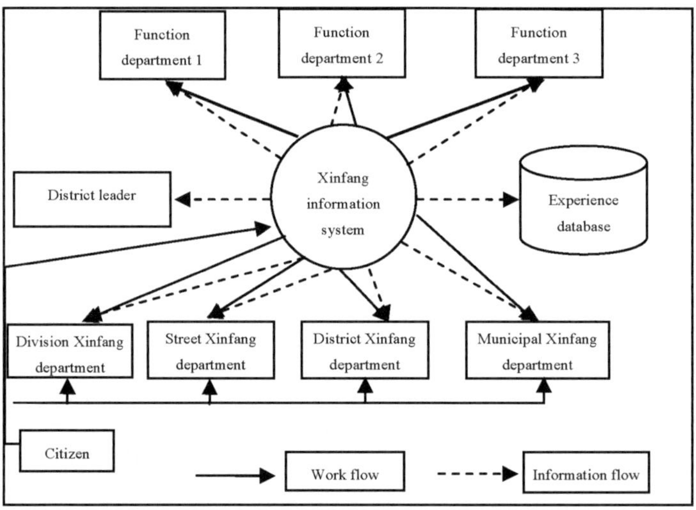

Figure 32-9. Business Process after the Implementation

Figure 32-10 shows the detailed case handling process. When a staff member receives a complaint letter, she inputs all the pertinent information from the letter and then classifies the case based on a predefined scheme. If this case is deemed particularly important and urgent, this case will be forwarded to her supervisor directly. For regular complaints, she will make suggestions about how to handle them and record the suggestions on the system. After that, the case will be sent to the supervisor and wait for input and approval. When the supervisor inputs his or her opinion, the case will continue to be processed based on the decisions about how it should be handled.

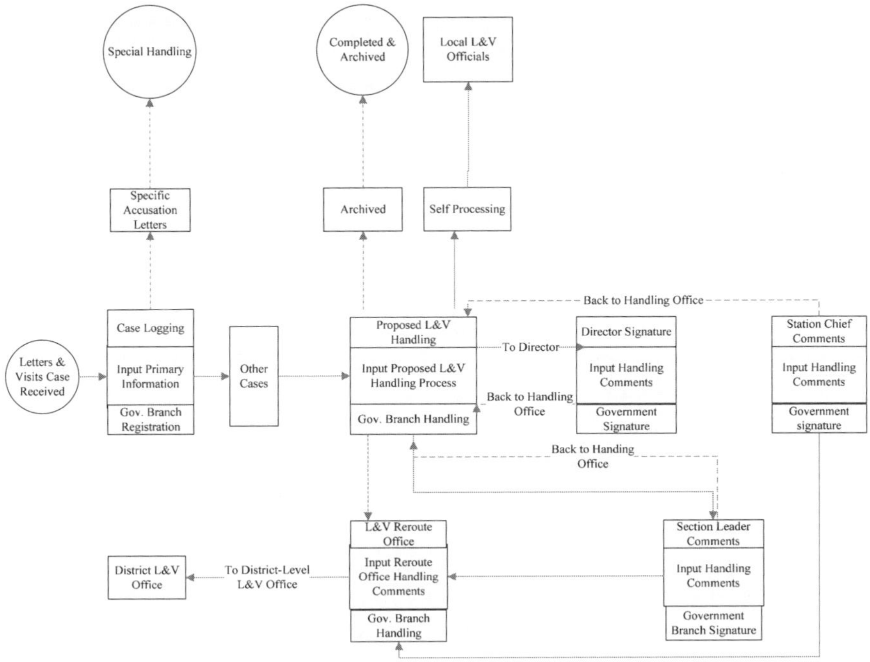

Figure 32-10. Complaint Handling Process

This Letters-and-Visits information system of the Xuhui District became operational in July 2005. It has been well-received by both citizens and government workers. Several other governments are developing their own Letters-and-Visits systems using the Xuhui system as a model. In a recent evaluation, it is concluded that most of its design objectives as discussed above are met. Also, it is worthwhile noting that this G2C application of Letters-and-Visits allows for both online (i.e., citizens can use the online version of the system directly for case reporting and tracking) and offline (i.e., government officials help process complaints received in mails or help visiting citizens enter their cases and update them about progress based on the same backend system) operations.

6. CONCLUDING REMARKS

In this chapter, we have discussed three e-government projects undertaken by Shanghai Municipal Government and two of its district governments. A running theme of our discussion is the need for the development of hybrid e-government projects, taking advantages of both online and offline systems. This form of hybrid e-government model is particularly important for developing countries where Internet and computer use are not as wide-spread as in developed countries. This e-government model also helps bridge the gap of the growing digital divide.

We conclude this chapter by discussing two key challenges of fully developing hybrid e-government systems.

First, to fully realize the potential of hybrid e-government systems, close coordination between and system integration (in the backend sense) across their online and offline components are a must. Unfortunately, due to a number of practical reasons, a lot of obstacles need to be overcome to implement this integration. Take the Qingpu case as an example. The Qingpu ASC has its own website with its own backend system support, separated from the online portal of the Qingpu District Government. No plans yet exist to integrate these systems because of administrative reasons. Such separation will lead to obvious problems with government operations and can cause a lot of confusion to the citizens served. Studying service integration, in particular, in a cross-channel context, is important from both research and implementation perspectives.

Second, information system adoption issues need to be seriously approached in the e-government setting. In the case of the Xuhui Letters-and-Visits system, we found that the use of its offline component exceeds substantially the use of its online Web component. Part of the reason could be the demographic distribution of the citizens filing the complaints. However, this reason alone cannot explain the observed phenomenon. We strongly suspect that psychological and social considerations also play a significant role. Studying these issues in a systematic manner can lead to fruitful findings.

ACKNOWLEDGEMENTS

This research was supported in part by the National Natural Science Foundation of China (NSFC) project No.70533030. The last author wishes to acknowledge support from an international collaboration grant (2F05NO1) from the Chinese Academy of Sciences, a 973 program grant (2006CB705500) from the National Natural Science Foundation of China, and a U.S. NSF Information Technology Research Grant (#IIS-0428241).

REFERENCES

Al-Tawil, K. M. and S. M. Sait (2002). E-Governance – Where We Stand? The World Bank Group The Fourth Mediterranean Development Forum. Amman, Jordan.

Backus, M. (2001). "E-Governance in Developing Countries." *IICD Research Brief*(1).

Carter, L. and F. Belanger (2004) "Citizen Adoption of Electronic Government Initiatives." *in* the 37th Hawaii International Conference on System Sciences (HICSS'04) - Track 5 Volume, 50119.3 DOI:

Chen, H. and Q. Zhang (2004). "Shanghai's E-Government: Implementation Strategies and A Case Study."

Fang, Z. (2002). "E-Government in Digital Era: Concept, Practice, and Development." *International Journal of The Computer, The Internet and Management* 10(2): 1 - 22.

Graafland-Essers, I., E. Ettedgui, et al. (2003). Benchmarking E-Government in Europe and the US.

Jiang, L., R. Wu, et al. (2006). "Research Frame on Service Quality Control of E - Government." *Information Science* 24(2): 310 - 315.

Lau, A. and R. Chu (2004). "A Study on the Constructs for Citizen utilization of E-Government Services in Hong Kong." *International Review of Law, Computers & Technology* 18(1): 109 - 132.

Layne, K. and J. Lee (2001). "Developing Fully Functional E-Government: A Four Stage Model." *Government Information Quarterly* 18(2): 122 - 136.

Lee, S. M., X. Tan, et al. (2005). "Current Practices of Leading E-Government Countries." *Communications of the ACM* 48(10): 99 -104.

Ndou, V. D. (2004). "E-Government for Developing Countries: Opportunities and Challenges." *The Electronic Journal on Information Systems in Developing Countries(EJISD)* 18(1): 1 - 24.

Reddick, C. G. (2004). "A Two Stage Model of E-Government Growth: Theories and Empirical Evidence for U.S. Cities." *Government Information Quarterly* 21(1): 51 - 64.

Ronaghan, S. A. (2002). Benchmarking E-government: A Global perspective. *American Society for Public Administration (ASPA) & United Nations Division for Public Economics and Public Administration*. New York.

Streib, G. and I. Navarro (2006). "Citizen Demand for Interactive E-Government:The Case of Georgia Consumer Services." *The American Review of Public Administration* 36(3): 288 - 300.

Wang, H. (2004). *Information Technology and e-Government: e-Government in the Information Age (Chinese)*, Tsinghua University Press.

Wei, X. and J. Zhao (2005). Citizens' Requirement Analysis in Chinese E-Government *in* Proceedings of the 7th International Conference on Electronic Commerce Xi'an, China, ACM Press: 525 - 528.

Zhao, X. (2003). "The Development Situations in Chinese Government Portals in 2003."

SUGGESTED READINGS

- "Better Services, Better Government---The Federal Government' E-government Strategy," Commonwealth of Australia, November 2002; downloadable from http://www.agimo.gov.au/. The document presents a policy framework within which Australian Federal departments and agencies pursue fully-fledged e-government applications to realize sustained benefits to citizens, business and government itself.

- "E-government and Developing Countries: An Overview," Subhajit Basu, International Review of Law, Computers & Technology, Volume 18, Number 1, pp. 109-132, March 2004. This paper provides an overview of legal and infrastructural issues related to e-government project development in developing countries.
- "Citizen Adoption of Electronic Government Initiatives," Lemuria Carter and France Belanger, in Proceedings of the 37th Hawaii International Conference on System Sciences (HICSS-2004), pp. 1-10. This paper reports a model building effort that integrates constructs from multiple technology adoption and acceptance theories to study a number of key factors that influence citizen adoption of e-government systems.

ONLINE RESOURCES

- "China Shanghai," www.shanghai.gov.cn. As discussed in Section 3, this website is the Web portal of the Shanghai Municipal Government.
- "Shanghai Qingpu Administrative Service Center," service.shqp.gov.cn. This website is the online portion of the Shanghai Qingpu Administrative Service, augmenting its offline operations.
- "Shanghai Qingpu District," www.shqp.gov.cn. This website is the Web portal of the Shanghai Qingpu District Government.

QUESTIONS FOR DISCUSSION

1. What are the key differences in citizen service requirements in developed versus developing countries from the point of view of e-government system requirement engineering?
2. Is the idea of hybrid e-government systems applicable to developed countries as well?
3. How can e-government projects benefit citizens who have no access to the Internet? How can e-government projects help bridge the digital divide?
4. What is special about G2C system development relative to the development of other types of e-government systems?
5. What are the key factors influencing adoption of G2C systems? Are they different from those studied in the context of Business-to-Consumer (B2C) systems?

AUTHOR INDEX

Acharya, Raj....................................377
Adam, Nabil R. 307
Adams, Nick.....................................487
Agouris, Peggy..................................353
Atluri, Vijay...................................307

Becker, Shirley Ann.............................141
Bederson, Benjamin B. 157
Boer, Alexander.................................223
Bornhövd, Christof..............................307
Borning, Alan...................................439
Brandt, Lawrence E..............................203
Breuker, Joost..................................223
Burke, G. Brian.................................421

Cai, Guoray.....................................395
Chen, Chen......................................615
Chen, Hsinchun..................263, 531, 585
Chun, Soon Ae...................................307
Coleman, Stephen..................................3
Conrad, Frederick G.............................157
Cooper, Jim.....................................307
Croitoru, Arie..................................353
Cullen, Rowena..................................647

Dawes, Sharon S. 103
Delcambre, Lois M. L............................561
Díaz, Walter, ...671

Fioravanti, Fabio...............................331
Förster, Ruth...................................439
Fortes, José A. B. 283
Fuhrmann, Sven..................................395

Gieber, Helene..................................467
Gil-Garcia, J. Ramon............................421
Glasmeier, Amy..................................377
Gregg, Valerie J. 203
Grönlund, Åke....................................61

Hanmer, Michael J. 157
He, Wei...615
Herrnson, Paul S. 157
Hovy, Eduard.................................43, 219
Hsu, Fang-Ming..................................585
Hu, Paul Jen-Hwa................................585

Janeja, Vandana P. 307
Johnston, Jim...................................487

Karr, Alan F. 503
Kaza, Siddharth.................................263

Leitner, Christine...............................467

MacEachren, Alan................................395
Macintosh, Ann...............................85, 487
Maier, David....................................561
Mao, Xiaoning...................................697
Matsunaga, Andréa...............................283
Myers, Wayne....................................377

Nardelli, Enrico................................331
Nielsen, Marianne Lykke.........................561
Niemi, Richard G. 157
Núñez-Molina, Mario.............................671

Orthofer, Gerti.................................467

Paczkowski, John................................307
Paliwal, Aabhas V...............................307
Pardo, Theresa A................................421

Patil, G.P. 377
Phoha, Shashi 377
Price, Susan 561

Rathbun, Stephen 377
Regan, Priscilla M. 127
Rivera-Vega, Pedro I. 671
Rodríguez-Martínez, Manuel 671

Schaper, Joachim 307
Scholl, Hans J. (Jochen) 21
Stefanidis, Anthony 353

Tang, Xieping 697
Tolle, Timothy 561
Traugott, Michael W. 157
Traunmüller, Roland 467
Tsugawa, Maurício 283

Valente, André 223
Van Engers, Tom M. 223
Vélez-Rivera, Bienvenido 671

Waddell, Paul 439
Weaver, Mathew 561
Whyte, Angus 181, 487
Winkels, Radboud 223

Xing, Chunxiao 615

Yan, Ping 531
Yang, Jijiang 615

Zeng, Daniel 531, 697
Zhang, Pengzhu 697
Zhang, Yong 615

SUBJECT INDEX

A

access control..... 286, 290, 534, 535, 536, 537, 552, 558, 685
administrative law 233, 235, 240, 241, 260
administrative license 638
Africa.. 212, 341
African American 171
agency performance... 585, 587, 592, 593, 595, 599, 607, 608, 613
air quality............ 228, 440, 451, 461, 570
archive management...589, 590, 591, 592, 594, 595, 596, 597, 607, 608
artificial intelligence......... 233, 268, 543, 551
Asians 665
assessment...... 24, 38, 72, 96, 98, 105, 107, 114, 120, 131, 147, 150, 152, 157, 165, 172, 183, 193, 307, 364, 392, 396, 399, 402, 412, 415, 440, 450, 457, 458, 468, 474, 480, 554, 558, 581, 587, 596, 598, 599, 600, 608, 669, 683
assistive technology.......... 143, 144, 145, 149, 151
Australia 67, 136, 212, 455, 590, 649, 650, 662, 666, 667
Austria 334, 335
authentication 95, 132, 134, 138, 139, 184, 292, 332, 333, 334, 335, 336, 337, 338, 339, 341, 342, 343, 345, 346, 347, 348, 349, 352, 573, 592, 657, 706

B

Beijing..... 615, 621, 622, 632, 633, 637, 638, 639, 640, 643
Belgium 335, 337, 348
best practice........ 92, 116, 352, 425, 471, 476, 478, 490, 587, 609, 669
biodiversity 214, 378, 444
bridging backbone.......331, 334, 349, 350
business and technology 586, 587, 591, 594, 599, 607, 608
business model.....22, 205, 627, 639, 640, 642, 643
business process.....39, 40, 104, 111, 113, 114, 120, 135, 204, 205, 287, 473, 591, 624, 638, 640, 641, 642, 713
business strategy.........592, 593, 594, 595, 596, 599, 608

C

call centers 601, 606, 607, 608
Canada......... 67, 212, 496, 513, 649, 650, 662, 666, 667
catalog system 627
causal dimensions 309, 310, 312, 313, 316, 321, 322, 325, 326
census forms.......649, 653, 654, 655, 656, 657, 658, 659, 663, 665, 666
central government.....588, 592, 597, 603, 616, 617, 618, 620
chief complaint...539, 540, 541, 542, 547, 548, 549, 554, 555, 556
China....553, 609, 615, 616, 617, 618, 619, 620, 621, 623, 626, 632, 637, 638, 643, 644, 645, 697, 699, 700, 701, 702, 704, 705, 706, 707, 709, 712, 713, 716, 717, 718
Chinese.......230, 549, 550, 553, 616, 619, 626, 644, 645, 697, 699, 701, 706, 713, 716, 717
citizen device 345, 347, 348
citizen participation......91, 92, 101, 186, 207, 490, 494, 500, 673, 676, 681
citizenship 13, 14, 102, 157, 176, 179, 336

city government... 37, 108, 602, 603, 683, 691
civil society...... 86, 87, 88, 89, 90, 92, 99, 102, 181, 182, 183, 184, 489, 494
cluster 24, 25, 29, 32, 49, 51, 68, 226, 303, 307, 377, 378, 379, 380, 391, 393, 394, 521, 522, 539, 545, 551, 555, 605
clustering 67, 69, 325, 392, 546, 551, 554, 557, 559
collusion distance metric based 321
compliance..........146, 147, 149, 150, 153, 308, 342, 417, 471, 474, 495, 589, 590, 599, 659, 664, 684
computer science... 23, 27, 30, 39, 46, 54, 82, 85, 98, 99, 100, 101, 104, 141, 157, 176, 179, 208, 215, 230, 279, 351, 373, 375, 377, 382, 418, 439, 446, 449, 453, 461, 462, 525, 556, 557, 579, 671, 672
controlled vocabularies...... 194, 221, 222, 563, 565, 566, 567, 576, 577, 581, 582, 583
county government..... 120, 131, 602, 603
court processes........................... 128, 251
court information 130
court records 130, 131
courts 158, 246, 251, 264, 441,
criminal justice .. 426, 427, 428, 431, 432, 436, 444
crisis management 208, 215, 395, 403,, 407, 415, 416, 417, 418
crisis response........ 45, 52, 214, 407, 408, 416, 418, 423, 429, 434
cross-boundary information sharing.. 421, 422, 426, 429, 436, 437, 438
cultural and technical logic.................. 13
cultural backgrounds 478
cultural beliefs 49
cultural development 616
cultural goals 284
cultural institutions 701
cultural issues...................................481
cultural norms 651
cultural politics....................................95
culture 8, 17, 18, 37, 50, 57, 66, 68, 110, 112, 421, 422, 431, 471, 476, 481, 488, 495, 496, 602, 613, 633, 708
cyber attacks.......................................390
cyberdemocracy 92
cyberinfrastructure 209, 213, 283, 284, 285, 299, 300, 390
cybernetics 5, 468
cybersecurity 390
cyberspace..17

D

data analysis.74, 107, 370, 533, 534, 538, 539, 543, 544, 548, 549, 551, 554, 557, 559, 713
data collection..55, 70, 73, 115, 116, 117, 118, 210, 219, 220, 221, 222, 223, 224, 225, 226, 227, 228, 304, 359, 375, 424, 504, 515, 531, 535, 537, 539, 540, 547, 549, 553, 588, 599, 648, 653, 655, 656
data integration...106, 210, 219, 221, 223, 285, 353, 354, 355, 356, 357, 358, 359, 370, 375, 376, 413, 429, 635, 653
data mining...97, 206, 278, 281, 309, 310, 325, 329, 365, 370, 373, 423, 527, 534, 536, 555, 556, 557, 558, 644
data quality........ 108, 110, 115, 117, 358, 371, 376, 397, 423, 504, 508, 509, 511, 525, 527, 529, 540, 652, 655, 663
data quality management 117, 358, 376
data sets 68, 117, 118, 120, 220, 227, 311, 312, 325, 328, 355, 356, 357, 358, 405, 503, 504, 513, 519, 520, 521, 522, 526
data source . 109, 117, 118, 119, 220, 221, 222, 223, 225, 229, 265, 268, 269, 273, 276, 278, 307, 326, 356, 358, 370, 375, 376, 511, 533, 539, 540, 543, 547, 634

database 106, 107, 115, 117, 132, 185, 186, 190, 222, 224, 225, 227, 228, 229, 230, 231, 264, 265, 266, 268, 270, 273, 276, 279, 280, 285, 291, 292, 293, 294, 296, 298, 300, 302, 308, 327, 338, 340, 344, 351, 353, 354, 359, 360, 363, 365, 370. 372, 373, 423, 428, 435, 455, 457, 477, 478, 484, 492, 493, 495, 505, 506, 507, 508, 509, 516, 524, 526, 527, 529, 532, 547, 556, 557, 573, 575, 583, 589, 592, 596, 609, 617, 627, 630, 631, 632, 635, 644, 645, 648, 649, 650, 655, 656, 658, 662, 672, 686, 689, 690, 698
decision makers 395, 396, 397, 399, 401, 403, 404, 413, 674, 682
decision support system..... 279, 377, 378, 416
decision-making process ... 86, 88, 89, 91, 183, 441, 446, 499
democratic process .. 5, 14, 86, 87, 88, 92, 440, 442, 445, 451, 488, 501
Denmark 473, 562, 565, 577, 580
Department of Environmental Protection............................... 387, 429
Department of Health 128, 137, 152, 155, 391, 393, 422, 428, 438, 549, 553, 603
Department of Health Services... 549, 553
Department of Homeland Security 278, 321, 398, 399, 400, 414, 418, 419, 438
Department of Justice 155, 266, 273, 275, 422, 427, 437, 438
developing countries.... 82, 463, 610, 612, 695, 697, 699, 700, 712, 716, 717, 718
development project 63, 64, 65, 79, 81, 684, 712
digital archive 600, 601, 606, 607
digital democracy . 89, 100, 197, 500, 695
digital government research program .. 53, 203, 205, 206, 208, 211, 214, 216
digital identity card............................ 339
digital libraries... 104, 230, 561, 562, 563, 564, 566, 576, 578, 579, 581, 582, 583, 682
digital signature.. 133, 333, 334, 335, 336, 337, 339, 340, 341, 342, 343, 492
discussion forum 487, 490, 492, 495, 496, 499
disease informatics..... 531, 532, 533, 549, 552, 557
disease outbreak . 379, 391, 532, 538, 554, 556, 557
disease surveillance.... 379, 533, 534, 537, 538, 547, 552, 554, 555, 556, 559
distance metric ... 227, 231, 311, 312, 321, 356, 363
district government 697, 699, 701, 706, 708, 709, 716
diversity.. 4, 109, 121, 476, 478, 479, 482, 585, 588
domain experts ... 273, 309, 316, 321, 329, 454, 566, 600, 623
domain model............................. 225, 226
domain-specific terminology 577, 583
Dominican Republic .. 283, 284, 293, 294, 295, 296, 301
Dutch administrative law 233, 235, 241
Dutch criminal law..... 233, 235, 251, 252, 253

E

e-citizenship 13
e-Court European project.... 232, 235, 248
e-democracy..... 85, 88, 89, 90, 92, 93, 94, 99, 100, 101, 182, 198, 473, 475, 500
E-GOV conferences 55, 61, 62, 57, 58, 75, 76, 78, 80, 81, 436
e-governance 3, 6, 8, 9, 10, 11, 12, 13, 14, 15, 16, 17, 19, 39, 181, 182, 184, 187, 197, 212, 717
e-government construction 615, 617, 618, 620, 621, 626, 637, 643
e-government initiative 58, 127, 129,

136, 586, 673, 674, 675, 676, 681, 699, 700, 705, 707
e-government resources..... 143, 151, 677, 678, 679, 680, 681, 682
e-government services... 17, 586, 588, 594, 597, 650, 676, 677, 678, 679, 681, 697
economics.... 25, 446, 449, 517, 616, 617, 620
elected assemblies 87, 183, 184, 188, 196,
elected representatives.. .... 85, 86, 87, 88, 89, 181, 182, 183, 184, 185, 186, 187, 188, 194, 196, 197, 199, 489, 499
electronic identity...... 332, 333, 334, 335, 337, 340, 341, 346, 347, 351, 352
electronic identity card...... 335, 336, 337, 338, 340, 341, 343, 344, 352
electronic record management... 585, 587, 590, 593, 600
Electronic Signature Law of PRC 617
electronic signatures... 133, 338, 346, 347
electronic voting. 157, 158, 176, 192, 214
electronic voting machines. 176, 177, 179
electronic voting records 178
electronic voting systems .. 157, 158, 176, 177, 192
emergency management.... 307, 314, 395, 396, 397, 398, 399, 400, 402, 403, 404, 406, 407, 408, 412, 413, 414, 415, 416, 417, 419, 420
emergency response... 365, 396, 398, 408, 416, 417, 427, 433, 437
emergency situations..........395, 396, 397, 398, 403, 407, 415, 481
England...................... 246, 496, 500, 662
enhanced semantic graph... 307, 309, 310, 312, 313, 324
enterprise architecture. 124, 302, 304, 590, 623, 643, 644, 645
environmental impact... ..... 124, 440, 444, 446, 451, 462
environmental impacts 124, 440, 442, 444, 446, 451, 462, 463, 562
environmental protection ...227, 387, 392, 423, 429, 460, 510, 703
e-Participation research..... 85, 88, 94, 95, 98, 101
epistemological framework...... 233, 242, 247, 254, 256, 257, 261
Estonia........................336, 337, 338, 348
Europe.... 4, 5, 14, 22, 50, 85, 86, 88, 90, 94, 98, 99, 181, 184, 186, 187, 191, 192, 193, 194, 209, 212, 233, 256, 333, 334, 336, 338, 339, 341, 468, 469, 470, 471, 473, 474, 476, 477, 478, 479, 481, 484, 485, 488, 489, 491, 582, 611, 662, 665
European Commission.5, 68, 94, 99, 197, 468, 469, 470, 471, 491
European E-Government Society .58, 217
European Union 24, 32, 334, 339, 351, 352, 437, 469, 470
exchange system........ 615, 621, 626, 629, 630, 631, 632, 634, 643, 645
exchange system architecture 629
execution environment.......287, 290, 293, 295, 299

F

federal agencies.......... 130, 142, 145, 146, 204, 205, 206, 209, 264, 267, 396, 428, 527
federal e-government 142, 143, 147, 150, 151, 154, 155
Federal Emergency Management Agency... 399, 416
Federal Enterprise Architecture.... ..... 124, 590, 623, 645
federal government 49, 123, 133, 137, 142, 146, 155, 207, 208, 210, 211, 214, 216, 336, 508, 536, 624, 717
federal statistical agencies..204, 211, 513, 526, 528
federal websites....150, 153,154, 505, 514

Forest Service (U.S.)......... 561, 562, 566, 571, 577, 578, 579, 580
Finland.................................. 94, 337, 338
France 338, 344

G

geographic information systems (GIS) 371, 372, 395, 396, 397, 403, 407, 415, 417, 418, 419, 420, 447, 534, 571, 583
geographic regions..... 378, 380, 428, 587, 605, 608
geographical information... 371, 408, 410, 656
geoinformation technology 395, 396, 397, 399, 400, 403, 404, 407, 412, 413, 414, 419
geospatial data ... 354, 359, 396, 399, 401, 403, 412, 413, 415
geospatial information....... 353, 361, 399, 400, 401, 403, 408, 416, 420, 630
Germany 26, 339, 344
government information resources.... 106, 615, 617, 621, 626, 627, 629, 630, 631, 632, 643
grounded theory. 69, 70, 71, 98, 426, 435, 436

H

Hasse diagram 378, 384, 385, 386, 393
Health Department............................. 118
health departments............. 433, 532, 535
homeland security...... 278, 281, 307, 321, 326, 328, 329, 365, 378, 390, 398, 399, 400, 414, 418, 419, 422, 432, 438, 526, 532, 555, 558
Homeless Management Information System 121
horizontal integration........ 127, 129, 135, 136, 698, 699, 709
hotspot detection and prioritization ...377, 378, 392
human-computer interaction 50, 57, 153, 165, 166, 176, 414, 416, 417, 418, 419, 461, 463, 610
humanitarian relief.....395, 397, 403, 410, 411, 414, 418, 420
Hungary.......................190, 191, 340, 342
Hurricane Katrina.......396, 397, 399, 400, 416, 417, 418
hybrid e-government...........697, 716, 718

I

identity management....95, 213, 214, 331, 332, 333, 334, 344, 346, 484
India 212, 397, 411
infectious disease........531, 532, 533, 534, 535, 537, 542, 546, 549, 551, 552, 554, 555, 556, 557
infectious disease informatics (IDI)....531
information and communication technology................................44, 488
information integration 104, 220, 221, 228, 231, 264, 265, 268, 269, 280, 282, 353, 354, 421, 422, 423, 424, 425, 426, 427, 428, 429, 430, 431, 432, 433, 434, 435, 436, 534
information management........ 25, 85, 99, 106 108, 109, 115, 116, 122, 183, 187, 188, 251, 258, 302, 327, 373, 424, 435, 585, 532, 533, 534, 582, 610, 611, 612, 619, 633, 647
information science.....23, 29, 38, 39, 40,, 98, 206, 207, 233, 371, 373, 377, 416, 417, 418, 527, 561, 581, 582, 717
information sharing....106, 114, 115, 123, 183, 187, 260, 263, 264, 265, 266,

267, 268, 269, 270, 277, 278, 279, 280, 281, 282, 293, 302, 303, 412, 413, 421, 422, 424, 426, 427, 428, 429, 432, 435, 436, 437, 438, 534, 550, 555, 571, 620, 624, 626, 640
institutional change.... 17, 37, 57, 38, 123, 436, 472, 610, 694
integration process..... 221, 296, 355, 358, 370, 375, 376, 423, 431
intelligence and security informatics. 278, 281
interdisciplinary collaboration............. 41
interdisciplinary research... 30, 32, 33, 38, 39, 41
interoperability 38, 222, 264, 265, 266, 268, 269, 270, 277, 280, 283, 285, 293, 302, 331, 332, 333, 334, 339, 340, 342, 343, 345, 346, 347, 348, 349, 350, 351, 399, 400, 415, 421, 422, 429, 430, 437, 535, 536, 537, 553, 582, 624, 645
Israel 456
Ireland....................................... 474, 488
Italy............ 340, 341, 344, 347, 348, 469

J

Journal of Public Administration... 18, 27, 82, 123, 137, 138
justice information system.. 268, 278, 431

K

knowledge acquisition........242, 247, 248, 258, 279, 281
knowledge base ... 24, 208, 234, 235, 257, 275, 276, 277, 314, 323, 527, 635
knowledge discovery......... 206, 256, 278, 307, 370, 373, 527
knowledge management 95, 233, 234, 238, 239, 240, 257, 258, 259, 278, 281, 418, 472, 485, 557, 591, 649
knowledge representation.. 234, 237, 257, 258, 259, 280, 371, 534
knowledge sharing.....279, 423, 482, 609, 649, 653, 662, 664
knowledge transfer.....212, 467, 468, 478, 483, 484, 486

L

land use and transportation 439, 442, 443, 444, 448, 451, 454, 457, 460
Latin America 212
law enforcement.263, 264, 266, 267, 268, 278, 279, 431, 534, 618
legal domain....... 186, 233, 236, 238, 247, 256, 257
legal knowledge .233, 237, 243, 244, 256, 258
legal ontologies ..237, 242, 256, 258, 259, 260, 261
legal reasoning 233, 238, 242, 257, 258
legal system....... 194, 238, 239, 242, 244, 246, 253, 257
Legislative Assembly of Queensland..491
legislative documents.. 189, 190, 192, 193
legislative process 181, 182, 183, 188, 191, 196
level of government 134, 135, 579, 713
linear extensions..........385, 386, 393, 394
local agencies.....267, 398, 562, 597, 603, 604, 605, 609
local e-democracy 92, 93, 473
local health departments 433

M

machine virtualization....... 287, 288, 292, 293, 298, 299, 300, 303
management information systems........28, 37, 263, 461, 463, 531, 534, 585, 610, 611, 616
mapping tools.....263, 264, 272, 273, 275, 278

maturity model... 61, 66, 75, 76, 623, 625, 626
mental models............. 211, 240, 410, 481
microeconomics.................................. 517
mobile devices... 190, 191, 337, 354, 407, 501
model cases......... 467, 478, 479, 481, 484
multimodal interface.. 395, 401, 402, 403, 404, 407, 414, 415, 417, 418, 419
Multnomah County Health Department 434
municipal government428, 615, 621, 637, 643, 645, 672, 695, 701, 704, 716, 718
mutual information 224, 226, 227, 230, 231, 280

N

National Archives...... 589, 590, 592, 609, 610, 612
National Research Council........ 132, 137, 138, 215, 354, 461, 528
National Science Foundation (U.S.).... 22, 37, 53, 57, 104, 122, 152, 175, 203, 204, 214, 216, 217, 327, 392, 414, 421, 422, 449, 460, 526, 553, 571, 580, 647
National Science Foundation (China)... 716
natural language. 104, 224, 238, 286, 292, 294, 295, 297, 414, 541
natural language processing 416, 541, 542, 554
Netherlands................ 235, 456, 469, 473
New York City Health Department... 391, 428
New Zealand...... 647, 648, 649, 650, 652, 653, 654, 655, 656, 657,
noncompliance............................ 148, 150
North Carolina... 138, 153, 301, 426, 428, 503, 505, 509, 510, 514, 528
Norway 649

O

online access 128, 131, 141, 142, 335, 339, 343, 352, 474, 491, 688
online transactions 133, 332, 343, 699, 703, 705, 706
ontology mapping 263, 264, 270, 271, 272, 273, 278, 279, 280
open source........ 212, 286, 455, 547, 548, 554, 579, 683, 686, 693
operating system........ 147, 204, 286, 288, 289, 290, 295, 296, 298, 301, 579, 654, 657
organizational boundaries .. 113, 117, 422, 424, 427, 429, 534, 698, 706
outbreak detection 534, 539, 543, 546, 547, 548, 551, 553, 554, 557, 558
outlier detection . 310, 311, 312, 316, 321, 322, 324, 325, 327, 329

P

Pacific Asia 700
Pacific Rim.. 212
paper ballot........ 158, 159, 160, 162, 165, 166, 169, 170, 180
paper trail ... 158, 161, 166, 174, 175, 179, 180
parent concept 317, 323
partial order......... 384, 385, 386, 387, 517
path-based terms........ 564, 565, 566, 569, 578
personal data 9, 88, 335, 338, 340, 341, 342, 344, 658, 659
personally identifiable information.... 129, 132, 134, 139
physical world..................... 249, 250, 256
planning processes 439, 441, 446, 449, 451, 452, 453, 458, 460, 598, 649, 656, 662, 664
Poland 342, 472, 496

policy issues..... ... 91, 128, 266, 276, 281, 475, 665
political participation....... 85, 87, 91, 490, 673, 674, 675, 678, 679, 681, 682
political parties 7, 85, 86, 95, 181, 182, 187, 192, 500, 674
political processes.... 6, 10, 85, 86, 87, 99, 182, 488, 489, 493, 494, 496, 499
political science..... 23, 29, 54, 56, 66, 67, 85, 100, 137, 157, 176, 177, 178, 672, 694
political scientists.... 5, 43, 44, 45, 46, 47, 53
presidential election... 158, 159, 162, 174, 176, 177, 179
privacy issues...... 95, 127, 129, 130, 131, 132, 133, 138, 139
private sector 105, 118, 134, 204, 205, 217, 344, 352, 377, 378, 591, 651, 669, 672
product description...... 55, 61, 62, 66, 69, 70, 71, 74, 75, 76, 79, 80
project management... 110, 116, 651, 653, 656, 659, 662, 666, 668, 669, 670, 699
public and private........ 37, 118, 145, 336, 344, 352, 586
public health surveillance .. 538, 539, 553, 554, 556, 557
public participation.... 101, 182, 198, 441, 490, 492, 500, 620
Public Petition Committee.................. 492
public policy...... 103, 104, 105, 109, 110, 158, 203, 423, 446, 504, 675
public records 130, 131, 139, 590, 611, 612
public safety agencies........ 266, 268, 276, 278, 281, 282
public safety information... 263, 264, 265, 266, 267, 268, 272, 277, 278, 279
public schools 505, 507, 512, 597, 601, 602, 604, 605
public servants.... 187, 188, 193, 198, 199
public service ... 6, 39, 105, 107, 182, 184, 207, 338, 339, 341, 468, 469, 470, 472, 473, 475, 484, 485, 618, 619, 620, 630, 639, 709
Puerto Rico........ 671, 672, 673, 675, 677, 678, 681, 693, 694

Q

Qingpu District...697, 699, 700, 701, 706, 716, 718

R

real estate 442, 447, 448, 450, 703
real world ... 154, 206, 233, 245, 255, 332, 349, 448, 451
reassessment................................108, 120
record management.... 534, 585, 587, 590, 592, 593, 595, 599, 600, 602, 607
reference model.. 266, 615, 621, 622, 623, 624, 625
regulations..... 4, 6, 11, 14, 109, 113, 128, 139, 186, 205, 231, 244, 265, 338, 339, 341, 342, 343, 440, 441, 481, 534, 588, 592, 595, 598, 617, 631, 637, 640, 642, 684, 691, 706
Rehabilitation Act.......142, 145, 146, 153, 505
remote access servers.........516, 522, 523, 524, 526
research and development......43, 63, 206, 229, 230, 329, 419, 552, 615, 643
research and practice....62, 85, 87, 88, 98, 103, 122, 125, 208, 534, 585, 588, 591
residual vote........159, 160, 176, 177, 178
resource allocation 392, 412, 421, 422, 433, 591, 601
resource management...27, 399, 562, 563, 566, 577, 621, 651
resource managers......562, 576, 577, 583, 628

response distributions 379, 380, 381
risk management....... 652, 659, 660, 664, 666, 667
Russian Federation 94

S

Salt Lake City, Utah .. 446, 450, 456, 457, 458, 459, 461, 463
San Diego, California........ 227, 267, 268, 278, 373, 393, 416, 418, 557
scan statistics 545, 548, 558, 559
science and technology..... 618, 633, 643, 708
Scotland 487, 488, 489, 491, 492, 493, 495, 496, 497
Scottish Parliament 487, 488, 489, 490, 491, 492, 495, 496, 499, 500
Section 508 (U.S.) 146
security and privacy..... 52, 129, 136, 177, 186, 346, 491, 651, 659
semantic centrality..... 310, 318, 319, 323, 324
semantic clique 310, 318, 319, 323
semantic components.................. 576, 577
semantic graph... 307, 309, 310, 311, 312, 313, 316, 321, 323, 324, 326, 329
semantic matching..... 208, 309, 310, 313, 315, 316, 322, 326
semantic relationships 309, 310, 312, 313, 315, 318, 319, 321, 322, 323, 325, 326
semantic web 97, 233, 234, 258, 259, 260, 275, 276, 277, 278, 279, 280, 327
semantic weights 307, 310, 318, 319, 320, 324
sensor networks......... 354, 356, 367, 370, 378, 388, 389, 390, 391
service delivery.... 96, 104, 109, 120, 203, 208, 425, 438, 473, 650, 660, 669, 698
Shanghai 699, 700, 701, 702, 704, 705, 707, 712, 713, 716
shape signature.................... 357, 368, 369
similarity metrics 359, 360, 363, 364, 369, 373
Slovakia... 86, 94
Slovenia...................................... 342, 343
social network 49, 97, 325, 326, 328
social science ... 32, 34, 35, 40, 45, 53, 85, 98, 104, 206, 207, 208
social security..... 185, 335, 336, 337, 338, 343, 516
Social Security 128, 132, 335, 703
software components 286, 290, 291, 293, 294, 295, 297, 298, 299, 621
software development....... 206, 209, 453, 579, 684, 688
software execution environments 287
Spain 343, 649
spatial data......... 353, 354, 355, 356, 357, 358, 359, 363, 372, 379, 397, 417
spatial scan statistic.... 379, 381, 393, 545, 554, 556
spatiotemporal.... 307, 309, 310, 312, 313, 318, 319, 322, 326, 359, 360, 361, 362, 363, 369, 375, 377, 378, 388, 392, 534
spatiotemporal data 353, 354, 355, 365, 366, 370, 373, 374, 376
spatiotemporal pattern....... 353, 365, 364, 365, 366, 367, 368
spectrum ... 21, 25, 30, 32, 34, 36, 41, 144, 237, 370, 543
statistical agencies...... 211, 513, 514, 516, 524, 525, 526, 527, 528, 662
statistical data..... 230, 231, 327, 526, 527, 528, 635, 653, 674, 683
statistical disclosure 516, 528
statistical information........ 211, 503, 504, 505, 512, 513, 527, 645
strategic alignments ... 585, 587, 591, 592, 593, 594, 595, 596, 597, 598, 599, 601, 604, 605, 606, 607, 608, 611
subject areas 562, 564, 566, 567, 578

Supreme Court (U.S.) 131
surveillance systems .. 367, 391, 392, 538, 552
syndrome categories .. 392, 539, 540, 541, 542, 546, 547
syndrome classification 539, 540, 541, 543, 547, 548, 549
syndromic surveillance systems........ 533, 537, 538, 539, 540, 541, 542, 545, 547, 553, 559

T

technology transfer 51, 106, 210, 561, 579, 671, 672, 673, 683
tele-democracy 85, 100, 487
theory testing ... 55, 62, 66, 68, 69, 71, 74, 75, 80
threat structure mining...... . 307, 309, 310, 311, 317, 320, 329
touch screens 158, 160, 161, 162, 165, 166, 169, 170, 174
transnational digital government (TDG) systems......... 284, 293, 294, 295, 296, 298, 299, 305
tripartite model 46, 47, 48, 49, 50, 51, 52, 53, 54, 56, 59

U

United Kingdom 344
United Nations ... 212, 397, 418, 420, 668, 669, 701, 717
universal access ... 45, 143, 145, 146, 148, 151, 155, 206, 213, 418
University of Maryland 157, 176, 275, 323, 373, 374, 506
urban models 439, 442, 443, 446, 447, 460, 461, 462
urban simulation . 443, 454, 457, 461, 462
usability......103, 110, 115, 117, 153, 155, 157, 158, 159, 161, 165, 166, 168, 169, 171, 172, 174, 175, 176, 179, 235, 366, 401, 402, 414, 442, 445, 457, 483, 527, 566, 571, 572, 573, 574, 580, 660
user access.... 91, 222, 345, 347, 396, 535, 537, 538, 552
user interfaces 115, 166, 172, 395, 397, 401, 413, 418, 420, 455, 547, 572, 573, 633, 655

V

value sensitive design..... 451, 452, 461, 463
verification systems ... 157, 158, 171, 172, 173
vertical integration 127, 129, 134, 135, 698, 699
virtual networks 291, 300, 303, 305
virtual state ... 11, 17, 38, 39, 57, 123, 436, 610, 694
virtualization technologies......... 283, 285, 287, 293, 299, 300, 304, 305
voting technology...... 160, 174, 176, 177, 178

W

Web accessibility....... 141, 142, 143, 145, 146, 147, 148, 149, 150, 152, 153, 154, 155
web accessibility 147, 153, 154
web design 143, 144, 148, 151, 152
web portal 49, 97, 142, 190, 196, 210, 275, 395, 397, 403, 410, 411, 412, 414, 415, 419, 513, 699, 701, 704, 706, 713, 718
West Nile Virus.. 426, 427, 434, 543, 549, 554, 557

X

Xuhui District Government. 697, 699, 701

Printed in the United States of America.